VOLUME II: THE RENAISSANCE TO THE PRESENT

The Western Humanities

SIXTH EDITION

Roy T. Matthews & F. DeWitt Platt

MICHIGAN STATE UNIVERSITY

McGraw Hill

Boston   Burr Ridge, IL   Dubuque, IA   Madison, WI   New York   San Francisco   St. Louis
Bangkok   Bogotá   Caracas   Kuala Lumpur   Lisbon   London   Madrid   Mexico City
Milan   Montreal   New Delhi   Santiago   Seoul   Singapore   Sydney   Taipei   Toronto

The McGraw·Hill Companies

Mc Graw Hill Higher Education

Published by McGraw-Hill, an imprint of The McGraw-Hill Companies, Inc., 1221 Avenue of the Americas, New York, NY 10020. Copyright © 2008. All rights reserved. No part of this publication may be reproduced or distributed in any form or by any means, or stored in a database or retrieval system, without the prior written consent of The McGraw-Hill Companies, Inc., including, but not limited to, in any network or other electronic storage or transmission, or broadcast for distance learning.

This book is printed on acid-free paper.

1 2 3 4 5 6 7 8 9 0 DOW/DOW 0 9 8 7

ISBN-13: 978-0-07-313638-7
ISBN-10: 0-07-313638-7

Editor in Chief: *Emily Barrosse*
Publisher: *Lisa Moore*
Marketing Manager: *Pamela Cooper*
Director of Development: *Lisa Pinto*
Developmental Editor: *Kristen Mellitt*
Project Manager: *Christina Gimlin*
Manuscript Editor: *Margaret Moore*
Art Director: *Jeanne Schreiber*
Design Manager: *Kim Menning*
Text Designer: *Glenda King*
Cover Designer: *Kim Menning*
Art Editor: *Robin Mouat*
Manager, Photo Research: *Brian Pecko*
Production Supervisor: *Randy Hurst*
Composition: *9.5/12 Palatino by Prographics*
Printing: *60# Sterling Gloss by RR Donnelley, Willard*

Credits: The credits section for this book begins on page C-1 and is considered an extension of the copyright page.

Library of Congress Cataloging-in-Publication Data
Matthews, Roy T.
    The Western humanities/Roy T. Matthews & F. DeWitt Platt.—6th ed.
        p. cm.
    Includes bibliographical references and index.
    ISBN 13: 978-0-07-313619-6 (alk. paper)
    ISBN 10: 0-07-313619-0 (alk. paper)
    1. Civilization, Western—History.   I. Platt, F. DeWitt. II. Title.

CB245.M375   2007
909'.09821—dc22
                                                                    2006046966

The Internet addresses listed in the text were accurate at the time of publication. The inclusion of a Web site does not indicate an endorsement by the authors or McGraw-Hill, and McGraw-Hill does not guarantee the accuracy of the information presented at these sites.

www.mhhe.com

There is nothing nobler or more admirable than when two people who see eye to eye keep house as man and wife, confounding their enemies and delighting their friends, as they themselves know better than anyone.

—HOMER, *Odyssey*

PREFACE

This new edition of *The Western Humanities* represents a personal and cultural milestone. We claim it as a personal milestone, because for more than twenty years we have been defined by this project (which we affectionately call, "the Book")—reading, researching, writing, revising, and refining the manuscript, attending concerts, plays, operas, films, lectures, exhibitions, and gallery openings, and discussing the meaning of the Western heritage with colleagues, students, friends, and family. We also claim "the Book" as a cultural milestone because when it existed only in outline form in 1985, academia was in the midst of a culture war in which the future of textbooks devoted exclusively to Western culture seemed in doubt. Throughout the course of five editions, however, *The Western Humanities* has established itself as a strong presence on the academic scene, and we hope that in some small way it has contributed to the revitalization of arts and humanities survey courses in colleges and universities. Its reach now extends around the world—the latest translation has been published in mainland China.

With this sixth edition, we continue in the same spirit with which we first approached our subject. In the first edition, we placed Western cultural achievements within their historical context. In the second and third editions, we expanded coverage of the contributions of women and other artists outside the traditional canon. In the fourth edition, we added a multicultural dimension, with the expectation that students would gain a greater appreciation of world cultures beyond the Western traditions. In the fifth edition, we expanded our coverage of Islamic civilization, as a way of helping students to better grasp contemporary political and cultural issues. For the sixth edition, we have made the most extensive revision yet, increasing the coverage of philosophy, science, music,

and religion, broadening the definition of creativity to embrace advances in technology, and enhancing our treatment of the history of film and photography. It is our hope that the sixth edition of *The Western Humanities* will continue to assist instructors in meeting today's teaching challenges, as well as help the next generation of students understand and claim their cultural heritage.

AIMS OF *THE WESTERN HUMANITIES*

In its origin *The Western Humanities* was an outgrowth of our careers as university teachers. Instructing thousands of undergraduate students throughout the years had left us dissatisfied with available textbooks. In our eyes, the existing books failed in one of two ways: They either ignored material developments and focused exclusively on cultural artifacts without context or perspective, or they stressed political, social, and economic history with too little or too disjointed a discussion of literature and the arts. Our goal in writing this book was to balance and integrate these two elements—that is, to provide an analysis and an appreciation of cultural expression and artifacts within an interpretive historical framework.

When we sat down to write the first edition of *The Western Humanities,* we feared that the world of the late twentieth century was in danger of being engulfed by present-minded thinking. Students merely mirror the wider society when they show little knowledge of, or even concern about, the great artistic and literary monuments and movements of the Western tradition, or about the political, economic, and social milestones of Western history. In *The Western Humanities,* we address the problem of present-mindedness by discussing not only the works that were produced in successive periods but also the prevailing historical and material conditions that so powerfully influenced their form and content. Our intention is to demystify the cultural record by showing that literature and the arts do not spring forth spontaneously and independently of each other, but reflect a set of specific historical circumstances. By providing this substantial context, out of which both ideas and artifacts emerge, we hope to give students a deeper understanding of the meaning of cultural works and a broader basis for appreciating the humanities.

We also emphasize the universal aspects of creativity and expression. People everywhere have the impulse to seek answers to the mysteries of human existence; to discover or invent order in the universe; to respond creatively to nature, both inner and outer; to delight the senses and the mind with beauty and truth; to communicate their thoughts and share their visions with others. Thus, another of our intentions is to demonstrate that the desire to express oneself and to create lasting monuments has been a compelling drive in human beings since before the dawn of civilized life. We believe that this emphasis will help students see that they are not isolated from the past but belong to a tradition that began thousands of years ago.

We also aim to help students prepare themselves for the uncertainties of the future. When they examine the past and learn how earlier generations confronted and overcame crises—and managed to leave enduring legacies—students will discover that the human spirit is irrepressible. In the humanities—in philosophy, religion, art, music, literature—human beings have found answers to their deepest needs and most perplexing questions. We hope that students will be encouraged by this record as they begin to shape the world of the twenty-first century.

ORGANIZATION AND CONTENT

The twenty-two chapters of this text provide a balanced treatment of history and culture. The chapters follow a consistent organization, as described below.

An interpretive context for the humanities. The first part of every chapter covers the material conditions of the era—the historical, political, economic, and social developments. We aim to capture the essence of complex periods and to fashion a coherent narrative framework for the story of Western culture.

Cultural expression. The remaining part of each chapter is devoted to cultural expression, both in the realm of ideas (philosophy, history, religion, science) and in the realm of cultural artifact (art, music, drama, literature, and film). In this part we describe and analyze the significant cultural achievements of the age, and we examine how creative individuals responded to the challenges presented to them by their society and how they chose values and forms by which to live.

Cultural legacy. Each chapter ends with a brief section describing the cultural legacy of that era. Students will find that some ideas, movements, or artistic methods with which they are familiar have a very long history. They will also discover that the meaning and ascribed value of cultural objects and texts can change from one time and place to another. Our goal is not only to help students establish a context for their culture but to show that the humanities have developed as a dynamic series of choices made by individuals in one era and transformed by individuals in other eras.

SPECIAL FEATURES

The Sixth Edition includes a variety of features to enhance student understanding of the humanities.

- **Enounter boxes.** A special feature introduced in the fifth edition was the **Encounter,** which recounts meetings between the West and other cultures. Through text and art, each Encounter focuses on critical interchanges that influenced both cultures. As we seek to nurture global awareness in today's students, these Encounters demonstrate that cultural encounters and exchanges are an enduring part of history, with both positive and negative consequences.

- **Slices of Life features.** Formerly known as Personal Perspectives, these boxes offer students the opportunity to hear voices from the past of those who witnessed or participated in the historical and cultural events described in the text. These excerpts from primary sources and original documents are designed to bring history to life for the reader.

- **Learning through Maps.** This feature encourages students to develop geographical skills—a highly desirable ability in this age of globalization. By performing map exercises and answering map-related questions, students learn to read maps and understand historical and cultural developments within a specific geographic setting.

- **Legacy sections.** Each chapter ends with a section that conveys the enduring legacy of the traditions described in the chapter. For example, in Chapter 8, the legacy section talks about the ongoing cultural influence of medieval Islam on both modern Islam and on the West.

In addition to the chapter features, each chapter offers several important features at its conclusion:

Terminology. In the text, when a new cultural term is introduced, it is boldfaced and defined immediately. At the end of each chapter, a list of **Key Cultural Terms** appears, serving as a handy review of important words for the student to know. The **Suggestions for Further Reading** is a list, in alphabetic order by author, of one or two literary works by the major writers discussed in the chapter. We provide this list—naming a readily available edition along with an assessment of its usefulness—so that students may do some additional reading on their own. The **Suggestions for Listening** feature offers a list, in alphabetic order by composer, of musical compositions covered in each chapter. The list, with brief annotations, is provided as a follow-up to the music discussion in the chapter, so that students may listen on their own.

CHANGES TO THE SIXTH EDITION

We have made several significant changes in this sixth edition of *The Western Humanities:*

Increased global emphasis. A new final chapter on the impact of globalization and terror on the arts, fourteen new Encounter features highlighting interactions between the West and other cultures, and the addition of numerous writers, artists, and philosophers from around the world (all discussed in detail below), strengthen the book's focus on the global roots of the Western humanities. The illustration program also includes new globally-oriented images, such as a map of the Silk Road in Chapter 7, and manuscript illuminations depicting the Crusades in Chapter 9.

Reorganization and expansion of final chapters. Chapter 21 now focuses on Late Modernism, from 1945 to 1970, while a brand-new Chapter 22 is devoted to Post-Modernism, from 1970 to the present. In Chapter 21, additions include Neo-Orthodoxy; Vatican II reforms; a new and extensive section on film; a new Encounter, "The Globalization of Popular Music"; and a new Slice of Life giving the words of the first astronauts as they recalled their impressions of being on the Moon. We also discuss many individuals not covered in previous editions, such as theologian Paul Tillich; and writers and artists who had not been previously included, such as painter Willem de Kooning, sculptor Eva Hesse, and architect Eero Saarinen. In Chapter 22, we stress both globalization and terrorism and their impact across global culture, as well as include enhanced treatment of science and technology; the birth of liberation theology; the papacy of Pope John Paul II; the rise of radical Islam; the maturation of woodwind chamber music; the rise of hip-hop culture in music; a film section; an Encounter about demography and migration and their impact on globalization; and a Slice of Life dealing with the sources of Islamic terrorism. New individuals covered include novelist Zadie Smith, poet Derek Walcott, playwrights Dario Fo and Franca Rame, painters Susan Rothenberg and Sam Gilliam, sculptor Maya Lin, architect Zaha Hadid, and composer Tan Dun.

Expanded coverage of selected cultural topics. Science, for example, now appears in ten chapters, including Hellenistic Greece and Post-Modernism. Similarly, philosophy is expanded to bridge gaps in our treatment of the history of thought, with the addition of Jean Bodin, David Hume, Paul Tillich, and Christian Existentialism. Medicine is now discussed in many chapters, beginning with the Mesopotamians and Egyptians and ranging from the Greeks—with the inclusion of Hippocrates—through the Romans, the Muslims and Renaissance Europe to Post-Modern times. Religion is now given more visibility, by focusing on the growth of evangelicalism in Protestantism and the Roman Catholic Church's hostile reaction to modernity, after 1850. This enhanced coverage of religion thus presents more clearly the history of the continuing dialogue between secular culture and religion—a central feature of Western life today. And music is now expanded to provide brief but intense discussions of 23 musical works. These music discussions also serve a secondary goal: They function as "mini-Listening Guides" for students who listen along with the Music CD that is part of the ancillary materials associated with our textbook. Other noteworthy additions to music include the Encounter "The Globalization of Popular Music" in Chapter 21, and an enlarged treatment of Post-Modern music, in Chapter 22.

Expanded coverage of Technology. Technology, which in earlier editions of *The Western Humanities* had been treated as the handmaid of the arts and humanities, is presented in this sixth edition as a form of creative expression whose roots go back to prehistoric times. We show that technology is subject to the same historical and cultural forces that operate on other creative achievements in each period of history. Our coverage of technology extends to most chapters, ranging from Stone Age culture to today's nanotechnology, with a focus especially on those technologies with transformative potential, such as machines, papermaking, food production, and power sources. Along with technology, we have included sections on warfare, which is central to the human experience, embracing the military, science, technology, and governments, and we also show warfare's impact on the wider culture.

New Encounters features. An Encounter feature now appears in all 22 chapters, resulting in an addition of fourteen new episodes for this sixth edition. The new Encounters include such major cultural exchanges as the invention of the alphabet by the ancient Phoenicians, which became the alphabet for virtually all Western languages; the creation of the Silk Road, linking ancient Rome and the Far East, the world's first attempt at globalization; and the development of the civil disobedience techniques of Gandhi, the father of Indian independence. We have made the Encounters more engaging by adding a set of questions at the end of each, entitled Learning from the Encounter, a pedagogical device meant to help students understand the historical and cultural significance of these meetings.

Enhanced Slices of Life features. We have revised the Slices of Life so that this feature reflects a rich variety of voices including people of diverse religious outlook, including Christian, Muslim, Jewish, and pagan. We have also added questions to each feature, entitled Interpreting this Slice of Life, which are meant to assist students in understanding each speaker.

Enhanced art program. About 115 new artworks are included. Every illustration in the book is discussed both in the text and in a detailed caption. The new illustrations include the Cylinder Seal of Queen Pu-abi, with Banqueting Scene; one of the Vaphio Cups; Horsemen, from the west frieze of the Parthenon; a Hunt Scene from the Piazza Armerina; Arches of the Great Mosque in Cordoba; manuscript illuminations of Crusaders Attacking a Muslim Fortress and Muslims Attacking Crusaders; Ghiberti's *Gates of Paradise*; Bellini's *Mehmet II*; Holbein's *Henry VIII*; Brueghel's *Netherlandish Proverbs*; Rembrandt's etching of *Christ Preaching*; Chambers' Pagoda in Kew Gardens, London; a Gillray caricature; Ingres's *Madame Rivière*; Solar's *Drago*; the Bauhaus Workshop; Moore's *Reclining Figure*; De Kooning's *Woman and Bicycle*; a still from Bergman's *The Seventh Seal*; Rothenberg's *Butterfly*; Richter's *Betty*; and Koolhaas' Seattle Public Library. We have also introduced students to less well-known artists, such as Gerard Ter Borch, Raoul Dufy, and Childe Hassam, through their paintings of historical events.

Increased coverage of women and people of diverse origins. These additions include Encounter 13, "Indigenous Peoples and New Spain"; DeIslas's portrait of Sor Juana Inès de la Cruz, the Mexican nun and early feminist; Slice of Life 17, the testimony of Elizabeth Bentley, a working class woman, before an English parliamentary commission; Inman's portrait of *Sequoyah*, the Cherokee leader, in Encounter 18; the rise of hip hop music; two women photographers (Margaret Bourke-White and Dorothea Lange); one woman film director (Leni Riefenstahl); two African American film directors (Melvin van Peebles and Spike Lee); one Iraqi-born woman architect, living in the U.K. (Zaha Hadid); one Chinese-American architect (I. M. Pei); one Chinese-American sculptor (Maya Lin); two women sculptors (Eva Hesse and Jeanne-Claude); two women painters (Bridget Riley and Susan Rothenberg); one African American painter (Samuel Gilliam); the Jamaican-British woman writer (Zadie Smith); one woman playwright-performer (Franca Rame); one West Indian-American poet (Derek Walcott); a woodwind ensemble composed of minority musicians (Imani Winds); and a Chinese-American actor (Bruce Lee).

TEACHING AND LEARNING RESOURCES

As instructors, we are keenly aware of the problems encountered in teaching the humanities, especially to large, diverse classes. This text comes with a comprehensive package of supplementary resource materials, designed to help solve those problems.

Instructor's Manual. The sixth edition of the Instructor's Manual has been revised and expanded. For each chapter the manual includes teaching strategies and suggestions; learning objectives; key cultural terms; film, reading, and Internet site suggestions; and a detailed outline revised to accompany the sixth edition of *The Western Humanities*. References to the accompanying anthology, *Readings in the Western Humanities*, are included in each chapter so that primary source material can be easily incorporated into each lesson. In addition to chapter-by-chapter materials, the Instructor's Manual offers five basic teaching strategies and seven lecture models in the preface. The Instructor's Manual is available on the Online Learning Center.

The Image Vault. A large percentage of images from the illustration program are available to adopting instructors in digital format in **The Image Vault**, McGraw-Hill's new Web-based presentation manager. Instructors can incorporate images from The Image Vault in digital presentations that can be used in class (no Internet access required), burned to CD-ROM, or embedded in course Web pages. See www.mhhe.com/theimagevault for more details.

Music selections. An audio CD that accompanies the sixth edition covers the broad spectrum of music discussed in the text and includes pieces by such composers as Hildegard of Bingen, J. S. Bach, Igor Stravinsky, and Philip Glass.

MyHumanitiesStudio. The student content for the Online Learning Center of this new edition of *The Western Humanities* has been reorganized and newly enriched. All of the Core Concepts content previously available on DVD-ROM has been converted so that students can access the information online. Students can watch videos about various art techniques and access interactive activities designed to strengthen their understanding of visual art, dance, music, sculpture, literature, theater, architecture, and film. They will also be able to use the guided Research in Action tool to enhance their understanding of time periods, genres, and artists. We hope that this online availability will strengthen student understanding of the humanities as well as spark their own creativity. All of this information is available at www.mhhe.com/mp6 when you click on the **MyHumanitiesStudio** link.

Readings in the Western Humanities. Selections in this anthology of primary source materials are arranged chronologically to follow the 22 chapters of the text, and are divided into two volumes. Volume I covers ancient Mesopotamia through the Renaissance; Volume II, the Renaissance into the 21st century. This anthology gives students access to our literary and philosophical heritage, allowing them to experience firsthand the ideas and voices of the great writers and thinkers of the Western tradition.

ACKNOWLEDGMENTS

We are grateful to many people for their help and support in this revision of *The Western Humanities.* We continue to appreciate the many insightful comments of students and former students at Michigan State University over the years. We thank Professor Michael Mackay for his suggestions on the topic of nanotechnology. We are also grateful for the many suggestions and comments provided to us by the following reviewers:

Peter Dusenbery, Bradley University
Bobby Hom, Santa Fe Community College
James Housefield, Texas State University—San Marcos
Susan Jones, Palm Beach Atlantic University
Vance S. Martin, Parkland College
Kevin R. Morgan, St. Petersburg College
Linda J. Nelson, Davenport University
Darrell G. Olges, Florida Community College—Jacksonville
Linda Smith Tabb, Parkland College
Stephen Thomas, Community College of Denver
Paul Van Heuklom, Lincoln Land Community College
Rennie VanKampen, International Academy of Design and Technology
Richard A. Voeltz, Cameron University
Bertha Wise, Oklahoma City Community College
Margaret Woodruff-Wieding, Austin Community College

This sixth edition, for reasons beyond our control, has been a challenge in preparation. We thank Alexis Walker for her early role in this project. And, we especially thank Clare Payton for her certain and steady guidance. It was Clare's vision that sustained us through the many months of this endeavor, and she proved to be a calm and wise influence for us both. Special thanks to Lisa Moore, and, especially, Lisa Pinto, Kristen Mellitt, and Christina Gimlin, and to the entire editorial and production team at McGraw-Hill.

CONTENTS

18
THE TRIUMPH OF THE BOURGEOISIE 1830–1871   *545*

19
THE AGE OF EARLY MODERNISM, 1871–1914   *579*

INTRODUCTION
Why Study Cultural History?

To be ignorant of what occurred before you were born is to remain always a child.

—CICERO, FIRST CENTURY B.C.E.

Anyone who cannot give an account to oneself of the past three thousand years remains in darkness, without experience, living from day to day.

—GOETHE, NINETEENTH CENTURY C.E.

The underlying premise of this book is that some basic knowledge of the Western cultural heritage is necessary for those who want to become educated human beings in charge of their own destinies. If people are not educated into their place in human history—five thousand years of relatively uninterrupted, though sometimes topsy-turvy, developments—then they are rendered powerless, subject to passing fads and outlandish beliefs. They become vulnerable to the flattery of demagogues who promise heaven on earth, or they fall prey to the misconception that present-day events are unique, without precedent in history, or superior to everything that has gone before.

Perhaps the worst that can happen is to exist in a limbo of ignorance—in Goethe's words, "living from day to day." Without knowledge of the past and the perspective it brings, people may come to believe that their contemporary world will last forever, when in reality much of it is doomed to be forgotten. In contrast to the instant obsolescence of popular culture, the study of Western culture offers an alternative that has passed the unforgiving test of time. Long after today's heroes and celebrities have fallen into oblivion, the achievements of our artistic and literary ancestors—those who have forged the Western tradition—will remain. Their works echo down the ages and seem fresh

in every period. The ancient Roman writer Seneca put it well when he wrote, in the first century C.E., "Life is short but art is long."

When people realize that the rich legacy of Western culture is their own, their view of themselves and the times they live in can expand beyond the present moment. They find that they need not be confined by the limits of today but can draw on the creative insights of people who lived hundreds and even thousands of years ago. They discover that their own culture has a history and a context that give it meaning and shape. Studying and experiencing their cultural legacy can help them understand their place in today's world.

THE BOUNDARIES OF THE WEST

The subject of this text is Western culture, but what exactly do we mean, first, by "culture" and, second, by the "West"? *Culture* is a term with several meanings, but we use it here to mean the artistic and intellectual expressions of a people, their creative achievements. By the *West* we mean that part of the globe that lies west of Asia and Asia Minor and north of Africa, especially Europe—the geographical framework for much of this study.

The Western tradition is not confined exclusively to Europe as defined today, however. The contributions of peoples who lived beyond the boundaries of present-day Europe are also included in Western culture, either because they were forerunners of the West, such as those who created the first civilizations in Mesopotamia and Egypt, or because they were part of the West for periods of time, such as those who lived in the North African and Near Eastern lands bordering the

Mediterranean Sea during the Roman and early Christian eras. Regardless of geography, Western culture draws deeply from ideals forged in these lands.

When areas that had been part of the Western tradition at one time were absorbed into other cultural traditions—as happened in the seventh century in Mesopotamia, Egypt, and North Africa when the people embraced the Muslim faith—then they are generally no longer included in Western cultural history. Because of the enormous influence of Islamic civilization on Western civilization, however, we do include in this volume both an account of Islamic history and a description and appreciation of Islamic culture. Different in many ways from our own, the rich tradition of Islam has an important place in today's world.

After about 1500, with voyages and explorations reaching the farthest parts of the globe, the European focus of Western culture that had held for centuries began to dissolve. Starting from this time, the almost exclusively European mold was broken and Western values and ideals began to be exported throughout the world, largely through the efforts of missionaries, soldiers, colonists, and merchants. Coinciding with this development and further complicating the pattern of change were the actions of those who imported and enslaved countless numbers of black Africans to work on plantations in North and South America. The interplay of Western culture with many previously isolated cultures, whether desired or not, forever changed all who were touched by the process.

The Westernization of the globe that has been going on ever since 1500 is perhaps the dominant theme of our time. What human greed, missionary zeal, and dreams of empire failed to accomplish before 1900 was achieved during the twentieth century by modern technology, the media, and popular culture. The world today is a global village, much of it dominated by Western values and styles of life. In our time, Westernization has become a two-way interchange. When artists and writers from other cultures adopt Western forms or ideas, they are not only Westernizing their own traditions but also injecting fresh sensibilities and habits of thought into the Western tradition. The globalization of culture means that a South American novel or a Japanese film can be as accessible to Western audiences as a European painting, and yet carry with it an intriguingly new vocabulary of cultural symbols and meanings.

HISTORICAL PERIODS AND CULTURAL STYLES

In cultural history, the past is often divided into historical periods and cultural styles. A historical period is an interval of time that has a certain unity because it is characterized by the prevalence of a unique culture, ideology, or technology, or because it is bounded by defining historical events, such as the death of a military leader like Alexander the Great or a political upheaval like the fall of Rome. A cultural style is a combination of features of artistic or literary expression, execution, or performance that defines a particular school or era. A historical period may have the identical time frame as a cultural style, or it may embrace more than one style simultaneously or two styles successively. Each chapter of this survey focuses on a historical period and includes significant aspects of culture—usually the arts, architecture, literature, religion, music, and philosophy—organized around a discussion of the relevant style or styles appropriate to that time.

The survey begins with prehistory, the era before writing was invented, setting forth the emergence of human beings from an obscure past. After the appearance of writing in about 3000 B.C.E., the Western cultural heritage is divided into three sweeping historical periods: ancient, medieval, and modern.

The ancient period dates from 3000 B.C.E. to 500 C.E. Timeline 1). During these thirty-five hundred years the light of Western civilization begins to shine in Mesopotamia and Egypt, shines more brightly still in eighth-century-B.C.E. Greece and Rome, loses some of its luster when Greece succumbs to Rome in 146 B.C.E., and finally is snuffed out when the Roman Empire collapses in the fifth century C.E. Coinciding with these historical periods are the cultural styles of Mesopotamia; Egypt; Greece, including Archaic, Classical (or Hellenic), and Hellenistic styles; and Rome, including Republican and Imperial styles.

The medieval period, or the Middle Ages, covers events between 500 and 1500 C.E., a one-thousand-year span that is further divided into three subperiods (Timeline 2). The Early Middle Ages (500–1000) is typified by frequent barbarian invasions and political chaos so that civilization itself is threatened and barely survives. No single international style characterizes this turbulent period, though several regional styles flourish. The High Middle Ages (1000–1300) is a period of stability and the zenith of medieval culture. Two successive styles appear, the Romanesque and the Gothic, with the latter dominating culture for the rest of the medieval period. The Late Middle Ages (1300–1500) is a transitional period in which the medieval age is dying and the modern age is struggling to be born.

The modern period begins in about 1400 (there is often overlap between historical periods) and continues today (Timeline 3). With the advent of the modern period, a new way of defining historical changes starts

Timeline 1   THE ANCIENT WORLD

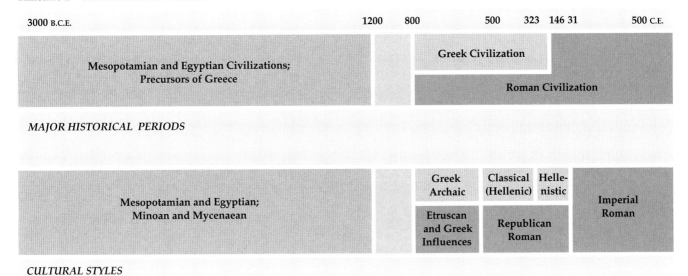

to make more sense—the division of history into movements, the activities of large groups of people united to achieve a common goal. The modern period consists of waves of movements that aim to change the world in some specific way.

The first modern movement is the Renaissance (1400–1600), or "rebirth," which attempts to revive the cultural values of ancient Greece and Rome. It is accompanied by two successive styles, Renaissance and Mannerism. The next significant movement is the Reformation (1500–1600), which is dedicated to restoring Christianity to the ideals of the early church set forth in the Bible. Although it does not spawn a specific style, this religious upheaval does have a profound impact on the subjects of the arts and literature and the way they are expressed, especially in the Mannerist style.

The Reformation is followed by the Scientific Revolution (1600–1700), a movement that results in the abandonment of ancient science and the birth of modern science. Radical in its conclusions, the Scientific Revolution is somewhat out of touch with the style of its age, which is known as the Baroque. This magnificent style is devoted to overwhelming the senses through theatrical and sensuous effects and is associated with the attempts of the Roman Catholic Church to reassert its authority in the world.

The Scientific Revolution gives impetus to the Enlightenment (1700–1800), a movement that pledges to reform politics and society according to the principles

Timeline 2   THE MEDIEVAL WORLD

500		1000	1150	1300	1500
Early Middle Ages			High Middle Ages		Late Middle Ages

MAJOR HISTORICAL PERIODS

Regional Styles		Romanesque	Gothic

CULTURAL STYLES

Timeline 3   THE MODERN WORLD

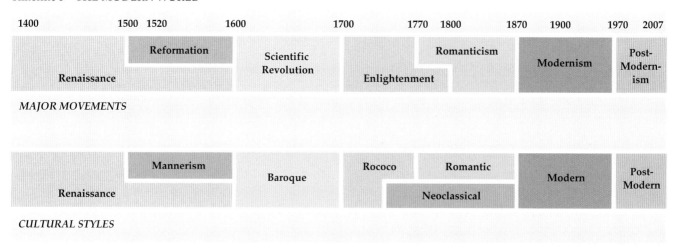

MAJOR MOVEMENTS

CULTURAL STYLES

of the new science. In stylistic terms the eighteenth century is schizophrenic, dominated first by the Rococo, an extravagant and fanciful style that represents the last phase of the Baroque, and then by the Neoclassical, a style inspired by the works of ancient Greece and Rome and reflective of the principles of the Scientific Revolution. Before the eighteenth century is over, the Enlightenment calls forth its antithesis, Romanticism (1770–1870), a movement centered on feeling, fantasy, and everything that cannot be proven scientifically. The Romantic style, marked by a revived taste for the Gothic and a love of nature, is the perfect accompaniment to this movement.

Toward the end of the nineteenth century, Modernism (1870–1970) arises, bent on destroying every vestige of both the Greco-Roman tradition and the Christian faith and on fashioning new ways of understanding that are independent of the past. Since 1970, Post-Modernism has emerged, a movement that tries to make peace with the past by embracing old forms of expression while at the same time adopting a global and multivoiced perspective.

Although every cultural period is marked by innovation and creativity, our treatment of them in this book varies somewhat, with more space and greater weight given to the achievements of certain times. We make these adjustments because some periods or styles are more significant than others, especially in the defining influence that their achievements have had on our own era. For example, some styles seem to tower over the rest, such as Classicism in fifth-century-B.C.E. Greece, the High Renaissance of sixteenth-century Italy, and Modernism in the mid–twentieth century, as compared with other styles, such as that of the Early Middle Ages or the seventeenth-century Baroque.

AN INTEGRATED APPROACH TO CULTURAL HISTORY

Our approach to the Western heritage in this book is to root cultural achievements in their historical settings, showing how the material conditions—the political, social, and economic events of each period—influenced their creation. About one third of each chapter is devoted to an interpretive discussion of material history, and the remaining two thirds are devoted to the arts, architecture, philosophy, religion, literature, and music of the period. These two aspects of history do not occur separately, of course, and one of our aims is to show how they are intertwined.

As just one example of this integrated approach, consider the Gothic cathedral, that lofty, light-filled house of worship marked by pointed arches, towering spires, and radiant stained-glass windows. Gothic cathedrals were erected during the High Middle Ages, following a bleak period when urban life had virtually ceased. Although religion was still the dominant force in European life, trade was starting to flourish once again, town life was reviving, and urban dwellers were beginning to prosper. In part as testimonials to their new wealth, cities and towns commissioned architects and hired workers to erect these soaring churches, which dominated the landscape for miles around and proclaimed the economic well-being of their makers.

We adopt an integrated approach to Western culture not just in considering how the arts are related to material conditions but also in looking for the common themes, aspirations, and ideas that permeate the artistic and literary expressions of every individual era. The creative accomplishments of an age tend to reflect a shared perspective, even when that perspective is not explicitly recognized at the time. Thus, each period possesses a unique outlook that can be analyzed in the cultural record. A good example of this phenomenon is Classical Greece in the fifth century B.C.E., when the ideal of moderation, or balance in all things, played a major role in sculpture, architecture, philosophy, religion, and tragic drama. The cultural record in other periods is not always as clear as that in ancient Greece, but shared qualities can often be uncovered that distinguish the varied aspects of culture in an era to form a unifying thread.

A corollary of this idea is that creative individuals and their works are very much influenced by the times in which they live. This is not to say that incomparable geniuses—such as Shakespeare in Renaissance England—do not appear and rise above their own ages, speaking directly to the human mind and heart in every age that follows. Yet even Shakespeare reflected the political attitudes and social patterns of his time. Though a man for the ages, he still regarded monarchy as the correct form of government and women as the inferiors of men.

THE SELECTION OF CULTURAL WORKS

The Western cultural heritage is vast, and any selection of works for a survey text reflects choices made by the authors. All the works we chose to include have had a significant impact on Western culture, but for different reasons. We chose some because they blazed a new trail, such as Picasso's *Demoiselles d'Avignon* (see Figure 19.22), which marked the advent of Cubism in painting, or Fielding's *Tom Jones*, one of the earliest novels. Other works were included because they seemed to embody a style to perfection, such as the regal statue called *Poseidon* (or *Zeus*) (see Figure 3.21), executed in the Classical style of fifth-century-B.C.E. Athens, or Dante's *Divine Comedy*, which epitomized

the ideals of the High Middle Ages. On occasion, we chose works on a particular topic, such as the biblical story of David and Goliath, and demonstrated how different sculptors interpreted it, as in sculptures by Donatello (see Figure 11.11), Verrocchio (see Figure 11.12), and Michelangelo (see Figure 12.20). Still other works caught our attention because they served as links between successive styles, as is the case with Giotto's frescoes (see Figure 10.20), or because they represented the end of an age or an artistic style, as in the haunting sculpture called *The Last Pagan* (see Figure 7.12). Finally, we included some works, especially paintings, simply because of their great beauty, such as Ingres's *Madame Rivière* (see Figure 17.7).

Through all the ages of Western cultural history, through all the shifting styles and tastes embodied in painting, sculpture, architecture, poetry, and song, there glows a creative spark that can be found in human beings in every period. This diversity is a hallmark of the Western experience, and we celebrate it in this book.

A CHALLENGE TO THE READER

The purpose of all education is and should be self-knowledge. This goal was first established by the ancient Greeks in their injunction to "Know thyself," the inscription carved above the entrance to Apollo's temple at Delphi. Self-knowledge means awareness of oneself and one's place in society and the world. Reaching this goal is not easy, because becoming an educated human being is a lifelong process, requiring time, energy, and commitment. But all journeys begin with a single step, and we intend this volume as a first step toward understanding and defining oneself in terms of one's historical and cultural heritage. Our challenge to the reader is to use this book to begin the long journey to self-knowledge.

A HUMANITIES PRIMER
How to Understand the Arts

INTRODUCTION

We can all appreciate the arts. We can find pleasure or interest in paintings, music, poems, novels, films, and many other art forms, both contemporary and historical. We don't need to know very much about art to know what we like, because we bring ourselves to the work: What we like has as much to do with who we are as with the art itself.

Many of us, for example, will respond positively to a painting like Leonardo da Vinci's *The Virgin of the Rocks*. The faces of the Madonna and angel are lovely; we may have seen images like these on Christmas cards or in other commercial reproductions. We respond with what English poet William Wordsworth calls the "first careless rapture," which activates our imaginations and establishes a connection between us and the work of art. However, if this is all we see, if we never move from a subjective reaction, we can only appreciate the surface, the immediate form, and then, perhaps subconsciously, accept without question the values it implies. We appreciate, but we do not understand.

Sometimes we cannot appreciate because we do not understand. We may reject Picasso's *Les Demoiselles d'Avignon*, for it presents us with images of women that we may not be able to recognize. These women may make us uncomfortable, and the values they imply may frighten us rather than please or reassure us. Rather than rapture, we may experience disgust; but when we realize that this painting is considered a groundbreaking work, we may wonder what we're missing and be willing to look deeper. (*The Virgin of the Rocks* and *Les Demoiselles d'Avignon* are discussed in the text on page 345 and pages 605–7, respectively.)

Leonardo da Vinci. *The Virgin of the Rocks.*

To understand a work of art (a building, a poem, a song, a symphony), we need to keep our "rapture" (our emotional response and connection) but make it less "careless," less superficial and subjective, less restricted to that which we recognize. We need to enrich our appreciation by searching for a meaning that goes beyond ourselves. This involves understanding the intent or goal of the artist, the elements of form present in the work, the ways in which those elements contribute to the artist's goal, the context within which the artwork evolved, and the connections of the work to other works. Understanding an artwork requires intellectual involvement as well as an emotional connection. The purpose of this primer is to provide you with some of the tools you will need to understand, as well as appreciate, literature, art, and music.

APPROACHES TO THE ANALYSIS OF LITERATURE, ART, AND MUSIC

When we analyze a work of art, we ask two questions: What is the artist trying to do, and how well is it done? We want to identify the intent of the work, and we want to evaluate its execution. To answer these questions, we can examine the formal elements of the work—an approach known as formalism—and we can explore its context—known as contextualism.

Formalism

A formal analysis is concerned with the aesthetic (artistic) elements of a work separate from context. This type of analysis focuses on medium and technique. The context of the work—where, when, and by whom a work was created—may be interesting, but is considered unnecessary to formalist interpretation and understanding. A formal analysis of a painting, sculpture, or architectural structure examines its line, shape, color, texture, and composition, as well as the artist's technical ability within the medium used; it is not concerned with anything extraneous to the work itself. A formal analysis of a literary work, such as a short story or novel, would explore the relationships among theme, plot, characters, and setting, as well as how well the resources of language—word choice, tone, imagery, symbol, and so on—are used to support the other elements. A formal analysis of a film would also explore theme, plot, characters (as developed both verbally and nonverbally), and setting, as well as how the resources of cinematography—camera techniques, lighting, sound, editing, and so on—support the other elements.

A formal analysis of *The Virgin of the Rocks* would examine the artist's use of perspective, the arrange-

PABLO PICASSO. *Les Demoiselles d'Avignon.*

ment of figures as they relate to each other and to the grotto that surrounds them, the technical use of color and line, the dramatic interplay of light and shadow (known as *chiaroscuro*). The same technical considerations would be explored in a formal analysis of *Les Demoiselles d'Avignon.* The fact that the two paintings were completed in 1483 and 1907, respectively, would be important only in terms of the technology and mediums available to the artists. In a formal analysis, time and place exist only within the work.

Contextualism

In contrast, a contextual analysis focuses on factors outside the work: why it was created, in response to what artistic, social, cultural, historical, and political forces, events, and trends; who the artist is, and what his or her intent and motives were in creating the work; how the work fits in with other works of the same genre of the same or different eras; and how the work fits in with the rest of the artist's body of work. Time and place are very important.

A contextual analysis of the da Vinci and Picasso paintings would include information about where and when each painting was completed; the conditions from which it arose; the prevailing artistic styles of the times; the life circumstances of the artists; and so on.

The paintings alone do not provide enough information for contextual inquiry. Similarly, contextual analysis of a novel by Dostoevsky would consider both his personal circumstances and the conditions in Russia and Europe when he wrote. A contextual analysis of a chorale and fugue by Bach would include information on Bach's life, his religious beliefs, and the political climate of Germany in the eighteenth century.

An Integrated Approach

In a strictly contextual analysis of an artwork, the work itself can sometimes be lost in the exploration of context. In a strictly formal analysis, important knowledge that can contribute to understanding may remain unknown. The most effective analyses, therefore, combine and integrate the two approaches, examining the formal elements of the work and exploring the context within which it was created. Such an approach is more effective and, in a sense, more honest than either the formal or the contextual approach alone. A work of art, whether a poem or a painting, a cathedral or a cantata, is a complex entity, as are the relationships it fosters between the artist and the art and between the art and its audience. The integrative approach recognizes these relationships and their complexity. This is the approach to artistic and cultural analysis most frequently used in *The Western Humanities.*

A Variety of Perspectives

Many students and critics of culture, while taking an integrative approach, are also especially interested in looking at things from a particular perspective, a set of interests or a way of thinking that informs and influences their investigations and interpretations. Common perspectives are the psychological, the feminist, the religious, the economic, and the historical.

People working from a psychological perspective look for meaning in the psychological features of the work, such as sexual and symbolic associations; they do a kind of retroactive psychological analysis of the artist. They might look for meaning in the facial expressions, gestures, and body positions of Mary and the angel in *The Virgin of the Rocks.* They might be interested in da Vinci's attitudes toward women and his relationships with them, and they might compare this painting with the *Mona Lisa* in a search for clues about who he was.

Someone working from a feminist perspective would examine the art itself and the context in which it arose from a woman's point of view. To take a feminist perspective is to ask how the work depicts women, what it says about women and their relationships in general, and how it may or may not reflect a patriarchal society. Many people have discussed the apparent hatred of women that seems to come through in Picasso's *Les Demoiselles d'Avignon.* At the same time, the work, in its size (8 feet by 7 feet 8 inches) and in the unblinking attitude of its subjects, suggests that these women have a kind of raw power. Feminist critics focus on such considerations.

Analysis from a religious perspective is often appropriate when a work of art originated in a religious context. The soaring spires and cruciform floor plans of medieval cathedrals reveal religious meaning, for example, as do Renaissance paintings depicting biblical characters. Many contemporary works of art and literature also have religious content. Religious analyses look to the use of symbolism, the representation of theological doctrines and beliefs, and intercultural connections and influences for meaning.

Someone approaching a work of art from an economic perspective focuses on its economic content—the roles and relationships associated with wealth. Often drawing upon Marx's contention that class is the defining consideration in all human relationships and endeavors, an economic analysis would examine both purpose and content: Was the work created as a display of power by the rich? How does it depict people of different classes? What is the artist saying about the distribution of wealth?

The historical perspective is perhaps the most encompassing of all perspectives, because it can include explorations of psychological, religious, and economic issues, as well as questions about class and gender in various times and places. Historical analysis requires an understanding of the significant events of the time and how they affect the individual and shape the culture. *The Western Humanities* most often takes a historical perspective in its views of art and culture.

The Vocabulary of Analysis

Certain terms and concepts are fundamental to the analysis of any artwork. We review several such general concepts and terms here, before moving on to a consideration of more specific art forms.

Any artwork requires a relationship between itself and its audience. **Audience** is the group for whom a work of art, architecture, literature, drama, film, or music is intended. The audience may be a single person, such as the Medici ruler to whom Machiavelli dedicated his political treatise *The Prince.* The audience can be a small group of people with access to the work, such as the monks who dined in the room where Leonardo da Vinci painted *The Last Supper* on the wall.

The audience can also be a special group of people with common interests or education; for example, films like *There's Something about Mary* and *Scream* are intended for a youthful audience. Sometimes the audience is limited by its own understanding of the art; we often feel excluded from what we don't understand. Consequently, some art requires an educated audience.

Composition is the arrangement of constituent elements in an individual work. In music, composition also refers to the process of creating the work.

Content is the subject matter of the work; content can be based on mythology, religion, history, current events, personal history, or almost any idea or feeling deemed appropriate by the artist.

Context is the setting in which the art arose, its own time and place. Context includes the political, economic, social, and cultural conditions of the time; it can also include the personal conditions and circumstances that shape the artist's vision.

A **convention** is an agreed-upon practice, device, technique, or form. A sonnet, for example, is a fourteen-line poem with certain specified rhyme schemes. A poem is not a sonnet unless it follows this formal convention. A convention of the theater is the "willing suspension of disbelief": We know that the events taking place before our eyes are not real, but we agree to believe in them for the duration of the play. Often, conventions in the arts are established as much by political powerbrokers as by artists. The Medicis and the Renaissance popes, for example, wanted portraits and paintings that glorified their reigns, and conventions in Renaissance art reflect these demands. Today, museum directors, wealthy individuals, and government funding agencies play a role in influencing the direction of contemporary art by supporting and showing the work of artists whose conventions they agree with or think are important.

Genre is the type or class to which a work of art, literature, drama, or music belongs, depending on its style, form, or content. In literature, for example, the novel is a genre in itself; the short story is another genre. In music, symphonies, operas, and tone poems are all different genres. Beginning in the Renaissance, genres were carefully distinguished from one another, and a definite set of conventions was expected whenever a new work in a particular genre was created.

The **medium** is the material from which an art object is made—marble or bronze, for example, in sculpture, or water colors or oils in painting. (The plural of *medium* in this sense is often *mediums;* when *medium* is used to refer to a means of mass communication, such as radio or television, the plural is *media*.)

Style is the combination of distinctive elements of creative execution and expression, in terms of both form and content. Artists, artistic schools, movements, and periods can be characterized by their style. Styles often evolve out of existing styles, as when High Renaissance style evolved into Mannerism in the sixteenth century, or in reaction to styles that are perceived as worn out or excessive, as when Impressionism arose to challenge Realism in the nineteenth century.

When we talk about **technique,** we are referring to the systematic procedure whereby a particular creative task is performed. If we were discussing a dancer's technique, we might be referring to the way he executes leaps and turns; a painter's technique might be the way she applies paint to a canvas with broad, swirling brushstrokes.

The dominant idea of a work, the message or emotion the artist intends to convey, is known as the **theme.** The theme, then, is the embodiment of the artist's intent. In a novel, for example, the theme is the abstract concept that is made concrete by character, plot, setting, and other linguistic and structural elements of the work. We often evaluate the theme of a work in terms of how well it speaks to the human condition, how accurate its truth is, how valuable its message or observation is. We usually make these judgments by exploring the extent to which the theme confirms or denies our own experience.

In addition to these general concepts and terms, each art form has its own vocabulary. These more specific terms will be introduced in the sections that follow on literary, artistic, and musical analysis, along with brief illustrative analyses in each area. These informal illustrations are meant not as definitive analyses but as examples of the kinds of productive questions you can ask as you approach a creative work. The analyses differ in their depth and level of detail.

✂ LITERARY ANALYSIS

Literary analysis begins with a consideration of various literary genres and forms. A work of literature is written either in **prose,** the ordinary language used in speaking and writing, or in **poetry,** a more imaginative and concentrated form of expression usually marked by meter, rhythm, or rhyme. Part of poetry's effect comes from the sound of words; it can often best be appreciated when spoken or read aloud. Prose is often divided into nonfiction (essays, biography, autobiography) and fiction (short stories, novels).

In literature, *genre* refers both to form—essay, short story, novel, poem, play, film script, television script—and to specific type within a form—tragedy, comedy, epic, lyric, and so on. According to Aristotle, a **tragedy** must have a tragic hero—a person of high stature who is brought down by his own excessive pride *(hubris);* he doesn't necessarily die at the end, but whatever his greatness was based upon is lost. A **comedy** is a story with a complicated and amusing plot; it usually ends with a happy and peaceful resolution of any conflicts. An **epic** poem, novel, or film is a relatively long recounting of the life of a hero or the glorious history of a people. A **lyric** poem is a short, subjective poem usually expressing an intense personal emotion. In a general sense, an epic tells a story and a lyric expresses an idea or feeling. Lyric poetry includes ballads (dramatic verse meant to be sung or recited, often by more than one singer or speaker), elegies (short, serious meditations, usually on death or other significant themes), odes (short lyric poems dealing with a single theme), and sonnets (formal fourteen-line poems identified by the arrangement of lines as either Italian [Petrarchan] or English [Shakespearean]).

In literature, the author's intent—the message or emotion the author wishes to convey—is usually discussed as the theme of the work. In an essay, the theme is articulated as the thesis: the idea or conclusion that the essay will prove or support. In a novel, story, or play, we infer the theme from the content and the development of ideas and imagery.

In fiction, the action of the story, what Aristotle calls "the arrangement of incidents," is the **plot.** There may be a primary plot that becomes the vehicle by which the theme is expressed, with subplots related to secondary (or even tertiary) themes. Plot can be evaluated by how well it supports the theme. Plot can also be evaluated according to criteria established by Aristotle in his *Poetics.* According to these criteria, the action expressed should be whole, with a beginning that does not follow or depend on anything else, a middle that logically follows what went before, and an end, or logical culmination of all prior action. The plot should be unified, so that every action is necessary and interrelated with all other actions. Few works of fiction adhere to these criteria completely; nevertheless, the criteria do provide a way of beginning to think about how a plot works.

Characters are also important both for themselves and for their effect on the plot and support of the theme. **Characters** provide the human focus, the embodiment, of the theme; they act out and are affected by the plot. The protagonist, or primary character, of the work is changed by the dramatic action of the plot and thus is a dynamic character; static characters remain unchanged throughout the story. An antagonist is a character in direct opposition to the protagonist. Some characters are stock characters, representing a type rather than an individual human being: the romantic fool, the nosy neighbor, the wise old woman, the vain beauty, the plain girl or dumb boy with a heart of gold.

Readers need to believe that characters' actions are authentic reactions to various events. The believability of a work of fiction—the writer's ability to express the truth—is called verisimilitude. Even in works of science fiction or fantasy, where events occur that could not occur in reality, readers must believe that what characters say and do make sense under the conditions described.

The background against which the action takes place is the **setting.** It can include the geographical location, the environment (political, social, economic) in which the characters live, the historical time in which the action takes place, and the culture and customs of the time, place, and people.

The story or poem is told from the point of view of the **narrator.** The narrator is not necessarily identical with the author of the work. The narrator (or **narrative voice**) can be examined and analyzed like any other element of the work. When a narrator seems to know everything and is not limited by time or place, the work has an omniscient point of view. Such a narrator tells us what everyone is thinking, feeling, and doing. When the story is told from the perspective of a single character who can relate only what he or she knows or witnesses, the work has a first-person point of view. Such a narrator is limited in his or her understanding. Thus, we need to consider the narrator in order to judge how accurate or complete the narrative is.

Sometimes a narrator proves to be unreliable, and we have to piece together an account of the story ourselves. Other times an author uses multiple narrators to tell a story from multiple points of view. William Faulkner uses this device in his novel *The Sound and the Fury* to show that a story can be fully told only when several different characters have a chance to speak. Japanese film director Akira Kurosawa uses a similar device in *Rashomon* to show that there are many equally valid—or invalid—versions of the truth.

A literary analysis of a drama, whether a play for the stage or a film script, will consider not only the elements already mentioned—theme, plot, character, setting, language, and so on—but also the technical considerations specific to the form. In theater, these would include the work of the director, who interprets the play and directs the actors, as well as stage design, light and sound design, costumes, makeup, and so on. In film, technical considerations would include direction, editing, cinematography, musical score, special effects, and so on.

Let's turn now to a poem by Shakespeare and see how to approach it to enrich our understanding. Identifying a poem's intent and evaluating its execution is called an *explication,* from the French *explication de texte.* An explication is a detailed analysis of a poem's meaning, focusing on narrative voice, setting, rhyme, meter, words, and images. An explication begins with what is immediately evident about the poem as a whole, followed by a more careful examination of its parts.

William Shakespeare (1564–1616) was not just a great playwright; he was also a great poet. His works portray human emotions, motives, and relationships that we recognize today as well as the conditions and concerns of his time. In this sense, they are an example of aesthetic universality, the enduring connection between a work of art and its audience.

Shakespeare's sonnets are his most personal work. Scholars disagree about whether they are generic love poems or are addressed to a specific person and, if the latter, who that person might be. Formally, an English (or Shakespearean) sonnet is a 14-line poem consisting of three 4-line stanzas, or quatrains, each with its own rhyme scheme, and a concluding 2-line stanza, or couplet, that provides commentary on the preceding stanzas. The rhyme scheme in a Shakespearean sonnet is abab cdcd efef gg; that is, the first and third lines of each quatrain rhyme with each other, as do the second and fourth lines, though the rhymes are different in each quatrain. The last two lines rhyme with each other.

The meter of most Shakespearean sonnets is iambic pentameter; that is, each line has five feet, or units ("pentameter"), and each foot consists of an iamb, an unaccented syllable followed by an accented syllable (as in *alone*). An example of iambic pentameter is, "My mistress' eyes are nothing like the sun"; each foot consists of an unaccented and an accented syllable, and there are five feet. Unrhymed iambic pentameter—the verse of most of Shakespeare's plays—is known as **blank verse.**

Sonnet 130 ("My mistress' eyes are nothing like the sun") is a poem that not only illustrates sonnet form but also showcases Shakespeare's wit and his attitude toward certain conventions of his time. The poem was originally written in Elizabethan English, which looks and sounds quite different from modern English. We reproduce it in modern English, as is customary today for Shakespeare's works.

Sonnet 130

My mistress' eyes are nothing like the sun;
Coral is far more red than her lips' red;
If snow be white, why then her breasts are dun;
If hairs be wires, black wires grow on her head.

I have seen roses damask'd, red and white,
But no such roses see I in her cheeks,
And in some perfumes is there more delight
Than in the breath that from my mistress reeks.

I love to hear her speak, yet well I know
That music hath a far more pleasing sound;

I grant I never saw a goddess go,
My mistress when she walks treads on the ground.

And yet, by heaven, I think my love as rare
As any she belied with false compare.

Because the poet's intent may not be immediately evident, paraphrasing each line or stanza can point the reader to the theme or meaning intended by the poet. Let's begin, then, by paraphrasing the lines:

My mistress' eyes are nothing like the sun;
 The speaker's lover's eyes are not bright.
Coral is far more red than her lips' red;
 Her lips are not very red, certainly not as red as coral.
If snow be white, why then her breasts are dun;
 Her breasts are mottled in color, not as white as snow.
If hairs be wires, black wires grow on her head.
 Her hair is black (not blond, as was the conventional beauty standard then, when poets referred to women's hair as "golden wires").

I have seen roses damask'd, red and white,
But no such roses see I in her cheeks,
 Her cheeks are not rosy.
And in some perfumes is there more delight
Than in the breath that from my mistress reeks.
 Her breath doesn't smell as sweet as perfume.

I love to hear her speak, yet well I know
That music hath a far more pleasing sound;
 Her voice doesn't sound as melodious as music.
I grant I never saw a goddess go,
My mistress when she walks treads on the ground.
 Although the speaker has never seen a goddess walk, he knows his lover does not float above ground, as goddesses are supposed to do, but walks on the ground, a mortal woman.

And yet, by heaven, I think my love as rare
As any she belied with false compare.
 His lover is as rare and valuable as any idealized woman glorified by false poetic comparisons.

Remember that to analyze a poem, we ask questions like, What is the theme of the poem, the poet's intent? How does Shakespeare support his point with specific images? From the paraphrased lines it is clear that the narrator is stating that his love is a real woman who walks upon the ground, not an unattainable ideal to be worshiped from afar. Idealized qualities are irrelevant to how he feels about her; the qualities he loves are the ones that make her human.

Closely examining each line of a poem helps to reveal the rhyme scheme (abab cdcd efef gg), the meter (iambic pentameter), and thus the form of the poem (sonnet). Explication of the formal elements of the poem would also include examining the use of language (such as word choice, imagery, comparisons, metaphors), the tone of the narrative voice, and so on.

To understand the context of the poem, we would consider the cultural climate of the time (was "courtly love" a prevalent cultural theme?); common contemporary poetic conventions (were many other poets proclaiming their eternal love for idealized women?); and the political, social, and economic conditions (what roles were open to women in Elizabethan England, and how were they changing? What influence might Queen Elizabeth have had on the poet's point of view? What comments about his society is Shakespeare making?)

Finally, we might consider how honest and accurate we find the emotional content of the poem to be, how relevant its truth. Are Shakespeare's observations germane to today, a time when the mass media present us with a nearly unattainable ideal as the epitome of female beauty?

✄ FINE ARTS ANALYSIS

As with literature, knowledge of a particular vocabulary helps us "speak the language" of art critics. The terms introduced here are in addition to those discussed earlier, such as *medium* and *technique*. They apply to all the visual arts, including drawing and painting, sculpture—the art of shaping material (such as wood, stone, or marble) into three-dimensional works of art—and architecture—the art and science of designing, planning, and building structures, usually for human habitation. In architecture, the critic would also pay attention to the blending of artistry and functionality (how well the structure fulfills its purpose).

Generally, art is more or less representational or more or less abstract. **Representational art** is true to human perception and presents a likeness of the world much as it appears to the naked eye. An important convention of representational art is **perspective,** the appearance of depth and distance on a two-dimensional surface. **Abstract art** presents a subjective view of the world, the artist's emotions or ideas; some abstract art simply presents color, line, or shape for its own sake.

The formal elements of visual art include line, shape, texture, color, composition, and so on. **Line** is the mark made by the artist, whether with pencil, pen, or paintbrush. Lines can be straight or curved, thick or thin, light or dark, spare or plentiful. **Color** is the use in the artwork of hues found in nature; **color** can enhance the sense of reality presented in a visual image, or it can distort it, depending on how it is used. The primary colors are red, blue, and yellow, and the secondary colors are orange (a combination of red and yellow), green (a combination of yellow and blue), and purple (a combination of blue and red). Blue, green, and purple hues are "cool" colors that appear to recede from the eye; red, yellow, and orange are "warm" colors that appear to move forward. Color has sym-

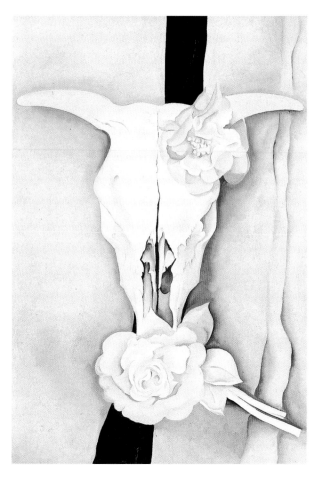

GEORGIA O'KEEFFE. *Cow's Skull with Calico Roses.*

bolic associations within specific historical and cultural settings. For example, in Western culture, white is a symbol of purity and is worn by brides. In Eastern cultures, white is a symbol of death; Chinese brides wear red to symbolize good luck.

How the artist arranges the work is referred to as the composition. Often the artist controls how the eye moves from one part to another by means of the composition. Through the composition the artist leads us to see the artwork in a particular way. The setting of an artwork is the time and place depicted in a representational work, as defined by visual cues—the people, how they are dressed, what they are doing, and so on.

With these terms in hand, let's consider *Cow's Skull with Calico Roses* by Georgia O'Keeffe (1887–1986), painted in 1931. What is the artist's intent? How well is that intent executed? Front and center we see the cow's skull, placed so the strong vertical line of the skull, accentuated by the skull's vertical midline crack, aligns with the center of the canvas. A broad band of black extending from the top of the canvas to the bottom behind the skull further reinforces the vertical axis, as do the wavy lines on the right. The skull's horns form a shorter, secondary horizontal line, creating a cross shape. At the bottom of the canvas, the black band seems to open; its expansion to the left is balanced by the rose stem in the lower right and the right-of-center rose at the top. The image overall is balanced and symmetrical, conveying a sense of stillness and repose rather than dynamic action.

The artist has not used broad or bold lines in her painting; rather, the lines of the skull and flowers are drawn delicately against the background; shading suggests contours and subtleties of lighting, and shadows blend softly. The surface is shallow and flat, conveying little sense of depth. The background material is ambiguous; is it cloth, paper, parchment, or some other material? The skull appears to float in front of this background. At the same time, the black band behind the skull seems to open into a mysterious space that recedes from the viewer.

The colors of the painting are muted, subtle, neutral—shades of black, gray, cream, and white. A slightly different color tone comes from the inside of the broken skull, where shades of tan and ochre are revealed. Within this world of muted tones, the white skull stands out rather starkly against the off-white background, and the flowers show up silvery gray against the white, beige, and black. The colors are quiet, almost somber, with a balance between the heavy black band and the other lighter-colored surfaces.

What are we to make of the image itself—a skull dressed up with cloth flowers? The animal almost appears to be eating or nuzzling one flower, and the other adorns its forehead. Many artists have used human skulls to remind us of our mortality, and in this painting suggestions of death and spirituality are reinforced, perhaps to the subconscious mind, by the cross shape that underlies the composition. In this context, the cow skull strikes an odd and discordant note. Cow skulls are often used to suggest the unforgiving nature of the desert, where animals and humans alike perish in a waterless, forbidding landscape. Here, the skull is transformed, first by its placement in an abstract setting and second by its adornment with artificial flowers. Is the image morbid, macabre? Is it humorous, playful, ironic? Or are we meant simply to see the skull in a new way, as a unique and interesting object, apart from the living animal it once was? Aged in the desert, bleached by the sun, the skull, though evocative of death, has its own stark beauty. The flowers too have their beauty; at the same time, the artist makes it clear that they are calico, not real. They are artificial, created by human hands to resemble living flowers.

Although the skull and flowers are painted realistically, the ambiguous background suggests that the artist is moving toward abstraction, toward an expression of feeling and mood rather than pure representation. The overall feeling evoked by the painting is one of contemplation, meditation. Faced with the juxtaposition of these incongruous objects, we are reminded of the intimate relationships between life and death, beauty and ugliness, art and nature.

How can we augment our appreciation and understanding of this painting with contextual knowledge? Georgia O'Keeffe grew up on a farm in Wisconsin, where she reveled in every detail of nature, bringing to it an attention and appreciation that would later be reflected in her paintings. She knew from an early age that she wanted to be an artist, and she studied art in Chicago and New York, developing a highly refined technique that quickly became recognized as uniquely her own. Among important early influences were the paintings and theories of Russian abstract artist Wassily Kandinsky, who believed that art and especially color had powerful spiritual effects. In 1929 O'Keeffe visited Taos, New Mexico, for the first time, where she became enraptured by the desert, the light, the colors of the landscape, the expanse of the sky. She was especially intrigued by bones—their form, shape, color, texture—and she shipped boxes of them back to her studio in New York to paint. Eventually she spent more and more time in the Southwest, developing a style that blended realism and abstraction. Her trademark was the selection and abstraction of an object or a view in nature, which she then transformed in accordance with her inner vision. She became known for her particular way of seeing and for her ability to enable others to see the same way.

When she painted *Cow's Skull with Calico Roses*, O'Keeffe was at a difficult time in her personal life. Perhaps depression led her to paint in subdued colors (rather than the brilliant colors of earlier and later paintings) and to focus on bones and other images of death (rather than the images of flowers for which she was already famous). Some have suggested that the seemingly suspended nature of the skull in this painting was suggestive of her own unsettled frame of mind. Whether or not personal details like these help us appreciate and understand the work, what is clear is that when we contemplate *Cow's Skull with Calico Roses*, we see not just the beauty of natural forms but also the power of nature to transform objects and the power of the artist to transform them once again.

MUSICAL ANALYSIS

Like literature and art, music has its own vocabulary, and we need to be familiar with it in order to analyze a composition. A basic distinction we can apply to music is the one between religious music, or **sacred music**—

such as Gregorian chants, Masses, requiems, and hymns—and **secular music**—such as symphonies, songs, and dances. Another distinction we can make is between vocal or choral music, which is sung and generally has lyrics (words), and instrumental music, which is written for and performed on instruments.

In music, composers choose among many different **forms,** or particular structures or arrangements of elements. Symphonies, songs, concertos, string quartets, sonatas, Masses, and operas are some of the many different forms in which composers may write their music. As in literature and the visual arts, various musical forms have been more or less popular according to the styles and fashions of the time. The madrigal, for example, was a popular vocal form of the Renaissance period; the church cantata was a common form in the Baroque period; and the symphony became the most important orchestral form beginning in the eighteenth century.

Music itself is a combination of tone, tempo, and texture. **Tone** is a musical sound of definite pitch (pitch is determined by the frequency of the air waves producing the sound). A set pattern of tones (or notes) arranged from low to high (or high to low) is known as a **scale.** The modern Western scale is the familiar do, re, mi, fa, sol, la, ti, do, with half steps in between the tones. In other cultures, more or fewer tones may be distinguished in a scale. The term tone can also refer to the quality of a sound. **Tempo** is the rate of speed of a musical passage, usually set or suggested by the composer. **Texture** describes the number and the nature of the voices or instruments employed and how the parts are combined. In music a theme is a characteristic musical idea upon which a composition is built or developed.

Melody is a succession of musical tones, usually having a distinctive musical shape, or line, and a definite rhythm (the recurrent alternation of accented and unaccented beats). **Harmony** is the simultaneous combination of two or more tones, producing a chord. More generally, harmony refers to the chordal characteristics of a work and the way in which chords interact with one another.

Music differs from literature and the visual arts in some important ways. First, unlike visual art, which does not change after the artist finishes it, music begins when the composition is complete. Like drama, music is lifeless until it is interpreted and performed. The written music represents the composer's intent, but the actual execution of the work is up to conductors and musicians.

A second difference is the fleeting, temporal nature of music. When we listen to live music, we hear it once and it's gone. We cannot study it like a painting or reread a passage as we can in a novel. Of course, recording devices and musical notation enable us to re-

visit music again and again, but by its very nature, music exists in time in a way that literature and the visual arts do not. For this reason, it is often particularly difficult to appreciate or understand a piece of music on first hearing; instead, we have to listen to it repeatedly.

Music is also more difficult to describe in words than literature or the visual arts. At best, words can only approximate, suggest, and refer to sounds. Sometimes it's helpful to use imagery from other sense modalities to describe a piece of music. What visual images does the work evoke? What colors? What textures? If you were to choreograph the work, how would the dancers move?

Finally, when we analyze a painting, we can reproduce it for our audience, and when we analyze a poem, we can reprint it. When we analyze music, we often have to hope that members of our audience know the work and can "hear" it in their heads. Alternatively, we can hope to generate enough interest in the work that they will want to make a point of hearing it themselves.

With these few basics in mind, let's consider a well-known musical work, *Rhapsody in Blue,* by George Gershwin (1898–1937). Even if you don't know this piece by name, it's very likely that you've heard it. It's been used in ads and in the sound tracks of numerous movies, including *Fantasia 2000;* it is also a standard accompaniment to images of New York City.

Imagine that you're seated in a concert hall and hearing this piece performed by a symphony orchestra (probably a "pops" orchestra, one that performs more popular classical music). When listening to a new piece of music or one you're not terribly familiar with, it's a good idea to simply try to get a sense of its general mood and character—again, focusing on the creator's intent. What emotions or ideas is the composer trying to convey? What musical elements does the composer use to execute that intent?

You'll notice, first of all, that the work is written for a small orchestra and a solo piano, the same instrumental configuration you would expect for a classical piano concerto (a concerto is a work for one or a few instruments and an orchestra, with much of its interest coming from the contrasts between the solo voice and the ensemble voice). But the opening notes of *Rhapsody in Blue* reveal something other than classical intentions: a solo clarinet begins low and sweeps up the scale in a seemingly endless "smear" of sound, finally reaching a high note, briefly holding it, and then plunging into the playful, zigzag melody that becomes one of the major themes of the work. Within moments, the orchestra enters and repeats the theme in the strings and brass, to be followed by the entry of the solo piano. Throughout the work, piano and orchestra alternate and combine to sing out beautiful melodies and create a varied and colorful texture. Variety also comes from different instrumentation of the themes and tunes, played first by a slinky muted trumpet, then by a sweet solo violin, later by a whole lush string section or a brash horn section.

You'll notice too the constant changes in tempo, now slower, now faster, almost as if the work is being improvised. Complex, syncopated, off-the-beat rhythms give the piece a jazzy feeling, and the combination of tones evokes the blues, a style of music in which certain notes are "bent," or lowered slightly in pitch, creating a particular sound and mood. The general feeling of the piece is upbeat, exciting, energetic, suggestive of a bustling city busy with people on the go. It may also make you think of Fred Astaire and Ginger Rogers movies you've seen on late-night TV— sophisticated, playful, casually elegant—and in fact, Gershwin wrote the music for some of their films.

What can we learn about this work from its title? Musical works often reveal their form in their title ("Fifth Symphony," "Violin Concerto in D," and so on). A rhapsody is a composition of irregular form with an improvisatory character. Although you may have heard themes, repetitions, and echoes in *Rhapsody in Blue,* you probably were not able to discern a regular form such as might be apparent in a classical sonata or symphony. The word *rhapsody* also suggests rapture, elation, bliss, ecstasy—perhaps the feelings conveyed by that soaring first phrase on the clarinet. *Blue,* on the other hand, suggests the melancholy of the blues. The dissonance created by the combination of the two terms—like the combinations and contrasts in the music—creates an energetic tension that arouses our curiosity and heightens our interest.

In making these observations about *Rhapsody in Blue,* we've been noticing many of the formal elements of a musical work and answering questions that can be asked about any composition: What is the form of the work? What kind of instrumentation has the composer chosen? What is the primary melodic theme of the work? What tempos are used? How do the instruments or voices work together to create the texture? What is the overall mood of the piece—joyful, sad, calm, wild, a combination?

Now, at your imaginary concert, there may be notes in the program that will provide you with some context for the work. You'll find that George Gershwin was a gifted and classically trained pianist who quit school at 15 and went to work in Tin Pan Alley, a district in New York City where popular songs were written and published. His goal in writing *Rhapsody in Blue* (1924) was to blend classical and popular music, to put the energy and style of jazz into a symphonic format.

Many listeners "see" and "hear" New York City in this piece. Gershwin created his own unique idiom, a fast-paced blend of rhythm, melody, and harmony that followed certain rules of composition but gave the impression of improvisation. He went on to write musicals, more serious compositions like the opera *Porgy and Bess,* and music for Hollywood films, all in his distinctive style. Information like this can help you begin to compare *Rhapsody in Blue* both with other works of the time and with other works by Gershwin. As in any analysis, integrating the formal and the contextual rounds out your interpretation and understanding of the work.

CONCLUSION

These three brief analyses should give you some ideas about how literature, art, and music can be approached in productive ways. By taking the time to look more closely, we gain access to the great works of our culture. This statement leads us to another issue: What makes a work "great"? Why do some works of art have relevance long beyond their time, while others are forgotten soon after their designated "fifteen minutes of fame"? These questions have been debated throughout history. One answer is that great art reflects some truth of human experience that speaks to us across the centuries. The voice of Shakespeare, the paintings of Georgia O'Keeffe, and the music of George Gershwin have a universal quality that doesn't depend on the styles of the time. Great art also enriches us and makes us feel that we share a little more of the human experience than we did before.

As both a student of the humanities and an audience member, you have the opportunity to appreciate and understand the arts. Despite the formal nature of academic inquiry, an aesthetic analysis is a personal endeavor. In looking closely at a creative work, seeking the creator's intent and evaluating its execution, you enrich your appreciation of the work with understanding; you bring the emotional reaction you first experienced to its intellectual completion. As twentieth-century composer Arnold Schoenberg once wrote, "You get from a work about as much as you are able to give to it yourself." This primer has been intended to help you learn how to bring more of yourself to works of art, to couple your subjective appreciation with intellectual understanding. With these tools in hand, you won't have to say you don't know much about art but you know what you like; you'll be able to say you know *about* what you like.

ARS VTINAM MORES
ANIMVMQVE EFFINGERE
POSSES PVLCHRIOR IN TER
RIS NVLLA TABELLA FORET
MCCCCLXXXVIII

11 THE EARLY RENAISSANCE
Return to Classical Roots
1400–1494

Believing they had broken radically with the past, Italian artists and intellectuals in the fifteenth century began to speak of a rebirth of civilization. Since the nineteenth century, the term *Renaissance* (meaning "rebirth") has described the cultural and artistic activities of the fifteenth and sixteenth centuries that began in Italy and spread northward. The Renaissance profoundly altered the course of Western culture, although scholars have differing interpretations of the significance of this first modern period.

THE RENAISSANCE: SCHOOLS OF INTERPRETATION

In the 1860s, Swiss historian Jacob Burckhardt, agreeing with the fifteenth-century Italians, asserted that the Renaissance was a rebirth of ideas after centuries of cultural stagnation. He maintained that a new way of understanding the world had emerged, as the Italians looked back to ancient Greece and Rome for inspiration and declared themselves part of a revitalized civilization that was distinctive and superior to the immediate past.

By the mid–twentieth century, Burckhardt's interpretation began to be viewed as too simplistic. According to some scholars, the Italians, after the fall of Rome, never lost sight of their Classical roots. These historians considered the revival of learning in the fifteenth century to be more of a shift in educational and cultural emphasis than a rediscovery of antiquity. They also noted that the Renaissance had at least two phases, the Early and the High, each with different contributions.

◀ **Detail** DOMENICO GHIRLANDAIO. *Giovanna degli Albizzi Tornabuoni.* Ca. 1489–1490. Tempera and (?) oil on panel, 29½ × 19¼". Madrid, Thyssen-Bornemisza Collection (cat. no. 46).

Figure 11.1 DOMENICO GHIRLANDAIO. *Old Man with a Child.* Ca. 1480. Panel 24½ × 18″. Louvre. *This double portrait summarizes many of the new secular values of the Early Renaissance, such as its human-centeredness and its preference for simple scenes. The work's subject, a man possibly with his grandchild, indicates the important role that the family played during the time. The age's commitment to direct observation of the physical world is evident in the treatment of the man's diseased nose (rosacea) and the landscape glimpsed through the open window.*

Since the 1960s, a third interpretation has dominated Renaissance studies. In this view, the Renaissance label should be used cautiously and only to describe what was happening in learning and the arts, not in politics and society. The authors of this book tend to agree with this third interpretation. In politics, economics, and society, Italy in the 1400s differed little from Italy in the 1300s; however, the Italians of the 1400s did start down a new *cultural* path (Figure 11.1).

This chapter examines the first phase of this new cultural style, the Early Renaissance (1400–1494); Chapter 12 is devoted to the brief High Renaissance (1494–1520) and to Early Mannerism (1520–1564), an anti-Classical phase of the Renaissance. Chapter 13 considers Northern Humanism, the Northern Renaissance, the early-sixteenth-century religious reformations, and Late Mannerism (1564–1603), when Renaissance style was slowly undermined by new trends (Timeline 11.1).

EARLY RENAISSANCE HISTORY AND INSTITUTIONS

For most of the fifteenth century, the city-states of northern Italy were prosperous and peaceful enough to sustain upper-class artists and writers. This supportive climate encouraged the innovations of Renaissance culture. By the end of the century, however, disputes among Italy's city-states and a shift in maritime trade from the Mediterranean to the Atlantic, coupled with the French invasion of Florence in 1494, had dimmed northern Italy's cultural preeminence.

Italian City-States During the Early Renaissance

The erratic fortunes of Italy's economy were a major factor in the region's politics in this period. The northern Italian city-states had emerged from the High Middle Ages in 1300 as Europe's leading commercial center and manufacturer of finished woolens (see Chapter 9), but by 1500 they had been eclipsed by various European nations to the north. In the 1300s, Italian population, productivity, and prosperity declined because of the Black Death and the birth of the English woolen industry. Although the Italians made a limited economic recovery in the 1400s, history was moving against them. Even their domination of international banking was challenged by German businessmen.

During the Early Renaissance, five Italian states competed for dominance: the Republic of Venice, the Duchy of Milan, the Republic of Florence, the Papal States, and the Kingdom of Naples (Map 11.1). Other small states, such as the artistic and intellectual centers of Ferrara and Modena, played minor but crucial roles. In the first half of the fifteenth century, the Italian states waged incessant wars among themselves, shifting sides when it was to their advantage.

The continuous warfare and the uncertain economy provided the conditions for the emergence of autocratic rulers called *signori,* who were from ruling families or elitist factions. Taking advantage of economic and class tensions, these autocrats pledged to solve local problems, and in so doing they proceeded to accumulate power in their own hands. What influence the guilds, the business leaders, and the middle class had wielded in the fourteenth century gave way to these despots, ending the great medieval legacy of republicanism in Venice, Milan, and Florence.

Under the *signori,* the conduct of warfare also changed. Technological developments improved weaponry, and battles were fought with mercenary troops led by *condottieri,* soldiers of fortune who sold their military expertise to the highest bidder. But the most significant change in Renaissance warfare was the

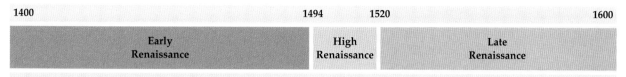

Timeline 11.1   STAGES OF THE ITALIAN RENAISSANCE

1400		1494	1520		1600
	Early Renaissance	High Renaissance		Late Renaissance	

Map 11.1   THE STATES OF ITALY DURING THE RENAISSANCE, CA. 1494
This map shows the many states and principalities of Italy in the Early Renaissance. **Consider** the size of each state with its role in competing for dominance of the Italian peninsula. **Notice** the large number of states in the north as compared with the small number in the south. **Notice** also the four forms of government—duchy, republic, kingdom, and papal states. **Identify** the major ports of the Italian state system. **What** geographic advantage made the Papal States such a force in Italian politics?

emergence of diplomacy as a peaceful alternative to arms, a practice that gradually spread throughout the Continent. The Italian regimes began sending representatives to other states, and it soon became customary for these diplomats to negotiate peace settlements. In turbulent fifteenth-century Italy, these agreements seldom lasted long—with the notable exception of the

Peace of Lodi. This defensive pact, signed in 1454 by Milan, Florence, and Venice, established a delicate balance of power and ensured peace in Italy for forty years.

The Peace of Lodi came apart in 1494, when a French army led by Charles VIII (r. 1483–1498) entered Italy in the hope of promoting French monarchic

Figure 11.2 PEDRO BERRUGUETE (?). *Federico da Montefeltro and His Son Guidobaldo.* Ca. 1476–1477. Oil on panel, 4′5⅛″ × 2′5⅞″. Galleria Nazionale della Marche, Urbino. *Urbino, under the Montefeltro dynasty, was transformed from a sleepy hill town with no cultural history into a major center of Renaissance life. Federico, the founder of the dynasty and one of the greatest condottieri of his day, was created duke of Urbino and captain of the papal forces by Pope Sixtus IV in 1474. Federico then devoted his energies to making Urbino a model for Italian Renaissance courts. In this portrait, the seated Federico wears the armor of a papal officer while reading a book—symbols that established him as both a soldier and a scholar, later the ideal of Castiglione's Courtier. At the duke's right knee stands his son and heir, Guidobaldo, wearing an elaborate robe and holding a scepter, a symbol of power. Federico's dream ended with his son, the last of the Montefeltro line.*

At the Urbino court, artists combined Flemish and Italian styles, as in this double portrait. The internal lighting, emanating from some unseen source on the left, is adopted from the tradition pioneered by Jan van Eyck; the profile portrait of the duke follows the Italian practice, based on portrait heads rendered on medals. This double portrait was probably painted by Pedro Berruguete, Spain's first great Renaissance artist, who studied painting in Naples and worked briefly in Urbino before returning to his homeland.

ambitions. Outside Italy, three events further weakened the region's prospects for regaining its position as a major economic power: the fall of Constantinople in 1453, Portugal's opening of the sea route around Africa to India at the end of the century, and Columbus's Spanish-sponsored voyage to the New World.

These three events shifted the focus of international trade from the Mediterranean to the Atlantic. The fall of Constantinople to the Ottoman Turks in 1453 temporarily closed the eastern Mediterranean markets to the Italian city-states. At the same time, by virtue of the wide-ranging global explorations they sponsored, some European powers—most notably Portugal and Spain—were extending their political and economic interests beyond the geographic limits of continental Europe.

Before the Italian city-states were eclipsed by other European powers, however, upper-class families enjoyed unprecedented wealth, which they used to cultivate their tastes in literature and art and thus substantially determine the culture of the Early Renaissance (Figure 11.2). One reason for the importance these families gave to cultural matters is that they put high value on family prestige and on educating their sons for their predestined roles as heads of family businesses and their daughters as loyal wives and successful household managers (Figure 11.3). The courts of the local rulers, or *grandi,* became places where educated men—and, on occasion, women—could exchange ideas and discuss philosophical issues.

Although the status of women did not improve appreciably, more were educated than ever before. Many ended up behind the walls of a convent, however, if their parents could not afford the costly dowry expected of an upper-class bride. The few upper-class women with an independent role in society were those who had been widowed young. The women at the ducal courts who exercised any political influence did so because of their family alliances. One of the most powerful of these women was Lucrezia Borgia [loo-KRET-syah BOR-juh] (1480–1519), the illegitimate daughter of Pope Alexander VI. Married three times before the age of twenty-one, she held court in Ferrara and was the patron of many writers and artists. Most women who tried to exercise real power, however, found it unattainable.

Florence, the Center of the Renaissance

Amid the artistic and intellectual activity occurring throughout Italy, Florence, the capital of the Tuscan region, was the most prominent of the city-states. After 1300 Florence's political system went through three phases, evolving from republic to oligarchy to family

Timeline 11.2   THE EARLY RENAISSANCE IN FLORENCE, 1400–1494

1400							1494
Early Renaissance							
1403–1424 Ghiberti's north doors, Florentine Baptistery	1425 Invention of linear perspective (Brunelleschi)	1424–1452 Ghiberti's east doors, Florentine Baptistery	1438–1445 Fra Angelico's *Annunciation*	1461 Completion of Pazzi Chapel by Brunelleschi	1473–1475 Verrocchio's *David*	1480s Botticelli's *Primavera* and *The Birth of Venus*	1483 Leonardo da Vinci's *The Virgin of the Rocks*
	1425–1428 Masaccio's frescoes for Santa Maria Novella	1430–1432 Donatello's *David*		1462 Founding of Platonic Academy, Florence			
		1435 Alberti's *On Painting*					

rule. During these turbulent political times, however, Florentine artists and writers made their city-state the center of the Early Renaissance (Timeline 11.2).

The republic, which began in the fourteenth century with hopes for political equality, fell into the hands of a wealthy oligarchy. This oligarchy, composed of rich bankers, merchants, and successful guildsmen and craftsmen, ruled until the early fifteenth century, when the Medici family gained control. The Medicis dominated Florentine politics and cultural life from 1434 to 1494, sometimes functioning as despots.

The Medicis rose from modest circumstances. Giovanni di Bicci de' Medici [jo-VAHN-nee dee BEET-chee day MED-uh-chee] (1360–1429) amassed the family's first large fortune through banking and close financial ties with the papacy. His son Cosimo

Figure 11.3 DOMENICO GHIRLANDAIO. *Giovanna degli Albizzi Tornabuoni.* Ca. 1489–1490. Tempera and (?) oil on panel, 29½ × 19¼". Madrid, Thyssen-Bornemisza Collection (cat. no. 46). *This likeness of Giovanna degli Albizzi Tornabuoni (1468–1486) embodies the Florentine ethos of family, city, and church. Her husband, Lorenzo Tornabuoni, a member of a prominent Florentine family, commissioned it as a memorial. Probably painted after his wife's death, it was much admired by Lorenzo, who, according to household records, kept it hanging in his bedroom, even after his remarriage. The subject's gold bodice is decorated with emblems—interlaced Ls and diamonds—which are symbolic of Lorenzo and his family. The brooch, the coral necklace, and the prayer book allude to Giovanna's high social status and piety. In the background, the Latin epigram "O Art, if thou were able to depict conduct and the soul, no lovelier painting would exist on earth" evokes the Renaissance ideal that equates physical beauty with moral perfection. The epitaph is based on a line from an ancient Roman poet.*

(1389–1464) added to the Medicis' wealth and outmaneuvered his political enemies, becoming the unacknowledged ruler of Florence. He spent his money on books, paintings, sculptures, and palaces, and, claiming to be the common man's friend, he was eventually awarded the title *Pater patriae,* Father of His Country—a Roman title revived during the Renaissance.

Cosimo's son, Piero, ruled for only a short time and was succeeded by his son Lorenzo (1449–1492), called the Magnificent because of his grand style of living. Lorenzo and his brother Giuliano controlled Florence until Giuliano was assassinated in 1478 by the Pazzi family, rivals of the Medicis. Lorenzo brutally executed the conspirators and then governed autocratically for the next fourteen years.

Within two years of Lorenzo's death, the great power and prestige of Florence began to weaken. Two events are symptomatic of this decline in Florentine authority. The first was the invasion by Charles VIII's French army in 1494. The invasion initiated a political and cultural decline that would eventually overtake Italy, whose small city-states could not withstand the incursions of the European monarchies. The French army drove the Medici family from Florence; they remained in exile until 1512.

The second event was the iconoclastic crusade against the city led by the Dominican monk Fra Savonarola [sav-uh-nuh-ROH-luh] (1452–1498). He opposed the Medicis' rule and wanted to restore a republican form of government. In his fire-and-brimstone sermons, he denounced Florence's leaders and the city's infatuation with the arts. He eventually ran afoul of the papacy and was excommunicated and publicly executed, but not before he had had an enormous effect on the citizens—including the painter Botticelli, who is said to have burned some of his paintings while under the sway of Savonarola's reforming zeal.

The Resurgent Papacy, 1450–1500

The Great Schism was ended by the Council of Constance in 1418, and a tattered Christendom reunited under a Roman pope (see Chapter 10). By 1447 the so-called Renaissance popes were in command and had turned their attention to consolidating the Papal States and pursuing power. Like the secular despots, these popes engaged in war and, when that failed, diplomacy. They brought artistic riches to the church but also lowered its moral tone by accepting bribes for church offices and filling positions with kinsmen. But above all, these popes patronized Renaissance culture.

Three of the most aggressive and successful of these church rulers were Nicholas V (pope 1447–1455), Pius II (pope 1458–1464), and Sixtus IV (pope 1471–1484). Nicholas V, who had been librarian for Cosimo de' Medici, founded the Vatican Library, an institution virtually unrivaled today for its holdings of manuscripts and books. He also continued the rebuilding of Rome begun by his predecessors. Pius II, often considered the most representative of the Renaissance popes because of his interest in the Greek and Roman classics and in writing poetry himself, rose rapidly through the ecclesiastical ranks. This clever politician practiced both war and diplomacy with astounding success. As a student of the new learning and as a brilliant writer in Latin, Pius II attracted intellectuals and artists to Rome. His personal recollections, or *Commentaries,* reveal much about him and his turbulent times.

Sixtus IV came from the powerful and scheming della Rovere family, and he increased his personal power through nepotism, the practice of giving offices to relatives. He continued the papal tradition of making Rome the most beautiful city in the world. The construction of the Sistine Chapel, later adorned with paintings by Botticelli and Michelangelo, was his greatest achievement (see Chapter 12).

THE SPIRIT AND STYLE OF THE EARLY RENAISSANCE

Drawing inspiration from ancient Greek and Roman models, the thinkers and the artists of the Early Renaissance explored such perennial questions as, What is human nature? How are human beings related to God? and What is the best way to achieve human happiness? Although they did not reject Christian explanations outright, they were intrigued by the secular and humanistic values of the Greco-Roman tradition and the answers they might provide to these questions. They also rightfully claimed kinship with certain fourteenth-century predecessors such as the writer Petrarch and the artist Giotto (see Chapter 10).

Those artists, scholars, and writers who are identified with the Early Renaissance and who embodied its spirit were linked, through shared tastes and patronage, with the entrepreneurial nobility, the progressive middle class, and the secular clergy. Until about 1450, most artistic works were commissioned by wealthy patrons for family chapels in churches and for public buildings; later, patrons commissioned paintings and sculptures for their private dwellings.

Even though artists, scholars, and writers stamped this age with their fresh perspectives, some of the old cultural traits remained. Unsettling secular values emerged in the midst of long-accepted religious beliefs, creating contradictions and tensions within the society. In other ways, however, the past held firm, and certain values seemed immune to change. For example, Early Renaissance thought made little headway in science, and church patronage still strongly affected the evolution of the arts and architecture, despite the growing impact of the urban class on artistic tastes.

The artists, scholars, and writers who flourished in the Early Renaissance were almost exclusively men, in contrast with the Middle Ages, when women occasionally played cultural roles. Recent scholarship has pointed out that women living in the Italian Renaissance were subjected to new constraints, especially in well-to-do families. For example, the learned Laura Cereta [che-RAY-tah] (1469–1499), daughter of a prominent family in Brescia, silenced herself at eighteen years of age, after meeting a firestorm of harsh criticism for her outspokenness. Nevertheless, a volume of her published letters has survived, in one of which she defended herself against her critics, asserting the right of women to be educated the same as men.

Humanism, Scholarship, and Schooling

Toward the end of the 1300s, Italy's educated circles became fascinated by ancient Roman civilization. Inspired by Petrarch's interest in Latin literature and language, scholars began to collect and translate Roman manuscripts uncovered in monastic libraries and other out-of-the-way depositories. There was a shift in emphasis from the church Latin of the Middle Ages to the pure Latin style of Cicero, the first-century B.C.E. Roman writer whose eloquent essays established a high moral and literary standard (see Chapter 5).

In the 1400s, these scholars spoke of their literary interests and new learning as *studia humanitatis.* They defined this term, which may be translated as "humanistic studies," as a set of intellectual pursuits that included moral philosophy, history, grammar, rhetoric, and poetry. At first, the men who studied these disciplines read the appropriate works in Latin, but after the Greek originals began to appear about 1400 and the study of ancient languages spread, they learned from the Greek texts as well.

In response to the demand for humanistic learning, new schools sprang up in most Italian city-states. In these schools was born the Renaissance ideal of an education intended to free or to liberate the mind—a liberal education. To that end, study was based on the recently recovered Latin and Greek works rather than on the more narrowly defined curriculum of scholasticism and Aristotelianism that had been favored in the Middle Ages.

The first Renaissance scholars, who were primarily searching for original Latin manuscripts, were philologists—that is, experts in the study of languages and linguistics. In time, they came to call themselves humanists because of their training in the *studia humanitatis.* These early humanists created a branch of learning, now called textual criticism, that compares various versions of a text to determine which one is most correct or authentic. They recognized that knowledge of the evolution of language was necessary to make a critical judgment on the authenticity of a text. As a result of their studies, they revealed writing errors committed by medieval monks when they copied ancient manuscripts—revelations that, in the case of religious documents, raised grave problems for the church.

The most spectacular application of textual criticism was made by Lorenzo Valla (1406–1457), who exposed the Donation of Constantine as a forgery. Throughout the Middle Ages, this famous document had been cited by the popes as proof of their political authority over Christendom. By the terms of the document, the Roman emperor Constantine gave the popes his western lands and recognized their power to rule in them. But by comparing the Latin of the fourth century, when Constantine reigned, with the Latin of the eighth century, when the document first came to light, Valla concluded that the Donation must have been produced then and not in the fourth century.

Other humanists played an active role in the life of their states, modeling themselves on the heroes of the Roman republic. Outstanding among them is Leonardo Bruni (1374–1444), who typifies the practical, civic humanist. A one-time chancellor, or chief secretary, of Florence's governing body, or *signoria,* Bruni also worked for both the Medicis and the papacy and wrote the *History of the Florentine People.* This work reflected his humanistic values, combining as it did his political experience with his knowledge of ancient history. To Bruni, the study of history illuminated contemporary events. Bruni and the other civic humanists, through their writings and their governmental service, set an example for later generations of Florentines and helped infuse them with love of their city. Moreover, by expanding the concept of humanistic studies, they contributed new insights to the ongoing debate about the role of the individual in history and in the social order.

An important consequence of humanistic studies was the rise of educational reforms. Vittorino da Feltre [veet-toe-REE-no dah FEL-tray] (1378–1446) made the most significant contributions. Vittorino favored a curriculum that exercised the body and the mind—the ideal of the ancient Greek schools. His educational theories were put into practice at the school he founded in Mantua at the ruler's request. At this school, called the Happy House, Vittorino included

SLICE OF LIFE
Battle of the Sexes, Fifteenth-Century Style

LAURA CERETA
In Defense of the Education of Women

In this letter, dated January 13, 1488, eighteen-year-old Laura Cereta responds fiercely to a male critic whose praise she finds patronizing to her as a woman. She then sets him straight about the intellectual needs of women of that time.

My ears are wearied by your carping. You brashly and publicly not merely wonder but indeed lament that I am said to possess as fine a mind as nature ever bestowed upon the most learned man. You seem to think that so learned a woman has scarcely before been seen in the world. You are wrong on both counts. . . .

I would have been silent, believe me, if that savage old enmity of yours had attacked me alone. . . . But I cannot tolerate your having attacked my entire sex. For this reason my thirsty soul seeks revenge, my sleeping pen is aroused to literary struggle, raging anger stirs mental passions long chained by silence. With just cause I am moved to demonstrate how great a reputation for learning and virtue women have won by their inborn excellence, manifested in every age as knowledge. . . .

Only the question of the rarity of outstanding women remains to be addressed. The explanation is clear: women have been able by nature to be exceptional, but have chosen lesser goals. For some women are concerned with parting their hair correctly, adorning themselves with lovely dresses, or decorating their fingers with pearls and other gems. Others delight in mouthing carefully composed phrases, indulging in dancing, or managing spoiled puppies. Still others wish to gaze at lavish banquet tables, to rest in sleep, or, standing at mirrors, to smear their lovely faces. But those in whom a deeper integrity yearns for virtue, restrain from the start their youthful souls, reflect on higher things, harden the body with sobriety and tri-als, and curb their tongues, open their ears, compose their thoughts in wakeful hours, their minds in contemplation, to letters bonded to righteousness. For knowledge is not given as a gift, but [is gained] with diligence. The free mind, not shirking effort, always soars zealously toward the good, and the desire to know grows ever more wide and deep. It is because of no special holiness, therefore, that we [women] are rewarded by God the Giver with the gift of exceptional talent. Nature has generously lavished its gifts upon all people, opening to all the doors of choice through which reason sends envoys to the will, from which they learn and convey its desires. The will must choose to exercise the gift of reason. . . .

I have been praised too much; showing your contempt for women, you pretend that I alone am admirable because of the good fortune of my intellect. . . . Do you suppose, O most contemptible man on earth, that I think myself sprung [like Athena] from the head of Jove? I am a school girl, possessed of the sleeping embers of an ordinary mind. Indeed I am too hurt, and my mind, offended, too swayed by passions, sighs, tormenting itself, conscious of the obligation to defend my sex. For absolutely everything—that which is within us and that which is without—is made weak by association with my sex.

Interpreting This Slice of Life **Describe** the ways Cereta responds to her critic. **What** are some of the types of women she lists? **How** does she portray herself? According to Cereta, **what** are some of the talents God has given to women? **Compare and contrast** Cereta's arguments with those used by modern feminists.

humanistic studies along with the medieval curriculum. A major innovation was the stress on physical exercise, which arose from his emphasis on moral training. At first, only the sons and daughters of Mantuan nobility attended his school, but gradually the student body became more democratic as young people from all classes were enrolled. Vittorino's reforms were slowly introduced into the new urban schools in northern Europe, and their model—the well-rounded student of sound body, solid learning, and high morals—helped to lay the foundation for future European schools and education.

Thought and Philosophy

The Italian humanists were not satisfied with medieval answers to the perennial inquiries of philosophy because those answers did not go beyond Aristotelian philosophy and Christian dogma. Casting their nets wider, the Renaissance thinkers concluded that the ancients had given worthwhile responses to many of the same issues as Christians and that they should not be dismissed simply because they were non-Christian.

Renaissance scholars came to advocate more tolerance toward unorthodox beliefs and began to focus on the important role played by the individual in society. Individual fulfillment became a leading Renaissance idea and remains a central notion in Western thought today. During the Renaissance, the growing emphasis on the individual resulted in a more optimistic assessment of human nature—a development that in time led to a rejection of Christianity's stress on original sin.

Throughout the 1400s, a small group of scholars from the Byzantine world, living and working in Rome, Florence, and Venice, actively gave shape to the Italian Renaissance. As teachers of Greek, these overseas scholars introduced Italy's first generation of humanists to the many ancient manuscripts not seen in the West for nearly a thousand years. Then, in 1453, with the fall of Constantinople to the Ottoman Turks, a fresh wave of Byzantine scholars, teachers, and intellectuals arrived in Italy, bearing more precious manuscripts (see Encounter in Chapter 10). Thereafter, the humanists began to focus increasingly on Greek language, literature, and, eventually, philosophy. The philosophy of Plato found a home in Italy in 1462 when Cosimo de' Medici established the Platonic Academy at one of his villas near Florence. Here, scholars gathered to examine and to discuss the writings of Plato as well as those of the Neo-Platonists. In turn, these scholars would reinterpret Platonism in ways that would later influence early Christian theology. The academy was under the direction of the brilliant humanist Marsilio Ficino [mar-SILL-e-o fe-CHEE-no] (1433–1499), whom Cosimo commissioned to translate Plato's works into Latin.

In two major treatises, Ficino made himself the leading voice of Florentine Neo-Platonism by harmonizing Platonic ideas with Christian teachings. Believing that Platonism came from God, Ficino began with the principle that both thought systems rested on divine authority. Like Plato, Ficino believed that the soul was immortal and that complete enjoyment of God would be possible only in the afterlife, when the soul was in the divine realm. Ficino also revived the Platonic notion of free will—the power of humans to make of themselves what they wish. In Ficino's hands, free will became the source of human dignity because human beings were able to choose to love God.

Ficino had the most powerful impact on the Early Renaissance when he made Plato's teaching on love central to Neo-Platonism. Following Platonism, he taught that love is a divine gift that binds all human beings together. Love expresses itself in human experience by the desire for and the appreciation of beauty in its myriad forms. Platonic love, like erotic love, is aroused first by the physical appearance of the beloved. But Platonic love, dissatisfied by mere physical enjoyment, cannot rest until it moves upward to the highest spiritual level, where it finally meets its goal of union with the Divine. Under the promptings of Platonism, the human form became a metaphor of the soul's desire for God. Many Renaissance writers and artists came under the influence of Ficino's Neo-Platonism, embracing its principles and embodying them in their works. Sandro Botticelli, for example, created several allegorical paintings in which divine love and beauty were represented by an image from pre-Christian Rome—Venus, goddess of love (Figure 11.4).

Ficino's most prized student, Pico della Mirandola [PEE-koh DAYL-lah me-RAHN-do-lah] (1463–1494), surpassed his master's accomplishments by the breadth of his learning and the virtuosity of his mind. Pico—a wealthy and charming aristocrat—impressed everyone with his command of languages, his range of knowledge, and his spirited arguments. His goal was the synthesis of Platonism and Aristotelianism within a Christian framework that also encompassed Hebraic, Arabic, and Persian ideas. Church authorities and traditional scholars attacked Pico's efforts once they grasped the implication of his ambitious project—that all knowledge shared basic common truths and that Christians could benefit from studying non-Western, non-Christian writings.

Pico's second important contribution—the concept of individual worth—had been foreshadowed by Ficino. Pico's *Oration on the Dignity of Man* gives the highest expression to this idea, which is inherent in the humanist tradition. According to Pico, human beings, endowed with reason and speech, are created as a microcosm of the universe. Set at the midpoint in the scale of God's creatures, they are blessed with free will, which enables them either to raise themselves to God or to sink lower than the beasts. This liberty to determine private fate makes human beings the masters of their individual destinies and, at the same time, focuses attention on each human being as the measure of all things—a Classical belief now reborn.

Architecture, Sculpture, and Painting

It was in architecture, sculpture, and painting that the Renaissance made its most dramatic break with the medieval past. The **Early Renaissance style** was launched in Florence by artists who wanted to make a complete break with the Late Gothic style (Figure 11.5). Led by the architect Filippo Brunelleschi [brunayl-LAYS-kee] (1377–1446), this group studied the ruins of Classical buildings and ancient works of sculpture to unlock the secrets of their harmonious style. They believed that once the Classical ideals were rescued from obscurity, new works could be fashioned that captured the spirit of ancient art and architecture without slavishly copying it.

Figure 11.4   SANDRO BOTTICELLI. *The Birth of Venus.* 1480s. Tempera on canvas, 5'8" × 9'1".
Uffizi Gallery, Florence. *With the paintings of Botticelli, the nude female form reappeared in
Western art for the first time since the Greco-Roman period. Botticelli's* Venus *contains many
Classical echoes, such as the goddess's lovely features and her modest pose. But the artist used
these pre-Christian images to convey a Christian message and to embody the principles of Fi-
cino's Neo-Platonist philosophy.*

Figure 11.5   LEONE BATTISTA ALBERTI. Tempio Malatestiano
(Malatesta Temple) (Church of San Francesco). Ca. 1450. Rimini, Italy. *Although unfinished, this church strikingly demonstrates the revolution in architecture represented by Early
Renaissance ideals. Nothing could be further from the spires of
Late Gothic cathedrals than this simple, symmetrical structure
with its plain facade, post-and-lintel entrance, rounded arches,
and Classical columns. Designed by the leading theoretician of the
new style, the Malatesta Temple served as a model for artists and
architects of the later Renaissance.*

Artistic Ideals and Innovations Guided by Brunelleschi's findings, architects, sculptors, and painters made the Classical principles of balance, simplicity, and restraint the central ideals of the Early Renaissance style. The heaviest debt to the past was owed by the architects, for they revived the Classical orders—the Doric, the Ionic, and the Corinthian. The new buildings, though constructed to accommodate modern needs, were symmetrical in plan and relied on simple decorative designs. The theoretician of Early Renaissance style and its other guiding light was Leone Battista Alberti [ahl-BAIR-tee] (1404–1472), who wrote at length on Brunelleschi's innovations and published a highly influential book on the new painting. Alberti believed that architecture should embody the humanistic qualities of dignity, balance, control, and harmony and that a building's ultimate beauty rested on the mathematical harmony of its separate parts.

Sculpture and painting, freed from their subordination to architecture, regained their ancient status as independent art forms and in time became the most cherished of the visual arts. Renaissance sculptors and painters aspired to greater realism than had been achieved in the Gothic style, seeking to depict human musculature and anatomy with a greater degree of credibility. Sculptors, led by this period's genius Donatello [dah-nah-TEL-lo] (about 1386–1466), revived Classical practices that had not been seen in the West for more than a thousand years: the freestanding figure; the technique of contrapposto, or a figure balanced with most of the weight resting on one leg (see Figure 3.22); the life-size nude statue; and the equestrian statue.

Whereas architecture and sculpture looked back to ancient Greek and Roman traditions, developments in painting grew from varied sources, including the Islamic world (see Encounter) and the Late Medieval world, though the most important influence was the art of the Florentine painter Giotto. In the early fourteenth century, Giotto had founded a new realistic and expressive style (see Chapter 10), on which Florentine painters began to build at the opening of the fifteenth century. Much of Giotto's genius lay in his ability to show perspective, or the appearance of spatial depth, in his frescoes, an illusion he achieved largely through the placement of the figures (see Figure 10.20). Approximately one hundred years after Giotto, painters learned to enhance the realism of their pictures by the use of linear perspective, the most significant artistic innovation of the age.

The invention of linear perspective was another of Brunelleschi's accomplishments. Using principles of architecture and optics, he conducted experiments in 1425 that provided the mathematical basis for achieving the illusion of depth on a two-dimensional surface (and, coincidentally, contributed to the enhancement of the status of the arts by grounding them in scholarly learning). Brunelleschi's solution to the problem of linear perspective was to organize the picture space around the center point, or **vanishing point.** After determining the painting's vanishing point, he devised a structural grid for placing objects in precise relation to each other within the picture space. He also computed the ratios by which objects diminish in size as they recede from view, so that pictorial reality seems to correspond visually with physical accuracy. He then subjected the design to a mirror test—checking its truthfulness in its reflected image.

When the camera appeared in the nineteenth century, it was discovered that the photographic lens "saw" nature according to Brunelleschi's mathematical rules. After the 1420s, Brunelleschi's studies led to the concept of Renaissance space, the notion that a composition should be viewed from one single position. For four hundred years, or until first challenged by Manet in the nineteenth century, linear perspective and Renaissance space played a leading role in Western painting (see Chapter 18).

A second type of perspective, atmospheric or aerial, was perfected by painters north of the Alps in the first half of the fifteenth century, although the Italian painter Masaccio was the first to revive atmospheric perspective in the 1420s, based on the Roman tradition. Through the use of colors, these artists created an illusion of depth by subtly diminishing the tones as the distance between the eye and the object increased; at the horizon line, the colors become grayish and the objects blurry in appearance. When atmospheric perspective was joined to linear perspective, as happened later in the century, a greater illusion of reality was achieved than was possible with either type used independently.

Again commenting on the innovations of Brunelleschi was Alberti, who published a treatise in 1435 that elaborated on the mathematical aspects of painting and set forth brilliantly the humanistic and secular values of the Early Renaissance. Alberti was an aristocratic humanist with both a deep knowledge of Classicism and a commitment to its ideals. In his treatise, he praised master painters in rousing terms, comparing their creativity to God's—a notion that would have been considered blasphemous by medieval thinkers. He asserted that paintings, in addition to pleasing the eye, should appeal to the mind with optical and mathematical accuracy. But paintings, he went on, should also present a noble subject, such as a Classical hero, and should be characterized by a small number of figures, by carefully observed and varied details, by graceful poses, by harmonious relationships among all elements, and by a judicious use of colors. These Classical ideals were quickly adopted by Florentine artists eager to establish a new aesthetic code.

Figure 11.6   FILIPPO BRUNELLESCHI. Cathedral Dome, Florence. 1420–1436. Ht. of dome from floor 367'. *After the dome of the Florence cathedral was erected according to Brunelleschi's plan, another architect was employed to add small galleries in the area above the circular windows. But the Florentine authorities halted his work before the galleries were fully installed, leaving the structure in its present state.*

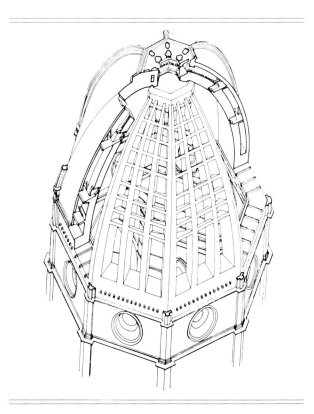

Figure 11.7   FILIPPO BRUNELLESCHI. Design for Construction of Dome of Florence Cathedral. *Brunelleschi designed the dome of the Florence cathedral with an inner and an outer shell, both of which are attached to the eight ribs of the octagonal-shaped structure. Sixteen smaller ribs, invisible from the outside, were placed between the shells to give added support. What held these elements together and gave them stability was the lantern, based on his design, that was anchored to the dome's top sometime after 1446.*

Architecture   In the High Middle Ages, most architects were stonemasons and were regarded as artisans, like shoemakers or potters. But by the fifteenth century, the status of architects had changed. Because of the newly discovered scientific aspects of their craft, the leading architects were now grouped with those practicing the learned professions of medicine and law. By 1450 Italian architects had freed architecture from Late Gothicism, as well as from the other arts. Unlike Gothic cathedrals adorned with sculptures and paintings, these new buildings drew on the Classical tradition for whatever simple decorative details were needed. This transformation became the most visible symbol of Early Renaissance architecture.

Although Brunelleschi established the new standards in architecture, most of his buildings have been either destroyed or altered considerably by later hands. However, the earliest work to bring him fame still survives in Florence largely as he had planned it—the dome of the city's cathedral (Figure 11.6). Although the rest of the cathedral—nave, transept, and

choir—was finished before 1400, no one had been able to devise a method for erecting the projected dome until Brunelleschi received the commission in 1420. Using the learning he had gained from his researches in Rome as well as his knowledge of Gothic building styles, he developed an ingenious plan for raising the dome, which was virtually completed in 1436.

Faced with a domical base of 140 feet, Brunelleschi realized that a hemispheric dome in the Roman manner, like the dome of the Pantheon, would not work (see Figure 5.14). Traditional building techniques could not span the Florentine cathedral's vast domical base, nor could the cathedral's walls be buttressed to support a massive dome. So he turned to Gothic methods, using diagonal ribs based on the pointed arch. This innovative dome had a double shell of two relatively thin walls held together by twenty-four stone ribs, of which only eight are visible. His crowning touch was to add a lantern that sits atop the dome and locks the ribs into place (Figure 11.7). The dome's rounded windows echo the openings in the upper nave walls, thereby ensuring that his addition would harmonize with the existing elements. But the octagonal-shaped dome was Brunelleschi's own creation and expresses a logical, even inevitable, structure. Today, the cathedral still dominates the skyline of Florence, a lasting symbol of Brunelleschi's creative genius.

Brunelleschi's most representative building is the Pazzi Chapel, as the chapter house, or meeting room, of the monks of Santa Croce is called. This small church embodies the harmonious proportions and Classical features that are the hallmark of the Early Renaissance style. In his architectural plan, Brunelleschi centered a dome over an oblong area whose width equals the dome's diameter and whose length is twice its width and then covered each of the chapel's elongated ends with a barrel vault. Double doors opened into the center wall on one long side, and two rounded arch windows flanked this doorway. A loggia, or porch, which Brunelleschi may not have designed, preceded the entrance (Figure 11.8). Inside the chapel, following the Classical rules of measure and proportion, Brunelleschi employed medallions, rosettes, **pilasters** (or applied columns), and square panels. In addition to these Classical details, the rounded arches and the barrel vaults further exemplify the new Renaissance style (Figure 11.9). His Classical theories were shared by Florence's humanist elite, who found religious significance in mathematical harmony. Both they and Brunelleschi believed that a well-ordered building such as the Pazzi Chapel mirrored God's plan of the universe.

The other towering figure in Early Renaissance architecture was Alberti. Despite the influence of his ideas, which dominated architecture until 1600, no completed building based on his design remains. A splendid unfinished effort is the Tempio Malatestiano in Rimini (see Figure 11.5), a structure that replaced the existing church of San Francesco. Rimini's despot, Sigismondo Malatesta (1417–1468), planned to have himself, his mistress, and his court buried in the refurbished structure, and he appointed Alberti to supervise the church's reconstruction.

Alberti's monument represents the first modern attempt to give a Classical exterior to a church. Abandoning the Gothic pointed arch, he designed this church's unfinished facade with its three rounded arches after a nearby triumphal arch. He framed the arches with Corinthian columns, one of his favorite decorative devices. Although the architect apparently planned to cover the church's interior with a dome comparable to Brunelleschi's on the Florentine cathedral, Malatesta's fortunes failed, and the projected temple had to be abandoned. Nevertheless, Alberti's unfinished church was admired by later builders and helped to point the way to the new Renaissance architecture.

Sculpture Like architecture, sculpture blossomed in Florence in the early 1400s. Donatello, the leader of the sculptural revival, was imbued with Classical ideals but obsessed with realism. He used a variety of techniques—expressive gestures, direct observation, and mathematical precision—to reproduce what his eyes saw. Donatello accompanied Brunelleschi to Rome to study ancient art, and he adapted linear perspective as early as 1425 into a small **relief** called *The Feast of Herod* (Figure 11.10). The subject is the tragic end of John the Baptist, Florence's patron saint, as recounted in Mark 6:20–29. In Donatello's square bronze panel, the saint's severed head is being displayed on a dish to King Herod at the left, while the scorned Salome stands near the right end of the table. A puzzled guest leans toward the ruler, who recoils with upraised hands; two children at the left back away from the bloody head; and a diner leans back from the center of the table—all depicted under the rounded arches of the new Brunelleschian architecture. The sculpture's rich details and use of linear perspective point up the horror of the scene and thus achieve the heightened realism that was among the artistic goals of this era. The scene's vanishing point runs through the middle set of arches, so that the leaning motions of the two figures in the foreground not only express their inner turmoil but also cause them to fall away from the viewer's line of sight.

Donatello also revived the freestanding male nude, one of the supreme expressions of ancient art. Donatello's bronze *David*, probably executed for Cosimo de' Medici, portrays David standing with his left foot on the severed head of the Philistine warrior Goliath—a pose based on the biblical story (Figure 11.11). This sculpture had a profound influence on later sculptors, who admired Donatello's creation but produced rival interpretations of David (Figure 11.12). Donatello and his successors used the image of David to pay homage to male power—a major preoccupation of Renaissance artists and intellectuals.

Like other Renaissance masters, Donatello owed debts to Classical artists, but he also challenged them by adapting their principles to his own times. For example, the Roman statue of Marcus Aurelius (see Figure 5.10) inspired Donatello's bronze called the *Gattamelata*, the first successful equestrian sculpture in over twelve hundred years (Figure 11.13). As Donatello's *David* portrays the subtleties of adolescent male beauty, his *Gattamelata* pays homage to mature masculine power. This work honored the memory of Erasmo da Narni, a Venetian *condottiere* nicknamed Gattamelata, or "Honey Cat." The warrior's pose resembles the Roman imperial style, but in almost every other way, the sculptor violates the harmonious ideas of ancient art.

Figure 11.8 (Inset), FILIPPO BRUNELLESCHI AND OTHERS. Exterior, Pazzi Chapel, Santa Croce Church. 1433–1461. Florence. *The Pazzi Chapel's harmonious facade reflects the Classical principles of the Early Renaissance style: symmetry and simplicity. By breaking the rhythm of the facade with the rounded arch, the architect emphasizes its surface symmetry so that the left side is a mirror image of the right side. Simplicity is achieved in the architectural decorations, which are either Greco-Roman devices or mathematically inspired divisions.*

Figure 11.10 DONATELLO. *The Feast of Herod.* Ca. 1425. Gilt bronze, 23½" square. Baptismal font, San Giovanni, Siena. *The first low-relief sculpture executed in the Early Renaissance style,* The Feast of Herod *is a stunning example of the power of this new approach to art. Its theatrical force arises from the successful use of linear perspective and the orderly placement of the figures throughout the three rooms.*

◀ **Figure 11.9** FILIPPO BRUNELLESCHI. Interior. Pazzi Chapel, Santa Croce Church. Ca. 1433–1461. 59'9" long × 35'8" wide. Florence. *Decorations on the white walls of the Pazzi Chapel's interior break up its plain surface and draw the viewer's eye to the architectural structure: pilasters, window and panel frames, medallions, capitals, and dome ribs. The only nonarchitecturally related decorations are the terra-cotta sculptures by Luca della Robbia of the four evangelists and the Pazzi family coat of arms, mounted inside the medallions.*

Figure 11.11 DONATELLO. *David.* Ca. 1430–1432. Bronze, ht. 62¼". Bargello, Florence. *The David and Goliath story was often allegorized into a prophecy of Christ's triumph over Satan. But Donatello's sculpture undermines such an interpretation, for his* David *is less a heroic figure than a provocative image of refined sensuality, as suggested by the undeveloped but elegant body, the dandified pose, and the incongruous boots and hat. Donatello's* David *is a splendid modern portrayal of youthful male power, self-aware and poised on the brink of manhood.*

Figure 11.12 ANDREA DEL VERROCCHIO. *David.* 1473–1475. Bronze, ht. 4′2″. Bargello, Florence. *Verrocchio's* David *inaugurated the tradition in Renaissance Florence of identifying the Jewish giant-killer with the city's freedom-loving spirit. A masterpiece of bravado, Verrocchio's boyish hero stands challengingly over the severed head of Goliath. In its virility, this work surpasses the sculpture that inspired it, Donatello's* David *(see Figure 11.11). Florence's ruling council liked Verrocchio's statue so much that they placed it in the Palazzo Vecchio, the seat of government, where it remained until Michelangelo's* David *(see Figure 12.20) displaced it. Verrocchio's* David *was restored in 2003, bringing back to the original the gold patina in the locks of hair, the borders of the clothes and boots, and the pupils of the eyes. With the restoration of the gold leaf gilding, restorers have concluded that the statue originally was intended for display indoors.*

Figure 11.13 DONATELLO. *Equestrian Monument of Erasmo da Narni, Called "Gattamelata."* 1447–1453. Bronze, approx. 11 × 13′. Piazza del Santo, Padua. *This equestrian statue of the condottiere was funded by his family but authorized by a grateful Venetian senate in honor of his military exploits. Conceiving of the dead military leader as a "triumphant Caesar," Donatello dressed him in Classical costume and decorated his saddle and armor with many allusions to antique art, such as flying cupids and victory depicted as a goddess.*

THE SPIRIT AND STYLE OF THE EARLY RENAISSANCE

Figure 11.14 DONATELLO. Detail of *"Gattamelata."* 1447–1453. Piazza del Santo, Padua. *Donatello deliberately designed the monument's stern, deeply lined, and serious face to conform to the Renaissance ideal of a strong military commander.*

Most significant, the rider's face owes its sharp realism—firm jawline, bushy eyebrows, widely set eyes, and close-cropped hair—to fifteenth-century sources, especially to the cult of the ugly, an aesthetic attitude that claimed to find moral strength in coarse features that did not conform to the Classical ideals (Figure 11.14). Since this work was commissioned after the hero's death and since Donatello had no way of knowing how the soldier looked, he sculptured the

Figure 11.15 LORENZO GHIBERTI. *The Annunciation.* Panel from the north doors of the Baptistery. 1403–1424. Gilt bronze, 20½ × 17¾". Florence. *Ghiberti's rendition of the Annunciation was typical of his panels on the north doors. Mary and the angel are placed in the shallow foreground and are modeled almost completely in the round. The background details, including a sharply foreshortened representation of God on the left, are scarcely raised from the metal. The contrast between these design elements enhances the illusion of depth.*

face to conform to his notion of a strong-minded general. The massive horse, with flaring nostrils, open mouth, and lifted foreleg, seems to be an extension of the soldier's forceful personality.

The only serious rival to Donatello in the Early Renaissance was another Florentine, Lorenzo Ghiberti [gee-BAIR-tee] (about 1381–1455), who slowly adapted to the new style of art. In 1401 he defeated Brunelleschi in a competition to select a sculptor for the north doors of Florence's Baptistery. The north doors consist of twenty-eight panels, arranged in four columns of seven panels, each depicting a New Testament scene. These doors, completed between 1403 and 1424, show Ghiberti still under the influence of the International Gothic style that prevailed in about 1400. Illustrative of this tendency is the panel *The Annunciation* (Luke 1:26–38), which depicts the moment when Mary learns from an angelic messenger that she will become the mother of Christ (Figure 11.15). The Gothic quatrefoil, or four-leafed frame, was standard for these panels, and many of Ghiberti's techniques are typical of the Gothic style—the niche in which the Virgin stands, her swaying body, and the angel depicted in flight. Nevertheless, Ghiberti always exhibited a strong feeling for Classical forms and harmony, as in the angel's well-rounded body and Mary's serene face.

The artistic world of Florence was a rapidly changing one, however, and Ghiberti adapted his art to conform to the emerging Early Renaissance style of Donatello. Between 1425 and 1452, Ghiberti brought his mature art to its fullest expression in the east doors,

the last of the Baptistery's three sculptured portals. These panels, larger than those on the north doors, depict ten scenes from the Old Testament. Most of the Gothic touches have been eliminated, including the framing quatrefoils, which are now replaced with square panels (Figure 11.16).

One of the sublime panels from the east doors is the one depicting the story of the brothers Cain and Abel (Figure 11.17), taken from the Book of Genesis. This panel shows, in many ways, Ghiberti's growing dedication to Classical ideals, seen, for example, in the graceful contrapposto of the standing figures and their proportional relationships. This work translates Albertian aesthetics into bronze by creating an illusion of depth. According to Ghiberti's *Commentaries,* the sculptor's purpose was not illusion for illusion's sake but, rather, an articulate visual presentation of the biblical story. Five incidents from the story of Cain and Abel are illustrated: (1) Cain and Abel as children with their parents, Adam and Eve, at the top left; (2) Cain and Abel making sacrifices before an altar, at the top right; (3) Cain plowing with oxen and Abel watching his sheep, in the left foreground and left middle, respectively; (4) Cain slaying Abel with a club, in the right middle; and (5) Cain being questioned by God, in the right foreground.

Painting The radical changes taking place in architecture and sculpture were minor compared with the changes in painting. Inspired by Classicism though lacking significant examples from ancient times, painters were relatively free to experiment and to define their own path. As in the other arts of the 1400s, Florentine painters led the way and established the standards for the new style—realism, linear perspective, and psychological truth (convincing portrayal of emotional states). This movement climaxed at the end

Figure 11.17 LORENZO GHIBERTI. *The Story of Cain and Abel.* Detail from the east doors of the Baptistery (the *Gates of Paradise*). 1424–1452. Gilt bronze, 31¼ × 31¼". Florence. *This exquisite panel from the Florence Baptistery's east doors is a testament to Ghiberti's absorption of Early Renaissance taste. He followed Brunelleschi's new rules for linear perspective by placing the vanishing point in the middle of the tree trunks in the center of the panel, and he adhered to Alberti's principle of varied details by adding the oxen, sheep, and altar.*

◀ **Figure 11.16** LORENZO GHIBERTI. *Gates of Paradise.* East doors of the Baptistery. 1424–1452. Gilt bronze, ht. approx. 17'. Florence. *The ten scenes depicted on these doors are based on Old Testament stories, taken from the books of Genesis through Kings. Reading from top left to right, then back and forth, and ending at bottom right, the panels begin with an illustration of the opening chapters of Genesis followed by others representing events in the lives of Cain and Abel, Noah, Abraham, Isaac and Jacob, Joseph, Moses, Joshua, David, and Solomon. Taking heed of medieval artistic tradition, Ghiberti placed several dramatic episodes from the life of each biblical character in a single panel. Each panel was formed into a wax model, then cast in bronze, and gilded with gold. According to Giorgio Vasari, the Renaissance artist and writer, Michelangelo, on first seeing the doors, described them as "worthy of Paradise"—the name by which they are still known—the* Gates of Paradise. *In 1991 Ghiberti's original doors were moved inside to Florence's Duomo Museum and duplicate doors replaced them on the Baptistery.*

of the century with the early work of Leonardo da Vinci.

After 1450 Florence's dominance was challenged by Venetian painters, who were forging their own artistic tradition. Venice, having won its freedom from the Byzantine Empire only in the High Middle Ages, was still in the thrall of Byzantine culture (see Chapter 7). As a result, Venetian painters and their patrons showed a pronounced taste for the stylized effects and sensual surfaces typical of Byzantine art. However, a distinct school of Venetian painters emerged, which eventually was to have a major impact on the course of painting in the West.

North of the Alps, a third Early Renaissance development was taking place in Burgundy and the Low Countries. There, the painters pursued an art more religious than that of Italy and closer in spirit to the Late Gothic. The northern artists concentrated on minute details and landscapes rather than on the problems of depth and composition that concerned Italy's painters. This survey confines itself to the major figures in the Florentine school, which is divided into two generations, and to the founder of the Venetian school.

The guiding genius of the revolution in painting in the earlier Florentine school was the youthful Masaccio [mah-ZAHT-cho] (1401–1428), whose career was

Figure 11.18 MASACCIO. *The Holy Trinity.* 1427 or 1428. Fresco, 21′10½″ × 10′5″. Santa Maria Novella, Florence. *Masaccio achieved a remarkable illusion of depth in this fresco by using linear and atmospheric perspective. Below the simulated chapel he painted a skeleton in a wall sarcophagus (not visible in this photograph) with a melancholy inscription reading, "I was once that which you are, and what I am you also will be." This* memento mori, *or reminder of death, was probably ordered by the donor, a member of the Lenzi family. His tomb is built into the floor and lies directly in front of the fresco.*

probably cut short by the plague. He adopted mathematical perspective in his works almost simultaneously with its invention by Brunelleschi. In the history of Western painting, Masaccio's *Holy Trinity* fresco is the first successful depiction in painting of the new concept of Renaissance space. His design for this fresco in the church of Santa Maria Novella, Florence,

shows that he was well aware of the new currents flowing in the art of his day. The painting offers an architectural setting in the style of Brunelleschi, and the solidity and vitality of the figures indicate that Masaccio had also absorbed the values of Donatello's new sculpture. Masaccio's fresco portrays the Holy Trinity—the three divine beings who make up the Christian idea of God—within a simulated chapel (Figure 11.18). Jesus' crucified body appears to be held up by God the Father, who stands on a platform behind the cross; between the heads of God and Jesus is a dove, symbolizing the Holy Spirit and completing the Trinitarian image. Mary and Saint John, both clothed in contemporary dress, flank the holy trio. Mary points dramatically to the Savior. Just outside the chapel's frame, the donors kneel in prayer—the typical way of presenting patrons in Renaissance art.

In the *Holy Trinity* fresco, Masaccio uses a variety of innovations. He is the first painter to show light falling from a single source, in this instance, from the left, bathing the body of Christ and coinciding with the actual lighting in Santa Maria Novella. This realistic feature adds to the three-dimensional effect of the well-modeled figures. The use of linear perspective further heightens the scene's realism. Finally, the perspective, converging to the midpoint between the kneeling donors, reinforces the hierarchy of beings within the fresco: from God the Father at the top to the human figures at the sides. In effect, mathematical tidiness is used to reveal the divine order—an ideal congenial to Florence's intellectual elite.

A second fresco by Masaccio, *The Tribute Money,* painted in the Brancacci Chapel of the church of Santa Maria del Carmine, Florence, is recognized as Masaccio's masterpiece (Figure 11.19). This fresco illustrates the Gospel account (Matthew 17:24–27) in which Jesus advises Peter, his chief disciple, to pay the Roman taxes. Because this painting depicts a biblical subject virtually unrepresented in Christian art, it was probably commissioned by a donor to justify a new and heavy Florentine tax. Whether the fresco had any effect on tax collection is debatable, but other artists were captivated by Masaccio's stunning technical effects: the use of perspective and **chiaroscuro,** or the modeling with light and shade.

The Tribute Money fresco follows the continuous narrative form of medieval art. Three separate episodes are depicted at the same time—in the center, Jesus is confronted by the tax collector; on the left, Peter, as foretold by Jesus, finds a coin in the mouth of a fish; and, on the right, Peter pays the coin to the Roman official. Despite this Gothic effect, the fresco's central section is able to stand alone because of its spatial integrity and unified composition. Jesus is partially en-

Figure 11.19   MASACCIO. *The Tribute Money.* Ca. 1425. Fresco, 8'2⅜" × 19'8¼". Santa
Maria del Carmine, Florence. *This fresco represents the highest expression of the art of Masac-*
cio, particularly in his realistic portrayal of the tax collector. This official, who appears twice, first
confronting Christ in the center and then receiving money from Peter on the right, is depicted
with coarse features—a typical man of the Florentine streets. Even his posture, though rendered
with Classical contrapposto, suggests a swagger—a man at home in his body and content with
his difficult occupation.

circled by his apostles, and the tax gatherer, viewed
from the back, stands to the right. In this central group,
the heads are all at the same height, for Masaccio
aligned them according to Brunelleschi's principles.
Fully modeled in the round, each human form occupies a precise, mathematical space.

Painters such as the Dominican friar Fra Angelico
(about 1400–1455) extended Masaccio's innovations.
Fra Angelico's later works, painted for the renovated
monastery of San Marco in Florence and partially
funded by Cosimo de' Medici, show his mature blending of biblical motifs in Renaissance space. The *An-*
nunciation portrays a reflective Virgin receiving the
angel Gabriel (Figure 11.20). Mary and Gabriel are
framed in niches in the Gothic manner, but the other
elements—the mastery of depth, the simplicity of gestures, the purity of colors, and the integrated scene—
are rendered in the new, simple Renaissance style.
The painting's vanishing point is placed to the right of
center in the small barred window looking out from
the Virgin's bedroom. The loggia [LOH-je-uh], or open
porch, in which the scene takes place was based
on a new architectural fashion popular among Florence's wealthy elite. Religious images abound in this
painting; the enclosed garden symbolizes Mary's vir-

ginity, and the barred window attests to the purity of
her life. Because of his gracious mastery of form and
space, Fra Angelico's influence on later artists was
pronounced.

One of those he influenced was Piero della Francesca [PYER-o DAYL-lah frahn-CHAY-skah] (about
1420–1492), a great painter of the second Florentine
generation, who grew up in a Tuscan country town
near Florence. His panel painting *The Flagellation* shows
the powerful though mysterious aesthetic effects of his
controversial style (Figure 11.21). The sunlight flooding
the scene unites the figures, but the composition places
them in two distinct areas. At the extreme left sits
Pilate, the judge, on a dais. The painting's subject—
the scourging of Christ before his crucifixion—is
placed to the left rear. Reinforcing this odd displace-
ment are the figures on the right, who are apparently
lost in their own conversation. Aesthetically this
strange juxtaposition arises because della Francesca
has placed the horizon line around the hips of the figures beating Christ, causing the three men on the right
to loom in such high perspective; thus the men in the
foreground appear to be indifferent to Christ and unaware of his importance. The effect is distinctly unsettling in a religious scene. The modern world, which

Figure 11.20   Fra Angelico. *Annunciation.* 1438–1445. Fresco, 7′6″ × 10′5″. Monastery of San Marco, Florence. *Fra Angelico's portrayal of the Virgin at the moment when she receives the news that she will bear the baby Jesus is a wonderful illustration of the painter's use of religious symbols. Mary's questioning expression and her arms crossed in a maternal gesture help to establish the painting's subject. Moreover, the physical setting of the scene, bare except for the rough bench on which she sits, suggests an ascetic existence—an appropriate detail for the painting's original setting, a monastery.*

loves conundrums, has developed a strong passion for the private vision of della Francesca as represented in his art.

Sandro Botticelli [baht-tuh-CHEL-lee] (1445–1510) is the best representative of a lyrical aspect of this second generation and one of the most admired painters in the Western tradition. One of the first Florentine artists to master both linear and atmospheric perspec-

tive, he was less interested in the technical aspects of painting than he was in depicting languid beauty and poetical truth.

Until the 1480s, Botticelli's art was shaped by the Neo-Platonic philosophy of the Florentine Academy, and thus he often allegorized pagan myths, giving them a Christian slant. Especially prominent in Neo-Platonic thought was the identification of Venus, the

Figure 11.21 PIERO DELLA FRANCESCA. *The Flagellation.* 1460s. Oil on panel, 23 × 32". Galleria Nazionale della Marche, Palazzo Ducale, Urbino. *A secondary religious message may be found in this work. In 1439 the Orthodox Church discussed union with Rome at the Council of Florence but later repudiated the merger when the Byzantine populace rioted in favor of Turkish rule. The hats on Pilate (seated at the left) and the third man from the right are copies of Greek headdresses that were worn at the council. In effect, these figures suggest that the Greek Church is a persecutor of true Christianity, for the papacy regarded the Greek Orthodox faith as schismatic.*

Roman goddess of love, with the Christian belief that "God is love." Botticelli, with the support of his patrons, notably the Medici family, made the Roman goddess the subject of two splendid paintings, the *Primavera* and *The Birth of Venus.* In this way, female nudes once again became a proper subject for art, though male nudes had appeared earlier, in Donatello's generation (see Figure 11.11).

Botticelli's *Primavera,* or *Allegory of Spring,* presents Venus as a Christianized deity, dressed in a revealingly transparent gown (Figure 11.22). At first glance, the goddess, standing just slightly to the right of center, appears lost amid the general agitation, but on closer view she is seen to be presiding over the revels. Venus tilts her head coyly and holds up her right hand, establishing by these commanding gestures that this

Figure 11.22   SANDRO BOTTICELLI. *Primavera.* Ca. 1482. Tempera on panel, 6'8" × 10'4".
Uffizi Gallery, Florence. *Botticelli's lyricism is evident in his refined images of human beauty.
His figures' elegant features and gestures, such as the sloping shoulders and the tilted heads, were
copied by later artists. The women's blond, ropelike hair and transparent gowns are typical of
Botticelli's style.*

orange grove is her garden and the other figures are
her familiars, or associates, all of them symbolically
linked with divine love.

Even though the *Primavera* is one of the most
beloved works of Western art, in technical terms the
painting shows that Botticelli was out of step with the
Early Renaissance. He has placed the scene in the near
foreground, stressing this area's extreme shallowness
by the entangled backdrop of trees and shrubs. The
figures are flattened, and the background appears
more decorative than real.

An even more famous work by Botticelli, and one of
the great landmarks of Western art, is *The Birth of Venus*
(see Figure 11.4). Painted in an even more flattened
style than the *Primavera,* this masterpiece was probably intended as a visual complement to it. In Neo-

Platonic terms, Venus is an image of beauty and love
as it is born and grows in the human mind; the birth of
Venus corresponds to the baptism of Jesus, because
baptism is a symbol of rebirth.

In the 1480s, Florentine art was moving toward its
culmination in the early works of Leonardo da Vinci
(1452–1519). Leonardo is the quintessential representative of a new breed of artist: the Renaissance man, who
takes the universe of learning as his province. Not only
did he defy the authority of the church by secretly
studying human cadavers, but he also rejected the
Classical values that had guided the first generation of
the Early Renaissance. He relied solely on empirical
truth and what the human eye could discover. His
notebooks, encoded so as to be legible only when read
in a mirror, recorded and detailed his lifelong curiosity

about both the human and the natural worlds. In his habits of mind, Leonardo joined intellectual curiosity with the skills of sculptor, architect, engineer, scientist, and painter.

Among his few surviving paintings from this period, the first version of *The Virgin of the Rocks* reveals both his scientific eye and his desire to create a haunting image uniquely his own (Figure 11.23). In this scene, set in a grotto or cave, Mary is portrayed with the infant Jesus, as a half-kneeling infant John the Baptist prays and an angel watches. The plants underfoot and the rocks in the background are a treasure of precise documentation. Nevertheless, the setting is Leonardo's own invention—without a scriptural or a traditional basis—and is a testimony to his creative genius.

Leonardo's plan of *The Virgin of the Rocks* shows the rich workings of his mind. Ignoring Brunelleschian perspective, he placed the figures his own way. He also developed a pyramid design for arranging the figures in relation to one another; Mary's head is the pyramid's apex, and her seat and the other three figures anchor its corners. Within this pyramid, Leonardo creates a dynamic tension by using gestures to suggest a circular motion: The angel points to John the Baptist, who in turn directs his praying hands toward Jesus. A second, vertical, line of stress is seen in the gesturing hands of Mary, the angel, and Christ. Later artists so admired this painting that its pyramidal composition became the standard in the High Renaissance.

No prior artist had used chiaroscuro to such advantage as Leonardo does in this work, causing the figures to stand out miraculously from the surrounding gloom. And unlike earlier artists, he colors the atmosphere, softening the edges of surfaces with a fine haze called **sfumato**. As a result, the painting looks more like a vision than a realistic scene. Leonardo's later works are part of the High Renaissance (see Chapter 12), but his early works represent the fullest expression of the scientific spirit of the second generation of Early Renaissance painting.

While the Florentine painters were establishing themselves as the driving force in the Early Renaissance, a rival school was beginning to emerge in Venice. The Venetian school, dedicated to exploring the effects of light and air and re-creating the sensuous effects of textured surfaces, was eventually to play a major role in the history of painting in Italy and the West. Founded by Giovanni Bellini, a member of a dynasty of painters, the Venetian school began its rise to greatness.

Giovanni Bellini (about 1430–1516), who trained in the workshop of his father, the Late Gothic painter Jacopo Bellini (about 1400–about 1470), made Venice a center of Renaissance art comparable to Florence and

Figure 11.23 LEONARDO DA VINCI. *The Virgin of the Rocks.* 1483. Oil on panel, approx. 6'3" × 3'7". Louvre. *Two slightly different versions of this work exist, this one dating from 1483 and a later one done in 1506 and on view in the National Gallery in London. The Louvre painting, with its carefully observed botanical specimens, is the culmination of the scientific side of the Early Renaissance. The painting's arbitrary features—the grotto setting and the unusual perspective—point ahead to the High Renaissance; the dramatic use of chiaroscuro foreshadows the "night pictures" of the Baroque period (see Figure 14.10).*

Rome. Ever experimenting, always striving to keep up with the latest trends, he frequently reinvented himself. Nevertheless, there were constants in his approach to painting. He combined the traditions of the Florentine school (the use of linear perspective and the direct observation of nature) and the Flemish school (the technique of oil painting, the use of landscape as background, and the practice of religious symbolism). Made aware of the importance of atmosphere by the Venetian setting, Bellini also experimented with a range of colors, variations in color intensity, and changes in light. In particular, Bellini perfected the

ENCOUNTER

The Influence of Islam on the European Renaissance

Can cultures learn from their enemies? Christian Europe and the Islamic world, despite mutually antagonistic religions, did engage in artistic borrowings in the period from 1300 to 1600. These borrowings, though modest for both cultures, were stronger and more enduring in Christian Europe, where Islamic influences helped give shape to the visual and decorative arts in the Renaissance, then in full flower.

Around 1400, at the beginning of the Early Italian Renaissance, Europe and Islam were locked in a centuries-old struggle, dating from the reign of Emperor Charlemagne in the early 800s. For Christian Europe, not only was Islam a false faith, but its leaders had unjustly conquered land, such as Spain and, especially, the Holy Land, or Palestine. For Islam, Christian Europe was the home of the infidel who refused to accept Muhammad as God's final revelation.

Intensifying the struggle between these cultures were their differing stages of economic growth. Islam, though past its Golden Age, was still flourishing, and its consumer goods appealed to Europe's elites. The West, whose industrial economy was in its infancy, was valued by the Islamic world only for its raw materials, such as furs and amber. Nevertheless, encounters occurred in the exchange of material goods—from the spoils of war, diplomatic gifts, and trade. These activities led to the acquisition of prized objects from both cultures, and this, in turn, inspired artistic borrowing between Islam and Europe.

Of these three types of encounters, conducting trade offered the best opportunity for cultural interchange, with Europe's taste for Islam's luxury goods turning the wheels of commerce. Venice led the way, followed by other Italian cities—Pisa, Lucca, and Siena—along with Sicily and southern Italy. These centers of commerce imported textiles, such as silks and embroidered cloth, carpets, metalwork, and other luxury goods from the Ottoman Empire (after 1453), Egypt, Syria, Iraq, and Persia.

These Islamic goods slowly changed the personal style of Europe's powerful and rich. For example, in 1003, Pope Sylvester II (pope 999–1003) was buried in a shroud made of Persian silk cloth. Islamic ceramic and metalwork goods became prestige objects, serving ritualistic purposes in churches and denoting the social aspirations of those who displayed them in their homes. The floors of royal and baronial courts, along with those of wealthy households, changed from being covered with rush matting to being dressed with woven carpets, especially in the Turkish and Persian styles. Carpets also were used as table covers and wall hangings.

As the Islamic luxury goods grew in popularity, Europe's decorative arts began to imitate them. In ceramics, southern Italian artisans copied Islamic models and motifs, such as geometric patterns, arabesques, and calligraphy that imitated Arabic writing. Venetian guildsmen imitated Ottoman models and designs in metalwork, varnished ware, and saddle decoration.

In the visual arts, painters began to incorporate elements, motifs, and design features from Islamic imported goods into both their secular and religious works—as symbols of opulence and high status. Italian painters started this trend, in the early 1300s, introducing images of carpets and some decorative motifs and patterns into their works. Artists across Europe followed their lead. For example, Hans Memling, in his painting *Madonna and Child with Angel*, depicts the Virgin and baby Christ, enthroned, with a Turkish carpet, identified as a "wheel carpet," placed before them (see Figure 10.24).

In contrast, Islam's borrowing from the West was more limited, confined to a few luxury goods, such as textiles, including velvets and cloths with gold and silver threads and pearls, from Florence, and undecorated glass, from Venice, to be finished with Islamic designs. However, one outstanding interchange between Islam and the West did occur during this time: the portrait of the Ottoman sultan who conquered

landscape format as a backdrop for foreground figures. A great teacher, Bellini founded a workshop where his methods were taught to young painters, including Giorgione and Titian (see Chapter 12).

An excellent example of Bellini's use of landscape may be seen in *St. Francis in Ecstasy* (Figure 11.24). This work, which depicts an ecstatic St. Francis displaying the stigmata (spontaneous appearance of open wounds, similar to those of the crucified Christ), shows Bellini's typical treatment of landscape. He divides the painting surface into zones, beginning with the area around the saint in the foreground, continuing through a second zone occupied by a donkey and a crane, to a third zone featuring Italian castles nestled into a hillside, and concluding with a fourth zone marked by a fortress and the sky. To heighten the realism, Bellini uses both a rich palette of colors and numerous objects to lead the viewer's eye into the vast distance. He adds to the realism by suffusing the scene with natural light. The landscape, with its vivid rendering of flora and fauna,

Constantinople, Mehmet II (r. 1444–1446 and 1451–1481), painted in about 1480 by the Venetian artist Gentile Bellini (Encounter figure 11.1). At that time, knowledge of the Renaissance art style was little known in Islam. Therefore, this portrait is a landmark, because it introduced Western perspective to the Ottoman court and its workshop of miniature painters.

Learning from the Encounter **Why** did Europe and Islam hold negative images of each other during the European Renaissance? **Compare and contrast** the economies of Europe and the Islamic world between 1300 and 1600. **Summarize** the influence of Islam on Europe during the Renaissance. **What** impact did the West have on Islam during the Renaissance? **Discuss** the interaction between the West and the Islamic world today.

Encounter figure 11.1 GENTILE BELLINI. *Mehmet II.* Ca. 1480. Oil on canvas, 27¾ × 20⅝". National Gallery, London. *Bellini's commission for this portrait grew out of a diplomatic exchange between Venice and the Ottoman Empire. As a condition of making peace with Venice after a war, the sultan requested that a Venetian portrait painter be sent to his court. Bellini's portrait blends Western technique—the oil medium, the seated subject in profile, and the perspective—with Islamic touches— the rounded arch with an elaborate design, the sumptuous fabric draped over the balustrade, the turban and fur-lined robe, and the black background.*

expresses the Franciscan belief that humankind should live in harmony with the natural world (see Chapter 9).

Music

The changes affecting the cultural life of fifteenth-century Europe naturally also affected the music of the time. The impetus for a new musical direction, however, did not spring from Classical sources, because ancient musical texts had virtually perished. Instead, the new music owed its existence to meetings between English and Continental composers at the church councils that were called to settle the Great Schism (see Chapter 10) and the Continental composers' deep regard for the seductive sound of English music. The English composer John Dunstable [DUHN-stuh-bull] (about 1380–1453) was a central figure in the new musical era that began with the opening of the fifteenth century. Working in England and in France, he wrote

Figure 11.24 GIOVANNI BELLINI. *St. Francis in Ecstasy.* 1470s. Oil in tempera on panel, 49 × 55⅞". Frick Collection, New York. *In the foreground, Bellini renders his vision of the grotto at Alvernia, a mountain retreat near Assisi, where St. Francis went to pray and fast for forty days, in imitation of Christ's forty days in the wilderness. The artist reinforces the scene's religious significance through various symbols, such as the grapevine and the stigmata, alluding to the sacrifice of Christ, and the donkey (in the middle distance), emblematic of Jesus' entry into Jerusalem before the Crucifixion.*

Figure 11.25 Mass at the Court of Philip the Good in Burgundy. Bibliothèque Royal Albert Ier, Brussels. Fifteenth century. *This miniature painting shows a Mass being conducted at the court of Philip the Good of Burgundy (r. 1419–1467). Philip's patronage of the arts and music attracted leading painters and musicians to his court, which he conducted in cities across his holdings in modern-day Holland, Belgium, and France. John Dunstable, a composer of the Franco-Netherlandish school, was, on occasion, at the duke's court. In the painting, the priest prepares the sacraments at the altar, with his attendant behind him. On the right, the choir, dressed in white robes and gathered in front of the music stand, sings the Latin Mass. In the center background, dressed in black, stands a member of the Burgundian royal court, attended by two servants.*

mainly religious works—motets for multiple voices and settings for the Mass—that showed his increasingly harmonic approach to polyphony. The special quality of his music is its freedom from the use of mathematical proportion—the source of medieval music's dissonance.

Dunstable's music influenced composers in France, in Burgundy, and in Flanders, known collectively as the Franco-Netherlandish school. This school, which became the dominant force in fifteenth-century music, blended Dunstable's harmonics with northern European and Italian traditions. The principal works of this group were Latin **Masses** (Figure 11.25), or musical settings of the most sacred Christian rite; **motets,** or multivoiced songs set to Latin texts other than the Mass; and secular *chansons,* or songs, with French texts, including such types as the French ballade and the Italian madrigal, poems set to music for two and six voices, respectively. Together, these polyphonic compositions established the musical ideal of the Early Renaissance: multiple voices of equal importance singing **a cappella** (without instrumental accompaniment) and stressing the words so that they could be understood by listeners.

Between 1430 and 1500, the Continent's musical life was guided by composers from the Franco-Netherlandish school, the most important of whom was the Burgundian Josquin des Prez [zho-SKAN day

PRAY] (about 1440–1521). Josquin was influential in his day and is now recognized as one of the greatest composers of all time. He was the first important composer to use music expressively so that the sounds matched the words of the text, thereby moving away from the abstract church style of the Middle Ages. One of his motets was described at the time as evoking Christ's suffering in a manner superior to painting. Josquin also began to organize music in the modern way, using major and minor scales with their related harmonies. All in all, he is probably the first Western composer whose music on first hearing appeals to modern ears.

Josquin's motet *Ave Maria . . . Virgo Serena (Hail, Mary . . . Serene Virgin,* 1502), a musical setting of a prayer to the Virgin Mary, shows the new expressive

Renaissance style as it breaks away from the abstract music of the Middle Ages. Based on a Gregorian chant, the opening section quickly gives way to an innovative melody. Divided into seven sections, the motet employs shifting voice combinations in each part. The opening section uses polyphonic **imitation,** a musical technique that functions like a relay race. The soprano begins with the phrase *Ave maria,* which, in turn, is restated by the alto, tenor, and bass. Next, there follows the second phrase, *gratia plena* ("full of grace"), sung to a different melody, which is also repeated among the voices. The musical effect in the first section is to create an overlapping tapestry of sound. The second section uses a duet of two upper voices, which is then imitated by the lower voices. Next, there is a four-voice ensemble, using expressive music that reflects the text, *nova laetitia* ("new joy"). Then, there follow four sections that shift voice groupings along with alterations in rhythms, ending with a brief pause. The motet ends with the group singing together in sustained chords: *"O mater Dei / memento mei. Amen,"* or "O Mother of God / remember me. Amen."

The Legacy of the Early Renaissance

Today, modern times are considered to begin with the Early Renaissance in Italy. This period saw the rebirth of the study and practice of the arts and the humanities and the rise of the idea of the "Renaissance man"—a term used today to define the supreme genius who makes all of human knowledge his province. Under the powerful stimulus of humanism, the liberal arts were restored to primacy over religion in the educational curriculum, a place they had not held for a thousand years, since the triumph of Christianity in the fourth century. With humanism also came a skeptical outlook that expressed itself in a new regard for the direct role of human causality in history and the rise of textual criticism. A new ingredient in Renaissance humanism was the drive to individual fulfillment, perhaps the defining trait of Western civilization from this point onward.

The greatest cultural changes took place in the arts and in architecture, largely under the spell of humanistic learning. Now freed from subordination to architecture, sculpture and painting became independent art forms. Fifteenth-century architects, inspired by the Greco-Roman tradition, adapted Classical forms and ideals to their own needs. For the next four hundred years, until the Gothic revival in the nineteenth century, Classicism was the ruling force in a succession of architectural styles. Sculpture also used its Classical roots to redefine its direction, reviving ancient forms and the practice of depicting male and female nudes. Of all the visual arts, painting was least influenced by the Classical tradition, except for its ideals of simplicity and realism. Perhaps as a consequence of its artistic freedom, painting became the dominant art form of this era and continues to hold first rank today.

KEY CULTURAL TERMS

Renaissance	chiaroscuro
studia humanitatis	*sfumato*
Early Renaissance style	Mass
vanishing point	motet
pilaster	a cappella
relief	imitation

SUGGESTIONS FOR FURTHER READING

CASSIRER, E., KRISTELLER, P. O., AND RANDALL, J., eds. *The Renaissance Philosophy of Man.* Chicago: University of Chicago Press, 1948. Selections from Pico, Valla, and other Renaissance scholars accompanied by a useful text.

PICO DELLA MIRANDOLA. *On the Dignity of Man.* Indianapolis: Bobbs-Merrill, 1956. A succinct statement on Renaissance thought by one of its leading scholars.

SUGGESTIONS FOR LISTENING

DUNSTABLE (or DUNSTAPLE), JOHN. Dunstable's sweet-sounding harmonies helped inaugurate Early Renaissance music. Predominantly a composer of sacred music, he is best represented by motets, including *Veni Sancte Spiritus—Veni Creator Spiritus* and *Sancta Maria, non est similis.* He also wrote a few secular songs, of which the two most familiar are *O Rosa bella* and *Puisque m'amour.*

JOSQUIN DES PREZ. Josquin's Masses, motets, and *chansons* all illustrate his skill at combining popular melodies with intricate counterpoint and his use of harmonies commonly heard today. The motet *Ave Maria,* the *chanson Faulte d'argent,* and the Mass *Malheur me bat* are good examples of his style.

12 THE HIGH RENAISSANCE AND EARLY MANNERISM 1494–1564

Between 1494 and 1564, one of the most brilliantly creative periods in Western history unfolded in Italy. During this span of seventy years, there flourished three artists—Leonardo da Vinci, Raphael, and Michelangelo—and a writer—Machiavelli—whose achievements became legendary. The works of these geniuses, and of other talented but less well-known artists and intellectuals, affected the basic Western concept of art and fundamentally influenced how we understand ourselves and the world (Figure 12.1).

The **High Renaissance,** lasting from 1494 to 1520, was the first phase of this creative period and was a time when the Classical principles of beauty, balance, order, serenity, harmony, and rational design reached a state of near perfection. The center of culture shifted from Florence, the heart of the Early Renaissance, to Rome, where the popes became the leading patrons of the new style in their desire to make Rome the world's most beautiful city. Florence even had to yield the services of Michelangelo, its favorite son, to the wealthy and powerful Roman pontiffs.

After 1520, however, the Renaissance veered away from the humanistic values of Classicism toward an antihumanistic vision of the world, labeled **Mannerism** because of the self-conscious, or "mannered," style adopted by its artists and intellectuals. Mannerist art and culture endured from 1520 until the end of the century, when the style was affected by religious controversy. This chapter covers the High Renaissance style and the Mannerist style through the end of its first phase in 1564, with the death of Michelangelo.

◄ **Detail** LEONARDO DA VINCI. *Mona Lisa.* 1503. Oil on panel, 30¼ × 21". Louvre.

THE RISE OF THE MODERN SOVEREIGN STATE

The most important political development in the first half of the sixteenth century was the emergence of powerful sovereign states in the newly unified and stabilized nations of France, England, and Spain. This process was already under way in the late fifteenth century (see Chapter 10), but it now began to influence foreign affairs. The ongoing rivalries of these aggressive national kingdoms led to the concept of balance of power—a principle that still dominates politics today.

From 1494 to 1569, Europe's international political life was controlled, either directly or indirectly, by France and Spain. France's central role resulted from the policies of its strong Valois kings, who had governed France since the early fourteenth century. Spain's fortunes soared during this period, first under the joint rule (1474–1504) of Ferdinand V and Isabella and then under Charles I (r. 1516–1556). In 1519 Charles I was also elected Holy Roman emperor as Charles V (he was of the royal house of Hapsburg), thus joining the interests of Spain and the Holy Roman Empire until his abdication in 1556. England kept aloof from Continental affairs during this time.

After 1591 the French and the Spanish rulers increasingly dispatched their armies and allies into the weaker states, where they fought and claimed new lands. As the sovereign monarchs gained power, the medieval dream of a united Christendom—pursued by Charlemagne, the popes, and the Holy Roman emperors—slowly faded away. These new states were strong because they were united around rulers who exercised increasing central control. Although most kings claimed to rule by divine right, their practical policies were more important in increasing their power. They surrounded themselves with ministers and consultative councils, both dependent on the crown. The ministers were often chosen from the bourgeois class, and they advised the rulers on such weighty matters as religion and war and also ran the developing bureaucracies. The bureaucracies in turn strengthened centralized rule by extending royal juris-

Figure 12.1   MICHELANGELO. *Dying Slave.* 1513–1516. Marble, approx. 7′5″. Louvre. *Michelangelo's so-called* Dying Slave *embodies the conflicting artistic tendencies at work between 1494 and 1564. The statue's idealized traits—the perfectly proportioned figure, the restrained facial expression, and the body's gentle S-curve shape—are hallmarks of the High Renaissance style. But the figure's overall sleekness and exaggerated arm movements—probably based on one of the figures in the first-century C.E.* Laocoön Group *(see Figure 4.19), which had recently been rediscovered—were portents of Early Mannerism.*

diction into matters formerly administered by the feudal nobility, such as the justice system.

The crown further eroded the status of the feudal nobles by relying on mercenary armies rather than on the warrior class, a shift that began in the Late Middle Ages. To pay these armies, the kings had to consult with representative bodies, such as Parliament in England, and make them a part of their regular administration.

The Struggle for Italy, 1494–1529

Italy's relative tranquility, established by the Peace of Lodi in 1454, was shattered by the French invasion in 1494. For the next thirty-five years, Italy was a battleground where France, Spain, and the Holy Roman Empire fought among themselves, as well as with the papacy and most of the Italian states.

The struggle began when France, eager to reassert a hereditary claim to Naples, agreed to help Milan in a controversy involving Naples, Florence, and the pope. The French king, Charles VIII, took Florence in 1494 and then advanced to Rome and Naples. But the Italians did not relinquish ground easily. Joined by Venice and the pope and supported by the Holy Roman emperor and the Spanish monarch, they drove out the French. In 1499 the French returned to Italy to activate their claim to Milan, and the Spanish and the Germans joined with the Italians to defeat the French. Over the next several decades, however, France continued to invade Italy intermittently. In the course of their campaigns, the French rulers, who were enamored of the Italian Renaissance, brought its artistic and intellectual ideals to northern Europe (Figure 12.2).

In 1522 full-scale hostilities broke out between France and the Holy Roman Empire over Italy's future, a struggle that pitted the old Europe against the new. The Holy Roman Empire, ruled by Charles V, was a decentralized relic from the feudal age. France, under the bold and intellectual leadership of Francis I (r. 1515–1547) of the royal house of Valois, was the epitome of the new sovereign state.

The first Hapsburg-Valois war was the only one fought in Italy. In 1527 the troops of Charles V ran riot in Rome, raping, looting, and killing. This notorious sack of Rome had two major consequences. First, it cast doubt on Rome's ability to control Italy—long a goal of the popes—for it showed that the secular leaders no longer respected the temporal power of the papacy. Second, it ended papal patronage of the arts for almost a decade, thus weakening Rome's role as a cultural leader. It also had a chilling effect on artistic ideals and contributed to the rise of Mannerism.

In 1529 the Treaty of Cambrai ended this first phase of the Hapsburg-Valois rivalry. Years of invasions and

Figure 12.2   JEAN CLOUET. *Francis I.* Ca. 1525. Oil on panel, 37¾ × 29⅛". Louvre. *During his thirty-two-year reign, Francis I was a major force in sixteenth-century European affairs. He also embarked on an extensive artistic program, inspired by the Italian Renaissance, to make his court the most splendid in Europe. Under his personal direction, Italian artworks and artists, including Leonardo da Vinci, were imported into France. Ironically, this rather stylized portrait by Jean Clouet, Francis's chief court artist, owes more to the conventionalized portraits of the Gothic style than it does to the realistic works of the Italian Renaissance.*

wars had left most of Italy divided and exhausted. Some cities had suffered nearly irreparable harm. Florence, because it had so much to lose, fared the worst. In the 1530s, the Medici rulers resumed ducal power, but they were little more than puppets of the foreigners who controlled much of the peninsula. The only Italian state to keep its political independence was Venice, which became the last haven for artists and intellectuals in Italy for the rest of the sixteenth century.

Charles V and the Hapsburg Empire

By 1530 the struggle between the Valois and the Hapsburgs had shifted to central Europe. The French felt hemmed in by the Spanish in the south, the Germans

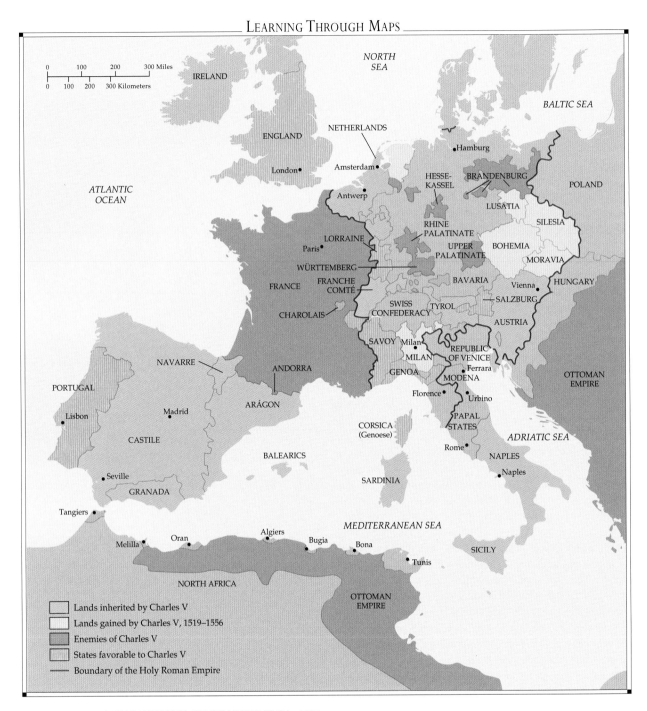

Map 12.1   EUROPEAN EMPIRE OF CHARLES V, CA. 1556
This map shows the extensive holdings of the Holy Roman emperor Charles V, also
known as King Charles I of Spain. **Notice** the lands inherited and the lands gained by
Charles V. **Identify** the boundaries of the Holy Roman Empire. **Who** were Charles V's
enemies within the Holy Roman Empire and elsewhere? **Consider** the challenges
Charles V faced in governing his widely scattered and culturally diverse empire. **What**
impact did geography have on France's attitude toward Charles V's empire?

to the east, and the Dutch to the north—peoples all
ruled by the Hapsburg emperor Charles V. In French
eyes, Charles had an insatiable appetite for power and
for control of the Continent. In turn, the Hapsburg

ruler considered the French king a land-hungry upstart who stood in the way of a Europe united under a
Christian prince—in other words, the dream of Christendom. In 1559, after a number of exhausting wars

and a series of French victories, the belligerents signed the Treaty of Cateau-Cambrésis, which ushered in a brief period of peace (Map 12.1).

Charles V, the man at the center of most of these events, lived a life filled with paradoxes (Figure 12.3). Because of the size of his empire, he was in theory one of the most powerful rulers ever to live; but in actuality, again because of the vastness of his lands, he never quite succeeded in gaining complete control of his empire. In some ways, he was the last medieval king; in other ways, he foreshadowed a new age driven by sovereign kings, standing armies, diplomatic agreements, and strong religious differences.

Charles V's unique position at the center of Europe's political storm was the result of a series of timely deaths and births and politically astute arranged marriages. These circumstances had permitted the Hapsburg rulers to accumulate vast power, wealth, and land. Charles was born in 1500 to a German father and a Spanish mother, and he was the grandson of both the Holy Roman emperor Maximilian I and the Spanish king Ferdinand V. He held lands in present-day Spain, France, Italy, Germany, and Austria—along with the unimaginable riches of the recently acquired lands in the New World. By 1519 Charles V—simultaneously Charles I of Spain—ruled the largest empire the world has ever known.

For most of his life, Charles traveled from one of his possessions to another, fighting battles, arranging peace treaties, and attempting to unify his empire by personal control and compromise. His attention was often divided, and he found himself caught between two powerful foes—especially the French to the west and the Ottoman Turks in the east—who drained both his personal energies and his imperial resources.

Within the Holy Roman Empire, the princes of the German principalities often took advantage of his prolonged absences and his preoccupation with the French and the Turks. Their ability to gain political power at the emperor's expense increased after Martin Luther's revolt and the beginning of the Protestant Reformation (see Chapter 13). Charles also weakened his own position by his contradictory policies. At times he angered the disaffected German princes by meddling in their affairs and condemning Lutheran doctrines, and at other times he angered the popes by making concessions to the Protestants.

Exhausted and disillusioned by his inability to prevail in Europe, Charles abdicated in 1556 and retired to a monastery. His brother Ferdinand (r. 1558–1564) took control of the German-Austrian inheritance and was soon elected Holy Roman emperor. His son Philip (r. 1556–1598) assumed control of the Spanish Hapsburg holdings, including Spain, the New World territories, and the Netherlands. Thus ended Charles's vision of a

Figure 12.3 TITIAN. *Charles V with a Dog.* Ca. 1533. Oil on canvas, 6′3″ × 3′8″. Prado, Madrid. *Titian's full-length, standing portrait of Charles V was painted when the Hapsburg emperor was at the height of his power. By rendering the "ruler of the world" in contrapposto, his fingers casually holding the collar of his dog, Titian endows the emperor with a natural grace. The lighting that illuminates Charles from the dark background and the breathless hush that seems to envelop the man and dog are trademarks of Titian's style.*

united Europe and Christendom, which had turned into a nightmare of endless meetings, gory battles, and false hopes of peace and unity.

ECONOMIC EXPANSION AND SOCIAL DEVELOPMENTS

By the end of the fifteenth century, Europe had nearly recovered from the impact of the plague; the sixteenth century continued to be a time of growing population and increasing prosperity. The center of commerce shifted from the Mediterranean to the Atlantic coast, making cities like London and Antwerp financial and merchandising centers. Skilled craftspeople turned out quality products, and enterprising merchants distributed these finished goods across much of northwestern Europe. The daring sailing expeditions and discoveries of the late fifteenth and early sixteenth centuries provided new raw materials from America. Innovative manufacturing methods spurred economic growth and expanded worldwide markets.

Demographics, Prosperity, and the Beginning of a Global World

Although the data are scattered and often unreliable, evidence indicates that the population of Europe increased from about forty-five million in 1400 to sixty-nine million in 1500 and to about eighty-nine million by 1600. There was a major population shift from rural to urban areas, and the number of cities with populations over one hundred thousand grew from five to eight between 1500 and 1600. Rome, for example, grew from about fifty thousand in 1526—the year before the sack—to one hundred thousand by the end of the century.

Prosperity brought a higher standard of living to most of the urban middle class, but throughout much of the century prices rose faster than wages. Those who were not profiting from increased economic growth, such as poor peasants or impoverished nobility living on unproductive farms, suffered the most. In areas of Europe hardest hit by inflation or agricultural and commercial stagnation, economic crises often became intertwined with social and religious matters that intensified long-standing regional and local differences.

Yet the boom offered economic opportunities to some. Many merchants made fortunes and provided employment for others. These merchants and the bankers who offered loans were also accumulating capital, which they then invested in other types of commercial activity. The campaigns of Charles V were financed by wealthy bankers operating in a well-organized money market. The amassing of surplus capital and its reinvestment ushered in the opening phase of commercial capitalism that laid the foundation for Europe's future economic expansion.

During the first half of the sixteenth century, the abundance of raw materials and the vast market potential of the New World had just begun to affect Europe's economy. South American gold and silver played an important role in the upward price spiral. After 1650 New World agricultural products, such as tobacco, cotton, and cocoa, were used in new manufactured goods and profoundly altered consumer habits.

In the late 1500s, a major economic change had occurred that would make it possible to bring the natural resources of the New World to Europe. Some Europeans, taking advantage of the institution of slavery and the existing slave trade in western Africa, mercilessly exploited the local Africans by buying them and shipping them to European colonies in the New World. The Africans were forced to work in the gold and silver mines of Central and South America and on the cotton and sugarcane plantations in the West Indies, where they became a major factor in the production of these new forms of wealth.

Technology

The High Renaissance was a period of economic and social transformation, stimulated by advances in technology. The heroes of this age were the explorers and adventurers who dared to sail beyond the confines of Europe's shores, along with the inventors whose devices and discoveries opened the world for exploration. One of the most powerful agents of change was improved firearms, which rendered old forms of warfare obsolete and, gradually, affected the balance of power among the rising nation-states.

Sailing   Europe, starting in 1492, began to explore and then conquer much of the world. The pretext was religion and the spread of the Christian faith, but the motivation was gold, commodities, and riches. Based on a wealth of knowledge of the sea and the winds, the technology was now advanced for navigational instruments, ships, sails, and guns. Other societies, of course, had their religious faiths; they searched for wealth; they sailed the oceans; they possessed weapons and conquered other groups through warfare. But it was the Europeans, through chance, circumstances, and design, who started the Age of Exploration and dominated much of the globe until the late twentieth century.

By the late fifteenth century, European sailors were using the magnetic compass (to determine direction) and the astrolabe (to determine latitude), two inventions that allowed them to crisscross the oceans. They soon learned the path of prevailing ocean winds, especially in the Atlantic, which would take them first westward and then, catching other wind currents, eastward. This type of navigation would carry them toward the coast of Africa. As the mariners learned other wind patterns, they were able to sail farther and farther from Europe. In the early sixteenth century, the Portuguese navigator Fernao de Magalhaes [mah-GAHL-yeesh] (in English, Ferdinand Magellan) (about 1480–1521), aware of these wind patterns and acquainted with earlier explorations, circumnavigated the globe.

New types of sailing vessels also made these dangerous journeys possible. By the fifteenth century, *galleys* (long warships powered by oars and sails and loaded with armed boarding parties) were being replaced by square-rigged sailing ships outfitted with cannons. The Portuguese and the Spanish used the *caravel* (a three-masted vessel with a small roundish hull and a high stern and bow) for ocean travel and exploration, because the caravel could both carry cargo and be equipped with deck guns. The *galleon*, a much larger vessel, with greater maneuverability and firepower, replaced the caravel starting in the mid–sixteenth century. The galleon proved to be the mainstay for commerce and navies until the eighteenth century. The success of the caravel and the galleon resulted from having cannons mounted on the main deck, facing outward, so that each could fire through an opening cut into the ship's hull. Rows of these larger guns were installed on each side of the main deck, with galleons equipped usually with fourteen or more pairs. So successful were these heavily armed ships that, by 1700, the outcome of Europe's wars was often determined by battles on the open seas, as in England's triumph over the Spanish Armada in 1588.

Warfare The firepower of the sailing vessels had been made possible by the evolution of the cannon, which first appeared in Europe in the early 1300s. The first ones were siege cannons, packed with gunpowder and stones or pieces of metal and used to batter down the walls of castles and towns. Both iron and bronze guns were in service, but the bronze cannon soon proved to be the better weapon. Although a bronze cannon cost more due to materials and labor, it was easier to cast, its barrel did not rust, and it weighed less than an iron cannon.

As Europe's kings began to create the first modern sovereign states, they quickly recognized the need for a new type of army and better weaponry. Arsenals and foundries, turning out guns and shot, sprang up around Europe, and those nations with access to raw materials and innovative and skilled technicians and gunsmiths soon possessed the best-equipped armies. By 1700 military commanders were beginning to make a distinction between heavy siege guns and lighter field artillery. Light, more easily portable cannons with smaller caliber (the diameter of the gun's bore) not only were effective as a tactical weapon but also were well suited for the new warships—the galleons. The Spaniards held the lead during the sixteenth century, but the Dutch and English moved ahead in the early 1700s. Europe was now experiencing its first arms race: Amassing weapons had become an increasingly central need for each sovereign state, while new strategies and tactics were reshaping the nature of warfare.

Figure 12.4 LEONARDO DA VINCI. *Men Struggling to Move a Large Cannon.* Ca. 1488. Pen and ink, drawing. Windsor, Royal Library. *Leonardo's drawing of men trying to move a large cannon is more than just a scene of a sixteenth-century iron foundry. While much can be learned from its details—the use of winches and pulleys, the tools and equipment, and the differing models and sizes of cannons—the artist is also showing how machines are coming to control their human creators. Leonardo was fascinated by the machines of war, but he also understood how this large cannon (above) could wreak havoc, when he wrote, "With its breath it will kill men and ruin cities and castles."*

Among those who understood how weaponry could transform warfare was the artist-scientist Leonardo da Vinci (see the section "Painting"). He designed catapults, giant crossbows, and cannons. He calculated the trajectories of missiles fired by mortars and cannons and drew plans for armed vehicles on land, underwater craft, and flying machines. As a military engineer, he advised city planners on fortifications. Leonardo's curiosity and quest for knowledge led him not only to invent engines of war but also to speculate on how these destructive devices brutalized humans and destroyed nature (Figure 12.4).

Science and Medicine

While less pronounced in their immediate impact than the technological innovations, advances in science during this age would have long-lasting effects.

In the study of natural science, Leonardo again surpassed his contemporaries, in observation, in practices, and in understanding. Leonardo's genius was directed toward the study of nature in all of its forms, especially the human body. In the knowledge that he gained, he perhaps surpassed all those who had gone before him. He dissected human cadavers, took meticulous notes, described organs, bones, and muscles, and drew detailed anatomical studies. Although his writings and anatomical drawings were not made public during his lifetime, Leonardo's contributions to the understanding of the structure of the human body and the function of its skeleton, muscles, and organs reflected the Renaissance's desire to understand ourselves and the world.

During much of the sixteenth century, Italy's schools of medicine continued to be among the best in Europe. Italy also took another innovative step in medical care through the creative work of local administrators in the largest cities, officials who personified another characteristic of the Italian Renaissance, **civic humanism.** Civic humanism was an outgrowth of the Renaissance's cultivation of the culture of ancient Greece and Rome. Italy's civic administrators—dedicated men who were trained in the Greek and Latin classics—saw themselves as modern equivalents of civil servants in an ancient *polis,* or city. As such, they tried to establish responsible and efficient city governments. One of their projects, for example, which had a strong impact on medical care, was the setting up of citywide health boards, composed of physicians and medical personnel, to deal with public health issues, especially plague and other contagious diseases. Although lacking knowledge of the germ theory of disease, the health boards, nevertheless, could build on successful practices that had worked in the past. For example, they used controls and quarantines to isolate plague and prevent the spread of this and other contagious diseases among the populace. Such preventive methods were pioneered in the 1400s. Once established, the new city health boards soon made their presence felt in the areas under their jurisdiction, such as keeping records of each death and its cause, inspecting food markets, regulating city health conditions, and supervising burials, cemeteries, hospitals, and even beggars and prostitutes.

FROM HIGH RENAISSANCE TO EARLY MANNERISM

The characteristics of High Renaissance style were largely derived from the visual arts. Led by painters, sculptors, and architects who worshiped ancient Classical ideals, notably those of late-fifth-century B.C.E. Greece, the High Renaissance was filled with images of repose, harmony, and heroism. Under the spell of Classicism and the values of simplicity and restraint, artists sought to conquer unruly physical reality by subjecting it to the principle of a seemingly effortless order.

Although the visual arts dominated the High Renaissance, literary figures also contributed to this era. From Classicism, the High Renaissance authors appropriated two of their chief aesthetic aims, secularism and idealism. Like their ancient predecessors, historians showed that contemporary events arose from human causes rather than from divine action—unmistakable evidence of a mounting secular spirit. Actually, secularism more deeply affected the writing of history than it did the arts and architecture, where church patronage and religious subjects still held sway. A rising secular consciousness can also be seen in the popular handbooks on manners that offered advice on how to become a perfect gentleman or lady. Although they have no counterpart in ancient literature, these books nevertheless have the Classical quality of treating their subject in idealized terms.

What distinguished the High Renaissance preoccupation with the Classical past from the Early Renaissance's renewed interest in ancient matters was largely a shift in creative sensibility. The Early Renaissance artists, in the course of growing away from the Late Gothic style, had invented new ways of recapturing the harmonious spirit of ancient art and architecture. The geniuses of the next generation, benefiting from the experiments of the Early Renaissance, succeeded in creating masterpieces of disciplined form and idealized beauty. The High Renaissance masters' superb confidence allowed them to produce works that were in harmony with themselves and the physical world—a hallmark of Classical art.

In spite of its brilliance, the High Renaissance existed for only a fleeting moment in the history of Western culture—from the French invasion of Italy in 1494 until the death of Raphael in 1520 (preceded by the death of Leonardo in 1519) (Timeline 12.1). In this era, the Renaissance popes spared no expense in their patronage of the arts and letters. After the disasters of the fourteenth century, the papacy seemed to have restored the church to the vitality that it had enjoyed in the High Middle Ages. In reality, however, the popes of the early sixteenth century presided over a shaky ecclesiastical foundation. To the north, in Germany, a theological storm was brewing that would eventually split Christendom and destroy the papacy's claim to rule over the Christian world. This religious crisis, coupled with increasing tendencies to exaggeration in High Renaissance art and with the sack of Rome in 1527, contributed to the development of Mannerism and its spread through Italy and later across western Europe (Figure 12.5).

Timeline 12.1   ITALIAN CULTURAL STYLES BETWEEN 1494 AND 1564

1494		1520					1564
	High Renaissance		Early Mannerism				
French invasion of Italy	1508–1512 Michelangelo's Sistine Chapel ceiling frescoes	1519 Death of Leonardo da Vinci **1520** Death of Raphael	1532 Publication of Machiavelli's *The Prince*	1536–1541 Michelangelo's *Last Judgment* fresco	1550 Palladio's Villa Rotonda		1564 Death of Michelangelo

Figure 12.5 *Pope Clement VII Besieged in Castel Sant' Angelo.* 1554. Engraving, 6¹⁄₆ × 9". Kunsthalle, Hamburg. *This engraving shows the imperial army of Charles V besieging Castel Sant' Angelo, one of the pope's palaces, during the sack of Rome in 1527. The engraver's sympathies with the pope are revealed by the huge statues of St. Peter (with keys, on the right) and St. Paul (with sword, on the left), who look on disapprovingly. Pope Clement VII, imprisoned in his own fortress, peers down on the scene from a balcony at the center top.*

Mannerist painters, sculptors, and architects moved away from two of the guiding principles of the High Renaissance: the imitation of nature and the devotion to Classical ideals. In contrast to the High Renaissance masters, Mannerist painters deliberately chose odd perspectives that called attention to the artists' technical effects and their individual points of view. Mannerist sculptors, rejecting idealism, turned and twisted the human figure into unusual and bizarre poses to express their own notions of beauty. Likewise, Mannerist architects toyed with the emotions and expectations of their audience by designing buildings that were intended to surprise. Behind the Mannerist aesthetic lay a questioning or even a denial of the inherent worth of human beings and a negative image of human nature, along with a sense of the growing instability of the world.

Literature

The leading writers of the High Renaissance in Italy drew their themes and values from the Greco-Roman classics. Their artistic vision sprang from the Classical virtue of *humanitas*—a term coined by Cicero in antiquity (see Chapter 5) that can be translated as "humanity," meaning the wisdom, humor, tolerance, and passion of the person of good sense. With some reservations, they also believed in Classicism's basic tenet that human nature is inherently rational and good. One of the finest expressions of Classicism in Renaissance literature was the poetry of the Venetian Gaspara Stampa, whose lyric verses, though devoted to obsessive sexual love, asserted the moral worth of the lover.

But even as High Renaissance literature was enjoying its brief reign, the Mannerist works of the

ENCOUNTER

Portuguese Exploration Sets the Stage for a New World

Starting in the mid–fifteenth century, Portugal led the first wave of Europeans to export their peoples, traditions, and culture overseas. In response to their daring deeds, the poet Luis Vaz da Camoes, following the lead of the ancient poet Vergil, wrote an epic poem celebrating his adventurous countrymen and heralding the new Age of Exploration.

Portugal, located at the end of the Eurasian land mass, was the first European country to open trade routes from Europe to Africa, India, and the Far East. Portugal's arrival in these areas launched a new phase of international trade and commerce, stimulated racial, ethnic, and cultural interchanges, and altered the course of world history.

During the fifteenth century, the Portuguese explored islands in the Atlantic and traded along the west coast of Africa for gold and slaves. By the 1490s, they were at the southern tip of Africa—the Cape of Good Hope—and were searching for sea routes to Asia, which would bypass the Muslim trade system in the Middle East. In 1497, Vasco da Gama [VAS-co da GAH-ma] (about 1460–1524) sailed from Lisbon, rounded the Cape of Good Hope, came up the east coast of Africa, crossed the Indian ocean—with the aid of a Muslim mariner—and landed at Calicut (modern Kolkata, formerly Calcutta), India. Da Gama returned to Portugal two years later, his ships laden with pepper and spices. The Portuguese soon set up trading posts and forts along the coasts of Africa, throughout the East Indies, and in China. They monopolized the spice and pepper markets and tried to control the in-

ternational sea routes between Europe and the Far East. For most of the 1500s, this minor country, small in size and population, was the richest nation in Europe. However, Portugal's wealth and power lasted hardly a century, as the Portuguese soon overextended their empire and found themselves challenged by the Spanish, Dutch, French, and English, who were entering the European Age of Exploration.

Portugal's age of greatness, personified by Vasco da Gama's heroic and daring adventures, was recorded and praised by the country's first renowned poet, Luis Vaz de Camoes [LU-ees VAZH th KAE-moish] (about 1524–1580) (Encounter figure 12.1), in his epic poem *The Lusiads*. Descended from the lesser nobility, Camoes's father was a sea captain whose travels probably inspired the son. Camoes attended a Portuguese university, which was just coming under the influence of Renaissance thought, where he studied Latin, mythology, history, and Greek literature. He enjoyed life in Lisbon for a short time before being banished—for unclear personal or political reasons—from the capital in 1546. His adventurous life now began: soldiering in North Africa, traveling to India, serving his government in the Far East, and, finally, returning home in 1570. *The Lusiads*, which he composed over the years of his wandering, was published in 1572. In recognition of his epic poem, he received a small stipend from the state and lived in modest circumstances until he died from the plague, in 1580.

The Lusiads, named for *Lusus*, the mythical founder of Portugal, was modeled on Vergil's *Aeneid*. In ten

Florentine author Niccolò Machiavelli began to appear, and at the heart of his thought is an anti-Classical spirit. Despite his education in Classicism and his strict rationalism, Machiavelli concluded that the human race was irremediably flawed. The contrast between the idealizing spirit of the High Renaissance and the anti-traditionalist views of Mannerism can be clearly seen by placing the work of the diplomat and courtier Baldassare Castiglione beside that of Machiavelli. Each wrote a book that can fairly be described as a manual of behavior—but there the resemblance ends.

Gaspara Stampa Gaspara Stampa (about 1524–1554) embraced the Classical tradition renewed by Petrarch in the 1300s; her work is thus typical of High Renaissance poetry. She adopted the Petrarchan sonnet as the preferred vehicle for her thoughts, and, like the earlier

poet, she used her poetic gifts to investigate the byways of love. Rather than glorifying the distant beloved, however, she asserted the moral worth of the suffering lover, thus transforming the essentially male Petrarchan ideal into a female point of view. Stampa poured out her heart in her verses, confessing vulnerability and lamenting abandonment. She portrayed the abandoned one as superior to the unresponsive loved one—the same lesson taught by Socrates in one of Plato's dialogues (see Chapter 3).

That Gaspara Stampa became a poet at all is testimony to the changing mores of Renaissance Venice, a city fabled for its love of luxury and pleasure. Her autobiographical poetry grew out of her situation in Venice's marginal world of writers, musicians, and artists, including aristocrats and high officials of church and state, who were notably indifferent to cantos, Camoes recounts Vasco da Gama's voyage to India. Along the route, da Gama and his men have many adventures. They encounter various enemies (usually Muslims), meet a friendly king to whom da Gama recounts the glorious history of Portugal, then sail across the Indian Ocean, establish trading outlets in India, and return home with their prizes and as triumphant heroes. As in the *Aeneid*, the author opens his tale *in medias res* (in the middle of events), with da Gama sailing up the east coast of Africa. Camoes then introduces the ancient Greek and Roman gods and goddesses, who play significant roles: Venus and Mars in aiding da Gama and Bacchus (the god of wine) in thwarting the explorer's journey.

Camoes was more than an accomplished storyteller: He was the voice of sixteenth-century Portugal and Europe. To him, Portugal had established itself as a great nation, acting as a harbinger for Europe's future, saving Europe from her enemies abroad, and helping spread the true Christian faith around the world. And, most important from a multicultural perspective, he linked Portugal's future, and, by extension, all of Europe's, to the hitherto little-known worlds overseas.

Learning from the Encounter **What** advantages enabled Portugal to become a nation of explorers? **What** were some consequences of the encounter between Portugal and the Far East? **Why** was Vasco da Gama seen as a hero? **Compare** *The Lusiads* with Vergil's *Aeneid*. **Discuss** the relationship between *The Lusiads* and the birth of a kind of multiculturalism in Europe.

Encounter figure 12.1   *Luis Vaz de Camoes.* Frontispiece from *The Lusiads*. 1655. *In this anonymous portrait, Luis Vaz de Camoes is dressed as a soldier and wears the laurel crown of the poet—an honorific symbol from Classical culture. The loss of his eye, he wrote, taught him about the expense of war and reminded him of the price he paid for adventure, heroism, fame, and his country's empire.*

Christian values. As a courtesan, or kept woman, she was a welcome member of this twilight world where sexuality was fused with art. Although she seems to have had several liaisons in her brief life, it was Count Collaltino di Collalto, a soldier, who won her heart. In time, Collaltino wearied of her, but Stampa transformed her hopeless love into some of the West's most touching poetry.

Castiglione   The reputation of Castiglione [kahs-teel-YOH-nay] (1478–1529) rests on *The Book of Courtier* or, simply, *The Courtier*, one of the most influential and famous books of the High Renaissance. Intended for Italian court society, *The Courtier* was published in 1528 and translated into most Western languages by the end of the century. It quickly became the bible of courteous behavior for Europe's upper classes and remained so

over the next two hundred years. Even today, at the beginning of the twenty-first century, Castiglione's rules for civilized behavior are still not completely outmoded.

A Mantuan by birth, Castiglione (Figure 12.6) based his guide to manners on life at the north Italian court of Urbino, where, between 1504 and 1517, he was the beneficiary of the patronage of its resident duke, Guidobaldo da Montefeltro (see Figure 11.2). Impressed by the graceful conversations of his fellow courtiers and especially taken with the charms of Urbino's duchess, Elisabetta, Castiglione was moved to memorialize his experiences in writing. *The Courtier* is composed as a dialogue, a literary form originated by Plato and favored by Cicero. Castiglione's dialogue is set in Urbino over a period of four evenings and peopled with actual individuals for whom he invents

Figure 12.6 RAPHAEL. *Baldassare Castiglione.* 1514. Oil on canvas, 32¼ × 26½". *Castiglione, author of a famous book on manners, was memorialized in this handsome portrait by Raphael, one of the great portrait painters of the High Renaissance. Elegantly groomed and completely at ease, Castiglione appears here as the age's ideal courtier—an ideal that he helped to establish.*

urbane and witty conversations that suit their known characters. Despite this realistic touch, his book's overall tone is definitely idealistic and hence expressive of High Renaissance style.

Castiglione's idealism shines forth most clearly in the sections in which the invited company try to define the perfect courtier, or gentleman. Under Duchess Elisabetta's eye, the guests cannot agree on which aspect of the ideal gentleman's training should take precedence: education in the arts and humanities or skill in horsemanship and swordplay. Some claim that a gentleman should be first a man of letters as well as proficient in music, drawing, and dance. In contrast, others believe that a courtier's profession is first to be ready for war, and hence athletics should play the central role. At any rate, both sides agree that the ideal

courtier should be proficient in each of these areas. A sign that the Renaissance had raised the status of painting and sculpture was the group's expectation that a gentleman be knowledgeable about both of these art forms.

The Courtier also describes the perfect court lady. In the minds of the dialogue participants, the ideal lady is a civilizing influence on men, who would otherwise be crude. To that end, the perfect lady should be a consummate hostess, charming, witty, graceful, physically attractive, and utterly feminine. She ought to be well versed in the same areas as a man, except for athletics and the mastery of arms. With these social attributes, the cultivated lady can then bring out the best in a courtier. But she must not seem his inferior, for she contributes to society in her own way.

Castiglione's book turned away from medieval values and led his followers into the modern world. First, he argued that social relations between the sexes ought to be governed by Platonic love—a spiritual passion that surpassed physical conquest—and thus he rejected medieval courtly love and its adulterous focus. Second, he reasoned that women in society should be the educated equals of men, thereby sweeping away the barrier that had been erected when women were excluded from the medieval universities. In the short run, the impact of Castiglione's social rules was to keep women on a pedestal, as courtly love had done. But for the future, his advice allowed women to participate actively in every aspect of society and encouraged their education in much the same way as men's.

Machiavelli   In contrast to Castiglione's optimism, the Florentine Machiavelli [mak-ee-uh-VEL-ee] (1469–1527) had a negative view of human nature and made human weakness the central message of his writings. If *The Courtier* seems to be taking place in a highly refined never-never land where decorum and gentility are the primary interests, Machiavelli returns the reader to the solid ground of political reality. His Mannerist cynicism about his fellow human beings sprang from a wounded idealism, for life had taught him that his early optimism was wrong. His varied works, by means of their frank assessments of the human condition, were meant to restore sanity to a world that he thought had gone mad.

Except for Martin Luther (see Chapter 13), Machiavelli left a stronger imprint on Western culture than any other figure who lived between 1494 and 1564. His most enduring contribution was *The Prince,* which inaugurated a revolution in political thought. Rejecting the medieval tradition of framing political discussions in Christian terms, Machiavelli treated the state as a human invention that ought not necessarily conform to religious or moral rules. He began the modern search for a science of politics that has absorbed political thinkers and policymakers ever since.

Machiavelli's career in sixteenth-century Italy, like that of many writers in antiquity, was split between a life of action and a life of the mind. Between 1498 and 1512, he served the newly reborn Florentine republic as a senior official and diplomat, learning statecraft firsthand. During these turbulent years, he was particularly impressed by the daring and unscrupulous Cesare Borgia, Pope Alexander VI's son. In 1512, after the fall of the Florentine republic to the resurgent Medici party, Machiavelli was imprisoned, tortured, and finally exiled to his family estate outside the city. There, as he recounts in one of his famous letters, he divided his time between idle games with the local farmers at a nearby inn and nightly communion with the best minds of antiquity in his study. From this background emerged in 1513 the small work known as *The Prince*, which circulated in manuscript until after his death. In 1532 it was finally published.

Machiavelli had several motives in writing this masterpiece. Despairing over Italy's dismemberment by the French and the Spanish kings, he hoped the book would inspire an indigenous leader to unify the peninsula and drive out the foreigners. Enlightened by his personal experience in Florence's affairs, he wanted to capture in writing the truth of the politics to which he had been a witness. And, of equal importance, by dedicating *The Prince* to the restored Medici ruler, he hoped to regain employment in the Florentine state. Like other writers in this age, Machiavelli could not live by his wits but had to rely on secular or religious patronage.

Machiavelli's work failed to gain its immediate objectives: The Medici despot brushed it aside, and Italy remained fragmented until 1870. But as a work that exposed the ruthlessness needed to succeed in practical politics, *The Prince* was an instant, though controversial, success. The book was denounced by religious leaders for its amoral treatment of political power and read secretly by secular rulers for its sage advice. In the prevailing climate of opinion in the sixteenth century, which was still under the sway of Christian ideals, the name "Machiavelli" became synonymous with dishonesty and treachery, and the word **Machiavellianism** was coined to describe the amoral notion that "the end justifies any means."

From the modern perspective, this negative valuation of Machiavelli is both too simplistic and too harsh. Above all else he was a clear-eyed patriot who was anguished by the tragedy unfolding in Italy. *The Prince* describes the power politics that the new sovereign states of France and Spain were pursuing in Italian affairs. Machiavelli realized that the only way to rid Italy of foreigners was to adopt the methods of its successful foes. Seeing his countrymen as cowardly and greedy, he had no illusions that a popular uprising would spring up and drive out Italy's oppressors. Only a strong-willed monarch, not bound by a finicky moral code, could bring Italy back from political chaos.

The controversial heart of Machiavelli's political treatise was the section that advised the ruler on the best way to govern. He counseled the prince to practice conscious duplicity, since that was the only way to maintain power and to ensure peace—the two basic goals of any state. By appearing virtuous and upright while acting as the situation demanded, the prince could achieve these fundamental ends. Machiavelli's startling advice reflected both his involvement in Italian affairs and his own view of human nature.

Painting

In the arts, the period between 1494 and 1564 was preeminently an age of painting, though several sculptors and architects created major works in their respective fields. The Classical values of idealism, balance, and restraint were translated by High Renaissance painters into harmonious colors, naturally posed figures with serene faces, realistic space and perspectives, and perfectly proportioned human bodies. After 1520, Mannerist tendencies became more and more evident, reflected in abnormal subjects, contorted figures with emotionally expressive faces, and garish colors.

Leonardo da Vinci   The inauguration of the High Renaissance in painting is usually dated from Leonardo's *The Last Supper*, which was completed between 1495 and 1498 (Figure 12.7). Painted for the Dominican friars of the church of Santa Maria delle Grazie in Milan, *The Last Supper* heralded the lucidity and harmony that were the essence of High Renaissance style. In executing the fresco, Leonardo unfortunately made use of a flawed technique, and the painting began to flake during his lifetime. Over the centuries, the work has been touched up frequently and restored seven times, with the most recent restoration completed in 1999. Nevertheless, enough of his noble intention is evident to ensure the reputation of *The Last Supper* as one of the best-known and most beloved paintings of Western art.

Leonardo's design for *The Last Supper* is highly idealized—a guiding principle of the High Renaissance. The fresco depicts the moment when Jesus says that one of the twelve disciples at the table will betray him. Ignoring the tradition that integrated this symbolic meal into an actual refectory, Leonardo separated the scene from its surroundings so that the figures would seem to hover over the heads of the clergy as they ate in their dining room. Idealism is also evident

Figure 12.7 LEONARDO DA VINCI. *The Last Supper.* (Restored.) 1495–1498. Oil-tempera on wall, 13'10" × 29'7½". Refectory, Santa Maria delle Grazie, Milan. *Classical restraint is one of the defining characteristics of this High Renaissance masterpiece. Instead of overwhelming the viewer with distracting details, Leonardo reduces the objects to a minimum, from the austere room in which the meal is being celebrated to the simple articles on the dining table. The viewer's gaze is thereby held on the unfolding human drama rather than on secondary aspects of the scene.*

in Leonardo's straightforward perspective. The artist makes Jesus the focal center by framing him in the middle window and locating the vanishing point behind his head. In addition, the arrangement of the banqueting party—Jesus is flanked by six followers on either side—gives the painting a balanced effect. This harmonious composition breaks with the medieval custom of putting the traitor Judas on the opposite side of the table from the others.

A final idealistic touch may be seen in the way that Leonardo hides the face of Judas, the third figure on Jesus' right, in shadow while illuminating the other figures in bright light. Judas, though no longer seated apart from the rest, can still be readily identified, sitting cloaked in shadows, reaching for the bread with his left hand, and clutching a bag of silver—symbolic of his treason—in the other hand. For generations, admirers have found Leonardo's fresco so natural and inevitable that it has become the standard version of this Christian subject.

Leonardo's setting and placement of the figures in *The Last Supper* are idealized, but his depiction of the individual figures is meant to convey the psychological truth about each of them. Jesus is portrayed with eyes cast down and arms outstretched in a gesture of resig-

nation, while on either side a tumultuous scene erupts. As the disciples react to Jesus' charge of treason, Leonardo reveals the inner truth about each one through bodily gestures and facial expressions: Beneath the visual tumult, however, the artistic rules of the High Renaissance are firmly in place. Since neither biblical sources nor sacred tradition offered an ordering principle, Leonardo used mathematics to guide his arrangement of the disciples. He divides them into four groups of three figures; each set in turn is composed of two older men and a younger one. In his conception, not only does each figure respond individually, but also each interacts with other group members.

Besides mastering a narrative subject like *The Last Supper*, Leonardo created a new type of portrait when he painted a half-length view of the seated *Mona Lisa* (Figure 12.8). As the fame of this work spread, other painters (and, later, photographers) adopted Leonardo's half-length model as a basic artistic format for portraits. This painting, perhaps the most famous portrait in Western art, was commissioned by a wealthy Florentine merchant. Avoiding the directness of *The Last Supper*, Leonardo hints at the sitter's demure nature through her shy smile and the charmingly awkward gesture of having the fingers of her right hand caress her left arm. In her face, celebrated in song and legend, he blends the likeness of a real person with an everlasting ideal to create a miraculous image. Further heightening the painting's eternal quality, the craggy background isolates the figure in space and time, in much the same way that the grotto functioned in Leonardo's *Virgin of the Rocks* (see Figure 11.23). Finally, he enhances the *Mona Lisa*'s mystery by enveloping the subject in the smoky atmosphere called *sfumato*—made possible by the oil medium—which softens her delicate features and the landscape in the background.

During the High Renaissance, Leonardo's great works contributed to the cult of genius—the high regard, even reverence, that the age accorded to a few select artists, poets, and intellectuals. *The Last Supper* earned him great fame while he was alive. The history of the *Mona Lisa* was more complicated, since it was unseen while he lived and found among his effects when he died in 1519. After his death, as the *Mona Lisa* became widely known, first as a possession of the king of France and later as a jewel in the Louvre collection, Leonardo was elevated to membership among the immortals of Western art.

Michelangelo   While Leonardo was working in Milan during most of the 1490s, Michelangelo Buonarroti [my-kuh-LAN-juh-lo bwo-nahr-ROH-tee] (1475–1564) was beginning a career that would propel him to the forefront of first the Florentine and later the Roman Renaissance, making him the most formidable artist of the sixteenth century. Michelangelo's initial fame rested on his sculptural genius, which manifested itself at the age of thirteen when he was apprenticed to the Early Renaissance master Ghirlandaio and then, one year later, taken into the household of Lorenzo the Magnificent, the Medici ruler of Florence. In time, Michelangelo achieved greatness in painting and architecture as well as in sculpture, but he always remained a sculptor at heart.

Michelangelo's artistic credo was formed early, and he remained faithful to it over his long life. Sculpture, he believed, was the art form whereby human figures were liberated from the lifeless prison of their surrounding material. In this sense, he compared the sculptor's creativity with the activity of God—a notion that would have been judged blasphemous in prior Christian ages. Michelangelo himself, unlike the skeptical Leonardo, was a deeply pious man given to bouts of spiritual anxiety. His art constituted a form of divine worship.

Central to Michelangelo's artistic vision was his most celebrated image, the heroic nude male. Like the ancient Greek and Roman sculptors whose works he studied and admired, Michelangelo viewed the nude male form as a symbol of human dignity. In the High

Figure 12.8   LEONARDO DA VINCI. *Mona Lisa*. 1503. Oil on panel, 30¼ × 21″. Louvre. *Leonardo's* Mona Lisa, *a likeness of the wife of the merchant Giocondo, illustrates the new status of Italy's urban middle class. This class was beginning to take its social cues from the fashionable world of the courts, the milieu described by Castiglione. Leonardo treats his middle-class subject as a model court lady, imbuing her presence with calm seriousness and quiet dignity.*

Renaissance, Michelangelo's nudes were based on Classical models, with robust bodies and serene faces. But in the 1530s, with the onset of Mannerism, the growing spiritual crisis in the church, and his own failing health, Michelangelo's depiction of the human figure changed. His later nudes had distorted body proportions and unusually expressive faces.

In 1508 Michelangelo was asked by Pope Julius II (pope 1503–1533) to decorate the Sistine Chapel ceiling. Michelangelo tried to avoid this commission, claiming that he was a sculptor and without expertise

Figure 12.9 MICHELANGELO. Sistine Chapel Ceiling. (Restored.) 1508–1512. Full ceiling 45 × 128'. The Vatican. *Michelangelo's knowledge of architecture prompted him to paint illusionistic niches for the Hebrew prophets and the pagan sibyls on either side of the nine central panels. Neo-Platonism inspired his use of triangles, circles, and squares, for these geometric shapes were believed to hold the key to the mystery of the universe. These various framing devices enabled him to give visual order to the more than three hundred figures in his monumental scheme.*

in frescoes, but the pope was unyielding in his insistence. The chapel had been built by Julius II's uncle, Pope Sixtus IV (pope 1471–1484), in the late 1400s, and most of the walls had already been covered with frescoes. Michelangelo's frescoes were intended to bring the chapel's decorative plan closer to completion.

The challenge of painting the Sistine Chapel ceiling was enormous, for it was almost 70 feet from the floor, its sides were curved downward, necessitating numerous perspective changes, and its area covered some 5,800 square feet. Michelangelo overcame all these difficulties, teaching himself fresco technique and working for four years on scaffolding, to create one of the glories of the High Renaissance and unquestionably the greatest cycle of paintings in Western art (Figure 12.9).

Michelangelo, probably with the support of a papal adviser, designed a complex layout (Figure 12.10) for the ceiling frescoes that combined biblical narrative,

theology, Neo-Platonist philosophy, and Classical allusions. In the ceiling's center, running from the altar to the rear of the chapel, he painted nine panels that illustrate the early history of the world, encompassing the creation of the universe, the fall of Adam and Eve, and episodes in the life of Noah. Framing each of these biblical scenes were nude youths, whose presence shows Michelangelo's belief that the male form is an expression of divine power.

On either side of the center panels, he depicted Hebrew prophets and pagan sibyls, or oracles—all foretelling the coming of Christ (Figure 12.11). The pagan sibyls represent the Neo-Platonist idea that God's word was revealed in the prophecies of pre-Christian seers. At the corners of the ceiling, he placed four Old Testament scenes of violence and death that had been allegorized as foreshadowing the coming of Christ. Michelangelo unified this complex of human and divine figures with an illusionistic architectural frame,

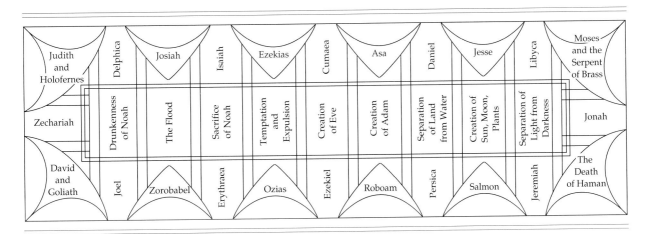

Judith and Holofernes	Delphica	Josiah	Isaiah	Ezekias	Cumaea	Asa	Daniel	Jesse	Libyca	Moses and the Serpent of Brass
	Drunkenness of Noah	The Flood	Sacrifice of Noah	Temptation and Expulsion	Creation of Eve	Creation of Adam	Separation of Land from Water	Creation of Sun, Moon, Plants	Separation of Light from Darkness	
Zechariah										Jonah
David and Goliath	Joel	Zorobabel	Erythraea	Ozias	Ezekiel	Roboam	Persica	Salmon	Jeremiah	The Death of Haman

Figure 12.10 Plan of Ceiling Frescoes, Sistine Chapel. 1508–1512. *The paintings on the Sistine Chapel ceiling may be grouped as follows: (1) the central section, which presents the history of the world from the creation (called "The Separation of Light from the Darkness") through the "Drunkenness of Noah"; (2) the gallery of portraits on both sides and at either end, which depict biblical prophets and pagan oracles; and (3) the four corner panels depicting Jewish heroes and heroines who overcame difficulties to help their people survive.*

Figure 12.11 MICHELANGELO. *The Libyan Sibyl.* (Restored.) Detail of the Sistine Chapel ceiling. 1508–1512. 12′11½″ × 12′6″. The Vatican. *Michelangelo, despite his manifold gifts as painter, sculptor, architect, and poet, always thought of himself as a sculptor, and this is quite evident in his portrait of the Libyan Sibyl, also known as Libica or Libyca (her Latin name). Her muscular back and shoulders are deviations from Classical sculptural ideals of feminine beauty and reflect, instead, Michelangelo's practice of using male models for female subjects. He was also fascinated by the anatomy of position, obvious in the Libyan Sibyl's rotated body, turned head, and outstretched arms. The Libyan Sibyl, according to the Sistine Chapel ceiling's Neo-Platonic plan, represented one of the Greek prophetesses often associated with Apollo. The church, by the end of the Middle Ages, had accepted twelve of these pagan seers. Like their counterparts—the prophets in the Old Testament—these adopted sibyls and their sayings foretold the coming of Jesus Christ. The book, which the Libyan Sibyl appears to be placing behind her, may symbolize these prophecies in writing.*

and he used a plain background to make the figures stand out.

The most famous image from this vast work is a panel from the central section, *The Creation of Adam* (Figure 12.12). In the treatment of this episode from the Book of Genesis, Michelangelo reduces the scene to a

Figure 12.12 MICHELANGELO. *The Creation of Adam.* Detail (restored) of the Sistine Chapel ceiling. 1511. 9′5″ × 18′8″. The Vatican. *One of the most celebrated details of this fresco is the outstretched fingers of God and Adam that approach but do not touch. By means of this vivid symbol, Michelangelo suggests that a divine spark is about to pass from God into the body of Adam, electrifying it into the fullness of life. The image demonstrates the restraint characteristic of the High Renaissance style. The Vatican's ongoing restoration of the Sistine Chapel frescoes has revealed the brilliant colors of the original, apparent in this detail.*

few details, in accordance with the High Renaissance love of simplicity. Adam, stretched out on a barely sketched bit of ground, seems to exist in some timeless space. Michelangelo depicts Adam as a pulsing, breathing human being. Such wondrous vitality in human flesh had not been seen in Western art since the vigorous nudes of ancient Greek art. In a bold move, Michelangelo ignored the Genesis story that told of God's molding Adam from dust. Instead, the artist paints Adam as half-awakened and reaching to God, who will implant a soul with his divine touch—an illustration of the Neo-Platonic idea of flesh yearning toward the spiritual.

By the 1530s, Michelangelo was painting in the Mannerist style, reflecting his disappointment with Florence's loss of freedom and his own spiritual torment. In this new style, he replaced his heroic vision with a fearful view of the world. A compelling example of this transformation is *The Last Judgment*, painted on the wall behind the Sistine Chapel's altar. This fresco conveys his own sense of sinfulness as well as humanity's future doom (Figure 12.13). Executed twenty-five years after the ceiling frescoes, *The Last Judgment*, with its images of justice and punishment, also reflects the crisis atmosphere of a Europe divided into militant Protestant and Catholic camps. In the center of the fresco, Michelangelo depicts Jesus as the divine and final judge, with right arm raised in a commanding gesture. At the bottom of the fresco, the open graves yield up the dead, and the saved and the damned (on Jesus' right and left, respectively) rise to meet their fate.

In this painting, Michelangelo abandons the architectural framework that had given order to the ceiling frescoes. Instead, the viewer is confronted with a chaotic surface on which a circle of bodies seems to swirl around the central image of Jesus. Michelangelo elongates the bodies and changes their proportions by reducing the size of the heads. There is no Classical serenity here; each figure's countenance shows the anguish provoked by this dreaded moment. Faced with judgment, some gesture wildly while others look beseechingly to their Savior. In this Mannerist masterpiece, simplicity has been replaced by exuberant abundance, and order has given way to rich diversity.

Raphael   The youngest of the trio of great High Renaissance painters is Raphael [RAFF-ee-uhl] Santi (1483–1520). Lacking Leonardo's scientific spirit and Michelangelo's brooding genius, Raphael nevertheless had such artistry that his graceful works expressed the ideals of this style better than did those of any other painter. Trained in Urbino, Raphael spent four years (from 1504 to 1508) in Florence, where he absorbed the local painting tradition, learning from the public

works of both Leonardo and Michelangelo. Inspired by what he saw, Raphael developed his artistic ideal of well-ordered space in which human beauty and spatial harmony were given equal treatment.

Moving to Rome, Raphael had an abundance of patrons, especially the popes. At the heart of Raphael's success was his talent for blending the sacred and the secular, and in an age when a pope led troops into battle or went on hunting parties, this gift was appreciated and rewarded. Perhaps Raphael's most outstanding work in Rome was the cycle of paintings for the *stanze*, or rooms, of the Vatican apartment—one of the finest patronage plums of the High Renaissance. Commissioned by Julius II, the *stanze* frescoes show the same harmonization of Christianity and Classicism that Michelangelo brought to the Sistine Chapel ceiling.

Raphael's plan for the four walls of the Stanza della Segnatura in the papal chambers had as its subjects philosophy, poetry, theology, and law. Of these, the most famous is the fresco devoted to philosophy called *The School of Athens* (Figure 12.14). In this work, Raphael depicts a sober discussion among a group of ancient philosophers drawn from all periods. Following Leonardo's treatment of the disciples in *The Last Supper*, Raphael arranges the philosophers in groups, giving each scholar a characteristic gesture that reveals the essence of his thought. For example, Diogenes sprawls on the steps apart from the rest—a vivid symbol of the arch Cynic's contempt for his fellow man. In the right foreground, Euclid, the author of a standard text on geometry, illustrates the proof of one of his theorems. In his careful arrangement of this crowd scene, Raphael demonstrates that he is a master of ordered space.

The School of Athens has a majestic aura because of Raphael's adherence to Classical forms and ideas. The architectural setting, with its rounded arches, medallions, and coffered ceilings, is inspired by Classical architectural ruins and also perhaps by contemporary structures. Perfectly balanced, the scene is focused on Plato and Aristotle, who stand under the series of arches at the painting's center. Raphael reinforces their central position by placing the vanishing point just above and between their heads. The two thinkers' contrasting gestures symbolize the difference between their philosophies: Plato, on the left, points his finger skyward, suggesting the world of the Forms, or abstract thought, and Aristotle, on the right, motions toward the earth, indicating his more practical and empirical method. Raphael also uses these two thinkers as part of his ordering scheme to represent the division of philosophy into the arts and sciences. On Plato's side, the poetic thinkers are gathered under the statue of Apollo, the Greek god of music and lyric verse; Aristotle's half includes the scientists under the statue of Athena, the Greek goddess of wisdom.

Figure 12.13 MICHELANGELO. *The Last Judgment.* 1536–1541. 48 × 44'. Sistine Chapel, the Vatican. *This* Last Judgment *summarizes the anti-Classicism that was sweeping through the visual arts. Other painters studied this fresco for inspiration, borrowing its seemingly chaotic composition, its focus on large numbers of male nudes, and its use of bizarre perspective and odd postures as expressions of the Mannerist sensibility. This fresco was recently cleaned (completed in 1994), its colors returned to the vivid primary colors of Michelangelo's original design and the draperies removed (they had been added during the Catholic Reformation).*

Figure 12.14   RAPHAEL. *The School of Athens.* 1510–1511. Fresco, 18 × 26'. Stanza della Segnatura, the Vatican. *Much of Raphael's success stemmed from the ease with which he assimilated the prevailing ideas of his age. For instance, the posture of the statue of Apollo in the wall niche on the left is probably derived from Michelangelo's* Dying Slave *(see Figure 12.1). For all his artistic borrowings, however, Raphael could be very generous, as indicated by the conspicuous way he highlights Michelangelo's presence in this fresco: The brooding genius sits alone in the foreground, lost in his thoughts and oblivious to the hubbub swirling about him.*

Of even greater fame than Raphael's narrative paintings are his portraits of the Virgin Mary, or his Madonna series. They set the standard for this form of portraiture with their exquisite sweetness and harmonious composition. Raphael's Madonnas clearly show the influence of Leonardo, whose Virgin and Christ child paintings were well known by then (see Figure 11.23). Like many of the Madonna series, Raphael's *Madonna of the Chair* (Figure 12.15) is organized in a pyramidal structure, a design he likely adopted from Leonardo. The Virgin and Christ child are not enthroned, as in the traditional setting, but are sitting, lovingly cuddled together, in a chair, as is hinted by the carved spindle (on the left). To the right stands the child John the Baptist, who looks up adoringly at the Virgin and her son. The Virgin's simple piety comes through in the way Raphael captures her beauty and tenderness in a lovely image. Unlike many religious paintings, the *Madonna of the Chair* does not deliver a theological message, preach a sermon, or tell a story. Because of its familial and domestic setting, this image is considered one of the most natural of Raphael's Madonnas and remains one of his most popular paintings today.

The Venetian School: Giorgione and Titian   Venice maintained its autonomy during the High Renaissance both politically and culturally. Despite the artistic pull of the Roman and Florentine schools, the Venetian artists stayed true to their Byzantine-influenced tradition of sensual surfaces, rich colors, and theatrical lighting. The two greatest painters of the Venetian High Renaissance were Giorgione [jor-JO-na] (about 1477–1510), who was acknowledged to be Venice's premier artist at the end of his life, and Titian [TISH-uhn] (about

Figure 12.15   RAPHAEL. *Madonna of the Chair.* Ca. 1515. Oil on wood panel, diameter 2′5″. Pitti Palace, Florence, Italy. *The Christ child caresses the Virgin's cheek—a conventional pose used by Renaissance artists for depicting the baby Jesus and Mary. Mary gazes at the viewer and seems to be contemplating her son's fate. Her head is covered in an oriental-inspired headdress (see Encounter in Chapter 11), and she wears a shawl over a red bodice. The Christ child sits on a blue pillow, the color mystically associated with the Virgin. The circular composition makes the three figures appear even more intimate, as it narrows the spaces between their bodies. Raphael probably painted the* Madonna of the Chair *for a church official.*

Figure 12.16   GIORGIONE. *The Tempest.* 1505. Oil on canvas, 31¼ × 28¾″. Galleria dell' Accademia, Venice. *Giorgione's mysterious painting evokes the period—called an "anxious hush"—that sometimes attends the prelude to a violent thunderstorm. He creates this tense mood through atmospheric effects that suggest a gathering storm: billowing clouds; a flash of lightning and its watery reflection; and, in particular, the stark color contrasts between the harshly lighted buildings and the somber hues of earth, sky, and river. The mood is also heightened by the presence of two vulnerable figures, especially the nursing mother who gazes quizzically at the viewer, about to be engulfed by the storm. The painting has a typical Venetian feature in its carefully rendered textures—flesh, cloth, wood, stone, and foliage. Giorgione's painting blazed the path for later artists, chiefly in northern Europe, who took the landscape as a subject.*

1488–1576), who in his later years was revered as Europe's supreme painter.

Little is known of Giorgione's life until the last years of his brief career. A student of Bellini, he won early fame, indicated by the rich private and public commissions he was awarded. Although only a few of his works survive, Giorgione's influence on the course of European art was substantial. His two major innovations, the female nude and the landscape, contributed to the growing secularization of European painting. These developments helped to make Venetian art distinctive from that of Rome and Florence.

The Tempest (Figure 12.16) is probably his best-known work. Breaking free of Bellini's influence, Giorgione created a dramatic landscape, framed on the left by a soldier and on the right by a partly clothed mother nursing a child, that did not allude to mythology, the Bible, or allegorical stories. Whereas Bellini's *St. Francis in Ecstasy* (see Figure 11.24) made the saint the focus of the painting, in *The Tempest* the framing figures are overshadowed by the menacing storm. Thus, Giorgione's landscape, freed of storytelling elements, becomes the subject and should be appreciated on its own terms.

Titian's paintings were prized not only for their easy grace and natural lighting—characteristics of the Venetian Renaissance—but also for their masterful use of color to create dramatic effects (see Figure 12.3). Titian's adherence to the principles of High Renaissance style is evident in such narrative paintings as his *Martyrdom of St. Lawrence* (Figure 12.17). According to tradition, St. Lawrence, a Spaniard, died in Rome in 258. As a deacon who was in charge of the church's treasures, he gave them to the poor. When ordered by the pagan Romans to turn this wealth over to the authorities, he assembled the poor and announced that here were the treasures of the church. For this act he was condemned to die, but he became the patron saint of the poor and poverty-stricken.

Titian's careful arrangement of this complicated scene of torture and martyrdom reflects his commitment to the principle of simplicity. In the foreground, he depicted St. Lawrence being roasted on a grill; to the right, Titian painted a pagan temple, rendered in sharply receding perspective, thereby framing the early Christian saint's death scene. The juxtaposition of the dying St. Lawrence and the Classical temple reminds the viewer that the pagan Romans had failed to eradicate Christianity. Typical of his works, Titian's subtle modulations of color to create a sense of harmony made him a leading "colorist"—someone concerned more with color than with form—and an inspiration to future generations of painters.

The School of Parma: Parmigianino Parma, in northern Italy, was another center of High Renaissance

Figure 12.17 TITIAN. *Martyrdom of St. Lawrence.* 1550s. Oil on canvas, 16′5½″ × 9′2″. Chiesa dei Gesuiti, Venice. *Even though Titian worked within the High Renaissance style, he was dissatisfied with the symmetry advocated by Classical rules and chose to deviate from their strict regularity in his works. In this painting, the temple's columns recede along a diagonal line, creating a sense of deep space in the foreground; within this space, he arranged objects in a triangular outline with the celestial light source at the apex. By using diagonal and triangular lines, as he often did in his religious works, Titian was able to achive dramatic and emotional effects without forfeiting coherence or meaning. He heightened this effect even further by bathing the human figures in the light from the sky and the glow from the torches and the fire underneath St. Lawrence.*

art, but the city's best-known artist is a founder of Mannerism, Parmigianino [pahr-mee-jah-NEE-noh] (1503–1540). The *Madonna with the Long Neck* shows Parmigianino's delight in ambiguity, distortion, and dissonance and his love of eccentric composition (Figure 12.18). Mary is portrayed with sloping shoulders and long arms in the manner of Botticelli, and her sensuous figure is not quite hidden under diaphanous draperies—a disturbing mix of sacred and profane

Figure 12.18 PARMIGIANINO. *Madonna with the Long Neck.* 1534–1540. Oil on panel, 7'1" × 4'4". Uffizi Gallery, Florence. *This Madonna by Parmigianino is one of the landmark works in the rise of the Mannerist style. Ignoring Classical ideals, Parmigianino exaggerates the Virgin's body proportions, especially the slender hands and long neck, and elongates the body of the sleeping Jesus. This anti-Classical portrait was greatly at odds with the prevailing High Renaissance image of the Madonna established by Raphael.*

love. A similar confusion exists in the depiction of the infant Christ: The bald baby Jesus appears more dead than alive, so that the subject invokes the Pietà image of the dead Christ stretched on his mother's lap along with the image of the Virgin and Christ child. On the left, five figures stare in various directions. In the background, unfinished columns and an old man reading a scroll, perhaps an allusion to biblical prophecies of Jesus' birth, add to the feeling of multiple focuses and contradictory scales. Unlike the art of the High Renaissance, which offered readily understood subjects, this Mannerist painting, with its uneasy blend of religious piety and disguised sexuality, is enigmatic.

Sculpture

Michelangelo's art is as central to the High Renaissance style in sculpture as it is in painting. An early sculpture that helped to inaugurate this style was the *Pietà* executed when he was twenty-one (Figure 12.19). The touching subject of the **Pietà**—Mary holding the body of the dead Christ—struck a responsive chord in Michelangelo, for he created several sculptural variations on the Pietà theme during his lifetime.

The first *Pietà*, executed in 1498–1499, about the same time as Leonardo's *Last Supper*, shows Michelangelo already at the height of his creative powers. He has captured completely a bewildering sense of loss in his quiet rendering of Mary's suffering. Everything about the sculpture reinforces the somber subject: the superb modeling of Jesus' dead body, with its heavy head and dangling legs; Mary's outstretched gown, which serves as a shroud; and Mary's body, burdened by the weight of her son. Like some ancient funeral

Figure 12.19 MICHELANGELO. *Pietà.* 1498–1499. Marble, ht. 5'8½". St. Peter's, the Vatican. *This Pietà is the only one of Michelangelo's sculptures to be signed. Initially, it was exhibited without a signature, but, according to a legend, when Michelangelo overheard spectators attributing the statue to a rival sculptor, he carved his signature into the marble strap that crosses Mary's chest.*

SLICE OF LIFE
Artists and Their Critics: Michelangelo's Strategy

GIORGIO VASARI
From *Life of Michelangelo*

The writer Giorgio Vasari (1511–1574) actually studied painting with Michelangelo, but he is known today primarily for his accounts of the lives of Renaissance artists, sculptors, and architects. Medieval artists had been categorized with guild members, who were little more than skilled craftspeople and not high up in the social hierarchy. In this telling excerpt, Vasari shows Michelangelo as a full-blown Renaissance artist: proud, confident, and ready to take on critics, even the head of the Florentine republic.

Some of his [Michelangelo's] friends wrote to him from Florence urging him to return there as it seemed very probable that he would be able to obtain the block of marble that was standing in the Office of Works. Piero Soderini, who about that time was elected Gonfalonier for life [head of the Florentine republic], had often talked of handing it over to Leonardo da Vinci, but he was then arranging to give it to Andrea Contucci of Monte Sansovino, an accomplished sculptor who was very keen to have it. Now, although it seemed impossible to carve from the block a complete figure (and only Michelangelo was bold enough to try this without adding fresh pieces) Buonarroti had felt the desire to work on it many years before; and he tried to obtain it when he came back to Florence. The marble was eighteen feet high, but unfortunately an artist called Simone da Fiesole had started to carve a giant figure, and had bungled the work so badly that he had hacked a hole between the legs and left the block completely botched and misshapen. So the wardens of Santa Maria del Fiore (who were in charge of the undertaking) threw the block aside and it stayed abandoned for many years and seemed likely to remain so indefinitely. However, Michelangelo measured it again and calculated whether he could carve a satisfactory figure from the block by accommodating its attitude to the shape of the stone. Then he made up his mind to ask for it. Soderini and the wardens decided that they would let him have it, as being something of little value, and telling themselves that since the stone was of no use to their building, either

botched as it was or broken up, whatever Michelangelo made would be worthwhile. So Michelangelo made a wax model of the young David with a sling in his hand; this was intended as a symbol of liberty for the Palace, signifying that just as David had protected his people and governed them justly, so whoever ruled Florence should vigorously defend the city and govern it with justice. He began work on the statue in the Office of Works of Santa Maria del Fiore, erecting a partition of planks and trestles around the marble; and working on it continuously he brought it to perfect completion, without letting anyone see it. . . .

When he saw the David in place Piero Soderini was delighted; but while Michelangelo was retouching it he remarked that he thought the nose was too thick. Michelangelo, noticing that the Gonfalonier was standing beneath the Giant and that from where he was he could not see the figure properly, to satisfy him climbed on the scaffolding by the shoulders, seized hold of a chisel in his left hand, together with some of the marble dust lying on the planks, and as he tapped lightly with the chisel let the dust fall little by little, without altering anything. Then he looked down at the Gonfalonier, who had stopped to watch, and said:

"Now look at it."

"Ah, that's much better," replied Soderini. "Now you've really brought it to life."

And then Michelangelo climbed down, feeling sorry for those critics who talk nonsense in the hope of appearing well informed.

Interpreting This Slice of Life   Why was Michelangelo eager to work on this particular block of marble? **What** does this story reveal about the character of Michelangelo? **Summarize** the exchange between Michelangelo and Soderini. **What** trick did Michelangelo play on Soderini? **Speculate** as to the motive behind Michelangelo's behavior. **Do** artists today show some of the same traits as those of Michelangelo in this piece? **Explain.**

monument, which the *Pietà* brings to mind, this sculpture of Mary and Jesus overwhelms the viewer with its sorrowful but serene mood.

In 1501, two years after finishing the *Pietà*, Michelangelo was given the commission by the city of Florence for the sculpture that is generally recognized as

his supreme masterpiece, the *David* (Figure 12.20). Michelangelo was eager for this commission because it allowed him to test himself against other great sculptors who had tackled this subject, such as Donatello in the Early Renaissance (see Figure 11.11). Moreover, Michelangelo, a great Florentine patriot, identified

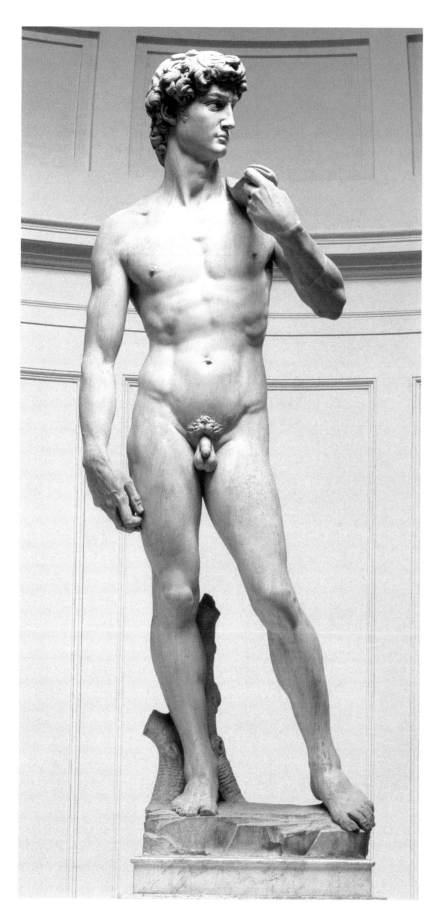

Figure 12.20 MICHELANGELO. *David.* 1501–1504. Marble, ht. 14′3″. Accademia, Florence. *Michelangelo's colossal David—standing more than 14 feet tall—captures the balanced ideal of High Renaissance art. The "closed" right side with its tensed hanging arm echoes the right leg, which supports the figure's weight; in the same way, the "open" left side with its bent arm is the precise counterpart of the flexed left leg. Further tension arises from the contrast between David's steady stare and the readiness of the right fist, which holds the stone. Through these means, Michelangelo reinforces the image of a young man wavering between thought and action.*

Figure 12.21 MICHELANGELO. *Pietà.* Before 1555. Marble, ht. 7′8″. Santa Maria del Fiore, Florence. *The rage that seemed to infuse Michelangelo's Mannerist vision in* The Last Judgment *appears purged in this* Pietà—*the work he was finishing when he died at the age of eighty-eight. Mannerist distortions are still present, particularly in the twisted body of the dead Christ and the implied downward motion of the entire ensemble. But the gentle faces suggest that serenity has been restored to Michelangelo's art.*

David with the aggressive spirit of his native city. Michelangelo's *David* was instantly successful, and the republic of Florence adopted the statue as its civic symbol, placing the work in the open square before the Palazzo Vecchio, the town hall. Damage to the statue through weathering and local unrest caused the civic leaders eventually to house Michelangelo's most famous sculpture indoors, where it remains today.

Michelangelo's *David*, rather than imitating Donatello's partly clothed and somewhat effete version, portrays the young Jewish warrior as a nude, Classical hero. Taking a damaged and abandoned block of marble, Michelangelo carved the colossal *David* as a muscular adolescent with his weight gracefully balanced

on the right leg, in Classical contrapposto. The *David* perfectly represents Michelangelo's conception of sculpture; imagining a human figure imprisoned inside marble, he simply used his chisel to set it free.

Michelangelo also made minor deviations from Classical principles in his rendition of David in the name of higher ideals, just as ancient artists had done. David's large hands, for example, are outside Classical proportions and suggest a youth who has yet to grow to his potential. And his furrowed brow violates the Classical ideal of serene faces but reflects his intense concentration.

Michelangelo's later sculpture is Mannerist in style, as are his later paintings. A second *Pietà*—with Christ,

Figure 12.22 BRAMANTE. Tempietto. After 1502. Marble, ht. 46'; diameter of colonnade 29'. San Pietro in Montorio, Rome. *Bramante's Tempietto is the earliest surviving High Renaissance building and an exquisite example of this style. Fashioned from pure Classical forms, the building is almost devoid of decoration except for architectural features, and the separate parts—dome, cylindrical drum, and base—are brought into a harmonious whole. The only significant missing feature (since High Renaissance buildings were always planned in relation to their enveloping space) is the never-finished courtyard.*

Mary, Mary Magdalene, and Joseph of Arimathea—shows the change in his depiction of the human form (Figure 12.21). In this somber group, Michelangelo's anti-Classical spirit is paramount. Jesus' body is elongated and unnaturally twisted in death; the other figures, with great difficulty, struggle to support his dead weight. But rather than detracting from the sculpture's impact, the awkward body adds to the scene's emotional interest—an aim of Mannerist art, which did not trust the viewer to respond to more orderly images. Joseph, the rich man who, according to the Gospel, donated his own tomb to Jesus, has Michelangelo's face—a face that is more a death mask than a human countenance.

Architecture

The architectural heir to Alberti in the early sixteenth century was Donato Bramante [brah-MAHN-tay] (1444–1514), who became the moving force behind the High Renaissance in architecture. Trained as a painter, Bramante rejected the reigning building style, called **scenographic**, in which buildings are composed of discrete, individual units. Instead, by concentrating on space and volume, Bramante created an architecture that was unified in all its components and that followed the rules of the Classical orders.

The clearest surviving expression of Bramante's architectural genius is the Tempietto, or little temple, in Rome (Figure 12.22). This small structure was designed both as a church, seating ten worshipers, and as a building marking the site of the martyrdom of St. Peter. Copied from the circular temples of ancient Rome, this small domed building became the prototype of the central plan church popularized in the High Renaissance and later.

Bramante's design for the Tempietto sprang from ancient Classical principles. Foremost was his belief that architecture should appeal to human reason and that a building should present a severe appearance and not seek to please through specially planned effects. Further, Bramante thought that a building should be unified like a piece of sculpture and that ornamentation should be restricted to a few architectural details.

In accordance with this artistic credo, the Tempietto functions like a work of sculpture; it is raised on a pedestal with steps leading up to its colonnaded porch. In the absence of sculptural decorations, the temple's ex-

Figure 12.23 MICHELANGELO. Dome of St. Peter's. View from the southwest. 1546–1564. (Completed by Giacomo della Porta, 1590.) Ht. of dome 452'. Rome. *Its harmonious design and its reliance on Classical forms made Michelangelo's dome an object of universal admiration when it was completed in 1590, after his death. From then to the present day, other architects have used his dome as a model, hoping to reproduce its Classical spirit.*

terior is accented with architectural details: the columns; the **balustrade**, or rail with supporting posts; and the dome with barely visible ribs. The proportions of its various features, such as the ratio of column widths to column heights, were based on ancient mathematical formulas. Unfortunately for Bramante's final conception, the plan to integrate the small temple into a circular courtyard of a nearby church was never completed. Despite the absence of this crowning touch, the Tempietto is one of the jewels of the High Renaissance.

Bramante had been commissioned by Pope Julius II to rebuild St. Peter's Basilica, the world's most famous church, but he died before his plans could be carried out. The supervision of the rebuilding of St. Peter's fell to other architects; eventually Michelangelo, at the age of seventy-one, was given this vital task. From 1546 until his death in 1564, Michelangelo, among his other artistic tasks, was occupied with St. Peter's, especially with the construction of the dome. Over the years, other building projects had come his way, but nothing could compare with the significance of this one. Although the dome was completed after his death and slightly modified, it remains Michelangelo's outstanding architectural monument and a splendid climax to his career.

Michelangelo's sculptural approach to architecture was similar to that of Bramante. In an attempt to integrate the dome of St. Peter's with the rest of the existing structure, Michelangelo used double Corinthian columns as a unifying agent. Because the facade of St. Peter's was altered in the 1600s, Michelangelo's dome is best observed from the southwest (Figure 12.23). Beginning at ground level, the Corinthian order provides the artistic cement that pulls the entire building together. Sometimes as columns, sometimes as pilasters, and sometimes as ribs, the double Corinthian units move up the walls, eventually up the dome's drum, and up the dome itself.

This plan for St. Peter's shows that Michelangelo the architect differed from Michelangelo the painter and sculptor. In painting and sculpture, he had by the 1530s become a Mannerist in his use of exaggeration and expressive effects. But in architecture, he stayed faithful to the High Renaissance and its ideal of harmonious design.

The preeminent architect of the Mannerist style was Andrea di Pietro (1508–1580), known as Palladio [pah-LAHD-yo], whose base of operations was Vicenza, in northern Italy. The name Palladio derives from Pallas, a name for Athena, the goddess of wisdom. Palladio's artistic creed was rooted in Classicism, but his forte

Figure 12.24 PALLADIO. Villa Rotonda (Villa Capra). Begun 1550. (Completed in about 1592 by Vincenzo Scamozzi [1548–1616].) Ht. of dome 70′; villa 80′ square. Vicenza. *Despite its harmonious proportions and Classical features, the Villa Rotonda belongs to the Mannerist style. Unlike High Renaissance buildings, which were designed to be integrated with their settings, this boxlike country house stands in an antagonistic relationship to its surrounding garden space. Furthermore, the Mannerist principle of elongation is apparent in its four long stairways. But the Villa Rotonda's most striking Mannerist feature is the surprise inherent in a plan that includes four identical porches.*

was the richly inventive way in which he could arrange the Classical elements of a building to guarantee surprise. He played with the effects of light and shadow, adding feature on top of feature, to create buildings that possess infinite variety in the midst of a certain decorative solemnity.

Palladio's most influential domestic design was the Villa Capra, more commonly called the Villa Rotonda because of its central circular area and covering dome (Figure 12.24). Inspired by ancient Roman farmhouses, the Villa Rotonda is a sixteenth-century country house built of brick and faced with stucco and located on a rise overlooking Vicenza. A dome provides a central axis from which four symmetrical wings radiate. Each of the four wings in turn opens to the outdoors through an Ionic-style porch raised on a pedestal. The porticoes, or covered porches supported by columns, then lead to the ground level through deeply recessed stairways. Statues stand on the corners and peak of

each of the four pediments, and others flank the four stairways.

Palladio's Mannerist spirit can be seen at work in the design of this building. Although the coldly formal porches are Classical in appearance, no Greek or Roman temple would have had four such identical porches, one on each side of the building (Figure 12.25). Palladio's design incorporates the unexpected and the contradictory within an apparently Classical structure.

Besides designing buildings, Palladio wrote about architecture in his treatise *Quattro libri dell'architettura*, or *The Four Books of Architecture*. Through its English translation, this work gained wide currency and led to the vogue of Palladianism in the English-speaking world. English aristocrats in the eighteenth century commissioned country houses built on Palladian principles, as did plantation owners in America's antebellum South.

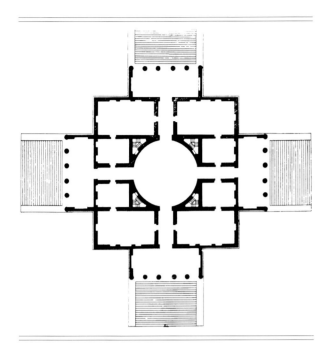

Figure 12.25 PALLADIO. Floor Plan of the Villa Rotonda. *Palladio designed the Villa Rotonda to further the social ambitions of its wealthy Venetian owner, so he made its most prominent interior feature a central circular area, or rotunda. Surmounted by a dome, this area was ideal for concerts, parties, and other entertainments. Palladio surrounded the rotunda with four identically shaped sets of rooms on two levels, where the family lived and guests were housed. Passageways led to the four porches, where villa residents could obtain relief from the summer's heat and enjoy diverting views of the surrounding countryside.*

Music

No radical break separates the music of the High Renaissance from that of the Early Renaissance. Josquin des Prez, the leading composer of the dominant Franco-Netherlandish school, had brought to a climax the Early Renaissance style of music while he was employed in Italy by the popes and the local aristocrats (see Chapter 11). Josquin's sixteenth-century pieces, which consist chiefly of religious Masses and motets along with secular *chansons*, or songs, simply heightened the ideal already present in his earlier works: a sweet sound produced by multiple voices, usually two to six, singing a cappella and expressing the feelings described in the text. Despite his interest in music's emotional power, Josquin continued to subordinate the song to the words—thus reflecting the needs of the church, the foremost patron of the age. This balancing act between the music and the words, resulting in a clearly sung text, was also evidence of the Classical restraint of his High Renaissance style. A striking feature of this style was the rich multichoral effect produced when the singing group was subdivided into different combinations of voices.

Experimentation with choral effects was carried into the next generation by Adrian Willaert [VIL-art] (about 1490–1562), a member of the Netherlandish school and a disciple of Josquin's. After the death of his mentor, Willaert was probably Europe's most influential composer. He made his mark on musical history from his post as chapel master of the cathedral of St. Mark's in Venice, and he is considered the founder

of the Venetian school of music. Taking advantage of St. Mark's two organs and the Venetian practice of blending instruments with voices, he wrote music for two choirs as well. By a variety of musical mechanisms, such as alternating and combining voices, contrasting soft and loud, and arranging echo effects, Willaert created beautiful and expressive sounds that were the ancestor of the splendid church concertos of the Baroque era. A benefit of Willaert's innovations was that the organ was released from its dependence on vocal music.

Missa Christus resurgens (Mass, the Risen Christ, about 1536), composed for four voices, shows Willaert's beautifully expressive style. Based on a short polyphonic work of the same name by the Franco-Flemish composer Jean Richafort (about 1480–about 1547), Willaert's Mass creates an appealing tapestry of sound, using melismas and imitation, but ensuring faultless understanding of the text—the essence of "modern" sacred polyphony, his legacy. The short Agnus Dei (Lamb of God) begins with all four voices forming an ever-shifting ground, from which the tenor voice emerges, soaring above the rest, giving an ethereal sound and acting as a musical metaphor for Christ's rebirth.

Except for the stylistic perfection achieved by Josquin and Willaert, the musical scene during this period witnessed only minor changes from that of the Early Renaissance. Instrumental music still played a secondary role to the human voice, though Josquin and Willaert composed a few pieces for specific instruments, either transposing melodies that originally had

Figure 12.26 GIOVANNI DI LUTERO, KNOWN AS DOSSO DOSSI. *Apollo and Daphne.* Ca. 1538. Oil on canvas, 6'2" × 3'9". Galleria Borghese, Rome. *Dosso Dossi (about 1490–1542), who lived in Ferrara and was influenced by Giorgione, Titian, and probably Raphael, painted many allegorical and mythological scenes. His sense of color and understanding of light added to the magic and fantasy of his works. Apollo, the patron of poetry and music and leader of the Muses, is placed in the foreground, while Daphne, whom he constantly chased, is in the middle ground, fleeing from her pursuer. An Italian city, perhaps Bologna (identified by its Twin Towers), fills in the background. Apollo, rather than playing the lyre, an ancient Greek string instrument, is holding a violin. This painting may be one of the first to feature the violin, since it had only appeared about 1510. By the 1570s, Andrea Amati, who is recognized as the designer of the first violin, was making the instrument at his workshop in Cremona, a city within eighty miles of Ferrara. Antonio Stradivari and Andrea Guarneri, two of the most famous violin makers in history, were pupils of Niccolo Amati, Andrea's grandson. Antonio Stradivari brought violin making to its highest level of perfection. He produced 540 violins along with many other string instruments. Today, a Stradivari violin is considered one of the most precious musical instruments in the world.*

been intended for singers or adapting music forms from dance tunes.

Still, one development was the appearance of the violin, which evolved from the Arabic *rebec* and the medieval fiddle and its Italian cousin (Figure 12.26). A bowed, stringed musical instrument, the violin is probably the most popular musical instrument in the world today. By the end of the sixteenth century, Italian violin makers had determined the instrument's basic size and shape, though the number of strings continued to vary for several decades.

The development that had the most promise for the future was the invention of families of instruments, ranging from the low bass to the high treble, which blended to make a pleasant sound. In most cases, these families, called **consorts**, consisted of either recorders or viols. The consorts represented the principle of the mixed instrumental ensemble, and from this beginning would emerge the orchestra. Recorders and viols could also be blended to make an agreeable sound; when human voices were added to the mixture, the conditions were ripe for opera.

The Legacy of the High Renaissance and Early Mannerism

From a contemporary perspective, the seventy-year period during which the High Renaissance and Early Mannerism flourished is the Golden Age of the West in certain artistic and humanistic areas. In the visual arts—painting, sculpture, and architecture—standards were set and indelible images created that have not been surpassed. In political theory, this age produced the Mannerist thinker Machiavelli, who is the founder of modern political thought.

Beyond those achievements, three other important steps were being taken on the road to the modern world. On a political level, the beginnings of the modern secular state may be seen in the changes taking place in France, Spain, and England. What was innovative, even revolutionary, for these countries in the early sixteenth century has become second nature to the states of the twenty-first century, both in the Western world and beyond. On a social level, a new code of behavior appeared in the Italian courts and was in time adopted throughout Europe. Not only did the rules of courtesy finally penetrate into the European aristocracy and alter their behavior, but also they eventually trickled down to the middle classes. By our day, the behavior of Castiglione's courtier and lady, though in diluted form, has become the model for all Western people with any shred of social ambition. On the international level, the first stirrings of multiculturalism were being felt, as Portugal, followed by Spain, England, France, and the Netherlands, began to initiate contacts with societies beyond Europe—thus initiating the process of globalization that defines our world today.

Another new idea was beginning to develop now as well. The Classical and the medieval worlds had praised what was corporate and public, in conformity with traditional, universal values. But in the 1500s a few artists and humanists, along with their patrons, began to revere what was individual and private. The supreme example of free expression and of the "cult of genius" in the High Renaissance was Leonardo da Vinci, whose encoded notebooks were meant for his personal use, not for general publication. Early Mannerism carried individual expression to extremes by finding merit in personal eccentricities and unrestrained behavior. That patrons supported the new works of these artists and humanists demonstrates the rise of the belief that free expression is both a social and a private good. Both the High Renaissance and Early Mannerism encouraged the daring idea of individualism and thereby introduced what has become a defining theme of Western culture.

KEY CULTURAL TERMS

High Renaissance
Mannerism
civic humanism
Machiavellianism

Pietà
scenographic
balustrade
consort

SUGGESTIONS FOR FURTHER READING

CASTIGLIONE, B. *The Book of the Courtier.* Translated by G. Bull. New York: Penguin, 1967. A flowing translation; includes a helpful introduction and descriptions of characters who participate in the conversations recorded by Castiglione; first published in 1528.

MACHIAVELLI, N. *The Prince.* Translated by G. Bull. New York: Penguin, 1971. The introduction covers Machiavelli's life and other writings to set the stage for this important political work; written in 1513.

SUGGESTION FOR LISTENING

WILLAERT, ADRIAN. Willaert is particularly noted for his motets, such as *Sub tuum praesidium,* which reflect the Renaissance humanist ideal of setting the words precisely to the music. His *Musica nova,* published in 1559 and including motets, madrigals, and instrumental music, illustrates the complex polyphony and sensuous sounds that made him a widely imitated composer in the second half of the sixteenth century.

1500

AD

Albertus Durerus Noricus
ipsum me proprijs sic effin
gebam coloribus ætatis
anno XXVIII.

13 NORTHERN HUMANISM, NORTHERN RENAISSANCE, RELIGIOUS REFORMATIONS, AND LATE MANNERISM

1500–1603

As the High Renaissance and Early Mannerism were unfolding in Italy (see Chapter 12), the rest of Europe was being transformed by three developments: a literary movement, two new artistic styles, and a religious crisis. The literary movement and the new artistic styles were partially inspired by the cultural changes under way in Italy. However, the religious crisis, in its early years, was unique to northern Europe; by midcentury, it had become intertwined with local and international politics. Northern (or Christian) humanism, as the literary movement was called, was inspired by both the Italian Renaissance, with its emphasis on Classical studies, and Late Medieval lay piety, with its focus on a simpler Christianity. Two distinct artistic styles now appeared in Europe: the Northern Renaissance, lasting from 1500 until about 1560, and Late Mannerism, enduring for the rest of the century. The course of these literary and artistic developments was, in turn, affected by the religious crisis that soon engulfed all of Europe (Timeline 13.1).

Germany became the epicenter of the spiritual earthquake called the **Reformation,** a movement that forever shattered the religious unity of the West. The Reformation, like the Renaissance, looked to the past for inspiration and ideas, but rather than focusing on the Classical world of Greece and Rome, the religious leaders of the Reformation looked to the early Christian church before it became hierarchical and bureaucratic. Almost immediately, these reformers met with unbending resistance from the contemporary church and its officials. From the confrontations between these hostile groups emerged the labels the two sides still wear today: the Protestants, who

◄ **Detail** ALBRECHT DÜRER. *Self-Portrait.* 1500. Oil on panel, 26¼ × 19¼″. Alte Pinakothek, Munich.

Timeline 13.1 THE SIXTEENTH CENTURY

1500					1545	1563			1600

The Reformation and Founding of the Protestant Order	Council of Trent	The Counter-Reformation

1509	1517	1521	1533	1540	1564	1586	1592–1594
Erasmus's *The Praise of Folly*	Luther's Ninety-five Theses	Independent Lutheran churches founded	Church of England founded	Jesuit order founded	Death of Michelangelo	El Greco's *Burial of Count Orgaz*	Tintoretto's *Last Supper*

1513 Dürer's *Knight, Death, and the Devil*

1541 Independent Calvinist churches founded

1566 Bruegel's *Wedding Dance*

1590–1610 Shakespeare's plays performed

wanted a complete renovation of the church, and the Roman Catholics, who were largely satisfied with the church as it was.

The Catholics did not oppose all change, however. In the second half of the sixteenth century, they conducted the **Counter-Reformation,** purifying the church and setting it on the path that it followed until the 1960s. In contrast, the Protestants disagreed over basic Christian doctrines and soon split into separate sects.

In the 1560s, the Counter-Reformation began to have a strong impact on culture, especially in Spain and Italy. Late Mannerism in the arts, architecture, and music flourished in these areas, until the Baroque style rose at the end of the century. One outstanding exception to this Late Mannerist trend was found in Spanish literature. Spanish writing, which had entered its Golden Age in about 1500, reached its zenith with the works of Cervantes.

NORTHERN HUMANISM

Northern humanism, also known as **Christian humanism,** shared some of the aesthetic values of the High Renaissance, such as idealism, rationalism, and a deep love for Classical literature. Unlike the humanist movement in Italy, however, the northern humanists were preoccupied with the condition of the church and the wider Christian world. For these northern thinkers, the study of Christian writings went hand in hand with research on the Greco-Roman classics, and their scholarship was meant to further the cause of ecclesiastical reform.

Like the lay pietists of the Late Middle Ages (see Chapter 10), from whom they drew inspiration, the northern humanists approached their faith in simple

terms. They taught that any Christian who had a pure and humble heart could pray directly to God. These scholars further strengthened the appeal of this simple creed by claiming that it was identical with Christ's scriptural message, which they were discovering in their vernacular translations of the New Testament.

The thinking of the Christian humanists, notably in Germany, was tinged with national feeling and hostility toward Italian interference in their local religious affairs. Their Christian humanism with its simple faith led them to believe that by imitating the early church—freed of corrupt Italian leaders—they could revitalize Christianity and restore it to its original purpose.

A notable French humanist was François Rabelais [RAB-uh-lay] (about 1494–1553), who wrote a five-part satire collectively titled *The Histories of Gargantua and Pantagruel.* In these works, Rabelais vigorously attacked the church's abuses and ridiculed the clergy and theologians. Beneath the satire, he affirmed the goodness of human nature and the ability of men and women to lead useful lives based on reason and common sense. However, his skepticism and secularism, as well as the ribald humor, obscene references, and grotesque escapades of his heroes, put Rabelais in a unique category, well outside the mainstream of northern humanism.

Another northern humanist outside the mainstream was Marguerite of Angoulême, queen of Navarre (1492–1549), sister of King Francis I. She was an important protector of Rabelais, Protestant reformers, and other free spirits. Most famously in literary history, Marguerite of Navarre—her usual name—was associated with the *Heptameron* (from the Greek word for "seven"), a collection of seventy frankly sexual tales in the style of Boccaccio's *Decameron* (see Chapter 10). Whether or not Marguerite actually wrote these tales is an unresolved topic of scholarly debate, although it is generally agreed that the stories were written for the French court. Based on the evidence of the stories, the French nobility welcomed outspokenness in sexual matters (the themes of the tales are rape, seductions bordering on rape, incest, and trespasses of the sexual and marital codes of aristocratic life) and condoned Protestant-like religious views (the tale's villains are often members of monastic orders and are consistently portrayed as gluttons, parasites, and rapists). The social matrix that spawned the *Heptameron* was northern humanism, a world hostile to the dying ethos of medieval monasticism.

The outstanding figure among the northern humanists—and possibly among all humanists—is the Dutch scholar Desiderius Erasmus (Figure 13.1). Erasmus (about 1466–1536) was fully prepared for the great role that he played in the Christian humanist movement. He studied in the pietistic atmosphere of a school run by the Brethren of the Common Life, where he was introduced to the Greek and Roman classics. He later completed his education at the University of Paris. This training was supposed to lead to a church career, but Erasmus never wore clerical garb or lived as a priest, although he was ordained. On the contrary, with the aid of patrons he patiently pursued a writing career, enjoying the comforts of a scholarly life. He also traveled widely throughout western Europe, eventually finding a second home in England among the intellectual circle gathered around Thomas More, England's lord chancellor and another well-known humanist.

As a humanist, Erasmus believed in education in the *humanitas* sense advocated by Cicero (see Chapter 5), emphasizing study of the classics and honoring the dignity of the individual. As a Christian, he promoted the "philosophy of Christ" as expressed in the Sermon on the Mount and in Jesus' example of a humble and virtuous life. Erasmus earnestly felt that the church could reform itself and avoid division by adopting the moderate approach that he advanced.

Despite a prodigious output of books that include treatises, commentaries, collections of proverbs, a manual for rulers, and a definitive edition of the Greek New Testament, Erasmus's fame rests on his most popular work, *The Praise of Folly*, written in 1509. This lively book, filled with learned humor, captures the gentle grace and good sense of the Christian humanists. Even this work's Latin title, *Encomium Moriae*, reflects a lighthearted spirit, for it is a punning reference to the name of Sir Thomas More—the English friend to whom the book is dedicated.

In this work, Erasmus pokes fun at the human race by making his mouthpiece a personified Folly—an imaginary creation who symbolizes human foolishness. In a series of sermons, Folly ridicules every social

Figure 13.1   HANS HOLBEIN THE YOUNGER. *Erasmus of Rotterdam.* Ca. 1523–1524. Oil on panel, 16½ × 121". Louvre. *This sensitive likeness of the great humanist was painted by one of the most successful Northern Renaissance portraitists, Hans Holbein. The artist conveys his subject's humanity and intellectual authority by depicting him engaged in writing one of his many treatises. The realistic detail, warm colors, and dramatic lighting are typical of Holbein's work.*

group, from scholars and lawyers to priests and cardinals. Erasmus's jolly satire, especially in its exposure of clerical hypocrisy, struck a responsive chord among educated people. But with the rapid growth of Protestantism, such cultivated criticism only got Erasmus into trouble. Roman Catholics felt betrayed by his mild barbs, and Protestants accused him of not going far enough. In the end, this mild reformer and gentle scholar sadly witnessed the breakup of his beloved church while being denounced by both sides.

For a time, Luther had hoped for the support of Erasmus in his reforming crusade. But that changed in 1524 when Erasmus asserted, contrary to Luther, that the human will was free; otherwise, according to Erasmus, the Bible would not have urged sinners to repent. Erasmus's argument so enraged Luther that he countered with a tract in which he declared that the human will was irrevocably flawed; in Luther's view, only

God's free grace could save any man or woman from the fires of hell. So intemperate was Luther's reply that the two scholars never communicated again. Erasmus's calm voice went unheeded amid the wild rhetoric and religious mayhem that characterized this age.

THE NORTHERN RENAISSANCE

While Italy was experiencing the High Renaissance and Early Mannerism, northern Europe was also bursting with cultural vitality. The cultural scene was affected by contemporary events in and outside northern Europe and by the last phase of the medieval world. The religious upheavals—the Reformation and the Counter-Reformation—split Europe into two camps and triggered wars across the Continent and within some of the emerging sovereign states. Late Medieval trends, such as Gothic forms and mysticism, manifested themselves in art and religion, while northern humanism shaped the minds and hearts of many thinkers, writers, and artists. The result of the religious and political conflicts and the dissimilar artistic tendencies meant that the **Northern Renaissance**—the term used to describe the culture of sixteenth-century northern Europe—was a period marked by competing styles. By midcentury, however, Early Mannerism was encroaching on the ideals of Renaissance painting and literature north of the Alps.

Northern Renaissance Thought and Science

As the Renaissance spread to northern Europe, it produced new attitudes for understanding the world, ranging from analyzing the nature and function of political institutions to the structure and organization of the human body. Jean Bodin's analysis of political systems and Andreas Vesalius's discoveries about the human body, while seemingly so different from one another, were indications of how the Renaissance was changing Europe. Both men were products of the new learning in the universities, they shared the Renaissance's goal of seeking to understand the worlds of nature and humanity, and they were heavily influenced by the political and religious events swirling around them.

Jean Bodin   Jean Bodin [ZHAHN bo-DAN] (1530–1596), the French political philosopher and author, lived through eight civil and religious wars that threatened to end the monarchy and to divide France into two religious factions. The Huguenots, or French Protestants, who coalesced into a political union composed of some of the French nobility and the rising middle class, fought the Catholic faithful and those loyal to the kings—mainly the peasants and the city of Paris. The wars—complicated by royal marriages, dynastic rivalries, and shifting alliances—lasted from about 1562 to 1598.

Bodin, born into a fairly prosperous working-class family, studied philosophy in Paris and civil law at the University of Toulouse. While teaching at that University, he came to appreciate and advocate Renaissance humanism as the best basis for an education. Later, he returned to Paris, where he entered government service, acting as councilor and adviser on religious and political issues for the French crown. In 1583, he moved to Laon, where he worked for the municipal government by day and at night wrote the theoretical works that made him the leading political thinker of this turbulent era.

As both a participant and observer of the period's wars and as a student of history and law, Bodin made it his lifes mission to understand the ideal state, which he set forth in his masterpiece of political philosophy, *Six Livres de la République (Six Books of the Commonwealth, or Republic)* (1576). According to Bodin, the basic issue in politics is sovereignty, that is, the political entity that has control of a state's internal and external affairs. And sovereignty, he further noted, is absolute and perpetual and resides always in the office of the monarchy. By claiming sovereignty to be inalienable—that is, not able to be shared, given away, or lost—Bodin, in effect, makes an argument for absolute monarchy. Within the context of absolute monarchy, Bodin allowed that there could be three different forms of government. First, there is the rule of one, or monarchy. Second, there is the rule of the few, or aristocracy. And, third, there is the rule of all, or democracy. Monarchs, by virtue of being naturally invested with absolute power, might choose to allow those who were the richest and from noble families to participate in government—thus creating an aristocracy. Similarly, monarchs might allow certain rights, including the ability to hold public office, to all subjects—thus making a democracy. Nevertheless, in both an aristocracy and a democracy, despite appearances, power ultimately remained in the hands of the monarch.

Bodin also distinguished among types of monarchies and explained the bases of their power. The absolute monarch, while not bound to the civil law, was bound to natural and divine law, and those who went against those laws—such as enslaving a people or seizing subjects' property—were tyrannical and should be opposed. Monarchs rule by divine right, because the Divine is looking out for the well-being of humanity—their lives and their property. And this is what a monarch does. Having witnessed the wars between Huguenots and Catholics, Bodin asserted that in a monarchy a uniform religious faith would be best, be-cause it would flourish and this would help ensure peace and harmony in the state. He concluded that a unity of religion and of country was the only way for a people to live.

Since Bodin, along with Machiavelli, was one of the first to focus on the ideal state in the modern world, his writings influenced the direction of later political theory. While attacking the last vestiges of the feudal system and all those elements in society that stand in opposition to royal power, Bodin's book is also a fore-cast of the future debate about the meaning of sover-eignty. Over the next two centuries, until the Age of Democratic Revolutions (see Chapter 17), political thinkers made sovereignty the central issue in their theories, raising questions about who possessed it and how best to use it in a civil society.

Andreas Vesalius   Andreas Vesalius [va-SAIL-yas] (1514–1564), like Bodin, personified the humanistic traits of the Renaissance. Both observed and analyzed the world around them, both looked to history for guidance, and both offered new ways to understand the human condition. However, Vesalius made his contributions in the sciences, while Bodin furthered the study of political science (a term attributed to him).

Born in Brussels, Vesalius came from a family of physicians who served at the court of the Holy Roman emperor. His studies took him to the elite universities of Europe: the University of Louvain (in modern Bel-gium), the University of Paris, and the University of Padua. The Paris years were critical, for it was there that he learned to dissect human cadavers and to ana-lyze human bones. His medical career began when he was appointed professor of surgery and anatomy at the University of Padua. There, based on his research, he discovered errors in the teachings of Galen, the renowned Roman physician whose findings in human anatomy had been the standard in medical training for the previous 1300 years (see Chapter 5). Indeed, Vesa-lius came to understand that Galen had only dissected apes, not human cadavers.

The young Vesalius, convinced that Galen's obser-vations were incorrect and that humans and animals do not share the same anatomy, first circulated some of his classroom drawings. Later, in 1543, he published his findings, *De Humani Corporis Fabrica (The Seven Books on the Structure of the Human Body)* or, as it was commonly known, *Fabrica.*

Fabrica's detailed and accurate descriptions, espe-cially illustrations of the human body, which were based on human dissections, transformed the study of anatomy (Figure 13.2). At the same time, Vesalius stirred up a fierce controversy among his contempo-raries, many of whom thought Galen was right, and

Figure 13.2   Andreas Vesalius. Drawing from *De Humani Corporis Fabrica.* 1543. *Vesalius wrote, illustrated, and super-vised the drawing, engraving, and printing of the first compre-hensive illustrated textbook on anatomy. The drawings of his dissections were engraved on wooden blocks and they, today, are considered to be some of the finest engraved art of the sixteenth century.* Fabrica *exceeded all previous medical texts in its clear and accurate illustrations, high standard of craftsmanship, and printing, layout, and organization. Vesalius, following a tradition of Renaissance anatomical drawings, placed his "muscle-men" in a landscape—with a village or Classical ruins in the background. He also gave each subject a Classical pose. None of his figures is a cadaver lying on a dissecting table. By rendering the human body in such settings, Vesalius made it easier for the viewer to accept what he had done, and, at the same time, these drawings also demonstrate that even medical illustrations are subject to the same cultural forces as the rest of a period's creative achievements.*

opposition from Catholic Church officials, who be-lieved that dissection of human cadavers flouted canon law. By proving Galen wrong, Vesalius did for anatomy what Copernicus did for astronomy in show-ing Ptolemy to be in error (see Chapter 15). Within a short time, Vesalius's writings were accepted in nearly all European medical schools, and his work came to in-fluence other sciences—physiology, biology, and the study of medicine.

With his reputation secure, Vesalius turned to medical practice and was appointed court physician to Emperor Charles V (see Figure 12.3)—thus following in the tradition of his forebears. He traveled with the emperor on many trips and campaigns. After Charles V abdicated in 1556, Vesalius served Philip II of Spain. Vesalius died in 1564 on his way home from a pilgrimage to Jerusalem.

Northern Renaissance Literature

The sixteenth century was truly an amazing period in literature, for the vernacular tongues now definitively showed that they were the equals of Latin as vehicles for literary expression. In the High Middle Ages, Dante led the way with his *Divine Comedy;* now, other authors writing in the vernacular found their voices. Montaigne, writing in French, and Shakespeare, writing in English, left such a rich legacy that, by common consent, each is revered as the outstanding writer of his respective tradition.

Michel de Montaigne   Like an ancient Roman senator, Michel de Montaigne [mee-SHEL duh mahn-TAYN] (1533–1592) balanced a public career with a life devoted to letters. While serving as a judge and a mayor, he worked on his lifelong project, which he called *Essays.* This collection of discursive meditations is essentially the autobiography of his mind and is thus representative of the individualistic spirit of the Renaissance. What emerges is a self-portrait of a man who is both intellectually curious and fascinated by his own mental processes and personality. He describes his contradictions, accidental as well as deliberate, though he writes that his loyalty is always to truth. What keeps the *Essays* from falling into sterile self-absorption is Montaigne's firm sense that in revealing himself he is speaking for others.

But the *Essays* are more than an early example of confessional literature. They also constitute, in the French tradition, the earliest work of *moralisme,* or moralism, and the beginning of modern skepticism. In terms of morality, Montaigne attached little importance to Christian ethics, since cruelty and barbarism in the name of religion were justified equally by Protestant and Catholic. His musings reflected France's chaotic condition during the religious wars, causing him to question the Renaissance's natural optimism. Montaigne searched for, without ever discovering, a moral code that was centered on a human world and that no one could deny. In his skeptical outlook, Montaigne rejected the Renaissance view of humanity as a microcosm of the universe. Indeed, he claimed that he saw nothing except vanity and insignificance in human beings and their reasoning. Montaigne, however, avoided total skepticism, for although he denied that humans could ever achieve perfect knowledge, he held that practical understanding was possible.

William Shakespeare   Montaigne wrote during a period when religious wars were disrupting France, but England at the same time was enjoying a relatively calm period of cultural exuberance, the Age of Elizabeth. Under Queen Elizabeth I, who reigned from 1558 to 1603, London rose to an eminence that rivaled that of Florence of the Early Renaissance. English playwrights rescued tragedy and comedy from the oblivion into which they had fallen with the collapse of Rome. As in ancient Greece, tragedy and comedy again became part of popular culture. A purely secular and commercial theater now emerged, with professional playwrights and actors, playhouses, and a ticket-buying public (Figures 13.3 and 13.4).

The revived popularity of the theater represented a dramatic reversal of a cultural outlook that had prevailed in the West since the time of Augustine in the fifth century (see Chapter 7). Christian scholars had condemned the stage for its wicked displays and seductive delights. On occasion, medieval culture had spawned morality plays and dramas with biblical themes, but those edifying works remained primitive in form, with little care given to language, character, or plot. A play like the fifteenth-century *Everyman,* for example, was intended mainly to reinforce Christian values and only incidentally to entertain or to provoke thought. Under Elizabeth, many able dramatists began to appear, such as Thomas Kyd (about 1557–1595) and Christopher Marlowe (1564–1593). These playwrights revolutionized drama in a single generation. However, first honors must be given to William Shakespeare, the greatest dramatist in the English language.

Shakespeare (1564–1616) was born in Stratford-upon-Avon, a market-town, and educated in its grammar school. By 1590 his plays were being performed on the London stage, and his active public career continued until 1610, when he returned home to Stratford to enjoy country life. His early retirement reflected the success that he had achieved as an actor, a theater owner, and a playwright. But it was as the age's leading dramatist that he earned undying fame, mastering the three different genres of history, comedy, and tragedy. His thirty-seven dramas constitute his legacy to the world. Just as tragedies ranked higher than comedies in ancient Greece, so have Shakespeare's tragedies enjoyed a reputation superior to that of his other writings. Of the eleven tragedies, many are regarded as masterpieces; *King Lear, Othello, Julius Caesar, Macbeth,* and *Romeo and Juliet* are constantly

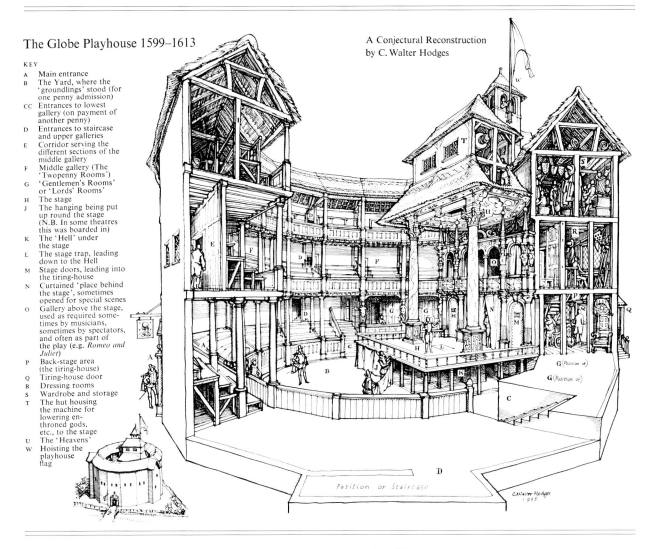

The Globe Playhouse 1599–1613

A Conjectural Reconstruction
by C. Walter Hodges

KEY

A   Main entrance
B   The Yard, where the 'groundlings' stood (for one penny admission)
CC   Entrances to lowest gallery (on payment of another penny)
D   Entrances to staircase and upper galleries
E   Corridor serving the different sections of the middle gallery
F   Middle gallery (The 'Twopenny Rooms')
G   'Gentlemen's Rooms' or 'Lords' Rooms'
H   The stage
J   The hanging being put up round the stage (N.B. In some theatres this was boarded in)
K   The 'Hell' under the stage
L   The stage trap, leading down to the Hell
M   Stage doors, leading into the tiring-house
N   Curtained 'place behind the stage', sometimes opened for special scenes
O   Gallery above the stage, used as required sometimes by musicians, sometimes by spectators, and often as part of the play (e.g. *Romeo and Juliet*)
P   Back-stage area (the tiring-house)
Q   Tiring-house door
R   Dressing rooms
S   Wardrobe and storage
T   The hut housing the machine for lowering enthroned gods, etc., to the stage
U   The 'Heavens'
W   Hoisting the playhouse flag

Figure 13.3   Reconstruction of the Globe Playhouse, 1599–1613. *When the Globe Playhouse of London was razed in 1644 to make way for new buildings, one of the most significant monuments of Renaissance England disappeared: the theater where most of Shakespeare's plays were first performed. This cutaway drawing, made by C. W. Hodges, a leading expert on the theaters of the period, attempts to depict the Globe Playhouse as it appeared in Shakespeare's day. As shown in the drawing, the Globe was a sixteen-sided structure with the stage erected in an open courtyard bounded on three sides by three tiers of seats.*

Figure 13.4   The Reconstructed Globe Playhouse. 1996. London, England. *Spurred by the vision of the American actor Sam Wanamaker, an international effort resulted in the construction of a modern Globe Playhouse, near the site of the original theater of Shakespeare's time. This theater, which staged its first performances in August 1996, is true to Elizabethan design and construction methods, including wooden nails and thatched roof. Performances are staged in the daytime, when weather permits—just as they were four centuries ago.*

performed on the stage and often presented in films, in English as well as other languages. Perhaps the Shakespearean tragedy that stands above the rest, however, and that is reckoned by many to be his supreme achievement, is *Hamlet*.

Hamlet is a **revenge tragedy,** among the most popular dramatic forms in the Elizabethan theater. The revenge play had its own special rules, consisting chiefly of a murder that requires a relative of the victim, usually with the prompting of a ghost, to avenge the crime by the drama's end. The origin of this type of play, with its characteristic violence and suspense, has been obscured by time, although Seneca's Roman tragedies, which were known and studied in England, are almost certainly a source.

The basic plot, characters, and setting of *Hamlet* are drawn from a medieval chronicle of evildoings at the Danish court. Elizabethan theatergoers had seen an earlier dramatized version (now lost) before Shakespeare's play was performed in 1600–1601. Shakespeare thus took a well-known story but stamped it with his own genius and feeling for character. In its basic conception, *Hamlet* is a consummate expression of Mannerist principles. Shakespeare presents Hamlet from shifting perspectives, preferring ambiguity, rather than portraying him from a single vantage point in accordance with the Classical ideal. By turns, Hamlet veers from madman to scholar to prince to swordsman, so that a unified, coherent personality is never exposed to the audience. Because of Hamlet's elusive character, he has become the most frequently analyzed and performed of all Shakespeare's heroes.

Another aspect of this play reminiscent of the Mannerist aesthetic is the self-disgust that seems to rule Hamlet's character when he is alone with his thoughts. Whereas the High Renaissance reserved its finest praise for the basic dignity of the human being, Hamlet finds little to value in himself, in others, or in life. Instead, he offers a contradictory vision:

> It goes so heavily with my disposition that this goodly frame, the earth, seems to me a sterile promontory; this most excellent canopy, the air . . . this majestical roof fretted with golden fire, why, it appears no other thing to me but a foul and pestilent congregation of vapours. What a piece of work is a man, how noble in reason, how infinite in faculty; in form and moving how express and admirable, in action how like an angel, in apprehension how like a god! the beauty of the world, the paragon of animals! And yet to me what is this quintessence of dust? Man delights not me.
>
> (Act 2, Scene 2)

In its construction, the tragedy of *Hamlet* is typical of Shakespeare's plays. All his dramas were written for commercial theater troupes and were not intended especially for a reading public. Only after Shakespeare's death were his plays published and circulated to a general audience and thus regarded as "literature."

Northern Renaissance Painting

The Northern Renaissance emerged during an era of cultural crisis. In about 1500, the Late Gothic style of the Flemish school was starting to lose its appeal, except for one extraordinary artist, Hieronymus Bosch. At the same time, growing numbers of artists were attracted to the new Italian art, especially to Mannerism. In the 1520s, the influence of the Protestant Reformation also began to become apparent in the arts. Individual tastes and styles became important, and secular subjects were acceptable, in part because some of the more fervent Protestants looked on enjoyment of the visual arts as a form of idol worship. They even destroyed some paintings, statues, and stained glass that portrayed religious subjects. The combined influences of Mannerism and Protestantism produced three artists of unique stature who reflected the turbulent world of post-Lutheran Europe in quite different ways: Dürer, Grünewald, and Bruegel.

Albrecht Dürer   Albrecht Dürer [AHL-brekt DYOU-ruhr] (1471–1528), the son of a goldsmith, pursued a career as an engraver and painter. After studying in Germany, he traveled widely in Italy, where he absorbed the lessons of Renaissance art. Between 1510 and 1519, he earned great fame for the works that he executed for the Holy Roman emperor, but he also discovered that his true artistic bent was for engraving, either on wood or on metal. His engravings, which were issued in multiple editions, enhanced his reputation, and as a result he received many commissions throughout Germany and the Netherlands. Near the end of his life, Dürer became a Lutheran, and some of his last paintings indicate his new faith.

Fully aware of himself and his place in the world, Dürer showed a Renaissance sensibility in introspective self-portraits, especially in the famous work in which he depicts himself as a Christ figure (Figure 13.5). In this stunning image—the intense stare suggests that it was painted while the artist was looking in the mirror—Dürer blends a dandified likeness of himself with a standard Flemish representation of Christ. Such an identification of his artistic self with Jesus' divine power would have been unthinkable before the Renaissance. Nevertheless, Dürer remained true to the spirit of the Middle Ages, for he was also following the tradition of mysticism in which he saw himself as striving to imitate the example of Christ.

Although Dürer's paintings brought him recognition and wealth in his day, his engravings constitute

Figure 13.5 ALBRECHT DÜRER. *Self-Portrait.* 1500. Oil on panel, 26¼ × 19¼". Alte Pinakothek, Munich. *The Northern Renaissance shared with the Italian Renaissance an emphasis on the individual, as shown in this self-portrait by the German artist Albrecht Dürer—one of the first artists to make himself the subject of some of his paintings. In a series of self-portraits, starting at the age of thirteen, he examined his face and upper torso and rendered them in precise detail, recording his passing age and moods. An unusual aspect of Dürer's self-portrait is that it suggests that he has taken on the role of artist in much the manner that Jesus had taken on the role of Savior.*

his greatest artistic legacy. At the time of Luther's revolt, Dürer engraved the scene called *Knight, Death, and the Devil* (Figure 13.6). This magnificent engraving shows a knight riding through a forest, ignoring both the taunts of Death, who holds up an hourglass to remind him of his mortality, and the fiendish Devil, who watches nearby. The knight is probably meant as a symbol of the Christian who has to live in the practical world.

Dürer's *Knight, Death, and the Devil* combines Late Gothic and Renaissance elements to make a disquieting scene. From the northern tradition are derived the exquisite details, the grotesque demon, and the varied landscape in the background. From Renaissance sources comes the horse, which Dürer copied from models seen during his Italian tour.

Matthias Grünewald A second major German artist in this period is Matthias Grünewald [muh-THI-uhs GREW-nuh-vahlt] (about 1460–1528), who was less influenced by Italian art and more northern in his techniques than Dürer. His paintings represent a continuation of the Late Gothic style rather than a northern development of Renaissance tendencies.

Figure 13.6 ALBRECHT DÜRER. *Knight, Death, and the Devil.* 1513. Engraving, approx. 9⅝ × 7 7/12". The Fogg Art Museum, Harvard University. Gift of William Gray from the Collection of Francis Calley Gray. *Dürer's plan for this work probably derived from a manual by Erasmus that advised a Christian prince on the best way to rule. In his version, Dürer portrays the Christian layman who has put on the armor of faith and rides steadfastly, oblivious to the various pitfalls that lie in his path. The knight is sometimes identified with Erasmus, whom Dürer venerated.*

Figure 13.7 MATTHIAS GRÜNEWALD. *The Crucifixion,* from the *Isenheim Altarpiece.* 1515. Oil on panel, 9′9½″ × 10′9″. Musée d'Unterlinden, Colmar, France. *Jesus' suffering and death were a central theme in northern European piety, particularly after the plague of the fourteenth century. Northern artists typically rendered Christ's death in vivid and gory detail. Grünewald's* Crucifixion *comes out of this tradition; Christ's broken body symbolizes both his sacrificial death and the mortality of all human beings.*

Grünewald's supreme achievement is the *Isenheim Altarpiece,* painted for the church of St. Anthony in Isenheim, Germany. The altarpiece includes nine painted panels that can be displayed in three different positions, depending on the church calendar. When the *Isenheim Altarpiece* is closed, the large central panel depicts the Crucifixion (Figure 13.7). In crowding the five figures and the symbolic lamb into the foreground and making Christ's body larger than the rest, Grünewald followed the Late Gothic style. This style is similarly apparent in every detail of Christ's tortured, twisted body: the gaping mouth, the exposed teeth, the slumped head, and the torso raked

by thorns. And Grünewald's Late Gothic emotionalism is evident in his treatment of the secondary figures in this crucifixion panel. On the right, John the Baptist points toward Jesus, stressing the meaning of his sacrificial death. John the Baptist's calmness contrasts with the grief of the figures on the left, including Mary Magdalene, who kneels at Jesus' feet, and the apostle John, who supports a swooning Mary. The swaying bodies of these three figures reinforce the anguish on their faces. One Renaissance feature in this otherwise Gothic painting is the low horizon line, which shows Grünewald's knowledge of Italian perspective.

Hieronymus Bosch Hieronymus Bosch [hi-uh-RAHN-uh-muhs BOSH] (about 1450–1516), whose personal life is a mystery, painted works that still puzzle modern experts. Treating common religious subjects in bizarre and fantastic ways, he earned a reputation even among his contemporaries for being enigmatic.

Much of Bosch's distinctive art may be explained by the changes under way in northern Europe during his day. In the late fifteenth century, political upheavals in Burgundy caused aristocratic patronage to decline, and, at the same time, a feeling of dread, born perhaps of the periodic ravages of the plague, stalked the land. In the early sixteenth century, serious religious trouble that would end with the revolt of Martin Luther was brewing. Influenced by the foregoing forces and also perhaps subjected to his own private demons, Bosch created a body of art that defies strict classification in the stylistic sense.

In his paintings, Bosch seems torn between the declining Late Gothic style and the soon-to-be-born Mannerist style. His addiction to precise detail and his frequent use of sweeping landscapes are clear signs of the debt he owed Flemish art and, in particular, the age's illuminated manuscripts; but his tendency to endow his works with ambiguous, or even cynical, moral messages points to the works of later Dutch artists, such as Pieter Bruegel the Elder. Perhaps the best way to look at Bosch is as an artist whose originality was so pronounced that he stands outside any historical period.

Of Bosch's thirty or more paintings, the best known and most controversial is *Garden of Earthly Delights*, a work in oil on three wood panels, called a **triptych** (Figure 13.8). When open, the triptych displays three separate but interrelated scenes, organized around the theme of the creation, fall, and damnation of the human race. Most confusingly, the center and right panels are crowded with tiny figures—mostly human, though some are grotesquely monstrous—performing a variety of peculiar actions. Although no scholarly consensus exists as to the ultimate meaning of this work, certain features can be identified that may help the viewer understand it.

The left panel of *Garden of Earthly Delights* shows the Garden of Eden, with Adam and Eve in the foreground and the first plants and animals (including "natural" animals but also weird monsters) scattered around. Contrary to the story in the Bible, Jesus holds the newly created Eve's hand and introduces her to Adam. Many scholars interpret this panel as making Eve the source of original sin.

The center panel—the dramatic focus of the triptych—depicts the sins of the flesh in lurid and metaphorical detail. In the top horizontal band, the waters of the earth converge to make a fountain, an image that has been identified as a false symbol of human happiness. In the middle band, naked young women cavort in a pool while a parade of naked youths riding animals—partly realistic, partly fantastic—encircles them. In the lower band, more naked men and women engage in various sex acts or are involved with huge birds, fruits, flowers, or fish. The diverse images in this central panel symbolize Bosch's perspective on the human condition: perpetual enslavement to the sexual appetite unleashed by Adam and Eve's first sin. Also worthy of note is that this crowded scene includes many black males and females, an early instance of nonwhites in Western art.

The triptych's right panel is a repulsive portrait of Hell and the pains human beings must suffer for their sins. A horrific scene of fiery ruins and grisly instruments of torture, this panel proclaims Bosch's hopeless vision of the futility of life on earth. For the artist, human beings cause their own destruction through wicked desires. Nowhere in the entire work is there a hint of salvation.

A few scholars reject this gloomy view of Bosch's message by trying to link the triptych to the beliefs of the Adamites, an underground, heretical sect. If their interpretation is correct, then the central panel may be understood as the Adamites' unusual vision of Paradise. Most scholars reject this view, however, and hold instead that Bosch was a stern moralist, mocking the corrupt society of his day.

Pieter Bruegel the Elder The life and work of Pieter Bruegel [BREW-gul or BROY-gul] the Elder (about 1525–1569) indicate the changes in northern European art in the mid–sixteenth century. The great German artists Dürer and Grünewald were now dead, and German art, which had dominated northern Europe in the early sixteenth century, was in decline. Protestant iconoclasm had taken its toll, and the demand for religious art had markedly diminished. Within this milieu, Bruegel chose a novel set of artistic subjects—landscapes, country-life scenes, and folk narratives—and in the process became the first truly modern painter in northern Europe. Bruegel's subjects, rooted in the Flemish tradition, were often devoid of overt religious content and presented simply as secular art, although he also painted a number of pictures on standard religious themes such as the adoration of the Magi.

Of Bruegel's forty or more surviving paintings, some of the most memorable are his scenes of peasant life or folk narratives. In them, he always depicted his peasant subjects in their natural settings, neither romanticizing nor patronizing them. He portrayed the common folk as types, never as individuals, and often as expressions or victims of the blind forces of nature.

Figure 13.8 HIERONYMUS BOSCH. *Garden of Earthly Delights*. Ca. 1510–1515. Oil on wood, center panel 86⅝ × 76¾"; each side panel 86⅝ × 38¼". Prado, Madrid. *Careful study of the minute details of this triptych has uncovered the major sources of Bosch's artistic inspiration—namely, medieval folklore, common proverbs, exotic learning, and sacred beliefs. For example, folklore inspired the ravens and owl (left panel), traditional emblems of nonbelievers and witchcraft, respectively; the Flemish proverb "Good fortune, like glass, is easily broken" is illustrated by the lovemaking couple under the glass globe; allusions to exotic learning may be seen in the egg shapes (all three panels), symbolic of the world and sex in the pseudoscience of alchemy; and Christian belief is evident throughout the triptych, but especially in the right panel, showing the punishment of sinners.*

In scenes of country weddings and dances, he could convey pessimism tinged with grudging admiration about human nature, as reflected in the peasants' simple, lusty behavior. Overall, though, he seemed more inspired by the timeless attitudes of the ordinary folk around him than by the prevailing intellectual thought of his times. This is most certainly the case in *Netherlandish Proverbs*, a depiction of proverbial sayings and moralizing allegories (Figure 13.9). **Proverbs** embody folk wisdom and, through repetition, have come to be regarded as wise sayings.

Bruegel's fascination with landscapes and village scenes are the backdrop for all of the sayings and stories he illustrates in *The Netherlandish Proverbs*. Bruegel views his subjects from above and they are loosely scattered across the tilted picture plane—a typical format for him. The nearly one hundred figures, either singly or in groups, represent a saying or a moral tale based on the Bible, folk tales, or popular culture. As in his other narrative paintings, he creates an organic harmony with splashes of color—yellows, browns, reds, blues, whites, and greens. And he uses the bold reds, blues, and greens to draw attention to a particular scene, as, for example, the man in the red cloak and red stockings (right foreground), who has a spinning globe on his left thumb ("He has the world on a string"). The painting also shows that Bruegel was, at the time, under the influence of Bosch (see Figure 13.8). Bosch's

Figure 13.9   PIETER BRUEGEL THE ELDER. *Netherlandish Proverbs.* 1559. Oil on panel, 3'10" × 5'4½". Staatliche Museen, Berlin. *Bruegel's satirical, ironic, and, ultimately, pessimistic view of human nature permeates his* Netherlandish Proverbs. *In Bruegel's "world turned upside down," human stupidity, folly, and vanity are depicted in nearly every scene. Many of these proverbs, or versions of them, have come down to modern times, such as the man in the lower left ("Don't butt your head against a brick wall"); the man in the center foreground ("Don't throw your roses before swine"); in the water ("Big fish eat the little fish"); and in the lower right corner ("Don't cry over spilled milk"). Many of the proverbs have sexual references, such as the woman in red (center foreground) who is putting a blue cloak on her husband. This act signifies she is unfaithful, and thus he is a cuckold.*

influence is evident in the complex narrative, the grotesqueness of some figures and scenes, and the general moralizing about the foolishness, absurdity, and sinfulness of human life.

A painting that illustrates Bruegel in a less dark attitude toward country folk is his lively *Wedding Dance* (Figure 13.10). The painting records the exuberant revels of the lusty men and the kerchief-wearing women. The bride and groom cannot be distinguished from the other dancers. Typical of Bruegel's style, there is a high horizon and a high point of view, so that we look at the

scene from above. This effect, along with the crude faces of the peasants, underscores the impression that these are types, not individuals. The painting's composition reinforces the sense of peasant types in the way that the swirling figures in the foreground are repeated in the background in ever-diminishing size.

Besides paintings, Bruegel is known for his sixty-one drawings, which were devoted to either fantastic or naturalistic subjects. About half of the drawings were made as preparations for engravings, and, as such, they establish Bruegel as the heir to the Netherlandish

Figure 13.10   PIETER BRUEGEL THE ELDER. *Wedding Dance.* 1566. Oil on panel, 47 × 62".
Detroit Institute of Arts. *Bruegel has made a sensuous arrangement out of the dancers and by-standers at this country wedding. The line of dancers winds from the foreground back through the trees, where it reverses itself and returns to its original starting point. The sense of lively movement is reinforced by the vivid red colors in the hats and vests and by the stomping feet and flailing arms.*

artists who developed the print as a new artistic me-dium in the Late Middle Ages (see Chapter 10). One of Bruegel's drawings, which was not intended for print-making, is *The Painter and the Connoisseur* (Figure 13.11). This work pioneered a new subject in art: a satiric view of the relations between an artist and an art expert. Bruegel depicts the painter as an eccentric visionary, and the connoisseur as a self-deluded igno-ramus who wears glasses and a ridiculous cap that covers his ears. Other details confirm this negative im-age of the connoisseur: the hairless face, the nonexis-tent lips, and the pinched expression.

THE BREAKUP OF CHRISTENDOM: CAUSES OF THE RELIGIOUS REFORMATIONS

Although the reasons for the breakup of Europe's reli-gious unity are complicated, two basic causes are clear: the radical reshaping of Western society and cul-ture that began about 1350 and the timeless spiritual yearnings of human beings. After 1500 these two forces came together in Germany to make conditions ripe for religious revolution. What made change virtu-ally inevitable was the combination of the historical

Figure 13.11 PIETER BRUEGEL THE ELDER. *The Painter and the Connoisseur.* Mid-1560s. Pen and gray-brown ink, with touches of light brown ink, 10 × 8½″. Graphische Sammlung Albertina, Vienna. *Bruegel's drawing was probably intended as an inside joke about the artistic community and not as an artwork to be engraved or sold. The painter, with his skullcap and bushy hair and beard, is depicted as a dreamer, his mind lost in thought as he stares into the distance. Behind him stands an art expert, who clutches the "money" pouch at his waist and stares in a different direction from that of the painter.*

trends occurring during the Late Middle Ages: the corruption and abuses inside the church, the rise of sovereign states, the decay of medieval thought, and the revival of humanism.

The church had been plagued with problems since the Avignon papacy and the Great Schism of the fourteenth century and the challenges to its time-honored practices posed by the growth of heretical groups like the Hussites (see Chapter 10). Without firm guidance from the popes, many clergy led less than exemplary lives, particularly those inside the monasteries. Lay writers, now unafraid of the church, delighted in describing clerical scandals, and the populace gossiped about their priests' latest sins. Everywhere anticlericalism seemed on the rise.

Perhaps the church could have reformed the clergy and stemmed the tide of a rising anticlericalism if the papacy had been morally and politically strong, but such was not the case. By 1500 the popes were deeply distracted by Italian politics and fully committed to worldly interests. The church also lost power to secular rulers, who were determined to bring all their subjects under state control. By 1500 the English and the French kings, to the envy of other European rulers, had made their national churches relatively free of papal control.

In Germany, however, where no unified nation-state had developed, the local secular leaders had no say about clerical appointments and were unable to control the ecclesiastical courts or prevent the church from collecting taxes—conditions that intensified anticlericalism and hatred of Rome. The German princes, who were already struggling to be free from the control of Charles V, made church reform a rallying cry and turned against Rome as well as the Holy Roman emperor. As events unfolded, the popes were incapable of preventing these princes from converting their lands into independent states outside papal jurisdiction (Map 13.1).

The Protestant Order

Protestantism first appeared in Germany, where Martin Luther led the founding of a new religious sect in the 1520s. In the 1530s a second generation of Protestants acted on the opportunity created by Luther. John Calvin, a French scholar, formed an independent church in Geneva, Switzerland, and King Henry VIII removed the English church from Roman rule (see Timeline 13.1).

Luther's Revolt One of the church's more glaring abuses was the selling of indulgences—pardons that reduced the amount of penance that Christians had to perform to atone for their sins—a practice that dated from the High Middle Ages. In 1517, in response to the archbishop of Mainz's sale of indulgences to raise

ENCOUNTER

Indigenous Peoples and New Spain

As religious wars in the 1500s were altering the map of Europe, the rise of European colonies in the New World, often inspired by religious motives, was changing the whole geography of Western culture. Spain led the way with its vast overseas empire covering much of North and South America. In 1535 Spain organized its overseas possessions into four viceroyalties—regional governments, each headed by a viceroy—to rule the conquered lands. New Spain was the northernmost viceroyalty, which, at its height, included all Spanish territories north of the Isthmus of Panama, Central America, Mexico, the Spanish islands in the Caribbean, and what is now the southwestern United States, California, and Florida, along with the Philippine Islands in the Pacific. The viceroyalty of New Spain held sway over much of its vast domain until 1821, when it collapsed in the wake of the wars of revolution that swept the Americas in the late eighteenth and early nineteenth centuries (see Chapter 17).

New Spain, over the course of its almost-400-year history, did bring its lands and peoples into the Western orbit, though with a distinctive character that reflected the ideas, rituals, beliefs, imagery, and traditions of indigenous populations. Spain's encounter with native peoples was reminiscent of that of ancient Rome's with the Greeks: The losing side gradually conquered the conquerors. The native cultures slowly permeated nearly all aspects of colonial life in New Spain, especially art and religion.

In a triumphal gesture the Spanish conquerors built the capital of New Spain, Mexico City, on the ruins of the Aztec capital, Tenochtitlán. Mexico City soon evolved into the grandest city of Spanish North America. From there, the viceroys carried out their plans to impose Western values and institutions on the native peoples: convert them to the Christian faith, establish schools and universities, and construct an economy based on mining, ranching, and farming. These policies at the local level were enforced through the *encomienda* system, in which Indians living within a geographic area were given to a landowner—an economic unit modeled on Europe's feudal past. The purpose of this economic system was to Christianize the native peoples, but it soon degenerated into oppression, exploita-

tion, and virtual slavery. Modern studies estimate that, from 1500 to 1600, the native population of New Spain declined sharply from twenty-five million to one million, because of overwork, harsh living conditions, and, most important, death from European diseases for which indigenous peoples had no immunity.

Although exploited by the Spanish ruling class, the descendants of the Native Americans quickly became the backbone of New Spain and the new emerging culture. The large numbers of mestizos (Spanish, "mixed"), persons of both European and Amerindian ancestry, with a 50:50 ratio—the result of intermarriage—stimulated a cross-cultural exchange. Once the feudal caste system of New Spain was swept away, in the new nation-states, after 1820, "mestizo" came to mean a person with any claim to both European and Amerindian ancestry. Currently, mestizos are believed to comprise 70 percent or more of the populations of most former lands of New Spain, including Mexico, Nicaragua, Panama, Honduras, and El Salvador. Mexico has embraced its mestizo heritage and looks upon the Spanish Conquest as "the painful birth of the mestizo nation." The ethnic traditions of these lands have been further enriched by the indigenas, purebred indigenous peoples, who adhere to their own dress, customs, and indigenous languages. In Mexico, for instance, indigenas account for about 10 percent of the populace.

Although Western styles were in the ascendant in art and sculpture, indigenous and mestizo influences were evident in the art and architecture of New Spain. Pre-Colombian crafts traditions, though greatly diminished in scale, survived in ceramics, embroidery, weaving, clothing, and pottery. Indigenous influences were highly visible, in subject matter, themes, and techniques. For example, manuscripts, composed in the glyph (symbolic figures or characters) writing of earlier indigenous peoples transformed into an alphabetic script and adorned with figural decoration, were produced for about fifty years after the Spanish Conquest.

In architecture, the conquerors dismantled the Indian temples and recycled the stones into churches, city buildings, and residences. Throughout New Spain, churches, monastic complexes, and schools were constructed for the new converts. The degree of Indian in-

Encounter figure 13.1   ANONYMOUS. *Our Lady of Guadelupe. A tangled web obscures the provenance of this image of Our Lady of Guadelupe. Nevertheless, it has captured the imagination of the faithful, many of whom crawl for miles on their knees to worship at her shrine. The image's meaning is twofold. For indigenous peoples, it represents the Virgin Mary defeating the chief Aztec gods (symbolized by the sun behind her and the moon at her feet). And for Christians, it depicts the Virgin as the woman in Revelation 12:1: "adorned with the sun, standing on the moon, and with the twelve stars on her head for a crown." Regardless of the image's ultimate meaning, the Virgin of Guadelupe's shrine is the most visited pilgrimage site in the Western Hemisphere.*

fluence on these new churches was often determined by a church's location. As new churches were built, often on the site of Indian temples, teams of artists were enlisted to assist with their ornamentation. The wealthy churches in Mexico City might import artists from Spain, but the poor rural parishes would have to make do with local artists. While the church had strict rules governing religious images, indigenous artists could follow their own taste, through personal ingenuity or the ignorance or connivance of the local priest, who himself might be mestizo or indigena.

Following a long tradition, stretching back to Roman days, the Catholic Church in New Spain embraced certain elements of local religions, such as building churches on indigenous holy sites and using Native American images for decoration. The major example of syncretism (blending) occurred during the conquest when the church appropriated the hill of Tepeyac—a holy site to the Aztec people, who believed it to be the home of Tonantzin, Mother of the Gods. There, in 1531, a series of miracles occurred, following an appearance of the Virgin Mary to an Indian convert named Juan Diego, later Saint Juan Diego. The Church of the Virgin of Guadelupe was soon built there, transforming an Aztec holy site into a Christian shrine. In time, the Virgin of Guadelupe (Encounter figure 13.1) became a symbol for all Mexican-born people, whether Creole, indigena, or mestizo. Her image rallied people to the independence movement in the early 1800s and to the cause of the Mexican Revolution in 1910. Today, the Virgin of Guadelupe is honored as the patron saint of Mexico and her shrine is part of Mexico City.

Learning from the Encounter   **What** was the class structure of New Spain? **Why** were indigenous peoples able to have such a strong impact on society and culture in New Spain? **Discuss** the influence of indigenous people on the art of New Spain. **What** was the significance of the syncretism that occurred between Christianity and indigenous faiths in New Spain?

LEARNING THROUGH MAPS

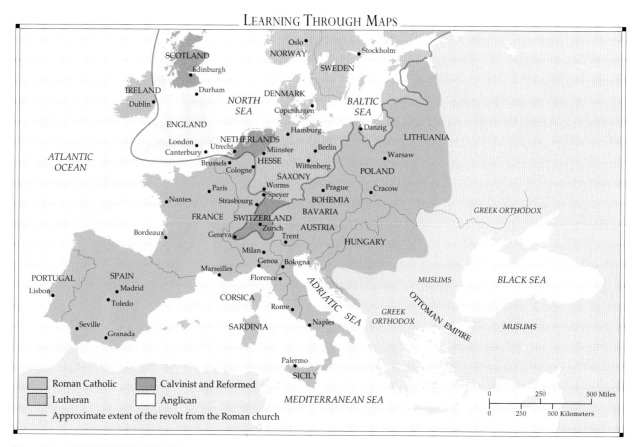

Map 13.1   THE RELIGIOUS SITUATION IN EUROPE IN 1560
This map shows the religious divisions in Europe in the middle of the sixteenth century.
Notice the line that separates Protestant Europe from Catholic Europe. **Which** of the two
areas is larger? **Identify** the three major Protestant religions and their locations. **Which**
Protestant religion covered the largest land area? **What** region was the most likely battleground between Protestants and Catholics? **Which** area of Charles V's empire (see Map
12.1) was most affected by the Protestant Reformation, as seen in this map?

money, Martin Luther (1483–1546), a monk teaching at
nearby Wittenberg University, published his famous
Ninety-five Theses (Figure 13.12). These were questions and arguments about the legitimacy of indulgences, and they implicitly challenged the sacraments
of confession and penance and the authority of the
pope. Luther had simply hoped to arouse a debate in
the university, but instead he ignited criticism against
the church and placed himself in the vanguard of a reform movement.

The church's response to Luther was initially hesi-
tant, but in 1520 Pope Leo X excommunicated him.
When Luther burned the papal document of excom-
munication in public, the church branded him a
heretic and an outlaw. Luther survived because he was
under the protection of his patron, Elector Frederick
the Wise of Saxony (r. 1486–1525), who had led the

German princes opposed to the Holy Roman emperor
(Figure 13.13).

LUTHER'S BELIEFS   Luther's attack on indulgences
arose from the spiritual quest to understand sin and
salvation that had led him to become a monk. Through
long study of the scriptures, he reached the understanding that salvation comes not from good works
but from God's unmerited love, or grace, or, as Luther
phrased it, "justification by faith alone." According to
Luther, salvation is achieved by faith in Jesus' sacrificial death; thus, buying indulgences is trying to buy
salvation—a direct contradiction of the biblical truth
Luther had experienced in his theological studies.

In his theology, which became known as **Lutheranism,** he tried to revive a Christianity based
on biblical precedents and reminiscent of the early

SLICE OF LIFE

The Conscience of Sixteenth-Century Christian Europe

BARTOLOMÉ DE LAS CASAS
A Short Account of the Destruction of the Indies

Bartolomé de las Casas (1484–1576), a Dominican friar, was an eyewitness to Spain's quest for empire. Outraged by the massacres committed during the 1502 conquest of Cuba, he eventually denounced Spain's entire overseas mission as misguided and even genocidal, in A Short Account of the Destruction of the Indies *(1542). By "Indies," he meant the lands of the Indians in the New World. In his short book, las Casas, speaking as the Christian conscience, called for justice for indigenous peoples.*

New Spain was discovered in 1517 and, at the time, great atrocities were committed against the indigenous people of the region and some were killed by members of the expedition. In 1518 the so-called Christians set about stealing from the people and murdering them on the pretence of settling the area. And from that year until this—and it is now 1542—the great iniquities and injustices, the outrageous acts of violence and the bloody tyranny of these Christians have steadily escalated, the perpetrators having lost all fear of God, all love of their sovereign, and all sense of self-respect. . . . This was . . . the pattern they followed in all the lands they invaded: to stage a bloody massacre of the most public possible kind in order to terrorize those meek and gentle peoples. What they did was the following. They requested the local lord to send for all the nobles and leading citizens of the city and of all the surrounding communities subject to it and, as soon as they arrived and entered the building to begin talks with the Spanish commander [Hernán Cortés (1485–

1546)], they were seized without anyone outside getting wind of what was afoot. Part of the original request was that they should bring with them five or six thousand native bearers and these were mustered in the courtyards when and as they arrived. One could not watch these poor wretches getting ready to carry the Spaniards' packs without taking pity on them, stark naked as they were with only their modesty hidden from view, each with a kind of little net on his shoulders in which he carried his own modest store of provisions. They all got down on their haunches and waited patiently like sheep. Once they were all safely inside the courtyard, together with a number of others who were also there at the time, armed guards took up positions covering the exits and Spanish soldiers unsheathed their swords and grasped their lances and proceeded to slaughter these poor innocents. Not a single soul escaped. . . . The Spanish commander gave orders that the leading citizens, who numbered over a hundred and were roped together, were to be tied to stakes set in the ground and burned alive.

Interpreting This Slice of Life What is las Casas's description of the indigenous people? **What** is his attitude toward the Spanish invaders? **What** appear to be las Casas's motives for writing? **Justify** your answer. Las Casas's book is dedicated to the Spanish king Philip II. **What** do you think las Casas wanted the king to do? **Why** do you think las Casas's call for justice went largely unheeded in his lifetime?

church. He believed that the sole source of religious authority was the Bible, not the pope or church councils, and that people could lead simple lives of piety and repentance without the need for priests to mediate with God. Luther also repudiated the mystical definition of the sacraments, the notion of purgatory, the adoration of the saints, and Masses for the dead; he retained only baptism and the Lord's Supper, as he called the Eucharist. Preaching in German became the heart of the liturgy, replacing the Latin Mass.

Luther's voluminous writings constitute the largest legacy of any German author. Among his vast output

of tracts, essays, and letters, his German translation of the Bible has had the most enduring influence. He introduced a new era in biblical scholarship by basing his translation on the original languages of the scriptures, the technique that had been developed by the northern humanists, particularly Erasmus. He also set the path followed by subsequent Protestant reformers in choosing what books to include in the Bible: Rejecting the Apocrypha of the Jewish Septuagint, Luther relied on the canonical books of the Hebrew Bible, or Old Testament, and the New Testament. Although nineteen German Bibles were in print by 1518,

Figure 13.12   Lucas Cranach the Elder. *Martin Luther.* 1520. Copper engraving, 5⁷⁄₁₆ × 3¹³⁄₁₆″. Courtesy of the Metropolitan Museum of Art. Gift of Felix Warburg, 1920. (20.64.21). *This portrait of Martin Luther, with its vivid rendering of his steel jaw and piercing eyes, shows some of the qualities that made him such a force during the Reformation. The admiring likeness was done by the German artist Lucas Cranach, a supporter of the new faith and a close friend of Luther's. At the time of this engraving, the Reformation was barely under way; the thirty-seven-year-old Luther was still in communion with the church in Rome and a member of a monastic order.*

Figure 13.13   Albrecht Dürer. *Elector Frederick the Wise.* 1524. Copper engraving, 7³⁄₈ × 4³⁄₄″. Print collection, Miriam and Ira D. Wallach Division of Art, Prints, and Photographs, The New York Public Library, Astor, Lenox, and Tilden Foundations. *Dürer's portrait captures the princely bearing of Frederick the Wise, the ruler of Electoral Saxony and Luther's great patron. Ironically, Frederick owned one of the largest collections of relics in Christendom. It has been estimated that the 17,443 artifacts in the elector's collection in 1518 could reduce the time in purgatory by 127,799 years and 116 days.*

Luther's version was the one that survived and left its stamp on the German language. His pithy style engaged the reader's emotions with realistic images and idiomatic speech.

SOCIAL AND POLITICAL IMPLICATIONS OF LUTHER'S REVOLT
The Ninety-five Theses circulated widely throughout Germany, and in 1521 Lutheran churches sprang up in most German towns. Simultaneously, radical followers of Luther fomented new problems, causing riots, driving priests from their homes, closing monasteries, and destroying religious images. Luther rejected this violence and advocated moderation. He did accept the abolition of monasticism, however, dropping the monk's habit in 1523 and marrying Katherine von Bora (1499–1552), a former nun, in 1525 (Figure 13.14). When he and Katherine had children, they created a familial tradition for Lutheran clergy, unlike the celibate tradition of Catholic Europe. Lutheran women thus seemed to make gains with the closing of con-

vents and the giving of new respectability to married life, but these steps proved illusory, since Luther affirmed male rule and female submission within the family.

Another area profoundly altered by Luther's beliefs was that of education. His supporters set up their own schools and universities, replacing Catholic foundations. Unlike church-run Catholic schools, the Lutheran schools were financed by taxes, so that teachers became state employees—a reflection of Luther's belief that church and state should work hand in hand. For Lutheran women, the changes in education created a dilemma. On the one hand, women were denied access to these schools, but, on the other hand, they were expected to know their Bibles, as both pious Lutherans and knowledgeable mothers capable of guiding their children's moral education.

Luther distanced himself from the anti-government political and social reforms espoused by some of his followers. In 1523 a brief Peasants' War erupted under

Figure 13.14 WORKSHOP OF LUCAS CRANACH. *Katherine von Bora. Ca. 1526. Oil on panel, 7½ × 5″. Wartburg-Stiftung, Germany. Katherine von Bora was one of a dozen nuns liberated from a convent near Wittenberg in the heady days of 1523. She joined the mixed collection who lived with Luther in the Black Cloisters, his old monastery given him by Frederick the Wise. Despite Luther's protests, she determined to become his wife, and she did. He treated her with great deference, calling her "My lord Kate," though he poked fun at her supposed greed for property. This small portrait was executed in the workshop of Lucas Cranach the Elder, who was also a witness to the marriage of Luther and Katherine von Bora.*

the banner of Luther's faith, but Luther urged suppression of the workers by the nobility, clearly showing his preference for the status quo. His reliance on Saxony's rulers for protection set the model for his religion; in the Lutheran faith, the church acted as an arm of the state, and the clergy's salaries were paid from public funds. Luther's revolt did not embrace individual rights in the political or social arena; indeed, the Protestant princes were more powerful than their predecessors, since their powers were not limited by Rome.

The Reforms of John Calvin Among the second generation of Protestant reformers, the most influen-

tial was John Calvin (1509–1564) (Figure 13.15). After earning a law degree in Paris, he experienced a religious conversion and cast his lot with the Reformation. Coming under the suspicion of the French authorities, he fled to Basel, Switzerland, a Lutheran center, where he began to publish *The Institutes of the Christian Religion*, which, in its final form, became a theological document of immense importance.

In his theology, Calvin, like Luther, advocated beliefs and practices having biblical roots. He differed from Luther over the nature of God, church–state relations, and Christian morals. Calvin's religious thought, called **Calvinism,** rested on his concept of an awesome, even angry, God, which led him to make

Figure 13.15 ANONYMOUS. *John Calvin.* 1550s. Bibliothèque
Publique et Universitaire de Geneva. *This anonymous portrait
of Calvin shows the way that he probably wanted to be viewed
rather than a natural likeness. Still, the angular features, the intense gaze, and the set mouth suggest that the reputation Calvin
had for strict discipline was justified. The well-trimmed beard and
somewhat extravagant fur collar, although typical of middle-class
fashion of the era, create an ironic contradiction in this otherwise
austere portrait.*

predestination (the belief that God predestines certain
souls to salvation and others to damnation) central to
his faith. Calvin also espoused a theocratic state in
which the government was subordinate to the church.
Within this state, he favored strict ethical demands,
regulating everything from laughter in church to public shows of affection between the sexes. Because of
such rules, which later became associated with the reform movement known as **Puritanism,** Calvinism acquired the reputation for being a joyless creed.

More important than the puritanical streak in
Calvin's theology was the impact of his thought on political, social, and economic life. Calvinism encouraged
thrift, industry, sobriety, and discipline—precisely the
same traits that made for business success. Calvin's
teachings spurred on the Christian capitalist in his ac-
cumulation of wealth, so that gradually there developed the idea that worldly success was tantamount to
God's approval and that poverty was a sign of God's
disfavor. In addition, of all the new sects, Calvinism
was the most international, and reformed congrega-

tions spread across Europe, especially in Scotland and
the Netherlands (see Map 13.1). The readiness of Calvin's followers to oppose tyranny with arms also
made them dangerous everywhere.

The Reform of the English Church   A second major
religious reformer in the 1530s was King Henry VIII (r.
1509–1547), who founded the Church of England (also
called the Anglican Church), largely out of political
considerations. In 1529 Henry asked the pope to annul
his marriage to Catherine of Aragon, who, though she
gave birth to a daughter, had failed to produce a male
heir. In Henry's eyes, Catherine's supposed failure
was a divine punishment for his sin of having married
his dead brother's widow—an incestuous union in the
eyes of the church. In favorable times, the pope might
have given Henry a dispensation, but the troops of
Holy Roman Emperor Charles V, Catherine's nephew,
had just sacked Rome and virtually imprisoned the
pontiff. Charles also opposed any step that would nul-
lify his aunt's marriage and make her daughter a bas-
tard. In 1533 Henry pushed through Parliament the
laws setting up the Church of England with himself as
the head and granting him a divorce (Figure 13.16).

Although **Anglicanism** was founded by Henry
VIII, the ground had been prepared locally by Christian humanists and English Lutherans. The work of
both groups led to the so-called Reformation Parliament (1529–1535), which had begun to reform the English church even before Henry made the decisive
break with Rome.

Religious turmoil followed Henry's death in 1547,
and the fate of the English Reformation stayed in
doubt until his daughter Elizabeth (r. 1558–1603) became queen and the head of the Anglican Church
(Figure 13.17). In 1559 Elizabeth resolved the crisis,
with the aid of Parliament, by steering a middle course
between Catholicism and Calvinism, which had
gained many English converts. Anglican beliefs were
summarized in the Thirty-nine Articles, and people
who wished to sit in Parliament, earn university degrees, or serve as military officers had to swear allegiance to them. Hence, Calvinists and Catholics were
excluded by law from English public life and remained so for about 275 years.

The Counter-Reformation

Before Martin Luther took his stand in Germany, a Roman Catholic reform movement had begun quietly in
isolated parts of Europe. Confronted with the surpris-
ing successes of the various Protestant groups, the Roman Catholic Church, as it was now called, struck
back with a Counter-Reformation. By 1600 this su-

Figure 13.16 HANS HOLBEIN THE YOUNGER. *Henry VIII.* Ca. 1540. Oil on wood panel, 34¾″ × 29½″. Galleria Nazionale d'Arte Antica, Rome. *Hans Holbein the Younger, like Erasmus, established his reputation in Europe before making his way to England. In 1537 Holbein became the court painter to Henry VIII, for whom he executed murals (now lost), designed jewelry, silver plate, and state robes, and painted easel portraits of the court, including the king. In this portrait, Holbein captured the power and majesty of his patron by centering him in a three-quarter, frontal pose so that the king's figure completely fills the frame with no props or objects to distract the viewer. The king's right upper arm is pushed out in an assertive manner, and he holds a glove in his clenched right hand. His Majesty's direct gaze and assured stance radiate self-confidence and speak of a sense of power and self-importance, which are reinforced by the bejeweled coat, puffed sleeves, decorated hat, and elaborate chain necklace. Holbein's painting sends a clear message about his subject's personal authority and high status, which contrasts nicely with his more intimate portrait of Erasmus, the Dutch scholar and man of ideas (see Figure 13.1).*

Figure 13.17 MARCUS GHEERAERTS THE YOUNGER. *Elizabeth I.* Late sixteenth century. Oil on panel, 7′11″ × 5′. National Portrait Gallery, London. *The so-called Ditchley portrait presented Queen Elizabeth in all her Renaissance finery. Following the Spanish fashion, the queen wears a neck ruff and yards of pearls, and she carries a fan. She stands atop a map of England, which she ruled for forty-five years with compassion and firmness, until her death in 1603.*

perbly organized campaign had slowed Protestantism and won back many adherents. The Catholics held on to southern and most of central Europe, halting Protestantism's spread in Poland, France, and Switzerland and limiting the movement to northern Europe. The Counter-Reformation moved forward on three fronts: a revitalized papacy, new monastic orders, and an effective reforming council. Together, these forces confronted the Protestant threat, purified the church of abuses, and reorganized its structure.

The Reformed Papacy With the reign of Paul III (pope 1534–1549), there appeared a series of reform-minded popes who reinvigorated the church. To counter the inroads made by Protestantism, Paul en-

listed the support of the full church by convening a council representing Roman Catholic clergy from all over Europe and launched new monastic orders.

Paul and his successors reclaimed the moral leadership of the church and reorganized the papal bureaucracy so that discipline was now enforced throughout the ecclesiastical hierarchy. Sensing that Protestantism would not go away and recognizing the increasing availability of written material now that the printing press had appeared, these popes tried to isolate the church from deviant ideas. A committee of churchmen drew up an Index of Forbidden Books, which listed writings that were off-limits to Roman Catholic readers because they were considered prejudicial to faith or morals. The first Index included the works of Luther,

Figure 13.18 JACOPINO DEL CONTE. *St. Ignatius Loyola.* 1556. Curia Generalizia, or Headquarters, of the Society of Jesus, Rome. *This portrait captures Loyola's humanness at the end of an active life. His energetic youth a distant memory, he now wears a serene and contemplative countenance. Not a life portrait, Jacopino del Conte's work was painted soon after Loyola's death. The artist probably had access to Loyola's death mask, so this portrait—unlike many that were painted years later—is as accurate a likeness of the founder of the Society of Jesus that exists.*

Calvin, and other Protestants. In the long run, this tactic failed to suppress hated ideas, but the Index continued to be updated until the 1960s.

New Monastic Orders The work of new monastic orders also contributed to the Counter-Reformation. Since the High Middle Ages, monastic reform had played only a small role in the life of the church. Suddenly, in the sixteenth century, new monastic groups arose to fill a variety of needs, such as preparing men and women to minister directly to the masses and reclaiming lapsed believers to the faith.

Typical of monastic reform for women in Counter-Reformation Europe was the fate of the Company of St. Ursula, or the Ursulines, founded in 1535 in Brescia, Italy, by Angela Merici [ma-REE-chee] (about 1470–1540). The Ursulines were named after a legendary British princess who, with eleven thousand virgin companions, was martyred on the way to her wed-

ding. Reflecting the same ideals as contemporary early Protestantism in stressing individual grace and keeping apart from clerical rule, the Ursulines were originally intended to be exclusively for laywomen, without any intrusion by male church officials. Merici's followers, divided into "daughters" and "matrons," were to live in their own homes, practice chastity without taking formal vows, serve the sick and the poor, and educate the young. In 1540, after Merici's death and under pressure from Protestantism, the Ursulines were reformed by church leaders, who cloistered the order and placed its members under male control. What happened to the Ursulines became the way of life for women in Catholicism: Laywomen were to be organized into formal structures under male supervision.

The most significant new order was the Society of Jesus, commonly known as the **Jesuits.** Recognized by Pope Paul III in 1540, the Jesuits had emerged by 1600 as the church's leading monastic order, with special blessings from the popes. The dedicated members helped to curb Protestantism in Europe, and their missionary efforts abroad represented the first steps in making Roman Catholicism a global faith. After a shaky beginning, their rise to power was quick, and their success was largely due to the order's founder, the Spaniard Ignatius Loyola (about 1493–1556) (Figure 13.18).

Loyola's life was imbued with more than a touch of medieval knight errantry. His first calling was as a professional warrior, defending his country from invaders. When in 1521 a battle injury to his leg left Loyola crippled for life, he underwent a religious conversion that led him to become a "soldier" in the army of Christ. Eventually, he founded the Society of Jesus, which resembled a military company in its rigid hierarchy, close discipline, and absolute obedience to the founder.

The Jesuits were initially concerned with working among the unchurched and the poor, focusing especially on teaching their children. But that mission was modified in the 1540s. Guided by the Spaniard Francis Xavier (1506–1552), they established outposts in the Far East and converted thousands to the Christian faith. Other Jesuits had similar success in missions to North and South America.

The Jesuits' special vow of loyalty to the pope set them apart from other monastic orders. Because of this connection and their expertise in education, the Jesuits soon became the church's chief weapon against the Protestants. In their writings, the Jesuits answered the church's critics, setting forth their orthodox beliefs in a clear and straightforward manner.

The Council of Trent The third force contributing to the Counter-Reformation was the reform established by the council conducted at Trent in northern Italy, meeting in three separate sessions between 1545 and 1563. Dominated by papal supporters, Italian delegates, and the Jesuits, the Council of Trent offered no sympathy to the Protestants and thus accepted the split in Christian Europe as an unfortunate fact of life. The council reaffirmed all the practices condemned by the Protestants, such as monasticism, the sale of indulgences, and the veneration of holy relics, although mechanisms were set in motion to eliminate abuse of these practices. In addition, the council initiated some clerical reforms, notably in the realm of education and training.

The council's unyielding position toward the Protestants was based on its belief that both the Bible and church tradition—not the Bible alone as advocated by the Protestants—were the bases of authority and the word of God. To the council, the Vulgate (including the Apocrypha of the Jewish Septuagint) was the official and only Bible; all other versions were rejected. The council reaffirmed that salvation should be sought by faith *and* by good works, not by faith alone; it also reaffirmed the seven sacraments. The moral, doctrinal, and disciplinary results of the Council of Trent laid the foundations for present-day Roman Catholic policies and thought.

Warfare as a Response to Religious Dissent, 1520–1603

As religious dissent spread, the secular rulers watched with mounting concern. Until 1530 compromise between the Lutheran rebels and the dominant faith seemed possible, but with the constant growth of mutually hostile sects, secular rulers increasingly relied on warfare to deal with the crisis.

War between Charles V's armies and the Lutheran forces erupted on German lands in 1546, the year Luther died, and lasted until 1555, when the Religious Peace of Augsburg brought it to an end. This armistice granted toleration to the Lutheran states, but on strict terms. The ruler's religion became the official faith of each territory; members of religious minorities, whether Roman Catholic or Lutheran, could migrate and join their coreligionists in nearby lands. But because the rights of other minority sects, such as the Calvinists, were ignored, the Peace of Augsburg contained the seeds of future wars.

In 1556 Philip II (r. 1556–1598) inherited the Spanish crown from Charles V and became the head of the Roman Catholic cause. Besides Spain, Roman Catholic regimes now ruled Italy, Portugal, and Austria; Protestants reigned in Scandinavia. Elsewhere the religious rivals vied for supremacy. For the rest of the century, until 1603, Germany was at peace, but western Europe suffered religious violence.

Financed by gold and silver from Mexico and Peru, Philip dominated European politics. His well-prepared armies enabled him to control much of Europe. He expelled suspected Muslims from Spain and defeated the Turks in the Mediterranean; he invaded Portugal and joined that country to Spain. But his fortunes declined when he launched a bloody campaign against the United Provinces in the northern Netherlands. (Eventually, in 1609, the United Provinces became an independent Protestant state.) As the Dutch war was winding down, Philip turned his attention to Protestant England, a supporter of the Dutch revolt. In Philip's eyes, only England stood between him and a reunited Christendom; moreover, Spain and England were rivals for the precious metals of the New World. Philip's solution was to attempt an invasion of England. In 1588 his scheme ended in disaster when the Spanish Armada was defeated by English sea power and a violent storm.

Philip II's dream of a reunited Christendom had been impossible from the beginning. The Protestant world was too dedicated, the growth of national consciousness too powerful, and the rise of a system of sovereign states too far advanced for any one monarch to succeed in unifying Europe under a single banner or cause. When Philip died in 1598, Spain was declining and Europe was divided into independent states and several religions.

LATE MANNERISM

The strongest impact of the Counter-Reformation on the arts, architecture, and music began after the Council of Trent, in 1563. Spain and the Italian states, the areas least attracted to Protestantism, were greatly influenced by the council's decisions. The council decreed that the arts and music should be easily accessible to the uneducated. In sacred music, for example, the intelligibility of the words should take precedence over the melody, and in architecture the building should create a worshipful environment. The church council envisioned paintings and sculptures that were simple and direct as well as unobjectionable and decent in appearance. Guided by this principle, the Counter-Reformation popes declared that some of the male nudes in Michelangelo's *Last Judgment* were obscene and ordered loincloths to be painted over them. General church policy now returned to the medieval ideal of an art and music whose sole aim was to serve and clarify the Christian faith.

Since the Roman Catholic Church after Trent wanted a simplified art that spoke to the masses, its artistic policy tended to clash with Mannerism, which embodied a self-conscious vision that was elitist and deliberately complex. Only with the rise of the Baroque

410

Figure 13.19 EL GRECO. *The Burial of Count Orgaz*. 1586. Oil on canvas, 16′ × 11′10″. Church of Santo Tomé, Toledo, Spain. *A Manneristic invention in* The Burial of Count Orgaz *was the rich treatment of the robe of St. Stephen, the first Christian martyr and, in this painting, the beardless figure supporting the body of the dead count. Sewn onto the bottom of this robe is a picture of the stoning of St. Stephen, an episode narrated in the New Testament. By depicting one event inside another, El Greco created an illusionistic device—a typical notion of Mannerist painters, who were skeptical about conventional reality.*

after 1600 was there a style that could conform to the church's need for art with a mass appeal. In the meantime, the general effect of Trent on the last stage of Mannerism was to intensify its spiritual values.

Late Mannerism, which emerged across Europe after 1564, dominated Spanish painting, but it had little influence on Spanish literature. Under the influence of the Renaissance, Spanish literature flourished with the revival of the theater and the birth of new literary genres.

Spanish Painting

No Catholic artist expressed the spirit of the Counter-Reformation better than El Greco (1541–1614) in his Spanish paintings after 1576. These visionary works epitomize the spirit of Late Mannerism. El Greco's real name was Domenikos Theotokopoulos [doh-me-NEEK-os TAY-o-toh-KOH-pooh-lohs]. A native of

Crete, he had lived in Venice, where he adopted the colorful style of Venetian painting. Unsuccessful in Venice, he also failed to find rich patrons in Rome, though he learned from the works of Michelangelo and the Mannerists. He arrived in Toledo, Spain, about 1576, and there he found an appreciative public among the wealthy nobility. But much to El Greco's despair, he never became a favorite of the Spanish ruler, Philip II, who found the Greek painter's works too bizarre.

For his select audience of aristocrats and Roman Catholic clergy, however, El Greco could do no wrong. They believed that his paintings of saints, martyrs, and other religious figures caught the essence of Spanish emotionalism and religious zeal—the same qualities that had led Loyola to found the Jesuits. In effect, El Greco's extravagant images gave visible form to his patrons' spiritual yearnings. In his paintings, he rejected a naturalistic world with conventional perspective, especially when a divine dimension was present or implied; his spiritualized vision came to be distinguished by elongated bodies, sharp lines in the folds of cloth, and luminous colors.

El Greco's masterpiece is *The Burial of Count Orgaz*, painted to honor the founder of the church of Santo Tomé in Toledo (Figure 13.19). This painting was designed to fit into a special place beside the church's high altar. Its subject is the miraculous scene that, according to legend, occurred during the count's burial, when two saints, Augustine and Stephen, appeared and assisted with the last rites.

From this legend, El Greco fashioned an arresting painting. The large canvas is divided into two halves, with the lower section devoted to the count's actual burial and the upper section focused on the reception of his soul in heaven. Except for a few men who tilt their faces upward, the town dignitaries seem unaware of what is happening just above their heads. El Greco has devised two distinct styles to deal with these different planes of reality. The dignitaries below are rendered in realistic terms, showing fashions of El Greco's era, such as the neck ruffs, mustaches, and goatees. The heavenly spectacle is depicted in the ethereal manner that he increasingly used in his later works.

El Greco also painted several portraits of church officials; the best known is *Cardinal Guevara* (Figure 13.20). This painting portrays the chief inquisitor, dressed in his splendid red robes. El Greco has captured the personality of this austere and iron-willed churchman who vigorously pursued heretics and sentenced them to die in an *auto-da-fé*, Portuguese for "act of faith"—that is, a public ceremony in which heretics were executed, usually by being burned at the stake. El Greco's likeness suggests much about the inner man: Cardinal Guevara seems to have an uneasy conscience, as betrayed by the shifty expression of the eyes, the left hand clutching the chair arm, and the general sense that the subject is restraining himself. Through these means El Greco created another model for Mannerist portraiture.

Another Mannerist artist-in-exile working in Spain in the late sixteenth century was Sofonisba Anguissola [an-gwee-SOL-uh] (about 1532–1625), a northern Italian from Cremona who, along with El Greco, is credited with helping to introduce the Italian school of painting into Spanish culture (Figure 13.21). Praised and encouraged by the aging Michelangelo, Anguissola began her rise to international fame when King Philip II of Spain chose her to be his court painter from 1559 to 1579. She painted mainly portraits, such as, for example, the *Portrait of Don Carlos* (Figure 13.22). In this three-quarter-length likeness of Spain's crown prince, Anguissola shows her mastery of the Mannerist style, including the challenging gaze of the young subject and the painting's highly polished surface and dark olive background. Portraits such as that of *Don*

Figure 13.20 El Greco. *Cardinal Guevara*. 1596–1600. Oil on canvas, 67¼ × 42½". Courtesy of the Metropolitan Museum of Art. The H. O. Havemeyer Collection. Bequest of Mrs. H. O. Havemeyer, 1929. (29.100.5). *El Greco's painting of Cardinal Guevara illustrates his mastery of Mannerist portraiture. Disturbing details are visible everywhere. Guevara's head is almost too small for his large body, made even grander by the cardinal's red robe, and the divided background—half wooden panel, half rich tapestry—sets up a dissonant effect. Even the cardinal's chair contributes to the air of uneasiness, for its one visible leg seems barely to touch the floor.*

Carlos made Anguissola a celebrity, the first internationally acclaimed Italian woman artist. Her painting career at the Spanish court ended in 1580, when she married a Sicilian nobleman and settled with him in Palermo, Sicily, where she lived and worked for much of the rest of her life. Most of her works are lost, but the surviving court portraits stand as vivid testaments to her brilliant gifts as an artist.

Anguissola's international acclaim was due, in part, to her aristocratic breeding and her education in Renaissance learning, rare for women of the times. This background, coupled with rich artistic gifts, enabled

Figure 13.21 SOFONISBA ANGUISSOLA. *Bernardino Campi Painting Sofonisba Anguissola. Ca. 1550. Oil on canvas, 43¹¹⁄₁₆ × 43⁵⁄₁₆". Pinacoteca Nazionale, Siena. Unusual for her time, the aristocratic Sofonisba Anguissola pursued a painting career, and, even rarer, she studied painting apart from her parents' household, under the artist Bernardino Campi (1522–1591), living in his home as a paying guest. From him, she learned the Mannerist style, as in this double portrait of herself and her mentor, both presented in three-quarter length. Within the painting, she depicts her likeness on a canvas supported by an easel. Campi, standing before her likeness, holds a paintbrush in his right hand, which is steadied by a hand rest (a device used to prevent smudges). The sharp contrasts of light and dark and the characteristic "square-U" shape to the hands are typical of Anguissola's Mannerist style. By depicting Campi at work, she also broke new ground in the portrait genre, which hitherto had focused on subjects seated or standing, but always in static situations (see Figures 12.2 and 12.8).*

Figure 13.22 SOFONISBA ANGUISSOLA. *(Formerly attributed to Alonzo Sánchez Coello.) Portrait of Don Carlos. Ca. 1560. Oil on canvas, 42¹⁵⁄₁₆ × 34³⁄₁₆". Prado, Madrid. This painting of Prince Don Carlos shows typical features of the artist's personal style. Like most women of the period, Anguissola was skilled in the needle arts, and she reveals this knowledge in the painstaking detail she has lavished on the prince's court costume—her trademark, according to one scholar. She also had a signature way of rendering hands—in a "square-U" pattern so that the index and little fingers are parallel and act as the raised portions of a "U" connected by an imaginary line—which may be seen in both of Don Carlos's hands.*

her to overcome the prejudices and guild restrictions that had previously kept women from pursuing careers in the arts. Sofonisba Anguissola was the ablest of the women artists who began to emerge in sixteenth-century Europe.

Spanish Literature

Known in Spanish as *Siglo de Oro*, or Golden Century, the sixteenth century is the high point in Spain's literary history. The writings were characterized by direct observation of life, satiric treatment of earlier epics and ballads, religious zeal, and Spanish themes, values, and subject matter; they also reflected minor influence from Renaissance humanism. Plays and novels were the most popular forms of literary expression.

As in England, theater was now revived in Spain for the first time in centuries. Spanish playwrights began to write dramas, including tragedies and comedies, and invent new dramatic forms, such as allegorical religious plays. The dramatist Lope de Vega [BAY-gah] (1562–1635), author of 426 secular plays and 42 religious dramas, is generally credited with almost single-handedly founding the Spanish national theater.

The **chivalric novel**, a Late Medieval literary form that presented romantic stories of knights and their ladies, was now challenged by the more realistic **picaresque novel**. The picaresque novel (Spanish *picaro*, "rogue") recounted the comic misadventures of a roguish hero who lived by his wits, often at the expense of those above him in society. Although having the hero question the social order was a revolutionary step, the novels were immensely popular in Spain and across Europe. The first picaresque novel was the anonymous *Lazarillo de Tormes*, published in 1554, in which the poor hero, Lazaro, encounters several masters, each of whom is a shady character suffering from self-deception. In translation, *Lazarillo de Tormes* found new audiences across Europe and influenced the writing of novels in England, France, and Germany for about two hundred years.

The Spanish novel was raised to new heights by Miguel de Cervantes Saavedra [sir-VAN-tez SAH-uh-VAY-drah] (1547–1616) in his masterpiece *Don Quixote* (part I, 1605; part II, 1615). Poet, playwright, and novelist, Cervantes is the greatest figure in Spanish literature and one of the most respected writers in the world. In *Don Quixote* he satirized the chivalric novel, mocking its anachronistic ideals. Although the long, rambling structure was borrowed from the chivalric novel, *Don Quixote* is the prototype of the modern novel, with its psychological realism, or probing into the motives of the main characters. These characters—the hero, Don Quixote, and his servant, Sancho Panza—whose lives are intertwined, embody the major themes of the work. The tormented Don Quixote, driven half-mad by his unreachable quest, represents the hopeless visionary, while the plodding Sancho Panza, never taken in by his master's madness, stands for the hardheaded realist. At one level, the characters signify the dual nature of the Spanish soul, the idealistic aristocrat and the down-to-earth peasant. At a higher level, the characters personify a universal theme, that idealism and realism must go hand in hand.

Late Mannerist Painting in Italy: Tintoretto

With the death of Michelangelo in 1564, Venice displaced Rome as the dominant artistic center in Italy. From then until the end of the century, Venetian painters carried the banner of the Italian Renaissance, bringing Mannerism to a brilliant sunset. The leading exponent of Late Mannerism in Italy was Tintoretto [tin-tuh-RAY-toe] (1518–1594). This Venetian artist created a feverish, emotional style that reflected impetuosity in its execution. With his haste, Tintoretto was reacting against his famous Venetian predecessor Titian, who had been noted for extraordinary discipline. But in other respects, he followed Titian, adopting his love of color and his use of theatrical lighting. The special quality of Tintoretto's art, which he achieved in his earliest paintings, was his placement of human figures in arrangements that suggest a sculptural frieze.

Tintoretto's rendition of the familiar biblical account of the Last Supper shows his feverish style (Figure 13.23). Unlike the serene, classically balanced scene that Leonardo had painted (see Figure 12.7), Tintoretto portrays an ethereal gathering, illuminated by eerie light and filled with swooping angels. The diagonal table divides the pictorial space into two halves; on the left is the spiritual world of Jesus and his disciples, and on the right is the earthly realm of the servants. Tintoretto's depiction of these different levels of reality is reminiscent of a similar division in El Greco's *The Burial of Count Orgaz* (see Figure 13.19). Especially notable is Jesus' body, including the feet, which glows as if in a spotlight. *The Last Supper*, finished in Tintoretto's final year, is a fitting climax to Mannerist painting.

Music in Late-Sixteenth-Century Italy and England

Unlike painting, Italian music remained under the sway of High Renaissance ideals, keeping to the path pioneered by Josquin des Prez (see Chapter 12). Nevertheless, the Council of Trent, along with other forces, led to the decline of the High Renaissance style and created the conditions for the rise of the Baroque. For one thing, the council ruled that the Gregorian chant was preferable to polyphony (two or more lines of melody sung or played at the same time) for church liturgy and that the traditional chants should be simplified to ensure that the words could be easily understood. Most composers, considering the chants to be barbarous, continued to use polyphony but pruned its extravagant effects. The best of these composers and the chief representative of Counter-Reformation music was Giovanni Pierluigi da Palestrina [pal-uh-STREE-nuh] (about 1525–1594). His controlled style established the Roman Catholic ideal for the next few centuries—polyphonic masses sung by choirs and with clearly enunciated and expressive texts.

Nevertheless, the future of Italian music lay outside the church. Ironically, secular vocal music was also moving toward an ideal in which the words took precedence over the sound, but secular composers, unlike those in the church, rejected polyphony because it did not allow the text to be fully understood. The move to make the words primary in secular music was triggered by Renaissance humanists who were convinced that ancient music's power stemmed from the expressive way that the setting suited the clearly articulated words of the text. The most evident signs of this humanistic belief were in the works of the Florentine Camerata, a group of musical amateurs. Rejecting

Figure 13.23   Tintoretto. *The Last Supper.* 1592–1594. Oil on canvas, 12′ × 18′8″. San Giorgio Maggiore, Venice. *Nothing better illustrates the distance between the High Renaissance and Mannerism than a comparison of Leonardo's* Last Supper *(Figure 12.7) with that of Tintoretto. Everything about Tintoretto's spiritualized scene contradicts the quiet Classicism of Leonardo's work. Leonardo's painting is meant to appeal to the viewer's reason; Tintoretto's shadowy scene is calculated to stir the feelings.*

polyphony, the Florentine musicians composed pieces for a text with a single line of melody accompanied by simple chords and sung in a declamatory (speechlike singing) style.

The trend to expressive secular music in Italy was reflected most completely in the **madrigal,** a song for four or five voices composed with great care for the words of the poetic text. The novelty of this vocal music was that it vividly illustrated the meanings and emotions in the words, rather than the structure of the music. Madrigals were first written in the 1520s, but their heyday was the second half of the sixteenth century. Late in the century, they were imported to England and quickly became the height of fashion there. The success of madrigals in England had to do with the vogue there for Italianate things, as is evident from the settings and sources of Shakespeare's plays and the translation into English of Castiglione's *The Book of the Courtier* during this period.

England's leading madrigal composer was Thomas Weelkes [WILKS] (about 1575–1623), whose works often made use of the technique called **word paintings,** or word illustrations, a musical illustration of the written text. For example, in the madrigal "As Vesta was from Latmos hill descending," Weelkes uses a descending scale for the word "descending," an ascending scale for the words "a maiden queen ascending," and a hill-shaped melodic phrase for the words "Latmos hill descending." Such clever fusing of music and lyrics appealed to listeners, many of whom, in the spirit of the Renaissance, were amateur musicians themselves (Figure 13.24)

Madrigals eventually achieved a European-wide popularity, but they ended with the Renaissance. Nevertheless, the technique of word painting continued to be a favorite of composers, down through Bach and Handel in the Baroque Age (see Chapter 14).

Figure 13.24   Martial Reymond. *Oval Dish: Apollo and the Muses: Fame.* 1599. Enamel on copper, diameter 21⅜". Henry Clay Frick Bequest. Frick Collection, New York. *This oval plate image represents Apollo, with a viol (center), and the nine Muses (four on the left, five on the right), playing sixteenth-century musical instruments that are little changed from late medieval times (see Figure 10.25). The lute, the portable organ or organetto, and the tambourine, for example, were still in popular use. This idealized scene depicts more than the popular instruments of the period. It is a forecast of a future direction in the making of art: exquisite objects for the ever-expanding art market. This particular dish was created by Martial Reymond, a skilled ceramicist, for a wealthy patron, probably as a display object. Limoges, France, where it was made, already had a reputation for superb enamelware, and in the next century, it would become one of the West's prime centers for fine porcelain and china.*

The Legacy of Northern Humanism, Northern Renaissance, Religious Reformations, and Late Mannerism

The period from 1500 until 1520 in northern Europe witnessed important developments in painting and literature. The German painters Grünewald and Dürer and the Flemish painter Bosch brought the Late Gothic style to its final flower, though Dürer was also influenced by the methods of the Italian Renaissance. In the Netherlands, Erasmus launched Christian humanism, and in France, Rabelais and Marguerite of Angoulême followed in this tradition. The movement was undermined by Luther's break with the Roman Catholic Church and was finally ended by the wars of religion.

The period from 1520 until 1603 brought to a close the third and final phase of the Renaissance. This eighty-three-year period, framed by the deaths of Raphael and Queen Elizabeth I, saw the foundations of early modern Europe move firmly into place. A world culture and economy, in embryo, began during this period. This momentous development was foreshadowed in the shift of Europe's commercial axis from the Mediterranean to the Atlantic, as well as in the start of Europe's exportation of peoples, technology, religions, and ideas to colonies in Asia, Africa, and the Americas.

Probably the most important material change during this era was the rise of a system of sovereign and mutually hostile states. No single state was able to assert its authority over the others; the pattern set by their struggles would govern Western affairs until the emergence of global politics in the twentieth century. The European state system also spelled the doom of a united Christendom.

The religious reformations further split Christian Europe, dividing it into Protestant and Catholic armed camps. As a result, religious wars afflicted this century and the next, fading away only by about 1700. On a lo-cal level, religious differences led to intolerance and persecution. Although Europe's religious boundaries today remain roughly the same as they were in 1600, it took over three hundred years for Protestants and Catholics to accept that they could live together in harmony.

The reformations also left different cultural legacies to their respective Christian denominations. From Protestantism came a glorification of the work ethic, Puritanism, and a justification for capitalism. At the heart of the Protestant revolution, despite its insistence on the doctrine of original sin, was the notion that human beings can commune directly with God without church mediation. Whereas Protestantism tended to view human beings as adrift in the universe, the Catholic Church tried to control the spiritual and moral lives of its members and to insulate them from the surrounding world. This policy eventually placed the church on a collision course with the forces of modernity, but it nevertheless was followed by most of the popes until after World War II.

In the aftermath of the religious crisis, the legacy of northern humanism—rational morals allied to a simple faith—went unheeded by Protestants and Catholics alike. Not until the eighteenth century and the rationalist program of the Enlightenment did Christian humanist ideas find a willing audience.

In the arts and humanities, however, the legacy was clear: This period left a rich and varied inheritance, including the work of Cervantes and the rest of Spain's Golden Age authors and the work of Shakespeare, the most gifted and influential individual writer in the history of Western civilization.

KEY CULTURAL TERMS

Reformation	Puritanism
Counter-Reformation	Anglicanism
Christian humanism	Jesuits
Northern Renaissance	Late Mannerism
revenge tragedy	chivalric novel
triptych	picaresque novel
proverb	madrigal
Lutheranism	word painting
Calvinism	

SUGGESTIONS FOR FURTHER READING

CALVIN, J. *Institutes of the Christian Religion.* Translated by F. L. Battles. Philadelphia: Westminster Press, 1960. A translation of Calvin's theological masterpiece.

CERVANTES, M. DE. *Don Quijote [Quixote].* Translated by B. Raffel with volume edited by D. de Armas Wilson. New York: Norton, 1999. An up-to-date translation of the first modern novel with accompanying commentary; another excellent volume in the Norton Critical Edition series.

ERASMUS, D. *Praise of Folly.* Translated by B. Radice. New York: Penguin, 1971. A lively translation of Erasmus's satire that ridiculed the hypocrisy of the age, especially in the church; originally published in 1509.

LUTHER, M. *Three Treatises.* Translations by various authors. Philadelphia: Fortress Press, 1960. Good versions of the short works that helped to make Luther an outstanding and controversial public figure in his day.

MONTAIGNE, ****M. DE. *Essays and Selected Writings.* Translated and edited by D. Frame. New York: St. Martin's Press, 1963. The *Essays* reveal Montaigne as one of the founders of French skepticism.

RABELAIS, F. *The Histories of Gargantua and Pantagruel.* Translated by J. M. Cohen. Franklin Center, Pa.: Franklin Library, 1982. An excellent modern version of this lusty masterpiece.

SHAKESPEARE. *Hamlet. Othello. King Lear. Romeo and Juliet. Antony and Cleopatra. Macbeth.* One of the best editions available of Shakespeare's tragedies is the New Folger Library, published by Washington Square Press. This series is inexpensive and profusely illustrated, and it offers extensive editorial notes.

SUGGESTIONS FOR LISTENING

PALESTRINA, GIOVANNI PIERLUIGI DA. A prolific composer of Masses, Palestrina is the major musical figure of the Counter-Reformation. Unlike the highly emotional style of Josquin, Palestrina's music is noted for its tightly controlled quality and its perfection of detail, as illustrated in such Masses as *Hodie Christus natus est, Assumpta est Maria,* and *Ave Maria.*

WEELKES, THOMAS. An English composer and organist, Weelkes is an important figure in Late Renaissance music. A composer of sacred vocal music and instrumental works for viols and harpsichord, he is best known for introducing the Italian madrigal to England and adapting it to the tastes of his compatriots. His madrigals are characterized by clever word paintings, as in "O, care, thou wilt despatch me" and "The Andalusian merchant" (both 1600).

14 THE BAROQUE AGE
Glamour and Grandiosity
1600–1715

As the Roman Catholic Church pursued its goal of eradicating Protestantism, and as powerful sovereign secular states became established in Europe, a new age—the **Baroque**—dawned in the early seventeenth century. It was a period characterized by grandeur, opulence, and expanding horizons. Baroque art and architecture provided spectacular and compelling images with which the church could reassert its presence and dazzle and indoctrinate the faithful. The Baroque also offered secular rulers a magnificence and vastness that enhanced their political power. Art became a propagandistic tool in a way that the individualistic Mannerist art of the previous period—with its focus on the distorted and the eccentric—never was.

The term *baroque* was coined by eighteenth-century artists and scholars whose tastes were attuned to Classical ideals. To them, much seventeenth-century culture was imperfect, or "baroque," a term probably derived from the Portuguese word *barroco,* meaning "irregular pearl." Not until the mid–nineteenth century did the word acquire a positive meaning, and now "Baroque" is a label for the prevailing cultural style of the seventeenth century.

The Baroque period was an era of constant turmoil, and until midcentury, Europe was plagued by religious warfare, a legacy of the Reformation. The conflicts of the second half of the century had secular motivations: territorial expansion and the race for overseas empires. The seventeenth century was also a period of great scientific discoveries and intellectual change. Because the Scientific Revolution, as this intellectual movement is called, so keenly influenced the making of the modern world, it is covered separately in Chapter

◄ **Detail** GIANLORENZO BERNINI. The Baldacchino. 1624–1633. Ht. approx. 100'. St. Peter's, Rome.

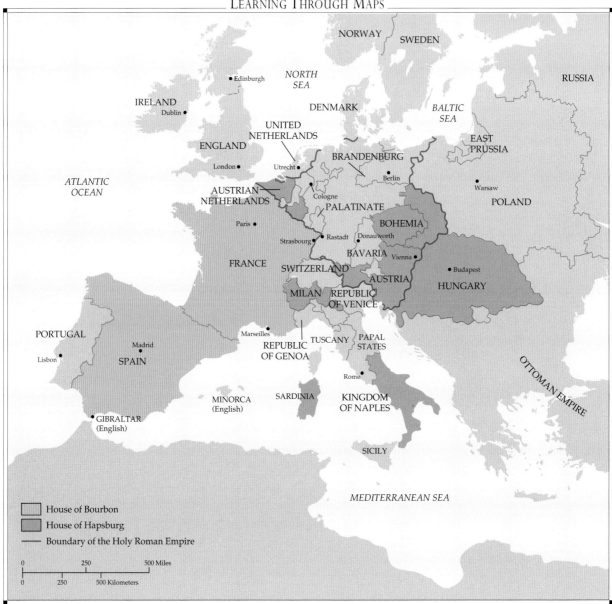

Map 14.1   EUROPE IN 1714
This map shows Europe in the early eighteenth century. **Compare** the lands of the Haps-burg dynasty in this map with the holdings of Hapsburg emperor Charles V in Map 12.1. **Compare** the Holy Roman Empire's size in this map with its size on Map 12.1. **Which** of the two dynasties—Bourbon or Hapsburg—had the larger land holdings in 1714? **How** did the size and location of England and the United Netherlands help make them major maritime powers? **Note** the large number of small states in central Europe and northern Italy.

15, along with related philosophical ideas. This chap-ter focuses on the art, literature, and music of the Baroque Age and their historical, political, and social contexts.

ABSOLUTISM, MONARCHY, AND THE BALANCE OF POWER

Although the Baroque style in art originated in Rome and from there spread across the Continent, the Italian city-states and the popes were no longer at the center of European political life. By the time Europe had re-covered from the first wave of religious wars in 1600, a new system of sovereign states had replaced the old dream of a united Christendom. By 1715 there was a balance of power in Europe among five great military states—England, France, Austria, Prussia, and Russia (Map 14.1). The rise of these states was due to a new breed of rulers fascinated with power. Known as *abso-lutists*, they wanted complete control over state affairs, unlike the medieval monarchs, who had to share au-thority with the church and the feudal nobles. Steeped in the works of Machiavelli, the new monarchs but-

Figure 14.1 ATTRIBUTED TO FRANÇOIS DE TROY. *Louis XIV and His Heirs.* Ca. 1710. Oil on canvas, 4′2¾″ × 5′3¾″. Wallace Collection, London. *Louis XIV's dynastic ambitions are reflected in this collective portrait of himself surrounded by his heirs. To his right stands his only legitimate son, the "Grand Dauphin," and the king's infant great-grandson, the duc de Bretagne, who is attended by a governess. To the king's left is his grandson, Louis, the duc de Bourgogne. Ironically, none of these heirs became king, because all of them died of illness within two years. In the painting, the Baroque love of grandeur is apparent in the opulent setting, the formal poses, and ornate dress. The king and the dauphin wear rich velvet suits and large, full-bottomed wigs, typical of seventeenth-century style. In contrast, the duc de Bourgogne represents the younger generation with his bright-colored suit and less formal wig. The wall painting within this portrait depicts the Greek sun god Helios, driving his chariot—a reference to Louis's claim to be the Sun King.*

tressed their claims to power with theories of divine right and natural law. France's greatest monarch, Louis XIV, was the most extreme in his claims, glorifying himself as the Sun King—a title derived from the Late Roman emperors (Figure 14.1).

In their bid for absolute power, these monarchs founded new institutions and reformed old ones. For example, administrative bureaucracies, which had existed since the High Middle Ages, were reformed to become the exclusive domain of university-trained officials drawn from the middle classes. These career bureaucrats began to displace the great lords who had previously dominated the kings' advisory councils. As a consequence, the authority of the feudal nobility began to diminish.

The absolute monarchs also established permanent diplomatic corps to assist in foreign policy. The great states of Europe set up diplomatic missions in the major capitals, staffed with trusted officials who served as their rulers' eyes and ears in foreign cities. Another new institution was the standing army funded from state revenues, led by noble officers, and manned by lower-class soldiers. New weapons—the flintlock rifle and the bayonet—and an improved breed of horse made these armies more efficient.

France: The Supreme Example of Absolutism

At the opening of the seventeenth century, France was ruled by Henry IV, the first of the Bourbon dynasty,

who had converted from Calvinism to Catholicism to restore peace to his largely Roman Catholic state. Like the medieval kings, Henry shared authority with the feudal nobles, though he began to reward middle-class supporters with high office. Henry was a pragmatist; he felt no need to force his adopted faith on the Huguenots, as the French Calvinists were called, and allowed them limited freedom of worship. The atmosphere changed when Henry was assassinated in 1610. Between then and 1715, France became the model absolutist state (Timeline 14.1).

Henry IV was succeeded by Louis XIII, but real authority passed to Cardinal Richelieu [REESH-lew] (1585–1642), who was the virtual ruler of France from 1624 until his death in 1642. Gifted with political acumen, Richelieu worked tirelessly to wrest power from the nobles. He was also a pragmatic statesman. For example, at home he restricted the freedom of his Protestant subjects, but abroad he allied himself with Swedish Protestants. His pragmatic policies were continued by his protégé and iron-fisted successor, Cardinal Mazarin [maz-uh-RAN] (1602–1661), who served as regent for the young Louis XIV. Mazarin's rule, during the 1640s and 1650s, moved France closer to absolutism, but it also coincided with the beginning of a golden age in France; for more than a century, French politics and culture dominated Europe, and French was the language of diplomacy.

When Mazarin died, Louis XIV, aged twenty-three, decided to rule France in his own right. Throughout his fifty-four-year reign, Louis made his private and

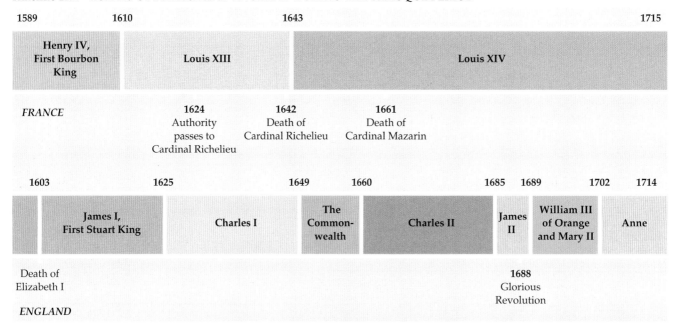

Timeline 14.1   RULERS OF FRANCE AND ENGLAND DURING THE BAROQUE PERIOD

FRANCE

1589	1610	1643	1715
Henry IV, First Bourbon King	Louis XIII	Louis XIV	

1624 Authority passes to Cardinal Richelieu

1642 Death of Cardinal Richelieu

1661 Death of Cardinal Mazarin

ENGLAND

Death of Elizabeth I

1688 Glorious Revolution

| 1603 | 1625 | 1649 | 1660 | 1685 | 1689 | 1702 | 1714 |

| James I, First Stuart King | Charles I | The Common-wealth | Charles II | James II | William III of Orange and Mary II | Anne |

public life the embodiment of the French state: *"L'État c'est moi"*—"I am the state"—is what he allegedly said about his concept of government. Determined that nothing should escape his grasp, Louis XIV canceled what freedom remained to the Huguenots, persecuting them until they converted to Roman Catholicism, fled into exile, or were killed. As king, he perfected the policies of his Bourbon predecessors, becoming the chief of a bureaucratic machine that regulated every phase of French life, from economics to culture. His economic policy was called mercantilism, a system that rested on state control. Through his ministers, Louis XIV regulated exports and imports, subsidized local industries, and set tariffs, customs duties, and quotas.

Louis XIV waged a spectacular campaign of self-glorification, and in so doing he made France the center of European arts and letters. His palace at Versailles became the symbol of his regal style (Figure 14.2). He also encouraged the work of the emerging academies, particularly the French Academy, founded in 1635 by Cardinal Richelieu to purify the French language and honor the state's most distinguished living authors, and the Royal Academy of Painting and Sculpture, founded by Cardinal Mazarin in 1648 to recognize the country's best artists. These seventeenth-century French academies became the models for similar institutions in other Western states.

England: From Monarchy to Republic to Limited Monarchy

Like France, England turned toward absolutism at the beginning of the seventeenth century. Following the

death of Elizabeth I, the new Stuart dynasty assumed the throne. King James I considered himself ruler by divine right, but certain aspects of English life held royal power in check. Specifically, the English property-owning classes served together in Parliament, with the upper nobility in the House of Lords and lesser lords and middle-class members in the House of Commons; Parliament met regularly and considered itself the king's partner rather than his enemy; and the country's Calvinist minority, called Puritans, were not despised by the Anglican majority, many of whom shared their religious zeal. When England became embroiled in a constitutional crisis between Parliament and the headstrong Charles I, Puritan leaders in Parliament led a successful civil war, toppling the monarchy and setting up a republic, called the Commonwealth, in 1649. But the Commonwealth soon lost its allure when its leader, the Puritan Oliver Cromwell, turned it into a military dictatorship.

Disappointed by the republic, the English restored monarchy in 1660, recalling Charles I's son from exile in France to become Charles II, an event known as the Restoration. The king's powers were now tempered by vague restrictions, but lack of clarity about the arrangement soon led to renewed conflicts between the crown and Parliament. In 1688 King James II, brother of Charles II, was expelled in a bloodless coup known as the Glorious Revolution, and his daughter and son-in-law, Mary II and William III of the Netherlands, became England's joint sovereigns. With their reign, England's constitutional crisis was finally resolved, for they understood that they could rule only if they recognized citizens' rights and Parliament's power over most financial matters. By 1715, England had become the classic example of limited monarchy

Figure 14.2 Louis Le Vau and Jules Hardouin-Mansart. Palace at Versailles. 1661–1688. Versailles, France. *As the seat of government and the center of fashionable society, Versailles was the greatest symbol of this age of kings. Here, nobles competed for Louis XIV's favors and a royal post. He shrewdly rewarded them with menial positions and lofty titles and thus undermined their political influence. At the height of Louis's power, this complex of buildings could house ten thousand people—members of the royal court, hangers-on, and servants.*

under written laws. In the ensuing years, political philosophers cited England's experience as a successful example of the principle that government should rest on the consent of the people.

Warfare in the Baroque Period: Maintaining the Balance of Power

Warfare was crucial in establishing the configuration of the great powers because the most successful states were those in which the king could marshal his country's resources behind his military goals. But when one state began to stand out from the rest, the other states pursued policies designed to hold it in check—that is, to keep a balance of power. This system had several consequences. For one, it prevented any single state from controlling the rest. For another, it was a practical way to discourage the ambition of empires like that of the Ottoman Turks, because the great powers were willing to unite to stop Turkish expansion. Finally, this system relegated many countries, such as Spain and Poland, to secondary-power status and spelled the end

of a significant international role for city-states like Florence and Venice.

The Thirty Years' War, 1618–1648   The first half of the seventeenth century was mired in the destructive Thirty Years' War (actually a series of four wars), the last great European-wide struggle between the Protestants and the Roman Catholics. Besides the great powers of Austria, France, and Brandenburg (soon to be Prussia), states involved at one time or another included Denmark, Sweden, Spain, Venice, the United Provinces of the Netherlands, and Poland. Germany suffered the most because the war was fought largely on its soil, wiping out a generation of Germans and inaugurating more than a century of cultural decline.

The Treaties of Westphalia, also known as the Peace of Westphalia, which ended the war in 1648, nullified the religious objectives that had caused the war and also created the conditions for the rise of Brandenburg-Prussia to great-power status. Germany itself remained divided; Calvinism was now tolerated, but true religious freedom did not appear, for the principle established at Augsburg in 1555 was retained: The religion

Figure 14.3   G ERARD T ER B ORCH. *The Swearing of the Oath of Ratification of the Treaty of Muenster, 15 May 1648. 1648. Oil on copper, 17⅞ × 25⁵⁄₁₆". National Gallery, London. The Treaty of Muenster, part of the Peace of Westphalia, ended the eighty-year war between the Spanish crown and the Dutch people. In the treaty, the United Provinces of the Netherlands was recognized as an independent republic, giving the Dutch their freedom and strengthening their position as a maritime power. In the painting, the Dutch Protestant delegates, left center, take the oath of allegiance by holding up their right hands, with two raised fingers, while the Catholic Spanish, right center, place their hands on the Bible and a cross. More than seventy people are crowded into the foreground, which is enclosed by three walls, while above stand three other groups of observers. The artist, depicted at the far left, gazes out to the viewer. Gerard Ter Borch [ge-RART ter BORK] (1584–1662), a very successful Dutch portrait painter and a master of domestic life scenes, helped establish, in this work, the tradition of painting contemporary historical events. Paintings commemorating important happenings, such as coronations (see Figures 17.6 and 19.6) or wars (see Figures 17.22 and 19.8) became popular later with the rise of nationalism and the emergence of art patrons who preferred secular to religious subjects.*

of each state was to be dictated by its ruler (see Chapter 13). A divided Germany served the interests of Brandenburg-Prussia and its rulers. Commencing with the Treaties of Westphalia, these Calvinist leaders began to amass additional territories, becoming kings of Prussia in 1701 and finally emperors of a united Germany in 1871.

The Thirty Years' War also had major consequences for the emerging system of great powers. The peace conference was the first in which decisions were arranged through congresses of ambassadors. Both the war and the conference revealed Spain's impotence, showing that it had fallen from its peak in the 1500s. In contrast, Sweden and the Netherlands gained advantages that made them major powers for the rest of the century (Figure 14.3). The Hapsburg rulers were forced to accept that Protestantism could not be turned back

in their German lands; henceforth they concentrated on their Austrian holdings, ignoring the Holy Roman Empire, which now seemed a relic of the feudal age.

France profited the most from the Thirty Years' War. By shifting sides to support first Roman Catholics and then Protestants, the French rulers demonstrated a particularly shrewd understanding of power politics. Even after the religious wars were over, France continued to struggle against Roman Catholic Spain until 1659. Having taken control of France in 1661, Louis XIV launched a series of aggressive wars four years later against various coalitions of European states that lasted until 1713.

The Wars of Louis XIV, 1665–1713   Louis XIV used various means, including marriage and diplomacy, to assert French might on the Continent, but it was

SLICE OF LIFE
Two Views of Power
Master (Louis XIV) and Servant (the Duke of Saint-Simon)

Louis XIV was the West's most powerful monarch during this age of kings. He made France the envy of other rulers, centralizing political power in his own hands, creating an efficient bureaucracy, fielding a well-armed army, and setting the cultural and artistic standards for the period. In contrast, the

soldier and courtier Duke of Saint-Simon, though an aristocrat, was little more than a servant to Louis XIV when both were in residence at Versailles, Louis's palatial home outside Paris.

LOUIS XIV
Reflections on Power

Kings are often obliged to do things against their natural inclination and which wound their natural goodness. They ought to love making people happy, and they must often chastise and condemn people whom they naturally wish well. The interest of the state must come first. One must overcome one's inclinations and not put oneself into a position of reproaching oneself, in something important, for not having done better because personal interests prevented one from doing so and distorted the views which one should have had for the grandeur, the good, and the power of the state. . . .

One must guard against oneself, guard against one's inclinations, and ever be on guard against one's own nature. The

king's craft is great, noble, and extremely pleasant when one feels oneself worthy of carrying out everything one sets out to do; but it is not exempt from pain, fatigue, cares. Uncertainty sometimes leads to despair; and when one has passed a reasonable amount of time in examining a matter, one must decide and choose the side believed to be best.

When one keeps the state in mind, one works for oneself. The good of the one makes the *gloire* of the other. When the former is happy, eminent and powerful, he who is the cause as a result is *glorieux* and consequently must savor more than his subjects, if the two are compared, all of the most agreeable things in life.

DUKE OF SAINT-SIMON
Memoirs

In everything [Louis XIV] loved splendor, magnificence, profusion. He turned this taste to a maxim for political reasons, and stilled it into his court on all matters. One could please him by throwing oneself into fine food, clothes, retinue, buildings, gambling. These were occasions which enabled him to talk to people. The essence of it was that by this he attempted and succeeded in exhausting everyone by making luxury a virtue, and for certain persons a necessity, and thus he gradually reduced everyone to depending entirely upon his generosity in order to subsist. . . . This is an evil which, once introduced, became the internal cancer which is devouring all individuals—because from the court it promptly spread to

Paris and into the provinces and the armies, where persons, whatever their position, are considered important only in proportion to the table they lay and their magnificence ever since this unfortunate innovation.

Interpreting This Slice of Life **What** is Louis XIV's thinking about his role as king? **How** does he think he should carry out his responsibilities? **In what ways** does Louis XIV see himself as the embodiment of the state? **How** does the duke of Saint-Simon view the king and his policies? **Why** does the Duke have his own point of view? **Which** of the two do you believe is telling the truth? **Explain.**

chiefly through warfare that he left his enduring mark. In his own mind, he fought for *la gloire* ("glory"), an elusive term that reflected his image as the Sun King but that in practice meant the expansion of France to imperial status.

Louis XIV fought the states of Europe in four separate wars and was finally defeated by a coalition that included virtually all of Europe's major and minor powers. Because of its wide-ranging nature, Louis's last struggle, the War of the Spanish Succession, is gen-

erally regarded as the first of the world wars—a new type of war. The Treaty of Utrecht, signed in 1713, not only settled this last war but also showed that the great-power system was working.

The peace constructed at Utrecht was a reaffirmation of the balance-of-power principle. The victors set aside Louis's most extravagant acquisitions of land, but they granted those additions that still serve as France's borders today. Brandenburg-Prussia gained territory, and England emerged with the lion's share of the spoils, acquiring Gibraltar and the island of Minorca from Spain and areas of Canada from France. From this augmented base, England became the leader of world trade in the 1700s.

Technology

While no dramatic breakthroughs occurred in the Baroque Age as would happen in the next century (see Chapter 17), this period saw a consolidation of trends, inherited from the near and distant past, along with a few important advances. The age's innovations, especially in warfare and household technologies, led to changes on the battlefield and in the home, thus affecting both public and private life. While widespread, their scope was limited by regional considerations, such as climate, habits, and availability of materials.

Warfare Technology By 1600 the cannon had modernized artillery warfare (see Chapter 12), and by 1700 several inventions in firearms had revolutionized infantry warfare. The Spanish, after 1450, invented the arquebus, or harquebus, a shoulder-fired gun. It rested on a small tripod and, after each shot, had to be reloaded and the fuse lit. The arquebus was difficult to maneuver and inaccurate most of the time. Nonetheless, Spanish, German, and Italian forces adopted it, but they did not abandon the pike—the medieval weapon of choice.

The musket, a muzzle-loading shoulder firearm, developed in Spain in the sixteenth century, soon replaced the arquebus. However, like the arquebus, the musket was cumbersome and inaccurate. In about 1630, the rifle—an improved musket, using a flintlock instead of a matchlock for ignition—appeared. Then, around 1670, the paper cartridge, which held the gunpowder, was invented, making rifles easier to manage. At about the same time, bayonets were affixed to the ends of rifles—a lethal weapon for close combat, which made pikemen obsolete and marked the end of medieval military equipment and infantry.

By 1700 gunpowder and shot, cannons, and firearms had revolutionized the way battles were planned and fought and wars were waged. In western Europe, armies were fighting with smaller and lighter cannons or field artillery, rifles, and bayonets—all supplied by the government, as regular standing armies grew more and more divorced from general society.

Household Technology In contrast to warfare technology, changes to household furniture, interior design, and heating arrangements moved at a glacial pace. Yet, between 1500 and 1700, significant advances occurred in wealthy households across the West.

Home furnishings during this time were descended from the Romans (see Chapter 5), including cupboards, tables, chairs, stools, and chests. Similarly, the tools used for furniture-making—axes, hatchets, chisels, mallets, hammers, and various lathes—even predated the Romans. Now, furniture began to lose its "Gothic" look, which was rough, large scale, and painted in showy colors. Italy led the way, perhaps because of its Roman heritage, with new types of furniture, especially chests with elaborate carvings, polished woods, and elegant shapes. Everywhere, furniture was given a more refined, finished look: waxed, varnished, and lacquered. Also contributing to the new taste for luxury was the fashion for imported Oriental goods, such as lacquered furniture and household goods (china, vases, and precious objects). Portugal (see Encounter in Chapter 12), Holland, and England helped bring about this change, after opening trade with India and the Far East. New furniture forms for specific purposes evolved: wardrobes, for clothing; dressers, with several levels for displaying valued objects; cupboards, for china and silver; and small cabinets, for writing materials, playing cards, and jewelry.

Similarly, home interiors evolved. In the Gothic era, furniture, ceilings, and walls had been painted in bright colors, perhaps to alleviate interior gloom, as houses had few windows. Inspired by the Italian Renaissance, Europe's elite opted for formal interiors with high ceilings and opulent displays, in effect, using their dwellings to assert their social status, real or imagined. Louis XIV's Versailles Palace is the quintessential example of this period's lavish Baroque style. Lesser royalty, nobility, and the bourgeoisie followed Louis XIV's lead as befitting their wealth and status (Figure 14.4).

The heating of palaces, courts, and residences changed between 1100 and 1700. Until about 1100, heat was supplied by open hearths, located in the center of a room, where the cooking was also done, making the kitchen the center of family life in winter. Other rooms used braziers, or charcoal-fired portable heaters—a health hazard, because of the danger of asphyxiation. In about 1100, wood-burning fireplaces, built into walls and with chimneys to vent the smoke, were introduced in Venice, as a refuge from the cold. From Venice, they spread north to all of Europe, except for Spain and Germany. In the Baroque era, fireplaces grew more complex, with the mantles carved into beautiful pieces of furniture, used for displaying status objects. In the 1630s, a French design improved the fireplace's efficiency, by introducing a complex system that drew air through passageways below the hearth and behind the grate and vented it through a grill in the mantle. England, because of a wood shortage, after about 1500, used coal in its fireplaces, making it

Figure 14.4 NICOLAES MAES. *The Eavesdropper.* 1657. Oil on canvas, 36⅜ × 48". The Netherlands Institute of Cultural Heritage, on loan to Dordrechts Museum, Dordrecht. *This Dutch painting accurately depicts the layout of a wealthy household. The high ceilings, tall banks of windows, rich draperies, and abundant use of carved wood for doors, columns, and arches attest to the owner's affluence. At the foot of the stairs, the lady of the house calls for silence, signaled by her slightly raised right forefinger. Having left the party upstairs (behind her), she has overheard her kitchen maid in an intimate moment with a young man. The guest's outer clothing is visible on the right. This satiric scene plays on the period's notion that maidservants had loose morals, thus necessitating close monitoring. As a respectable matron, the lady of the house was expected to keep a watchful eye on her household. Privacy was not a concern of this period, as reflected in this scene as well as the openness of the house's interior. Note the map on the wall (right), which may be interpreted as a sign of the globalism embraced by Holland's middle-class elite.*

unique among European nations. Nonetheless, fireplaces remained notoriously inefficient, as a 1695 letter reports on conditions inside Versailles' Hall of Mirrors: "At the king's table the wine and water froze in the glasses." This being the period's most palatial room, it should come as no surprise that people across the West wore furs and heavy robes indoors in winter, to fortify themselves from the cold.

Stoves, with ovens—for heating and cooking—appeared in Germany in 1490 and soon inspired models in Russia, Poland, Hungary, and Scandinavia. Stoves were made of stone, brick, and clay. A German model was built with earthenware tiles that were then richly decorated, and a popular Russian model added a set of flues—heat ducts—so that four rooms could be heated at once.

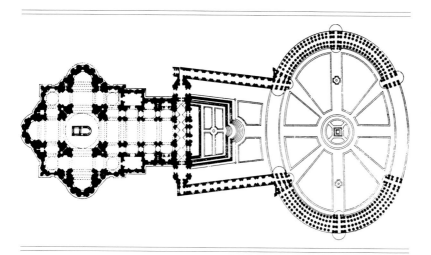

Figure 14.5 Carlo Maderno and Gianlorenzo Bernini. Plan of St. Peter's Basilica with Adjoining Piazza. 1607–1615 and 1665–1667. *This plan of St. Peter's Basilica shows the design of Maderno for the church (left), dating from 1607–1615, and the adjoining piazza and colonnade (right) by Bernini, dating from 1665–1667.*

THE BAROQUE: VARIATIONS ON AN INTERNATIONAL STYLE

The Baroque mentality originated in a search for stability and order in a restless age. Encouraged by the Catholic Church, artists and writers sought to reveal the order they believed lay beneath the seeming chaos of life. In this, they shared certain aims with the artists of the High Renaissance. But although both styles were devoted to order, they differed in their concept of how harmony was best achieved. High Renaissance artists valued repose, a single, static perspective, and designs that were complete in themselves. Baroque artists, on the other hand, created dynamic, open-ended works that threaten to explode beyond their formal boundaries. These exuberant works are characterized by grand, sweeping gestures; flowing, expansive movement; and curving lines and oval and elliptical shapes. Reflecting the excitement of overseas explorations and of the new discoveries in astronomy, Baroque artists were fascinated with the concept of infinite space.

Despite religious differences among various regions of Europe, the Baroque style spread readily from its origin in Rome to the entire Continent and to England. Lines of communication—through trade, diplomacy, and marriage—facilitated its spread, as did the persistence of Latin as the common language of scholarly works and diplomatic exchanges. Travel was also a factor in the export of Baroque ideals to the rest of Europe. Many Protestant families in northern and western Europe sent their sons, and sometimes their daughters, on grand tours of the Continent to "complete their education." English travelers to Rome and other Catholic bastions included such faithful Protes-

tants as poet John Milton and architect Christopher Wren.

Although the Baroque was an international style, it was reinterpreted in different regions, so that three distinct manifestations of the style emerged. The Florid Baroque, dominated by Roman Catholic religious ideals and motivations, was a product of the Counter-Reformation. This style developed in Italy and flourished there and in Spain and central Europe. The Classical Baroque, aristocratic and courtly, was a more subdued interpretation of Baroque ideals. This style was associated with French taste, which had been guided by the values of simplicity and harmony since the early 1500s, when Renaissance culture was first introduced into France. The French preference for the Classical fit well with the absolutist policies of Louis XIV, who promoted the adoption of strict rules in all aspects of cultural life as a way to reinforce his own obsession with order and control.

The third manifestation of this style was the Restrained Baroque, which arose in the middle-class United Provinces of the Netherlands and aristocratic England. Repelled equally by Catholicism and French absolutism, the artists and writers of the Restrained Baroque cultivated a style in keeping with their own Protestant values, a style simpler and less ornate than either the Florid or the Classical Baroque.

The Florid Baroque

The most important formative influence on the evolution of the Baroque style in the arts and architecture was the Council of Trent (see Chapter 13). In this series of sessions held between 1545 and 1563, church lead-

Figure 14.6 GIANLORENZO BERNINI. *Piazza of St. Peter's. 1665–1667. The Vatican. Bernini's plan for the piazza leading up to St. Peter's was instrumental in making exterior space a major concern of Baroque architects. The ancient Romans had integrated buildings into their urban settings, as had High Renaissance planners, but no architect had ever achieved such a natural blending of a monumental structure with its surroundings as Bernini did in this design.*

ers had reaffirmed all the values and doctrines rejected by the Protestants and called for a new art that was geared to the teaching needs of the church and that set forth correct theological ideas easily understood by the masses. To achieve these goals, the popes of the late sixteenth century began to hold a tighter rein on artists and architects and to discourage the individualistic tendencies of the Mannerist style.

The seventeenth-century popes used their patronage powers to bring to life the **Florid Baroque style.** Once again, as in the Middle Ages, aesthetic values were subordinated to spiritual purposes. The popes enlisted architects, painters, and sculptors to glorify the Catholic message. Architects responded with grand building plans and elaborate decorative schemes that symbolized the power and richness of the church. Painters and sculptors represented dramatic incidents and emotion-charged moments, particularly favoring the ecstatic visions of the saints and the suffering and death of Jesus. They portrayed these subjects with a powerful realism intended to convey the physical presence and immediacy of the church's holiest figures. In everything, vitality and theatrical effects were prized over such Classical elements as restraint and repose.

Architecture The church of St. Peter's in Rome became the age's preeminent expression of the Florid Baroque building style. First conceived in the early

1500s by Donato Bramante (see Chapter 12) as a High Renaissance temple in the shape of a Greek cross, St. Peter's was now redesigned to conform to the ideals of the Council of Trent. Rejecting the Greek cross as a pagan symbol, Pope Paul V commissioned Carlo Maderno [mah-DAIR-noh] (1556–1629) to add a long nave, thereby giving the floor plan the shape of a Latin cross (Figure 14.5). Not only did the elongated nave satisfy the need to house the large crowds drawn to the mother church of Roman Catholicism, but also the enormous size of the building signified the church's power.

St. Peter's exterior was basically finished after Maderno designed and built the building's facade, but the popes wanted to integrate this huge church into its urban setting—a Classical ideal that was now adapted to Baroque taste. For this task, Pope Alexander VII commissioned Gianlorenzo Bernini [bayr-NEE-nee] (1598–1680). Bernini's solution was a masterstroke of Florid Baroque design in which he followed the principle of abolishing all straight lines. He tore down the buildings around St. Peter's and replaced them with a huge public square where the faithful could gather to see and hear the pope. Bernini then outlined this keyhole-shaped space with a sweeping colonnade topped with statues of saints (Figure 14.6). For worshipers assembled in the square, the curved double colonnade stood as a symbol of the church's welcoming arms.

From its origin in Rome, the Florid Baroque style in architecture spread to Spain, Austria, and southern

ENCOUNTER

Japan Closes Its Doors, Nearly

Historically, when societies feel threatened by contact with foreigners, they react in predictable ways: They strengthen their defenses and build up their military; they safeguard their political and economic systems; they regulate rival religious faiths and monitor subversive ideas; and, when all else fails, they expel the foreigners. These acts of self-defense may be more intense if the society is already under stress, as was the case in Japan when Westerners first arrived in about 1550. The Japanese initially welcomed them, but after about a century, they closed Japan's doors to the world. They concluded that Western customs and thought threatened the Japanese way of life, so they ejected nearly all foreigners and limited contacts with the outside world for the next two hundred years.

Sixteenth-century Japan was embroiled in a costly and bloody civil war, which undermined the old feudal order, challenged the power of regional military governors, or *shoguns*, and further weakened an already-moribund imperial system. The new military technology adopted during the war reduced the role of the warrior class and made way for the rise of a new feudal system dominated by regional lords. Each lord, or *daimyo*, derived his wealth and power from his land-holdings, variable in size, which were passed down through the line of male heirs. With the support of vassals, the *daimyos* controlled the local economy and kept the peace.

After 1550, power was seized by a few powerful *daimyos* until Japan was unified under three successive shoguns—the final victor being Tokugawa Ieyasu [toe-kug-ah-wah ee-yas-u] (r. 1603–1616). The emperor remained the titular head of state, but actual power was in the hands of the shogun. After a series of power struggles with rival *daimyo* families, Ieyasu moved the capital from Heian (modern Kyoto) to Edo (modern Tokyo) and assumed full control of the country, opening trade with the West and giving access to Christian missionaries. And, most important, he established the Tokugawa *shogunate*, or government, which lasted until 1867, though its zenith was from the 1640s to the 1750s.

The Tokugawa shogunate had two goals: to prevent civil war and to stabilize the country. This meant controlling domestic and foreign affairs. At home, it brought the powerful *daimyo* class under its supervision by interfering in local disputes, organizing the *daimyo* domains, and requiring each *daimyo* to attend the shogun's court in Edo every other year—a practice called "alternate attendance." To further ensure loyalty, a *daimyo's* chief wife had to live in Edo all the time. Like France's King Louis XIV, Japan's Tokugawa rulers required court attendance as a way of keeping watch over their aristocratic supporters, looking for signs of rebellion, and forcing them to spend their wealth on a lavish lifestyle. The shogunate also created a class of elite warriors or retainers, known in the West as *samurai*, whose mission was to protect the rulers in Edo.

At the height of the civil war, in 1543, the first Westerners—Portuguese traders (see Encounter in Chapter 12)—arrived in Japan, bringing Roman Catholicism and guns. Trade soon commenced, and by 1549 Jesuit missionaries were on the scene. At first, the Japanese did not see Christianity as a threat, and Christian missionaries were usually welcomed in the ports. By 1603, the year of the founding of the Tokugawa shogunate, nearly three hundred thousand Japanese had converted to Christianity. About this time, however, some voices around the shogunate were raised about the threat posed by Christians in their midst. These negative voices knew that Spanish forces had conquered the Philippines, followed by waves of traders and Christian missionaries. Thus, these skeptics reasoned that Christian missionaries and traders might be only the first wave of Europeans, preparatory to destabilizing their recently unified country. They also feared that the foreigners might attract disgruntled *daimyos* as allies, or that Christian converts might be more loyal to the pope than to the shogun. Starting with a few isolated persecutions, the Tokugawa regime, in 1612, inaugurated a campaign to drive out the Christian missionaries and to force converts to renounce their new faith or face execution. In 1638 the persecutions reached a climax when about twenty thousand peasants, in revolt against the persecutions, were put to death.

At the same time, the shogun issued a series of Exclusion Decrees (1633, 1636), regarding trade and travel. The decrees made it a crime for Japanese to go abroad and declared that those who did would be executed on their return. To further ensure isolation, no large ships were to be built. Rules also were laid down regarding treatment of foreign vessels in Japanese ports. Only Chinese and Dutch traders were permitted to trade, and then only through the port of Nagasaki (Encounter figure 14.1). In 1640, when a Portuguese ship entered Nagasaki Bay, most of the crew was executed—a clear warning to the West. But, by allowing the Dutch to keep a center at Nagasaki, the Japanese were able to receive some news from the outside world. Thus, a small circle of Japanese thinkers began to focus on "Dutch Learning"—their name for Western culture. In the following decades, these scholars and writers advocated more contacts between Japan and the West and imported some Western knowledge, particularly in science and technology.

Learning from the Encounter   **How** do societies react when they feel threatened from the outside? **What** were some consequences of the civil wars in sixteenth-century Japan? **How** and **why** did the Japanese come to see the Westerners as threats? **Evaluate** the Japanese response to these perceived threats. **How** has the United States, during its history, reacted to outside threats? Give an **example. Evaluate** the American policy you offered as an example.

Encounter figure 14.1   Nagasaki in the Kanban Era (1661–1673). Folding screens, 50⅗" × 124". Nagasaki Museum of History and Culture. *The Dutch ships appear in the lower part of the picture, near their warehouses and living quarters. The Chinese ships are in the upper part of the scene. Japan's rulers regarded merchants and businessmen with contempt, and the Dutch suffered their disapproval—as long as they could make some guilders. Life on Deshima Island was miserable, and most of its inhabitants were simple sailors or tradesmen. Yet, over the years, the Dutch passed on to the Japanese much information and knowledge about life in the West.*

Figure 14.7 GIANLORENZO BERNINI. The Baldacchino. 1624–1633. Ht. approx. 100'. St. Peter's, Rome. *This magnificent canopy reflects the grandiose ambitions of its patron, Pope Urban VIII, a member of the Barberini family. The Barberini crest was the source for the huge stylized bees displayed on the flaps of the bronze canopy. In his desire for worldly immortality, this pope shared a common outlook with the secular rulers of the Baroque age.*

Germany. By 1650 this lush style had appeared in Spanish and Portuguese colonies in the Americas, and there it flourished until well into the nineteenth century.

Sculpture During the Baroque period, sculpture once again became a necessary complement to architecture, as it had been in medieval times. This change was hastened by the Council of Trent's advocacy of religious images to communicate the faith as well as the need to decorate the niches, recessed bays, and pedestals that were part of building facades in Florid Baroque architecture. The demand for sculpture called forth an army of talented artists, of whom the most outstanding was Bernini, one of the architects of St. Peter's.

Bernini brought the Florid Baroque to a dazzling climax in his sculptural works. His pieces, executed for such diverse projects as churches, fountains, and piazzas, or squares, often combined architecture with sculpture. His sculptural ideal was a dynamic composition that used undulating forms to delight the eye. His sensuous sculptures with their implicit movement were the perfect accompaniments to Florid Baroque structures with their highly decorated walls.

Bernini's most famous sculptures are those he made for the interior of St. Peter's—including altars, tombs, reliefs, statues, and liturgical furniture—during a fifty-year period, commencing in 1629. His masterpiece among these ornate works is the **baldacchino** [ball-duh-KEE-no], the canopy, mainly bronze and partly gilt, that covers the spot where the bones of St. Peter are believed to lie—directly under Michelangelo's dome. Combining architectural and sculptural features, the baldacchino is supported by four huge columns whose convoluted surfaces are covered with climbing vines (Figure 14.7). Bernini crowned this colossal work with a magnificent display of four large angels at the corners, four groups of cherubs in the centers of the sides, and behind the angels four scrolled arches that rise to support a ball and cross at the top.

The baldacchino's twisting columns were modeled on the type that by tradition supported Solomon's Temple in Jerusalem and had been used in the old St. Peter's Basilica. Thus these columns symbolized the church's claim to be the true successor to the Jewish faith. So popular was Bernini's Solomonic canopy that

THE BAROQUE: VARIATIONS ON AN INTERNATIONAL STYLE

Figure 14.8 GIANLORENZO BERNINI. *The Ecstasy of St. Teresa.* 1645–1652. Marble, glass, metal, life-size. Cornaro Chapel, Santa Maria della Vittoria, Rome. *Even though this sculpture captures an ecstatic vision, its portrayal reflects the naturalism that was central to the Baroque style. Bernini based this work on the saint's personal account, in which she described how an angel pierced her heart with a golden spear—a mystical moment the tableau faithfully reproduces. The sculpture's subject, St. Teresa of Avila (Spain) (1515–1582), founded the Carmelite order of nuns (1562); she recorded her mystic visions in works such as* Camino de perfección (The Road to Perfection).

in southern Germany it inspired many imitators and became the standard covering for altars for the next two centuries.

The sculpture that marks the highest expression of Bernini's art is *The Ecstasy of St. Teresa* (Figure 14.8). Using marble, metal, and glass, he portrayed the divine moment when the saint receives the vision of the Holy Spirit—symbolized here by the arrow with which the angel pierces her heart. In his conception, Bernini imagines the pair floating on a cloud and bathed by light from a hidden source; the light rays seem to turn into golden rods that cascade onto the angel and the saint. The intensity of the saint's expression, the agitation of the draperies, and the billowing clouds all contribute to the illusion that the pair are sensuously real. By depicting St. Teresa's supernatural experience in physical terms, Bernini intended to force the viewer to suspend disbelief and accept the religious truth of the scene.

Painting   In the Baroque period, painting once again became an essential part of church decoration. In pursuit of church ideals, the painters of this tradition tended to use rich color and unusual lighting effects to depict spectacular or dramatic moments. They represented nature and the human form realistically to make art intelligible and meaningful to the ordinary viewer.

The earliest great Florid Baroque painter was Michelangelo Merisi (1573–1610), better known as Caravaggio [kahr-ah-VAHD-jo]. Caravaggio rejected the antinaturalism of Mannerism in favor of a dramatic realism. His concern with realism led him to pick his models directly from the streets, and he refused to idealize his subjects. To make his works more dramatic and emotionally stirring, he experimented with light and the placement of figures. His paintings offer startling contrasts of light and dark—the tech-

nique known as chiaroscuro—and he banished landscape from his canvases, often focusing on human figures grouped tightly in the foreground.

A superb example of Caravaggio's work is *The Conversion of St. Paul* (Figure 14.9), which is paired with his *Crucifixion of St. Peter* in a Roman church. The two works were part of a commission to paint the founders of the Church of Rome, who, according to the New Testament, preached in the city. Caravaggio's revolutionary use of chiaroscuro emphasizes the dramatic event of Paul's conversion. The light, coming from the upper right, focuses on St. Paul and part of the horse's body. This makes the background nearly indistinct except for the groomsman, on the right, who holds the reins of the horse. St. Paul's head is thrown toward the viewer, and his eyes are shut as he is blinded by the light of the presence of Jesus, who, as recorded in the New Testament (Acts 9:3–9), did not appear in human form but only as light.

Caravaggio had an enormous influence on other painters both in Italy and elsewhere, notably France,

Figure 14.9 CARAVAGGIO. *The Conversion of St. Paul.* 1600–1601. Oil on canvas, approx. 7'5" × 5'8". Cerasi Chapel, Santa Maria del Popolo, Rome. *Caravaggio's paintings made monumentality an important feature of the Florid Baroque. By presenting St. Paul's figure in close-up, and giving full weight and presence to both him and the horse, the artist filled the canvas not only to capture a turning point in St. Paul's life and in the history of Christianity but also to teach the faithful a lesson about forgiveness and the power of God. Saul of Tarsus, the persecutor of Christians, will now become St. Paul, the convert who has been chosen to bring Jesus' message to the Gentiles.*

Spain, and the Netherlands. Perhaps the most original of Caravaggio's Italian disciples—known as Caravaggisti—was Artemisia Gentileschi [ahrt-uh-MEEZ-e-uh jain-teel-ESS-key] (1593–1653), his only female follower. Unlike most women artists of the early modern period, who limited their art to portraits, such as the late-sixteenth-century painter Sofonisba Anguissola (see Chapter 13), Gentileschi concentrated on biblical and mythical subjects, as many male artists did. Trained by her painter-father Orazio, himself a disciple of Caravaggio, Gentileschi adapted the flamboyant and dramatic style of Caravaggesque realism and made it her own. In almost thirty surviving paintings, she followed this style's preference for "night pictures," dark scenes whose blackness is illuminated by a single internal light source.

What distinguishes Artemisia Gentileschi's art from that of the rest of the Caravaggisti is its female as-

sertiveness, a highly unusual quality in the Baroque period, when women artists were still making their way without guild support or access to nude modeling. Female assertiveness is expressed throughout her works in an androgynous (having female and male characteristics) ideal, as may be seen in *Judith and Her Maidservant with the Head of Holofernes* (Figure 14.10), which depicts a scene from an apocryphal book of the Old Testament, the Book of Judith. The painting's central figure—Judith—is decidedly female (as shown in the vulnerable throat and fleshy body) and yet exhibits masculine strength (as shown in the commanding gesture accentuated by the firmly grasped sword). Judith, often treated in Italian painting and sculpture in the Renaissance and Baroque eras, is a perfect subject for Gentileschi, since the biblical story describes a woman of destiny. In the story, Judith saves the Jewish people by beheading their enemy Holofernes after having

Figure 14.10 ARTEMISIA GENTILESCHI. *Judith and Her Maidservant with the Head of Holofernes.* Ca. 1625. Oil on canvas. Detroit Institute of Arts. *Gentileschi's style in this painting is strongly indebted to the style of Caravaggio: The natural background is painted black and thus virtually eliminated, the central figures are shown in tight close-up, and the action is frozen like a single frame in a film sequence. The aesthetic impact of this cinematic method is to draw viewers into the scene and to personalize the figures. The artist's interest in the personal psychology of her characters is part of the trend toward naturalism that characterized Baroque culture in general.*

seduced him. In the painting, Holofernes' bloody head, partly visible in the basket, starkly dramatizes the point that Judith is a forthright woman who plans and acts, just as men do. Gentileschi's Judith typifies a heroic female ideal who is endowed with the traits of that fuller humanity that by tradition had been allowed only to male figures. Through such dramatic works as this, Gentileschi helped to spread the Caravaggesque style in Italy.

About the same time that Caravaggio was creating his dramatic works, a new form caught the imagination of painters in the Florid Baroque tradition—the illusionistic ceiling fresco. In these paintings, artists constructed imaginary continuations of the architectural features already present in the room, expanding up through layers of carefully foreshortened, sculptured figures and culminating in patches of sky. Looking up as if at the heavens, the viewer is overawed by the superhuman spectacle that seems to begin just overhead.

The superb example of this **illusionism** is the nave ceiling of the church of Sant' Ignazio (St. Ignatius) in Rome, painted by Andrea Pozzo [POE-tzo] (1642–1709). In this fresco, entitled *Allegory of the Missionary Work of the Jesuits,* Pozzo reveals a firm mastery of the technique of architectural perspective (Figure 14.11). The great nave ceiling is painted to appear as if the viewer were looking up through an immense open colonnade. Figures stand and cling to the encircling architectural supports, and, in the center, an expansive vista opens to reveal St. Ignatius, the founder of the Jesuit order, being received by an open-armed Christ. The clusters of columns on either side are labeled for the four continents—Europe, Asia, America, and Africa—symbolizing the missionary zeal of the Jesuits around the globe. Pozzo was motivated by spiritual concerns when he painted this supernatural vision. He believed that the illusion of infinite space could evoke feelings of spiritual exaltation and even religious rapture in the viewer. Illusionism, infinite space, and

Figure 14.11   ANDREA POZZO. *Allegory of the Missionary Work of the Jesuits.* Ca. 1621–1625. Ceiling fresco. Sant' Ignazio, Rome. *The meaning of Pozzo's fresco is based on* ignus, *Latin for "fire," a pun on the name of St. Ignatius (Loyola), the founder of the Jesuit order. In church tradition, the saint and the Jesuit mission are linked with the power of fire and light. At the fresco's center, Christ, holding the cross, emits rays of light from his wounded side, which pierce the figure of Ignatius (sitting on the cloud bank nearest Christ), who acts as a mirror; from him the light then radiates to the four corners, symbolic of the four continents. Thus, Ignatius and his missionary followers mediate Christ's saving light to the whole earth, as commanded by the scriptures.*

spectacular effects make this a masterpiece of the Florid Baroque. To see the dramatic differences between Baroque and High Renaissance ideals, compare this ceiling fresco with the ceiling of the Sistine Chapel by Michelangelo (see Figure 12.9).

Outside Italy, the principal centers of Florid Baroque painting were the studio of Velázquez in Spain and the workshop of Rubens in Flanders (present-day Belgium). Whereas Velázquez softened the Florid Baroque to his country's taste, Rubens fully embraced this sensual style to become its most representative painter.

The work of Diego Velázquez [vuh-LAS-kus] (1599–1660) owes much to the tradition of Caravaggio but does not have the intense drama of the Italian's painting. Velázquez also used chiaroscuro, but he avoided the extreme contrasts that made Caravaggio's paintings controversial. Velázquez's greatest work is *Las*

Meninas, or *The Maids of Honor* (Figure 14.12). In his role as official artist to the Spanish court, Velázquez painted this group portrait of the Infanta, or princess, surrounded by her maids of honor (one of whom is a dwarf). What makes this painting so haunting is the artful play of soft light over the various figures. In the background, a man is illuminated by the light streaming through the open door, and even more abundant sunshine falls on the princess from the window on the right.

Velázquez also plays with space and illusion in this painting. On the left side, he depicts himself, standing before a huge canvas with brush and palette in hand. The artist gazes directly at the viewer—or is he greeting the king and queen, who have just entered the room and are reflected in the mirror on the rear wall? The princess and two of her maids also look attentively out of the picture, but whether at the artist painting their portrait, at the royal couple, or at the viewer is left unclear. This fascination with illusion and with the effects of light and shade reveals Velázquez's links with Caravaggio and the art of the Florid Baroque.

In contrast to Velázquez's devotion to the ideal of grave beauty, the work of Peter Paul Rubens (1577–1640) is known for its ripe sensuality and the portrayal of voluptuous female nudes. Rubens had already forged a sensuous style before he sojourned in Italy for eight years, but his encounters with Caravaggio's tradition impressed him deeply, causing him to intensify his use of explosive forms and chiaroscuro. From the Venetian painters, especially Titian, he derived his love and mastery of gorgeous color. In his mature works, he placed human figures in a shallow foreground, bathed them in golden light with dark contours, and painted their clothes and flesh in sensuous tones.

As the most sought-after artist of his day, Rubens was often given commissions by the kings of the great states, and he produced works for royalty, for the church, and for wealthy private patrons. As official painter to the French court before the ascendancy of Louis XIV, who preferred the Classical style, Rubens was commissioned to paint a cycle of works glamorizing the life of Queen Marie de' Medici, widow of

Figure 14.12 VELÁZQUEZ. *Las Meninas (The Maids of Honor).* 1656. Oil on canvas, 10′5″ × 9′. Prado, Madrid. *Velázquez uses the mirror on the back wall, reflecting the Spanish king and queen, to enhance the dynamic feeling of the scene. This illusionistic device explodes the pictorial space by calling up presences within and outside the painting.*

Henry IV and powerful regent for her son, Louis XIII. One of the typical works from this series is *The Education of Marie de' Medici* (Figure 14.13). In this huge canvas, Rubens used Roman mythological figures to transform a mundane episode in the life of a queen into a splendid pageant of the French monarchy. All action is centered on the kneeling future queen. Minerva, the goddess of wisdom, offers instruction in reading and writing; Mercury, the god of eloquence, hovers overhead and offers his blessing; Apollo (or Orpheus, or Harmony) plays a stringed instrument,

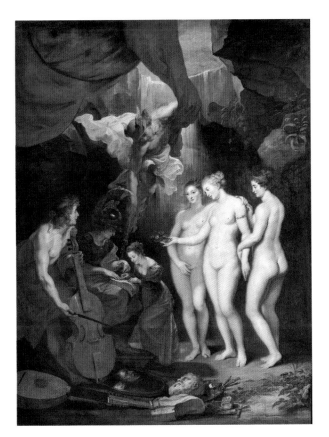

Figure 14.13 PETER PAUL RUBENS. *The Education of Marie de' Medici.* 1621–1625. Oil on canvas, 12′11″ × 9′8″. Louvre. *The Medici cycle, of which this work is a superb example, not only established the artist's European-wide reputation but also defined historical narrative—the combining of a historical event with mythological motifs—as one of the great themes of Baroque art. By 1715 the French Academy had created a ranked set of painting subjects, of which historical narrative occupied the highest level.*

Figure 14.14 André Le Nôtre, Landscape Architect, and Various Sculptors. Versailles Gardens. The Pool of Latona with adjacent parterres. 1660s. Versailles, France. *This fountain, composed of four concentric marble basins, is named for its crowning statue of Latona, the mother of the sun god Apollo, who was the inspiration for Louis XIV's reign. On either side of the fountain are parterres, or flower gardens with beds and paths arranged into patterns. Beyond the fountain stretches an avenue flanked by wooded areas that culminates in the grand canal, which extends the view into infinity. The rich profusion of this scene is a hallmark of Baroque design.*

thereby inculcating a love of music; and the three Graces, attendants of the goddess Venus, encourage the perfection of feminine grace. A waterfall cascades in the background, a drapery billows above, and various images of Greco-Roman culture (a mask of tragedy and a musical instrument) are displayed in the foreground. Rubens's mastery of both spiritual and secular subjects and the turbulent drama of his works made him the finest artist of the Florid Baroque.

The Classical Baroque

Although the Baroque originated in Rome, the pronouncements of the church had little effect on the art and architecture of France. Here, the royal court was the guiding force in the artistic life of the nation. The rulers and the royal ministers provided rich commissions that helped to shape the **Classical Baroque,** giving this style a secular focus and identifying it with absolutism. A second powerful influence on the Baroque in France was the pervasiveness of the Classical values of simplicity and grave dignity. Accordingly, after Louis XIV became king, French artists and architects found the Florid Baroque alien and even offensive; their adaptation of the Baroque was more impersonal, controlled, and measured.

Architecture The palace of Versailles was the consummate architectural expression of the Classical Baroque. Versailles, a former hunting lodge, was transformed by Louis XIV into a magnificent royal residence that became the prototype of princely courts in the West. At Versailles, where all power was concentrated in the royal court, were collected the best architects, sculptors, painters, and landscape architects as well as the finest writers, composers, and musicians

that France could produce. The duty of this talented assemblage was to use their gifts to surround Louis XIV with the splendor appropriate to the Sun King.

The redesign of Versailles gave Louis XIV the most splendid palace that has ever been seen in Europe. The chief architects of this revamped palace were Louis Le Vau [luh VO] (1612–1670) and Jules Hardouin-Mansart [ar-DWAN mahn-SAR] (1646–1708), but the guiding spirit was the Sun King himself. When finished, the palace consisted of a huge central structure with two immense wings (see Figure 14.2). The architecture is basically in the style of the Renaissance, with rounded arches, Classical columns, and porticoes inspired by Roman temples, but the overall effect is a Baroque style that is dignified yet regal.

The most striking aspect of Versailles is its monumentality: The palace is part of an elaborate complex that includes a royal chapel and various support structures, all of which are set in an elaborate park over two miles long. The park, designed by André Le Nôtre [luh NOH-truh] (1613–1700), is studded with a rich display of fountains, reflecting pools, geometric flower beds, manicured woods, exotic trees, statues, urns, and graveled walks—a gorgeous outdoor setting for royal receptions and entertainments (Figure 14.14).

The most famous room in Versailles Palace is the Hall of Mirrors, a central chamber with a tunnel-vaulted ceiling (Figure 14.15). The grandiose design of this hallway reflects its original function as the throne room of Louis XIV. Named for its most prominent feature, this long hall is decorated with Baroque profusion, including, in addition to the mirrors, wood parquetry floors of intricate design, multicolored marbles, ceiling paintings depicting military victories and other deeds of Louis XIV, and gilded statues at the base of the paintings. In modern times, major political events have taken place in the Hall of Mirrors: The

Figure 14.15 Charles Lebrun and Jules Hardouin-Mansart. Hall of Mirrors, Palace at Versailles. 1678–1684. Versailles, France. *The French architects Lebrun and Mansart designed this enormous hall to overlook the vast park at Versailles—the court and showplace of the French king, Louis XIV, the most powerful ruler in seventeenth-century Europe. Viewed through the floor-to-ceiling windows, which are placed along the width of the room, the majestic park outside becomes an extension of the interior space. The inside space in turn is enlarged by the tall mirrors that match the windows, echoing the exterior views.*

Germans proclaimed their empire from here in 1871 after having vanquished the French, and the peace treaty that ended World War I was signed here in 1919.

Painting   Classical values dominated Baroque painting in France even more completely than architecture. In pursuit of ancient Roman ideals, Classical Baroque artists painted mythological subjects, stressed idealized human bodies, and cultivated a quietly elegant style. The outstanding Classical Baroque artist was Nicolas Poussin [poo-SAN] (1594–1665). Ironically, except for two disappointing years in Paris, Poussin spent his professional life in Rome, the home of the Florid Baroque. Although he was inspired by Caravag-

gio's use of light and dark, the style that Poussin forged was uniquely his own, a detached, almost cold approach to his subject matter and a feeling for the unity of human beings with nature.

A beautiful example of Poussin's detached style is *Et in Arcadia Ego,* a painting in which the human figures are integrated into a quiet landscape (Figure 14.16). In ancient mythology, Arcadia was a land of pastures and flocks. In Poussin's painting, four shepherds, modeled on ancient statuary and clothed in Roman dress, are portrayed standing around a tomb, evidently absorbed in a discussion provoked by the Latin words carved into the tomb: *Et in Arcadia Ego,* that is, "I too once dwelled in Arcadia." One shepherd

Figure 14.16 NICOLAS POUSSIN. *Et in Arcadia Ego.* Ca. 1640. Oil on canvas, 34 × 48". Louvre. *In sacred art, painters expressed the theme of the inevitability of death in portraits of the sufferings of Jesus and the saints, and in secular art, in depictions of skeletons and death's heads, or images of human skulls. But Poussin, whose art was fired by Classical ideals and who was thus more reflective than others of his age, treated death in a much more detached way, as in this painting. Poussin's puzzled shepherds are a gentle reminder that the reality of death always comes as a surprise in the midst of everyday existence.*

traces the letters with his finger, spelling out the words. The magnificent stillness, the mythological subject, and the gentle melancholy evoked by this reminder of death were central to Poussin's art and evidence of his Classical spirit. Typically Baroque are the use of chiaroscuro, which makes the exposed limbs and the faces of the shepherds stand out vividly from the shadowy middle ground, and the sensual tones and rich colors.

The Restrained Baroque

The Protestant culture of northern and western Europe created simpler works that humanized Baroque exuberance, appealed to democratic sentiments, and reflected common human experience. This style of art is called the **Restrained Baroque,** and it was founded by the painters and architects of the Netherlands and England.

Painting   The Calvinist Netherlands pointed the way in the arts in Protestant Europe until 1675. The Dutch Republic was ruled by a well-to-do middle class whose wealth was based largely on their dominant role in international shipping. Led by these sober-minded burghers, as the townspeople were called, the Netherlands was briefly one of Europe's great powers. During the middle of the century, the Dutch virtually controlled northern Europe, using their military and

naval might to fight England, check French ascendancy, and destroy Spanish sea power. Amsterdam became one of Europe's largest cities, and an important school of painting flourished there. In about 1675, a series of military disasters ended the Netherlands' economic expansion, and the state's fortunes declined sharply. By this time, the great days of Dutch art were over.

During the heyday of the Dutch Republic, a school of painters arose whose works defined the Restrained Baroque. Attuned to the sober values of their religion and sympathetic to the civic ideals of the republic, these artists created a secular style that mirrored the pious outlook of the ruling middle class. An important development that helped to shape the course of Dutch painting was the rise of an art market. Venice had shown some tendencies in this direction in the 1500s, but in the Netherlands in the 1600s the first full-fledged art market made its debut. The impact of this market on the Dutch school was instantaneous and dramatic. Driven by a demand for home decoration, especially small works to hang on the wall, the market responded with specific subjects—still lifes, landscapes, portraits, and genre, or "slice-of-life," scenes. Paintings were sold by dealers as wares, and buyers speculated in art objects. The market dictated success or failure; some painters pursued other careers as a hedge against financial ruin.

The greatest artist of the Dutch school and probably one of the two or three greatest painters of Western art

Figure 14.17　REMBRANDT VAN RIJN. *The Night Watch (The Militia Company of Captain Frans Banning Cocq).* 1642. Oil on canvas, 12′2″ × 14′7″. Rijksmuseum, Amsterdam. *Because of its murky appearance, this painting acquired its nickname,* The Night Watch, *in the nineteenth century. But a cleaning of the painting's deteriorated surface showed that it was actually set in daylight. Restored to its original conception, this work now reveals Rembrandt's spectacular use of light and dark.*

was Rembrandt van Rijn (1606–1669). His early genius lay in his subtle and dramatic use of lighting and his forceful expressiveness—both qualities that reflected the distant influence of Caravaggio. He also was supremely gifted in his ability to portray the range of moods and emotions he found in humanity, as expressed through the ordinary people he used as models.

The culmination of Rembrandt's early style is a painting entitled *The Militia Company of Captain Frans Banning Cocq* but commonly known as *The Night Watch* (Figure 14.17). The painting was commissioned by one of Amsterdam's municipal guard troops in a typical display of Dutch civic pride. Instead of painting a con-

ventional group portrait, however, Rembrandt created a theatrical work filled with exuberant and dramatic gestures and highly charged chiaroscuro effects. He gave the composition added energy by depicting the guardsmen marching toward the viewer. The militia is led by Captain Cocq, the black-suited figure with the red sash and white ruff who marches with arm outstretched in the center foreground. On his left marches his attentive lieutenant, dressed in yellow, with his halberd in his hand. Behind them, the members of the surging crowd, engaged in various soldierly activities and looking in different directions with expressive faces, seem ready to burst forth from

Figure 14.18   REMBRANDT VAN RIJN. *Susanna and the Elders*. 1647. Oil on mahogany panel, 2′5″ × 4′. Gemäldegalerie Staatliche Museen, Berlin. *The scene is the garden of Susanna's wealthy husband, Joacim, whose palace looms in the upper left background. As Susanna steps into the pond, the two Elders appear. The first one lunges after her, trying to disrobe her, while the other stands nearby and leers. Rembrandt's masterful command of chiaroscuro, his placement of the three figures so as to make the scene more threatening, and his deployment of light on Susanna's body heighten the dramatic incident.*

the space in which they are enclosed. Of Rembrandt's vast repertory, this painting is one of his most representative.

However, by 1647, five years after *The Night Watch*, Rembrandt's reputation was in decline, and by 1656 he was bankrupt. During these years, his paintings and etchings, which often had a religious theme, began to express his deepest emotions and convictions. He also often illustrated moral lessons, as he did in *Susanna and the Elders* (Figure 14.18).

The story of Susanna is found in chapter 13 of the biblical book of Daniel, a chapter considered canonical by Roman Catholics and Greek Orthodox, but part of the noncanonical Apocrypha by Protestants. Jews also consider this chapter of Daniel outside their biblical canon. In Susanna's tale, Daniel is presented as a young, learned Jew who is deported from Israel to Babylon. There, through his storytelling ability and predictions, he becomes an adviser to Babylon's ruler, Nebuchadnezzar. As the story unfolds, Daniel chal-

Figure 14.19   REMBRANDT VAN RIJN. *Self-Portrait*. 1669. Oil on canvas, 23¼ × 20″. Mauritshuis, The Hague. *In this last self-portrait, Rembrandt's eyes reveal the personal anguish of a man who has outlived wife, beloved mistress, and children. By this means, Rembrandt expresses one of the most popular themes of Baroque art, that of pathos—the quality that arouses feelings of pity and sorrow.*

lenges two powerful Jewish Elders, who are also jurists, to save the life and reputation of an innocent young Jewish married woman, Susanna, who is charged with adultery—a capital offense under the old Jewish law code. The two Elders, filled with lust, spy on Susanna while she is bathing in an enclosed garden. They demand that she yield to them or they will swear that they have seen her having sex with a young man. Susanna refuses to succumb to their advances and calls for her servants. The next day, in a jumped-up trial, the Elders repeat their accusation against her. Because of their standing in the community, the crowd believes them until Daniel appears and demands a new trial for Susanna. Daniel shows, through his cross-examining of the witnesses, that the Elders have lied. The men are condemned to death and Susanna is exonerated. Innocence and honor are vindicated, and false testimony given by the powerful is proven worthless when exposed to the truth and God's sense of right and wrong. Rembrandt, the devout Protestant, understood the meaning of the story and, in his painting, captured the climactic moment when the elders

startle the naked Susanna, who appears vulnerable and helpless.

In the later work painted in the mid-1640s, Rembrandt's style became more personal and simpler. His paintings now expressed a stronger naturalism and an inner calm, a change that paralleled the rise of the quieter Classical Baroque. This final stage of his art is most beautifully and movingly rendered in his last self-portrait (Figure 14.19). During his career, he had often painted his own likeness, coolly revealing the effects of the aging process on his face. The last self-portrait is most remarkable for the expressive eyes, which, though anguished, seem resigned to whatever happens next. Rembrandt's pursuit of truth—inspired by his own meditations—is revealed here with clarity and acceptance. Looking into this time-ravaged face, the viewer recognizes the universality of growing old and the inevitability of death.

Besides being a master painter, Rembrandt was a giant in printmaking, creating thousands of extant prints and influencing the field for generations to come. Beginning in the 1640s, when he was beset with personal woes (the death of his first wife, Saskia) and a series of financial crises, he was able to keep himself afloat financially through sales of his prints. While prints generally sold for lower prices than paintings, Rembrandt, through his mastery of the print medium, was able to command higher prices for his prints than for his paintings, which were not selling. Fashioned with a deft hand and a clinical eye, the prints showed the same mastery of chiaroscuro and understanding of character as his paintings. The methods Rembrandt used were either etchings or drypoint—both techniques from Late Medieval times (see Chapter 10)—and his subjects included landscapes, Amsterdam street scenes, self-portraits, and religious scenes.

The religious prints reflected his personal faith, which was centered on a compassionate, personal savior rather than a stern, distant God. Rembrandt's simple religious scenes, in sharp contrast to the grandeur and splendor of the Italian Florid Baroque, often portray Christ, dressed in simple clothes, mingling with the common folk, as he heals, preaches, and brings hopes to the poor and downtrodden (Figure 14.20). Pious Protestants, who bought religious art for their homes, found Rembrandt's prints appealing because of their simple treatment of Christian themes.

Another great Dutch artist was Jan Vermeer [yahn ver-MEER] (1632–1675), who specialized in domestic genre scenes. His works reveal a calm world where ordinary objects possess a timeless gravity. Color was important for establishing the domesticity and peacefulness of this closed-off world; Vermeer's favorites were yellow and blue. These serene works evoked the

Figure 14.20 REMBRANDT VAN RIJN. *Christ Preaching.* Ca. 1648–1650. Etching, 11 × 15½″. Rijksmuseum, Amsterdam. *Rembrandt's command of the etcher's tools shines forth in this scene, based on a verse from the biblical book of Matthew, depicting Christ preaching in the street. Christ stands in the center, bathed in light, while surrounded by the poor and the lame, their figures fading into the shadows on the right. On the left are gathered the Pharisees—a sect that interpreted Jewish laws strictly. Recognizable by their finery and showy hats, the Pharisees engage in conversation, perhaps debating what to make of this street preacher. Rembrandt created characters not from his imagination but from real people he encountered in the streets of Amsterdam. This etching is often called the Hundred Guilder Print, because of the high price (est. $1,300, today) it brought at an auction in the seventeenth century.*

fabled cleanliness of Delft, the city where he lived and worked.

One of the most beautiful of his domestic scenes is *The Lacemaker* (Figure 14.21). Like most of his thirty-five extant paintings, *The Lacemaker* depicts an interior room where a single figure is encircled by everyday things. She is lit by a clear light falling on her from the side, another characteristic of Vermeer's paintings. The composition (the woman at the table and the rear wall parallel to the picture frame), the basic colors (yellow and blue), and the subject's absorption in her task typified Vermeer's works. *The Lacemaker* also has a moral message, for a woman engaged in household tasks symbolized the virtue of domesticity for Vermeer.

One of the few Dutch female artists was Judith Leyster (1609–1660), who, like her male colleagues, was a member of an artists' guild (in Haarlem) and painted for the art market. Beginning in about 1300, women were able to join artists' guilds in the Netherlands—

working in embroidery and other crafts—but it was the explosive growth of the art market in the 1600s, with the increased demand for artworks in the home by the Dutch burghers, that made artistic careers such as Leyster's possible. Leyster opened her own studio, where she also instructed aspiring artists. Leyster's specialties were genre scenes, portraits, and still lifes. Her *Self-Portrait* (Figure 14.22), painted when she was about twenty, demonstrates early mastery of artistic technique. Leyster's skill at genre painting enabled her to experience modest success in her profession.

England also contributed to the creation of the Restrained Baroque, but conditions there led to a style markedly different from that of the Dutch school. Unlike the Netherlands, England had no art market, was dominated by an aristocracy, and, most important, had as yet no native-born painters of note. Painting in England was controlled by aristocratic patrons who preferred portraits to all other subjects and whose taste

Figure 14.21 JAN VERMEER. *The Lace-maker.* Ca. 1664. Oil on canvas, 9⅝ × 8¼". Louvre. *Unlike Rembrandt, Vermeer was not concerned with human personality as such. Rather, his aim was to create scenes that registered his deep pleasure in bourgeois order and comfort. In* The Lacemaker, *he gives his female subject generalized features, turning her into a social type, but renders her sewing in exquisite detail, giving it a monumental presence. The painting thus becomes a visual metaphor of a virtuous household.*

Figure 14.22 JUDITH LEYSTER. *Self-Portrait.* Ca. 1630. Oil on canvas, 29 × 25½". National Gallery of Art, Washington, D.C. Gift of Mr. and Mrs. Robert Wood Bliss. Photo by Lorene Emerson. (1949.6.1). *Leyster's* Self-Portrait *shows her command of the painting tradition in which she was trained. The casual pose—a model turned in a chair with an arm resting on its back—was pioneered by the Dutch artist Franz Hals (see Figure 15.9), who may have been Leyster's teacher in Haarlem. Her smiling, open mouth represents a "speaking portrait," a frequent pose in this period, in which the subject seems to be wanting to make a statement. The merrymaking fiddler in the easel painting within the portrait was a popular genre subject among the Dutch art-buying public.*

Figure 14.23 ANTHONY VAN DYCK. *Lords John and Bernard Stuart.* Ca. 1639. Oil on canvas, 7'9⅓" × 4'9½". National Gallery, London. *Van Dyck has depicted these dandies in the carefully disheveled style preferred by the era's aristocrats. Their doublets (jackets) are of plain, muted colors and slashed on the chest and sleeves to allow a contrasting color to show. The deliberately casual look is especially prominent in the unbuttoned doublet worn by Lord John (left) and the cloak thrown over the shoulder of Lord Bernard (right). Both men wear the soft leather boots, partly rolled down the legs, that were now replacing the shoes of an earlier time.*

was courtly but restrained. The painter whose style suited these aristocratic demands was a Flemish artist, Anthony van Dyck [vahn DIKE] (1599–1641). A pupil of Rubens, van Dyck eventually settled in England and became court painter to Charles I.

Van Dyck's elegant style captured the courtly qualities prized by his noble patrons. He depicted his subjects' splendid costumes in all their radiant glory, using vibrant colors to reproduce their textures. He in-

vented a repertory of poses for individual and group portraits that showed his subjects to their greatest advantage. But van Dyck did more than cater to the vanity of his titled patrons. With superb sensitivity, he portrayed their characters in their faces, showing such qualities as intelligence, self-doubt, and obstinacy. His psychological insights make his courtly portraits genuine works of art.

Van Dyck's fluent style is clearly shown in his double portrait of Lords John and Bernard Stuart, two of the dandies of the court of Charles I (Figure 14.23). This painting indicates the artist's mastery of the society portrait. The subjects' fashionable dress and haughty expressions establish their high social status. Van Dyck skillfully renders the play of light on the silk fabrics of their clothing. He creates an interesting design by placing their bodies opposite each other, but this positioning also offers psychological insight into their characters as the mirrorlike pose suggests that they are vain young men. Van Dyck's deftness at creating elegant likenesses set the standard for English portraiture and influenced French artists well into the eighteenth century.

Architecture The architecture of the Restrained Baroque drew strongly on the Classical tradition. One of the most influential English architects of this period was Sir Christopher Wren (1632–1723), whose Baroque style had two sources. From the Classical Baroque of Versailles came his love of rich ornamentation, and from Bramante's High Renaissance style came his devotion to pure Classical forms, such as the dome and the Classical orders. Following those traditions, Wren created his own unique style, with spacious interiors and elaborately decorated facades.

Although Wren created many brilliant secular works, he is best known for his churches, which he built in the aftermath of the Great Fire of London in 1666. His masterpiece is St. Paul's cathedral in London (Figure 14.24). Intended as a Protestant rival to St. Peter's in Rome, St. Paul's has a longitudinal floor plan similar to St. Peter's but with Gothic features in the interior, including transept and choir and a dome reminiscent of Bramante's Tempietto (see Figure 12.22). The church has many Classical elements, such as the pairs of columns on two levels, the symmetrical towers and decorations, and the elaborate pediment. At the same time, its Baroque nature is revealed in the ornate facade punctuated by niches, the robust twin steeples with their shadowy recesses and staggered columns, and the dramatic play of light across the face of the building. The most outstanding feature of St. Paul's is the magnificent dome, inspired by the one designed by Michelangelo for St. Peter's (see Figure 12.23), with its encircling colonnade. This elegant

Figure 14.24 CHRISTOPHER WREN. St. Paul's Cathedral. 1675–1710. London. *Wren was a true child of the Baroque Age. An astronomy professor at Oxford University, he made discoveries that brought him to the attention of the age's greatest scientist, Isaac Newton. When opportunity called and Wren was given the royal commission to rebuild the churches of London, he approached this task with the same passionate love of geometry that had motivated his scientific researches. St. Paul's design united his sense of beauty with his mathematical bent.*

dome still dominates central London's skyline, a splendid reminder of Baroque glory.

Literature

The Council of Trent's decrees, which had such a powerful impact on artists and architects, were hardly felt by seventeenth-century writers. Nevertheless, a style of literary expression arose that is called Baroque and that became international in scope. The most enduring literary legacy of this period is drama. Baroque audiences delighted in works that blended different forms, and drama mixed literature, costume design, set painting, and theatrical spectacle. Tragedy, based on Roman models, was the supreme achievement of the Baroque stage, but comedies of all types, including satires, farces, and sexual comedies, were also important. After centuries of neglect, tragedy and comedy had been brilliantly revived in Elizabethan England, and their appearance in France was evidence of the continuing growth of secular consciousness. Another ancient literary genre that gained wide favor was the epic, a reflection of the love of power typical of the age. Finally, Baroque literature began to acknowledge the world outside Europe, as may be seen in the rise of writings with a non-Western dimension. These non-Western aspects included settings (for example, Mexico in the poetry of the Mexican nun Sor Juana Inés de la Cruz [1648–1695]) (Figure 14.25), characters (for example,

Figure 14.25 ANDRES DE ISLAS. *Sor Juana Inés de la Cruz.* 1772. Museo de America, Madrid. *This portrait, painted seventy-seven years after the subject's death, is based on an earlier (now lost) likeness. Sor Juana is depicted in a conventional pose for a writer-intellectual (see Figure 13.1)—seated before an open book, writing implement in hand. She wears the Hieronymite habit of the Order of St. Jerome—a white tunic under a full-length scapular in a color that varied by region. In Mexico City, the scapulars were black or blue. Around her neck is a nun's shield—in Spanish,* escudo de monja*—typically a painting on copper of a religious scene of spiritual importance to the wearer. Sor Juana's shield shows the Annunciation, the moment when the Angel Gabriel reveals to Mary her destiny as the Mother of God. This painting is by the Mexican artist Andres de Islas (active 1753–1775), whose specialty was the documentation of the ethnic life of colonial Mexico.*

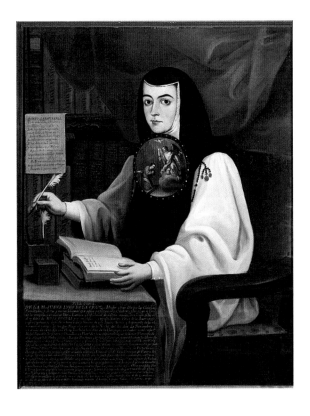

the Aztec ruler Montezuma, the hero of the play *The Indian Emperor* [1665], by John Dryden [1631–1700]), and themes (especially the comparison of Western and non-Western customs in travel literature, as in *A New Voyage Round the World* [1697], by William Dampier [1652–1715], and *Travels in Persia* [1686], by Jean Chardin [1643–1713]).

Despite the variety of their works, the Baroque writers had common characteristics, including a love of ornate language and a fascination with characterization, either of individuals or of types. Baroque authors often dealt with emotional extremes, such as gross sensuality versus pangs of conscience. With such emotionally charged themes, Baroque writers could and did employ dramatic rhetoric, slipping occasionally into empty bombast.

Baroque Literature in France   Drama was France's greatest contribution to the literature of the Baroque period. Secular drama revived under the patronage of Louis XIII in the 1630s and reached a climax during Louis XIV's reign. Strict control was exercised over the plays staged at the royal court, although comic playwrights were given more freedom, as long as they did not offend common decency or good taste.

The tragic playwrights were expected to obey the rules of literary composition identified by the French Academy and based on the theories of Aristotle (see Chapter 3). The ideal play had to observe the unities of time, place, and action—that is, it had to take place during a twenty-four-hour time span, have no scene changes, and have a single uncomplicated plot. Furthermore, the plays were supposed to use formal language and to focus on universal problems as reflected in dilemmas experienced by highborn men and women. Because of the playwrights' strict adherence to these rules, it is sometimes claimed that the dramas of this period are expressive of a Classical style. But the French preference for order, gravity, and severity was evidence of a Baroque sensibility—just as was the case in the French style of Baroque painting and architecture.

The two great French tragedians of the Baroque period were Pierre Corneille [kor-NAY] (1606–1684) and Jean Racine [ra-SEEN] (1639–1699). Corneille wrote tragedies in verse based on Spanish legends and Roman themes. Drawing on the Hellenistic philosophy of Stoicism, his dramas stressed the importance of duty, patriotism, and loyalty—ideals that appealed to his courtly audience. His finest work is *Le Cid*, based on a legendary figure of Spanish history and concerned with the hero's choice between personal feelings and honor.

In Racine, drama found a voice whose refined language and penetrating psychological insight have never been equaled in the French theater. Preoccupied with the moral struggle between the will and the emo-

tions, Racine created intensely human characters in classically constructed plays. A subject that intrigued Racine was the doomed woman who was swept to her destruction by obsessive sexual passion. This Baroque theme was most perfectly expressed in his masterpiece, *Phèdre (Phaedra)*, his version of the Greek tale of incestuous love first dramatized by Euripides in the fifth century B.C.E. Where Euripides makes fate a central reason for the heroine's, Phèdre's, downfall, Racine portrays the unfortunate woman as a victim of her passion for her stepson. Even though he explored other types of love in his plays, such as mother love and even political passion, it was in his study of sex as a powerful motive for action that Racine was most original.

The Baroque period in French drama also produced one of the comic geniuses of the Western theater, Jean Baptiste Poquelin, better known as Molière [mole-YAIR] (1622–1673). Molière analyzed the foibles of French life in twelve penetrating satirical comedies that had the lasting impact of tragedy. He peopled his plays with social types—the idler, the miser, the pedant, the seducer, the hypochondriac, the medical quack, the would-be gentleman, the pretentiously cultured lady—exposing the follies of the entire society. To create his comedic effects, Molière used not only topical humor and social satire but all the trappings of farce, including pratfalls, mistaken identities, sight gags, puns, and slapstick, as well.

Molière was appointed official entertainer to Louis XIV in 1658; even so, he made many enemies among those who felt they were the butt of his jokes. When he died, for example, the French clergy refused to give him an official burial because they believed some of his plays to be attacks on the church. The testament to Molière's enduring brilliance is that many of his comedies are still performed today, including *Tartuffe, The Miser, The Would-Be Gentleman,* and *The Misanthrope,* and they are still enormously entertaining.

Baroque Literature in England   The outstanding contribution in English to the literature of the Baroque period was provided by John Milton (1608–1674), a stern Puritan who held high office in Cromwell's Commonwealth. The deeply learned Milton had a grand moral vision that led him to see the universe as locked in a struggle between the forces of darkness and the forces of light. Only an epic was capable of expressing such a monumental conception.

His supreme literary accomplishment was to Christianize the epic in his long poem *Paradise Lost.* Inspired by Homer's and Vergil's ancient works, but also intended as a Protestant response to Dante's *Divine Comedy,* Milton's poem became an immediate classic. His grandiose themes in *Paradise Lost* were the rebellion of the angels led by Lucifer, the fall of Adam and Eve in the Garden of Eden, and Christ's redemption of humanity.

An astonishing aspect of *Paradise Lost* is Milton's portrait of Lucifer, which some readers have seen as a Baroque glamorization of evil. Lucifer is characterized as a creature of titanic ambition and deceitful charm. Despite his powerful presence, however, this epic story has moral balance. At the end, Adam, the author of original sin, is saved instead of being condemned to Hell. Adam's redemption occurs when he accepts Jesus as Lord. Adam's choice reflected Milton's belief in free will and the necessity of taking responsibility for one's actions.

In addition to its grand theme, *Paradise Lost* is Baroque in other ways. The mixing of Christian legend and ancient epic, for example, is typical of Baroque taste. Milton's convoluted style is Baroque with its occasionally odd word order, Latinisms, and complex metaphors. Most of all, Milton's epic is Baroque in its lofty tone and exaggerated rhetoric—literary equivalents, perhaps, of Rubens or Rembrandt.

A secondary achievement of the literary Baroque in England was that literature began to reflect the West's overseas expansion, as in the publishing of travel books, memoirs, and letters describing real and fictional contacts with peoples and lands around the globe. Part of a European-wide trend, the growth of English literature with a non-European dimension expressed the Baroque theme of pushing against the boundaries of life and art. A pioneering work on this Baroque theme was the short prose story *Oroonoko* (1688) by Aphra Behn (1640–1689), an English writer who exploited her firsthand experiences as a resident of Surinam (modern Suriname) to provide a vivid, exotic setting. Situated in South America and told with a blend of realism and romance, *Oroonoko* condemns the culture of slavery through the story of the doomed love affair between a black slave-prince and a slave woman. The author portrays the black hero as untutored in Western ways yet polished and educated on his own terms, and, above all, superior to the natural depravity of the European characters. This is an early version of the myth of the noble savage, the cultural archetype that reached its climax in the Romantic era (see Chapter 17). England's first woman to earn her living as a writer, Behn also wrote about twenty comedies for the stage and a poem collection, but *Oroonoko* is her chief claim to renown.

Music

Unlike the Renaissance, when a single musical sound prevailed (see Chapter 12), the Baroque had no single musical ideal. Nonetheless, four trends during the Baroque period give its music distinctive qualities. First, the development of major and minor tonality, which had been prefigured in Josquin des Prez's music in the early 1500s, was a central feature of the works of this time, making it the first stage in the rise of modern music. Second, the mixing of genres, which has been noted in literature and the arts, also occurred in Baroque music. Third, the expressiveness that had entered music in the late 1500s now became even more exaggerated, being used to stress meanings and emotions in the musical texts that otherwise might not have been heard. And last, this was an age of **virtuosos,** master musicians, especially singers, who performed with great technical skill and vivid personal style, and of a growing variety of musical instruments (Figure 14.26). The musical form that drew these trends together was **opera,** making it the quintessential symbol of the age.

Opera Opera originated in Italy in the late sixteenth century among a group of Florentine musicians and poets with aristocratic ties. The first great composer of opera was Claudio Monteverdi [mon-teh-VAIR-dee] (1567–1643), whose earliest opera, *Orfeo* (1607), was based on the legend of the ancient Greek poet-musician Orpheus. *Orfeo* united drama, dance, elaborate stage mechanisms, and painted scenery with music. Monteverdi wrote melodic arias, or songs, for the individual singers, and he increased the opera's dramatic appeal by concluding each of its five acts with a powerful chorus. His setting truly mirrored the text, using musical phrases to serve as aural symbols and thus to enhance the unfolding of events.

By the 1630s, opera began to shed its aristocratic origins and become a popular entertainment. This change did not affect opera's focus on ancient myths and histories about noble men and women, nor did it halt the trend to brilliant singing called *bel canto*, literally "beautiful song." However, to appeal to a wider audience, operatic composers added elements from Italy's popular comic theater, such as farcical scenes and stock characters, notably humorous servants. By the end of this age, the operatic form was stylized into a recipe, including improbable plots, inadequate motivations for the characters, and magical transformations—signs of its Baroque nature.

Opera became immensely popular in Europe, especially in Italy, where it remains so today. By 1750, opera houses had been built in many major cities; Venice led the way with more than a dozen establishments. The rise of opera in Italy during the 1600s, like the founding of a commercial theater in London in the 1500s, presaged the downfall of the aristocratic patronage system and the emergence of entertainments with mass appeal.

Figure 14.26 JAN BRUEGEL. *Hearing.* Ca. 1620. Oil on canvas, approx. 2′3″ × 3′6″. Prado, Madrid. *One of a series of allegorical paintings representing the five senses, this work by Jan Bruegel depicts the sense of hearing. Set in a Renaissance interior framed by three rounded arches, it shows a variety of sources that make sounds pleasing to the human ear. Most prominent are the musical instruments, which collectively constitute an anthology of the instruments used in Baroque music.*

The winding down of the Thirty Years' War allowed Italian opera to be exported to the rest of Europe. Only in France were composers able to defy the overpowering Italian influence and create an independent type of opera. This development was made possible by the grandeur of Louis XIV's court and by French taste, which was more restrained than the opulent Italian. Nevertheless, French opera was founded by an Italian, Jean-Baptiste Lully [loo-LEE] (1632–1687), who later became a French citizen and Louis's court composer. Under Lully's direction, French opera developed its identifying features: dignified music, the full use of choruses, the inclusion of a ballet, and, most important, a French text. Lully's patron, the Sun King, sometimes performed in the opera's ballet sequences himself, dancing side by side with the composer. Lully's works, which dominated French music until 1750, ensured a powerful role for French music in the Western tradition.

Bach, Handel, and Vivaldi Baroque music reached its climax after 1715. Three composers were responsible for this development: in Protestant northern Europe, the Germans Bach and Handel, and in Roman Catholic Italy, Vivaldi.

JOHANN SEBASTIAN BACH The greatest of these Late Baroque masters was Johann Sebastian Bach (1685–1750). A devout Lutheran who worked for German noble courts and municipalities far from the major cities, Bach created a body of sacred music that transcends all religious creeds and nationalities. Employing all the Baroque musical genres, his works are distinguished by their inventiveness and complete mastery of major and minor tonality. His most memorable achievements are the Passions, the musical settings of the liturgy to be performed on Good Friday—the most tragic day in the Christian calendar. Composed in about 1727, the *St. Matthew Passion* expresses the collective grief of the Christian community for the death of Jesus. Bach used a German text with arias and choruses, making the music bring out all the emotional implications of the words. Thus, the *St. Matthew Passion* is more dramatic than most operas and a sublime religious experience in itself.

Although Bach's religious music is his greatest legacy, he also left a body of secular music, including orchestral works and works for various instrumental groups. A musician's musician, Bach composed *The Well-Tempered Clavier* as an ordered set of studies in all the major and minor keys. The forty-eight preludes and fugues in this work set a heroic challenge for keyboard performers and are still an essential part of the piano repertoire today. (A **clavier** is an early keyboard instrument; a **fugue** is a polyphonic composition in which a theme is introduced by one instrument and then repeated by each successively entering instrument until a complicated interweaving of themes, variations, imitations, and echoes results.) This work contributed to the standardization of the pitches of the notes of the musical scale and of the tuning of keyboard instruments.

Bach's Organ Fugue in G Minor ("Little Fugue"; about 1709) is a classic of the fugue genre. A fugue may be written for a group of instruments, voices, or a single keyboard instrument, in this instance, an organ. Bach's organ fugue is scored for four melodic lines, soprano, alto, tenor, and bass. It opens with the "voices" playing "follow the leader": the soprano line announces the **subject**—the main musical theme, followed by its imitation in the alto, tenor, and bass lines. However, before the alto line can complete its part, the soprano line begins the **countersubject**—a variation of the subject that will now be played in tandem with the subject, either above it or below it. The bass line, recognizable by its deep plush tones, concludes the opening sequence.

A short transitional section, known as an **episode,** leads to another round of follow the leader, with each melodic line taking a turn. Episodes may be fresh music or phrases taken from the subject. Throughout the remainder of this piece, the subject and countersubject are in constant dialogue, with episodes added after each recurrence of the subject. Sustained notes and **trills**—rapid alternation of two notes, a step apart—are two means Bach used to embellish the increasingly active melody. The Little Fugue, though in a minor key, has some episodes and restatements of the subject in a minor key, and it concludes with a glorious major chord—a typical Baroque ending.

Of Bach's secular works, the most popular today are probably the six *Brandenburg Concertos* (written for the duke of Brandenburg), whose tunefulness and rhythmic variety the composer rarely surpassed. The concertos were composed for the type of ensemble found in the German princely courts of the time—a group of string players of average ability along with a few woodwind and brass instruments, perhaps a total of twenty to twenty-five musicians. Bach's dominant idea in these concertos was to demonstrate the interplay between individual soloists and the larger group. As in most of his work, the composer wove different melodic lines and different harmonies together into elaborate, complex structures of tremendous variety, power, and scope.

GEORGE FRIDERIC HANDEL   The other great Late Baroque German master, George Frideric Handel (1685–1759), was renowned for his Italian-style operas. More cosmopolitan than Bach, Handel eventually settled in London, where he composed thirty-six operatic works. His operas succeeded in their day because of the brilliant way in which the music allows the singers to show their virtuosity, but they are generally not to the taste of modern audiences and have not found a place in the standard operatic repertory. In contrast, his mastery of sacred music, particularly the **oratorio**—an operalike form but without any stage action—which he perfected, has made his name immortal. Of the oratorios, *Messiah,* based on biblical texts and sung in English, holds first place. Its popularity stems from its Baroque qualities: the emotionally stirring choruses and the delightful embellishments the soloists are permitted in their arias. As a result, *Messiah* is probably the best-known work of sacred music in the English-speaking world.

One of *Messiah*'s great arias, which shows Handel's expressive music to perfection, is "Ev'ry Valley Shall Be Exalted," for tenor, strings, and basso continuo. Handel's exuberant music matches the exuberant text, based on Isaiah 40:4, a verse that envisions an earth transformed by the coming of the Messiah.

Ev'ry valley
Ev'ry valley shall be exalted,
and ev'ry mountain
and hill made low,
the crooked straight,
and the rough places plain.
Ev'ry valley shall be exalted,
and ev'ry mountain and hill
made low, the crooked straight,
and the rough places plain.
The crooked straight,
And the rough places plain.

Through word painting, a popular Baroque musical technique, Handel makes the text come alive. For example, the word *exalted (raised up)* (in line 2) becomes a rising musical phrase made up of forty-six rapid notes. High tones are used to depict *hill* and *mountain*, and certain words are given musical equivalents, such as *crooked* (two notes a half step apart, repeated), *straight* (sustained tone), and *plain* (long sustained note). The aria begins and ends in the Baroque style with a **refrain** (in Italian, *ritornello*), a short instrumental passage.

ANTONIO LUCIO VIVALDI   Antonio Lucio Vivaldi (1678–1741), the Late Baroque Italian composer and violinist, set a new standard for instrumental music. Unlike Bach and Handel, who worked almost exclusively within secular settings, Vivaldi supported himself through church patronage, serving as both a priest (briefly) and a musician and composer (mainly) at a church orphanage for females in Venice. He also was a freelance composer, producing works for patrons and customers across Europe. Employing diverse musical genres, he wrote nearly fifty operas, of which about sixteen survive complete; about forty cantatas; fifty sacred vocal works; ninety **sonatas** (a sonata is a work for a small group of instruments); and nearly five hundred **concertos** (a concerto is a piece for solo instrument and orchestra), of which nearly half were written for solo violin. Vivaldi's music is little performed today except for the concertos, whose innovations and style raise him to the first rank of composers. His innovations include a three-movement form, arranged in a fast-slow-fast pattern, and, most important, the use of a refrain, that is, a recurring musical phrase, in combination with brief passages performed by a solo instrument, which together provide a unifying thread to the work. Vivaldi's concerto form influenced the Late Baroque works of Bach and helped to set the standard for Classical music in general (see Chapter 16).

The best known of Vivaldi's concertos are those collectively titled *The Four Seasons* (1725), a set of four violin concertos, each named after a season of the year, beginning with spring. Using both major and minor tonality, Vivaldi's music passionately evokes a feeling of each passing season. This work established the tradition of **program music,** or music that represents a nonmusical image, idea, or story without the use of words. Later, Beethoven made program music a central feature of his music (see Chapter 17).

Vivaldi's lively "La Primavera" ("Spring"), from *The Four Seasons*, is a masterful evocation of springtime. A work in a major key usually conveys optimism, and this concerto certainly does. Typical of Baroque concerti, "Spring" opens with an orchestral *ritornello,* expressed in two phrases, which are repeated twice, first loudly and then softly. The *ritornello* theme, or at least parts of it, becomes a recurring motif. After the opening, violin solos alternate with the orchestral *ritornello.* To conjure up the complex sounds of spring, Vivaldi uses word painting, for both solo violin and the orchestra's string section: bird songs (high trills and repeated high notes), murmuring brooks (running notes alternating with sustained notes), and thunder and lightning (string **tremolos**—the rapid repetition of a pitch or chord) and upward rushing scales. "La Primavera" is probably Vivaldi's most popular single work.

The Legacy of the Baroque Age

The Baroque period left a potent legacy to the modern world in politics, economics, religion, and the arts. The system of great states governed by a balance of power dominated European affairs until 1945. Standing armies, divorced from general society, became a central feature of life among Europe's great powers until 1790. From the Baroque period date the roles of France and England as Europe's trendsetters, both politically and culturally. The concept and practice of "world war" also date from this period. The economic system known as mercantilism originated during the Baroque period and prevailed in Europe into the nineteenth century. The religious orientation of the European states became well established in the seventeenth century, along with the division of the vast majority of Westerners into Protestant and Catholic camps. In the Netherlands, artists operated in an open market, painting works for wealthy citizens, thus launching the trend toward today's commercial art world. The Baroque idea of spectacle is a thread that runs throughout the culture of this period and helps to explain not only the propagandistic aspects of politics and religion but also the theatrical elements in the arts and entertainment. Culturally, the Baroque is still with us, even though much about this style seems excessive to modern taste. Although Baroque operas are not often performed, the idea of opera originated in this age of spectacle. Other Baroque musical works, notably the majestic oratorios of Handel and the powerful compositions of Bach for church and court, are part of the regular concert repertoire in the West today. Some of the most admired and enduring artworks in Western history were created during this time, including Bernini's *Ecstasy of St. Teresa* and the paintings of Rembrandt. Many cities of Europe are still showcases of Baroque splendor. The church of St. Peter's in Rome, St. Paul's cathedral in London, and the palace and gardens at Versailles are but three of the surviving monuments of this period, reminding us of the grand religious and political ideals of a very different age.

KEY CULTURAL TERMS

Baroque
Florid Baroque style
baldacchino
illusionism
Classical Baroque style
Restrained Baroque style
virtuoso
opera
bel canto
clavier
fugue

subject
countersubject
episode
trill
oratorio
refrain
sonata
concerto
program music
tremolo

SUGGESTIONS FOR FURTHER READING

BEHN, A. *Oroonoko and Other Stories*. Edited and introduced by M. Duffy. London: Methuen, 1985. An edition of Behn's stories, with a useful introduction; these short works prepared the way for the novel genre, born after 1700. *Oroonoko* was first published in 1678.

CORNEILLE, P. *The Cid*. Translated by V. J. Cheng. Newark: University of Delaware Press, 1987. A version of Corneille's drama, recounting the story of a hero torn between honor and love; imitates the poetic form of the original, first staged in 1636.

MILTON, J. *Paradise Lost*. New York: Norton, 1975. Milton's Baroque epic about rebellion—Lucifer's revolt in heaven and Adam and Eve's defiance on earth; Scott Elledge provides a useful introduction and notes to the text, which was first published in 1667.

MOLIÈRE (POQUELIN, J. B.). *The Misanthrope*. Translated by R. Wilbur. London: Methuen, 1967. A good translation by a leading American poet. Useful English versions by various translators of Molière's other frequently performed comedies are also available, including *The Miser* (New York: Applause Theatre Book Publishers, 1987), *Tartuffe* (London: Faber and Faber, 1984), and *The Bourgeois Gentleman (The Would-Be Gentleman)* (New York: Applause Theatre Book Publishers, 1987).

RACINE, J. B. *Phaedra [Phèdre]*. Translated by R. Wilbur. New York: Harcourt Brace Jovanovich, 1986. A solid translation of this French tragic drama.

SOR JUANA INÉS DE LA CRUZ. *Poems, Protest, and a Dream*. Translated by M. S. Peden. New York: Penguin, 1997. A selection of Sor Juana's writings, including ironic, courtly poems and the first defense by a New World author of the right of women to be educated, *La Respuesta de la poetisa a la muy ilustre Sor Filotea de la Cruz (Response to the Most Illustrious Poetess Sor Filotea de la Cruz)*, first published in 1691. With a helpful introduction by I. Stavans.

SUGGESTIONS FOR LISTENING

BACH, JOHANN SEBASTIAN. The greatest composer of the Baroque era, Bach is best known for his sacred music, which has tremendous emotional power. His church music for voices includes more than two hundred cantatas, or musical settings of biblical and choral texts, such as *Jesu der du meine Seele (Jesus, Thou Hast My Soul), Wachet Auf (Sleepers Awake)*, and *O Haupt voll Blut und Wunden (O Sacred Head Now Wounded)*; six motets, such as *Jesu meine Freude (Jesus, My Joy)*; two Passions, or musical settings of biblical passages and commentaries on the Easter season (the *St. Matthew Passion* and the *St. John Passion*); and a Mass, the Mass in B Minor. He also composed instrumental church music, notably about 170 organ chorales required by the liturgy for the church year. Besides sacred music, Bach wrote secular music, including the "Little" Fugue in G Minor, the *Brandenburg Concertos,* and *The Well-Tempered Clavier* (1722; 1740), a collection of works for keyboard that consisted of one prelude and fugue for each of the twelve major and minor keys.

HANDEL, GEORGE FRIDERIC. The German-born Handel, who lived and worked mainly in England, made eighteenth-century England a center of Baroque music. Of the thirty-six Italian-style operas that he composed and produced in London, three of the best known are *Rinaldo* (1711), *Giulio Cesare* (1724), and *Serse* (1738). His oratorios—including *Messiah*—were performed in public theaters rather than churches and especially appealed to the rising middle classes. Handel also produced a body of instrumental music, of which the most significant are the two suites known as the *Fireworks Music* (1749) and the *Water Music* (about 1717) and six concertos for woodwinds and strings.

LULLY, JEAN-BAPTISTE. Lully's eleven operas helped to define the operatic genre in France, giving it an opening overture and a ballet movement. Of his operas, the best known are probably *Theseus* (1675) and *Amadis* (1684). Especially appealing to modern ears are the massed choruses and rhythmic dances of his operas.

MONTEVERDI, CLAUDIO. A prodigious composer of madrigals and sacred music, Monteverdi is best remembered as a pioneer of opera. He composed his operas in a highly expressive style that matched the spirit of the music to the meaning of words in the text, as in *Orfeo* (1607) and *The Coronation of Poppea* (1642).

VIVALDI, ANTONIO LUCIO. Vivaldi's concertos—scored for a solo instrument (including violin, bassoon, cello, oboe, or flute) and orchestra—perfected the form for later composers. Rhythmical and full of feeling, these works often were given picturesque or evocative titles, as in *The Four Seasons* (1725), a cycle of four violin concertos, named for the seasons of the year. One of the most popular works of serious music, *The Four Seasons* was part of a larger suite of twelve, known as *The Trial Between Harmony and Invention.*

15 THE BAROQUE AGE II
Revolutions in Scientific and Political Thought 1600–1715

The Baroque Age was more than a time of political upheaval and artistic spectacle. It was also the period when the Scientific Revolution took place. As centuries-old beliefs were challenged by discoveries in astronomy and physics, a whole new way of viewing the universe emerged. In England, a revolution in political philosophy was also occurring, leading to the notion that states ought to be governed by the people rather than by paternalistic rulers. These momentous changes added to the pervasive restlessness of the times.

The term *Scientific Revolution* applies chiefly to astronomy and physics, although major advances were also made in medical science, and changes occurred in chemistry, biology, and embryology. In addition, the Scientific Revolution gave rise to a type of literature that considered the impact of the new science on secular and religious thought. A few scholars composed literary works that redefined the place of human beings in the cosmos and the purpose of human life. The chief result was to bring to a climax the separation of philosophy from theology, a gap that had been widening since the 1300s (see Chapter 10). From this point, philosophy begins to address secular concerns, and theology is relegated to a minor cultural role.

The climax of this revolutionary age occurred between 1685 and 1715, a period that witnessed what one twentieth-century historian called "the crisis of the European conscience." For a handful of scholars, the balance tipped from traditional ideas to modern views. These early modern scientists and philosophers countered faith with reason, dogma with skepticism, and divine intervention with natural law. They made mathematics their guiding star in the

◄ **Detail** *Tycho Brahe in His Observatory.* Engraving, from Brahe's *Astronomiae Instauratae Mechanica.* 1598. Joseph Regenstein Library, University of Chicago.

Timeline 15.1 REVOLUTIONS IN SCIENTIFIC AND POLITICAL THOUGHT

1543		1600					1700	1715
		The Scientific Revolution and Early Modern Political Philosophy						

1543	1570–1600	1609	1625	1637	1651	1687	1690
Copernicus's *Revolutions of the Heavenly Bodies*	Brahe's observations	Kepler's *On the Motion of Mars*	Grotius's *The Law of War and Peace*	Descartes's *Discourse on Method*	Hobbes's *Leviathan*	Newton's *Mathematical Principles*	Locke's *Two Treatises of Government* and *An Essay Concerning Human Understanding*

1610	1632
Galileo sights four moons of Jupiter	Galileo's *Dialogues on the Two Chief Systems of the World*

search for truth, accepting as true those things that could be proven mathematically and rejecting as untrue those that could not. Their new philosophy eventually concluded that the universe was like a great clock that operated according to universal laws. Although we today tend to discount this clockwork image, we still owe a debt to these thinkers, who set Western culture on its present course and brought modernity into being (Timeline 15.1).

THEORIES OF THE UNIVERSE BEFORE THE SCIENTIFIC REVOLUTION

The Scientific Revolution was both an outgrowth and a rejection of the Aristotelian cosmology that had held Western thinkers in thrall for two thousand years. The Aristotelian system, named for the fourth-century B.C.E. philosopher, was developed by the ancient Greeks and transmitted to the West through Roman and Islamic culture and the medieval scholastic tradition. The fundamental principle of this cosmology is **geocentrism,** the theory that the universe is earth centered. Around the earth revolved the five known planets (Mercury, Venus, Mars, Jupiter, and Saturn) and the sun and the moon, each held aloft by a crystalline sphere. The earth, which did not move, was not considered a planet. Nearest the earth was the moon, and there was a complete division between the supralunar world, the region beyond the moon, and the sublunar world, the region beneath the moon (Figure 15.1). In the supralunar world, the planets moved in circular orbits and were made of an incorruptible el-

Figure 15.1 PETER APIAN. Geocentric Diagram of the Universe, from the *Cosmographia*. 1539. The Bancroft Library, University of California, Berkeley. *This schematic diagram illustrates the geocentric universe in the pre-Copernican era. The unmoving earth is at the center and is surrounded by ten moving spheres, containing, in sequential order, the moon, Mercury, Venus, the sun, Mars, Jupiter, Saturn, the fixed stars, the aqueous or crystalline heaven, and the empty sphere called the primum mobile. The ninth sphere, the crystalline heaven, was added by medieval scholars to address a problem raised by the account of creation in Genesis. The tenth sphere, the primum mobile, was logically necessary in Aristotle's theory because it moved first and brought the other nine into motion. Beyond the tenth sphere was the Empyrean, home of the Unmoved Mover in philosophy or of God in theology.*

ement, aether; in the sublunar world, change was constant, motion was rectilinear, and matter was composed of the four elements, earth, air, fire, and water. This system had an absolute up and down: "Up" referred to the area beyond the spheres inhabited by the Unmoved Mover—Aristotle's philosophical term for the source of all celestial motion—and "down" referred to the center of the earth.

In the second century C.E., the Egyptian scholar Ptolemy updated Aristotle's geocentric theory with new astronomical data and improved mathematical calculations. During the golden age of Muslim culture (800–1100 C.E.), Arab intellectuals preserved this geocentric legacy, improving and refining it to reflect new planetary sightings. In the High Middle Ages (1000–1300), Western scholars recovered the Ptolemaic heritage—with its Muslim additions—and gave it a Christian interpretation: Medieval Christian scientists began to identify the Unmoved Mover as God and the space beyond the spheres as heaven. More important, the church became attached to the geocentric theory because it seemed to validate the doctrine of original sin: The corrupt earth—inhabited by fallen mortals—corresponded to the sublunar world of decay and constant change.

At the University of Paris in the 1300s, a more self-assured and skeptical outlook arose among a few thinkers. Unconvinced by Aristotle's solution to the problem of motion (which was to attribute the forward motion of a projectile to air movement), the Parisian scholars offered an alternative explanation. They asserted that a projectile acquired "impetus," a propulsive quality that gradually diminished as the projectile moved through space. The theory of "impetus" commanded scholars' attention for centuries, leading them to consider a new range of scientific problems.

From the modern perspective, it matters little that the theory of "impetus" was untrue. It was a first step away from the Aristotelian tradition because it made Western scientists aware that the great Greek thinker was not always right. And scholars at Paris and other universities began to advocate applying mathematics to practical problems as well as directly observing nature—in other words, collecting data (**empiricism**) and framing hypotheses from observable facts (**inductive reasoning**).

Aristotle had also used empirical data and inductive logic, but his writings had become so revered that for generations scholars did not examine his methodology and were afraid to tamper with his conclusions. Indeed, his followers relied on **deductive reasoning;** that is, they only explored the ramifications of accepted truths. But with the new critical spirit that appeared in the Late Middle Ages, scholars began to look at the world with new eyes. In time, this spirit led to

the greatest achievement of Baroque science, the Scientific Revolution, which overturned the geocentric Ptolemaic system and established **heliocentrism,** the theory that the universe is centered on the sun.

THE MAGICAL AND THE PRACTICAL IN THE SCIENTIFIC REVOLUTION

The Scientific Revolution is notable for the paradoxes and ironies that the movement gave rise to, some of which will be discussed in a later section of this chapter. A paradox that should be noted at the outset, however, is that this revolution in human thought, which ushered in modern science, was rooted in both magical beliefs and practical technological achievements. With one or two exceptions, the makers of the Scientific Revolution were motivated by two divergent and rather contradictory sets of beliefs. On the one hand, they followed the lead of Late Medieval science by collecting empirical data, reasoning inductively, and using mathematics to verify results (Figure 15.2). Significantly, the most startling changes occurred in those areas where mathematics was applied to long-existing intellectual problems, namely in astronomy, physics, and biology.

On the other hand, the makers of the Scientific Revolution were entranced by Neo-Platonism, the philosophy that revived the ancient Greek philosophy in the Early Renaissance (see Chapter 11). Like Late Medieval science, Neo-Platonism stressed the role of mathematics in problem solving, but Neo-Platonism also had a mystical streak—a legacy from Pythagoras—that led its devotees to seek harmony through numbers (see Chapter 2). Thinkers who followed Neo-Platonism believed that simplicity was superior to complexity in mathematical figuring because simplicity was the supreme sign that a solution was correct. This belief has become a guiding ideal of modern science, although other aspects of Neo-Platonism are rejected today, such as the attribution of mysterious powers to the sun. One effect of Neo-Platonism's occult side was to tighten the link between astronomy and astrology, a connection as old as Greek science. Most of those who made the revolution in science supported this linkage, and a few even cast horoscopes for wealthy clients.

As for the role of technology in the Scientific Revolution, many of its achievements would have been impossible without the telescope and the microscope, both of which were invented in about 1600 in the Netherlands. Without them, scholars would have simply remained "thinkers," as they had been since the time of the ancient Greeks. But with the telescope and the microscope, they could penetrate deep into hitherto

Figure 15.2 MARIA SIBYLLA MERIAN. *Insect Metamorphoses in Surinam.* 1705. Hand-colored engraving. (Reprinted in F. Schnack, *Das Kleine Buch der Tropenwander.* Leipzig: Insel-Verlag, 1935. Plate 11. 4¾ × 7".) *A painter and a scientist, the German-born Maria Sibylla Merian (1647–1717) traveled to the South American Dutch colony of Surinam, where, for two years, she collected and raised insects and made notes and illustrations. Her illustration of the metamorphosis of a moth, from caterpillar through pupa (covered by a cocoon) to mature adult, along with a flowering branch of an orange tree, captures the exotic character of the New World, adds to the growing body of scientific knowledge, and reflects the high standards of seventeenth-century Dutch art.*

inaccessible areas—outer space and the inner workings of the human body. Henceforward, scholars with a scientific bent allied themselves with the crafts tradition, becoming experimenters and empiricists.

Astronomy and Physics: From Copernicus to Newton

The intellectual shift from the earth-centered to the sun-centered universe was almost 150 years in the making and involved an international community of scholars. Heliocentrism, the new model of the world, was first broached in modern times by the Polish

thinker Copernicus in 1543, and incontrovertible mathematical calculations to prove this view were published by the English scholar Newton in 1687. Between those dates, major steps in the revolution in science were taken by Tycho Brahe of Denmark, Johannes Kepler of Germany, and Galileo Galilei of Italy. Isaac Newton spoke the truth when he claimed that he "stood on the shoulders of giants" (see Timeline 15.1).

Nicolas Copernicus When Nicolas Copernicus (1473–1543) published *Revolutions of the Heavenly Bodies* in 1543, he was reviving the discarded heliocentric theory of the third-century B.C.E. Greek thinker Aristarchus (see Chapter 4). In this highly technical work, Copernicus launched a head-on assault against Ptolemaic geocentrism. The main issue between Copernican astronomy and the older worldview was not one of mathematical precision, for both were mathematically solid and thus equally able to predict planetary positions and solar and lunar eclipses. Rather, the basic question between the two systems was which one was simpler. Copernicus reasoned that a more convincing picture of the universe could be achieved by transposing the positions of the sun and the earth. Instead of the Ptolemaic notion of a finite world centered on a fixed earth, Copernicus envisioned a vastly expanded, but not infinite, universe with the planets orbiting the sun (Figure 15.3).

Recognizing the revolutionary nature of his hypothesis, Copernicus delayed printing his ideas until he was dying. In an attempt to mollify clerical critics, he dedicated his book to the pope, Paul III. Later the religious establishment concluded that heliocentrism was dangerous and contrary to scripture; they therefore condemned it as a false system. What disturbed them was that when the earth was removed from the center of the universe, the place of human beings in the divine order was also reduced. In effect, human beings were no longer the leading actors in a cosmic drama staged for them alone.

Catholics and Protestants alike denounced the ideas of Copernicus. Lutheran and Calvinist authorities condemned his views as unbiblical, and in 1610 the pope placed *Revolutions of the Heavenly Bodies* on the Index, the list of forbidden books created during the Counter-Reformation. Eventually, the two religious groups came to a parting of the ways over Copernican ideas. For more than two hundred years, until 1822, the Roman Catholic Church, with all of its considerable power and influence, opposed the sun-centered theory, thus reversing a centuries-old tradition of being open to innovative scientific thought. However, in Protestantism—where authority was not centralized as it was in Roman Catholicism—some sects slowly accepted and adapted their beliefs to the new astronomy.

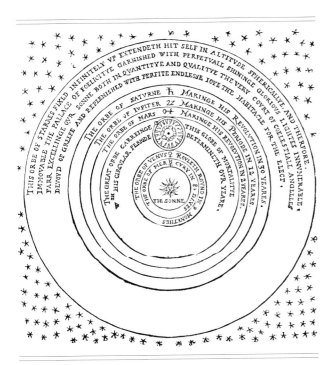

Figure 15.3 THOMAS DIGGES. The Sun-Centered Universe of Copernicus, from *A Perfit Description of the Celestiall Orbes.* 1576. The Huntington Library, San Marino, California. *This diagram drawn by the Englishman Thomas Digges agrees with the Copernican system except in one major way. Copernicus believed the universe was a finite, closed system, but Digges represents it as infinite, expressed in the stars scattered outside the orbit of fixed stars.*

Figure 15.4 *Tycho Brahe in His Observatory.* Engraving, from Brahe's *Astronomiae Instauratae Mechanica.* 1598. Joseph Regenstein Library, University of Chicago. *Tycho Brahe, the Danish astronomer who contributed to the Scientific Revolution, is shown in his observatory at Uraniborg, on the island of Ven, in Denmark. With right hand pointing upward, he instructs his assistants in the use of the wall quadrant, the semicircular, calibrated instrument (on his left) he developed for measuring the position of stars. In the background, other assistants work with various astronomical instruments and perform chemical experiments.*

Johannes Kepler The reception of Copernican astronomy by the scientific community was neither immediate nor enthusiastic. For example, the great Danish astronomer Tycho Brahe [TEE-ko BRAH-hee] (1546–1601) adopted a modified Copernicanism, believing that the other planets moved around the sun but that the earth did not. Brahe nevertheless contributed to the ultimate triumph of heliocentrism through his copious observations of planetary movement. So accurate were his sightings (without the aid of a telescope) that they set a new standard for astronomical data (Figure 15.4).

Among Brahe's assistants was Johannes Kepler (1571–1630), a brilliant mathematician who dedicated his life to clarifying the theory of heliocentrism. When the Danish astronomer died, Kepler inherited his astronomical data. Inspired by Neo-Platonism to make sense of the regular and continuous sightings of Brahe, Kepler in 1609 published *On the Motion of Mars,* setting forth his solution to the problem of what kept the planets in their orbits. His findings were expressed in two scientific laws that were elegant in their simplicity. In the first planetary law, Kepler substituted the ellipse

for the circle as the descriptive shape of planetary orbits. And his second planetary law, which was set forth in a precise mathematical formula, accounted for each planet's variable speed within its respective orbit by showing that nearness to the sun affected its behavior—the closer to the sun, the faster the speed, and the farther from the sun, the slower the speed. Together, these laws validated sun-centered astronomy.

Kepler continued to manipulate Brahe's undigested data, convinced that other mathematical laws could be derived from observations of the heavens. In 1619 he arrived at a third planetary law, which relates the movement of one planet to another. He showed that the squares of the length of time for each planet's orbit

are in the same ratios as the cubes of their respective mean distances from the sun. Through this formula, he affirmed that the solar system itself was regular and organized by mathematically determined relationships. This was the first expression of the notion that the universe operates with clocklike regularity, an idea that became an article of faith by the end of the Baroque Age. Kepler took great pride in this discovery, because it confirmed his Neo-Platonist belief that there is a hidden mathematical harmony in the universe.

Galileo Galilei While Kepler moved in the rarefied realm of theoretical, even mystical, science, one of his contemporaries was making major breakthroughs with experiments that relied on precise mathematics and careful logic. This patient experimenter was Galileo Galilei (1564–1642), whose most valuable contributions were his accurate celestial observations and his work in terrestrial mechanics, the study of the action of forces on matter. Inspired by news that Dutch lens grinders had made a device for viewing distant objects, in 1609 Galileo made his own telescope, which enabled him to see stars invisible to the naked eye.

With these sightings, Galileo demonstrated that the size of the universe was exponentially greater than that computed on Ptolemaic principles. Further, his observations of the moon's rough surface and the sun's shifting dark spots provided additional proofs against the ancient arguments that the heavenly bodies were perfectly formed and never changed. But his most telling discovery was that the planet Jupiter has moons, a fact that contradicted the Ptolemaic belief that all celestial bodies must move about a common

center. Galileo's research affirmed that Jupiter's four satellites rotated around it in much the same way that the six planets orbited the sun. These telescope observations hastened the demise of geocentrism.

Similarly, Galileo's research in terrestrial mechanics proved conclusively that both Aristotle and his fourteenth-century critics in Paris were wrong about one of the central questions of earthly motion—that is, the behavior of projectiles. Aristotle had claimed that projectiles stayed in flight because of the pushing motion of the air, and the Parisian scholars had countered with the theory of "impetus." Through experimentation, Galileo showed that a mass that is moving will go on moving until some force acts to stop it—the earliest expression of the modern law of inertia.

Galileo was probably the first scientist to make a clock a basic means for measuring time in his experiments. Like his contemporary Kepler, he reported his findings in the form of simple mathematical laws. Galileo's work was later validated by Newton, who proved that the laws of mechanics on earth were the same as the laws of mechanics in the sky.

At the same time that Galileo was conducting the experiments that would make him a hero of modern science, he ran afoul of the religious authorities, who brought his career to a humiliating end. The church, as noted previously, had by now abandoned its relative openness to ideas and was moving to stifle dissent. In 1633 Galileo was arrested by the Inquisition, the church court created in the 1200s to find and punish heretics. The great astronomer was charged with false teachings for his published support of the idea that the earth moves, a notion central to Copernicanism but untrue according to Aristotle and the church. Threatened with torture, Galileo recanted his views and was released. Despite living on for several years, he died a broken man. This episode abruptly ended Italy's role in the burgeoning revolution in science (Figure 15.5).

Isaac Newton Building on the research of the heirs to Copernicus, including Kepler's laws of planetary motion and Galileo's law of inertia, the English mathematician Isaac Newton (1642–1727) conceived a model of the universe that decisively overturned the Ptolemaic scheme and finished the revolution in astronomy begun by Copernicus. In Newton's world picture, there is uniform motion on earth and in the heavens. More significant, Newton presented a satisfactory explanation for what held the planets in their orbits. Newton's solution was the force of gravity, and this topic formed the heart of his theory of the universe (Figure 15.6).

In a precise mathematical formula, Newton computed the law of universal gravitation, the formula whereby every object in the world exerts an attraction to a greater or a lesser degree on all other objects. By

◄ **Figure 15.5** PIETRO DA CORTONA. *Glorification of the Reign of Urban VIII.* 1633–1639. Fresco. Palazzo Barberini, Rome. *Pope Urban VIII (pope 1623–1644), born Maffeo Barberini, a member of the powerful Barberini [bar-baa-RE-nee] family of Italy's Tuscan region, was active in state and church affairs, a patron of the arts (he supported Bernini's projects to beautify Rome), a poet and man of learning, and a longtime friend of Galileo. However, Galileo could not rely on his friend when he found himself before the Inquisition. Indeed, Pope Urban VIII sanctioned the Inquisition's second condemnation of Galileo. In this illusionistic ceiling painting, Pietro da Cortona [pe-EH-tro dah kor-TOE-nah] (1596–1669) depicted Urban VIII's reign as a golden age—in the tradition of art used as propaganda. The ceiling design is a complex blend of religious, artistic, and dynastic symbols. Mythological figures, whose heyday predated the Christian era, are portrayed in the shadows—symbolic of their pagan roots. And the illuminated figures in the center represent people who have been exposed to the truth of Christianity. Near the top of the frame floats the personification of Religion, holding symbols of the papal office—the triple crown and two crossed keys. Below Religion, angelic figures and cherubs carry a giant laurel wreath—the Roman emblem of triumph—and inside the wreath are three huge bees—part of the Barberini coat of arms.*

Figure 15.6 GODFREY KNELLER. *Sir Isaac Newton.* 1702. Oil on canvas, 29¾ × 24½". National Portrait Gallery, London. *As the most celebrated intellectual of his generation, the middle-class Newton was given star treatment in this portrait by the reigning society painter in England. Decked out fashionably in an elaborate Baroque wig, Newton peers somewhat uncomfortably at the viewer. The likeness tends to support Newton's reputation for vanity and ostentation.*

this law, the sun held tightly in its grip each of the six planets, and each in turn influenced to a lesser degree the sun and the other planets. The earth and its single moon as well as Jupiter and its four satellites similarly interacted. In effect, because of gravity, the heavenly bodies formed a harmonious system in which each attracted the others.

Having described gravity and asserted its universal nature, Newton declined to speculate about what caused it to operate. For him, the universe behaved precisely as a machine, and his law was nothing but a description of its operation. Because Newton refused to speculate beyond what mathematics could prove, he has been called a "mind without metaphysics." Modern scientists have followed Newton's lead, preferring to ignore the *why* of things and to concentrate on the *how* and *what.*

Newton's views were set forth in his authoritative work *Mathematical Principles of Natural Philosophy.* Known more familiarly as the *Principia* (the first word of its Latin title), this book quickly gained an authority

that made Newton the modern world's equivalent of Aristotle. By the eighteenth century, the English poet Alexander Pope could justifiably write:

Nature and Nature's Laws lay hid in Night;
God said, *Let Newton be!* and All was *Light.*

Even though his work was the culmination of the revolution that brought modern science into being, Newton was not fully free of older attitudes. True, he believed that the discovery of scientific truth was simply a matter of using methodical principles. He made mathematics his guiding ideal and used patient and careful observation. But Newton cared little for his own scientific achievement, believing that his lasting monument would be his religious writings. A pious Christian, he devoted his last years to demonstrating that the prophecies in the Bible were coming true.

Newton also invented a form of calculus, a mathematical method of analysis that uses a symbolic notation. This breakthrough had huge potential for solving problems in physics and mechanics by providing a tool for computing quantities that had nonlinear variations. Simultaneously and independently of Newton, Gottfried Wilhelm von Leibniz [LIBE-nits] (1646–1716), a German thinker, invented a more useful version of calculus. By 1800 Leibniz's symbols had become the universally accepted language of calculus.

Medicine and Chemistry

At the same time that Western understanding of the universe at its outer limits was being radically altered, another breakthrough involved anatomical knowledge and the discovery of the true circulation of the human blood. Unlike developments in astronomy, this breakthrough in medical science happened largely without the aid of technology. Only during the last step in the solving of the mystery of the blood's circulation did early modern scientists use the newly invented microscope.

In 1600 anatomical knowledge was extremely limited, primarily because the church forbade the violation of corpses, a position based on the teaching that the body would be resurrected from the dead. Biological research had been limited to the dissection of animals, with generalizations then applied to the human body, leading to a great deal of misinformation and half-truths. Besides, in biology as in astronomy and physics, the authority of ancient Greek thinkers reigned supreme—Aristotle since the fourth century B.C.E. and Galen since the second century C.E. Galen's vast researches covering nearly all aspects of ancient medicine were lost in the fall of Rome, but some works were preserved by Arab scholars and were translated

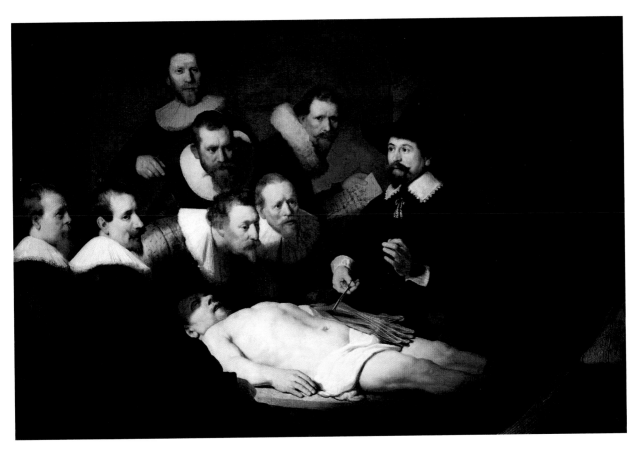

Figure 15.7   REMBRANDT VAN RIJN. *The Anatomy Lesson of Dr. Tulp.* 1632. Oil on canvas,
66¾ × 85¼". Mauritshuis, The Hague. *The pioneering work of Vesalius made the study of
anatomy a central concern of medical science in the seventeenth century. In this painting, Rembrandt depicts Dr. Nicholas Tulp of Amsterdam as he demonstrates the dissection of the left arm.
Rembrandt's use of Baroque effects, such as the dramatic light on the corpse, the contrast between
Dr. Tulp's calm demeanor and the inquisitive faces of his pupils, and the flayed arm of the corpse,
make this an arresting image.*

from Arabic into Latin by Western scholars from the eleventh century onward (see Chapter 8). Though of-fering rival theories, Aristotle and Galen shared many false ideas, namely the notions that air ran directly from the lungs into the heart, that blood flowed from the veins to the outer part of the body, and that differ-ent types of blood coursed in the arteries and the veins.

The problem of the circulation of the blood was eventually resolved by scientists at the University of Padua in Italy, the most prominent of whom was An-dreas Vesalius. Vesalius's anatomical studies first proved Galen's explanation of the body's structure and muscle system to be wrong (see Chapter 13). And later, through his meticulous observations, Vesalius also came to the conclusion that Galen's theory about the circulation of the blood—that it passed from one side of the heart to the other through the septum, an impermeable membrane—was incorrect (Figure 15.7).

The research of Vesalius and his successors set the stage for William Harvey (1578–1657), an English sci-entist who studied and taught at the University of Padua. In 1628 Harvey published his groundbreaking work, which produced the correct view of circulation, including the roles of the heart, the lungs, the arteries, and the veins. Mathematical calculation played a deci-sive role in this scientific triumph, just as it had in Newton's gravitation theory. Using arithmetic, Harvey proved that a constant quantity of blood continuously circulated throughout the body, thereby invalidating Galen's ebb-and-flow theory. However, Harvey lacked knowledge of the capillaries, the connectors between the arteries and the veins. In 1661 the Italian scientist Marcello Malpighi [mahl-PEE-gee] (1628–1694) identi-fied these tiny vessels with the aid of the microscope, and with this critical piece of information an essen-tially correct, modern description of the blood's circu-lation was complete.

Chemistry did not become a separate discipline in the Baroque Age, but the English physicist Robert Boyle (1627–1691) did establish the groundwork for modern chemistry. A major aspect of Boyle's thought linked him to Newton, for both believed that the universe is a machine. Boyle believed that the workings of nature could be revealed only through experimental study—the inductive method. Boyle's zeal for experimentation led him to study the behavior of gases and to formulate the famous law that bears his name.

Boyle was also one of the first to distinguish chemistry from alchemy, a set of magical practices that had been allied with chemistry since the time of the ancient Greeks. In medieval Europe, alchemy had led scholars to search vainly for the "philosopher's stone" that would miraculously turn a base metal such as lead into gold. Rejecting alchemy's assumptions and methodology, Boyle sought to understand only those chemical reactions that happened naturally and could be analyzed in mathematical terms.

Technology

Galileo's studies of celestial and terrestrial motion and Newton's explanation of gravity may be difficult to understand, but their experiments led to inventions, in particular, the pendulum clock, that directly impacted life in seventeenth-century Europe. This improved clock, which measured time more precisely and accurately than any other heretofore, soon determined how people conducted business, performed religious duties, and planned their daily lives. The clock became a metaphor for the human condition, symbolizing both the brevity of life and all its graduated moments filled with unexplored potential.

Humans had built instruments for measuring time for millennia. All of the ancient devices, such as sundials, water clocks, and hourglasses, were inherited by medieval Europeans, but none of them could keep accurate time. That changed after the fall of Rome, as pressure to measure time more precisely came from an unexpected direction: the church. The church, with its monasteries, nunneries, schools, and cathedrals, needed devices to set schedules for prayer, work, lessons, and daily activities. While some scholars claim that an Italian church official invented a weight-driven clock in the tenth century, other records confirm that the earliest clocks were installed in English cathedrals by the thirteenth century. By 1335 Milan, Italy, had the first public clock and during the fourteenth century several cities, including Paris and Rouen, France, had municipal tower clocks. In each, the clock mechanism was driven by heavy weights that were attached to

cords around a drum and regulated by a circular escapement mechanism and sets of gears.

Clocks grew smaller around 1500. Then, a German locksmith, Peter Henlein (1480–1542), invented the coil spring clock, which reduced the size and weight of the timekeeping mechanism—thus allowing for table clocks and eventually watches. Henlein's early timepieces, four to five inches in diameter, could be carried around or placed on a table. Further advances throughout the sixteenth and seventeenth centuries improved clocks' accuracy and dependability. By 1600 clocks were all given an upright design, though they remained bulky and difficult to regulate.

The development of the pendulum clock came in two stages: the work of Galileo and Christian Huygens [HOI-genz] (1629–1695). In the 1580s, Galileo, while studying the properties of motion, observed that the period of oscillation of a swinging pendulum was always the same. Later, he used the pendulum in some of his experiments. Although he recognized the importance of the pendulum, he failed to design a pendulum clock. That achievement belongs to Huygens, the Dutch mathematician, physicist, and astronomer. While studying the heavens, Huygens needed an accurate time instrument to calibrate his findings. He then discovered that the swinging pendulum could regulate a clock. He built a vertical clock with a pendulum, which kept time more accurately than any other clock then on the scene. The pendulum clock had an error rate of less than a minute a day. The time required for a "natural" period of oscillation was steady and dependable. Through experimentation, Huygens determined the ideal dimensions for a pendulum, relative to the clock mechanism (Figure 15.8).

A few years later an English clockmaker devised the "seconds" pendulum and improved the escapement mechanism. The two pendulums—one for the hours, the other for the seconds—and other parts of the clock were encased in wood—thus creating the so-called grandfather clock. This invention made it possible to place clocks anywhere—in palaces, courts, homes, offices, businesses, shops, laboratories, and schools. Mechanical clocks were now on their way to becoming part of the collective consciousness of modern life.

The Impact of Science on Philosophy

The Scientific Revolution had a profound influence on Western thought and also gave rise to a type of literature that reflected the impact of science on the wider culture. Three prominent contributors to this literature were the English jurist and statesman Francis

Figure 15.8 A Reconstruction of Huygens's 1656 Clock. Science Museum, London. *Huygens's clock used the old-fashioned escapement mechanism, but he added a pair of gear wheels to adjust for the precise swinging of the pendulum, to ensure accurate timekeeping. On the main dial, the hour hand is the shorter one, rotating twice every day. The longer hand was the second hand, and it required five minutes to revolve. This reconstruction also shows a minute hand in the small dial at the bottom, which rotated anticlockwise once every hour.*

Figure 15.9 FRANZ HALS. *René Descartes.* After 1649. Oil on canvas, 30¾ × 26¾". Louvre. *In this likeness, Frans Hals, the great Dutch portrait artist and contemporary of Rembrandt, has captured the complex personality of the great French philosopher and mathematician. Descartes's piercing gaze shows his skeptical spirit. His disdainful presence and rough features reveal his early background as a soldier. Hals apparently felt no need to flatter his sitter in this compelling portrait.*

Bacon and two brilliant French mathematicians, René Descartes and Blaise Pascal, whose speculative writings continued the French rationalist tradition begun by Montaigne in the 1500s (see Chapter 13).

Francis Bacon Francis Bacon (1561–1626) owes his fame to his ability to write lucid prose about science and its methodology. In a field that was dominated by scholars whose writings were accessible only to those learned in mathematics, Bacon's clear prose informed a curious and educated public. In the process of clarifying the techniques and the aims of the new science, he became the spokesman for the "experimenters," those who believed that the future of science lay in discarding Aristotle. Condemning Aristotle for relying on deductive reasoning and unproven axioms, Bacon advocated the inductive method, the procedure that embraced the conducting of experiments, the drawing of conclusions, and the testing of results in other experiments. His claims were not new, but they were forcibly and memorably expressed; few scholars exhibited Ba-

con's optimism about the usefulness of science. Bacon sincerely believed that the march of science inevitably led to mastery over the natural world, a view summarized in the famous phrase attributed to him, "Knowledge is power."

René Descartes An outstanding critic of the belief that the experimental method was the correct path to knowledge was René Descartes [day-KAHRT] (1596–1650), a philosopher who urged a purely mathematical approach in science (Figure 15.9). Descartes's love of numbers came from a mystical side of his personality, as illustrated by his confession that a dream had inspired his belief that mathematics holds the key to nature. Descartes was the founder of analytic geometry, that branch of mathematics that describes geometric figures by the formulas of algebra, and the author of a widely influential philosophical treatise, *Discourse on Method*, published in 1637.

In the *Discourse on Method*, Descartes outlined four steps in his approach to knowledge: to accept nothing as true unless it is self-evident; to split problems into manageable parts; to solve problems starting with the

465

simplest and moving to the most complex; and to review and reexamine the solutions. He used deductive logic in his method, making inferences only from general statements. But more important than his stress on deductive reasoning was his insistence on mathematical clarity: He refused to accept anything as true unless it had the persuasiveness of a proof in geometry.

Descartes's most influential gifts to Western philosophy were skepticism and a dualistic theory of knowledge. He rejected the authoritarian method of medieval scholasticism and began with universal doubt in order to determine what was absolutely certain in the universe. Step-by-step, he questioned the existence of God, of the world, and of his own body. But he soon established that he could not doubt the existence of his own doubting self. He reached this absolute conclusion in the oft-quoted phrase *Cogito ergo sum*—"I think, therefore I am." Having first destroyed the age-old certainties, he then, through deduction, reestablished the existence of his own body, the world, and, finally, God.

Descartes's speculations were aimed at identifying clear and distinct ideas that were certain for everyone, but his efforts had a deeply ironic result: In the long run, his thought fostered the growing awareness among the educated elite that absolute truth was not possible. Many who read his *Discourse* were unimpressed by his rational arguments, but they nevertheless accepted his radical doubt, and some even became atheists. That his work contributed to the rise of atheism would have horrified Descartes, since, to his own way of thinking, he had proven the existence of God. He had used skepticism merely as a means of achieving certainty.

Descartes's other great legacy, dualism, made a division between the material world and the human soul or mind. According to him, mathematics permitted natural truths to be revealed to the human understanding. He thought, however, that the mind itself was beyond mathematical knowing and hence was not a fit subject for study. From this dichotomy arise two contrasting traditions: the scientists who reduce the natural world to order through mathematics and the thinkers who focus on human psychology. The second group—the psychologists—represent another ironic legacy, for through the study of such topics as depth psychology and alienation they want to prove that Descartes was wrong and that the human self is knowable in all its irrationality.

Even though Descartes's speculations were aimed at achieving certainty, his focus on deductive logic has not withstood the test of time. This is because modern scientists think that inductive reasoning—building a model of truth on the facts—is more valid. But Descartes was proven correct in assigning to mathematics its paramount role in establishing precision and certainty in science. Today, those sciences that have the greatest degree of mathematical rigor have better reputations for accuracy and believability than those sciences whose formulations cannot be achieved mathematically.

Descartes made another contribution to the Scientific Revolution when he applied his method to terrestrial mechanics. It was he, rather than Galileo, who gave final expression to the law of inertia. He concluded that a projectile would continue to move in a straight line until it was interrupted by some force. With this language Descartes finally debunked the myth of circular motion, and his definition of the law of inertia became part of the scientific synthesis of Newton.

Blaise Pascal   Descartes's work was barely published before it elicited a strong reaction from Blaise Pascal [BLEHZ pas-KAHL] (1623–1662), an anguished thinker who made radical doubt the cornerstone of his beliefs. Like Descartes, Pascal left his mark in mathematics, notably in geometry and in the study of probability. Pascal was a Jansenist, a member of a Catholic sect that to some observers was Calvinistic because it stressed original sin and denied free will. Pascal's Jansenism permeates his masterpiece, the *Pensées*, or *Thoughts*, a meditative work of intense feeling published in 1670, eight years after his death.

In the *Pensées*, Pascal went beyond Descartes's skepticism, concluding that human beings can know neither the natural world nor themselves. Despite this seemingly universal doubt, Pascal still reasoned that there were different levels of truth. Regarding science, he thought that what he called the geometric spirit—that is, mathematics—could lead scholars to a limited knowledge of nature. Pascal's most controversial opinions, however, concerned human psychology. He felt that the passions enabled human beings to comprehend truths about God and religion directly. He summed up this idea in his often quoted words "The heart has reasons that reason does not know." In another passage, he justified his continued belief in God, not by intellectual proofs in the manner of Descartes, but by a wager—a notion he derived from his probability studies. Pascal claimed his faith in God rested on a bet: If God exists, then the bettor wins everything, but if God does not exist, then nothing is lost. Pascal's fervent belief in God in the face of debilitating doubt makes him a forerunner of modern Christian existentialism (see Chapter 21).

Ironies and Contradictions of the Scientific Revolution

Ironies abound in the seventeenth century's most characteristic development, the Scientific Revolution. To begin with, it must be remembered that only a handful of thinkers contributed to the scientific changes, that the vast majority of the populace remained unaware of their findings, and that they could not have understood them even if they had been informed of them. Furthermore, those who made the scientific discoveries were engaged primarily in solving practical problems rather than in trying to build a new model of the universe. They also believed that what they were doing was entirely within an orthodox Christian framework (although some were aware that religious leaders might think otherwise), and few foresaw that their efforts would eventually lead to a conflict between religion and science.

Another irony was that the scientific advancements were not always completely original creations but were rooted in Late Medieval rationalism and the Renaissance revival of Classical learning. Indeed, the new thinkers were often more concerned with working out minor inconsistencies in the calculations of medieval scholars than in overturning the accepted picture of the universe.

Not only did seventeenth-century science have roots in medieval science, but it was also influenced by superstitions and mystical beliefs. During the Scientific Revolution, even the greatest intellectuals still held firmly to nonrational medieval views. Brahe and Kepler, for example, supported their research by pursuing careers as court astrologers. Harvey imagined that the heart restored a "spirituous" quality to the blood during circulation. Newton and Boyle were both involved in secret experiments with alchemy. A mystical experience lay behind Descartes's mathematical zeal, and Neo-Platonism motivated the thought of Copernicus, Kepler, and Galileo. Many scholars were conventionally devout in their religious convictions, and Newton tried to correlate biblical prophecy with history. Despite their medieval roots, these scholars did point European thought in a new direction. In the next century, a new generation of intellectuals constructed a set of beliefs based on the achievements of the Scientific Revolution and their implications for the improvement of humanity.

THE REVOLUTION IN POLITICAL PHILOSOPHY

Political philosophy reflected the nature of the shifting political, economic, social, scientific, and religious institutions of the seventeenth century. The Thirty Years' War, the wars of Louis XIV, and the English Civil War (see Chapter 14) forced political theorists to reconsider such basic themes as the nature of government, the relations between rulers and subjects, the rivalries among sovereign states, and the consequences of war on society and the individual.

Political writers, stimulated by the rise of the nation-state in the 1500s, addressed themselves in the 1600s to the fundamental questions of who holds the final sovereignty in a state and how power should be exercised. Realizing that new states were rapidly extinguishing the rights held by the feudal estates, these theorists tried to define the best form of government. They all supported their arguments with the same sources—the Bible, the concept of natural law, scientific discoveries, and their own views of human nature—but they came to widely differing conclusions.

Natural Law and Divine Right: Grotius and Bossuet

Hugo Grotius [GRO-she-us] (1583–1645) thought that natural law should govern the relations between states. He arrived at this belief chiefly because of his personal sufferings during the Thirty Years' War and the intolerance that he observed in religious disputes. A Dutch citizen but also an ambassador for Sweden, he saw at first hand the ambiguity of diplomatic relations between the great powers.

Drawing on the idea of natural law as set forth by the ancient Stoic thinkers, Grotius urged that the states follow a law that applied to all nations, was eternal and unchanging, and could be understood by human reason. Like the Stoics, Grotius was convinced that natural law was founded on human reason and was not the gift of a loving God. He rejected original sin, believing instead that human beings were not motivated merely by selfish drives. He thought that because all mortals were rational, they wanted to improve themselves and to create a just and fair society. In his treatise *The Law of War and Peace,* he applied this rational view of human nature to his description of sovereign states. He concluded that nations, like individuals, should treat each other as they would expect to be treated. Today, the writings of Grotius are recognized as the starting point of international law.

Taking a contrary point of view to Grotius was Bishop Bossuet [bo-SWAY] (1627–1704), who defended the theory that kings rule by divine right. This French church leader echoed the opinions of James I of England, who maintained that God bestowed power on certain national monarchs. The French bishop avowed that absolutism, as ordained by God in past societies, was now manifested in the rule of Louis XIV, king of France. Louis, as God's chosen vessel on earth, had the power to intervene in the lives of his subjects, not because of natural law, but by divine right. According to this theory, for corrupt and sinful humans to rebel against the king was to go against God's plan. The bishop believed that the age's conflicts made autocratic rule a political necessity. Bossuet's belief in

SLICE OF LIFE
Innocent or Guilty? A Seventeenth-Century Witch Trial

SUZANNE GAUDRY
Trial Court Records, June 1652

Suzanne Gaudry, an illiterate old woman, was accused of witchcraft—of renouncing "God, Lent, and baptism," worshiping the devil, attending witches' Sabbaths, desecrating the Eucharist wafer, and committing other crimes. Questioned by the local court at Rieux, France, she confessed to some charges but later recanted. Because confession was necessary for conviction, she was subjected to torture, and once again she confessed. She was then condemned and sentenced to be tied to a gallows, strangled to death, and to have her body burned.

On [June 27], . . . this prisoner [Suzanne Gaudry], before being strapped down, was admonished to maintain herself in her first confessions and to renounce her lover [the devil].

—Said that she denies everything she has said, and that she has no lover. Feeling herself being strapped down, says that she is not a witch, while struggling to cry.[1] . . .

—Says . . . she is not a witch. And upon being asked why she confessed to being one, said that she was forced to say it.

Told that she was not forced, that on the contrary she declared herself to be a witch without any threat.

—Says that she confessed it and that she is not a witch, and being a little stretched [on the rack] screams ceaselessly that she is not a witch, invoking the name of Jesus and Our Lady of Grace, not wanting to say any other thing. . . .

The mark having been probed by the officer, in the presence of Doctor Bouchain, it was adjudged by the aforesaid doctor and officer truly to be the mark of the devil.[2]

Being more tightly stretched upon the torture-rack, urged to maintain her confessions.

—Said that it was true that she is a witch and that she would maintain what she has said.

Asked how long she has been in subjugation to the devil.

—Answers that it was twenty years ago that the devil appeared to her, being in her lodgings in the form of a man dressed in a little cow-hide and black breeches. . . .

Asked if her lover has had carnal copulation with her, and how many times.

—To that she did not answer anything; then, making believe that she was ill, not another word could be drawn from her.

_____

[1] Not crying was thought to be a sign of witchcraft.
[2] Perhaps a birthmark or other skin blemish. It was commonly believed that witches were marked by the devil, as a sign of their intimate union, and when the mark was pricked, no pain would occur nor any blood flow out.

Interpreting This Slice of Life What were the charges against Suzanne Gaudry? **How** did she respond to the charges? In **what** ways does the official court record reveal the attitudes and reactions of that time and place? **Did** Suzanne Gaudry receive a fair trial? **Explain. Compare and contrast** this trial with the treatment of suspect criminals today.

autocracy was shared by the Englishman Thomas Hobbes, although he explained absolute rule in different terms.

Absolutism and Liberalism: Hobbes and Locke

Thomas Hobbes (1588–1679) grew up in an England increasingly torn by religious, social, and political discord. A trained Classicist and a student of the new science, Hobbes came to believe that everything, including human beings and their social acts, could be explained by using mechanistic, natural laws to describe various states of motion or movement.

Hobbes's efforts to synthesize a universal philosophy founded on a geometric design and activated by some form of energy culminated in his best-known work, *The Leviathan,* published in 1651 (Figure 15.10). *The Leviathan* sets forth a theory of government based on the pessimistic view that individuals are driven by two basic forces, the fear of death and the quest for power. Hobbes imagined what life would be like if these two natural inclinations were allowed free rein and there were no supreme power to control them. Hobbes described human life under these circumstances as "solitary, poor, nasty, brutish, and short."

Hobbes thought that human beings, recognizing the awfulness of their situation, would decide to give up such an existence and form a civil society under the rule of one man. This first step in the evolution of government was achieved by means of a **social contract** drawn up between the ruler and his subjects. By the

Figure 15.10 Frontispiece of *The Leviathan*. 1651. The Bancroft Library, University of California, Berkeley. *The original illustration for Hobbes's Leviathan conveys the political message of this controversial work in symbolic terms. Towering over the landscape is the mythical ruler, whose body is a composite of all his subjects and in whose hands are the sword and the scepter, symbols of his absolute power. Below this awesome figure is a well-ordered and peaceful village and countryside—Hobbes's political dream come true.*

terms of this covenant, the subjects surrendered all their claims to sovereignty and bestowed absolute power on the ruler. The sovereign's commands were then to be carried out by all under him, including the religious and civic leaders. Armed with the sword, the sovereign would keep peace at home and protect the land from its enemies abroad.

Hobbes made no distinction between the ruler of a monarchy and the head of a commonwealth, for he was less concerned with the form of government than with the need to hold in check destructive human im-

pulses. In the next generation, Hobbes's pessimistic philosophy provoked a reaction from John Locke, who repudiated absolutism and advocated a theory of government by the people.

Despite their contradictory messages, Hobbes and John Locke (1632–1704) had been subjected to similar influences. Both adapted ideas from the new science, witnessed the English Civil War, and sought safety on the Continent because of their political views. But Locke rejected Hobbes's gloomy view of humanity and his theory of absolutism; he taught instead that human nature was potentially good and that human beings were capable of governing themselves. The two thinkers originated opposing schools of modern political thought: From Hobbes stems the absolutist, authoritarian tradition, and from Locke descends the school of liberalism. Their works represent two of the most significant legacies of the Baroque Age to the modern world.

Locke set forth his political theories in his *Two Treatises of Government,* which he published anonymously in 1690. In the *First Treatise* he refuted the divine right of kings, and in the *Second Treatise* he laid out the model for rule by the people. The latter work has become the classic expression of early **liberalism.** In it Locke described the origins, characteristics, and purpose of the ideal political system—a government limited by laws, subject to the will of its citizens, and existing to protect life and property.

Locke's treatise shared some of Hobbes's ideas, such as the view that human life is violent and disorderly in the state of nature, that human beings must form civil governments to protect themselves, and that a social contract is the necessary basis of civil society. But Locke believed that basic rights, including life and property, exist in the state of nature. He also believed that human beings possess reason, are fundamentally decent and law abiding, and are slow to want change. From these principles, he concluded that human beings would contract together to create a limited government that had no other purpose than the protection of the basic natural rights of life and property.

Locke rejected the idea that by making a social contract citizens surrender their sovereignty to a ruler. He argued instead that the people choose rulers who protect their rights in a fiduciary trust; that is, they expect their rulers to obey the social contract and govern equitably. If the rulers break the agreement, then the people have the right to revolt, overthrow the government, and reclaim their natural rights. Unlike Hobbes, Locke asserted that rulers possess only limited authority and that their control must be held in check by a balanced governmental system and a separation of powers. In later years, Locke's tract influenced American and French political thinkers and patriots who used its ideas to justify the right to revolt against a tyrant and to establish a government of checks and balances.

Locke was not only a political theorist but also the preeminent English philosopher of his day. He grappled with many of the same problems as Descartes, although his conclusions were radically different from the French thinker's. In his important philosophical work *An Essay Concerning Human Understanding,* published in 1690 (the same year he published *Two Treatises of Government*), Locke addressed the question,

How is knowledge acquired? Descartes had proposed that the germs of ideas were inborn and that people were born knowing certain truths, such as mathematical principles and logical relationships; education required nothing more than the strenuous use of the intellect without concern for new information from the senses.

Locke repudiated these views and described the mind at birth as a **tabula rasa** (blank tablet) on which all human experiences were recorded. Locke maintained that all that human beings can know must first be received through their senses (a basically Aristotelian viewpoint) and then recorded in their minds. The raw sensory data are manipulated by the mental faculties, such as comparing and contrasting, so that abstract concepts and generalizations are formed in the mind. As a result, reason and experience are united in human thought and together determine what is real for each person. Locke's explanation of the origin of ideas is the basis of modern-day empiricism—the theory that all knowledge is derived from or originates in human experience. His influence has been so great that many of his ideas seem to the modern reader to be just "common sense."

EUROPEAN EXPLORATION AND EXPANSION

The exploration begun in the late fifteenth century had led to a series of encounters with new peoples that slowly eroded the isolation and self-absorption of Europe. In the sixteenth century, the pace of exploration quickened and the globe was circumnavigated—events that intensified rivalries among the European states, increased the Continent's economic power, and diffused European culture and customs around the world.

The greatest success of European expansion was achieved through a series of permanent settlements in North and South America and by the opening of new trade routes to the Far East (Map 15.1). Expansion and colonization affected Europe in numerous ways: the introduction of new foodstuffs and other products, the establishment of innovative business methods, the disruption of old economic and social patterns, the introduction of novel ways of looking at the world, and the adoption of new symbols and themes in the arts. Whatever may have been the beneficial or harmful effects of these changes on European life, the negative impact on non-Europeans tended to outweigh the good that came with the introduction of Western culture. In Africa, the Europeans expanded the slave trade; in North, Central, and South America and the Caribbean, they annihilated many native tribes; and

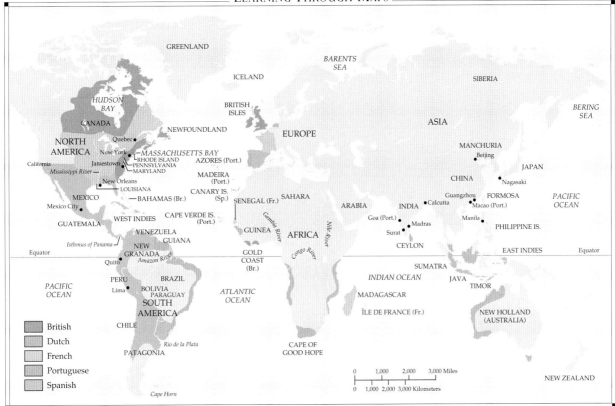

Map 15.1   EXPANSION OF EUROPE, 1715
This map shows the presence of Europeans around the globe in the early eighteenth century. **Notice** the overseas holdings of the five European countries identified on the map.
Observe the differing encounter patterns—coastal and inland—on the various continents.
Which country has the largest number of overseas holdings? On **which** continent is there
the greatest European presence? **Where** are conflicts among European powers most likely
to occur? **Which** areas of the world seem less touched by European expansion?

everywhere they forced trade agreements favorable to
themselves on the local people.

The earliest leaders in the European penetration of
the Western Hemisphere were Portugal and Spain (see
Encounters in Chapters 12 and 13). Since the 1500s,
these two states had claimed South and Central America and the southern reaches of North America. Where
possible, they mined the rich gold and silver veins,
flooding Europe with the new wealth and gaining
power and influence for themselves. But during the
seventeenth century, the mines were nearing exhaustion and the glory days were a thing of the past.

While Spain's and Portugal's ties with the New
World languished during the Baroque Age, England,
France, and the Netherlands were accelerating theirs,
especially with North America (Table 15.1). In 1607
English farmers settled along the Atlantic seaboard in
Virginia, ready to exploit the land, and in 1620 English

Puritans emigrated to New England in search of religious freedom (Figure 15.11). To the north, French explorers, missionaries, and fur traders founded Quebec
in 1608 and then spread along the St. Lawrence River
valley and southward into the Great Lakes region. At
the same time, the French moved into the Caribbean
basin, occupying many islands in the West Indies. After 1655 the English worked their way into the southern part of the Atlantic coast and the West Indies.
These newly arrived colonists eventually either drove
out the Spaniards or drastically reduced their influence. Meanwhile, the Dutch set up their own colonies
in North America, on the banks of the Hudson River
and in scattered areas of the mid-Atlantic region (Figure 15.12).

The English, French, and Dutch recognized the economic advantages of sending more explorers and families abroad and encouraged the founding of colonies.

Table 15.1	SETTLEMENTS IN THE NEW WORLD DURING THE BAROQUE AGE		

LOCATION	DATE OF FOUNDING	SETTLERS
Jamestown (Virginia)	1607	English
Quebec (Canada)	1608	French
Plymouth (Massachusetts)	1620	English
St. Kitts (West Indies)	1623	English
New Amsterdam (New York)	1624	Dutch
Barbados	1627	English
Brazil	1632–1654	Dutch
Curaçao (West Indies)	1634	Dutch
Martinique (West Indies)	1635	French
Saint Lucia (West Indies)	1635	French
Honduras (Belize)	1638	English
Saint Domingue (Haiti)	1644	French
Bahamas (West Indies)	1648	English
Jamaica (West Indies) (captured from Spain)	1655	English

Relying chiefly on state or royal charters, they created large overseas settlements that soon led to a brisk trade in which raw products from the New World were exchanged for finished goods from the Old World. William Penn (1644–1718) founded Pennsylvania in 1681 on the basis of such a charter from England.

In the Far East, colonial developments relied less on charters than on joint-stock companies, a private enterprise technique exploited by both England and the Netherlands. The English East India Company and the Dutch East India Company were the means whereby England and the Netherlands, respectively, opened trade routes and secured markets in the Far East (see Encounters in Chapters 14 and 15). The two companies made lucrative contracts with Indian princes and Japanese and Chinese state officials (Figure 15.13).

RESPONSES TO THE REVOLUTIONS IN THOUGHT

The scientific discoveries, the growth of skepticism, the new political theories, and the overseas explorations provoked a variety of responses among the artists, intellectuals, and educated public of the 1600s. In the aristocracy, for example, a new social type appeared— the **virtuoso,** a person who dabbled in the latest science and gave it respectability. A new type of literature also appeared, in which scientific concepts and discoveries were popularized for the consumption of an educated elite. Overall, the innovations and changes of the seventeenth century found ample creative expression in the attitudes and images of the period.

The Spread of Ideas

In the exciting dawn of the Scientific Revolution, some scientists and intellectuals realized that new scientific

Figure 15.11 HOLLAR. *Indian of Virginia, Male.* 1645. Etching, 4 × 3". Courtesy of the New York Public Library. *This engraving portrays a Native American male, who was probably one of many brought to London in the early seventeenth century. Whether his presence abroad was voluntary or involuntary is unknown, but the artist depicts him as a proud man with dignity. A translation of the Latin inscription reads, in part: at the upper left, "An American from Virginia. Age 23," and, at the upper right, "W. Hollar . . . made from Life 1645." W. Hollar is Wenceslaus Hollar (1607–1677), an artist from what is now the Czech Republic, who lived in London in the mid–seventeenth century and worked for aristocratic patrons with ties to the English court.*

Figure 15.12 ANONYMOUS. *Dutch Shipyard.* Engraving. Seventeenth century. *The Dutch were successful traders, explorers, and colonists because of their business practices and maritime technology. In the Dutch Republic, leaders encouraged entrepreneurial projects such as the Dutch East Indies Company, founded in 1602. This joint stock company—a trading company of investors who pooled their funds and shared the risk to make money in an overseas venture—made many very rich. To transport their cargoes overseas, the Dutch built spacious and fast merchant ships. Dutch sailors and crews ranked at the top, rivaled only by the English. Dutch naval vessels, or men-of-war, were well-constructed, seaworthy, and armed. Although they were smaller than the heavier Portuguese and Spanish galleons, they were easier to maneuver, required less wind to sail, and subsequently drove those ships off the high seas.*

findings needed to be given the widest dissemination possible, since the information would be of inestimable value to others who were engaged in their own research. Their enthusiasm for this task led them to share ideas. At first, they exchanged information informally through personal contacts or by chance encounters in the universities. But by midcentury, the scientific society had become the usual method for communicating new knowledge. The first one was in England, where King Charles II gave a charter to the Royal Society in 1662. Only a few years later, in 1666, Louis XIV supported the creation of the French Academy of Science (Figure 15.14), and in 1700 German scientists instituted the Berlin Academy of Science.

Figure 15.13 *A Chinese Interpretation of Dutch Traders.* Porcelain. Ch'ing dynasty, K'ang-hsi period, seventeenth century. Formerly owned by the Dutch East Indies Company. *As Europeans spread Western culture around the globe in the seventeenth century, they were sometimes confronted with images of themselves created by artists in other cultures, as in these Chinese representations of Dutch traders. These figures express a stereotype of a European man, dressed in the costume of the day (long coat, knee breeches, and hat) and with distinctive features (marked cheekbones, curly hair [wig?], and smiling face). Dating from the reign of China's Emperor K'ang-hsi (1661–1722), these porcelains were made as "curiosities" for the European market. They are enameled glaze porcelains, in which green, yellow, purple, and white enamels were applied to a prefired, or biscuit, body and then given a second firing.*

ENCOUNTER

The Sinews of Trade

In 1616 Sir Thomas Roe (about 1581–1644), King James I's ambassador, paid homage, with gifts, to Jahangir [je-HAN-ger] (1569–1617), or the Great Mogul, at his court in Agra, India (Encounter figure 15.1). Roe, through his strong personality, patience, and palace intrigues, managed to gain a trade outlet, or "factory," for the English trading business venture the East India Company at Surat on India's west coast. This seemingly insignificant encounter linked together one of the richest and most powerful empires in the world and a small island kingdom whose futures would be intertwined until the mid–twentieth century.

The English, as the Portuguese and the Dutch before them, were interested only in turning a profit from Indian goods and products. They held in contempt or viewed with amazement the rich, eclectic Mogul civilization of Persian, Indian, and central Asian elements that had emerged in the aftermath of the Mongol invaders and rulers of the thirteenth century. As Christians they were offended by many of the Hindu and Muslim religious practices and beliefs. Although unimpressed with the Moguls' achievements in architecture and technology, in the metal arts, and in much of their fine arts and jewelry, they immediately recognized the economic value of Indian textiles, especially cotton goods. English merchants began to import linen cloth from the Gujarat area of western India to be made into household goods and, later in the seventeenth century, into wearing apparel. Madras cotton cloth, from the town of Madras, and chintz, a type of printed cotton cloth, along with Persian silks also became popular.

During the 1600s, the East India Company forced more concessions from the Mogul rulers, and as the Mogul empire collapsed in the early 1700s, the English meddled in local political affairs. In the mid–eighteenth century they drove out their remaining rival, the French, and gained control of the country through a network of princes and by economic pressures. In the nineteenth century the Industrial Revolution in Europe ruined the Indian textile industry, for the British could now ship their own finished cotton goods to India and sell them at a profit. India still remained vital to British interests for her raw materials and as a market for English manufactured products, becoming the mainstay of Great Britain's worldwide holdings. Her central role in the British Empire became self-evident in 1876 when Queen Victoria was made empress of India. Yet, within seventy-five years, in 1947, India, led by the Indian nationalist and spiritual leader Mahatma Gandhi [ma-HAT-ma GAN-de] (1869–1948), gained its independence, emerging as the most populous democracy in the world. Its independence also initiated the beginning of the dismantling of the British Empire (see Encounter in Chapter 20).

Learning from the Encounter Why did the Portuguese, Dutch, and English go to India? **What** did India gain from its encounter with the English? **How** did the English react to the Indian culture and religions? In **what** ways did the original trade agreements between the English and India evolve into an imperial relationship? **Discuss** how trade affects relationships between the United States and other countries.

Encounter figure 15.1 BICHTIR. *Allegorical Representation of the Emperor Jahangir.* Seventeenth century. Color and gold on paper, ht. 10½". Courtesy of the Freer Gallery, Smithsonian Institution, Washington, D.C. (42.15V). *In this delicate miniature painting, Jahangir (r. 1605–1627), whose name means "World Seizer," sits on an hourglass throne, perhaps a reference to the fleeting of time and the brevity of his reign. Jahangir's head is encircled in a halo with the sun and the moon. Before him stands a mullah, or Islamic teacher, to whom the ruler is handing a book. The two figures who are placed below the mullah—a symbolic ranking to show Jahangir's preference for spiritual over worldly matters—have been identified by art historians as the Ottoman sultan (with a black beard) and James I of England (with the neck ruff). At the lower left, the man holding a painting may be Bichtir, the famous court artist who painted this miniature.*

At the same time, many intellectually curious men and women, who wanted to learn more about the changes taking place in science and mathematics but who lacked specialized training, turned to writers who could demystify the new discoveries and explain them in popular language. One who responded to this interest was the French thinker Bernard de Fontenelle [fon-tuh-NELL] (1657–1757), the long-lived secretary of the Academy of Science. His *Conversations on the Plurality of Worlds* set the early standard for this type of popular literature. With learning and wit, Fontenelle created a dialogue between himself and an inquiring countess in which Newtonian physics and the new astronomy were explained in an informative and entertaining way. Through publicists like Fontenelle, the new theories and ideas became available to a general public and entered the broader culture.

Another French publicist, Pierre Bayle [BEL] (1647–1706), launched the intellectual fashion for arranging ideas in systematic form, as in dictionaries and encyclopedias. Bayle's great popularizing work was called the *Historical and Critical Dictionary,* and it was probably the most controversial book of the Baroque Age. For this encyclopedic work, Bayle wrote articles on biblical heroes, Classical and medieval thinkers, and contemporary scholars, many of which challenged Christian beliefs. Each article was a little essay with a text and lengthy footnotes. He approached the work with the aim of setting forth rival and contradictory opinions on each topic; if the result proved to be offensive to the pious, he pointed out that he himself was only following the Bible and the teachings of the Christian faith. Many readers responded to the essays by becoming skeptical about the subjects, as Bayle

Figure 15.14 J. GOYTON after a painting by S. Leclerc. *Louis XIV at the Academy of Science.* 1671. Engraving. Bibliothèque Nationale, Paris. *Science became fashionable during the Baroque Age, and rulers provided funds to advance the new discoveries. Louis XIV, king of France, is shown here visiting the Royal Academy of Science, the premier organization of scientists in France. From this period dates the close alliance between science and government, a linkage based on mutual self-interest.*

clearly was. Others questioned Bayle's motives and accused him of atheism. The controversy over his works did not cease with his death. By 1750 his *Dictionary* had been reprinted many times and had spawned many imitations.

Bayle's *Dictionary* marked a new stage in the history of literature for two reasons. First, the work was sold to subscribers, which meant that royal, aristocratic, or ecclesiastical patronage was no longer necessary to publish a book. Second, the extravagant success of his venture showed that a literate public now existed that would buy books if they appealed to its interests. Both of these facts were understood very well by authors in the next generation, who freed writing from the patronage system and inaugurated the world of modern literature with its specialized audiences.

Impact on the Arts

The innovations in science and philosophy coincided with and fostered a changed consciousness not only in the educated public but also in artists and writers. New attitudes, values, and tastes reflecting these ideas are evident in the creative works of the Baroque period, many of which are discussed and illustrated in Chapter 14. Central among the new ideas was the belief that there is a hidden harmony in nature that may be expressed in mathematical laws. In the arts, this belief was expressed by order and wholeness beneath wild profusion, such as the geometric order that organizes the gardens and grounds of Versailles or the theme of redemption that unifies Milton's sprawling epic, *Paradise Lost.*

A second reflection of the Scientific Revolution, and particularly of the discoveries in astronomy, is the feeling of infinite space that pervades Baroque art. The love of curving lines, elliptical shapes, and flowing contours may be related to the new, expansive views of the planets and the universe. The ultimate expression of these interests and feelings, of course, is the illusionistic ceiling painting (see Figure 14.11).

A final effect of the Scientific Revolution was the elevation of analytic reasoning skills to a position of high esteem in the arts. Just as Newton's genius led him to grasp concepts and laws that had eluded others, so artists and humanists were inspired to use their powers of analysis to look below the surface of human life and search out its hidden truth. Racine's plays, for example, reveal acute insight into human psychology, as do the political philosophies of Hobbes and Locke; and Rembrandt's cycle of self-portraits shows his ability and his desire to reveal his innermost feelings. Baroque art and literature demonstrate that although the Scientific Revolution may have displaced men and women from the center of the universe, an optimistic view of the human predicament was still possible.

The Legacy of the Revolutions in Scientific and Political Thought

One historian of science claims that the Scientific Revolution "outshines everything since the rise of Christianity and reduces the Renaissance and Reformation to the rank of mere episodes . . . within the system of medieval Christendom." Although other scholars hesitate to go that far in praise of this singular event, enough evidence exists to show that the revolution in science caused a dramatic shift in the way people viewed themselves and their world. The Newtonian system became the accepted view of the universe until the twentieth century. Likewise, the new methodology—collecting raw data, reasoning inductively to hypotheses, and verifying results with mathematics—remains the standard in modern science. Out of the gradual spread of this method of reasoning to other areas of thought have emerged the modern social sciences. Even certain disciplines in the humanities—such as linguistics, the study of language—use scientific methods to the extent that is possible.

At the same time that science held out the promise that it could unlock the secrets of nature, it was also contributing to a dramatic upsurge in skepticism. Since the end of the Baroque Age, virtually everything in Western culture has been subjected to systematic doubt, including religious beliefs, artistic theories, and social mores. Although many causes besides science lie behind this trend to question all existing standards, the Scientific Revolution created a highly visible model and ready tools for universal doubt. In effect, because Aristotle's and other ancient thinkers' ideas were proven false, modern scholars were inclined to question all other beliefs received from the past. This trend has encouraged the intellectual restlessness that is perhaps the most prominent feature of modern life.

The legacies left by the innovations in Baroque political thought and the expansion of European culture cannot compare with the effects of the rise of modern science. Nevertheless, the changes in political theory and in the relations of Europe with the rest of the world did have strong consequences for modern life. In general, the new political theories gave rise to two rival heritages, the authoritarian tradition, which claims that a strong centralized government is the best way to ensure justice for all citizens, and the liberal tradition, which holds that citizens are capable of ruling themselves. From this time forward, politics in the West has been organized around the conflicting claims of these two points of view. From 1945 to 1989, the symbol of this development was the division of the world between the supporters of the authoritarian Soviet Union and the supporters of the democratic United States.

The colonizing efforts in the New World during the 1600s served to extend the geographic limits of the West. As a result, Western ideas and technology may be found today even in the most far-flung reaches of the globe. A negative consequence of the opening of the New World was that slavery, an institution that had virtually died in Europe in the early Middle Ages, was reintroduced, with destructive consequences for the non-Western people who became enslaved. We in the modern age are reaping the bitter harvest of this development.

KEY CULTURAL TERMS

Scientific Revolution
geocentrism
empiricism
inductive reasoning
deductive reasoning

heliocentrism
social contract
liberalism
tabula rasa
virtuoso

SUGGESTIONS FOR FURTHER READING

BACON, F. *The Essays.* New York: Penguin, 1985. Judiciously edited version of Bacon's highly readable text, dating from 1625, which contributed significantly to the rise of modern scientific thinking.

BAYLE, P. *Historical and Critical Dictionary: Selections.* Translated by R. H. Popkin and C. Brush. Indianapolis: Bobbs-Merrill, 1965. Typical and controversial excerpts from one of the first modern dictionaries, originally published in 1697.

DESCARTES, R. *Discourse on Method.* Edited and translated by E. Anscombe and P. T. Geach. Indianapolis: Bobbs-Merrill, 1971. A lucid translation of one of the key tracts of modern philosophy; Descartes's arguments and evidence are relatively easy to understand. First published in 1637.

GALILEI, G. *Dialogue Concerning the Two Chief World Systems—Ptolemaic and Copernican.* Translated by S. Drake, foreword by A. Einstein. Berkeley: University of California Press, 1953. Written in a conversational style, this work—first published in 1632—aligned Galileo with the supporters of the Copernican system and led to his trial by the Roman Catholic authorities.

HOBBES, T. *The Leviathan.* Buffalo, N.Y.: Prometheus Books, 1988. Hobbes's most important work—first issued in 1651—advocating absolutist government without any restraint by the people; this work has inspired many modern forms of authoritarian rule.

LOCKE, J. *An Essay Concerning Human Understanding.* New York: Collier Books, 1965. A good edition, introduced by M. Cranston, of Locke's essay arguing that the mind is shaped by the environment, an assertion that made the progressive theories of the modern world possible; first published in 1690.

———. *Two Treatises of Government.* Cambridge: Cambridge University Press, 1967. An excellent edition with introduction and notes by the distinguished scholar P. Laslett; Locke's *Second Treatise,* making the case for the doctrine of government by consent of the governed, has become the bible of modern liberalism.

16 THE AGE OF REASON
1700–1789

The scientific discoveries and philosophic ideas that made the seventeenth century so intellectually exciting bore fruit in the eighteenth century, a period often referred to as the Age of Reason. The great revelations of the Scientific Revolution led thinkers in the 1700s to believe they were living in a time of illumination and enlightenment. Committed to scientific methodology, mathematical reasoning, and a healthy skepticism, they fervently believed their knowledge could lead to the improvement of both the individual and society.

The Age of Reason was marked by four different trends. The first was the growing concentration of political power in the great states, a process that had begun during the Baroque era. France was the most powerful state, followed by Great Britain (the new name of a unified England and Scotland in 1707), Prussia, Austria, Russia, and the Netherlands (Map 16.1). The second trend was the return of the aristocracy to prominence after a century or more of decline. In time, the ostentatious culture spawned by the resurgent aristocrats proved to be their swan song, as the French Revolution, at the end of the century, destroyed their bases of power (see Chapter 17). The third trend was the rise to political and cultural eminence of the middle class who supported those progressive thinkers who advocated social equality, social justice, and a thorough revamping of society. The intellectual and cultural movement spawned by these thinkers is called the **Enlightenment,** which constitutes the fourth and most important trend that helped to reshape Western life in the 1700s.

At the same time that these political and social trends were occurring, a new style in art, architecture, and music was developing in France in reaction

◄ **Detail** Étienne Aubry. *Paternal Love.* Ca. 1775. Oil on canvas, 30 × 39″. The Trustees of the Barber Institute of Fine Arts, The Uiversity of Birmingham, England.

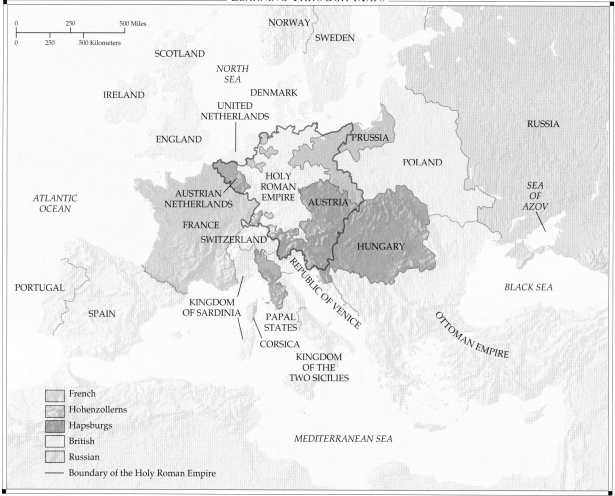

Map 16.1 EUROPE, 1763–1789
This map shows the political divisions of Europe in the mid–eighteenth century. **Locate** the territories of France, Great Britain, Russia, the Hohenzollern dynasty, and the Hapsburg dynasty—the five great powers. **Which** great power has the most compact state? **Which** great power has the most widely dispersed lands? **How** would geography and cultural diversity influence a state's ability to maintain great-power status? **Notice** the vastness of the Ottoman Empire, a Muslim state, in the southeast corner of Europe.

to the excesses of the Baroque. This style, known as Rococo, was more informal and graceful, less ponderous and oppressive than the Baroque (Figure 16.1). After about 1750, in reaction to both the Rococo and the Baroque, a very different style—the Neoclassical—developed. Unlike the Rococo, the Neoclassical style in art and architecture spread widely throughout Europe and the United States. In music, a refined and elegant Classical style developed, graced by the incomparable presence of Mozart, arguably the greatest musical genius who ever lived.

THE ENLIGHTENMENT

Eighteenth-century thinkers derived their ideals and goals from a variety of sources. Following the example of ancient Greece and Rome, they rejected superstition, sought truth through the use of reason, and viewed the world from a secular, human-centered perspective. Drawing on the Renaissance, they embraced humanism—the belief that a human being becomes a better person through the study and practice of literature, philosophy, music, and the arts. And from the

Timeline 16.1   THE AGE OF REASON

1700	1714		1740	1748	1756	1763		1776	1783	1789
War of Spanish Succession			**War of Austrian Succession**		**Seven Years' War**			**American Revolution**		

		1740 Richardson's *Pamela*	**1750** First volume of the *Encyclopédie*	**1759** Voltaire's *Candide*	**1776** Smith's *Wealth of Nations*	**1786** Mozart's *Marriage of Figaro*

1762 Rousseau's *Social Contract*

1785 David's *Oath of the Horatii*

1771–1773 Fragonard's *Lover Crowned*

seventeenth-century revolutions in science and philosophy, particularly the works of Newton, Bacon, Descartes, and Locke, they derived a reliance on rationalism, empiricism, skepticism, and the experimental method, along with a belief in human perfectibility through education and unlimited progress.

Despite the power of these ideas, they reached a relatively small percentage of Europe's population. The Enlightenment had its greatest effect in the cultural capitals of France and Great Britain—Paris, London, and Edinburgh. Many aristocrats read the works of Enlightenment writers, as did many members of the middle class, particularly educators, lawyers, journalists, and clergymen. Ultimately, enough literate and influential people were converted to the goals of the Enlightenment to have an effect on the revolutionary events that occurred later in the eighteenth century (Timeline 16.1).

The *Philosophes* and Their Program

The central figures of the Enlightenment were a small band of writers known as *philosophes*, the French word for "philosophers." Not philosophers in a formal

Figure 16.1 SIR JOSHUA REYNOLDS. *Mrs. Siddons as the Tragic Muse.* 1784. Oil on canvas, 7'9" × 4'9". Huntington Art Gallery, San Marino, California. *The Rococo portrait painter Sir Joshua Reynolds painted many English personalities of his day, including Sarah Siddons. Mrs. Siddons, who came from a theater family, won the applause of England's knowledgeable and discerning audiences to emerge as the most famous actress of tragic drama in the late eighteenth century. Reynolds distances Mrs. Siddons from the viewer and surrounds her with elaborate scenery as if she were on a proscenium stage in a darkened theater. The two figures behind her represent Aristotle's definitions of tragedy—pity and terror.*

sense, the *philosophes* were more likely to be popularizers who wanted to influence public opinion. They avoided the methods of academic scholars, such as engaging in philosophical debates or writing only for colleagues, and tried to reach large audiences through novels, essays, pamphlets, plays, poems, and histories. In this they were following the lead of Fontenelle, who had popularized the new astronomy in his *Conversations on the Plurality of Worlds* (see Chapter 15). When possible, they openly attacked what they deemed to be the evils of society and supported those rulers who favored change, the so-called enlightened despots. When the censors threatened, however, the *philosophes* disguised their radical messages or else published their criticisms in the Netherlands—the most liberal state in Europe at the time.

The Enlightenment was essentially a product of French cultural life, and Paris was its capital. The principal *philosophes* were Voltaire, Diderot, Montesquieu—all French—and by adoption the French-speaking Swiss writer Rousseau. But major *philosophes* appeared elsewhere in Europe, notably in Great Britain, and in Britain's North American colonies. The most influential of these voices were the English historian Edward Gibbon, the American writer Benjamin Franklin, and two Scottish thinkers, the economist Adam Smith and the philosopher David Hume.

The *philosophes,* though never in complete agreement and often diametrically opposed, shared certain assumptions. They had full confidence in reason; they were convinced that nature was orderly and fundamentally good and could be understood through the empirical method; they believed that change and progress would improve society, since human beings were perfectible. Faith in reason led them to reject religious doctrine, in particular Roman Catholic dogma; to denounce bigotry and intolerance; and to advocate freedom of religious choice. Maintaining that education liberated humanity from ignorance and superstition, the *philosophes* called for an expanded educational system independent of ecclesiastical control.

The *philosophes* thought that the political, economic, and religious institutions should be reformed to bring "the greatest happiness for the greatest numbers"—a phrase that expresses a key Enlightenment ideal and that, in the nineteenth century, became the battle cry of the English thinker and reformer Jeremy Bentham (see Chapter 18). These theorists anticipated a general overhaul of society, leading to universal peace and a golden age for humanity. In effect, they preached a secular gospel that happiness need not be delayed until after death but, instead, could be enjoyed here on earth.

Envisioning a rejuvenated society that guaranteed natural rights to its citizens, the *philosophes* were almost unanimous in thinking exclusively in terms of men and not of women. They still considered women their intellectual and physical inferiors and thus in need of male protection or guidance. Not until the late eighteenth century were voices raised on behalf of women's rights and only then under the inspiration of the French Revolution.

One of those thinkers moved by the revolutionary winds blowing from France was the English writer Mary Wollstonecraft (1759–1797), who, in *A Vindication of the Rights of Woman* (1792), used Enlightenment ideals to urge the liberation of her own sex. Like Rousseau, Wollstonecraft was a democrat and opposed to hierarchy in all forms: in the aristocracy, the military, and the clergy to the extent that promotion was based on obsequiousness. Unlike Rousseau, she was dedicated to the rights of women, whom she repeatedly called "one-half of the human race." Rejecting the "Adam's rib" explanation of woman's inferiority as being simply a male fabrication, she claimed that women were as rational as men and thus should be treated the same. The heart of this latter-day *philosophe*'s argument was that women should abandon feminine artifice and cunning, especially the all-consuming need to be socially pleasing, and through education become equal partners with educated men. Starting in the nineteenth century, reformers gradually began to take up Wollstonecraft's challenge, particularly her call for female education and women's suffrage.

Religion

During the Age of Reason, the Deist religion appealed to a small but influential group of thinkers and writers, while new offshoots of Protestantism attracted many followers at all levels of society in Europe and the New World. Both trends generated controversy and social tensions at the time, and their lingering effects are still felt in the West today.

Deism   Newtonian science implied that God had set the universe in motion and then left it to run by its own natural laws. The *philosophes* accepted this metaphor of God as a clockmaker, and in place of traditional Christianity some thinkers now offered a version of Christianity called **Deism.** Deists focused on the worship of a Supreme Being, a God who created the universe and set the laws of nature in motion but who never again interfered in natural or human matters. Believing in this idea of a clockmaker God, the Deists rejected the efficacy of prayer and reduced the role of Jesus from that of savior to that of a good moral example.

Deism was espoused by only a relatively small percentage of Westerners, however, such as Benjamin

Franklin in the British colony of Pennsylvania. Although it did not find wide acceptance, Deism's appeal marked another shift in religious attitudes and was added evidence of the growing secularization of European consciousness in the 1700s.

Popular Religion The two most important popular religious movements of the 1700s were **Pietism** in Europe and the **First Great Awakening** in England's American colonies. Both movements emerged from mainline Protestantism, and the two were loosely interconnected and shared certain traits. Both thought established churches had lost contact with their membership, by becoming too closely identified with the rich and powerful. Both also believed that the church's mission should be to help resolve pressing social and economic issues, such as poverty and social inequality, rather than accepting the status quo, as seemed to be the case with established churches in England and Germany. And both also urged a personal living faith based on strict adherence to the Scriptures, rather than a focus on ritual and liturgy, as was done in the established churches.

Pietism began in Germany among the Lutherans in the late 1600s and flourished until the 1760s. It spread into central Europe in the early 1700s under a number of different leaders and spawned several new sects. One branch sent a missionary to England's American colonies, while another branch, the Moravians (in the modern Czech Republic), founded settlements there. The Moravians also sent missions to England, where they had a ready audience among those disaffected from the Church of England. John Wesley (1703–1791), the founder of Methodism, was influenced by the Moravians both in England and in the Georgia colony, which he visited in his early life. Wesley called for a spiritual renewal, demanding of his followers that they be "born again," that is, renounce their sinful ways and choose Jesus Christ as personal savior—a belief that remains central to the evangelical movement today. Wesley's movement—which had special appeal to both urban workers drawn to the factories of this first Industrial Age and to the rural poor—grew rapidly in England and America. Although he initially did not want to secede from the Church of England, Wesley gradually recognized that the differences between his teachings and the Church of England were irreconcilable. The formal break did not come until 1784, the official date of the founding of the Methodist church.

Methodism and German Pietism became catalysts for the First Great Awakening in Colonial America. A wave of preaching and revivalism swept over the English colonies, from New England to Georgia. As in the Protestant Reformation (see Chapter 13), this movement stressed human sinfulness and the gift of God's grace, the central role of Jesus Christ as savior, the Bible as the ultimate source of religious authority, and the need to be "born again." Two of its key leaders were Jonathan Edwards (1703–1758), the theologian and spellbinding preacher, operating in New England, and George Whitfield (1714–1770), a fire-and-brimstone preacher and member of Wesley's inner circle, who led revivals in Georgia and other southern colonies, as well as in cities along the East Coast.

While the First Great Awakening soon died out in New England, it showed great staying power along the westward-moving frontier, in the countryside, and throughout the southern colonies—laying the foundation for what became the Bible Belt of the United States. By reaching out to the poor, to women, and even to slaves and free blacks, this movement tended to democratize religion in colonial life. It also led to the founding of a number of colleges, which, by educating young men and training ministers, ensured that the religious, moral, and cultural values of the First Great Awakening would be perpetuated for generations to come. As a strong rival to the Church of England and other mainline Protestant sects, the movement tended to weaken the ties of the established churches with local British officials. This development had social and political implications, which surfaced on the eve of the American Revolution (see Chapter 17). While the First Great Awakening peaked in the 1760s, its influence remained strong, and it became the prototype of religious revivals in America's later history.

The *Encyclopédie*

The message of the *philosophes* was communicated by a variety of means: through pamphlets, essays, and books, through private and public discussions and debates, through the new journalistic press, and, especially in France, through the salon—the half-social, half-serious gatherings where the fashionable elite met to discuss ideas. But the principal work of the *philosophes* was the *Encyclopédie*—the monumental project that remains the summation of the Enlightenment. Two earlier works, Chambers's *Cyclopedia* in England (1728) and Bayle's *Dictionary* in France (1697) (see Chapter 15), paved the way for the *Encyclopédie*. Begun in 1750 and completed in 1772, the original work comprised seventeen text volumes and eleven books of plates and illustrations (Figure 16.2). More than 161 writers wrote articles for this educational venture, which was intended as a summary of existing knowledge in the arts, crafts, and sciences.

The editor of the *Encyclopédie* was Denis Diderot [DEED-uh-roh] (1713–1784), one of the giants of the

Figure 16.2 Illustration from the *Encyclopédie: Cotton Plantation in the French West Indies. 1751–1765. As principal editor of the* Encyclopédie, *Diderot adopted Francis Bacon's notion that all knowledge is useful. Thus, the articles and the illustrations for this reference work focused on practical data such as soapmaking, human anatomy, and military drill. In this drawing, for example, the readers could peruse the romanticized plantation scene to discover how raw cotton was prepared for shipment to European mills.*

Enlightenment. Diderot was constantly in trouble with the authorities because of the work's controversial essays, which he asserted were meant "to change the general way of thinking." Publication was halted in 1759 by the state censor but resumed secretly with the collusion of other government officials. Unlike most publications of the period, the project was funded by its readers, not by the crown or the church, and private circulating libraries rented the volumes to untold numbers of customers.

The Physiocrats

Under the broad umbrella of Enlightenment ideas, the *philosophes* were joined by a group of French writers concerned with economic matters—the **Physiocrats,** as they called themselves. (The term is a coined word, from Greek, meaning "rule of, or from, the earth.") The Physiocrats examined the general nature of the economy and, in particular, the strengths and weaknesses of mercantilism, the prevailing economic system, in which the state regulated trade and production for its own benefit. In their eyes, this state-run system had hindered the growth of the economies of the various European countries. Contrary to its goals, mercantilism had lowered the productivity of workers, especially farmers, and had led to labor unrest and riots.

Guided by Enlightenment doctrine that "natural laws" governed society, the Physiocrats assumed that

similar "laws" applied to economic growth and decline. After a thorough analysis of the French economy, they concluded that certain fundamental economic principles did exist, such as the law of supply and demand, and that these laws operated best when free from governmental interference. Accordingly, they recommended the dismantling of mercantilism and the adoption of *laissez-faire*, French for "to let alone"—in other words, an economy where the self-regulating laws of free trade were in effect. In addition, they argued that unrestricted enjoyment of private property was necessary for individual freedom. These French thinkers concluded that both the individual and the entire society automatically benefited when all people were allowed to serve their own self-interest instead of working for the good of the state.

At about the same time, the Scottish economist Adam Smith (1723–1790) was developing similar ideas. He reported his conclusions in *An Inquiry into the Nature and Causes of the Wealth of Nations* (1776), a book that became the bible of industrial capitalism and remains so today. In this work, Smith blamed mercantilism for the economic woes of his time, identified the central role played by labor in manufacturing, and called for open and competitive trade so that the "invisible hand" of a free-market economy could operate. Smith's ideas were quickly absorbed by budding entrepreneurs and had an immediate impact on the changes being generated by the Industrial Revolution (see Chapter 17).

Figure 16.3 ÉTIENNE AUBRY. *Paternal Love.* Ca. 1775. Oil on canvas, 30 × 39". The Trustees of the Barber Institute of Fine Arts, The University of Birmingham, England. *Paternal Love is a symbol of French rural bourgeois life. It depicts a father, probably returned home from a trip, greeting his three children, wife, and father (the children's grandfather). Although the room's amenities—stone floor, fireplace, and solid walls—signal financial security, the simple and sturdy furniture and the scanty display of household effects indicate that the family is merely middle class and not upper class (see Figure 16.5). Nevertheless, the painter's moral lesson is evident: Parental love makes a family strong—a sentiment that would appeal to moralistic middle-class taste. Aubry (1745–1781) was a popular artist, praised by the writer-critic Diderot and famous for his "moral genre" paintings, such as this.*

THE GREAT POWERS DURING THE AGE OF REASON

In comparison with the seventeenth century, the period between 1715 and 1789 was relatively peaceful; national conflicts were few and brief. In addition, Europe experienced a slow but steady economic expansion that was supported by a continuing increase in population. The prosperity fueled the rise of the middle classes, especially in Great Britain and Holland. In France, however, the middle class made only modest gains, and in central and eastern Europe they were a small fraction of the population.

Society: Continuity and Change

A major consequence of the century's modest economic growth was the growing urbanization of society. Although most Europeans still followed traditional livelihoods on farms and in villages, cities and towns offered increasing opportunities for ambitious folk. The rural-to-urban shift originated in England, the home of the Industrial Revolution, and to a lesser extent in France. Only in the next century did it slowly spread to some parts of central and eastern Europe.

The traditional social hierarchy kept each class in its place. The aristocracy constituted only about 3 percent of the total population, but it possessed tremendous

power and wealth. The upper middle class—encompassing rich merchants, bankers, and professionals—normally resided in the rapidly expanding urban areas and influenced business and governmental affairs. In the broad middle class were the less wealthy merchants, shopkeepers, skilled artisans, and bureaucrats, and substantial rural families (Figure 16.3). Beneath the middle ranks were the lesser artisans and craftspeople, and below them, the metropolitan poor, who performed menial labor and were often unemployed, and rural laborers. In the countryside, the nobility and the prosperous farmers owned large sections of the land and controlled the rural populace. The small cultivators, tenant farmers, landless workers, and indentured contract laborers constituted a complex group whose legal, social, and personal rights varied widely across Europe. Next were the peasants, whose status ranged from freedom in western Europe to serfdom in Russia. (Serfs were bound to the land they worked, but they had customary rights, and strictly speaking they were not slaves.) These impoverished people often bore the brunt of the taxes and the contempt of the other classes.

With few exceptions, such as the upper-middle-class women who played influential roles in the salons, women remained subordinate to men. As mentioned earlier, the *philosophes*, who thoroughly critiqued society, failed to recognize women's contributions or champion their rights. Even Jean-Jacques Rousseau, who was often at odds with his fellow writers, agreed with the *philosophes* that women were inferior to men and should be submissive to them.

Another group who gained little from the Enlightenment were the African slaves in Europe's overseas colonies. During the eighteenth century, ships from England, France, and Holland carried about six million Africans to enslavement in the New World. Efforts to abolish the slave trade or even to improve the conditions of the slaves proved futile despite the moral disapproval of the *philosophes* and the pleas of English Christians.

Absolutism, Limited Monarchy, and Enlightened Despotism

The eighteenth century was the last great age of kings in the West. In most countries, the royal rulers followed traditional policies even in the face of criticism or opposition. Supported by inefficient bureaucracies and costly armies, they controlled the masses through heavy taxes and threats of brutality while holding in check the privileged groups. Although a few rulers attempted reforms, by the end of the century most of the monarchies were weakening as democratic sentiments continued to rise.

In France, the kings struggled to hold on to the power they inherited from Louis XIV. In Great Britain, the kings fought a losing battle against Parliament and the restrictions of constitutional monarchy. In Prussia and Austria, so-called enlightened despots experimented with reforms to strengthen their states, while in Russia the czars found new ways to expand absolutism. By midcentury, the Continent had undergone a series of brief wars that ended the several relatively peaceful decades Europe had enjoyed (see Timeline 16.1). For France and England, the Continental conflicts soon escalated into global commercial, territorial, and colonial rivalries that were resolved only with the outcome of the American Revolutionary War (1775–1783).

France: The Successors to the Sun King   No French ruler was able to recapture the splendor of Louis XIV. Louis XV (r. 1715–1774), who succeeded to full political control at age thirteen and never acquired a strong will to rule, only compounded the problems of the French state. Those he chose as his subordinates were not always talented or loyal, and he permitted his mistresses, who were not trained in government, to influence his decisions about official matters. When Louis XV, despairing over a military defeat, expressed his misgivings about the future of France to his royal favorite, Madame de Pompadour (1721–1764), she re-

portedly replied with the prophetic words *"Après nous le déluge"* ("After us, the flood").

Life at Louis XV's court could not be sustained in the grand manner of the late Sun King, and the nobles began to leave Versailles for Paris. Whether at Versailles or elsewhere, educated aristocrats were becoming fascinated by Enlightenment ideas, and they and their wives read the *Encyclopédie* and studied the writings of the *philosophes*. Upper-class women played influential roles in presiding over salons, where the enlightened thinkers and their admirers gathered to dine and converse. Two of the best-known salons were conducted by Madame du Deffand [day-FAHN] (1679–1780) and Julie Lespinasse [les-pee-NAHS] (1732–1776). For a number of years, Madame du Deffand (Marie de Marquise du Deffand) claimed Voltaire as her most prominent literary celebrity, and his presence ensured that other *philosophes* would attend her gatherings. Julie de Lespinasse, serving first as companion to Madame du Deffand, broke away to found her own salon, where Jean d'Alembert (1717–1783), coeditor of Diderot's *Encyclopédie*, was a favored guest.

Even though the French elite debated the merits of reform and the more controversial topics raised by the *philosophes*, Louis XV clearly did not accept the movement's call for change. It is ironic that the country where the Enlightenment began failed to undertake any of its progressive reforms. Indeed, when changes were finally introduced under Louis XVI (r. 1774–1792), they were too little and too late.

Handicapped by the weak Louis XV, France found its preeminent position in foreign affairs challenged by Great Britain, Austria, and Prussia. As a result of the Seven Years' War, which began in 1756, France suffered defeats in Europe and lost its holdings in North America and India. During the American Revolution, France sided with the colonists against Great Britain, its foe at home and overseas. France's aid to the Americans further diminished the government's financial resources and forced the nation deeper into debt.

France's kings also failed to solve the nation's domestic problems, the consequence of their own failures of leadership and that of the royal officials called *intendants*, who were supposed to coordinate the loose federation of provinces into a functioning French state. Meanwhile, the tax collectors failed to provide adequate revenues for the state because of the corrupt tax system. And, most important, the crown was faced with a resurgent aristocracy determined to recover the feudal privileges it had lost under Louis XIV. Rather than joining the king's efforts to reform the judicial system, the nobility blocked the crown at every step. The middle class combined forces with some sympathetic aristocrats, transforming what had been a feudal issue into a struggle for freedom in the name of the people. In 1789, during the reign of Louis XVI, France started on a revolutionary course that united most of French society against the crown and that culminated in the French Revolution (1789–1799) (see Chapter 17).

Great Britain and the Hanoverian Kings To the *philosophes*, Great Britain was the ideal model of a nation. To them, Britain seemed more stable and prosperous than the states on the Continent, a success they attributed to the limited powers of the English monarchy imposed by Parliament during the Glorious Revolution of 1688. Britain's laws guaranteed to every Englishman certain political and social rights, such as free speech and fair and speedy trials. Britain's economy was strong as well. Prompted by enterprising merchants and progressive landowners, the nation was dominant in an expanding global market; at home, the standard of living was rising for the growing population.

After the death of Queen Anne in 1714, the English crown was inherited by George I, a great-grandson of James I and the Protestant ruler of the German principality of Hanover. The first two Hanoverian kings seemed more interested in events in Germany than in those in England, leading to a decline in their powers, and eventually the kings reigned in splendid isolation at the royal court. George I (r. 1714–1727) allowed Parliament to run the country. Under George II (r. 1727–1760), Britain was drawn into the Seven Years' War but emerged victorious, the dominant presence in world trade. From this pinnacle of international power, Great Britain occupied center stage until the outbreak of World War I in 1914.

Nevertheless, Great Britain faced serious domestic problems under George III (r. 1760–1820) because he sought to restore royal powers lost to Parliament by his predecessors. This internal struggle affected foreign policy when the king and Parliament offered differing proposals to control the economic development of the American colonies through export and import quotas, duties, and taxes. The differences between the two proposals hastened the onset of the American Revolution and probably contributed to Britain's eventual defeat.

Enlightened Despotism in Central and Eastern Europe The system of European states underwent some modifications during the Age of Reason. Great Britain and France now dominated western Europe; the less populous countries of Holland and Sweden declined in power; Spain turned increasingly inward and all but disappeared from Continental affairs; and Italy, under Austrian and papal control, remained economically depressed. Meanwhile, Prussia, Austria, and Russia jockeyed for control of central and eastern Europe. Un-

der their absolutist rulers, these states pursued aggressive policies, seizing territories from one another and their weaker neighbors. Although these rulers portrayed themselves as enlightened despots, their regimes were generally characterized by oppressive and authoritarian policies.

By 1740 Prussia, ruled by the Hohenzollern dynasty, had a solid economic base, a hardworking bureaucracy, and an efficient army. Capitalizing on these advantages, Frederick II, known as Frederick the Great (r. 1740–1786), turned Prussia into a leading European power. A pragmatic diplomat, a skilled military tactician, and a student of the Enlightenment and French culture, Frederick was an enlightened despot of the type beloved by the *philosophes*. He even attempted (though failed) to reform his state's agrarian economy and social system in accordance with the rational principle that all individuals have the natural right to choose personally the best way to live.

Prussia's chief rival in central Europe was Austria. Throughout the 1700s, Austria's rulers struggled to govern a multiethnic population that included large numbers of Germans, Hungarians, Czechs, and Slovaks along with Poles, Italians, and various Slavic minorities. At the same time, the emperors tried, with mixed success, to assert Austria's role as a great power, both politically and culturally. Schönbrunn Palace in Vienna, for example, was built as a rival to France's Versailles (Figure 16.4). Two rulers stand out—the Hapsburg emperors Maria Theresa and Joseph, her son, whose combined reigns lasted from 1740 to 1790.

Unlike Frederick II of Prussia, Maria Theresa (r. 1740–1780) was not attracted to the ideas of the *philosophes*. More important was her Roman Catholic faith, which led her to portray herself to her subjects as their universal mother. She was perhaps the most beloved monarch in this age of kings. Maria Theresa's reforming zeal sprang not from philosophic principle but from a reaction against Austria's territorial losses during military defeats. She used all her royal prerogatives to overhaul the political and military machinery of the state. Along with universal military conscription, increased revenues, and more equitable distribution of taxes, she wanted a general reorganization of society that gave more uniform treatment to all citizens. Her efforts were not wasted, for her son Joseph II took up her uncompleted task and became the ultimate personification of enlightened despotism.

During his brief reign, from 1780 to 1790, Joseph II launched far-reaching changes to raise farm production and to provide more economic opportunities for the peasants. Convinced that his country's economic and social institutions had to be fully modernized if it was to survive, he abolished serfdom and passed

488

Figure 16.4 JOHANN FERDINAND HETZENDORF VON HOHENBERG. Gloriette, or "The Temple of Fame." Schönbrunn Palace Gardens. 1768. Vienna. *The Gloriette, a triumphal arch flanked by colonnaded screens, is situated on the highest point within the vast gardens of Schönbrunn Palace. Designed by Johann Ferdinand Hetzendorf von Hohenberg (1732–1816), court architect to Empress Maria Theresa, it is the crowning touch of his beautification campaign for the palace grounds. It functioned as a theatrical backdrop for court rituals and receptions. Constructed partly from the ruins of a castle near the site, the Gloriette uses Classical features (colonnades, balustrades, and statuary and urns) though its style is Baroque (profuse decorative details and the reflecting pool).*

decrees guaranteeing religious toleration and free speech. In the 1790s, much of what he had accomplished was undone by his successors, who, fearing the excesses of the French Revolution, restored aristocratic and ecclesiastic control and privileges.

Russia was the newest member of the family of great powers, having achieved this stature during the reign of Peter the Great (r. 1682–1725). Abroad, Peter had made Russia's presence known, and at home he had begun to reform political, economic, and social institutions along Western lines. Most of his eighteenth-century successors were ineffective, if not incompetent, until Catherine the Great (r. 1762–1796) became empress. She pursued the unifying policies of Peter, but unlike him she was able to win the powerful support of the large landowners. A patron of the Enlightenment, Catherine sought the advice of a few *philosophes*, including Diderot. She also attempted to improve the low farm productivity and the nearly enslaved condition of the peasants, but the vastness of Russia's problems and the reactionary autocratic government defeated any genuine reforms.

CULTURAL TRENDS IN THE EIGHTEENTH CENTURY: FROM ROCOCO TO NEOCLASSICAL

Even though the eighteenth century was dominated by the Enlightenment, other cultural trends also held sway. The Rococo style in the arts mirrored the taste of

the French nobility; the succeeding Neoclassical style was adopted and supported by the progressive writers, artists, intellectuals, and ambitious members of the middle class. Meanwhile, innovations in literature were pointing the way toward the modern world.

The Rococo Style in the Arts

Conceived on a more intimate scale than the Baroque and committed to frivolous subjects and themes—the dominant ideas of a work—the **Rococo style** arose in France in the waning years of the Sun King's reign. With his death in 1715 and the succession of his five-year-old heir, Louis XV, the nobility were released both from Versailles and from the ponderous Baroque style. Paris once again became the capital of art, ideas, and fashion in the Western world. There, the Rococo style was created for the French elite almost single-handedly by the Flemish painter and decorator Jean-Antoine Watteau.

The Rococo gradually spread to most of Europe, but its acceptance was tied to religion and class. It was embraced by the aristocracy in Germany, Italy, and Austria; Roman Catholic nobles in Austria developed a version of Rococo that was second in importance only to that of France. The English, on the other hand, rejected the Rococo, possibly because its erotic undercurrent and sexual themes offended the Protestant middle-class sensibility. Consequently, Rococo style is a purely Continental phenomenon; there is no English Rococo.

Figure 16.5 JEAN-ANTOINE WATTEAU. *Departure from Cythera*. 1717. Oil on canvas, 4'3" ×
6'4½". Louvre. *Watteau's aristocratic lovers, savoring a last few moments of pleasure, represent
the idealized image that the eighteenth-century elite wanted to present to the world. No hint of
the age's problems is allowed to disturb this idyllic scene. From the court costumes to the hovering cupids, this painting transforms reality into a stage set—the ideal of Rococo art.*

Rococo Painting Jean-Antoine Watteau [wah-TOE]
(1684–1721) specialized in paintings that depict *fêtes
galantes,* or aristocratic entertainments. In these
works, Watteau portrays the intimate world of the
aristocracy, dressed in sumptuous clothing, grouped
in parks and gardens, and often accompanied by costumed actors, another of Watteau's favorite subjects.
He filled these bucolic settings with air and lightness
and grace—all of which were a contrast to the occasionally heavy-handed Baroque. Mythological allusions made Watteau's works depictions of Classical
themes rather than merely scenes of aristocratic life.

In 1717 Watteau became the first Rococo painter to
be elected to membership in the Royal Academy of
Painting and Sculpture in Paris. As required by the
terms of election, he submitted as his diploma piece
Departure from Cythera (Figure 16.5). The setting is
Cythera, the legendary island of Venus, whose bust on
the right is garlanded with her devotees' roses. Forming a wavering line, the lovers express hesitation as
they make their farewells: The couple under the statue

are lost in reverie as a clothed cupid tugs at the
woman's skirt; beside this group a suitor assists his
lady to her feet; and next to them a gentleman accompanies his companion to the waiting boat as she long-
ingly gazes backward. This melancholy scene, signified by the setting sun and the departing lovers,
represents Watteau's homage to the brevity of human
passion.

In *Departure from Cythera*, many of the new values
of the Rococo style can be seen. Where the Baroque favored tumultuous scenes depicting the passions and
ecstasies of the saints, the Rococo focused on smaller,
gentler moments, usually involving love of one variety
or another, whether erotic, romantic, or sentimental.
Where the Baroque used intense colors to convey feelings of power and grandeur, the Rococo used soft
pastels to evoke nostalgia and melancholy. The monumentality and sweeping movement of Baroque art
were brought down to a human scale in the Rococo,
making it more suited to interiors, furniture, and architectural details than to architecture itself. *Departure*

Figure 16.6 Jean-Antoine Watteau. *The Sign for Gersaint's Shop.* Ca. 1720. Oil on canvas, 5'11⅝" × 10'1⅛". Stiftung Preussischer Kulturbesitz, Schloss Charlottenburg, Berlin. *This painting of a shop interior illustrates the social dynamics of the emerging art market in the eighteenth century. The aristocratic customers act as if they own the place, turning it into a genteel lounge. The shop employees, on the other hand, have clearly inferior social roles; one brings forward a heavy painting for inspection, another holds a miniature work up to view, and a third stands downcast at the left. Through such details, Watteau reveals the social gulf between classes that was implicit in the Rococo style.*

from Cythera shows the Rococo to be a refined, sensual style, perfect for providing a charming backdrop to the private social life of the eighteenth-century aristocracy.

In one of his last works, *The Sign for Gersaint's Shop*, Watteau removed all mythological and idyllic references (Figure 16.6). His subject, a shop where paintings are sold (François-Edmé Gersaint [1696–1750] was one of the outstanding art dealers of the eighteenth century), indicates the importance of the new commercial art market that was soon to replace the aristocratic patronage system. Art collecting in the Age of Louis XIV had been restricted largely to kings, princes, and nobles. Within Gersaint's shop, elegantly dressed customers browse, flirt, and study the shopkeeper's wares. The sexual motifs in the pictures on the walls and in the oval canvas on the right reinforce the sensuous atmosphere of this painting. But Watteau also makes this Parisian scene dignified by giving equal focus to the human figures and the role each plays in the overall composition.

Watteau's painting is a telling metaphor of the end of one age and the beginning of another. This meaning can be interpreted in the crating of the portrait of Louis XIV (on the left), a punning metaphor for the demise of the old political order and the style of Louis XIV. In effect, the painting shows that, in the Rococo period, many new collectors came from the world of the upper bourgeoisie and shopped in commercial galleries like Gersaint's shop.

Watteau's paintings convey a dreamy eroticism, but those of François Boucher [boo-SHAY] (1703–1770) are characterized by unabashed sexuality. Boucher was the supreme exponent of the graceful Louis XV style, becoming official painter to the French crown in 1765. His voluptuous nudes, which were made more titillating by their realistic portrayal without Classical trappings, appealed to the king and to the decadent court nobility. Boucher's *Nude on a Sofa* is probably a study of one of Louis XV's mistresses (Figure 16.7). The casually suggestive pose, the rumpled bedclothes, and the

Figure 16.7 FRANÇOIS BOUCHER. *Nude on a Sofa.* 1752. Oil on canvas, 23⅜ × 25⅜". Alte Pinakothek, Munich. *The trend toward the secularization of consciousness that had been building since the Late Middle Ages reached a high point in this nude by Boucher. Boucher's frank enjoyment of sensual pleasure and his desire to convey that feeling to the viewer represented a new stage in the relationship between artists and the public. By portraying his subject without any justification except eroticism, Boucher embodied a new artistic sensibility.*

delicate pastel shades are all designed to charm and to seduce. Boucher's art, though masterful, epitomizes the lax morals of French noble life that were becoming increasingly offensive even to other Rococo artists.

A different focus is evident in the Rococo portraits of Elisabeth-Louise Vigée-Lebrun [vee-ZHAY-luh-BRUHN] (1755–1842), who became the leading society painter of the later eighteenth century and one of the relatively few women to gain fame as an artist. In 1787, she painted a famous family portrait of Louis XVI's queen, Marie Antoinette, whom she served as court painter (Figure 16.8). With this work, Vigée-Lebrun solidified her status as the equal of the best court portraitists of the century. Elements of the Rococo style can be seen in this elegant portrait of the queen and her children in the dainty colors, the graceful gestures, and the feeling of domestic intimacy. The queen's role as mother is the focus as she sits with the baby Duke of Normandy in her lap, the small Madame Royale at her side, and the little Dauphin pointing at the empty cradle. Vigée-Lebrun's depiction of Marie Antoinette dressed as a lady of fashion instead of in the traditional trappings of royalty reflects the queen's well-known fondness for simplicity. Stifled by the formality of court life, the queen promoted a more relaxed social code at Le Hameau, a rustic hideaway she had built for herself at Versailles, where all rules of court etiquette were set aside.

The last great French Rococo painter, Jean-Honoré Fragonard [frag-uh-NAHR] (1732–1806), revived Watteau's graceful, debonair themes, as in *The Lover Crowned* (Figure 16.9). A young woman crowns her kneeling lover with a wreath of flowers, while an artist in the lower right corner sketches the enraptured pair. The man's red suit and the woman's yellow dress cause them to stand out dramatically from the setting in which they are placed. The terrace setting is rich in sensual, if not erotic, details, including rose blossoms, boxed orange trees, two guitars, and sheet music. The statue of a sleeping cupid, mounted on a pedestal, presides over this erotic episode.

What is fresh in Fragonard's art and prefigures Romanticism is his finely detailed treatment of the natural background, which, although resembling the idealized backgrounds of Watteau, has a vivid, luxuriant life of its own. In Fragonard's painting, nature seems almost to threaten the couple's romantic idyll. Despite his interest in landscape, however, Fragonard remained faithful to the Rococo style even after it fell out of fashion. His paintings continued to focus on the playful themes of flirtation and pursuit in a frivolous, timeless world.

Rococo Interiors The decorative refinement and graceful detail of the Rococo style made it well suited to interior design. A major Rococo design element was *rocaille:* fanciful stucco ornaments in the shape of ribbons, leaves, stems, flowers, interlaces, arabesques, and elongated, curving lines applied to walls and ceilings. The effect of *rocaille* was to make solid surfaces look like fleeting illusions. Mirrors further deceived the senses, and chandeliers provided jewel-like lighting;

492

Figure 16.8 Elisabeth-Louise Vigée-Lebrun. *Marie Antoinette and Her Children.* 1787. Oil on canvas, 9'1¼" × 7'⅝". Musée National du Château de Versailles. *Like the greatest court painters, Vigée-Lebrun was able to provide psychological insight into her highborn subjects while flattering them. Here, Marie Antoinette, though surrounded by adoring children, seems uncomfortable in a maternal role. Instead, with her head held in an imperious manner and her face a beautiful mask, she looks every inch the lady of fashion, which she indeed was. Vigée-Lebrun has muted this psychological insight by providing rich distractions for the viewer's eye, such as the shiny surfaces of the queen's attire (satin gown, pearls, and hat) and the elegant room (carpet, chest, and tasseled cushion).*

Figure 16.9 Jean-Honoré Fragonard. *The Lover Crowned.* 1771–1773. Oil on panel, 10'5⅛" × 7'11¾". The Frick Collection, New York. *This painting was one of a series of four panels known as* The Progress of Love, *commissioned by Madame du Barry, Louis XV's mistress and rival to Madame de Pompadour. Intended to adorn a pavilion nicknamed the "sanctuary of pleasure" at her palace, the panels were rejected by Madame du Barry, for reasons unknown, before they were installed. Like the other panels in this series,* The Lover Crowned *is a symbolic allegory. In effect, the couple's love has been consummated, as symbolized by the floral wreath and the sleeping cupid. All that remains is for the artist, a reference to Fragonard himself, to transform the lovers' passion into a work of art.*

Figure 16.10 GERMAIN BOFFRAND. Salon de la Princesse, Hôtel de Soubise. Ca. 1735–1740. Paris. *The Salon de la Princesse was a reception room designed for the apartment of the Princess de Soubise. The graceful undulations of Boffrand's design represent the exquisite style of the Louis XV era. A typical Rococo design element is the blurring of the line between the walls and the ceiling.*

all elements worked together to create a glittering, luxurious setting for an ultrarefined society.

Germain Boffrand [bo-FRAHN] (1667–1754), France's royal architect, helped to establish Rococo's popularity with his "Salon de la Princesse" in the Hôtel de Soubise in Paris (Figure 16.10). Exploiting the room's oval shape, Boffrand eliminated the shadows and omitted Classical details such as pilasters and columns, which had been elements of decoration since the Renaissance. The floor-to-ceiling windows admit light freely, and the strategically placed mirrors reinforce the airy feeling. Instead of using a large overhead fresco, Boffrand divided the ceiling into many panel pictures. The characteristically nervous Rococo line—seen in the intricate designs of the gold edging—integrates the interior into a harmonious whole. The overall effect of airiness, radiance, and grace is worthy of a Watteau setting of aristocratic revelry.

German decoration followed the French lead. The Residenz, a palace commissioned by the prince-bishop of the German city of Würzburg, is an example of Baroque architecture with Rococo interiors. Designed chiefly by Balthasar Neumann [NOI-mahn] (1687–1753), the building's glory is the main reception room, called the Kaisersaal, or Emperor's Room (Figure 16.11). The ceiling frescoes are by Giovanni Battista Tiepolo [tee-AY-puh-loh] (1696–1770), an Italian-born

Rococo master. His paintings combine the theatricality of the Italian Florid Baroque and the love of light and color characteristic of Rubens and the Flemish school (see Chapter 14). But Tiepolo's frescoes are only one facet of the riotous splendor of this room, which abounds in crystal chandeliers, gilt ornamentation, marble statues, Corinthian capitals and arabesques, gold-edged mirrors, and cartouches, or scroll-like frames. In rooms such as this, the age's painters and decorators catered to their patrons' wildest dreams of grandeur.

The English Response In Great Britain, where the Rococo was condemned as tasteless and corrupt, the painter William Hogarth (1697–1764) won fame as a social satirist, working in a style quite different from that of his French contemporaries. Even though his mocking works appealed to all social groups, the Protestant middle class most enthusiastically welcomed his biting satires. In the paintings, which sometimes ridicule idle aristocrats and always take a moralistic view of life, his bourgeois admirers discovered the same values that caused them to embrace the English novel. Taking advantage of his popularity, Hogarth made engravings of his paintings, printing multiple copies—the first major artist to take this step to reach a new clientele.

Figure 16.11 BALTHASAR NEUMANN AND OTHERS. Kaisersaal, the Residenz. View toward the south wall. 1719–1744. Würzburg, Germany. *In this magnificent room, the ceiling fresco by Tiepolo is gorgeously framed with multicolored marble curtains pulled back by stucco angels. Other sumptuous details include ornate framed paintings, cartouches, and mirrors; gilded Corinthian capitals and arabesques; and crystal chandeliers suspended low over a polychrome marble floor.*

Among the most popular of Hogarth's moral works was the series of paintings that depict the course of a loveless marriage between a profligate nobleman and the daughter of a wealthy middle-class businessman. Entitled *Marriage à la Mode*, this series comprises six scenes that show in exquisite detail the bitter consequences of an arranged marriage by following the husband and the wife to their untimely deaths. In the fourth episode, called *The Countess' Levée*, or *Morning Party*, Hogarth portrays the wife plotting a rendezvous with a potential lover (Figure 16.12). In this scene, which was typical of the age's aristocratic entertainments, the hostess is having her hair curled while the would-be suitor lounges on a sofa, charming her with conversation. Nearby, guests, servants, and musicians play their supporting roles in this sad tale. Hogarth, never willing to let the viewers draw their own conclusions, provides the moral lesson. In the right foreground, a black child-servant points to a small horned creature—a symbol of the cuckold, or the deceived husband—thus alluding to the wife's planned infidelity. Even the paintings on the walls echo Hogarth's theme of sexual abandon.

The Challenge of Neoclassicism

Soon after the middle of the eighteenth century, the Rococo began to be supplanted by a new style, known as **Neoclassical.** With its backward glance to the restrained style of antiquity, the Neoclassical had its origins both in a rejection of the Rococo and in a fascination with the new archeological discoveries made at midcentury. Knowledge about Pompeii and Herculaneum—the Roman cities buried by Mt. Vesuvius in 79 C.E., with excavations beginning in 1738 and 1748, respectively—had greatly heightened the curiosity of educated Europeans about the ancient world. At the same time, scholars began to publish books that showed Greek art to be the original source of ancient Classicism. The English authorities James Stuart and Nicholas Revett pointed out the differences between Greek and Roman art in *The Antiquities of Athens*, published in 1762. In 1764, the German Johann Joachim Winckelmann (1717–1768) distinguished Greek sculpture from the Roman in his *History of Art*—a study that led to the founding of the academic discipline of art history. The importance of Neoclassicism is indicated by the decision made in 1775 by the Paris Salon—the exhibition (biennial to 1831 and annual thereafter) that introduced the latest paintings to the public—to rebuff works with Rococo subjects and to encourage those with Classical themes.

Neoclassical Painting   In 1775, the same year the Salon began to promote Neoclassicism, Louis XVI appointed Joseph-Marie Vien to head the Académie de France in Rome, a leading art school. A strict discipli-

Figure 16.12 WILLIAM HOGARTH. *The Countess' Levée,* or *Morning Party,* from *Marriage à la Mode.* 1743–1745. Oil on canvas, 27 × 35". Reproduced by courtesy of the Trustees, The National Gallery, London. *Hogarth's painterly techniques—learned in France—have transformed a potentially banal topic into a glittering social satire. On the left, a pig-snouted singer is used to ridicule the popular* castrati—*men who were emasculated as youths to preserve their boyish tenor voices. Hovering over the* castrato *is a flutist—his coarse features demonstrating the artist's loathing for this social type. Other rich details, such as the tea-sipping dandy in hair curlers and the female guest who is gesticulating wildly, confirm Hogarth's contempt for the entire gathering.*

narian, Vien returned the study of art to the basics by instructing his students to focus on perspective, anatomy, and life drawing, efforts that resulted in the purified style of Jacques-Louis David [dah-VEED] (1748–1825), the principal exponent of the Neoclassical style.

David's response to a commission from Louis XVI for a historical painting was *Oath of the Horatii,* a work that electrified the Salon of 1785 (Figure 16.13). Taking a page from the history of the early Roman republic,

this painting depicts the brothers Horatii vowing to protect the state, even though their stand means killing a sister who loves one of Rome's enemies. The patriotic subject with its tension between civic duty and family loyalty appealed to the *philosophes,* who preferred Neoclassicism, with its implicitly revolutionary morality, to the Rococo, with its frivolous themes.

David's *Oath of the Horatii* established the techniques and ideals that soon became typical of Neoclassical painting. His inspirational model was the

Figure 16.13 JACQUES-LOUIS DAVID. *Oath of the Horatii.* 1785. Oil on canvas, 10'10" × 14'. Louvre. *David achieved a Classical effect in his works by arranging the figures so that they could be read from left to right as in a sculptural frieze and by giving them the idealized bodies of Classical art. He further enhanced the sense that his central figures had been sculptured instead of painted by omitting distracting details. The resulting stark images contrast sharply with Rococo paintings and their luxuriant backgrounds (see Figures 16.5 and 16.9).*

ENCOUNTER

Chinoiserie: Fantasy of the East

Cultural borrowing usually means cultural adaptation, rather than "pure" appropriation, because receiving cultures tend to process new ideas according to traditional tastes and habits of thought. Such was the situation in the eighteenth century, when the Chinese style took the West by storm. **Chinoiserie** *[shen-WAZ-uh-ree] (French, Chinois, "China"), as the Chinese style was called, was not a pure style but a Western fantasy of the East—an early version of what has come to be called Orientalism. The West's taste for Chinese culture embraced mainly the decorative arts and, to a lesser extent, Chinese writings.*

In the 1700s, Chinoiserie became a fashionable style for the West's rich and powerful, including those in the English colonies in the New World. This style, with its elaborate decoration and intricate patterns, was used for interior design, furniture, pottery, textiles, and garden design. While its roots dated from the age of Marco Polo (late thirteenth century), the heyday of Chinoiserie was about 1740 to 1770. The style lingered on until about 1850, dying out with the arrival in the West of more reliable information about Chinese culture.

Not historically accurate, Chinoiserie was inspired by travelers' accounts (see Encounter in Chapter 12), imported wares from the Far East, particularly in countries with East India companies—England (1600), Holland (1602), and France (1664)—or trade depots in China (Portugal, in Macao [1553]), and the vivid imagination of Western craftspeople, artists, and designers, who drew freely on Chinese decorative design. In the 1600s, Chinese goods, such as cabinets, porcelain vessels, and embroideries, flooded the European market. Soon, new centers specializing in Chinese-style wares but cheaper than the imports sprang up across Europe. In Delft, the Netherlands, tin-glazed earthenware, sometimes called delftware, began to be manufactured in about 1600, and shortly thereafter, the blue-and-white pattern became the town's signature style, in imitation of blue-and-white Ming dynasty (1368–1644) porcelain. Except for novelty items, delftware—tiles, china, jugs, basins, vases, and various vessels—is free of figures in its design. In Meissen, Germany, near Dresden, Europe's first hard-paste porcelain factory, using only hand labor, was established in 1710. Having mastered the secret Chinese formula for porcelain—clay fired into a vitrified, or glasslike, form—the Meissen workers created Chinese

shapes for dishes, vases, and tea sets, handpainting them with fanciful designs, such as mountain scenes with a solitary figure, dragons and phoenixes, outdoor pavilions and pagodas, and monkeys gamboling along intricate borders (Encounter figure 16.1).

The Chinoiserie fad influenced both interior and exterior design. Style-conscious people designated a Chinese room, with lacquered furniture, decorated screens, and precious objects, in their palaces or townhouses, as did France's King Louis XIV at Versailles in 1671. Louis XIV's example set the pace until the rise of Neoclassicism in the late eighteenth century. Chinese design merged seamlessly with the Rococo, to create what has been called the **Chinese Rococo**—characterized by gilding and lacquering, Oriental shapes and

Encounter figure 16.1 Cup. Meissen Factory, Germany. Ca. 1725. Approx. 1.7 × 3". Cleveland Museum of Art. 1919.1022. *This cup is an early example of Meissen ware, produced in the first twenty years after the 1710 founding of the porcelain factory. The design—a stooped, full-length Chinese man portrayed against a cloudless sky, carrying a full tray, flanked by an interlocking foliate pattern on the left and right, and the scene topped by a pagoda-style "roof"—shows a European interpretation of a Chinese scene. The gilt and enamel design stands out starkly against the pure white background of the translucent porcelain—the signature look of Meissen in the early eighteenth century. After 1770, European subjects were supplanting Oriental themes in Meissen ware.*

themes, and unusual perspectives. The Chinese garden, with its irregular shapes that imitate the irregularity of nature and its curved roof pagodas, or towers, and gazebos, influenced garden design. In England, the homegrown English garden, so carefully planned to look "unplanned," was merged with the Chinese version to create the Anglo-Chinese garden. Kew Gardens, outside London, is an elegant, surviving example of the Anglo-Chinese garden (Encounter figure 16.2).

The fashion for all things Chinese reflected the global yearnings of the West's elite classes. At a time when cross-continental travel was difficult if not impossible, and international trade was a precarious but profitable undertaking, sophisticated people eagerly sought knowledge of exotic lands, along with acquiring status products from those regions—as evidence of their cultivated taste. Chinese culture was especially admired for its philosophical, literary, and artistic traditions, which sometimes seemed in advance of the West. A sign of the West's high regard for Chinese literature was the successful play *Orphan of China*, by Voltaire, the Age of Reason's leading writer. Based on a play by Chi Chun-hsiang during the Mongol dynasty (1279–1368), *Orphan of China* opened in Paris in 1755. With Chinese-style sets and costumes, this drama has been described as the first historic spectacle in Western theater. Just as Chinoiserie represented Chinese taste adapted to Western palates, Voltaire similarly altered the Chinese source to suit his political purposes. He made the hero Genghis Khan a stand-in for France's Louis XV, showing him to be a power-mad ruler. Voltaire was fond of this play, and he even acted the part of Genghis Khan in amateur productions at Ferney, Switzerland, his home when in exile from Paris. There, in 1757, the English historian Gibbon judged Voltaire's performance thus: "I was . . . struck with the ridiculous figure of Voltaire at seventy acting a Tartar Conqueror with a hollow broken voice, and making love to a very ugly niece of about fifty."

Learning from the Encounter Define *Chinoiserie.* **What** are the distinguishing characteristics of the "Chinese style"? **Discuss** the impact of Chinese influence on Western interior design, garden design, literature, pottery, and furniture. **How** does "pure" Chinese style differ from Chinoiserie? **What** are some of the reasons for the adoption of Chinese influences by Westerners in the 1700s? **Discuss** Chinoiserie today in the West, in films, commerce, and food.

Encounter figure 16.2 WILLIAM CHAMBERS. The Pagoda. 1761. Ht. 163'; lowest story 49' diameter. Kew Gardens, United Kingdom. © Copyright Colin Smith and licensed for reuse under this Creative Commons License. TQ1876. *The architect William Chambers (1723–1796) was unusual for this period, because he had traveled to the Chinese port of Guangzhou (Canton) in his youth. Thus, his design for the Pagoda at Kew Gardens—one of several garden buildings he designed there—was actually based on firsthand knowledge, rather than the fanciful imaginings of other artists and designers of the time. An imitation of an actual Chinese pagoda, Chambers's Pagoda stands ten stories tall, with projecting roofs on each level and dragons (eighty in all) positioned at each of the roof angles. The structure has been heavily restored, because of damage from bombs during World War II. Originally a private preserve, Kew Gardens became a royal garden in 1759.*

Figure 16.14 JACQUES-LOUIS DAVID. *The Death of Socrates.* 1787. Oil on canvas, 4'11" × 6'6". Metropolitan Museum of Art. Wolfe Fund, 1931. *Neoclassicism usually relied on ancient literature and traditions for inspiration, as in this painting by David. The scene is based on Plato's dialogue* Phaedo, *though David has chosen to depict Plato present (at the foot of the bed), unlike in the literary account. Two of the domestic details, the lamp and the bed, are modeled on artifacts uncovered at Pompeii. The shackles and cuffs under the bed refer to the fact that Socrates was in chains just before drinking the hemlock.*

seventeenth-century French artist Poussin, with his Classical themes and assured mastery of linear perspective. Rejecting the weightless, floating images of Rococo painting, David portrayed his figures as frozen sculptures, painted in strong colors. The Classical ideals of balance, simplicity, and restraint served as a basis for many of David's artistic choices.

David showed his mastery of these techniques and ideals in *The Death of Socrates*, which was exhibited in the Salon of 1787 (Figure 16.14). Like Jesus in scenes of the Last Supper, Socrates is portrayed shortly before his death, encircled by those men who will later spread his message. Just as in *Oath of the Horatii*, David's arrangement of the figures reflected the Classical ideal of balance. Surrounded by grieving followers, the white-haired Socrates reaches for the cup of poison and gestures toward his heavenly goal—serene in his willingness to die for intellectual freedom.

The Print   As demands for art grew in England and France, prints became popular among the middle class. These new patrons wanted art for collecting and for decorating their homes, but they could not afford original paintings. Prints, which had been produced since the mid–fifteenth century (see Chapter 10), turned out to be the solution. And the prints now available were for the first time in color, though only to a limited degree. Color prints dated from Rembrandt's era, when some Dutch printmakers pioneered the mezzotint and the aquatint. Both types of prints came into their own in the eighteenth century.

The **mezzotint** (half-tone), which requires several stages of cutting and scraping the metal plate with special tools to make an image, allows for subtle gradations of shadings along with precise lines to give greater definition. In the late 1600s, Dutch engravers arrived in London, where they trained a generation of

Figure 16.15 PHILIBERT-LOUIS DEBUCOURT. *The Public Promenade.* 1792. Etching, engraving, and aquatint, 14⅜ × 23¼". The Elisha Whittelsey Collection, The Elisha Whittelsey Fund, Metropolitan Museum, New York. *Aquatints, such as this, appealed to the middle class, because the prints, besides being relatively inexpensive, were able to imitate the look of a watercolor painting, with their subtle shadings of color and shadow. The blues are set among spots of pink and white, and the darker trees around the periphery frame the scene. In the center, vivid colors highlight this gathering of fashionable society on parade. The artist Debucourt [de-BOO-cour] (1755–1832) satirizes his subjects, through their opulent dress and haughty manners, as they disport themselves in the gardens of the Palais Royale—an eighteenth-century public area only in the sense that it was reserved for the social elite.*

artists in the mezzotint technique. In the 1700s, William Hogarth and other English printmakers popularized mezzotint prints by making inexpensive reproductions of original paintings and copies of their own works. Connoisseurs and art patrons collected the more valuable first-run mezzotints, while the less wealthy middle classes bought the cheaper mass-produced prints.

In comparison to the mezzotint, aquatints fell out of favor soon after their first appearance. However, in the late eighteenth century, Jean-Baptiste Le Prince (1734–1781) wrote a manual on the technique and began to print aquatints in France. Other printmakers soon joined him in Paris. Across the channel, Paul Sandby (1730–1809), a watercolorist—famous for his landscapes—was the first English painter to replicate

his drawings in aquatints. An attempt to create the effect of a watercolor, **aquatints** were labor intensive and time-consuming to make. First, the image was cut into the copper plate with a metal tool. Then, the plate was dusted with a resin and the plate heated. As the resin melted, an irregular pattern of open and closed spaces was formed over the plate's image. Next, the plate was subjected to an acid wash (*aqua fortis,* nitric acid—the source of the name *aquatint*), etching only those areas around the solid resin and creating a fine, grainy pattern, capable of holding color. Finally, watercolor was applied by hand, either to the plate or to the print itself. By 1800, English and French collectors were purchasing aquatints (Figure 16.15). With the rise of improved methods of color printing after 1830, the aquatint process soon faded away.

Figure 16.16   ROBERT ADAM. Kenwood House. 1764. Exterior, the north front. London. *Adam's restrained style in the late eighteenth century represented a strong reinfusion of Classical principles into the English tradition. His style, with its reliance on the Classical orders and principles of balance and proportion, appealed to all classes but especially to the sober-minded middle class.*

Neoclassical Architecture No other painter could compare with David, but the Scotsman Robert Adam (1728–1792) developed a Neoclassical style in interior decor that was the reigning favorite from 1760 until 1800. Classicism had dominated British architecture since the 1600s, and Adam reinvigorated this tradition with forms and motifs gathered during his archeological investigations. Kenwood House in London shows his application of Roman design to the exterior of a domestic dwelling, combining Ionic columns, a running frieze, and a triangular pediment to form a graceful portico, or porch, in the manner of a Roman temple (Figure 16.16). In the library, Adam mixed Classical elements with the pastel colors of the Rococo to produce an eclectic harmony (Figure 16.17). To continue this theme, he borrowed from Roman buildings with his barrel-vaulted ceiling and adjoining apse.

French architects too began to embrace the Neoclassical style in the late 1700s. The leader of this movement was Jacques-Germain Soufflot [soo-FLOH] (1713–1780), who designed buildings based on Roman temples. Soufflot's severe Neoclassicism is characterized by its reliance on architectural detail rather than on sculptural decoration. Avoiding Adam's occasional intermingling of Rococo and Classical effects, Soufflot preferred pure Roman forms. The most perfect expression of Soufflot's style is the Pantheon in Paris. Soufflot's Classical ideal is mirrored in the Pantheon's basic plan, with its enormous portico supported by huge Corinthian columns (Figure 16.18). Except for the statues in the pediment, the building's surface is almost devoid of sculptural detail. The only other decoration on the stark exterior is a frieze of stone garlands around the upper walls. For the dome, Soufflot found his inspiration not in Rome but in London—a sign that English architecture had come of age: The Pantheon's spectacular dome, with its surrounding Corinthian colonnade, is based on the dome of St. Paul's cathedral (see Figure 14.24).

Philosophy

The Age of Reason proved to be a seminal period in the history of Western thought. During this period, the philosophy of David Hume, one of the founders of modern philosophy, appeared, and two landmark books in the history of political thought were published.

Figure 16.17 ROBERT ADAM. Library, Kenwood House. Begun in 1767. London. *Adam designed the library of Kenwood House with several basic elements of Classical architecture: columns, pilasters, and apses. By and large, he followed the Renaissance dictum of letting the architectural elements determine the chamber's decorative details. Nonetheless, he achieved a dazzling effect by his daring addition of mirrors and color.*

Political Philosophy Modern political theory continued to evolve after its founding in the seventeenth century. Absolutism, the reigning form of government in the eighteenth century, still had many staunch defenders. Voltaire, convinced that the people lacked political wisdom, advocated enlightened despotism. But the other leading *philosophes* of the Age of Reason rejected absolutism and supported alternative forms of government.

The Enlightenment's chief political theorists were Baron de Montesquieu and Jean-Jacques Rousseau, whose contrasting social origins probably to some extent account for their radically different definitions of the ideal state. Montesquieu, a titled Frenchman and a provincial judge, believed that rule by an enlightened aristocracy would ensure justice and tranquility. Rousseau, an impoverished citizen of the Swiss city-state of Geneva, advocated a kind of pure democracy. Rousseau's ideas about who should control the state were more far-reaching and revolutionary than Montesquieu's.

Montesquieu [mahnt-us-KYOO] (1689–1755) most persuasively expressed his political ideas in *The Spirit of the Laws* (1748), a work that compares systems of government in an effort to establish underlying principles. He concludes that climate, geography, religion, and education, among other factors, account for the world's different types of laws as well as governmental systems. Despite his misunderstanding of the roles of climate and geography, Montesquieu's analytical approach identified influences on governments that had not been considered before. One enduring idea in *The Spirit of the Laws* is that a separation of governmental powers provides an effective defense against despotic rule. Montesquieu was an admirer of England's parliamentary democracy and of the work of the English political philosopher John Locke (see

Chapter 15), whose influence is evident here. American patriots adopted this principle of the separation of powers in the 1780s when they framed the Constitution, dividing the federal government's power into executive, legislative, and judicial branches.

In contrast to the conservative Montesquieu, Jean-Jacques Rousseau [roo-SOH] (1712–1778) framed his

Figure 16.18 JACQUES-GERMAIN SOUFFLOT. The Pantheon. 1755–1792. Paris. *By 1789, advanced thinkers in France had begun to appropriate Classical images for their movement, with David's Neoclassical paintings leading the way. When the revolution began, its leaders determined to build a suitable monument to house the remains of those* philosophes *whose works had furthered the cause of reform. Hence, it was natural that the revolutionary government turn Soufflot's Classical church—with its portico modeled from Roman styles—into a patriotic shrine.*

political theories within a more libertarian tradition. Rousseau set forth his model of the ideal state in *The Social Contract,* published in 1762. He agreed with John Locke that human beings are free and equal in nature, but he defined the "state of nature" as a paradoxical condition in which individuals can follow any whim and hence possess no moral purpose. On the other hand, the state, which is founded on a social contract (an agreement among people), gives its citizens basic civil rights (freedom, equality, and property) and a moral purpose—precisely the things that they lack in nature. That morality arises within the civil state is a function of the "General Will," Rousseau's term for what is best for the entire community. If each citizen is granted the right to vote, and if each citizen votes on the laws in accord with the General Will, then the laws will embody what is best for the whole society. Thus, in Rousseau's thinking, citizens who obey the laws become moral beings. (It should be noted that who defines and implements the General Will and how it affects individual freedom remain ambiguous in *The Social Contract.*)

In contrast to Locke's form of democracy, whereby a representative group such as a legislature acts in the name of the people, Rousseau's asserted that the people themselves collectively personify the state through the General Will. Rousseau's ideal state, therefore, has to be relatively small so that all citizens can know and recognize one another. His model for the ideal state was based on his experience as a citizen of the tiny Genevan republic. Nevertheless, Rousseau has had an incalculable influence on thinkers and politicians concerned about much larger states. Indeed, his impact in the nineteenth century extended far beyond democratic circles. Nationalistic philosophers such as G. W. F. Hegel borrowed Rousseau's theory of the all-encompassing state, and radical theorists such as Karl Marx adopted his doctrine of the General Will (see Chapters 17 and 18).

David Hume   David Hume (1711–1776), a close friend of fellow Scotsman Adam Smith (see page 484), was a philosopher and historian. His *History of England,* in six volumes, became the standard for generations. From 1763 to 1766, he served at the British embassy in Paris, where he was honored by the French *philosophes.* He later returned to Edinburgh, where he was the leader of the Scottish Enlightenment.

Hume first laid out his philosophy in *A Treatise of Human Nature* (1739–1740), which he continued to revise over the rest of his life. His argument in this treatise is subversive, as he undermines that which he claims to defend. He begins in the critical spirit of the Age of Reason and ends up advocating skepticism. He follows the empirical ("knowledge comes from experi-

ence") method of the English thinker John Locke. However, revising Locke's dictum that all "ideas" in the mind are first in the senses, he denies the existence of "the mind," holding that it is simply a grab-bag of mental images. He then shows that Locke's dictum leads, not to certainty, but to **solipsism,** the belief that all that can be known is one's own mental world. Hume reached this controversial conclusion by breaking down "ideas" into (a) sense impressions and (b) mental images formed as a result of these impressions. Thus, two worlds exist: the subjective world, which can be known and worked with but which contains no guarantee of its objective truth; and the external world, which is perceived, if at all, through a screen of "ideas."

Hume also applied his empirical-skeptical method to **causality**—the idea that one event in the world "causes" another. He knew that such reasoning was typical of human thinking on empirical matters. In the end, he concluded that cause and effect is not communicated to the mind through the senses; it is merely an assumption made about the world. In other words, the notion of causality rests on habit. Later thinkers have found it difficult to refute Hume's skepticism.

Hume was also controversial for his religious views. His known skepticism kept him from a professor's chair at Edinburgh University. To live in peace, he arranged to have printed after his death the *Dialogues Concerning Natural Religion* (1779), an atheistic work that called God "an empty hypothesis."

Literature

Western literature in the Age of Reason was dominated by French authors and the French language, which now replaced Latin as the international language of scholarship, diplomacy, and commerce. French writers made common cause with the progressive *philosophes,* sharing their faith in a glorious future. They wrote for the growing middle-class audience that was replacing the aristocratic patrons. Because these authors were under the constant threat of state censorship, they were often forced to disguise their more barbed social criticisms or to sugarcoat their beliefs. Those restrictions did not, however, deter them from their mission to liberate the consciousness of their readers and usher in an enlightened society.

French Writers: The Development of New Forms
The two political philosophers discussed earlier—Montesquieu and Rousseau—were also prominent figures in French literature. Early in his career, Montesquieu wrote *Persian Letters,* a cleverly devised, wide-ranging critique of French institutions and cus-

toms in the guise of letters purporting to be written by and to Persian travelers during a trip to Paris. Through the eyes of the "Persians," Montesquieu ridiculed the despotism of the French crown, the idleness of the aristocracy, and the intolerance of the Roman Catholic Church. His device of the detached observer of Western life was a safeguard against censorship, as was the decision to print *Persian Letters* in the Netherlands. Montesquieu's publication inspired a new type of literature, a genre in which a "foreign" traveler voices the author's social criticisms.

Rousseau foreshadowed the Romantic sensibility of the next century with his intensely personal autobiography, *The Confessions*. Published after his death, this work was the frankest self-revelation that had yet been seen in print. It narrated Rousseau's lifelong follies and difficulties, including sexual problems, religious vacillation, a mismatched marriage, and his decision to place his five offspring in an orphanage as soon as each was born. Not only did he reveal his personal secrets, but he also tried to justify his failings, pleading with his audience that they not judge him too harshly. The revelations shocked many readers, but others praised him for his emotional truthfulness and were willing to overlook his rather self-serving treatment of a number of the facts of his own life. After Rousseau's candid admissions, the genre of autobiography was never the same again.

The third great French writer of the eighteenth century was François-Marie Arouet, better known by his pen name, Voltaire (1694–1778)—the outspoken leader of the Age of Reason and the *philosophe* who best personifies the Enlightenment (Figure 16.19). A restless genius, Voltaire earned success in many forms, including dramas, essays, poems, histories, treatises, novels, a philosophical dictionary, letters, and the first work of history—the *Essay on Customs*—to survey civilization from a world perspective.

Of Voltaire's voluminous writings, only one work is still widely read today: the novel *Candide*, published in 1759. The most popular novel of the Age of Reason, *Candide* exhibits Voltaire's urbane style, his shrewd mixture of philosophy and wit, and his ability to jolt the reader with an unexpected word or detail. Beneath its frivolous surface, this work has the serious purpose of ridiculing the fashionable optimism of eighteenth-century thinkers who, Voltaire believed, denied the existence of evil and insisted that the world was essentially good.

At one time an optimist himself, Voltaire altered his beliefs about evil after the 1755 Lisbon earthquake, a calamity that figures prominently in *Candide*. This comic adventure tale recounts the coming of age of the aptly named Candide, who is introduced to optimism by Dr. Pangloss, a caricature of a German professor.

Figure 16.19 JEAN-ANTOINE HOUDON. *Voltaire*. 1780. Lifesize. Bibliothèque Nationale, Paris. *Houdon's Neoclassical portrait in plaster of Voltaire shows the sculptor's determination to portray his subject as an ancient Roman. Houdon seated Voltaire in an armchair copied from ancient models and draped him in an ample robe that suggested Roman dress (but was actually based on the robe worn by the great* philosophe *to keep out the cold). He endowed his sculpture with a vivid sense of life, as may be seen in the fine details and the expressive face.*

The naive hero suffers many misfortunes—war, poverty, religious bigotry, trial by the Inquisition, shipwreck—and through them all holds fast to Pangloss's teaching that "this is the best of all possible worlds." But finally, faced with mounting incidents of pain and injustice, Candide renounces optimism. The story ends with the hero's newly acquired wisdom for combating the evils of boredom, vice, and want: "We must cultivate our garden."

Neoclassicism in English Literature   In England, the presence of a Protestant middle class, which was growing larger and increasingly literate, created a demand for a literature that was decorous, conservative, and basically moralistic and religious in tone, even if that religion were little more than deference to nature and nature's God. The poetry of Alexander Pope and the monumental historical work of Edward Gibbon are typical of this style of literature, which is referred to as Neoclassical.

Alexander Pope (1688–1744) is the most representative voice of the English Neoclassical style. His poems celebrate the order and decorum that were prized by the middle classes—the social group from which he sprang. He became his age's leading spokesman for humane values such as reason, Classical learning, good sense and good taste, and hatred of hypocrisy and ostentation. His verses, marked by their satirical tone and sophisticated wit, made Pope the supreme inspiration of the Age of Reason until the Romantics, led by William Wordsworth in the 1790s, turned away from the Neoclassical ideal.

Pope wrote many kinds of poetry—pastorals, elegies, and satires, among others—but the work closest to the spirit of the Age of Reason is his *Essay on Man,* a didactic work combining philosophy and verse, published in 1733–1734. Issued in four sections and composed in rhymed couplets, this poem brings together one of the age's central ideas, optimism, and some notions inherited from antiquity. In the first section of this poem, Pope argues that God in his infinite power has created the best possible world—not a perfect universe—and that God's design rests on the concept of the great chain of being: Reaching from God to microscopic creatures, this chain links all living things together. Human beings occupy the chain's midpoint, where the human and animal species meet. Because of this position, two different natures fight in the human breast: "Created half to rise, and half to fall; / Great lord of all things, yet a prey to all."

Since humanity's place is unchanging, human reason is limited, and God does not make mistakes, humans should not question the divine plan. Pope concludes that "whatever is, is right." From this fatalistic principle it follows that what humans perceive as evil is simply misunderstood good. This qualified optimism was satirized by Voltaire in *Candide* through the character of Dr. Pangloss.

Having established a fatalistic outlook in the first section of *Essay on Man,* Pope became more optimistic in the remaining sections. Although God's ways may be unknowable, he reasoned that some truths may still be learned by human beings: "The proper study of mankind is man." From this belief he concluded that a paradise could be created on Earth if human beings would think and act rationally—an attitude dear to the hearts of the *philosophes.*

Edward Gibbon's (1737–1794) *History of the Decline and Fall of the Roman Empire* appeared in six volumes between 1776 and 1788. Gibbon's recognition was instant and universal; he was hailed across Europe both for the breadth of his historical knowledge and for the brilliance of his style. His subject, the history of Rome, appealed to the age's Classical interests, and his skepticism, notably regarding the Christian faith, echoed the sentiments of the *philosophes.* Although Gibbon's

authority as a scholar was eclipsed in the next century because of the progress of historical science, his work remains one of the Enlightenment's genuine literary masterpieces.

Gibbon's massive work reflects both the ancient historical tradition and the ideals of the Enlightenment. Following the ancient historians, Gibbon wrote with secular detachment and offered reasons for historical change based on human motives and natural causes. From the Enlightenment, he determined that history should be philosophy teaching through example. These influences come together in his history when he attributes Rome's decay to an unpatriotic and subversive Christian faith along with the Germanic invasions. In effect, Gibbon's history praises secular civilization and covertly warns against the perils of religious enthusiasm.

The Rise of the Novel   Despite the contributions of Pope and Gibbon to Western letters, the most important literary development in England during the Age of Reason was the rise of the modern novel. The hallmark of the early English novel was its realism. In the spirit of the Scientific Revolution, the new authors broke with the past and began to study the world with fresh eyes. Previous writers had based their plots on historical events or fables, but now individual experience became the keystone of the writer's art, and authors turned away from traditional plots in favor of an accurate representation of real-life events.

The English novel was realistic in several ways. It focused on individual persons rather than universal types and on particular circumstances rather than settings determined by literary custom. Furthermore, its plots followed the development of characters over the course of minutely observed time. The sense of realism was complete when the author adopted a narrative voice that contributed to the air of authenticity.

The novel captured the wholehearted attention of the reading public, including many women. The works of Samuel Richardson and Henry Fielding especially appealed to these new readers. The writings of these two Englishmen helped to define the modern novel and at the same time set the standards for later fiction. For centuries, tragedy, with its plots about aristocratic heroes and heroines, had been regarded as the highest literary form. But since the age of Richardson and Fielding, the novel, with its focus on ordinary people, has been and remains the dominant literary genre.

The novels of Samuel Richardson (1689–1761) focus on love between the sexes. For more than a thousand pages in *Pamela, or Virtue Rewarded* (1740) and almost two thousand pages in *Clarissa Harlowe* (1747–1748), he tells the contrasting stories of two young women whose virtue is sorely tested by repeated seduction attempts. Pamela, a resourceful and somewhat calculat-

SLICE OF LIFE
How to Manipulate the System

LADY MARY WORTLEY MONTAGU
Letter, 25 March 1744

Lady Montagu (1689–1762) was one of the great letter writers in the Western tradition. A free spirit and a keen observer, this Englishwoman lived apart from her husband, Lord Edward Wortley Montagu, for about twenty years, four of which were spent in Avignon, France. In this letter to her husband, Lady Mary explains how she was able to save a group of French Protestant Huguenots from being galley slaves.

I take this opportunity of informing you in what manner I came acquainted with the secret I hinted at in my letter of the 5th of Feb. The Society of Freemasons at Nîmes presented the Duke of Richelieu, governor of Languedoc, with a magnificent entertainment. It is but one day's post from hence, and the Duchess of Crillon with some other ladies of this town resolved to be at it, and almost by force carried me with them, which I am tempted to believe an act of Providence, considering my great reluctance and the service it proved to be to unhappy, innocent people.

The greatest part of the town of Nîmes are secret Protestants, which are still severely punished according to the edicts of Louis XIV whenever they are detected in any public worship. A few days before we came they had assembled; their minister and about a dozen of his congregation were seized and imprisoned. I knew nothing of this, but I had not been in the town two hours when I was visited by two of the most considerable of the Huguenots, who came to beg of me with tears to speak in their favour to the Duke of Richelieu, saying none of the Catholics would do it and the Protestants durst not, and that God had sent

me for their protection, [that] the Duke of Richelieu was too well bred to refuse to listen to a lady, and I was of a rank and nation to have liberty to say what I pleased. They moved my compassion so much I resolved to use my endeavours to serve them, though I had little hope of succeeding.

I would not therefore dress myself for the supper, but went in a domino to the ball, a mask giving opportunity of talking in a freer manner than I could have done without it. I was at no trouble in engaging his conversation. The ladies having told him I was there, he immediately advanced towards me, and I found from a different motive he had a great desire to be acquainted with me, having heard a great deal of me. After abundance of compliments of that sort, I made my request for the liberty of the poor Protestants. He with great freedom told me that he was so little a bigot, he pitied them as much as I did, but his orders from Court were to send them to the galleys. However, to show how much he desired my good opinion he was returning and would solicit their freedom (which he has since obtained).

Interpreting This Slice of Life   **What** is Lady Mary Wortley Montagu's motive for acting as she does? **What** is the religious situation in the town of Nîmes? **How** does Lady Montagu prevent the Huguenots from becoming galley slaves? **Compare** the tone and style of this letter with the way we write letters (or e-mails or text messages) today. **How** would you describe Lady Montagu?

---

ing maidservant, eventually finds happiness in marriage to her prosperous would-be seducer. Clarissa, from a higher social class but of weaker mettle, runs off with her seducer and dies of shame.

In contrast to Richardson's sentimental domestic dramas, the novels of Henry Fielding (1707–1754) depict a robust world of comedy and adventure. His best work is *The History of Tom Jones, a Foundling* (1749), a comic masterpiece that has been called the finest English novel. Tom, the hero, is a high-spirited young man who makes little effort to resist the temptations that come his way. His wealthy guardian rejects him for his immoral behavior, but Tom is shown to be good-hearted and honest and thus worthy of the good fortune that befalls him at the novel's end when he has

learned the virtues of moderation. The novel contains a great deal of amusing satire, aimed particularly at the upper classes.

Music

The standard in music in the early part of the eighteenth century was set by the French, as it was in art and decoration. Rococo music, like Rococo art, represented a reaction against the Baroque. Instead of the complex, formal structure of Baroque music, eighteenth-century French composers strove for a light and charming sound with graceful melodies over simple harmonies. Known as the *style galant* (gallant style), this music was particularly fashionable during the reign of Louis XV.

The perfect instrument for Rococo music was the harpsichord, a keyboard instrument whose strings are plucked, giving it a delicate, refined sound. At the same time, improved instruments, such as brasses and woodwinds, were joining the musical family, and the violin was perfected by Antonio Stradivari. The piano was invented in the first decade of the eighteenth century by Bartolomeo Cristofori, who installed a mechanism in a harpsichord that would strike the strings with hammers rather than pluck them. With this new instrument, a player could vary the loudness of the sound depending on the force exerted on the keys, something impossible to do on the harpsichord—thus the name **pianoforte,** from the Italian for "soft" and "loud."

The two outstanding composers of Rococo music were the Frenchmen François Couperin and Jean-Philippe Rameau. Couperin [koop-uh-RAN] (1668–1733) set the tone in court society for the early part of the eighteenth century. His finest works were written for the harpsichord; many contain dance pieces and are noted for their rhythmic virtuosity. His highly ornamented compositions are the perfect musical counterpart to Watteau's painting.

Rameau [rah-MOH] (1683–1764) shared Couperin's fascination with the harpsichord and small-scale works, but his major achievement was as a composer of dramatic operas. Following in the footsteps of the French-Italian operatic composer Jean-Baptiste Lully (see Chapter 14), he made a ballet sequence with a large corps of dancers a central feature of his operatic works. The best of his operas was *Hippolyte and Aricie* (1733), based on the French playwright Racine's tragedy *Phèdre.* Rameau heightened the tension of the gripping plot through his expressive music, underscoring the sexual tension between the doomed heroine and her stepson.

Like Rococo art, Rococo music was supplanted in the second half of the eighteenth century by the new **Classical style,** in which more serious expression seemed possible. An important characteristic of Classical music was its emphasis on form and structure. The most versatile and widely used form to emerge was the **sonata form,** in which a musical piece is written in three main sections, known as the exposition, the development, and the recapitulation. In the first, melodies and themes are stated; in the second, the same material is expanded and changed in various ways; and in the third, the themes are stated again but with richer harmonies and more complex associations for the listener.

The sonata form was also used as the basis for whole compositions, including the **symphony** (a com-position for orchestra), the concerto (a piece for a solo instrument and orchestra), and the sonata (a work for a small group of instruments). Such pieces often had three movements varying in **key, tempo,** and **mood.** The first was usually the longest and had a quick tempo. The second was slow and reflective, and the third was as quick as the first if not quicker. If there were four movements, the third was either a minuet, based on a French dance, or a **scherzo,** a lively Italian form. The sonata form provided general principles of composition that governed each movement and yet allowed composers to express their own ideas. Classical music retained the Rococo love of elegant melodic lines and clear, simple harmonies, but by using the sonata form, composers were able to add length and depth to their works.

A second basic form that helped define the Classical style was **theme and variations,** a technique in which a musical idea is stated and then repeated in variant versions. The theme and its variations are each about the same length, but each variation is unique and may vary in mood from the basic theme. Variations may diverge from the first theme in several ways, including changes in rhythm, dynamics, harmony, key, accompaniment, and **tone color**—the quality of the sound, determined by the overtones. The theme and a variation may be heard together, or played overlapping, or separated by pauses. Main themes may be inventions of a composer or a borrowed melody from an existing work. The theme and variations form has been used in independent works or for a single movement in a symphony, sonata, or chamber work.

Franz Joseph Haydn [HIDE-un] (1732–1809) was the first master of the Classical style. Haydn spent almost thirty years as music director at the palace of a Hungarian noble family, where his status was that of a skilled servant of the reigning prince. At his death, however, he was both comfortably well-off and famous throughout Europe. He is largely responsible for the development of the sonata form, and his 104 symphonies helped to define the standard, four-movement symphony. Despite their formal regularity, the symphonies show Haydn's inventiveness and sense of freedom as he experimented with a large and imaginative variety of moods and structures.

Haydn's most popular symphony today is Symphony No. 94 in G Major, generally known as the *Surprise* Symphony. First performed during Haydn's first visit to London in 1791, this work helped to establish Haydn's name with the concertgoing public there. The second movement, marked *andante* (Italian, "moderate speed"), is in the theme and variations form. The opening theme, evocative of the children's nursery rhyme "Twinkle, Twinkle, Little Star," begins softly but ends with a crashing chord—the *surprise* that

Figure 16.20 Performance of a Haydn Opera. *This print depicts a scene from Haydn's* L'in-contro improvviso, *or* The Chance Meeting, *staged around 1775 at Esterháza, the summer castle of the Esterházy family, his patron and employer. Dignitaries and music lovers flocked to Esterháza to hear Haydn's latest works and to walk the grounds. In the print, the proscenium stage, the painted scenery, the costumed singers, and the orchestra below in the pit indicate that the presentations of operas have not changed much over the past 230 years. Some scholars assert that Haydn is playing the harpsichord, at the lower left. Although isolated at Esterháza, Haydn's reputation grew, and his symphonies and concertos were performed across Europe.*

gives this symphony its nickname. Four variations follow, achieved through shifts in tone color, dynamics, rhythm, and melody. The movement concludes with a restatement of the core theme, as a dissonant accompaniment seems to mock the piece's lighthearted mood. Haydn's more than seventy string quartets, each composed for first and second violins, viola, and cello, became the accepted norm for this type of chamber music. His supreme innovation was to allow each instrument to show its independence from the rest. Although the first violin has the most prominent role, the musical effect of a Haydn quartet is of four persons conversing. His operas (about twenty), popular in his day, are now seldom performed (Figure 16.20).

However prodigious Haydn's efforts, they are overshadowed by the greatest exponent of the Classical style, Wolfgang Amadeus Mozart (1756–1791). From the age of six, he wrote music, alternating composing with performing. His travels around Europe as a child prodigy exposed him to the musical currents of his day, which he eagerly adapted into his own works. For

nine years of his adult life, he was a court musician in the service of the archbishop of Salzburg, a post that caused him great anguish because of its low social position. Unlike Haydn, he would not accept the conventional position of musician as a liveried (uniformed) servant of a wealthy patron. The last decade of his life was spent as a freelance musician in Vienna, where he died in extreme poverty. Despite his brief and tragic life, Mozart left a huge body of music that later generations have pronounced sublime.

Mozart's gift was not for creating new musical forms; Mozart already had at hand the sonata, the opera, the symphony, the theme and variations, and the quartet. Rather, his inimitable talent was for composing music with a seemingly effortless line of melody, growing naturally from the opening bars until the finale. His disciplined and harmonious works embody the spirit of the Enlightenment.

The transparency of Mozart's composing technique allowed him to give a unique stamp to every type of music that he touched, and he composed in every genre available to him. In vocal music, he composed religious works (such as Masses, oratorios, and an unfinished Requiem Mass) and dramatic works (for example, operas and a ballet). In instrumental music, he wrote orchestral and ensemble music, including symphonies, serenades, divertimentos, marches, minuets, and German dances; concertos for piano, violin, horn, flute, trumpet, and clarinet; chamber music for strings and winds; violin sonatas; and keyboard sonatas.

The light touch, which makes Mozart such a beloved composer, is nowhere more evident than in the work for small string orchestra *Eine Kleine Nachtmusik* (*A Little Night Music;* 1787), K. 525, one of his most often heard works today. Classified as a **serenade,** this lighthearted piece, in four movements, was composed for an evening's entertainment. The third movement is a **minuet and trio,** a Classical music form derived from a French court dance, also called the minuet. It begins with a stately melody whose loud staccato tones summon up images of the courtly bowings and curtsies of the dance's origin. As the minuet unfolds, each section is repeated. The minuet then yields to a quieter, smoothly flowing trio, also written as a dance-like melody with repeated phrases. The movement ends with a repeat of the opening stately melody and a concluding staccato phrase.

The fullest expression of Mozart's genius was reached in his operas, especially his comic operas, where he gave free rein to the playful side of his temperament, blending broad humor with dramatic characterization. His masterpiece in this genre is probably *The Marriage of Figaro,* based on a play by the French *philosophe* Pierre Beaumarchais [boh-mahr-SHAY] (1732–1799). Since its first performance in 1786, *Figaro's* knockabout humor and rich musical texture have made it one of the most popular works in the entire operatic repertory. Beneath the farcical scenes and the enchanting melodies, however, lies a serious theme: By allowing the servant Figaro to outwit his arrogant master, Mozart joined the growing ranks of those who criticized the privileged classes and attacked the injustices of their times. In Mozart's other music, his personal presence was always obscured. But in *Figaro,* the disgruntled servant-musician who chafes at his hard lot speaks with Mozart's authentic voice.

The Legacy of the Age of Reason

After the Enlightenment, Western civilization was never the same. By the end of the period, the prevailing form of government—absolutism—was on the defensive, facing condemnation from all sides. Supporters of absolutism argued for enlightened despotism, aristocratic critics advocated a division of centralized rule into rival branches, and democrats wanted to abolish monarchy and give the power to the people. Under these assaults, absolutist governments began to crumble.

Another development in the eighteenth century with long-term consequences was the emergence of the middle classes as a potent force for change. By and large, the Enlightenment reflected their political, social, and economic agenda, though their advocates claimed to speak for all people regardless of background. The rise of the middle classes also opened the door to popular forms of culture, such as the novel. Today, this democratizing tendency continues and is one of the hallmarks of modern civilization.

Many of the ideas and principles of the Enlightenment are now articles of faith in the Western heritage. From it come the beliefs that governments should rest on the consent of the people, that the least amount of state interference in the lives of citizens is best, and that all people are created equal. More fundamentally, from the Enlightenment come the views that human nature is good and that happiness is the proper goal of human life.

Although the Enlightenment pointed the way to the future, we must not be misled by the modern-sounding language of the times. The *philosophes* wrote endlessly in support of free speech and religious toleration, and yet censorship and bigotry remained the normal condition of existence for most Europeans. Despite their brave words, most of these enlightened thinkers did not move from ideas to action, believing that ideas would triumph because of their inner logic and inherent justice. Moreover, they thought that the ruling classes would surrender their privileges once reason had shown them the error of their ways. The Enlightenment was the last era in which such simplistic beliefs held sway. The world in 1789 stood poised on the brink of an era in which ideas became politicized through action, war, and social agitation. In the postrevolutionary world, the radical power of ideas would be understood by all.

KEY CULTURAL TERMS

Enlightenment	causality
philosophes	*style galant*
Deism	pianoforte
Pietism	Classical style (in music)
First Great Awakening	sonata form
Physiocrats	symphony
Rococo style	key
fête galante	tempo
rocaille	mood
Neoclassical style	scherzo
Chinoiserie	theme and variations
Chinese Rococo	tone color
mezzotint	serenade
aquatint	minuet and trio
solipsism	

SUGGESTIONS FOR FURTHER READING

DIDEROT, D. *The Encyclopedia: Selections*. Edited and translated by S. J. Gendzier. New York: Harper & Row, 1967. Well-chosen selections from the most influential work of the Enlightenment; originally published between 1750 and 1772.

FIELDING, H. *The History of Tom Jones, a Foundling*. Middletown, Conn.: Wesleyan University Press, 1975. The rollicking novel about an orphan who through personal charm, good looks, and honesty survives misadventures and is finally restored to his rightful inheritance; first issued in 1749.

GIBBON, E. *The History of the Decline and Fall of the Roman Empire*. Abridged by M. Hadas. New York: Putnam, 1962. One of the landmarks of the Enlightenment, Gibbon's history attributes the fall of Rome to the rise of Christianity; published between 1776 and 1788.

HARDT, U. H. *A Critical Edition of Mary Wollstonecraft's "A Vindication of the Rights of Woman, with Strictures on Political and Moral Subjects."* Troy, N.Y.: Whitston, 1982. An authoritative text of one of the books that helped launch the modern feminist movement.

MONTESQUIEU, BARON DE. *The Persian Letters*. Translated by G. R. Healy. Indianapolis: Bobbs-Merrill, 1964. An excellent English version of this epistolary novel that satirizes European customs through the eyes of fictional Persian travelers; the original dates from 1721.

———. *The Spirit of the Laws*. Translated and edited by A. M. Cohler, B. C. Miller, and H. S. Stone. New York: Cambridge University Press, 1989. A good English version of this groundbreaking work that claims people's choices are influenced by such matters as climate, geography, and religion.

POPE, A. *An Essay on Man*. Edited by M. Mack. London: Methuen, 1964. A poetic statement of the ideals of the Enlightenment by the leading English poet of the age.

RICHARDSON, S. *Pamela*. London: Dent, 1962. A modern edition of one of the earliest novels in the English language, recounting the tale of a servant girl whose fine moral sense enables her to prevail over adversity and rise to the top of aristocratic society.

ROUSSEAU, J.-J. *Basic Political Writings*. Translated and edited by D. A. Cress. Indianapolis: Hackett, 1987. Includes selections from *First Discourse* (1750), *The Social Contract* (1762), *Émile* (1762), and other writings.

———. *Confessions*. Translated by J. M. Cohen. New York: Penguin, 1954. A highly original book, the first in the tradition of confessional autobiographies; bridges the Enlightenment and the Romantic period.

SMITH, A. *The Wealth of Nations: Representative Selections*. Indianapolis: Bobbs-Merrill, 1961. The basic writings that set forth the theory of free-market economics; first published in 1776.

VOLTAIRE. *Candide*. Translated by L. Bair. New York: Bantam Books, 1981. The most popular novel of the eighteenth century; first published in 1759.

SUGGESTIONS FOR LISTENING

COUPERIN, FRANÇOIS. The harpsichord, with its delicate and lively sounds, was the signature instrument of Rococo music; Couperin's more than two hundred harpsichord works, composed usually in highly stylized and stately dance rhythms, helped to define the Rococo musical style. Typical works are *La visionaire (The Dreamer)* and *La mystérieuse (The Mysterious One)*, both from 1730.

HAYDN, FRANZ JOSEPH. Over a long and laborious career, Haydn honed his approach to music, moving from Late Baroque forms until he established the sonata form of composition as the basic ingredient of the Classical musical style. Of the string quartets, those in Opuses 17 and 20, composed respectively in 1771 and 1772, show his pure Classical style; the quartets he wrote in the 1790s (Opuses 76 and 77) illustrate his later style, bursting with rhythmic vitality and harmonic innovation. Good examples of his more than one hundred symphonies are Symphony No. 45 (*Farewell*) (1772), Symphony No. 85 (*La reine*, or *The Queen*) (1785), Symphony No. 94 (*Surprise*) (1791), and Symphony No. 103 (*Drum Roll*) (1795). Besides instrumental music, Haydn composed religious works, notably the oratorios for orchestra and massed chorus, *The Creation* (1798) and *The Seasons* (1801)—inspired by Handel's *Messiah*.

MOZART, WOLFGANG AMADEUS. The most gifted composer of the period, Mozart helped to define the Classical style in virtually all forms of musical expression, including the symphony, the piano sonata, the concerto for piano and orchestra, the string quartet, and the comic opera. Mozart's religious music includes Masses, motets, and settings of sacred songs, such as *Solemn Vespers of the Confessor* (1780), with its serene "Laudate Dominum" section, as well as the *Epistle Sonatas* for organ and orchestra, composed between 1767 and 1780 as part of the Mass. Among his best-loved compositions are his last two symphonies, Nos. 40 and 41, composed in 1788; the six concertos for piano and orchestra written in 1784; the six string quartets in Opus 10 (1785), dedicated to Haydn; the opera *Don Giovanni* (1787) in Italian, combining comic and dramatic elements; and the comic operas *The Marriage of Figaro* (1786) and *Cosi fan Tutte (They All Do It This Way)* (1790) in Italian and *Die Zauberflöte (The Magic Flute)* (1791) in German.

RAMEAU, JEAN-PHILIPPE. Rameau's musical fame rests largely on his operas, which combine Late Baroque forms with Rococo elegance and grace. His best-known operas include *Hippolyte et Aricie* (1733), *Les Indes galantes (The Gallant Indies)* (1735), and *Castor et Pollux* (1737).

17 REVOLUTION, REACTION, AND CULTURAL RESPONSE 1760–1830

The Age of Reason was a time of radical talk and little action, but by the end of the eighteenth century, three revolutions had changed the Western world forever—and today the period between 1760 and 1830 is considered a historical watershed. The Industrial Revolution created an industrialism that replaced agriculture as the soundest basis for the economic well-being of a state. The American Revolution demonstrated that government by the people was a workable alternative to monarchy. And the French Revolution forced sweeping changes in the distribution of political power in Europe (Figure 17.1).

These changes were not welcomed by all, and many groups tried to prevent the spread of revolutionary political ideas. However, the middle class, known as the *bourgeoisie*, benefited the most from these revolutions. The emboldened middle class asserted itself as the new standard-bearer of culture, first embracing Neoclassicism and then shifting favor to the powerful new spirit and style of the age—Romanticism.

THE INDUSTRIAL REVOLUTION

Even before the Industrial Revolution, agricultural innovations in England made industrialization possible. The shift toward enclosure, whereby common lands were fenced off by their wealthy owner and consolidated into one large estate, brought hardship to smaller farmers but resulted in increased farm productivity. Improvements in farming techniques increased crop yields and farm income. Better technology also led to improved tools and farm implements, such as the iron plow and the reaper.

◀ **Detail** LOUIS-LEOPOLD BOILLY. *Simon Chenard as a Sans-culotte*. 1792. Oil on canvas, 13⅙ × 8⅝″. Musée Carnavalet, Paris.

511

Figure 17.1 Jean-Auguste-Dominique Ingres. *Napoleon I.* 1806. Oil on canvas, 8′6″ × 5′4″. Musée de l'Armée, Paris. *Napoleon, emperor of France, 1804–1815, is depicted on a throne in the style of an ancient ruler but with references that link him to the French monarchy. He wears a wreath, a Greek symbol of victory, and in his right hand he holds a long rod topped by a gold fleur-de-lis, or French lily—France's national symbol since the Middle Ages. His left hand holds the ivory hand of justice, an image adopted by France's kings in 1314 and revived by Napoleon at his coronation in 1804. Ingres's portrait helped to establish Napoleon's authority and image.*

Industrialization in England

By the mid–eighteenth century, changes at home and abroad had created conditions that steered England toward industrialization. A population increase provided both a labor force and a consumer market. Money to invest was available because of surplus capital generated by sound fiscal practices. Several decades of peace had created an atmosphere conducive to economic growth, and the government's policies promoted further expansion. Free of internal tariffs or duties, goods moved easily throughout Britain, and Britain's acquisition of colonies gave merchants access to raw materials and new overseas markets.

Three economic changes were necessary before these conditions could combine to produce industrial-

ism: the substitution of machines for manual labor; the replacement of animal and human power with new sources of energy such as water and steam (the steam engine, patented by James Watt in 1769, transformed the generation of power); and the introduction of new and large amounts of raw materials, such as iron ore and coal. By 1800 these changes had taken place (Figure 17.2).

The changes in the cotton cloth industry dramatically illustrate the impact of the Industrial Revolution. Local woolen producers, threatened by competition from cotton, persuaded Parliament to prohibit the importation of inexpensive cotton goods from India; but still the demand grew. The English industry tried to meet the demand for cotton through the putting-out system—a method of hand manufacture in which

Figure 17.2 MICHAEL ANGELO ROOKER. *The Cast Iron Bridge at Coalbrookdale.* 1782. Approx. 15½ × 24½". Aberdeen Art Gallery, Aberdeen, Scotland. *The earliest iron bridges, made from the superior grade of iron that was being produced in the new factories, were molded and cast to look like wooden bridges. The first iron bridge, located at Coalbrookdale, became a favorite subject for many artists. Architects did not begin to use iron in building construction until the early 1800s.*

workers wove the fabric in their homes—but this medieval technique proved hopelessly outdated. As a result industrialists developed the factory system to speed manufacturing; flying shuttles and power looms were located under one roof, and this building was situated near a swiftly flowing stream that supplied the water for the steam engines that drove the massive equipment.

The laborers had to adjust their entire lives to the demands of the factory system. No longer could most rural workers stay at home and weave at their own pace. Towns near the factories rapidly expanded, and new ones sprang up in the countryside next to the mills. In both cases, employees were crowded into miserable living quarters, with little regard given for the basic amenities of human existence.

With the factories came the "working class." A realigned class system—with the capitalists and the workers at either extreme—transformed the social order, created new indicators of wealth and success, and established different patterns of class behavior. The earlier cooperation between the gentry and small farmers was replaced by increasingly strained relations between the factory owners and the working class.

Classical Economics: The Rationale for Industrialization

Although industrialization did not produce a school of philosophy, it did generate serious thinking about the newly emerging economic system. Much of this thought could be interpreted as a rationale for industrialization and a justification for profit-seeking. The

French Physiocrats and the Scotsman Adam Smith both advocated the abolition of mercantilism—the economy at the service of the state—and its replacement with a laissez-faire system—the economy at the service of the individual entrepreneur. In England, Smith's ideas attracted a band of thinkers who became known as the Classical economists and included Thomas Malthus and David Ricardo.

Smith's key contribution to Classical economics was his advocacy of a free-market system based on private property that would automatically regulate prices and profits to the benefit of all. He focused his *Wealth of Nations* (1776) on agriculture and commerce, while only glancing at manufacturing. As manufacturing gained power in the English economy, however, businessmen read into his work a rationale for their activities. Smith argued that entrepreneurs acting mutually in enlightened self-interest would not only raise the standard of living for all but also get rich—if the government left them alone. Such an argument was welcome news to businessmen, factory owners, and other capitalists.

Thomas Malthus (1766–1834) and David Ricardo (1772–1823) also lent support to the changes wrought by the Industrial Revolution. In his *Essay on the Principle of Population* (1788), Malthus forecast a world burdened with misery that would worsen if the human population continued to increase. Since the population grew at a geometric rate and the food supply advanced at an arithmetical rate, the number of human beings would soon far exceed the amount of food, leading Malthus to conclude that famines, plagues, and wars were necessary to limit the world's population. His gloomy prediction persuaded most of the middle classes that laborers were victims of their own

SLICE OF LIFE
Life Inside a "Satanic Mill" in 1815

ELIZABETH BENTLEY
Report of Parliamentary Committee on the Bill to Regulate the Labour of Children in Mills and Factories, 1832

The poet William Blake (1757–1827) called England's new factories "dark, Satanic mills." Blake's image was less poetic license than a statement of objective truth. In 1832 the British House of Commons convened a parliamentary commission to study factory conditions, and its report confirmed the hellish environment in which male, female, and child workers labored. The interview with Elizabeth Bentley, a former child laborer, dealing with conditions in about 1815, was part of the commission's final report.

What age are you?
Twenty-three.
What time did you begin work at the [flax] factory?
When I was six years old [in 1815].
What was your business in that mill?
I was a little doffer.
What were your hours of labour in that mill?
From 5 in the morning till 9 at night, when they were thronged.
What were the usual hours of labour when you were not so thronged?
From six in the morning till 7 at night.
Do you consider doffing a laborious employment?
Yes.
Explain what you had to do?
When the frames are full, they have to stop the frames, and take the flyers off, and take the full bobbins off, and carry them to the roller, and then put empty ones on, and set the frame going again.
Does that keep you constantly on your feet?
Yes, there are so many frames and they run so quick.
Your labour is very excessive?
Yes, you have not time for anything.
Suppose you flagged a little, or were late, what would they do?
Strap us.
Have you ever been strapped?
Yes.
Is the strap used so as to hurt you excessively?
Yes it is. . . . I have seen the overlooker go to the top end of the room, where the little girls hug the can to the backminders; he has taken a strap, and a whistle in his mouth, and sometimes he has got a chain and chained them, and strapped them all down the room.
Had you a clock?
No, we had not.
Were you generally there in time?
Yes, my mother has been up at 4 o'clock in the morning, and at 2 o'clock in the morning; the colliers [coal workers] used to go to their work at 3 or 4 o'clock, and when she heard them stirring she has got up out of her warm bed. . . . I have sometimes been at Hunslet Car at 2 o'clock in the morning, when it was streaming down with rain, and we have had to stay till the mill was opened.
You are considerably deformed in person as a consequence of this labour?
Yes I am.
And what time did it come on?
I was about 13 years old when it began coming, and it has got worse since; it is five years since my mother died, and my mother was never able to get me a good pair of stays to hold me up, and when my mother died I had to do for myself, and I got me a pair.
Were you perfectly straight and healthy before you worked at a mill?
Yes, I was as straight a little girl as ever went up and down town.
Do you know of anybody that has been similarly injured in their health?
Yes, in their health, but not many deformed as I am.
Where are you now?
In the poorhouse.

Interpreting This Slice of Life Based on this Slice of Life, **describe** factory conditions in England before the factor reform acts of the 1830s. **Would** you expect Elizabeth Bentley to have attended school during her youth? **Note** the absence of child labor laws, worker's compensation, factory safety legislation, and factory hour regulation. **Compare and contrast** factory conditions then and now.

Timeline 17.1   REVOLUTION, REACTION, AND CULTURAL RESPONSE

1760	1775	1783	1789	1799	1815	1830
Industrial Revolution in England	**American Revolution**			**French Revolution**	**Napoleon and the French Empire**	**Restored Bourbon Monarchy in France**

1769 Watt's steam engine	**1776** Smith's *Wealth of Nations*			**1793** David's *Death of Marat*	**1803** Beethoven's Third Symphony	**1808** Goethe's *Faust* (Part 1)	**1818** Géricault's *Raft of the "Medusa"*	**1830** Berlioz's *Symphonie fantastique*

1774 Goethe's *The Sorrows of Young Werther*

1798 Wordsworth and Coleridge's *Lyrical Ballads*

1813 Austen's *Pride and Prejudice*

1821 Constable's *Hay Wain*

thoughtless habits, including unrestrained sexuality, and could not be helped.

In *Principles of Political Economy and Taxation* (1821), David Ricardo maintained that wages for laborers would always hover around the subsistence level and that workers would never be able to improve their standard of living beyond that level—his "iron law of wages." Tying Malthus's conclusion to his own, he argued that the working class was inevitably mired in poverty. Thus, the theories of the Classical economists provided the rationales for the business classes as they sought arguments to justify the methods of industrialization and the degradation it brought to workers.

POLITICAL REVOLUTIONS, 1760–1815

During the approximately fifty years between the Treaty of Paris (1763) and the Battle of Waterloo (1815), Europe saw monarchies fall and old societies swept away. By 1830 Europe was divided into a conservative eastern Europe and a progressive western Europe that included the former colonies in the New World. This twofold division persisted well into the twentieth century (Timeline 17.1).

The American Revolution

Although Great Britain was leading the way to industrialization, it was also suffering from an outmoded tax structure and from debts contracted in the Seven Years' War. The royal ministers tried numerous schemes and taxes to make the American colonists share in the burden of empire. The colonists, calling the British government's new taxes on sugar, stamps, and tea unconstitutional, claimed immunity from im-

perial taxation because, they asserted, they were not represented in the British Parliament.

Protests and violence succeeded in nullifying the parliamentary taxes and uniting the colonies in a common cause. In 1774 the colonists convened a Continental Congress in Philadelphia, which spoke for the American people against the "foreign power" of Great Britain. In April 1775, conflict between British troops and colonists in Massachusetts triggered a war. The congress in Philadelphia proclaimed the American goals in the Declaration of Independence, signed on July 4, 1776: government by consent of the governed and the rights to life, liberty, and the pursuit of happiness. The American Revolution lasted until 1783 and resulted in victory and independence for the colonies.

To realize their democratic goals, the Americans developed two new ideas: the constitutional convention and a written constitution. Wary of centralized power, the framers of the United States Constitution met in Philadelphia in 1787 and created three coordinated branches of government—legislative, judiciary, and executive—with specified powers delegated to each. (The idea of a balance of powers is derived from the works of both the English political theorist John Locke and the French *philosophe* Montesquieu [see Chapters 15 and 16].) The central government could assess and collect its own taxes, regulate commerce, and make and enforce laws. The framers also limited the government's role in everyday life by accepting the superior claims of human rights.

The founders failed to extend rights to slaves, whose existence was barely noted, and women were not given the right to vote. Still, the Constitution made America the most democratic society of its day and the first successful democracy since Athens in the fifth century B.C.E. As an exemplary democracy, America offered hope to the oppressed, and the successful

Table 17.1 SHIFTS IN THE FRENCH GOVERNMENT, 1789–1830	
July 1789–September 1792	Limited constitutional kingdom; the Assembly
September 1792–August 1795	First Republic; Reign of Terror (1793–1794)
August 1795–November 1799	Directory
November 1799–May 1804	Consulate
May 1804–June 1815	First Empire
June 1815–July 1830	Restored Bourbon monarchy

struggle for independence provided a model for future revolution.

The French Revolution

Despite the importance of the American Revolution, the revolution in France overshadowed it. Because of its dramatic break with the past and its lasting worldwide effects, the French Revolution is a key event of modern times.

When Louis XVI took the throne in 1774, the French crown was confronted with a challenge from two sides: the aristocrats, who were resurgent after the death of Louis XIV, and the emerging bourgeoisie, who were clamoring for power. The affluent bourgeoisie aligned themselves with the nobles in supporting laissez-faire economics, but they joined the king in calling for an end to the feudal privileges of the aristocracy.

The peasant farmers endured burdensome taxes and continued to be subjected to feudal claims. In urban France, the lower middle class, consisting of small shopkeepers, salaried workers, and semiskilled artisans, had little opportunity to escape their bleak existence. Below them existed wage earners, menial workers, and the marginal groups who drifted in and out of the criminal world. Oppressed by high taxes and harboring ill-disguised hatred for the classes above them, the lower orders schemed to stay one jump ahead of the tax collector.

In the 1780s, France began to develop a huge national debt, fueled by its support of America in its revolution. In 1789 Louis XVI finally agreed to convene the Estates-General, a representative body similar to the English Parliament, which had last met in the early 1600s. When this body gathered, the middle-class representatives shunted aside the nobles and the church leaders and formed themselves into the National Constituent Assembly. The Assembly then proceeded to end royal despotism and to turn France into

a limited, constitutional kingdom similar to England (Table 17.1).

This first phase of the revolution lasted from 1789 until September 1792. Dominated by the well-to-do middle classes, the Assembly embraced laissez-faire, restricted the vote to property owners, overhauled the legal system, and introduced representative government. Especially impressive was this body's approval of *The Declaration of the Rights of Man and Citizen* (1789), a document that guaranteed both natural and civil rights and that has served as the basis of subsequent French regimes. In framing the constitution of 1791, the Assembly attempted to embody the slogans of the revolution—liberty, equality, and fraternity—but class hatred made fraternity more an ideal than a reality. This stage of the revolution failed, however, because Louis XVI proved to be untrustworthy and forces inside France were pressing its leaders for increasingly radical reforms. In 1792 the constitution of 1791 was suspended along with the monarchy.

The revolution entered its second and most violent phase, which lasted from September 1792 to August 1795. This phase was dominated by leaders from the lower bourgeois and working classes, who executed the king, founded the French Republic, and briefly replaced Christianity with a state religion organized on rational ideals (Figure 17.3). Full voting rights were given to all males, including blacks and Jews, state education was opened to all, conquered people were allowed to vote on their future, and the slave trade was abolished. Women, however, were denied the vote and citizenship, but they acquired certain rights, including equal treatment of both sexes in marital law, equal rights of inheritance for male and female children, and the legal age for marriage raised to twenty-one. (These advances were short-lived, as they were all swept away later by the Napoleonic Law Codes, after 1804.)

Such far-reaching reforms alarmed many who supported the monarchy, church, and old social order, and soon the fledgling Republic faced civil war at home and invasions from abroad, which in turn set off more domestic political and financial crises. These events led to the year-long Reign of Terror (1793–1794), the controversial period in which suspected enemies of the revolution were executed. Its excesses overshadowed many of the Republic's accomplishments and discredited the idea of revolution among many of its early supporters. In August 1795, a more moderate republic, known as the Directory, was instituted, in which power was shared between two legislative houses and five directors.

The Directory lasted only four years. Although this government favored the commercial middle classes, it

Figure 17.3   Louis-Leopold Boilly. *Simon Chenard as a Sans-culotte.* 1792. Oil on canvas, 13⅙ × 8⅝″. Musée Carnavalet, Paris. *As French workers came into their own during the second phase of the revolution, their clothing became fashionable. The men dressed in short jackets and baggy trousers, rather than in the aristocratic costume of waistcoats and breeches, or culottes, with silk stockings. Because of the long trousers, these workers were known as* sans-culottes *("without breeches"). The artist Boilly, a supporter of the revolution, sought to glorify the* sans-culottes *in this portrait of a typical worker—actually his friend, the actor Simon Chenard. Clad in worker's attire, including wooden shoes, and holding the tricolor (the red, white and blue banner of the revolution), Chenard strikes a heroic pose, as if ready to defend his newly won rights. Boilly has placed Chenard in the foreground so that he towers over the landscape, just as the newly enfranchised workers dominated the political scene.*

remained revolutionary. Its leaders faced nearly insurmountable problems, such as a growing counterrevolution, the collapse of the currency, and a breakdown in law and order. The directors appealed to the military for aid against their enemies, and in November 1799 General Napoleon Bonaparte staged a coup d'état (French, literally, "a stroke of state," a sudden, violent overthrow of government) that abolished the Directory and established the Consulate.

With the rise of Napoleon (1769–1821), events had come full circle, in effect returning France to a monarchy. Napoleon was a dictator and military genius who embodied the enlightened despotism of his century and at the same time anticipated modern totalitarianism. Above all, he was heir to the French Revolution.

Although the cost of Napoleonic rule between 1799 and 1815 was the loss of political liberty for the French, in exchange France received internal peace and a consolidation of most of the revolution's policies. Napoleon kept careers "open to talent" (Napoleon's term meaning jobs for the people with the proper ability and not for those with aristocratic connections), suppressed aristocratic privilege, rewarded wealthy property owners, and refashioned public education. He welcomed home revolutionaries who had emigrated—provided they were loyal to his regime. He restored relations with the papacy, though his efforts failed to achieve religious harmony. He also ended the civil war that had raged for more than a decade, and he stabilized the economy.

Napoleon's most enduring legacy was the law code he helped draft. Intended for universal application, the Napoleonic Code introduced rational legal principles and legitimized the idea of the lay state. The code rested on reforms of the revolutionary era, such as the abolition of serfdom, the guilds, and feudal property. Despite its reactionary ideas of paternal rule and the subservience of women—thus reversing the small gains made by women in the revolutionary era—the code remains the basis of civil law in both France and its former colonies.

Napoleon's military conquests and diplomatic successes soon eclipsed his domestic achievements. A brilliant field general before he seized power, Napoleon launched a series of victorious wars once he became emperor in 1804 (see Figure 17.1). When not winning battles, he managed to make the coalitions allied against him fall apart by exploiting his foes' basic distrust of one another. In particular, he worked to keep Great Britain out of Continental affairs while he crushed Prussia and Austria, who then sued for peace. Simultaneously, he annexed land for France and established satellite kingdoms ruled by members of his family or by his generals. As the self-proclaimed heir of the Age of Reason and the French Revolution,

LEARNING THROUGH MAPS

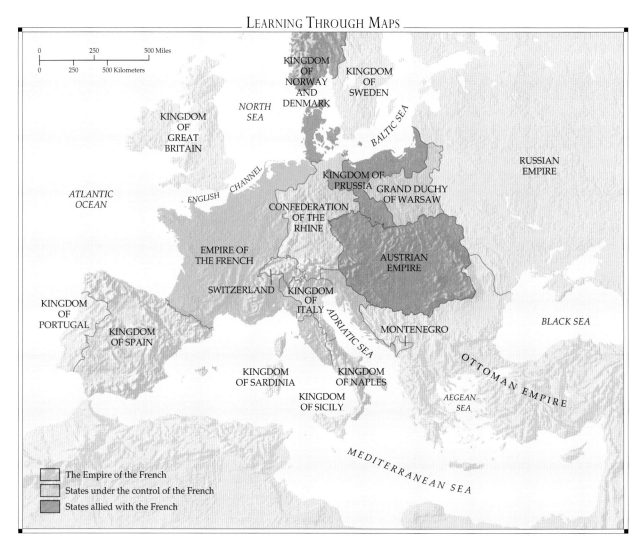

Map 17.1   EUROPE AT THE HEIGHT OF NAPOLEON'S POWER, 1810–1811
This map shows the maximum expansion of Napoleonic power across the map of Europe. **Compare** the borders of the French Empire in this map with those of France in Map 16.1, Europe, 1763–1789. **Identify** the states now under the control of France. **Which** states were allied with the French? **Notice** the various states that appear in Map 14.1 but no longer exist or have new names in Map 17.1. **Consider** the influence of geography in helping make Great Britain and Russia the enemies of Napoleon.

Napoleon reorganized his newly conquered territories along the lines of France. At first, many local reformers welcomed the French, but they soon learned the high costs of occupation and began to resist their "liberators" (Map 17.1).

Napoleon's empire upset the European balance of power at a basic level, so that ultimately the other nations united to defeat him once he was proven vulnerable in battle by the failure of his invasion of Russia in 1812. An alliance of Great Britain and the European states defeated Napoleon in June 1815 at Waterloo (in modern Belgium). Exiled to an island in the South Atlantic, Napoleon died there in 1821, but his spirit hovered over France and Europe for much of the nineteenth century.

Technology

The wars of this era—the American Revolution, the French Revolutionary Wars, and the Napoleonic Wars—were blends of the old and new. Waged with both proven and new weapons, they were fought with traditional and innovative tactics and strategies and subjected to varied influences, far from the scenes of battle. By about 1750, most of Europe's Great Powers had created an early version of the military-industrial complex. While these systems varied by country, their basic infrastructure was the same: tax systems to pay for armies and navies, contracts to supply arms and materials, and bureaucracies to oversee funds, goods, and services. Officers still came from the upper class, with rank-and-file soldiers and sailors from the lower class. With most countries at military parity, victory often hinged on technology, innovative thinking, and resources as the scale and complexity of warfare increased.

Among the new weapons was the field artillery cannon. In the 1730s, the French started to cast cannons as a solid piece of metal, which was then bored out to make the barrel. This method made cannons more accurate, safer, and easier to move in the field. By the 1770s, most nations had adopted the French innovation, but older-type siege guns also remained in use. Nevertheless, victory still depended on battle tactics: how the generals placed their troops and best managed their firepower.

A major change during the French Revolutionary Wars was the founding of the first "citizens' army." In 1793 the French raised an army from its citizenry, the *levée en masse*—a mobilization of all Frenchmen. The *levée en masse* transformed the army and the nature of warfare. For the moment, other European countries continued to rely on traditional recruiting practices, such as mercenary troops and press gangs (roving government officials who forced unsuspecting men into military service). By World War I, however, most Western countries had followed the French example, using nationwide conscription to bring large segments of their male citizenry into the military.

Naval warfare during this period was basically a contest between France and Great Britain. The fleets of potential rivals—Portugal, Spain, and Holland—had been swept from the high seas by 1800, along with the loss of their overseas colonies. And other European countries had no need for a navy, as their borders were landlocked. France itself was defeated by Britain in the Seven Years' War (1756–1763), but soon thereafter began to rebuild its navy, entering a rivalry that it could not win.

France's weakness was fundamental: It valued the army over the navy. This attitude was evident in the French use of privateers—private gunboats—to supplement its regular navy. In contrast, the British placed the Royal Navy first, giving it strong financial backing in Parliament and making it part of an emerging national identity (Figure 17.4). Britain's naval superiority was manifest in its better-trained officer corps, the use of copper sheathing to protect its wooden men-of-war, and its invention of the carronade—a destructive cannon at close range. The Royal Navy's man-of-war be-

came an awesome fighting machine, with a hundred guns or more stacked on three decks. Although the French navy helped the American colonists achieve independence, the British beat the French decisively in the Napoleonic Wars, thus establishing British naval supremacy, which lasted until World War I (see Chapter 19).

REACTION, 1815–1830

After 1815 the victorious nations tried to restore Europe to its prerevolutionary status, but the forces of change had already altered the future of Western—and world—history. As heirs of the Enlightenment notion that they were citizens of the world, the French largely ignored the traditions of the peoples whom they had conquered, believing that the principles of their revolutionary society represented what was best for humanity. Ultimately, however, the French were not as successful as they had hoped in exporting their revolution. The European states and Great Britain shared a conservative agenda that aimed to suppress the advance of liberal ideas. At the Congress of Vienna in 1815, the victors stripped France of most of its conquests, restored the balance of power, halted or reduced reform programs, and inaugurated a period of reaction.

Despite this redesign of the map, many Napoleonic reforms remained in force until 1830 and beyond. Even in France, where the allies restored the Bourbons, Louis XVIII (r. 1815–1824) issued a charter that guaranteed a constitutional regime resembling the limited monarchy of 1791. Most western European states now had governments elected by their citizens and civil law based on the Napoleonic Code. In contrast, Prussia, Russia, and Austria remained basically untouched by democracy and representative government.

The fate of reform in Europe between 1815 and 1830 varied from modest changes in England to repression in Russia. In the immediate postwar period in Great Britain, the government resisted attempts to reform Parliament or to institute free trade, but in the 1820s, Britain began to modernize itself. France regressed toward absolutism as the restored Bourbon monarchy chipped away at the revolutionary heritage. By 1830, resistance to the crown was mounting, and in the July Revolution the people revolted and replaced the Bourbon monarchy with Louis Philippe, the Duke of Orléans (r. 1830–1848). Constitutional government now put the middle class in power.

In central Europe, Austria kept liberal sentiments under tight control at home and within the region. Prussia, which had made important liberal reforms in the Napoleonic era, now seemed more interested in

ENCOUNTER

Slavery and the French Revolution

Slavery and the slave trade are as old as civilization. In ancient Mesopotamia, Egypt, Israel, Greece, and Rome, men, women, and children fell into this terrible system in varied ways: by conquest (conquerors enslaved their captured enemies), by sale (parents could sell children for economic gain), by debt (to settle a debt), by court sentence (a judicial punishment), and by kidnapping (gangs of slave traders preying on the weak). Slaves were required to perform the most arduous and dangerous tasks, had no rights or privileges, and were entrenched at the bottom of society. Slavery and the slave trade remained unchallenged in the Western world until about 1750.

When African slaves were introduced into the West Indies and North America, many whites accepted slavery as embedded in history, sanctioned by the Bible, and necessary to large-scale agricultural production. After 1750 those attitudes were challenged, as thinkers and religious groups, especially the Quakers, began to question slavery's legitimacy. The turning point came later, during the French Revolution, when whites, struggling to overthrow repressive regimes in France, inspired slaves in the French West Indies to fight for their freedom—and the ideals of the French Revolution: liberty, equality, and brotherhood.

By the 1780s, New World slave owners were importing nearly seventy-five thousand slaves a year, many of them destined for the sugar plantations in the French colony of St. Domingue or modern Haiti. St. Domingue, at that time, formed the western half of the island of Hispaniola; the eastern half was Spain's

colony of Santo Domingo. The slaves in French St. Domingue, with no rights, were at the bottom of a rigid social and racial system. Above them were the free people of color—those of mixed blood who had some rights but were still subject to discrimination. Next, constituting a group of second-class citizens, were less-influential whites, who served as plantation overseers and ran the small but necessary businesses. At the top stood the white plantation owners, prosperous merchants, some French noblemen, the clergy, and government officials. In 1789, when news of the outbreak of the French Revolution reached St. Domingue, the colony's old social and racial order began to crumble.

In the opening phases of the French Revolution, the upper-class whites on St. Domingue set up their own government, sent delegates to the Estates-General in France (Encounter figure 17.1), and pressed for more economic freedom. From 1790 to 1794, a series of revolts by the free people of color, the poorer whites, and the slaves occurred and spread to the Spanish side of the island. The island's revolutionary government abolished slavery in 1793, and the French government did likewise in 1794. By then, Toussaint L'Ouverture [TOO-san LOO-ver-tchur] (1743–1803), an ex-slave who was literate and familiar with the writings of the French *philosophes*, had emerged as a military and political leader. In 1801, after defeating both British and French forces, he ruled the island as a military dictator—the first black-led government in the New World. A year later Toussaint was arrested and sent to France, where he died in prison.

efficiency than in modernizing the state. Russia became increasingly reactionary and repressive. Until the 1860s, Russia's autocratic regime and Austria's domination of central Europe widened the gulf between eastern and western Europe.

REVOLUTIONS IN ART AND IDEAS: FROM NEOCLASSICISM TO ROMANTICISM

The makers of the French Revolution had at hand an artistic style that was perfectly suited to their purposes—the Neoclassical. In contrast to the frivolous Rococo, this style was high-minded, ethical, and serious. Neoclassical artists and architects followed the ancient Greco-Roman ideals of balance, simplicity, and restraint, principles that were thought to embody the

underlying order of the universe. Truth was seen as eternal, unchanging, the same for one and all. Art and literature created according to Classical principles were believed to be both morally uplifting and aesthetically satisfying.

In England, Classicism lingered on in the novels of Jane Austen. Untouched by the revolutions that dominated this age, Austen created fictional works that took England's deep countryside for their setting and dealt with the lives of the less wealthy gentry, an essentially middle-class world that appealed to her audience.

Advanced thinkers in France made the Neoclassical paintings of David a symbol of the new rational order they wanted to introduce into the world. The revolution intensified devotion to Classical ideals, and David became its official artist. Later, when the revolution lost its way and France began to see itself as a new Rome, Napoleon made David his court painter. After

Encounter figure 17.1 *Jean-Baptiste Bellay [buh-LAY] joined the slave revolt led by Toussaint L'Ouverture before being elected as one of three delegates to the constitutional assembly, or Convention, in 1793. He lost his seat in 1797, returned home, and faded into history. Elegantly dressed and wearing the French tricolor in his sash and on his hat, Bellay leans against the bust of Abbé Raynal [re-NAHL], the French* philosophe *whose antislavery writings inspired Toussaint and probably Bellay. Including and relating a dead person to the individual in the portrait was a popular device in eighteenth-century paintings. The background on the right represents the Haitian countryside.*

Out of the mixing of an economic enterprise to supply slave labor for an expanding plantation system for Europeans, a debate among European intellectuals over human rights and freedom, and a series of revolutions in France and wars in Europe, an independent republic emerged, in 1803, on the island of Haiti. This government was the first black republic in history and the second republic in the New World. A new society had been born, and its future now rested in the hands of an emancipated and self-governing people.

Learning from the Encounter   What was the socioeconomic system in the French West Indies at the end of the eighteenth century? **How** did ideas and events of the French Revolution affect conditions in the French West Indies? **What** were the outcomes of the Haitian revolt? **Discuss** the issues raised by the revolt and its results. **How** did other countries confront slavery in the nineteenth century? **Have** slavery and the slave trade been fully eliminated from the world today?

1800 David transformed Neoclassicism into an imperial style that lingered on in France and on the Continent long after the French emperor was exiled from Europe in 1815.

Even earlier, starting about 1770, a new movement was emerging across Europe, one that was to have lasting effects on the Western consciousness. **Romanticism** was a whole new way of thinking that came to dominate European arts and letters in the nineteenth century. Rejecting Neoclassicism as cold and artificial, the Romantics glorified unruly nature, uncontrolled feeling, and the mysteries of the human soul. They claimed that their ideals were more in tune with human nature than the order, reason, and harmony of Classicism. Certain ideas and elements of Romanticism have permeated our Western way of thinking and become articles of faith in the modern world.

Neoclassicism in Literature After 1789

During her brief life, Jane Austen (1775–1817) wrote six novels that together rank as the finest body of fiction produced in this period. Austen approached novel writing in a Classical spirit, portraying her characters as inhabiting a serene environment reminiscent of the quiet domestic scenes of the seventeenth-century Dutch painter Vermeer (see Chapter 14). Calling herself a miniaturist, she concentrated her author's eye on a vanishing world where the smallest important unit was the family and the most significant problems involved the adjustment of social relationships.

In the hands of a lesser writer, such a literary program might have failed by being too narrow, but Austen transcended her limited framework. She did this through clear writing, ironic understatement, and,

Figure 17.4   JAMES GILLRAY. *John Bull bother'd:—or—the Geese Alarming the Capitol.* 1792. Hand-colored etching and aquatint, 12¼ × 15¼". British Museum, London. *As the French Revolution grew more radical, British observers became increasingly alarmed. James Gillray (1756–1815), the master caricaturist of England's "Golden Age of Caricaturing," shows William Pitt, the prime minister, peering through a telescope with John Bull—the symbol of Great Britain—standing beside him. At this time, national symbols were taking shape across the West. In this caricature, Pitt thinks the geese are the French* sans-culottes *about to descend on Great Britain and overthrow the government. John Bull, the personification of the common man, is bothered (a word derived from "both eared"), not knowing what to believe since he sees only geese, and, like many Englishmen in 1792, he is confused. To emphasize his dilemma, his hat reads "God Save the King" while his French cockade has "Vive la liberté"— "Long Live Liberty." The balloons—a typical feature of these caricatures—above Pitt and John Bull convey Pitt's fears and John Bull's mixed feelings. This Gillray work typically has more than one meaning, as it is also a sly protest against the British government's campaign to whip up fear about events in France. When collected by admirers, prints like this became part of what has been called the public sphere of British life, which included coffeehouses and print shops, where public discourse occurred among the politically aware. This work also shows Gillray to be a master of the aquatint.*

above all, beautifully realized descriptions of the manners and little rituals of provincial life: the balls attended, the letters and conversations, the visits to relatives, and the unexpected social breakdowns, such as an elopement, a betrayed confidence, or a broken engagement. She was especially sensitive to the constraints her society imposed on women, depicting with great wit a world in which women were given lit-

tle access to formal education, confined to the domestic sphere, kept economically dependent on men, and socialized to be weak and sentimental. The best known of Austen's novels is *Pride and Prejudice* (1813), a gently satirical work whose plot revolves around the problems that arise when the Bennets—a shabby genteel family—try to find suitable husbands for five daughters.

Neoclassical Painting and Architecture After 1789

Jacques-Louis David founded Neoclassicism in painting in the 1780s and remained its consummate exponent until his death in 1825. As official artist of the French Revolution, he rendered contemporary events in the ancient manner. David's most successful painting from this period was his study of the revolution's famous martyr Jean-Paul Marat [muh-RAH], who was assassinated while seated in his bath (Figure 17.5). Himself an ardent supporter of the revolution, David meticulously planned this work to give universal meaning to a specific moment in French history. The setting is historically accurate because Marat suffered from a skin disorder and often conducted official business while seated in the bathtub. Once having established the scene, David suppressed every detail that did not contribute to the general impression of tragedy. As a result, the few details take on a highly charged quality. The figure of Marat resembles a piece of Classical sculpture against the stark background.

His torso is twisted so that the bleeding wound and the peaceful face are fully visible. The pen and the inkwell remind the viewer that Marat was killed while serving the revolution. In effect, David has portrayed Marat as a secular saint.

Barely escaping the revolution's most violent phase, David survived to become court painter to Napoleon, and modifications in the cause of political propaganda now appeared in his art. Napoleon, to enhance his image as a new Augustus, encouraged David to make his painting reflect the pomp and grandeur of the Napoleonic court. *The Coronation of Napoleon and Josephine* is typical of David's imperial paintings (Figure 17.6). This pictorial record of the investiture conveys the opulent splendor and theatrical ceremony that Napoleon craved as a way of validating his empire in the eyes of Europe's older monarchs, who regarded him as an upstart. Napoleon's family members, who had been made kings, princes, princesses, and so on, are depicted in elaborate court dress. In addition, David's treatment of the coronation reveals the modern conception of political power. Instead of being crowned by the pope, Napoleon placed the crown on his own head. This painting shows Napoleon preparing to crown his empress, who is kneeling. Virtually ignored in this splendid moment for the Bonaparte family is the pope, who is seated at the right.

The only Neoclassical painter comparable to David was his pupil Jean-Auguste-Dominique Ingres [ANG-gruh] (1780–1867). Ingres inherited the mantle of Neoclassicism from David, but he lacked his teacher's moral enthusiasm. As a result, Ingres's Classicism is almost cold-blooded and stark in its simple images.

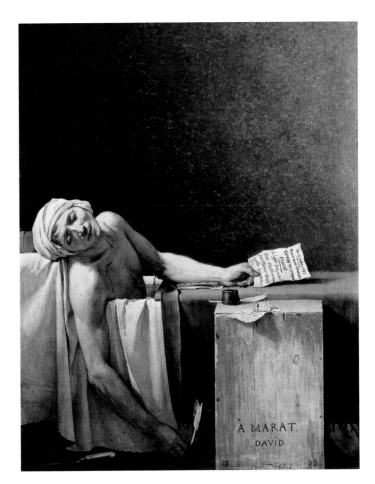

Figure 17.5 JACQUES-LOUIS DAVID. *Death of Marat.* 1793. Oil on canvas, 65 × 50½". Musées Royaux des Beaux-Arts, Brussels. *David's presentation of figures in the nude in his Neoclassical history paintings was often denounced by literal-minded critics as unrealistic, but David defended this choice as consistent with "the customs of antiquity." The critics were silenced by David's depiction of the Marat murder scene, since in this case the nudity was true to life. In this painting, David's Classical principles and the demands of realistic portrayal combined to produce a timeless image.*

Figure 17.6 JACQUES-LOUIS DAVID. *The Coronation of Napoleon and Josephine.* 1805–1808. Oil on canvas, 20′ × 30′6½". Louvre. *Napoleon orchestrated his own coronation and then guided David in painting it. For instance, Napoleon's mother did not attend, probably because of her disapproval of her son's grandiose ambitions, but Napoleon insisted that David depict her seated prominently at the center of the festivities. David also shows the pope's hand raised in benediction, contrary to the report of eyewitnesses who described him sitting with both hands resting on his knees.*

The finest expressions of Ingres's art are his portraits. With clean lines drawn with a sure and steady hand, he created almost photographic images of his subjects. Of Ingres's many portraits, one of the most exquisite is that of Madame Rivière [reev-yehr], the wife of Philibert Rivière, an official in Napoleon's government (Figure 17.7). While not probing deeply into the inner self, this portrait does convey the sitter's high social position, stressing her poise and alluding to her wealth through her jewelry and dress. Madame Rivière's portrait and that of Napoleon (see Figure 17.1), were among those Ingres showed in the 1806 Salon, where their acclaim helped elevate the young artist's reputation, at age twenty-six, to new heights. In his own way, Ingres gave members of the new bourgeois aristocracy in the Napoleonic Empire the same glamorous treatment that had been accorded prerevolutionary nobles in Rococo portraits.

After 1789 the Neoclassical style in architecture spread to the European colonies, notably to the former British territories in North America. In the United States, the middle-class founders of the new republic made Neoclassicism synonymous with their own time, which is known as the Federal Period. They graced their capital, Washington, with the Classical architecture that symbolized devotion to republican and democratic sentiments.

The most profound influence on America's Classical heritage was exercised by Thomas Jefferson (1743–1826), the coauthor of the Declaration of Independence and the third president of the United States. Jefferson was also a master architect. Like other architects in this era, he was deeply indebted to the principles of the Italian Andrea Palladio (1508–1580), whose book on architecture he had read. Palladio's Villa Rotonda near Vicenza served as the model for Jefferson's home at Monticello near Charlottesville, Virginia (Figure 17.8). Like the Villa Rotonda (see Figure 12.24), Monticello is a country dwelling arranged around a domed central area, though it features only two symmetrical connecting wings. Executed in brick with wooden trim, Monticello has inspired so many imitations that it has come to symbolize the American dream of gracious living.

Just as Jefferson's plan for his personal residence influenced American domestic architecture, his design for Virginia's state capitol in Richmond has deeply influenced public architecture (Figure 17.9). From his plan for the Virginia statehouse arose the tradition of building public structures in the form of ancient temples. His model for the capitol was the Maison Carrée (see Figure 5.12), a Roman temple dating from the first century C.E. Though small by today's standards for public buildings, Jefferson's statehouse has a strong presence and is a marvel of refined elegance and simple charm. The most pleasing part of his original

Figure 17.7 JEAN-AUGUSTE-DOMINIQUE INGRES. *Madame Rivière.* 1805. Oil on canvas, oval, 45 × 36". Louvre. *Ingres was the last great painter of portraits in a field that was taken over by the camera after 1840. A keen observer of the human face and form, Ingres was able to render intense, idealized but realistic likenesses, as evidenced in Madame Rivière's portrait. Ingres conveys his subject's physical presence by centering her in the foreground, highlighting her physical features and the color of her flesh, and depicting the gleaming surfaces of her clothing and the pillow on which she leans. The patterned shawl—probably an expensive accessory—accentuates the oval shape of the portrait by covering the subject's right arm, curling around her shoulders, and hanging over the chair.*

design is the central building, with its perfectly proportioned features—columns, pediment, and windows. Even though two smaller wings were added later, they enhance rather than detract from Jefferson's symmetrical and harmonious plan.

Romanticism: Its Spirit and Expression

In contrast to Neoclassicism, Romanticism stood for everything that was unbounded and untamed. The Romantics' patron saint was Rousseau, whose emotionalism and love of nature had made him out of step with his own time. Like Rousseau, the Romantics preferred to be guided by emotion and intuition.

Figure 17.8   THOMAS JEFFERSON. Monticello. 1770–1784; remodeled 1796–1806. Charlottesville, Virginia. *The Palladio-inspired architecture of Monticello reflected Jefferson's ethical
vision. Its portico in the plain style of a Roman temple mirrored his admiration for the Roman republic and its ideals of simplicity and order. Its overall devotion to mathematical principles and
unobtrusive details were expressions of his commitment to disciplined living. Though built for
one of America's elite, Monticello was conceived on a modest scale as a visual rebuke to the luxurious palaces of Europe's aristocrats.*

Figure 17.9   THOMAS JEFFERSON. State Capitol of Virginia.
1785–1796. Richmond, Virginia. *Jefferson described the Maison
Carrée, the model for this statehouse, as "the most perfect and precious remain of antiquity in existence." Political considerations
also influenced Jefferson's choice, for he identified this Roman temple as a symbol of Roman republican values. Like Monticello, Jefferson's statehouse design was an outgrowth of his ethical vision.
It is currently undergoing its third major renovation and is scheduled to reopen in 2007. Plans call for correcting damages to the
foundation, repairing the columns, walls, and roof, updating all
utilities, and constructing an underground exhibition hall and vis-
itor's center.*

Figure 17.10   PHILIP JACQUES DE LOUTHERBOURG. *Coalbrookdale by Night.* 1801. Oil on canvas, 26¾ × 42″. Science and Society Picture Library, London. *At first glance, this painting seems to portray the world engulfed in a flaming inferno. Only gradually does the meaning of the scene—a depiction of one of England's new industrialized towns—emerge. As a terrifying symbol of industrialism, the painting helps to explain what Romantic art was rebelling against.*

Following these guides, they conjured up an image of the world that was deeply personal and alive with hidden meanings. Nature itself became God for many Romantics, who spiritualized nature so that divinity was expressed through bucolic scenes as well as terrifying natural forces. To characterize the latter face of nature they invented the term *Sublime* to convey the awesome and majestic power of earthquakes, floods, and storms.

The Romantic reverence for nature stemmed partly from a desire to escape from the effects of the Industrial Revolution, which was altering the countryside for the worse (Figure 17.10). Not surprisingly, England, the first home of industrialization, became the center of a movement that exalted the Middle Ages, creating a world of natural sentiment that existed only in imagination. The Romantics' rejection of the industrial world had many other consequences, including a preoccupation with the exotic East and the domains of the imagination, dreams, drugs, and nonrational mental states.

Another formative force in Romanticism was the French Revolution. Many early Romantics willingly saw in this awesome upheaval Europe's future. The revolutionary watchwords "liberty," "rights of man," "the individual," and "equality" became the basis of a moral and humanitarian viewpoint that could be applied beyond the orbit of the French Revolution. When Greece declared its independence from the feeble Ottoman Empire and fought for its freedom in the 1820s, for example, many Europeans, influenced by revolutionary principles, declared their solidarity with the rebels. Among them was the English Romantic poet Lord Byron, who died in Greece while aiding in the cause of Greek independence.

The French Revolution also sparked a strong negative reaction among some Romantics, who criticized its seemingly random violence. They likewise deplored Napoleonic imperialism, which squeezed the life out of other cultures by conquering them and then imposing French customs. These conservative Romantics renounced the French Revolution's stress on abstract ideas and natural rights and focused their attention on history and the rights and traditions native to each country. They especially disagreed with the revolution's international spirit and advocated instead a nationalistic point of view.

At first, Romantic nationalism was little more than a rejection of foreign influences and a reverence for those unique aspects of culture that are created by the common people—folk dancing, folk sayings, folk tales, folk music, and folk customs. This benign nationalism later developed into an aggressive attitude that insisted on the moral superiority of one people over all others and expressed unrelenting hostility toward outsiders. In its extreme form, militant nationalism encouraged the expulsion of "alien" groups who were not recognized as members of the national heritage. Aggressive nationalism lasted almost a century, from 1848 to 1945, climaxing in Nazi Germany, and still remains a potent force today.

The Romantics also generated a cult of nonconformity and held in great esteem outlaws, gypsies, and those who lived outside middle-class society. This hostility toward middle-class life has an ironic twist because those who professed it generally came from this class and sought its patronage. The unruly presence of Romanticism coincided with the rise to political dominance of the middle class. Out of the love-hate relationship between Romantics and the middle class emerged another familiar emblem of modern life, the anti-bourgeois bourgeois—that is, middle-class people who scorn their own social origins. From the dawn of the Romantic period until the present day, modern culture has been filled with middle-class rebels in revolt against their class.

France played a central role in Romanticism because of its culturally strategic position, and England also produced major figures in Romanticism, particularly in poetry and painting. Notwithstanding these achievements, the heart of Romanticism was German-speaking Europe. The French writer Madame de Staël (1766–1817) helped popularize German culture and writers with her book *On Germany* (1810). So great was the German cultural response that Romanticism is often called a German invention.

The Romantic Movement in Literature

Romanticism in literature was foreshadowed in the German literary movement known as **Sturm und Drang,** or Storm and Stress. This movement flourished briefly in the 1770s and early 1780s, arising as a revolt against Classical restraint and drawing inspiration from Rousseau's emotionalism. On a positive level, this literary movement idealized peasant life and the unconventional, liberated mind. The Sturm und Drang writers attacked organized religion because of its hypocrisy and followed Rousseau in finding God in nature. These middle-class authors objected to the formality and tedium of eighteenth-century life and letters and valued free expression in language, dress, behavior, and love. By the mid-1780s, the movement had settled down, drained of its rebelliousness. The most influential members became fully integrated into the German literary scene.

The Sturm und Drang movement's outstanding writer was Johann Wolfgang von Goethe [GUHR-tuh] (1749–1832), the greatest of German writers. In 1774, while still in his twenties, Goethe acquired a European-wide reputation with *The Sorrows of Young Werther,* a novel in which the young hero commits suicide because of disappointment in love. So successful was this novel that it led to Wertherism, the social phenomenon in which young men imitated the hero's emotionalism, sometimes even to the point of killing themselves. Werther is a complex character: passionate and excitable, given to inappropriate outbursts, moved by the innocence of children, attracted to social misfits, and overwhelmed by God's presence in nature. He embodies many characteristics of Romanticism.

With the publication in England in 1798 of *Lyrical Ballads* by William Wordsworth (1770–1850) and Samuel Taylor Coleridge (1772–1834), a turning point in the history of literary style was reached, and Romanticism truly began. Rejecting what they considered to be the artificiality of the Neoclassicists, the two poets turned to more natural types of verse, Coleridge

to ballad forms and Wordsworth to simple lyrics of plain folks, voiced in the common language of the "middle and lower classes of society." Henceforth many Romantic writers, both in poetry and in prose, sought to reproduce the language of customary speech—a literary revolution that was the equivalent of the coming of democracy.

The task Wordsworth assigned himself in *Lyrical Ballads* was to compose verses about the pleasures of everyday existence. He responded to this challenge with poems filled with deep feeling, which were mainly about finding wisdom in simple things. A famous poem from this collection entitled "Lines Composed a Few Miles Above Tintern Abbey" shows Wordsworth's pantheism, or the belief that God lives in nature. In it, speaking to his sister Dorothy, he recalls the strong emotions he felt in his early life when he "bounded o'er the mountains, by the sides / of the deep rivers, and the lonely streams, / wherever nature led." Now he describes himself as subdued but still "a worshipper of Nature." Wordsworth's nature is a world of overgrown hedgerows, meadows, orchards, and peasant cottages. The beauty of the ordinary became Wordsworth's lifelong preoccupation; he is regarded as the English language's most stirring poet of nature.

Soon after the appearance of *Lyrical Ballads,* Goethe published his verse play *Faust* (Part I, 1808). Goethe's Werther had been a social rebel, the prototype of the anti-bourgeois bourgeois. But his Faust was a universal rebel, unwilling to let any moral scruple stand in the way of his spiritual quest for the meaning of life. Faust's two distinguishing marks are his relentless pursuit of knowledge and his all-consuming restlessness. Having exhausted book learning, Faust hopes that experience will satisfy his spiritual hunger, and thus he turns to the Devil (Mephistopheles), who proposes to give Faust all the exciting experiences that have so far been lacking in his life. If Faust finds any moment satisfying, then his immortal soul is forever condemned to hell. Under such conditions Faust signs the compact, in his blood, with Mephistopheles.

Mephistopheles helps Faust recover his youth and involves him in a series of adventures that include drunkenness, sexual excess, seduction, and murder. His mistress kills their illegitimate child and perishes in despair. *Faust,* Part I, concludes with Faust more dissatisfied than when he began and no nearer to his goal. Goethe later added Part II (1832) to his drama, in which God redeems Faust because of his willingness to sacrifice his life for others, but lacking the emotional intensity of the first part, this second half failed to reach a large audience.

Goethe's *Faust,* Part I, however, proved irresistible. His drama became the most often performed

Figure 17.11 RICHARD WESTALL. *George Gordon, Lord Byron.* 1813. Oil on canvas, 36 × 28". National Portrait Gallery, London. *Westall's portrait of Lord Byron captures the brooding and dark good looks that made him the exemplar of the Romantic hero. Gazing intently into the distance while resting his chin on his hand, Byron seems lost in thought. His isolation is heightened by the overall darkness except for his face, hand, and shirt collar. It was this image of Byron—a person coiled tight as a spring—that caused one female admirer to describe him as "mad, bad, and dangerous to know."*

German-language play in the world. It inspired numerous paintings and several works of music. The word **Faustian** came into use to characterize one who is willing to sacrifice spiritual values for knowledge, experience, or mastery.

Another powerful voice in Romantic literature was the English poet George Gordon, Lord Byron (1788–1824). Better known on the Continent than his compatriots Wordsworth and Coleridge, Byron was called by Goethe the "herald of world literature." The personality of Byron has fascinated successive generations of Western artists and thinkers. At a time when the middle classes were ruled by a restrictive code of respectability, he created a model for rebellious youth with his flowing hair, open shirt collar, and love of ungovernable forces (Figure 17.11). His greatest Romantic creation was probably himself—the "Byronic hero," who was moody, passionate, absorbed in exploring and expressing his innermost self.

Yet the English treated Byron as a pariah and drove him into exile for his unconventional life. Perhaps in retaliation, Byron, in his most admired poem, *Don Juan* (1819–1824), presented the notorious seducer as a virtuous hero—a literary device intended to expose the

hypocrisy of society. Like Goethe's *Faust,* Byron's *Don Juan* was a study in moral duality and reflected the author's fascination with subterranean drives in human nature.

Byron was the best known of the trio of Romantic poets whose enduring lyrical works helped to define the period from 1810 to 1824 as England's great Age of Poetry. The other two poets were Byron's friend Percy Bysshe Shelley (1792–1822), famed for poetry that was often charged with radical politics, and John Keats (1795–1820), who drew on a tragic personal history to create works of quiet beauty and stoic calm. That all three writers led tragically shortened lives—Byron dying at age thirty-six, Shelley at twenty-nine, and Keats at twenty-five—contributed in later years to their Romantic image as doomed poets.

English Romanticism also produced two of the most pervasive figures of Western culture—Frankenstein and his manufactured monster. Made familiar through countless films and cartoons, these two fictional characters first appeared in the novel *Frankenstein* (1818) by Mary Wollstonecraft Shelley (1797–1851). Shelley was well connected to two of the most unconventional literary families of the day; she was the daughter of Mary Wollstonecraft, a founder of modern feminism (see Chapter 16), and she was the wife of Percy Bysshe Shelley. In Shelley's novel, Dr. Frankenstein, having thoughtlessly constructed a humanlike being with no prospect for personal happiness, is eventually hunted down and killed by his own despairing creature. Part of the Romantic reaction against Enlightenment rationalism, which began with Rousseau (see Chapter 16), Shelley's novel presented Frankenstein as a man driven by excessive and obsessive intellectual curiosity and the monster as a tragic symbol of science out of control. Written in the optimistic dawn of the industrialized age, when humanity seemed on the verge of taming the natural world, Shelley's *Frankenstein* is one of the earliest warnings that scientific research divorced from morality is an open invitation to personal and social disaster.

Romantic Painting

Romanticism in painting was a European-wide art style, in which artists of all countries shared many subjects (for example, landscape scenes and literary subjects) and themes (for example, love of the exotic and the cult of the hero). But there were also national variations within this international style, as reflected in the images created by the leading painters in England, Germany, Spain, and France.

England Romanticism in painting appeared first in England, manifesting itself as part of a cult of nature

2

529

Figure 17.12 JOHN CONSTABLE. *The Hay Wain.* 1821. Oil on canvas, 51¼ × 73". Reproduced by courtesy of the Trustees, The National Gallery, London. *Although the pastoral subject was alien to them at the time, French Romantic painters recognized in Constable a kindred spirit when* The Hay Wain *was exhibited at the Paris Salon of 1824. The scene's informality, the strong colors, and the natural lighting converted them, and a later French school of landscape painters was influenced by Constable.*

with two distinct aspects, the pastoral and the Sublime. Painters of pastoral scenes specialized in landscapes in which peasant life was equated with the divine order of things, thus forging a moral link between human beings and the natural environment. The painter John Constable was the chief exponent of the pastoral. In contrast, painters of Sublime subjects focused on devastating natural or human-made calamities, reflecting a world order beyond mortal control or understanding. The leading exponent of the Sublime was the painter J. M. W. Turner.

Like the Dutch masters of the 1600s, John Constable (1776–1837) preferred to paint simple country landscapes. But more important than the Dutch influence on his art was the Romantic "cult of nature." Constable's landscapes, like Wordsworth's poetry, reflected the sense of God's universal presence in nature. Wordsworth claimed that nature aroused feelings that "connect the landscape with the quiet of the sky." In his canvases, Constable tried to awaken the viewer to the divinity in nature by focusing on ordinary scenes such as one might see on a country walk. Constable

had an almost holy vision that was true to nature without using what he called tricks or crass emotional appeals.

Constable's landscapes often convey a feeling of having been painted right on the spot. In actuality, he liked to sketch on a site and then transform his impressions into a finished painting that preserved the feeling of immediacy. This two-step method resulted in a style that was both solid and sensitive to the natural world. Constable's innocent and sincere style was meant to convey the feeling that his vision sprang from a mystical communion with nature, rather than being an artificial scene conceived in an artist's studio.

Although Constable's art was not fully appreciated by his contemporaries, a few works won acclaim and helped to redefine the way that the public looked at nature. Of these the most famous is *The Hay Wain* (Figure 17.12). Over the years, this painting has been reproduced so often that it is sometimes dismissed as "calendar art," but when it first appeared, it excited admiration at home and in Paris. The freshness of the simple images attracted viewers to the beauty of the

Figure 17.13 JOHN CONSTABLE. *Cloud Study.* 1821. Oil on paper on panel, 8⅜ × 11½". Yale Center for British Art, New Haven. Paul Mellon Collection. *As Constable made his cloud paintings, he kept precise records of the weather conditions. For example, in this* Cloud Study, *he recorded the date and time, September 21, 1821, between 2 and 3 P.M., and noted: "strong Wind at west, bright light coming through the Clouds which are laying one on the other." Thus, these paintings combine the scientist's meticulous eye with the artist's sensitive response to nature.*

scene. *The Hay Wain* added many features of everyday rural life to the repertoire of Romantic motifs, including a thatch-roofed cottage, a gently flowing stream, a dog running along a riverbank, cows grazing in the background, and overhead the ever-changing English sky.

The sky, for Constable, served as the unique source of light. In 1821–1822, he conducted a program that he called "skying," capturing on canvas the cloud-filled English sky as it moved from sunshine to rain and back again (Figure 17.13). Dissatisfied with earlier artists who used artificial means to represent nature, Constable worked as a naturalist to record the truth in nature. Constable's cloud studies echoed Romantic poets, like Goethe and Wordsworth, who identified clouds as a symbol of various themes, such as loneliness and the fleeting quality of life. In his attempt to portray the out-of-doors in its lively colors and ever-changing light, Constable was an important influence on the nineteenth-century Impressionists.

As for the Sublime, Joseph Mallord William Turner (1775–1851) created a new type of subject, "the sublime catastrophe," in which he specialized from 1800 until about 1830. He was the most original artist of his age, prefiguring the Impressionists with his virtuosic use of color and anticipating modern abstract painting in his depictions of wild nature. An example of Turner's sublime catastrophes is *Snowstorm: Hannibal and His Army Crossing the Alps* (Figure 17.14). Although inspired by an episode from Roman history, this paint-

ing is more about the fury of nature than it is about the Carthaginian general Hannibal. The actual subject is the snowstorm, whose sweeping savagery threatens to annihilate everything, including soldiers and horses. No artist before Turner had handled paint in the way that he does here. He turns the sky, which occupies at least three-fourths of the canvas, into an abstract composition, a series of interpenetrating planes of differently colored light.

Turner also dealt with another aspect of the Sublime theme, the notion that all human endeavor is doomed, in *The Bay of Baiae, with Apollo and the Sibyl* (Figure 17.15). Inspired by his first visit to Italy, he portrays Classical motifs in a Romantic landscape. In ancient Rome, the imperial court built splendid villas and baths at the Bay of Baiae (near Naples), which by Turner's time stood in ruins. The painter, using artistic license, rearranged the actual scene to make this vista much more appealing. By placing Apollo and the Sibyl in the foreground, Turner alludes to a Greek myth associated with the nearby port of Cumae, the home of the Cumaean Sibyl.

Germany About the time the Sublime developed in England, it also was launched in Germany by Caspar David Friedrich (1774–1840), a painter who specialized in brooding landscapes, usually with a few human figures to give them a spiritual scale. A lifelong resident of Pomerania on northern Europe's Baltic coast, he drew artistic inspiration from his homeland's deserted

Figure 17.14 JOSEPH MALLORD WILLIAM TURNER. *Snowstorm: Hannibal and His Army Crossing the Alps.* 1810–1812. Oil on canvas, 4'9½" × 7'9½". Tate Gallery. *Hannibal and his troops, stretching from left to right in the bottom third of the painting, are almost invisible; above them and dominating the scene is a raging snowstorm, through which may be glimpsed a ghostly sun. This painting, based on a Gothic novel of the time, was less about the ancient struggle between the Carthaginian general Hannibal and Rome than about the French general Napoleon and England in the 1800s; thus, this work implicitly reflects the period's political climate—a rare occurrence in Turner's art.*

Figure 17.15 JOSEPH MALLORD WILLIAM TURNER. *The Bay of Baiae, with Apollo and the Sibyl.* 1823. Oil on canvas, 57¼ × 94". Tate Gallery. *Turner has deftly focused the viewer's eye on the painting's center by means of a circular arrangement of objects (boats, ruins, and rocks) and the use of shadows and light. Within this space, Turner places Apollo making overtures to the Sibyl, a tactic whose outcome is symbolized by the rabbit and the snake. The rabbit (center) represents love, referring to Apollo's pursuit of the Sibyl, and the snake (lower right) alludes to lurking evil, perhaps a reference to the Sibyl's fate for spurning Apollo. The god curses her so that she will grow old but never die—just as the ruins at the Bay of Baiae are reminders of Rome's former glory.*

Figure 17.16   CASPAR DAVID FRIEDRICH. *Monk by the Sea.* 1808–1810. Oil on canvas, 43¼ × 67½". Stiftung Preussischer Kulturbesitz, Schloss Charlottenburg, Berlin. *This painting is revolutionary in form and content. In form, it violates Classical perspective by using a low horizon line to create a sky of limitless space; it also rejects traditional design by reducing figures and setting to a minimum level. In content, the meaning is left deliberately ambiguous. These simplifications make the painting a nearly abstract image, and thus it points the way to Modern art (see Chapter 19).*

beaches, dense forests, and chalky cliffs. What sets his landscapes apart from those of earlier artists on the same subject is his desire to turn natural scenes into glimpses of the divine mystery. Avoiding traditional Christian subjects, Friedrich invented his own symbols for conveying God's presence in the world.

In *Monk by the Sea* (Figure 17.16), the setting is the stark Baltic seacoast, where a hooded figure stands on the dunes before a great wall of sky. This figure—the "monk" of the title—forms the only vertical line in an otherwise horizontal painting. Below is the angry sea, but the sky is calm except for a bank of clouds lit by the moon or perhaps the coming dawn. By showing the monk from the back—he rarely painted faces—Friedrich encourages the viewer to see what the monk sees and to feel what he feels. Perhaps, filled with optimism, he awaits a new day. Or perhaps, despairing,

he watches the descent of night. Or perhaps he feels insignificant when confronted with the limitless sky and sea. Infrared photographs have revealed that Friedrich originally included two ships struggling against the waves in the painting. Ships are often present in Friedrich's works, symbolic of a divine messenger to the human realm. By painting them out, Friedrich removed an optimistic note that may have guided the viewer's interpretation. Nevertheless, the finished painting represents twin Romantic themes and favorites of Friedrich's—love of solitude and fascination with the infinite.

Spain   In Spain, Romanticism flourished in the anti-Classical paintings of Francisco Goya (1746–1828), a major figure in Spanish culture. Reflecting a nightmarish vision of the world, his art ranges from Rococo fantasies to sensual portraits to grim studies of human folly to spiritual evil and finally to scenes of utter hopelessness. Various reasons have been suggested for Goya's descent into despair, but certainly his dashed hopes for the regeneration of Spain's political and social order were central to his advancing pessimism, as was his slow decline into deafness.

In the 1790s, Goya was serving as court painter to King Charles IV, and signs of the artist's political disaffection can be detected in his revealing portrait of the royal family (Figure 17.17). He depicts the queen (center) as a vain, foolish woman and the king (right, front) as a royal simpleton. History has judged Goya's interpretations to be accurate, for this was a corrupt and stupid court. Perhaps the lace-covered gowns, the glittering medals, and the general elegance of the ensemble allowed him to get away with such unflattering portraits and survive within this dangerous environment.

In 1797 Goya published a collection of etchings that set forth his savage indictment of the age's social evils and established him as an outstanding humanitarian artist. The title of this series was *Caprichos*, or *Caprices*, a Romantic genre that allowed artists to express their personal feelings on any subject. One of the eighty *caprichos*, *The Sleep of Reason* was intended as the series' frontispiece and is the key to Goya's artistic purpose (Figure 17.18). The inscription on the desk reads, "The sleep of reason brings forth monsters," a statement that conveys the need for eternal vigilance against cruelty and superstition. The nocturnal creatures—bats, owls, and cats—symbolize the dark forces that continually threaten rationality.

Napoleon's conquest of Spain and the subsequent Spanish war of liberation form the background to Goya's masterpiece, *The Execution of the Third of May, 1808* (Figure 17.19). This protest against French imperialism is one of the world's most compelling depictions of the horrors of war. It shows Spanish captives being executed by a French firing squad. The French troops are a faceless line of disciplined automatons,

Figure 17.17 FRANCISCO GOYA. *The Family of Charles IV.* 1800. Oil on canvas, 9'2" × 11'. Prado, Madrid. *Following a well-established Spanish tradition, Goya has painted himself into the canvas on the left, from which vantage point in the shadows he observes the royal family. Velázquez had followed this tradition 150 years earlier (see Figure 14.12), which this painting echoes. Goya portrayed the ravaged face of the king's sister on the left as a reminder of the fleeting nature of human beauty.*

Figure 17.18 FRANCISCO GOYA. *The Sleep of Reason.* 1797. Etching and aquatint, approx. 8½ × 6". Courtesy, Museum of Fine Arts, Boston. Bequest of William P. Babcock. *Goya's artistic technique in the* Caprichos *series is aquatint, a process that uses acid on a metal plate to create subtle shades of light and dark. The absence of color in the resulting engravings heightens the moral message of these works. The nocturnal creatures—bats, owls, and the lynx—symbolize the dark forces that continually threaten rationality. The lynx, noted for its sharp eyes, is identified with occult knowledge.*

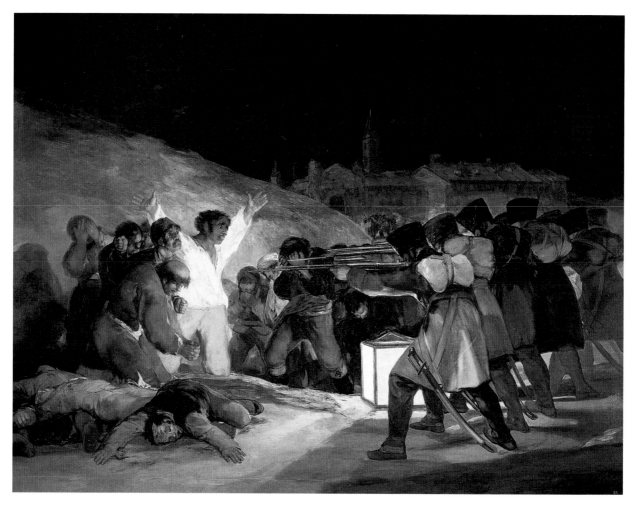

Figure 17.19 Francisco Goya. *The Execution of the Third of May, 1808*. 1814–1815. Oil on canvas, 8′9″ × 13′4″. Prado, Madrid. *A comparison of this painting by Goya with David's portrait of the assassinated Marat (see Figure 17.5) shows the difference in tone between Romantic and Neoclassical art. David makes Marat's death a heroic sacrifice despite its tragic circumstances. In contrast, Goya's passionate portrayal of the Spanish martyrs shows that there is nothing heroic about their deaths; their cause may be just, but the manner of their death is pitiless and squalid.*

and the Spanish soldiers a band of ill-assorted irregulars. The Spanish patriots are arranged in three groups: Those covered with blood and lying on the ground are already dead, those facing the firing squad will be dead in an instant, and those marching forward with faces covered are scheduled for the next round. The emotional center of this otherwise somber-hued painting is the white-shirted man bathed in brilliant light. With his arms outstretched, he becomes a Christ figure, symbolizing Goya's compassion for all victims who die for a "good cause."

France Romantic painting arrived in France in 1818 with the appearance of *The Raft of the "Medusa,"* a work by Théodore Géricault [zhay-rih-KOH] (1791–1824)

that was based on an actual incident (Figure 17.20). The *Medusa*, a sailing ship, had foundered in the South Atlantic, and it was believed that all aboard were lost. Then, after almost two months, a handful of survivors were rescued from a makeshift raft. From their story came shocking details of mutiny, crimes by officers, murder, cannibalism, and a government cover-up.

Géricault was attracted to this incident in which a few men outwitted death against all odds. Focusing on the precise moment of their rescue, he depicts these ordinary humans as noble heroes nearly overwhelmed by the terrible forces of nature. The nude and partially clad bodies in the foreground convey a powerful sense of dignity and suffering. From here, the figures surge upward toward the black youth who is hoisted

Figure 17.20 THÉODORE GÉRICAULT. *The Raft of the "Medusa."* 1818. Oil on canvas, 16′1″ × 23′6″. Louvre. *Other artists, including Turner and Friedrich, painted shipwrecks and their victims (see Figure 18.3), but Géricault's enormous canvas is probably the best known. He so vividly caught his subjects' desperation and hope that his work received instant praise, regardless of the controversies surrounding the subject and its relationships to social and political issues. With his usual thorough preparation, Géricault made over fifty studies of the incident, rearranging the figures on the raft until he had created a pyramidal structure, moving from the lower left corner to the center and upper right.*

aloft and waving a flag at the unseen rescue ship. Géricault wanted his painting to convey a political statement about the government and to be as realistic as possible—he interviewed survivors and had a replica of the raft constructed—but at the same time, he imbued it with expression and pathos. The result was a highly emotional work that embodied the spirit of Romanticism.

Géricault's *Raft of the "Medusa"* also illustrates Romanticism's connection to liberal political ideas. The devastated humanity on the raft underscored the breakdown in civilization that the entire *Medusa* incident came to represent. The painting itself became a rallying point for the critics of the restored Bourbon monarchy, who saw in the portrayal of a crew cast adrift a metaphor for the French nation. Many of Géricault's ideas were taken up by Eugène Delacroix [del-uh-KWAH] (1798–1863), who became the leader of a school of Romantic painting that was in open rivalry with Ingres and the Neoclassicists. Like Géricault, Delacroix was a humanitarian who drew artistic inspiration from his violent times. In the 1820s, he identified with Greek freedom fighters in their war of independence against the Turks, expressing his support in *Massacre at Chios* (Figure 17.21). Delacroix painted it immediately after the Turks killed twenty thousand Greek inhabitants of the Aegean island of Chios in 1822. Chios, which claims to be the birthplace of Homer, was linked in European minds with the glories of Classical culture. Delacroix's painting of this

Figure 17.21   Eugène Delacroix. *Massacre at Chios.* 1824. Oil on canvas, 13'10" × 11'7".
Louvre. *Delacroix uses vivid colors and vulnerable bodies to express the horror of the historic
event—a typical technique for him. Dead and dying Greeks fill the foreground, while two Turkish
soldiers (in turbans) continue to slaughter the innocents. In the middle background, another group
of Greeks is being killed, and, in the far left, distant smoke rises from a burning village. The dark
blue sea in the background and the yellowish blue sky overhead add a threatening mood to the
scene of carnage. The unearthly yellow of the sky is echoed in the skin tones of the victims in the
foreground.* Massacre at Chios, *when exhibited in the 1824 Salon, was a popular success. The
French government bought it for six thousand francs—a common practice in this period, which
linked the art world and the state, creating a kind of "official art." When Impressionism was born
in the 1870s, it would be in reaction against "official art" (see Chapter 19).*

Figure 17.22 EUGÈNE DELACROIX. *Liberty Leading the People*. 1831. Oil on canvas, 8'6" × 10'8". Louvre. *Delacroix's canvas bears some meaningful resemblances to Géricault's* Raft of the "Medusa." *Each painting takes a contemporary event as its subject and transforms it into a symbol of France. Moreover, Delacroix's placement of two dead male figures, one partially nude and the other clothed, echoes similar figures in Géricault's work. Delacroix's portrayal of the people triumphant thus seems to be an optimistic response to Géricault's image of France adrift.*

massacre scene is a rarity in the history of Western art: It is a great work of art and simultaneously a piece of political propaganda.

Delacroix's *Liberty Leading the People* was also inspired by a political incident, the July Revolution of 1830, which resulted in the establishment of a constitutional government (Figure 17.22). The painting combines realism and allegory, depicting revolutionaries on the barricades led by an idealized, bare-breasted goddess of liberty. Surrounding Liberty are three central figures who symbolize the various classes that constitute "the People": The man in the tall hat represents the middle classes, the chief beneficiaries of the revolution; the kneeling figure in the cap stands for the working-class rebels; and the boy brandishing the twin pistols is an image of the street urchin, among the lowest social groups.

The focal point of the painting is the tricolor, the revolutionary flag adopted in the revolution of 1789, outlawed from 1815 until 1830 and now restored as France's unifying symbol. The flag's red, white, and blue determine the harmony of color in the rest of this painting. Completed soon after the 1830 revolution, this work was purchased by the new king as a fitting tribute to the struggle that brought him to power. It was quickly hidden away, however, for the bourgeois establishment found the revolutionary heritage an embarrassment. Only later, with the creation of the Second Republic in 1848, did the French public see the painting.

Science and Philosophy

Science, having been part of natural philosophy since ancient Greece (see Chapter 2), grew more independent during this period, with each field of study going its separate way. Science, based on a blend of empiricism, experiment, and rationalism, now held sway in western Europe, especially among French and British thinkers. But, east of the Rhine, German thinkers, rejecting what they judged to be the materialism and skepticism of the new science (see "David Hume," Chapter 16), began developing an alternative approach to truth—German Idealism, which assigned a central role to spiritual values. Still, most people in the West remained ignorant of these shifts in science and thought. They found comfort and assurance in popular religion, especially in those movements that had emerged in the early eighteenth century (see Chapter 16).

Science   Between 1760 and 1830, the educated classes of Europe embraced the Scientific Revolution, making its findings part of the bedrock of Western thought (see Chapter 15). Although this period did not witness any dramatic breakthrough equal to the Scientific Revolution or Newtonian synthesis, the world of science was changing in many ways. The scientific spirit gave birth to new journals devoted to research, national academies of science, modeled after that of France, and public recognition of scientific achievements. The practice of science itself grew more organized, often with the support of state funds.

Instead of "science," it now became customary to speak of "the sciences." The sciences, as such, comprised the biological sciences, the physical sciences, and the natural sciences. Each area of scientific study, in turn, began to splinter into distinct and specialized disciplines, such as botany, zoology, chemistry, and electricity. As more scientific discoveries were made, the new knowledge was soon integrated into the mainstream of Western thought and culture and spread around the world (Figure 17.23)—a trend that continues today.

Modern chemistry, one of the new sciences born in the eighteenth century, was founded through the efforts of primarily one scientist—Antoine-Laurent Lavoisier [AN-twan-lo-RAHN lahv-WAHZ-yeh] (1743–1794). Trained as a chemist, he conducted experiments

Figure 17.23   Frontispiece, *Journal du voyage fait par ordre du roi à l'Équateur (Journal of the Voyage to the Equator, by Order of the King).* 1751. *This frontispiece, taken from a thesis defense, was dedicated to three French scholars who set out to measure the equator in 1742. Such expeditions preceded the establishment of schools and colleges in Europe's South American colonies in the eighteenth century. The images in the frontispiece blend Classical themes with the new science. Minerva, the Roman goddess of wisdom, sits enthroned and surrounded by* putti, *angelic figures associated with the Roman goddess Venus. The* putti *are using scientific instruments—microscopes and magnifying glasses—to examine plants, study the globe, calculate distances, and experiment with fire. In the left background is a telescope and, in the left foreground, a pendulum clock. The illustration's message is clear: Scientific knowledge is spreading around the world.*

with air, gas, and heat, which led, in turn, to many discoveries, including his explanation for combustion. At about the same time, the first chemical element—oxygen—was identified by the English scientist and theologian Joseph Priestly (1733–1804). Later, Lavoisier, through his experiments, discovered the life-sustaining role played by oxygen for plants and animals. Lavoisier also broke water down into its two basic elements, oxygen and hydrogen, though he did not identify hydrogen by name. For the discipline of chemistry, he coauthored its classification system and established the ground rules for conducting chemical experiments.

Lavoisier also was active in government affairs and dedicated his expertise to improving the French economy and society. However, because of his government service for the French crown, he became a victim of the Reign of Terror and was guillotined.

The study of electricity, which began in the mid-1600s, advanced with the English physicist Robert Boyle (see Chapter 15). Boyle was one of the first to recognize that electricity had mutual attraction and repulsion characteristics. In the 1740s, the American Benjamin Franklin (1706–1790) conducted experiments with electric phenomena, testing the properties of what he called the "electric fluid." Soon he was able to distinguish between positive and negative charges and between conductors and nonconductors of electricity. Franklin wrote several articles explaining his experiments, which made his reputation as a "man of science" in Europe. His famous and dangerous 1752 kite episode proved that electricity was identical with lightning. Later, he invented the pointed iron lightning rod, which protected a building from lightning by transmitting an electrical charge by wire into the ground. His contributions to the understanding of electricity made Franklin a central figure in the emergence of this new scientific field.

The Swedish botanist, explorer, and collector Carl Linnaeus [ley-NEE-eus] (1707–1778) laid out the modern taxonomic system for plants, animals, and minerals in his *Systema Naturae* (1753). Taxonomy is the science of the classification of living organisms or extinct beings. Linnaeus also established the basic botanical nomenclature (names), along with the rules for their use. In his system, the plant and animal worlds are divided into a hierarchy: beginning at the top, class, order, genus, and species. In his nomenclature, he used a binomial method (two names, both in Latin: first the genus and then the species—for example, *Equus caballus,* for the domestic horse). His system became part of modern science, though aspects of it have been updated, supplemented, and modified.

Philosophy   German thought stood in stark contrast to the Anglo-French Enlightenment. German Idealism, which espoused a spiritual view of life, was closely related to the Romantic spirit and its expressions. From Kant through Hegel, German thinkers constructed Idealism as a philosophic alternative to conventional religion.

In the 1790s, Immanuel Kant [KAHNT] (1724–1804) began the revolution in German thought when he distinguished the world of phenomena ("appearances") from the world of noumena ("things-in-themselves," or spirit). In Kantian terms, the phenomenal world may be understood by science, but the noumenal world may be studied, if at all, only by intuitive means.

Kant's followers, nonetheless, tried the impossible when they began to map out the spiritual realm. Johann Gottlieb Fichte [FICK-tuh] (1762–1814) found reality in the World Spirit, a force having consciousness and seeking self-awareness. Friedrich Wilhelm Joseph von Schelling [SHEL-ing] (1775–1854) equated nature with the Absolute, his name for ultimate reality. He also was the first to espouse the Romantic belief in the religion of art by claiming that artists reveal divine truths in inspired works. Schelling's teaching on art influenced the English poet Coleridge and through him English Romanticism in general.

The climax of Idealism came with Georg Wilhelm Friedrich Hegel [HAY-guhl] (1770–1831), who explained human history as the record of the World Spirit seeking to know its true nature. Self-knowledge for the World Spirit arose only through a dialectical struggle. In the first stage, the Spirit developed a thesis that in turn produced an antithesis; in the second stage, a conflict ensued between these two ideas that led to a synthesis, or a new thesis, which in turn gradually provoked new strife—a third stage, and so on ad infinitum. Hegel's theory of history ignored individuals because humans in the mass became tools of the World Spirit in its quest for freedom. In this view, wars, riots, and revolts were merely evidence of spiritual growth. For this reason, Hegel characterized Napoleon and his wars as embodiments of the World Spirit.

Hegelianism had a tremendous impact on later Western thought. Revolutionaries such as Karl Marx borrowed Hegel's dialectical approach to history. Conservatives, especially in Germany, used his thought as a justification for a strong centralized state, and nationalists everywhere drew inspiration from his thought. Other thinkers rejected his denial of human responsibility and founded existentialist philosophies that glorified the individual (see Chapter 20).

The Birth of Romantic Music

As the middle class gained political power between 1789 and 1830, they converted the musical scene into a marketplace; that is, laissez-faire economics and music became intertwined. Replacing elite forms of patronage, programs that the bourgeoisie now attended required admission fees and paid performers. Salaries and the demand for performances freed musicians from the patronage system. With their newly won independence, they became eccentric and individualistic—attitudes that were encouraged by the Romantic cult of the artist. Music grew more accessible as democracy progressed, and new industrial techniques and production allowed more people to own inexpensive musical instruments.

Figure 17.24 FERDINAND GEORG WALDMÜLLER. *Ludwig van Beethoven.* 1823. Oil on canvas, approx. 28⅓ × 22⅝". Archiv Breitkopf and Härtel, Leipzig, Germany. Original destroyed in World War II. *Beethoven in his later years was the embodiment of the Romantic genius, disheveled, singing to himself as he strolled Vienna's streets, mocked by street urchins; once, he was even arrested by the police as a tramp. In this 1823 portrait, Waldmüller suggests Beethoven's unkempt appearance, but through the strong expression, fixed jaw, and broad forehead he also conveys the great composer's fierce determination and intelligence.*

The most gifted composer of this period, and one of the greatest musical geniuses of all time, was Ludwig van Beethoven [BAY-toe-vuhn] (1770–1827), a German who spent most of his life in Vienna. He personified the new breed of musician, supporting himself through concerts, lessons, and the sales of his music (Figure 17.24). His works represent both the culmination of Classical music and the introduction of Romantic music. Working with the standard Classical forms—the sonata, the symphony, and the string quartet—he created longer works, doubling and even tripling their conventional length. He also wrote music that was increasingly expressive and that showed more warmth and variety of feeling than Classical music, particularly his program music—that is, music that portrays a particular setting or tells a story. He made several other significant musical innovations, including the use of choral voices within the symphonic form and the composing of music that expressed the power of the human will.

Beethoven's career may be divided into three phases, but his extreme individualism left his unique stamp on everything that he composed. In the first phase, from the 1790s until 1803, he was under the shadow of Haydn, with whom he studied in Vienna. His First Symphony (1800) may be termed a Classical work, but in it he reveals a new spirit by lengthening the first and third movements and making the middle movement more lively than usual.

In the second phase, from 1803 until 1816, Beethoven's genius gave birth to Romantic music. He began to find his own voice, enriching and deepening the older forms. The Third Symphony (1803), which Beethoven called the *Eroica* ("Heroic"), is the most characteristic work from this second stage. The composer originally dedicated this symphony to Napoleon, whom he admired as a champion of democracy. But when the French ruler declared himself emperor in 1804, Beethoven angrily tore up the dedication page and dedicated the work instead "to the memory of a great man." In the Third Symphony, Beethoven substantially expanded the musical material beyond the limits characteristic of earlier symphonies, making it longer and more complex. The music is grand, serious, and dignified, a truly heroic work.

From the second phase also comes Beethoven's most famous work, Symphony No. 5 in C Minor, Op. 67 (1808). The highly emotional Fifth Symphony, filled with bold harmonies and rich color contrasts, begins with a conflict-laden movement and concludes with an exultant final movement. The first movement opens with four notes—three short and one long—which have been described as the most memorable musical phrase of all time. During World War II their similarity to the Morse code made them symbolic of "V for Victory," and the Fifth Symphony was played at concerts to rally support for the Allied troops. In the first movement, this musical phrase is endlessly repeated, passed back and forth among the various instruments, played by a single instrument, or group of instruments, or the full orchestra. This phrase is also given shifting tone colors, ranging from harsh to lyrical, from soft to loud, along with dynamic changes in rhythm. The four notes function as a unifying motif in the first movement, and they return as a pervasive presence throughout the other three movements.

In his third phase, from 1816 until 1827, Beethoven's music became freer and more contemplative, reaching its culmination in the Ninth Symphony (1822–1824), the last of his large-scale works. In the last movement of this work, Beethoven included a choral finale in which he set to music the poem "Ode to Joy" by the German Romantic poet Friedrich von Schiller [SHIL-uhr] (1759–1805). Despite a life of personal adversities that included deafness from the age of thirty, Beethoven affirmed in this piece his faith in both humanity and God—"Millions, be you embraced! For the universe, this kiss!" The magnificent music and the idealistic text have led to the virtual canonization of this inspirational work.

Across these three phases, Beethoven was a prolific composer in all musical genres; many of these works are unrivaled in their expressiveness and originality. Besides the nine symphonies, he wrote two Masses, two ballets, one opera *(Fidelio),* sixteen string quartets, thirty-two piano sonatas (most notably the *Pathétique* and *Moonlight* sonatas), five concertos for piano, one concerto for violin, and numerous chamber and choral compositions.

Vienna contributed another outstanding composer in Franz Schubert [SHOO-bert] (1797–1828), who was famous for the beauty of his melodies and the simple grace of his songs. He lived a rather bohemian life, supporting himself, like Beethoven, by giving lessons and concerts. But unlike Beethoven, Schubert wrote mainly for the living rooms of Vienna rather than for the concert hall and is most famous for perfecting the **art song,** called *lied* (plural, *lieder*) in German. The emergence of this musical form in the Romantic period was tied to the revival of lyric poetry. Schubert composed the music for over six hundred *lieder,* with texts by Goethe ("Gretchen at the Spinning Wheel"), Shakespeare ("Who Is Sylvia?"), and other poets. His efforts raised the song to the level of great art.

One of Schubert's best-known songs is "Erlkönig" ("The Erlking"), a musical setting of a narrative ballad by Goethe. Filled with Romantic imagery, the poem tells of a distraught father, carrying his dying son in his arms while riding horseback through a storm-filled night. During the hectic ride, the boy has visions of the Erlking—in German folklore, the king of the elves, and, in Goethe's poem, the symbol of death. Schubert sets the text against a musical background that represents the horse's galloping hooves: pulsing, triplet rhythms. The song requires the soloist to give voice to each of four characters: narrator, father, son, and Erlking. Appropriate music is written for each, such as, for example, upper register, with discordant notes, for the boy; and cajoling tunes for the Erlking. Three times the boy cries out, "My father, my father!" The song ends with the narrator speaking in recitative: "In seinen Armen das Kind war tot,"or, in English, "In his arms the child was dead."

A final composer of significance in this first period of Romanticism was the Frenchman Hector Berlioz [BAIR-lee-ohz] (1803–1869). His most famous work is the *Symphonie fantastique (Fantastic Symphony)* (1830), a superb example of program music. Subtitled "Episode of an Artist's Life," this symphonic work illustrates musically a story that Berlioz described in accompanying written notes. In the tale, which takes the form of an opium dream, an artist-hero hopelessly adores an unfaithful woman and eventually dies for her. Relatively conventional in form, the symphony is most original in its use of a recurring musical theme, called an **idée fixe,** or "fixed idea," that becomes an image of the hero's beloved. Because every section contains the *idée fixe* in a modified form, it unifies the symphony in an innovative way. For example, in the fifth movement, subtitled "Dream of a Witches' Sabbath," he uses the *idée fixe* to introduce the Witches' Dance—a favorite pseudo-Gothic subject for Romantic composers and artists. Berlioz based the dance on the *Dies Irae (Days of Wrath)* from the Catholic Mass, thus making it emblematic here of a black mass, or devil worship. The *Dies Irae* theme, made up of long, evenly sustained notes, is first stated by low woodwinds and horns, accompanied by chimes. The theme becomes part of a musical conversation, being played in a rapid staccato, by high woodwinds, giving it a mocking sound. Variations of the theme are played by various groups of instruments, sometimes overlapping, and with frequent shifts in rhythm and tone color. The success of this Berlioz symphony helped to strengthen the fashion for program music in the Romantic period.

The Legacy of the Age of Revolution and Reaction

During this period of revolution and reaction, the West turned away from the past, with its monarchical forms of government, its hierarchical society dominated by aristocratic landowners, its glacial rate of change, and its patronage system ruled by social, ecclesiastical, and political elites. Three events in particular—the Industrial Revolution and the American and the French Revolutions—have left an indelible stamp on the modern world. The Industrial Revolution, which continues today, has gradually made humanity master of the earth and its resources while accelerating the pace of life and creating the two leading modern social groups, the middle class and the working class. The Industrial Revolution also spawned Classical economics, the school of economists who justified the doctrine of laissez-faire that is still held to be the best argument for capitalism and continuous industrial growth. This same doctrine altered the patronage system, subjecting the creative works of modern artists, writers, musicians, and humanists to the law of the marketplace.

The American Revolution produced the first successful modern democracy, one that today stands as a beacon of hope for those oppressed by authoritarian regimes. The French Revolution contributed the idea of an all-encompassing upheaval that would sweep away the past and create a new secular order characterized by social justice and fairness. Although viewed with skepticism by some people, for multitudes of others the notion of such a revolution became a sustaining belief. From the French Revolution also arose the idea that race and religion should not be used to exclude people from the right to vote—a reflection of its emphasis on the "brotherhood of man." Further, the French Revolution contributed the idea of a citizens' army, based on national conscription—a development that led to the savagery of modern warfare. And the French Revolution gave birth to the Napoleonic Code, the law code that is used in the French-speaking world today.

Both the French and the American Revolutions contributed certain beliefs that have become basic statements of Western political life, such as the idea that constitutions should be written down and that basic human liberties should be identified. Indeed, the progressive expansion of natural and civil rights to embrace all of society is an outgrowth of these two revolutions.

Other enduring legacies of this late-eighteenth- and early-nineteenth-century period are the Neoclassical buildings in Washington, D.C., and in most of the state capitals of the United States, the body of music of the Romantic composers, and the paintings of the Neoclassical and early Romantic schools. An ambiguous legacy of this period has been nationalism, the belief in one's own country and its people. At its best, nationalism is a noble concept, for it encourages people to examine their roots and preserve their collective identity and heritage. At its worst, it has led to cutthroat behavior, dividing the people of a country against one another and leading to the disintegration of nations. Both forms of nationalism remain potent forces in the world today.

On a more personal level, this period saw the development of the Romantic view of life, an attitude that stresses informality, identification with the common people, the importance of feeling and imagination, and enjoyment of simple pleasures. Perhaps more than any other legacy of this period, the Romantic outlook has helped to shape the way that most Western men and women live in today's world.

KEY CULTURAL TERMS

Romanticism   Faustian
Sublime   art song (lied)
Sturm und Drang   idée fixe

SUGGESTIONS FOR FURTHER READING

AUSTEN, J. Pride and Prejudice. Sense and Sensibility. Introduction by D. Daiches. New York: Modern Library, 1950. Both novels deal with English provincial life. Pride and Prejudice (1813) focuses on the proud Mr. Darcy, who must be humbled before the "prejudiced" Elizabeth Bennet can take his marriage proposal seriously; Sense and Sensibility (1811) uses practical-mindedness ("sense") to expose the self-indulgence of the "picturesque" spirit ("sensibility"), an aspect of genteel taste in the late eighteenth century.

BYRON, G. G., Lord. Don Juan. Edited by T. G. Steffan, E. Steffan, and W. W. Pratt. New York: Penguin, 1973. One of Byron's most admired works, full of autobiographical references; dates from 1819–1824.

FICHTE, J. G. Addresses to the German Nation. Translated by R. F. Jones and G. H. Turnbull. Chicago: Open Court, 1923. The work that helped to launch German nationalism when first published in the early 1800s.

GOETHE, J. W. v. Faust. Part I. Translated by M. Greenberg. New Haven, Conn.: Yale University Press, 1992. A good English version of Goethe's drama of a man prepared to sacrifice his soul for the sake of knowledge based on feeling; originally published in 1808.

———. *The Sorrows of Young Werther.* Translated by E. Mayer and L. Bogan. Foreword by W. H. Auden. New York: Vintage, 1990. The 1774 Romantic novel that brought Goethe his earliest European-wide fame, translated by modern poets.

HEGEL, G. W. F. *Reason in History.* Translated and with an introduction by R. S. Hartman. New York: Liberal Arts Press, 1953. The best source for Hegel's theory that history moves through a dialectical process; first published in 1837.

KANT, I. *Critique of Pure Reason.* Introduction and glossary by W. Schwarz. Aalen, Germany: Scientia, 1982. A good version of Kant's difficult work that tried to establish what human reason can know apart from experience; dates from 1781.

MALTHUS, T. *On Population.* Edited and with an introduction by G. Himmelfarb. New York: Random House, 1960. This influential essay, first published in 1788, identified the modern dilemma of keeping population growth in equilibrium with food production.

RICARDO, D. *On the Principles of Political Economy and Taxation.* New York: Penguin, 1971. Ricardo's "iron law of wages"—that wages tend to hover around the subsistence level—became a central tenet of nineteenth-century laissez-faire theory.

SCHELLING, F. W. J. v. *Ideas for a Philosophy of Nature.* Translated by E. E. Harris. New York: Cambridge University Press, 1988. An excellent translation of Schelling's 1799 work, which helped shape Romantic thinking by claiming to find God both in nature and in the human intellect.

SHELLEY, M. *Frankenstein.* With an introduction by D. Johnson. New York: Bantam Books, 1991. The original source of the Frankenstein legend, published in 1818 when Shelley was twenty-one years old; inspired by an evening of reading and discussing ghost stories.

WORDSWORTH, W. *Lyrical Ballads.* Edited by R. L. Braett and A. R. Jones. London: Routledge and Kegan Paul, 1988. A well-annotated edition of the original volume (1798) by Wordsworth and Coleridge that initiated the age of Romantic poetry in England; contains informative introductory material.

SUGGESTIONS FOR LISTENING

BEETHOVEN, LUDWIG VAN. Composing mainly in Classical forms, notably the symphony and the string quartet, Beethoven moved from a Classical style in the manner of Haydn and Mozart to a Romantic style that was his own. The First Symphony (1800) shows his Classical approach; the Third Symphony, the *Eroica* (1803), inaugurated his Romantic style with its intense emotionalism and rich thematic variations. Of special note is the Ninth Symphony (1822–1824), a semimystical work whose final section blends full orchestra with a massed chorus. The emotional nature of the Violin Sonata No. 9 (*Kreutzer* Sonata, 1803) inspired the Russian writer Leo Tolstoy to use the piece as a catalyst for murder in his story "The Kreutzer Sonata." Beethoven's stylistic development can also be traced in his sixteen string quartets: The first six quartets, dating from 1800, reflect the grace of Haydn and Mozart, and the last five, Nos. 12 through 16 (1823–1826), are technically difficult to play, enormously long, and characterized by mood shifts from light to tragic and unusual harmonic juxtapositions. The familiar piano piece "Für Elise" (1808) is a fine example of the rondo form.

BERLIOZ, HECTOR. Berlioz was typically Romantic in going beyond the forms of Classicism and stressing the emotional possibilities of his music. For example, his *Requiem* (1837) is less a religious work than a dramatic symphony for orchestra and voices; its inspiration was the tradition of patriotic festivals originated during the French Revolution. Similarly, his opera *Damnation of Faust* (1846) is not an opera in a conventional sense but a series of episodes based on Goethe's play, a form that allowed the composer to focus on those scenes that seemed full of theatrical potential. Finally, the *Symphonie fantastique* (1830) is more than a symphony; it has been called "a musical drama without words"—the prototype of Romantic program music.

SCHUBERT, FRANZ. Though a prolific composer of symphonies, operas, and piano sonatas, Schubert is most famous for perfecting the art song, or *lied.* Two of his best-known songs, with texts by Goethe, are "Gretchen am Spinnrade" ("Gretchen at the Spinning Wheel," 1814) and "Erlkönig" ("The Erlking," 1815). One of Schubert's most celebrated chamber works, a quintet for piano and strings, is "Die Forelle" ("The Trout," 1821), in which the lively, fluid music suggests the energetic movements of a swimming fish.

18 THE TRIUMPH OF THE BOURGEOISIE
1830–1871

The French and American Revolutions offered the hope of political power to all disenfranchised groups, and the Industrial Revolution promised material gains to the impoverished. Those expectations remained largely unfulfilled in Europe, however, as the nineteenth century unfolded. Benefits were reaped mainly by one group—the middle class, especially its wealthiest sector.

Left behind was a new group created by industrialization—the proletariat, or working class. These urban workers expressed their frustrations through political uprisings and social movements, and often the lower middle class joined them in demanding universal suffrage and a fairer distribution of power and wealth. Against the liberalism of the bourgeoisie, some of the workers set forth the ideals of socialism. But reform was limited at best, and successive waves of revolutionary uprisings failed to win significant improvements (Figure 18.1).

These changes were echoed in the cultural realm. From its brief peak in the 1820s, Romanticism declined and finally faded away. Embraced by the middle class, it gained respectability and lost much of its creative fire. By mid-century, a new, realistic style was emerging that reflected changing political and social conditions. Realism focused on ordinary people and attempted to depict in objective terms "the heroism of everyday life." At the same time, industrialization continued to spread, and people's ideas about themselves and the world were being challenged by everything from the theories of Charles Darwin to the invention of the camera (Timeline 18.1).

◄ **Detail** GUSTAVE COURBET. *Interior of My Studio: A Real Allegory Summing Up Seven Years of My Life as an Artist.* 1855. Oil on canvas, 11′9¾″ × 19′6⅝″. Louvre.

Timeline 18.1   THE AGE OF THE BOURGEOISIE

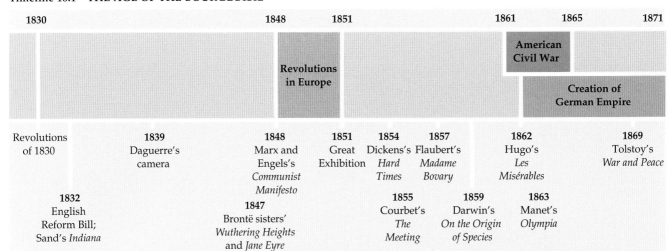

1830		1848	1851		1861	1865	1871
		Revolutions in Europe			**American Civil War**		
						Creation of German Empire	

Revolutions of 1830	**1839** Daguerre's camera	**1848** Marx and Engels's *Communist Manifesto*	**1851** Great Exhibition	**1854** Dickens's *Hard Times*	**1857** Flaubert's *Madame Bovary*	**1862** Hugo's *Les Misérables*	**1869** Tolstoy's *War and Peace*
1832 English Reform Bill; Sand's *Indiana*		**1847** Brontë sisters' *Wuthering Heights* and *Jane Eyre*		**1855** Courbet's *The Meeting*	**1859** Darwin's *On the Origin of Species*	**1863** Manet's *Olympia*	

Figure 18.1   FRANÇOIS RUDE. *The Departure of the Volunteers.* 1833–1836. Approx. 42 × 26′. Paris. *This group sculpture, depicting a crowd of warriors inspired by the winged Liberty, symbolizes the French people on the march during the revolution of 1830, the first of a series of revolutions in nineteenth-century Europe. Designed for the Arch of Triumph in Paris, the work came to be known affectionately as* La Marseillaise, *the name of the French national anthem.*

THE POLITICAL AND ECONOMIC SCENE: LIBERALISM AND NATIONALISM

The powerful forces of liberalism and nationalism drove many nineteenth-century events. The basic premise of liberalism was that the individual should be free from external control, a notion that resonated with the American and French Revolutions and the need of the bourgeoisie to liberate themselves from aristocratic society. The liberal political agenda included constitutionally guaranteed political and civil rights such as free speech, religious toleration, and voting rights for the propertied classes. Perhaps most important, liberalism embraced the laissez-faire economic ideals that allowed the wealthy middle class to maximize their profits in the business world. Liberalism was most successful in England, France, and Belgium; it failed to take root in Italy and central and eastern Europe, and Russia remained reactionary.

The other driving force of this era, nationalism, emphasized cooperation among all of a country's people who shared a common language and heritage. Overlooking class divisions, nationalists advocated humanitarian values, stressing the concept that all members of a nation are brothers and sisters. As nationalism spread, these concepts were often expanded to include liberal ideals, republican principles, and even democratic beliefs. Nationalism became a force in central, southern, and eastern Europe, where the states of what would become Germany and Italy were still little more than "geographic expressions" (Map 18.1). After 1848 nationalism became increasingly militant.

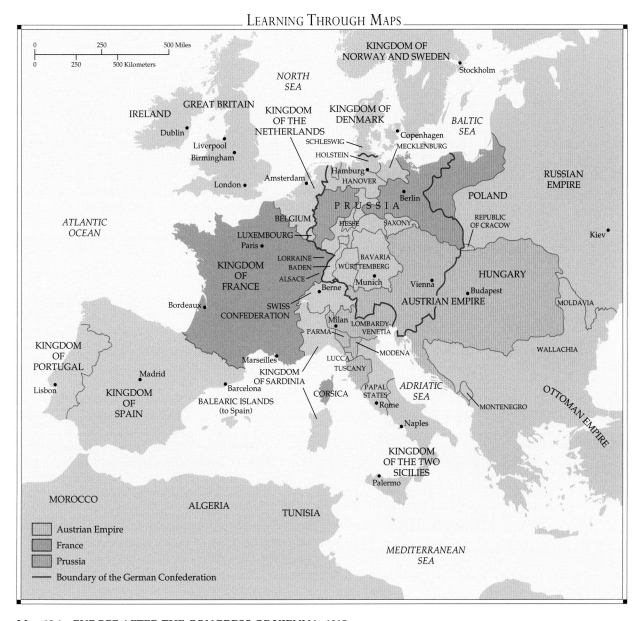

Map 18.1   EUROPE AFTER THE CONGRESS OF VIENNA, 1815
This map shows the political divisions of Europe after the defeat of Napoleon. **Compare** this map with Map 17.1, Europe at the Height of Napoleon's Power. **Notice** the trend toward larger but fewer states. **Which** states improved their territorial holdings at the Congress of Vienna? **Which** states were the losers at the congress? **Identify** the German Confederation and its boundary. **Which** state, Austria or Prussia, was better positioned to emerge as leader of the German Confederation?

The Revolutions of 1830 and 1848

The repressive policies imposed by the Congress of Vienna in 1815 were challenged in 1830 by a series of uprisings, beginning with the July Revolution in France and the French overthrow of the Bourbon monarchy and the installation of Louis Philippe (r. 1830–1848), who pledged to uphold a liberal constitution. This regime increasingly became the tool of the rich middle

class at the expense of the workers, however. Voting was limited to wealthy male property owners, and laws favored unregulated economic expansion. Having gained political dominance, the middle class intended to keep the benefits of the liberal agenda for themselves.

Liberal revolutions followed elsewhere, including in Belgium and areas of central and southern Europe, but they were unsuccessful. In central Europe, local

Table 18.1 MAJOR POLITICAL EVENTS OF THE 1815–1871 PERIOD

EVENT AND DATE	OUTCOME
Congress of Vienna, 1815	Inaugurates an era of repression
July Revolution in France, 1830	Ends the Bourbon dynasty and installs the bourgeois monarchy
First English Reform Bill, 1832	Extends voting rights to wealthy middle-class males
Revolution in France, 1848	Ends the bourgeois monarchy and installs the Second Republic, with Louis-Napoleon as president
Revolutions in Europe, 1848–1851	Their failure leads to an era dominated by realpolitik
Creation of Second French Empire, 1851	Louis-Napoleon becomes Napoleon III and leads empire until 1870
Kingdom of Italy, 1860	Sicily joins Piedmont
Creation of German Empire, 1862–1871	Engineered by Bismarck using a policy of "blood and iron"; unites German states around Prussia
American Civil War, 1861–1865	Preserves national union and abolishes slavery
Second English Reform Bill, 1867	Extends voting rights to working-class males
Franco-Prussian War, 1871	Destroys the Second French Empire, proclaims the German Empire, and leaves a legacy of French bitterness toward Germany

conservatives backed by Austrian troops quickly crushed the liberal uprisings of 1830 and punished rebels, imposed martial law, reinstituted censorship, and took control of the school systems. Although liberals continued to hope for moderate reforms, conservatives made it difficult for them. Across central and eastern Europe, the one force emerging as a rallying point was nationalism, focusing as it did on ethnic identity and common cultural heritage.

In 1848 accumulated dissatisfactions and frustrations erupted in another series of uprisings across Europe (Table 18.1), starting with demonstrations and riots in February 1848 in Paris. The rebellions were propelled by liberal ideals and nationalistic goals, but their immediate causes were declining production, rising unemployment, and falling agricultural prices. By the spring of 1848, the path of revolution ran from Paris through Berlin to Vienna, and all along this route varied groupings of bourgeoisie, intellectuals, workers, students, and nationalists toppled kings and ministers. Temporary governments, led by liberals and reformers, drove out foreign troops and set up constitutional monarchies, republics, or democracies with universal male suffrage. A few governments—influenced by the new movement known as socialism—addressed economic problems by passing laws to stimulate productivity, improve working conditions, and aid the poor with relief or employment programs.

By the fall of 1848, the conservatives—the army, aristocrats, and church—had rallied to defeat the often disorganized revolutionaries, and by January 1849 many of the old rulers had reclaimed power. After 1848 the idealism of the liberals, social reformers, and nationalists gave way to an unsentimental vision of politics and diplomacy backed by pragmatic use of force. This perspective came to be known as *realpolitik*, a German term that means "practical politics," a tactful way of saying "power politics."

European Affairs in the Grip of Realpolitik

From 1850 to 1871, realpolitik guided the European states as conservative regimes turned to strong and efficient armies, short, fierce wars, and ambiguously written agreements to resolve the various problems that had surfaced in the 1848 revolts. Otto von Bismarck (1815–1898), the prime minister of Prussia and future architect of German unification, mocked the failure of the liberals' parliamentary reforms and asserted that his country's fate would be settled not with speeches but with "blood and iron." Nationalists in Austrian-occupied Italy learned that Italian unity could be achieved only by military force and clever diplomacy. The Russian czars, seldom supporters of any type of reform, became even more committed to the belief that if any change did come, it would begin at the top, not the bottom, of society.

Limited Reform in France and Great Britain One of the most astute observers of the 1848 revolutions was Louis-Napoleon Bonaparte, nephew of the former French emperor. He became Emperor Napoleon III (r. 1852–1870) of the Second French Empire by appealing to both the bourgeoisie and the working class. A benign despot, he ruled over a sham representative government supported by a growing middle class made prosperous by the expanding industrial base. He also provided the poor with social services, and with an economic plan and subsidies, he enabled most urban workers and farmers to maintain a high standard of living.

Figure 18.2   CHARLES BARRY AND A. W. N. PUGIN. *The Houses of Parliament. 1836–1860. Big Ben (right) 320' high; Victoria Tower (left) 336' high; riverfront width 800'. London.*
In contrast to the revolutionary tradition on the Continent, Great Britain struggled to respond to changing political and social realities through debate and reform. To many observers in England and abroad, Parliament symbolized the success of liberalism and the representative legislative system. The Gothic spires of the Houses of Parliament rose in the mid–nineteenth century after the old buildings burned. Along with the neighboring clock tower known as "Big Ben" (a name applied originally only to the bell), they still stand today as the most recognizable image of modern London.

In Great Britain, a liberal coalition of landed and business interests pushed a reform bill through Parliament in 1832 over the protests of the conservatives. This new law redrew the political map of England to reflect the tremendous shift in population resulting from industrialization, and it enfranchised thousands of new male voters by lowering the property qualifications for voting, although millions of British citizens were still denied the vote. In 1867 a second reform bill extended voting rights to working-class males. With Queen Victoria (r. 1837–1901) on the throne and political forces balanced evenly between liberals and conservatives, Great Britain reached its apex of economic power and prestige (Figure 18.2).

Wars and Unification in Central Europe   Among the German-speaking states, the small principalities tended to discard liberalism and embrace militant nationalism. Their concerns were overshadowed, however, by the power struggle between Prussia and Austria for control of central Europe. William I became king of Prussia in 1861, and Bismarck was appointed his prime minister. Over the next few years, Bismarck built the Prussian army into a fierce fighting machine, at the same time ignoring liberal protests and the Prussian assembly and its laws. Nationalism replaced liberalism as the rallying cry of the Prussians, and Bismarck used this shift to unite the Germans around the Prussian state at the expense of France and of Austria (see Map 18.1).

Bismarck achieved his goal by neutralizing potential enemies through deft diplomacy and, failing that, through force. By 1866 he had united the German states into the North German Confederation, a union that excluded Austria. In 1870 he engineered a diplomatic crisis that forced France to declare war on Prussia. Costly French defeats brought the Franco-Prussian War to an abrupt end later that year, toppled the Second Empire of Napoleon III, and resulted in France's humiliation in the treaty signed at Versailles in 1871, proclaiming the German Empire. The seeds of World War I were sown by this crucial turn of events (Map 18.2).

On the Italian peninsula, most of which was ruled by Austrian princes, liberalism and nationalism were also causes of disruption. In the 1830s, Italian liberals inspired by the revolutionary writings of Giuseppe Mazzini [maht-SEE-nee] (1805–1872) banded together to form Young Italy, a nationalistic movement, and the independent Italian state of Piedmont-Sardinia emerged as the hope of liberals. Piedmont was a constitutional monarchy that honored its subjects' civil and political rights. Its economy was well balanced between farming and trade, and under Prime Minister Count Camillo Benso di Cavour [kuh-VOOR] (1810–1861), the standard of living was raised for many Piedmontese, especially middle-class merchants and manufacturers.

Between 1859 and 1871, Piedmont expelled most of the Austrians. As part of his grand strategy to unite

Map 18.2   EUROPE IN 1871
This map shows the political divisions of Europe in the third quarter of the nineteenth century. **Compare** this map with Map 18.1, Europe After the Congress of Vienna. **Notice** the sacrifice of the small states in the German Confederation and on the Italian peninsula to the unified countries of Germany and Italy. **Observe** the changes in the European holdings of the Ottoman Empire. **Consider** how the unification of Germany threatened the dominance of France in Europe. **Which** states divided Poland among themselves?

Italy, Cavour, with the encouragement of Napoleon III of France, annexed parts of central and southern Italy. Further assistance came from the fiercely patriotic soldier Giuseppe Garibaldi [gahr-uh-BAHL-dee] (1807–1882), who, with his personal army of a thousand "Red Shirts," invaded and liberated the Kingdom of the Two Sicilies (see Map 18.1) from its Spanish Bourbon ruler. In 1860 Sicilians voted overwhelmingly to join Piedmont in a Kingdom of Italy, and soon thereafter the Italian mosaic fell into place. In 1866 Austria gave up Venetia, and in 1870 Rome fell to nationalist troops and became Italy's capital.

Civil War in the United States

Paralleling the turbulent unification of the modern states of Italy and Germany, the United States was also undergoing expansion and centralization, processes that carried within themselves the seeds of conflict. The economy was mixed and regionally divided. On one side stood the Northeast, the national leader in commerce, trade, and banking and the site of a growing factory system; on the other side was the South, dominated by huge cotton plantations cultivated by thousands of black slaves. The unsettled western lands formed a third region.

After 1830 the economic issues that divided the northern and southern states became intensified over the question of slavery (Figure 18.3). As settlers moved west, the debate over the spread of slavery into these new territories and states aggravated sectional interests. In 1861 the southern states seceded from the Union, provoking a civil war.

Unlike Europe's contemporaneous wars, which were short and resulted in relatively few deaths, the

Figure 18.3 JOSEPH MALLORD WILLIAM TURNER. *The Slave Ship (Slavers Throwing Overboard the Dead and Dying, Typhoon Coming On). Ca. 1840. Oil on canvas, 35¾ × 48¼". Courtesy, Museum of Fine Arts, Boston. Henry Lillie Pierce Fund. Turner was motivated, in part, to paint* The Slave Ship *because of the famous* Zong *trial of 1783. The captain of the* Zong, *a British slave ship, in a ploy to collect insurance on his "property," claimed that because the ship was running out of water, he ordered the crew to throw the sick slaves overboard. At the trial, testimony proved that there was no water shortage on the ship. However, the court saw the incident as a civil insurance issue, not a criminal case, and the insurance company eventually had to pay for the loss of property— that is, the value of the slaves who had died. By the time he painted* The Slave Ship *(ca. 1840), Parliament had, in the 1830s, abolished slavery in the British colonies. Turner's terrifying image of natural calamity and human cruelty reflected the humanitarian values that had surfaced during the parliamentary and national debates about slavery. The ghoulish scene, painted in Turner's unique Romantic style, depicts the castaway bodies of the dead and dying, encircled by hungry fish, as they sink into the stormy sea.*

American Civil War lasted four years and resulted in huge losses on both sides (Figure 18.4). The northern victory in 1865, engineered by President Abraham Lincoln (in office 1861–1865), saved the Union and guaranteed freedom for the slaves. But animosity between the North and the South continued to smolder during the war's aftermath, called Reconstruction (1865–1876), and relations remained strained, particularly over racial matters, for more than a century.

Industrialism, Technology, and Warfare

Underlying the political upheavals of the nineteenth century were rapid changes in industrialism, technology, and warfare. The three became more closely related and interdependent as they spread across Europe and the Atlantic Ocean. They affected the personal lives of vast numbers of people at every social stratum.

Larger factories, with their huge machines, gave work to more workers and increased urban population growth. Inventions and innovations in transportation and communications shortened travel time and accelerated the dissemination of information. Industrialism and technology transformed the makeup of armies and navies and how campaigns were planned and wars fought.

Industrialism: The Shrinking Globe After its eighteenth-century beginnings in England (see Chapter 17), industrialism started to take root in France in the 1830s, and a short time later Belgium entered the industrial age. For the next forty years, Belgium and France were the chief economic powers on the Continent, with factory and railway systems radiating from Paris and Brussels to Vienna and Milan by 1871. The expansion of rail lines meant that factories no longer needed to be near coal mines or clustered in urban

Figure 18.4 ÉDOUARD MANET. *The Battle of the U.S.S.* Kearsarge *and the C.S.S.* Alabama. 1864. Oil on canvas, 54¼ × 50¾". John G. Johnson Collection, 1917. Philadelphia Museum of Art. *The American Civil War was also fought on the high seas. The C.S.S.* Alabama *was built in England in 1862 and, for twenty-two months, this commercial raider attacked Union merchant ships until the U.S.S.* Kearsarge *sank it off the French coast in 1864. Many bystanders on shore witnessed the battle, and reports quickly reached Paris, where Manet, after reading about the event, painted his imagined version of the conflict. He not only caught the drama of naval warfare but also documented its technological changes—the combining of steam with sail. His painting started a trend among French artists to travel to the coast and paint seascapes. In the 1870s, the Impressionists (see Chapter 19) painted many marine scenes, which helped establish their reputation.*

areas. Inventions in communications, such as the telegraph, made it easier for industrialists to take advantage of distant resources and markets, and in 1866 engineers laid a transatlantic telegraph cable, linking Europe and America.

New Technologies   Rapid advances in technology confirmed that the industrial revolution had launched a period of constant innovation. The steam engine, dating from 1769 (see Chapter 17), was soon adapted to many uses. Steamboats, with paddle wheels, dominated commerce, transport, and agriculture in Middle America from 1816 to 1870, when they were surpassed by an improved rail system. Steam locomotives were perfected in 1830 by the English father and son team George (1781–1848) and Robert Stephenson (1803–1859), who designed the Liverpool and Manchester Railway, the first rail service with a timetable. From then dates the Age of the Railroad, which continued until World War II. Steam engine technology was applied to watermills, leading to the invention of the water turbine (1820s), which was used first in sawmills and textile mills. In 1882, the world's first hydroelec-

tric plant, using the water turbine, was built in Appleton, Wisconsin, with many others soon to come. Other power sources also appeared. Gas lighting, with coal gas, began in the early 1800s in Great Britain, and by 1870 most cities and towns in Europe were illuminated by the glow of gaslights. Oil was discovered in Pennsylvania, with the first "gusher" in 1859. For now, oil was important only as a source for kerosene, the preferred fuel for lamps. Gasoline, though it had a bright future, was viewed only as a waste by-product. And, in communications, new technologies were linking the world closer together: the previously mentioned telegraph and the world's first uniform postal system (Great Britain, 1839). Similarly, the industrialization of war accelerated from the 1840s to 1914. Every nation-state and its military had to adopt the new and improved technologies if they expected to win wars. Steam-powered boats and railway engines were militarized, using, respectively, iron-clad hulls and powerful locomotives to haul troops, horses, and supplies. In particular, the Prussians integrated the rail system into their plans against Austria in 1866 and, against the French in 1870, in the Franco-Prussian War.

Figure 18.5 W. P. Frith. *The Railway Station.* Ca. 1862. Oil on canvas, 3'10" × 8'5". Royal Holloway College and Bedford New College, Surrey, England. *London was the hub of England's economy long before the Industrial Revolution, and with the coming of the railroads its position was enhanced. The massive new railway stations, often constructed of glass and iron, symbolized the changing business and leisure habits of life. In this painting of one of London's new rail stations, Frith's well-dressed middle-class citizens convey the excitement of travel as well as its novelty and uncertainty.*

This strategy hastened the defeat of the much larger, but less mobile, French army. Bismarck commemorated Prussia's strategy in his famous "blood and iron" metaphor. The Prussian army also relied on the "needle gun," a breech-loading rifle that discharged a cartridge as opposed to a muzzle-loading musket that shot a ball. And the industrial-military complex continued to evolve, as mass-produced weapons began to be made with interchangeable parts, manufactured with precision machine tools. By 1870 Germany—formerly Prussia—was setting the pace in strategy and weaponry for Europe, and other nations planned future wars to be quick and short.

The Spread of Industrialism In 1830 Great Britain passed into a new phase of the Industrial Revolution. It continued to build ships, to construct factories, and to lay rail lines; by 1850 all its major cities were linked by rail (Figure 18.5). In England and on the Continent, the mining of new coal and iron deposits and the rise of imports in materials for textiles and other goods kept the machines of industry humming. British financiers, joined by Continental bankers, made loans to fledgling companies for new factories, warehouses, ships, and railways, thereby generating more wealth for capitalists who had surplus funds to invest.

Symbols of the Bourgeois Age: The Crystal Palace and the Suez Canal As Europe's economy grew, two marvels of the industrial age—the Crystal Palace in London and the Suez Canal in Egypt—captured the world's imagination. The iron and glass Crystal Palace housed the Great Exhibition of 1851—in effect, the first world's fair (see Slice of Life, p. 560). In a structure that used advanced architectural methods and building materials, the newest inventions and machine-made goods were displayed for everyone, rich and poor alike. Although other nations displayed products and inventions, Britain's exhibits were the most impressive and proved that it was the world's leading industrial and agricultural power (Figure 18.6).

The second marvel was the digging of the Suez Canal to link the Gulf of Suez and the Red Sea with the Mediterranean Sea. Funded by a French company and opened in 1869, the canal shortened the distance

Figure 18.6   JOSEPH NASH. Detail of *The Crystal Palace*. 1851. Color lithograph with watercolor, approx. 21½ × 29⅝". Victoria and Albert Museum, London. *This detail illustrates the splendor and pageantry surrounding the moment when Queen Victoria opened the Great Exhibition. After the fair closed, the Crystal Palace was disassembled and rebuilt in a suburb in south London, where it stood as an arts and entertainment center until it was destroyed by fire in 1936. Nevertheless, the "prefab" construction principles of the Crystal Palace foreshadowed modern building methods.*

Figure 18.7   A French Frigate in the Suez Canal. 1869. © The Hulton Picture Company, London. *Just as Great Britain showed the world what it could achieve through industry and agriculture, so France demonstrated its technological and engineering genius in digging the Suez Canal. The Suez Canal Company, headed by the French entrepreneur Ferdinand de Lesseps [duh lay-SEPS] (1805–1894), began its work in 1859 and completed the canal ten years later. The French vessel pictured here was one of the first to navigate this waterway linking the Mediterranean with the Orient.*

between Europe and India, thus enabling steamships to ferry passengers and goods around the globe more quickly and comfortably (Figure 18.7).

The Crystal Palace, the Suez Canal, and other wonders of the age were made possible by the labor of millions of workers—men, women, and children. On the Continent, the working and living conditions of this group were no better than the squalid circumstances found in Great Britain in the first stage of the Industrial Revolution. The social costs of industrialism, notably the rapid growth of cities that threw poor and ill-trained people into slums and ghettos, were part of its negative side. The slums became breeding grounds for class hatred and offered ready audiences for revolutionaries and socialists advocating revolt and social changes. The rebellions that flashed across the Continent in 1848 were caused partly by the mounting frustrations in these working-class areas.

Even a large segment of the middle class remained cut off from economic and political power. In the United States, all white males were granted suffrage in the 1820s, and in England voting rights were granted to working-class males in the Reform Act of 1867. The revolutions of 1830 and 1848 widened the franchise for French, Italian, German, and Austrian men, although important government posts were always reserved for aristocrats. Women still could not vote in 1871, nor could wage earners (except for British and American workers) and members of the lower middle class. Universal suffrage was not yet a reality.

NINETEENTH-CENTURY THOUGHT: PHILOSOPHY, RELIGION, AND SCIENCE

The period 1830 to 1870 was rich in intellectual discourse. Liberalism, based on the ideas of Locke, Montesquieu, Rousseau, and Voltaire, and tested and proven in the American and French Revolutions, was now redefined. Socialism, born in reaction to industrialism and liberal economic theory, emerged as a galvanizing force for change among the working classes. Popular religion, in protest against the embryonic secular state, gave rise to "evangelicalism," a conservative movement dedicated to biblical authority. And breakthroughs in science and thought challenged traditional ways of understanding the world and human history.

Liberalism Redefined

At the heart of the debate over liberalism was the question, Which is primary, the individual or the group? Liberalism glorified the value of free expression for each human being, and capitalists used liberal arguments to justify their economic policies. But the corollaries of these policies seemed to be poverty, degradation, and injustice for workers, and new voices began to be raised in support of approaches that promised antidotes to the injustices of industrial capitalism. Primary among these were a variety of socialisms, forms of political and social organization in which material goods are owned and distributed by the community or the government.

In the late eighteenth century, English philosopher and social theorist Jeremy Bentham (1748–1832) had developed a variant of liberalism known as **Utilitarianism.** Bentham made "utility" his supreme moral principle, meaning that what gave pleasure to both the individual and society was right and what gave pain was wrong. Utility for society was always identified with "the greatest happiness for the greatest number"—a view that reflected Bentham's commitment to democracy. Accepting liberalism's laissez-faire ideal, yet tempering it with the principle of utility, Bentham pushed for a renovation of the repressive and outmoded governments of his time, including reform of the legal system, prisons, and education.

After 1830 Bentham's ideas were eloquently reinterpreted by bourgeois liberalism's strongest defender, the English philosopher John Stuart Mill (1806–1873). Growing to maturity in the second phase of the industrial age, Mill became increasingly fearful that the masses and a powerful state would ultimately destroy individual rights and human dignity. In his essay *On Liberty* (1859), Mill argued that the continued existence of the "civilized community" required the fullest freedom of speech, discussion, and behavior that was possible among all citizens, as long as no person was physically harmed. Mill's essay represents the high point of English liberalism.

After having advocated laissez-faire economics in his 1848 edition of the *Principles of Political Economy,* in later editions Mill embraced a mild form of socialism. Condemning unbridled economic competition, he reasoned that though production was subject to economic laws, distribution was not, and thus humans should divide the benefits of industrialism along rational lines. Mill also campaigned for religious toleration and minority rights and became a staunch supporter of women's right to vote and own property. In many of his writings, Mill collaborated with Harriet Taylor, his wife.

Socialism

Liberalism provided support for bourgeois values, but **socialism** seemed to many European workers and intellectuals to be the irresistible wave of the future. Socialism began as a reaction to industrialism and came to be its most severe critic, holding out a vision of what society might become if only certain fundamental reforms were made. Two main groups spoke for socialism in the 1800s: the utopian socialists and the Marxists. The utopians, who had their greatest impact before 1848, believed that the ills of industrial society could be overcome through cooperation between workers and capitalists. In contrast, the Marxists, who flourished after 1848, held the utopians in contempt as naive idealists and called for revolutions, violence, and the inevitable triumph of scientific socialism.

The principal utopian socialists—Robert Owen (1771–1858) (himself a wealthy industrialist), Comte de Saint-Simon [san-see-MOH(N)] (1760–1825), and Charles Fourier [FOOR-ee-ay] (1772–1837)—shared the belief that a more just society could be introduced using the discoveries about society made in communal associations that served as laboratories for their philosophical ideas. All three thinkers were concerned more about the consumption of the fruits of industrialism than they were about the creation of goods. To them, the workers were simply not receiving a fair share for their efforts and were being victimized by a ruthless, competitive system. To solve these problems, the utopian socialists proposed a number of alternatives, but their often impracticable schemes had little chance

ENCOUNTER

The Tragedy of the Cherokee Nation

Cultural encounters are unpredictable, with neither side able to foresee the long-range outcome of their meetings. Such was the case when the Cherokees, a tribe of Native Americans, decided to organize themselves and their lands, preparatory to petitioning to become a state in the United States. While they were amazingly successful in adopting American values and traditions, they failed in their ultimate goal.

When the first European settlers were establishing colonies on the Atlantic coast, the Cherokees lived farther inland, in farming villages surrounded by hunting and fishing lands, in western Virginia and the Carolinas, eastern Kentucky and Tennessee, and northern Alabama and Georgia. Their villages, composed of five hundred to two thousand people each and ruled by chiefs and priests, were fairly independent, though linked in loose regional federations. Although they had contact with the settlers, the Cherokees kept to the traditions of their ancestors.

However, as whites moved west after 1700, their impact on Cherokee landholdings was devastating. During the Revolutionary War era, when the Cherokees sided with the British, American forces broke their power and forced them to surrender much of their land. Additional land was lost in the Georgia colony when the Cherokees were forced to give up two million acres to pay off debts to white traders. By 1800 they were confined to parts of northern Georgia, the western Carolinas, and eastern Tennessee. The Cherokee population, however, remained the same—about twenty-two thousand people—as it had been in 1650.

Recognizing their inability to stem the tide of white settlement, Cherokee leaders devised a strategy for survival: They would forsake the old ways and Westernize their culture. Cherokee leaders and their people

Encounter figure 18.1 Chief Vann House. 1804. Courtesy, Historic Preservation Section, Georgia Department of Natural Resources. *James Vann, a Cherokee chief, built this three-story brick house in northern Georgia during the period when the Cherokees were emulating white culture. In 1834 Vann's son and heir, Joseph Vann, was dragged from this house by white men who seized the surrounding property. The Vann estate included eight hundred acres of farmland, peach trees, apple trees, forty-two cabins, six barns, five smokehouses, assorted shops, and a trading post. Houses for rank-and-file Cherokees were more modest in appearance and layout.*

adopted white techniques of farming and home construction and began to acquire property (Encounter figure 18.1). They fought alongside Americans in wars against other Native Americans and the British. Most important, Sequoyah (b. between 1760 and 1770, d. 1843), a Cherokee, invented a writing system, called a syllabary, for his native tongue (Encounter figure 18.2).

of succeeding in an age that was becoming more scientific and realistic.

The utopian socialists and their supporters quickly faded from view once Karl Marx (1818–1883) appeared on the scene. As a student at the University of Berlin, Marx studied Hegel's dialectical explanation of historical change, but as an atheist he rejected Hegel's emphasis on Spirit. Since Marx's radical politics made a teaching post untenable in reactionary Prussia, he became editor of a Cologne newspaper. When the police shut down the paper, Marx sought refuge abroad. From Brussels, he and Friedrich Engels (1820–1895), his lifelong friend and coauthor, were asked to develop a set of principles for a German workers' society.

The resulting pamphlet, *The Communist Manifesto* (1848), became the bible of socialism. Both men played minor roles in the 1848 revolts, seeing in them the first steps of a proletarian revolution. Marx spent his last years in London, writing his major work, *Capital* (volume 1, 1867; volumes 2 and 3, completed by Engels, 1885–1894), and founding an international workers' association to implement his ideas.

Marx's approach to historical change differed radically from the utopian view. According to Marx, history moved in a dialectical pattern as the Hegelians had argued, but not in rhythm with abstract ideas or the World Spirit. Instead, Marx thought that material reality conditioned historical development; the

Encounter figure 18.2   HENRY INMAN, after Charles Bird King. *Sequoyah.* Ca. 1830. Oil on canvas, 35¼ × 30½″. National Portrait Gallery, Smithsonian Institution. NPG.79.174. *This portrait depicts Sequoyah wearing white man's clothing, except for the exotic turban. Smoking a clay pipe, he wears a peace medal and holds a tablet displaying the Cherokee alphabet he invented—symbolic of his efforts to accommodate his people to mainstream society. Henry Inman's (1801–1846) portrait is a copy of one painted by Charles Bird King (1785–1862) in 1828 for the Commissioner of Indian Affairs in Washington, D.C., in an effort to create a record of prominent Native Americans. A legendary figure in American history, Sequoyah lives today through the name of the genus of California's giant redwood trees.*

The syllabary quickly enabled many Cherokees to read and write. In 1827 tribal leaders established the Cherokee Nation (northern Georgia), with separate legislative, executive, and judicial branches, a bill of rights, and a written constitution—based on the U.S. model. A bilingual newspaper, *The Cherokee Phoenix,* began publishing in 1828.

Despite their efforts to Westernize, the Cherokees soon learned that this was not enough. In 1830 the Cherokees, along with other tribes, were ordered to move to the Oklahoma Indian Territory. The Cherokee Nation sued to protect their lands, and the U.S. Supreme Court sided with them, but President Andrew Jackson (in office 1828–1836) refused to enforce the court's decision. Jackson's refusal is bitterly ironic, for he said his goal was "to reclaim [Native Americans] from their wandering habits and make them a happy, prosperous people"—the same goal sought by the Cherokees. In 1838–1839, American soldiers evicted the Cherokees from their homes and lands, and more than four thousand died on the 116-day journey to Oklahoma, a trek that became known as the Trail of Tears. In Oklahoma they joined with other southeastern tribes—the Creek, the Chickasaw, the Choctaw, and the Seminole, all of whom had been forcibly relocated earlier.

Learning from the Encounter   Compare and contrast Cherokee life before and after the American Revolution. **What** led the Cherokees to Westernize themselves and their culture? **Identify** the steps taken by the Cherokees to emulate white settlers. **Explain** the role of Sequoyah. **What** happened to the Cherokee Nation? **Why** did the Cherokees' plan fail? **Can** you relate the ordeal of assimilation experienced by the Cherokees to the experiences of today's immigrants?

various stages of history, which were propelled by class conflicts, unfolded as one economic group replaced another. For example, the bourgeoisie, which had emerged out of the collapse of the feudal system, represented only a moment in history, destined dialetically to bring forth its own gravedigger, the proletariat, or the urban working class. Moreover, the institutions and ideas of a society constituted a superstructure erected on the foundation of economic reality; governments, law, the arts, and the humanities merely reflected the values of a particular ruling class.

Marx then forecast a revolt by the proletariat, who would install a classless society. Marx believed that the workers' revolution would be international in scope

and that communist intellectuals would assist in bringing an end to bourgeois rule. Elaborating on his political, economic, and social theories, Marx's followers created Marxism and, inspired by his ideal society, organized to abolish the capitalist system, although their impact before 1871 was minimal.

From the first, socialism appealed especially to women, because it condemned existing social relations and called for universal emancipation. The ideal classless society would be free of every inequality, including sexual inequality. Utopian socialists were the most welcoming to supporters of female rights. For example, Fourier claimed that female freedom was the touchstone for measuring human liberation everywhere;

Owen espoused a new moral order in which sexual and class differences would be overcome in cooperative, loving communities; and Saint-Simon preached the moral superiority of women, though he preferred sexual complementarity to sexual equality.

Marx and Engels's views on women were ambiguous. They urged the full integration of women into the workforce as a condition of female emancipation but insisted that freedom for male workers was key to radical social change. So, they encouraged women to curb their aspirations in the name of the greater good—that is, for an ideal Marxian workers' society.

Religion and the Challenge of Science

The rise of **evangelicalism** was probably the major religious development of the Age of the Bourgeoisie. Evangelicalism, a distinctively Protestant movement, grew out of the Methodist tradition, with its focus on personal salvation (belief that one must be "born again") and sanctification (ability of the Holy Spirit to redeem sinners and create new lives) (see Chapter 16). In the United States, all mainline Protestant sects except for the Lutherans and the Episcopalians became evangelicals, while, in England, the Methodists formed the movement's core, along with a strong wing of Anglicans. The evangelicals wanted to transform society, one person at a time, and their methods included revivalism and the **holiness** movement—which stressed sanctification, or a holy life, after being "born again." They also were involved in the founding of nonsectarian self-help and personal uplift organizations, all in Great Britain: the Young Men's Christian Association (1844), the Young Women's Christian Association (1855), and the Salvation Army (1865).

The evangelicals were called conservative, because of their insistence on the paramount authority of the Holy Scriptures—a position that set them apart from liberal Protestants, who adopted many Deist ideas, and from traditional Protestants, such as Episcopalians and Lutherans, who stressed ritual and the sacraments. Grounded in their biblical faith, the evangelicals tried to hold the line against new developments in thought and science that contradicted their beliefs and values.

While the evangelicals tried to hold back the secular tide that was washing over the West, the Roman Catholic Church committed to a war against modernity itself. The once liberal Pius IX (pope 1846–1878), made captive briefly by revolutionaries in the 1848 uprising in Rome, became one of the most reactionary popes in history. In 1864 he issued an encyclical, the *Syllabus of Errors*, in which he denounced, as contrary to the faith, about eighty modern ideas, including public schooling, liberalism, democracy, socialism, religious toleration, and

civil marriage. Then, in 1870, he proclaimed the doctrine of papal infallibility, by which the pope cannot err when he speaks *ex cathedra* (Latin, "from the chair")—that is, when speaking officially as pope. This decree, which was made retroactive, led to a schism with some disaffected Catholics in the Netherlands, Germany, and Switzerland, but which slowly faded from prominence. Until 1963 the Catholic Church seemed self-isolated and opposed to all progressive ideas.

Meanwhile, in a development that alarmed some Christians, a group of Protestant scholars in Germany began to study the Bible not as a divinely inspired book incapable of error but simply as a set of human writings susceptible to varied interpretations. In Germany, this movement to treat the Bible like any other book was called **higher criticism.** Scholars began to try to identify the author or authors of each of the biblical books rather than relying on old accounts of their origins, to study each text to determine its sources rather than treating each book as a divine revelation, and, most important, to assess the accuracy of each account rather than accepting it as God's final word. By 1871 orthodox Christians were engaged in intellectual battles with the higher critics, some of whom portrayed Jesus not as God's son but as a mythological figure or a human teacher.

While the higher critics chipped away at Christianity from within, science assaulted it from outside. Geologists first discredited the biblical story of creation, and then biologists questioned the divine origin of human beings. The challenge from geology was led by the Englishman Charles Lyell [LIE-uhl] (1797–1875), whose fossil research showed that the earth was much older than Christians claimed. By treating each of God's six days of creation as symbolic of thousands of years of divine activity, Protestant Christians were able to weather this particular intellectual storm. Not so easily overcome, however, was biology's threat to biblical authority.

Following the Bible, the church was clear in its explanation of humanity's origin: Adam and Eve were the first parents, having been created by God after he had fashioned the rest of the animate world. Paralleling this divine account was a secular argument for evolution. Based on Greek thought, but without solid proofs, it remained a theory and nothing more for centuries. In 1859, however, the theory of **evolution** gained dramatic support when the Englishman Charles Darwin (1809–1882) published *On the Origin of Species*. Marshaling data to prove that evolution was a principle of biological development rather than a mere hypothesis, Darwin showed that over the course of millennia modern plants and animals had evolved from simpler forms through a process of natural selection.

In 1871, in *Descent of Man,* Darwin applied his findings to human beings, portraying them as the outcome of millions of years of evolution. Outraged clergy attacked Darwin for his atheism, and equally zealous Darwinians heaped ridicule on the creationists for their credulity. Today, the theory of evolution is one of the cornerstones of biological science, despite some continuing criticism.

Other advances in science were helping to lay the groundwork for the modern world. In the 1850s, French scientist Louis Pasteur [pass-TUHR] (1822–1895) proposed the germ theory of disease, the notion that many diseases are caused by microorganisms. This seminal idea led him to important discoveries and proposals for change. Claiming that germs were responsible for the spread of disease, he campaigned for improved sanitation and sterilization and thus paved the way for antiseptic surgery. He demonstrated that food spoilage could be prevented by killing microorganisms through heating, a discovery that resulted in the "pasteurization" of milk. His studies of rabies and anthrax led him to the first use of vaccines against these diseases. As the founder of bacteriology and an important figure in the development of modern medicine, Pasteur is the embodiment of Francis Bacon's seventeenth-century assertion that "knowledge is power."

In chemistry, a fruitful way of thinking about atoms was finally formulated, moving beyond the simplistic notions that had been in vogue since fifth-century B.C.E. Greece. In about 1808 the Englishman John Dalton (1766–1844) invented an effective atomic theory, and in 1869 the Russian Dmitri Mendeleev [men-duh-LAY-uhf] (1834–1907) worked out a periodic table of elements, based on atomic weights, a system that, with modifications, is still in use. By 1871 other chemists had moved from regarding molecules as clusters of atoms to conceiving of them as structured into stable patterns. Nevertheless, without means and equipment for studying the actual atoms, atomism remained merely a useful theory until the twentieth century.

Advances in chemistry also led to changes in anesthetics and surgery. In the 1840s, chemists introduced nitrous oxide, chloroform, and other compounds that could block pain in human beings. Use of these new painkillers in obstetrics increased after Queen Victoria was given chloroform to assist her in childbirth in 1853. These desensitizers revolutionized the treatment of many diseases and wounds and made modern surgery possible.

CULTURAL TRENDS: FROM ROMANTICISM TO REALISM

In its triumph, the middle class embraced both Neoclassical and Romantic styles in the arts. In Neoclassicism, the bourgeoisie found a devotion to order that appealed to their belief that the seemingly chaotic marketplace was actually regulated by economic laws. In Romanticism, they found escape from the sordid and ugly side of industrialism.

But both styles slowly grew routinized and pretentious under the patronage of the middle class, partly because of the inevitable loss of creative energy that sets in when any style becomes established and partly because of the conversion of the cultural arena into a marketplace. Because they lacked the deep learning that had guided many aristocratic patrons in the past, the new bourgeois audiences demanded art and literature that mirrored their less refined values. Catering to this need, artists and writers produced works that were spectacular, sentimental, and moralistic. Simply put, successful art did not offend respectable public taste.

Adding to this bourgeois influence was the growing ability of state institutions to control what was expressed in art and literature. The most powerful of these was France's Royal Academy of Painting and Sculpture, founded in 1648 for the purpose of honoring the nation's best painters. After 1830 its leaders became obsessed with rigid rules, thus creating what was called "official art." Those artists who could not obtain the academy's approval for exhibiting their works in the annual government-sponsored Paris Salons, or art shows, were virtually condemned to poverty unless they had other means of financial support. Rejected artists soon identified the Royal Academy as a defender of the status quo and an enemy of innovation. No other Western state had a national academy with as much power as France's Royal Academy, although in other European countries similar bodies tried to regulate both art and literature.

In reaction to the empty, overblown qualities of official art, a new style began to appear in the 1840s. Known as **Realism,** this style focused on the everyday lives of the middle and lower classes (Figure 18.8). The Realists depicted ordinary people without idealizing or romanticizing them, although a moral point of view was always implied. Condemning Neoclassicism as cold and Romanticism as exaggerated, the Realists sought to convey what they saw around them in a serious, accurate, and unsentimental way. Merchants, housewives, workers, peasants, and even prostitutes replaced kings, aristocrats, goddesses, saints, and heroes as the subjects of paintings and novels.

Many forces contributed to the rise of Realism. In diplomacy, this was the era of Bismarck's realpolitik, the hard-nosed style that replaced more cautious and civilized negotiation. In science, Darwin demystified earthly existence by rejecting the biblical view of creation and concluding that the various species, including human beings, evolved from simpler organisms. The spread of democracy encouraged the Realists to

SLICE OF LIFE
Observing Human Behavior: The Classes and the Masses

This Slice of Life tells the tale of the two Englands: the world of the well-to-do classes, who were visiting the 1851 Great Exhibition—as reported by Charlotte Brontë (1816–1855), the novelist; and the world of the masses, the lower and working classes, who were observed on the grounds at the annual Derby Day Horse Races, in 1861—as described by Hippolyte Taine (1828–1893), the French philosopher, historian, and critic.

CHARLOTTE BRONTË
The First World's Fair, 1851

Yesterday I went for the second time to the Crystal Palace. We remained in it about three hours, and I must say I was more struck with it on this occasion than at my first visit. It is a wonderful place—vast, strange, new, and impossible to describe. Its grandeur does not consist in *one* thing, but in the unique assemblage of *all* things. Whatever human industry has created you find there, from the great compartments filled with railway engines and boilers, with mill machinery in full work, with splendid carriages of all kinds, with harness of every description, to the glass-covered and velvet-spread stands loaded with the most gorgeous work of the goldsmith and silversmith, and the carefully guarded caskets full of real diamonds and pearls worth hundreds of thousands of pounds. It may be called a bazaar or a fair, but it is such a bazaar or fair as Eastern genii might have created. It seems as if only magic could have gathered this mass of wealth from all the ends of the earth—as if none but supernatural hands could have arranged it thus, with such a blaze and contrast of colours and marvellous power of effect. The multitude filling the great aisles seems ruled and subdued by some invisible influence. Amongst the thirty thousand souls that peopled it the day I was there not one loud noise was to be heard, not one irregular movement seen; the living tide rolls on quietly, with a deep hum like the sea heard from the distance.

HIPPOLYTE TAINE
A Day at the Races, 28 May 1861

Races at Epsom: it is the Derby Day, a day of jollification; Parliament does not sit; for three days all the talk has been about horses and their trainers. . . .

Epsom course is a large, green plain, slightly undulating; on one side are reared three public stands and several other smaller ones. In front, tents, hundreds of shops, temporary stables under canvas, and an incredible confusion of carriages, of horses, of horsemen, of private omnibuses; there are perhaps 200,000 human heads here. Nothing beautiful or even elegant; the carriages are ordinary vehicles, and toilettes are rare; one does not come here to exhibit them but to witness a spectacle: the spectacle is interesting only on account of its size. From the top of the Stand the enormous antheap swarms, and its din ascends. But beyond, on the right, a row of large trees, behind them the faint bluish undulations of the verdant country, make a magnificent frame to a mediocre picture. Some clouds

take an interest in ordinary people, and the camera, invented in the 1830s, probably inspired the Realists in their goal of truthful accuracy. All these influences combined to make Realism a style intent on scientific objectivity in its depiction of the world as it is.

Literature

In literature, the Romantic style continued to dominate poetry, essays, and novels until midcentury, when it began to be displaced by Realism. The Romantic authors were concerned with the depth of their characters' emotions and had great faith in the power of the individual to transform his or her own life and the lives of others. The Realists, in contrast, tended to be determinists who preferred to let the facts speak for themselves. They rejected the bourgeois world as flawed by hypocrisy and materialism and denounced the machine age for its mechanization of human relationships. Realism in literature flourished between 1848 and 1871, chiefly in France, England, and Russia. A special contribution to Realistic literature was made by African American writers who found their voices during the slavery controversy preceding the Civil War.

as white as swans float in the sky, and their shadow sweeps over the grass; a light mist, charged with sunshine, flits in the distance, and the illuminated air, like a glory, envelops the plain, the heights, the vast area, and all the disorder of the human carnival.

It is a carnival, in fact; they have come to amuse themselves in a noisy fashion. Everywhere are gypsies, comic singers and dancers disguised as negroes, shooting galleries where bows and arrows or guns are used, charlatans who by dint of eloquence palm off watch chains, games of skittles and sticks, musicians of all sorts, and the most astonishing row of cabs, barouches, droskies, four-in-hands, with pies, cold meats, melons, fruits, wines, especially champagne. They unpack; they proceed to drink and eat; that restores the creature and excites him; coarse joy and open laughter are the result of a full stomach. In presence of this ready-made feast the aspect of the poor is pitiable to behold; they endeavour to sell you penny dolls, remembrances of the Derby; to induce you to play at Aunt Sally,[1] to black your boots. Nearly all of them resemble wretched, hungry, beaten, mangy dogs, waiting for a bone, without hope of finding much on it. They arrived on foot during the night, and count upon dining off crumbs from the great feast. Many are lying on the ground, among the feet of the passers-by, and sleep open-mouthed, face upwards. Their countenances have an expression of stupidity and of painful hardness. The majority of them have bare feet, all are terribly dirty, and most absurd-looking; the reason is that they wear gentlemen's old clothes, worn-out fashionable dresses, small bonnets, formerly worn by young ladies. The sight of these cast-off things, which have covered several bodies, becoming more shabby in passing from one to the other, always makes me uncomfortable. To wear these old clothes is degrading; in doing so the human being shows or avows that he is the off-scouring of society. Among us [the French] a

peasant, a workman, a labourer, is a different man, not an inferior person; his blouse belongs to him, as my coat belongs to me—it has clothed no one but him. The employment of ragged clothes is more than a peculiarity; the poor resign themselves here to be the footstool of others.

One of these women, with an old shawl that appeared to have been dragged in the gutter, with battered head-gear, which had been a bonnet, made limp by the rain, with a poor, dirty, pale baby in her arms, came and prowled round our omnibus, picked up a castaway bottle, and drained the dregs. Her second girl, who could walk, also picked up and munched a rind of melon. We gave them a shilling and cakes. The humble smile of thankfulness they returned, it is impossible to describe. They had the look of saying, like Sterne's[2] poor donkey, "Do not beat me, I beseech you—yet you may beat me if you wish." Their countenances were burned, tanned by the sun; the mother had a scar on her right cheek, as if she had been struck by a boot; both of them, the child in particular, were grown wild and stunted. The great social mill crushes and grinds here, beneath its steel gearing, the lowest human stratum.

[1]A game played at fairs, featuring an effigy of an old woman smoking a pipe, at which fairgoers threw missiles to win prizes.
[2]Laurence Sterne (1713–1768), British novelist.

Interpreting This Slice of Life **Compare and contrast** what Brontë and Taine say about the different groups they meet. **Why** are their descriptions so different? **What** do their observations reveal about life in mid-nineteenth-century England and about their own attitudes? **How** would you describe public behavior in the United States, and **what** does that tell us about our society?

The Height of French Romanticism In France, the leading exponent of Romanticism was the poet, dramatist, and novelist Victor Hugo (1802–1885). His poetry established his fame, and the performance of his tragedy *Hernani* in February 1830 solidified his position as the leader of the Romantic movement. Enlivened with scenes of rousing action and by characters with limitless ambition, this play seemed with one stroke to sweep away the artificialities of Classicism. Its premiere created a huge scandal. When the bourgeois revolution erupted in July 1830, many French people believed that Hugo's *Hernani* had been a literary prophecy of the political upheaval.

Hugo became something of a national institution, noted as much for his humane values as for his writing. Because of his opposition to the regime of Napoleon III, he was exiled from France for eighteen years, beginning in 1851. While in exile, he published his most celebrated novel, the epic-length *Les Misérables (The Wretched)* (1862), which expresses his revulsion at the morally bankrupt society he believed France had become after Napoleon I.

The hero and moral center of the book is the pauper Jean Valjean, who is imprisoned for seventeen years for stealing a loaf of bread. He escapes and becomes a prosperous, respectable merchant, but the law is

Figure 18.8 ÉDOUARD MANET. *A Bar at the Folies-Bergère.* 1882. Oil on canvas, 3'1½" × 4'3". Courtauld Institute Galleries, London (Courtauld Collection). *The Folies-Bergère was the grandest of the glorified beer halls, or cafés-concerts, which sprang up in Paris after 1850, offering drinks and raucous stage entertainment. Catering initially to a lower middle class prospering from the booming economy, these cafés-concerts soon became classless settings in which all strata of society could anonymously rub elbows. In this painting, Manet captures the spectacle of the cafés-concerts: the ghastly white light, the crush of customers, the stoic barmaid, the trapeze artist whose green feet are just visible in the top left corner. Most of these details are shown in the mirror behind the barmaid. The painting presents a problem in the impossibly placed mirror; the barmaid appears to be looking at the viewer but is also standing before the top-hatted man reflected in the mirror.*

unrelenting in its pursuit of him, and he is forced into a life of hiding and subterfuge. Hugo makes Valjean a symbol of the rising masses' will to freedom, and his bourgeois readers were fascinated and horrified at the same time by Valjean's ultimate triumph.

Another popular Romantic literary figure was the French novelist and playwright George Sand (1804–1876), who was forced by need to become a writer. Amandine-Aurore-Lucie Dupin took the name George Sand in part to keep from embarrassing her own and her estranged husband's families and in part to assert herself in the male literary world; she was addressed by her friends as Madame George Sand.

Sand has been called "the first modern, liberated woman." She courted controversy as she engaged in highly public sexual liaisons with leading men of the times, including Romantic composer and pianist Frédéric Chopin [SHO-pan] (1810–1849). She often dressed as a typical bourgeois gentleman: coat and vest, cravat, trousers, steel-tipped boots, and top hat. Sand was the first Western woman to play an active part in a revolutionary government. In the Paris uprising of 1848, she sat on committees, delivered speeches and debated issues, and wrote in support of the short-lived radical socialist regime.

Because her father was descended from Polish royalty and her mother was the daughter of a Parisian bird-seller, Sand found herself in a socially equivocal position in class-conscious France. Thus, she was predisposed to focus her writings on people without power, such as women, artists, and laborers. Her novels and plays, with their strong political undertones, illustrate Victor Hugo's claim that Romanticism was "liberalism in literature." For Sand, idealism simply meant another way to call for social reform.

Sand's first novel, *Indiana* (1832), is usually regarded as her best and is praised for its multifaceted characters and its accurate depiction of the constraints imposed on married women at that time. Indiana, the nineteen-year-old heroine, is unhappily married to an older man; she seeks true love apart from her spouse and in a relationship of equals. Unfortunately, because of her lover's treachery and society's inflexible marital code, she has to flee from France and scandal to Bourbon Island (modern Réunion), then a French colony in the Indian Ocean. There she finds a soul mate with whom she settles down in a Rousseau-like paradise. Critics read the work as an attack on France's Napoleonic Code, which placed wives under their husband's control (see Chapter 17). *Indiana* made Sand's reputation, and she followed it with about eighty more novels and twenty plays, a book of travel writings, and two volumes of children's stories.

Romanticism in the English Novel   In England, Romanticism found its most expressive voices in the novels of the Brontë sisters, Charlotte (1816–1855) and Emily (1818–1848). Reared in the Yorkshire countryside far from the mainstream of cultured life, they created two of the most beloved novels in the English language. Their circumscribed lives seemed to uphold the Romantic dictum that true artistic genius springs from the imagination alone.

Emily Brontë's *Wuthering Heights* (1847) creates a Romantic atmosphere through mysterious events, ghostly apparitions, and graveyard scenes, but it rises above the typical Gothic romance. The work is suffused with a mystical radiance that invests the characters and the natural world with spiritual meanings beyond the visible. A tale of love and redemption, the story focuses on a mismatched couple, the genteel Catherine and the outcast Heathcliff, who are nevertheless soul mates. In the uncouth, passionate Heathcliff, Brontë creates a Byronic hero who lives outside conventional morality. Her portrayal of him as a man made vengeful by cruel circumstances has led some to label this the first sociorevolutionary novel.

Charlotte Brontë published *Jane Eyre* in the same year *Wuthering Heights* appeared. A dark and melancholy novel, the work tells the story of a governess's love for her brooding and mysterious employer. Her hopes for happiness are crushed by the discovery that the cause of his despair is his deranged wife, kept hidden in the attic. Narrated in the first person, the novel reveals the heroine's deep longings and passions as well as her ultimate willingness to sacrifice her feelings for moral values. Recognized at the time as a revolutionary work that dispensed with the conventions of sentimental novels, *Jane Eyre* was attacked by critics but welcomed by the reading public, who made it a best-seller.

Romanticism in American Literature   Romanticism reached a milestone with the American literary and philosophical movement known as **Transcendentalism.** Flourishing in New England in the early and middle part of the nineteenth century, this movement was critical of formal religions and drew inspiration from the belief that divinity is accessible without the necessity of mediation. Unlike the God of traditional religion, the divine spirit (Transcendence) manifested itself in many forms, including the physical universe, all constructive practical activity, all great cultural achievements, and all types of spiritual expression. In their goal of seeking union with the world's underlying metaphysical order, the Transcendentalists followed in the steps of the German Idealists (see Chapter 17). Of the Transcendentalists, Henry David Thoreau (1817–1862) was probably the most influential. His most celebrated book, *Walden* (1854), the lyrical journal of the months he spent living in the rough on Walden Pond, is virtually the bible of today's environmental movement. Thoreau's *On the Duty of Civil Disobedience* (1849), an essay on the necessity of disobeying an unjust law, was one of the texts that inspired Martin

Luther King Jr.'s protests of the 1950s and 1960s against America's segregated social system.

American poetry now became a major presence in Western literature with the writings of Emily Dickinson and Walt Whitman. Both poets worked within the Romantic style, drawing on intimate histories, in the manner of other Romantic poets. They also adopted offbeat verse forms and punctuation, that have greatly influenced twentieth-century poets. Today, Dickinson and Whitman are regarded as two of the most innovative poets of nineteenth-century American literature. Dickinson, a virtual recluse in her day, published only seven poems during her lifetime. Since her death, her reputation has increased dramatically, based on the almost 1,800 poems that make up the Dickinson canon. Whitman, vilified at first by the establishment, lived long enough to see himself become an American icon, the model of the good gray-haired poet. During his career, he effected a revolution in American poetry by creating a body of works based on his experience as an American, written in a specifically American language.

Realism in French and English Novels   Realism began in France in the 1830s with the novels of Honoré de Balzac [BAHL-zak] (1799–1850). Balzac foreshadowed the major traits of Realism in the nearly one hundred novels that make up the series he called *The Human Comedy.* Set in France in the Napoleonic era and the early industrial age, this voluminous series deals with the lives of over two thousand characters, both in Paris and in the provinces. Balzac condemns the hollowness of middle-class society, pointing out how industrialism has caused many people to value material things more than friendship and family, although there are virtuous and sympathetic characters as well.

France's outstanding Realist was Gustave Flaubert [floh-BAIR] (1821–1880), who advocated a novel free from conventional, accepted moral or philosophical views. His masterpiece is *Madame Bovary* (1857), which caused a scandal with its unvarnished tale of adultery. In contrast to Balzac's broad sweep, Flaubert focused on a single person, the unhappy and misguided Emma Bovary. In careful detail, he sets forth the inner turmoil of a frustrated middle-class woman trapped by her dull marriage and her social standing. By stressing objectivity and withholding judgment, Flaubert believed he was following the precepts of modern science. As a social critic, he portrays everyday life among the smug members of this small-town, bourgeois society. Notwithstanding the scandal it caused, *Madame Bovary* was an instant success and established the new style of Realism. For most readers, Emma Bovary became a poignant symbol of people whose unrealistic dreams and aspirations doom their lives to failure.

English novelists also wrote in the new Realist style. Like their French counterparts, they railed against the vulgarity, selfishness, and hypocrisy of the middle class, but unlike the French, who were interested in creating unique characters, they spoke out for social justice. England's most popular writer of Realist fiction was Charles Dickens (1812–1870), who favored stories dealing with the harsh realities of urban and industrial life. Writing to meet deadlines for serialized magazine stories, Dickens poured out a torrent of words over a long literary career that began when he was in his twenties.

In early works, such as *Oliver Twist* (1837–1839) and *David Copperfield* (1849–1850), Dickens was optimistic, holding out hope for his characters and, by implication, for society in general. But in later novels, such as *Bleak House* and *Hard Times,* both published between 1851 and 1854, he was pessimistic about social reform and the possibility of correcting the excesses of industrialism. Dickens's rich descriptions, convoluted plots with unexpected coincidences, and topical satire were much admired by Victorian readers, and his finely developed and very British characters, such as Mr. Pickwick, Oliver Twist, and Ebenezer Scrooge, have survived as a memorable gift to literature.

Realist fiction in England was also represented by important female writers. The two most successful were Elizabeth Gaskell (1810–1865) and Mary Ann Evans (1819–1880), better known by her pen name, George Eliot. Both wrote novels about the hardships imposed on the less fortunate by England's industrial economy. Gaskell's *North and South* (1855) underscores the widening gap between the rich, particularly in England's urban north, and the poor, concentrated in the rural south, within the context of the rise of the labor unions. Typically, her themes involve contrasts, contradictions, and conflicts, such as the helplessness of the individual in the face of impersonal forces and the simultaneous need to affirm the human spirit against the inequalities of the factory system. Similarly, in *Middlemarch* (1872) and other novels, George Eliot explores the ways human beings are trapped in social systems that shape and mold their lives, for good or ill. Eliot's outlook is less deterministic, however, stressing the possibility of individual fulfillment despite social constraints as well as the freedom to make moral choices.

The Russian Realists During the Realist period, Russia for the first time produced writers whose works received international acclaim: Leo Tolstoy [TOHL-stoy] (1828–1910) and Feodor Dostoevsky [duhs-tuh-YEF-skee] (1821–1881). Like English and French Realists, these Russians depicted the grim face of early industrialism and dealt with social problems,

notably the plight of the newly liberated serfs. Their realism is tempered by a typically Russian concern: Should Russia embrace Western values or follow its own traditions, relying on its Slavic and Oriental past? Significantly, Tolstoy and Dostoevsky transcend Western Realism by stressing religious and spiritual themes.

In his early works, Tolstoy wrote objectively, without moralizing. The novel *Anna Karenina* (1875–1877) describes the unhappy consequences of adultery in a sophisticated but unforgiving society. *War and Peace* (1865–1869), his greatest work, is a monumental survey of Russia during the Napoleonic era, portraying a huge cast of characters caught up in the surging tides of history. Although Tolstoy focuses on the upper class in this Russian epic, he places them in realistic situations without romanticizing them. In these early works, he was a determinist, convinced that human beings were at the mercy of forces beyond them. But in 1876, after he had a religious conversion to a simple form of Christianity that stressed pacifism, plain living, and radical social reform, he repudiated all art that lacked a moral vision, including his own. Tolstoy devoted the rest of his life to this plain faith, following what he believed to be Jesus' teachings and working for a Christian anarchist society.

Feodor Dostoevsky was a powerful innovator who introduced literary devices that have become standard in Western letters. For example, *Crime and Punishment* (1866), written long before Sigmund Freud developed psychoanalysis, analyzes the inner life of a severely disturbed personality. In *Notes from Underground* (1864), the unnamed narrator is the first depiction of a modern literary type, the anti-hero, the character who lacks the virtues conventionally associated with heroism but who is not a villain.

In *The Brothers Karamazov* (1879–1880), Dostoevsky reaches the height of his powers. Like Flaubert in *Madame Bovary*, Dostoevsky sets his story in a small town and builds the narrative around a single family. Each of the Karamazov brothers personifies certain traits of human behavior, though none is a one-dimensional figure. Using the novel to address one of life's most vexing questions—If God exists, why is there suffering and evil in the world?—Dostoevsky offers no easy solution. Indeed, he reaches the radical conclusion that the question is insoluble, that suffering is an essential part of earthly existence and without it human beings can have no moral life.

Realism Among African American Writers In the 1840s, as public opinion in the United States became polarized over slavery, a new literary genre, the **slave narrative,** emerged. The narratives, whether composed by slaves or told by slaves to secretaries who wrote

Figure 18.9 Jean-Auguste-Dominique Ingres. *The Turkish Bath.* Ca. 1852–1863. Oil on canvas, diameter 42½″. Louvre. *Interest in Oriental themes was a continuous thread in France's nineteenth-century bourgeois culture. In his rendering of a Turkish bath, Ingres used a harem setting in which to depict more than twenty nudes in various erotic and nonerotic poses. The nudes nevertheless are portrayed in typical Classical manner, suggesting studio models rather than sensual human beings.*

them down, were filled with gritty, harsh details of the unjust slave system; these stories in turn influenced Realist fiction and also fueled the fires of antislavery rhetoric. Many slave narratives were eventually published, but probably the most compelling was the *Narrative of the Life of Frederick Douglass* (1845), written by Douglass (1817–1895) himself, which launched this literary tradition. Douglass's narrative described a heroic struggle, starting from an early awareness of the burden of being a slave, continuing through successful efforts to educate himself, and concluding with a bolt to freedom and a new life as a spokesman for abolition. This eloquent narrative was one of the first great modern books in the West to be written by a person of color. Besides establishing a new genre, Douglass made a splendid addition to the old genre of autobiography and opened the door to a more inclusive world literature free from the racial segregation that had characterized the varied literatures of the world since the fall of Rome.

Another African American who contributed to the Realist tradition was Sojourner Truth (1795–1883). Given the slave name of Isabell ("Bell") Hardenberg at birth, she won her freedom and took a new name, symbolic of her vow to "sojourn" the American landscape and always speak the truth. Truth's voice, captured by her secretary, Olive Gilbert, is both colloquial and eloquent, teasing and sincere, homespun and filled with biblical knowledge. Her actual voice electrified

listeners, causing Truth to be remembered as one of the most natural orators in the nineteenth-century United States. Sojourner Truth's "Ain't I a Woman?" speech, delivered in 1851 before the Women's Rights convention in Akron, Ohio, shows the simple eloquence that made her a legend in her own time.

Art and Architecture

Realism in art grew up alongside an exaggerated version of Romanticism that persisted well beyond midcentury. Even Neoclassicism was represented in the official art of France throughout this period. Both styles found favor with the wealthy bourgeoisie.

Neoclassicism and Romanticism After 1830 Jean-Auguste-Dominique Ingres, who had inherited the position of Neoclassical master painter from Jacques-Louis David, virtually controlled French academic art until his death in 1867. He understood the mentality of the Salon crowds, and his works catered to their tastes. What particularly pleased this audience—composed almost exclusively of the wealthy, educated middle class—were chaste nudes in mythological or exotic settings, as in *The Turkish Bath* (Figure 18.9). The women's tactile flesh and the abandoned poses, though superbly realized, are depicted in a cold, Classical style and lack the immediacy of Ingres's great portraits.

Figure 18.10   EUGÈNE DELACROIX. *Hamlet and Horatio in the Graveyard*. 1839. Oil on canvas, 32 × 26″. Louvre. *Shakespeare's* Hamlet, *a tragedy of doomed love, became a touchstone for Romantic artists and poets. Delacroix, after having seen* Hamlet *performed in Paris, was so taken by the graveyard scene that he created at least three lithographs and two paintings of it. In this painting, he has reduced the scene to its bare essentials: The two gravediggers (foreground) confront Hamlet and Horatio (middle ground), while a cloud-filled sky takes up nearly half of the canvas. He makes the dark skull the focus of the painting by having all four figures gaze at it and placing it against the light sky. Dynamic tension is added by the diagonal line running from the upper right to the lower left side of the painting, a line made up of the descending hill and the gravedigger's upraised arm.*

Eugène Delacroix, Ingres's chief rival, remained a significant force in French culture with almost comparable artistic power. Delacroix perfected a Romantic style filled with superb mastery of color and human feeling. One of his finest works from this period is *Hamlet and Horatio in the Graveyard,* based on Act 5, Scene 1, of Shakespeare's drama (Figure 18.10). In the painting, one of the gravediggers holds up a skull to Hamlet and Horatio. Delacroix, faithful to the Shakespearean text, captures the men's differing reactions: Hamlet, on the right, seems to recoil slightly, while Horatio appears more curious. In this and later paintings, Delacroix tried to work out the laws governing colors—especially the effects that they have on the viewer. The results in *Hamlet and Horatio in the Graveyard* are somber hues that reinforce the melancholy atmosphere. Later, the Impressionists based some of their color theories on Delacroix's experiments (see Chapter 19).

Romantic painting, especially of landscapes, became popular in the United States as Americans pushed westward. The grandeur, vastness, and beauty of the new country and God's presence in Nature, as explained by the Transcendental poet and essayist Ralph Waldo Emerson (1803–1882), inspired landscape artists to glorify Nature, to portray Nature as Sublime, and to relate the individual to the natural world. One group of artists, known as the Hudson River School

(ca. 1825–1870), specialized in images of the mountains and valleys of New England and New York. For them, following Emerson's teachings, God and Nature were one, and they attempted to infuse their works with a mystical quality while also showing that the individual had a role to play in understanding and affecting Nature. A second generation of the Hudson River School ushered in **luminism,** an art movement that emphasized Nature rather than the individual, whom they often depicted in small scale or omitted entirely from their paintings (Figure 18.11).

Like Romantic painting, nineteenth-century architecture tended to be romantically nostalgic, intrigued by times and places far removed from the industrial present. Particularly appealing were medieval times, which were considered exotic and even ethically superior to the present. Patriotism also contributed to the trend among Romantic architects to adapt medieval building styles, notably the Gothic, to nineteenth-century conditions, since the Middle Ages was when the national character of many states was being formed.

In London, when the old Houses of Parliament burned to the ground in 1834, a decision had to be made about the style of their replacement. Since English rights and liberties traditionally dated from the Magna Carta in 1215, during the Middle Ages, a parliamentary commission chose a Gothic style for the

Figure 18.11 JOHN FREDERICK KENSETT. *Lake George.* 1869. Oil on canvas, 44 × 66¼″. The Metropolitan Museum of Art. Bequest of Maria DeWit Jesup. *John Frederick Kensett (1816–1872), one of the fashionable landscape artists of his day, traveled, studied, and painted in Europe and England during the 1840s; and in 1848 he opened his studio in New York City. Kensett belonged to the luminists, as the second generation of the Hudson River School were called. The luminists focused on pristine images of Nature, emphasizing the play of light over the natural scene and downplaying any human presence. In* Lake George, *Kensett positions the mountains in the background and the trees and rocks in the foreground to frame the still lake as if not a single breeze were blowing.*

new building (see Figure 18.2). Designed by Charles Barry (1795–1860) and A. W. N. Pugin (1812–1852), the Houses of Parliament show a true understanding of the essential features of the Gothic style, using pointed arches and picturesque towers. Despite these features, this building is not genuinely Gothic, for it adheres to Classical principles in the regularity of its decorations and its emphasis on the horizontal.

The Rise of Realism in Art Dissatisfied with the emotional, exotic, and escapist tendencies of Romanticism, a new breed of painters wanted to depict the real-life events they saw around them. In 1848 the jury of the Salon, influenced by the democratic sentiments unleashed by the social revolutions during the year, allowed a new kind of painting to be shown. The artist most identified with this new style was Gustave Courbet [koor-BAY] (1819–1877), a painter renowned for his refusal to prettify his works in the name of an aesthetic theory. His provocative canvases outraged middle-class audiences and made him the guiding spirit of militant Realism. Until about 1900, most painters in

one way or another followed in Courbet's footsteps. A man of the people, a largely self-taught painter, and a combative individual, Courbet began to attract notice in 1849 by painting common people engaged in their day-to-day activities. Above all, he strove for an art that reflected the conditions of ordinary life.

Courbet's art was not readily accepted under France's Second Empire. Salon juries rejected his pioneering works, such as *The Meeting,* or *"Bonjour Monsieur Courbet,"* a visual record of an encounter between the painter and his wealthy patron, Alfred Bruyas (1821–1877) of Montpellier (Figure 18.12). With an expansive gesture, the well-dressed Bruyas (center) greets Courbet (right), as a manservant (left) stands with head bowed. The painter's informal costume—with painting equipment and belongings strapped to his back—helped promote Courbet's image as a carefree artist serving the cause of Realism. With Bruyas's financial backing, Courbet installed this painting at the Realism Pavilion, next door to the official Salon of 1855. Critics ridiculed *The Meeting,* claiming it had no narrative, dramatic, or anecdotal subject, and accused

Figure 18.12 GUSTAVE COURBET. *The Meeting*, or *"Bonjour Monsieur Courbet."* 1855. Oil on canvas, 50¾ × 58⅝″. Musée Fabre, Montpellier. *This painting is an allegory of the artistic and financial pact made between Courbet and his wealthy patron, Bruyas. Deeply attracted to Fourier's socialist ideas, both men thought they had found the solution, a Fourierist term, to the problem of uniting genius, capital, and work for the benefit of all. Published letters between the two show them involved in a mutual compact: for Bruyas, greater access to art circles and society, and for Courbet, the gaining of spiritual and economic freedom. Despite their partnership, the figural placement in the painting proclaims the preeminence of the artist: With his head tilted haughtily, the painter is privileged, placed nearest the viewer and isolated from the other two figures.*

Courbet of self-promotion and narcissism. Relishing the controversy, Courbet remained true to his vision and continued to make art from his own life—an ideal that influenced Manet and the Impressionists (see Chapter 19).

Another of Courbet's paintings rejected by the 1855 Salon jury and exhibited in the Realism Pavilion was his masterpiece, *Interior of My Studio* (Figure 18.13). An intensely personal painting that visually summarizes his approach to art until this time, this work uses realistic contemporary figures to convey allegorical meaning. Its subtitle suggests Courbet's intent: *A Real Allegory Summing Up Seven Years of My Life as an Artist.* At the center of this canvas is the artist himself, in full light and painting a landscape while he is watched by a naked model and a small boy. The model and the fabric may be ironic references to the Salon's preference for nudes and still lifes. To the left of this central group, in shadow, are depicted those who have to work for a living, the usual subjects of Courbet's paintings, including peasants (the hunter and his dog) and a laborer. To the right, also in shadow, are grouped those for whom he paints, including his friends and mentors, each representing a specific idea. For example, the man reading a book is the poet Charles Baudelaire [bohd-LAIR], a personification of lyricism in art. As a total work, *Interior of My Studio* shows Courbet as

the craftsman who mediates between the ordinary people pursuing everyday lives and the world of art and culture, bringing both to life in the process.

Although Courbet is considered the principal founder of the Realist style in art, he had a worthy predecessor in Honoré Daumier [DOH-m'yay] (1808–1879), a painter of realistic scenes before Realism emerged as a recognized style. Daumier chronicled the life of Paris with a dispassionate eye. In thousands of satirical lithographs, from which he earned his living, and hundreds of paintings, he depicted its mean streets, corrupt law courts, squalid rented rooms, ignorant art connoisseurs, bored musicians, cowardly bourgeoisie, and countless other urban characters and scenes. His works not only conjure up Paris in the mid-century but also symbolize the city as a living hell where daily existence could be a form of punishment.

Daumier is a master of the lithograph print. Lithography, invented in 1798 in Germany, is based on the resistance between water and grease. In early lithography, the artist drew an image on a flat stone surface using a greasy substance—applied with brush or crayon—and then poured a special chemical to adhere the image to the stone. He then dampened the stone with water, which saturated the nongreasy areas. The artist next applied an oily ink with a roller, which held fast only to the greasy image, while the blank sections

Figure 18.13 GUSTAVE COURBET. *Interior of My Studio: A Real Allegory Summing Up Seven Years of My Life as an Artist.* 1855. Oil on canvas, 11'9¾" × 19'6⅝". Louvre. *Romanticism and Realism are joined in this allegorical work. The subjects—the artist and artistic genius— were major preoccupations of the Romantic era, as was the use of allegory. But undeniably Realist is Courbet's mocking attitude toward academic art and society. This painting's fame rests on its deft three-part composition, its allegorical biography of the artist, and its painterly technique, which captures the sensuosity of different textures, such as the female model's skin, a lace shawl, and a dog's ruffled fur.*

were protected by the thin layer of water. Next, paper was laid on the stone, which was then run through a press, thus transferring the image to the paper. Today's lithography makes use of zinc or aluminum surfaces instead of stone.

In Daumier's prints, no one and nothing was safe from his gaze. For example, in *The Freedom of the Press,* he depicts a muscular printer, symbolic of free ideas, ready to fight oppressive regimes (Figure 18.14). On the right, Charles X, attended by two ministers, has been knocked down—a reference to the role of the press in the king's fall from power in the 1830 revolution. On the left, top-hatted Louis Philippe threatens the printer with an umbrella, egged on by two attendants. For such satire, Daumier was awarded a six-month prison term in 1832, but to his adoring audience he was a hero. Daumier often included printers in his political drawings until tighter censorship laws were passed in 1835.

One of Daumier's well-known paintings is entitled *The Third-Class Carriage* (Figure 18.15). In Paris, third-class coach was the cheapest sort of rail travel, and the resulting accommodations were cramped and plain. In Daumier's scene the foreground is dominated by three figures—a mother with her sleeping child, an old

woman, and a sleeping boy. Behind them are crowded other peasants and middle-class businessmen, the latter recognizable by their tall hats. Although caricature is hinted at in this painting, it is a realistic portrayal of the growing democratization of society brought on by the railway.

In contrast to Daumier with his urban scenes, Jean-François Millet [mee-YAY] (1814–1875) painted the countryside near Barbizon, a village south of Paris where an artists' colony was located in the 1840s. Millet and the Barbizon school were influenced by the English Romantic Constable, whose painting *The Hay Wain* had been admired in the Paris Salon of 1824 (see Figure 17.12). Unlike Constable, who treated human beings only incidentally in his landscapes, Millet made the rural folk and their labors his primary subject.

One of Millet's early Barbizon paintings was *The Sower,* which he exhibited in the Salon of 1850 (Figure 18.16). This work depicts a youth casting seeds onto a freshly plowed field; dimly visible in the background are a flock of birds and two oxen with a plowman. Ordinarily, such a pastoral scene would have been a romantic idyll symbolizing the dignity of human work, but in Millet's canvas the monotonous toil degrades the laborer. Millet forces attention on the solitary

Figure 18.14 HONORÉ DAUMIER. *The Freedom of the Press.* Caption: "Watch It!!" ["*Ne vous y Frottez Pas!!*"]. 1834. Lithograph, 16½ × 11½". British Museum, Department of Prints and Drawings, London. *Daumier's career as a caricaturist was made possible by technological advances associated with the industrial era. After drawing a cartoon, he reproduced it for the ever-expanding popular market using the lithographic process, the first application of industrial methods to art. Daumier's prints reflect his liberal politics, as shown in this defense of a free press. And their design elements—a blend of figures and words, the use of metaphors, and the lack of reverence for authority—make them the progenitors of today's political cartoons.*

Figure 18.15 HONORÉ DAUMIER. *The Third-Class Carriage.* Ca. 1862. Oil on canvas, 25¾ × 35½". Metropolitan Museum of Art. Bequest of Mrs. H. O. Havemeyer, 1929. *Close study of this oil painting reveals Daumier's genius for social observation: the mother's doting expression, the old woman's stoicism, and the melancholy profile of the top-hatted man in the shadows at the far left. None of the figures is individualized, however, for all represent social types. Despite the cramped quarters, Daumier stresses the isolation of individual travelers.*

peasant, isolated from the world in a desolate landscape. The resulting image is that of a hulking presence, powerfully muscled and striding boldly across the canvas. Salon critics reacted by calling the picture "savage" and "violent," and its artist a "socialist."

However, Realist painters could focus on rural life and not be accused of socialism, as the career of Rosa Bonheur [boh-NURR] (1822–1899) reveals. Specializing in animal subjects, Bonheur enjoyed success with critics and public alike, starting with the Salon of 1841, when she was nineteen. In 1848 the Salon jury awarded Bonheur a Medal First Class for an animal scene. In 1853 *The Horse Fair* (Figure 18.17)—portraying spirited horses and their handlers at a horse market—made her an international celebrity, after a lithograph copy sold well in France, Britain, and the United States. What makes Bonheur's horses different from those painted by the Romantic Delacroix was her accuracy in depicting anatomy and movement—a reflection of her Realist faith in science. To prepare for this painting, Bonheur, dressed as a man, visited a horse market twice a week for two years to make sketches. Today, the work is considered her master-

Figure 18.16 JEAN-FRANÇOIS MILLET. *The Sower.* 1850. Oil on canvas, 40 × 32½". Courtesy, Museum of Fine Arts, Boston. Gift of Quincy Adams Shaw through Quincy A. Shaw Jr. and Mrs. Marian Shaw Haughton. *Like Daumier's peasant travelers, Millet's farmhand is depicted as a social type rather than as an individual. But Millet's Realist vision of peasant life is less forgiving than that of Daumier. He portrays the sower as little more than an animal and places him in a dark, nearly monochromatic landscape. Whereas Daumier's caricatures had provoked laughter or anger, Millet's painting produced fear.*

Figure 18.17 ROSA BONHEUR. *The Horse Fair.* 1853. Oil on canvas, 8′ × 13′4″. Metropolitan Museum of Art. Gift of Cornelius Vanderbilt, 1867. *Artists specializing in animal scenes usually painted their subjects in loving detail but only sketched in the background—perhaps reflecting lack of landscape technique. In contrast, Bonheur fully renders the setting of* The Horse Fair, *including the feathery trees and dusty cobblestones. So precise is her design that the cupola in the distance has been identified as that of La Salpêtrière hospital in Paris—a landmark near a midcentury horse market. Such realism led to the work's favorable reception from Napoleon III, which in turn helped promote Bonheur as one of France's best painters. In 1864 Bonheur became the first woman to receive the Legion of Honor, France's highest award. However, the award was bestowed privately by the empress, for the emperor refused to give the medal to a woman in a public ceremony.*

piece, both for its impressive scale and for its knowledgeable portrayal of nineteenth-century country life.

If the Parisian art world was gratified by the paintings of Bonheur, it was outraged by the work of Édouard Manet [mah-NAY] (1832–1883), a painter whose style is difficult to classify. He contributed to the events that gradually discredited the Salon and the Academy, encouraging painters to express themselves as they pleased, and thus was a bridge between the Realists of the 1860s and the group that became known in the 1870s as the Impressionists. His notoriety arose in 1863 when Napoleon III authorized a Salon des Refusés (Salon of the Rejects) for the hundreds of artists excluded from the official exhibit. An audacious painting by Manet in this first of the counter-Salons made him the talk of Paris and the recognized leader of new painting.

In the official Salon of 1865, Manet exhibited *Olympia,* painted two years earlier, which also created a scandal (Figure 18.18). The painting presents a nude woman on a bed, a subject established by the painter Titian in the sixteenth century, but which Manet now modernized. Titian presented his nude as the goddess

Venus in an idealized setting, but Manet rejected the trappings of mythology and depicted his nude realistically as a Parisian courtesan in her bedroom. The name Olympia was adopted by many Parisian prostitutes at the time, and Manet has portrayed her as being as imperious as a Greek goddess from Mount Olympus. Manet's Olympia is neither demure nor flirtatious; she gazes challengingly at the observer in a mixture of coldness and coyness. Her posture speaks of her boldness, as she sits propped up by pillows and dangles a shoe on her foot. She is attended by a black maid, whose deferential expression is in sharp contrast to Olympia's haughty demeanor. At her feet lies a black cat, an emblem of sexuality and gloom, perhaps inspired by a poem by the artist's friend Baudelaire.

More important than these historical connections, however, are Manet's artistic theories and practices, which strained against the boundaries of Realism. Unlike the other Realists, whose moral or ideological feelings were reflected in the subjects they painted, Manet moved toward a dispassionate art in which the subject and the artist have no necessary connection. Manet's achievement was revolutionary, for he had discarded

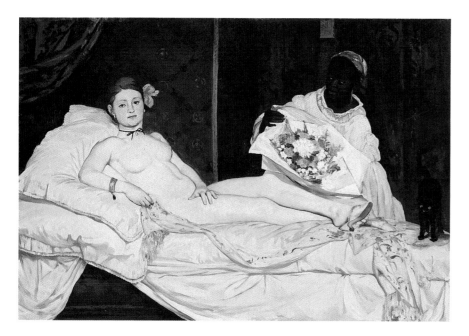

Figure 18.18 Édouard Manet. *Olympia.* 1863. Oil on canvas, 51¼ × 74¾". Musée d'Orsay, Paris. *Despite its references to traditional art,* Olympia *created a furor among the prudish and conservative public and critics. Parisian bourgeoisie expected to see nudes in the official Salon, but they were shocked by the appearance of a notorious prostitute, completely nude. The art critics, likewise, found the painting indecent and also condemned Manet's harsh, brilliant light, which tended to eliminate any details of the room's interior. Regardless of its initial negative reception,* Olympia *today is admired as a work that made a break with traditional art practices and opened the way for a modern art centered on the painter's own theories.*

the intellectual themes of virtually all Western art: reliance on anecdote, the Bible, Christian saints, politics, nostalgia, Greece and Rome, the Middle Ages, and sentimental topics. With his work, he opened the door to an art that had no other purpose than to depict what the artist chose to paint—that is, "art for art's sake." In sum, Manet was the first truly modern painter.

Photography

One of the forces impelling painting toward a more realistic and detached style of expression was the invention of the camera. Two types of camera techniques were perfected in 1839. In France, Louis-Jacques-Mandé Daguerre [duh-GAIR] (1787–1851) discovered a chemical method for implanting images on silvered copper plates to produce photographs called daguerreotypes. In England, William Henry Fox Talbot (1800–1877) was pioneering the negative-positive process of photographic images, which he called "the pencil of nature." Not only did the camera undermine the reality of the painted image, but it also quickly created a new art form, photography. From the beginning, many photographers began to experiment with the camera's artistic potential, though only recently has photography received wide acceptance as serious art.

Among the early photographers were the American Mathew Brady (about 1823–1896) and the English Julia Margaret Cameron (1815–1879). Both made important contributions to photography, but their techniques and results were quite different. Brady at-

tempted, through a sharp focus, to capture his subject in a realistic manner, whereas Cameron, by using a soft focus, delved into the personality and character of the individual in a near-mystical way.

Brady's reputation today is based mainly on his pictorial record of the American Civil War. Before the war, he operated a spacious studio and gallery in New York City, and there, in February 1860, he photographed Abraham Lincoln, who was campaigning to be the Republican nominee for president (Figure 18.19). This portrait introduced Lincoln to the East Coast public, who previously had thought the midwesterner to be a coarse, backwoods politician. The original photograph achieved wide circulation when it was printed on a *carte-de-visite,* a 2½-inch print that was mounted as a calling card or collected as a personal memento. After Lincoln was elected president, he acknowledged to Brady that the photograph had been instrumental in securing his victory.

While Brady and his staff were photographing battlefield scenes as well as portraits, Cameron, in 1863, at age forty-eight, began to photograph her family and friends—many of whom were prominent Victorians (Figure 18.20). Within two years her talent was recognized, and soon she was exhibiting her works and winning awards. Her photographs document her conventional views of a woman's place in society, her deep Christian faith, and the impact of the Romantic movement. In her effort to catch the consciousness of each sitter, Cameron experimented with lighting, used props and costumes, tried different cameras, and often developed her own plates.

Figure 18.19 MATHEW BRADY. *Abraham Lincoln.* 1860. Library of Congress. *Urged by his supporters in New York City, Lincoln hastily arranged to have Brady photograph him. Typical of the* carte-de-visite, *Lincoln is shown standing in a three-quarter-length frontal pose, a position influenced by the Western tradition of portrait painting. Dressed in the proper attire of the successful attorney that he was, Lincoln looks steadily at the viewer while resting his left hand lightly on a stack of books. This photograph enhanced the Honest Abe image, with its dignity, seriousness, and air of calm resolve. On the left is the photographer's logo: Brady N.Y.*

Music

Originating shortly after 1800, Romantic music reigned supreme from 1830 until 1871. Romantic works grew longer and more expressive as composers forged styles reflecting their individual feelings. To achieve unique voices, Romantic composers adopted varied techniques such as shifting rhythms, complex musical structures, discordant passages, and minor keys. In addition, with the spread of nationalistic feelings across Europe, especially after 1850, composers began to incorporate folk songs, national anthems, and indigenous dance rhythms into their music. Nonetheless, throughout this era Romantic composers stayed true to the established forms of Classical music composition—the opera, the sonata, and the symphony.

Although a Baroque creation, opera rose to splendid heights under Romanticism. The bourgeois public, bedazzled by opera's spectacle and virtuoso singers, eagerly embraced this art form. Operatic composers sometimes wrote works specifically to show off the vocal talents of particular performers. So prolific were these musicians that they wrote over half of the operas performed today.

Concerts also flourished under Romanticism. As the middle class grew wealthier, they used culture, especially music, to validate their social credentials. They founded orchestras, whose governing boards they ran, turned concerts into social rituals with unwritten codes of dress and behavior, and made musical knowledge a badge of social worthiness (Figure 18.21).

Figure 18.20 JULIA MARGARET CAMERON. *Beatrice.* 1866. Victoria and Albert Museum, London. *Cameron photographed many women representing religious, historical, Classical, and literary females. Turning to* The Divine Comedy, *Cameron tries to capture the compelling beauty of Beatrice, who was one of the guiding inspirations of Dante's famous work. The light, coming in from the upper right, accentuates Beatrice's contemplative pose and her allure. In 1864, eight years before Cameron took this picture and when she was beginning her career, she wrote that she wanted to ennoble photography "by combining the real & Ideal and sacrificing nothing of Truth by all possible devotion to Poetry and beauty."*

Figure 18.21   Covent Garden Theater, London. 1846. Engraving. University of Southampton Library. *This engraving shows a concert at London's Covent Garden Theater, with the famous French conductor Louis Jullien (1812–1860) leading an orchestra and four military bands. Note the fashionable clothes: "poke" bonnets and elegant dresses with low necklines for the women; evening wear and "stovepipe" hats for the men; and formal or military dress for the musicians. An event such as this came to be called a "promenade" concert, or "proms," the equivalent of a pop concert, with a blend of lighter and classical music. Jullien is credited with introducing "proms" concerts to London, and they remain an essential feature of musical life there today.*

Romanticism had an important impact on opera. The orchestras for operas became larger, inspiring composers to write long, elaborate works requiring many performers. Composers also began to integrate the entire musical drama, creating orchestral music that accentuated the actions and thoughts of the characters onstage. Most important, the form of opera itself was transformed. At first, composers imitated the form that they had inherited, writing operas in which a series of independent musical numbers—that is, **arias** (melodious songs)—alternated with recitatives (text either declaimed in the rhythms of natural speech with slight musical variations or sung with fuller musical support). The Italian composer Verdi brought this type of opera to its peak, advancing beyond the mechanical aria-recitative alternation. But even as Verdi was being lionized for his operatic achievements, a new style of opera was arising in Germany in the works of Wagner, which were written not as independent musical sections but as continuous musical scenes.

Giuseppe Verdi [VAYR-dee] (1813–1901), Italy's greatest composer of opera, followed the practice of the time and borrowed many of his plots from the works of Romantic writers filled with passion and full-blooded emotionalism.

One of the operas that brought him international fame was *Rigoletto* (1851), based on a play by Victor Hugo. What makes it such a favorite with audiences are its strong characters, its beautiful melodies, and its dramatic unity—features that typify Verdi's mature works. A study in Romantic opposites, this work tells of a crippled court jester, Rigoletto, deformed physically but emotionally sensitive, coarse in public but a devoted parent in private. The jester's daughter, Gilda, is also a study in contrasts, torn between love for her father and attraction to a corrupt noble.

In *Rigoletto,* Verdi continues to alternate arias with sung recitatives, but overall his music for the orchestra skillfully underscores the events taking place onstage. In addition, he employs musical passages to illustrate the characters' psychology, using convoluted orchestral backgrounds to accompany Rigoletto's monologues, for example, or shifting from simple to showy musical settings to demonstrate Gilda's conflicted nature. In Act III, the lighthearted aria "La donna e mobile" ("Woman Is Fickle") is sung by the Duke of Mantua, expressing perfectly his cynical view of women. Following a brief orchestral section, the duke sings a four-line refrain, which is reprised two more times, in between two verses with different words. The theme of this tenor aria is "Woman is deceitful, always changeable in word and thought." Verdi underscores the irony by setting this famous aria in a low dive—a decaying inn—where the count has been lured by Maddalena, a loose woman. When the aria ends, Rigoletto, who has been eavesdropping on the Duke of Mantua, exchanges words, in recitative, with Maddalena's brother, a hired killer.

Other operas followed, enhancing Verdi's mounting celebrity: *La Traviata* in 1853, based on a play written by the French Romantic writer Alexandre Dumas [doo-MAH] the younger, and *Aïda* in 1871, commissioned by Egypt's ruler and first performed in the Cairo opera house.

Romantic opera reached its climax in the works of Richard Wagner [VAHG-nuhr] (1813–1883), who sought a union of music and drama. A political revolutionary in his youth and a visionary thinker, Wagner was deeply impressed by the Romantic idea that the supreme expression of artistic genius occurred only when the arts were fused. To that end, he not only composed his own scores but also wrote the **librettos,** or texts, frequently conducted the music, and even planned the opera house in Bayreuth, Germany, where his later works were staged.

Wagner's major musical achievement was the monumental project entitled *The Ring of the Nibelung* (1853–1874), a cycle of four operas—or **music dramas,** as Wagner called them—that fulfilled his ideal of fusing music, verse, and staging. In these works, the distinction between arias and recitatives was nearly erased, giving a continuously flowing melodic line. This unified sound was marked by the appearance of recurring themes associated with particular characters, things, or ideas, known as **leitmotifs.** Perhaps the best-known Wagnerian motif is that identified with the valkyrie—the mythic blond women warriors who administered to the fallen heroes in Valhalla, the Norse heaven. They were the subject of Wagner's second opera in the *Ring* cycle, *Die Walküre (The Valkyrie)* (1856). Act III of that opera begins with "Ride of the Valkyries," an exciting evocation of a wild cosmic ride, which builds to a thrilling climax, interspersed with quiet **pianissimos**—very soft sounds—and crashing **crescendos**—increases in volume—and shifts in rhythm and tone color. The work, written as an orchestral prelude, unfolds with the curtain rising before its finish, to reveal a stage filled with blond maidens carrying dead warriors to their heavenly rest. Today, it is sometimes heard in films, as in the helicopter scene in *Apocalypse Now,* Francis Ford Coppola's 1979 epic about the Vietnam War.

Based on a popular Romantic source—the medieval Norse myths—the *Ring* also reflected Wagner's belief that opera should be moral. The *Ring* cycle warns against overweening ambition, its plot relating a titanic struggle for world mastery in which both human beings and gods are destroyed because of their lust for power. Wagner may have been addressing this warning to the Faustian spirit that dominated capitalism in the industrial age—a message that went unheeded.

Another German, Johannes Brahms (1833–1897), dominated orchestral and chamber music after 1850 in much the same way that Wagner did opera. Unlike Wagner, Brahms was no musical innovator. A classical Romanticist, he took up the mantle vacated by Beethoven, and he admired the Baroque works of Bach. In Vienna, his adopted home, Brahms became the hero of the traditionalists who opposed the new music of Wagner. Neglecting the characteristic Romantic works of operas and program music, he won fame with his symphonies and chamber music. His characteristic sound is mellow, always harmonic, delighting equally in joy and melancholy.

Despite his conservative musicianship, Brahms's work incorporates many Romantic elements. Continuing the art-song tradition established by Schubert (see Chapter 17), he introduced folk melodies into his pieces. In his instrumental works, he often aimed for the expressiveness of the human voice, the "singing" style preferred in Romanticism. He was also indebted to the Romantic style for the length of his symphonies, the use of rhythmic variations in all his works, and, above all, the rich lyricism and songfulness of his music.

Despite the dominance of Classical musical forms, this period was the zenith of Romantic *lieder,* or art songs. The continuing popularity of *lieder* reflected bourgeois taste and power, since amateur performances of these songs were a staple of home entertainment for the well-to-do, especially in Germany and Austria. In the generation after Schubert, the best composer of *lieder* was the German Robert Schumann (1810–1856), a pianist who shifted to music journalism and composition when his right hand became crippled in 1832. Splendid fusions of words and music, his songs are essentially duets for voice and piano.

Schumann's *lieder* are often parts of song cycles held together with unifying themes. One of his best-known song cycles is *Dichterliebe (A Poet's Love)* (1840), set to verses by Heinrich Heine (1797–1856), Germany's preeminent lyric poet. This song cycle superbly illustrates the Romantic preoccupation with program music. For instance, the song "Im Wunderschönen Monat Mai" ("In the Marvelously Beautiful Month of May") conveys the longing of Heine's text through ascending lines of melody and an unresolved climax. The passion in this song cycle was inspired by Schumann's marriage to Clara Wieck (1819–1896), a piano virtuoso and composer in her own right.

The Legacy of the Bourgeois Age

We in the modern world still live in the shadow of the bourgeois age. The revolutions of 1830 and 1848 demonstrated that uprisings could bring about change but not always the desired results and that more drastic methods might be necessary in the future. These failed revolutions inspired the amoral concept of realpolitik, a guiding principle in much of today's politics. Realpolitik also contributed to the unification of Germany in 1871, which upset the balance of power on the Continent, unleashed German militarism, and led to France's smoldering resentment of Germany. The two world wars of the twentieth century had their seeds in these events.

With liberalism in the ascendant, the middle-class values of hard work, thrift, ambition, and respectability became paramount, as did the notion that the individual should take precedence over the group. However, the utopian socialists and the Marxian socialists, in criticizing liberalism and the industrial system, offered alternative solutions to social and economic problems. Their proposals foreshadowed approaches such as labor unions, mass political parties, and state planning. The intellectual and artistic developments of this age had far-reaching repercussions. There is still interest in Marx's controversial analysis of history, despite the collapse of global communism; Darwin's theory of evolution, though intensely debated, is central to modern thought; Pasteur's contributions in immunology and microbiology have helped make the world a safer place; higher criticism, by challenging the Hebrew Bible and the New Testament, has diminished the notion of religious revelation itself; and the evangelical movement, with its faith-based rejection of arguments grounded in science, history, and textual analysis, has become a fixture in the American political landscape.

Romanticism, although under siege from other modes of thought after 1850, has not disappeared from the West, even today. Realism, its immediate successor, became the reigning style until 1900, partly because of the development of the camera and the art of photography. London's Crystal Palace inaugurated the high-tech tradition in art and architecture, and inventions and new techniques in printing and publishing laid the foundation for a mass market in the visual arts. Perhaps the most significant artistic development during this time was Manet's adoption of the credo "art for art's sake," which terminated the debate over the representational nature of art. Most artists in the post-1871 period followed Manet's bold move.

KEY CULTURAL TERMS

Utilitarianism	slave narrative
socialism	luminism
evangelicalism	aria
holiness	libretto
higher criticism	music drama
evolution	leitmotif
Realism	pianissimo
Transcendentalism	crescendo

SUGGESTIONS FOR FURTHER READING

BALZAC, H. DE. *Cousin Bette.* Translated by M. A. Crawford. New York: Penguin, 1972. A representative novel from the *Human Comedy* series, Balzac's monumental commentary on French bourgeois society in the post-Napoleonic era.

———. *Père Goriot.* Translated by J. M. Sedgwick. New York: Dodd, Mead, 1954. Another of the best known of Balzac's almost one hundred novels in the *Human Comedy* series.

BRONTË, C. *Jane Eyre.* Edited and with an introduction by M. Smith. London: Oxford University Press, 1973. A classic of Romanticism, this novel deals with a theme dear to the hearts of nineteenth-century women readers, the life and tribulations of a governess.

BRONTË, E. *Wuthering Heights.* Edited and with an introduction by I. Jack. New York: Oxford University Press, 1983. A classic of Romanticism, this novel recounts the doomed affair of the socially mismatched but passionate soul mates Heathcliff and Catherine.

DICKENS, C. *Hard Times.* London: Methuen, 1987. A depiction of life in the new industrialized cities, this grim tale of forced marriage and its consequences reveals what happens when practical, utilitarian thinking replaces human values.

———. *Oliver Twist.* London: Longman, 1984. Dickens's moving tale of the orphan Oliver and his experiences among London's poor in the sordid conditions of the 1830s.

DICKINSON, E. *Complete Poems of Emily Dickinson.* Edited by T. H. Johnson. Boston: Little Brown & Co., 1976. Excellent gathering of the complete corpus—all 1,775 works—of Dickinson's poetry, arranged in chronological order from awkward juvenilia to the morbid, hell-obsessed verses of her later years. Compiled by a respected Dickinson scholar.

DOSTOEVSKY, F. *The Brothers Karamazov.* Translated by D. Magarshack. New York: Penguin, 1982. In his novel, Dostoevsky deals with broad metaphysical and psychological themes, such as the right of human beings to reject the world made by God because it contains so much evil and suffering. These themes are dramatized through the actions and personalities of the brothers and their father.

———. *Crime and Punishment.* Translated by S. Monas. New York: New American Library, 1980. A masterpiece of psychological insight, this gripping tale of murder explores the themes of suffering, guilt, redemption, and the limits of individual freedom.

DOUGLASS, F. *Narrative of the Life of Frederick Douglass, an American Slave, Written by Himself.* Introduction by Henry Louis Gates. Bedford Books in American History. Bedford Press, 1993. A heartbreaking, but ultimately uplifting, autobiography of perhaps the most influential and celebrated African American of the nineteenth century. Originally published in 1845, this work launched the literary genre known as the slave narrative. A reprint of the 1960 Harvard University Press publication.

ELIOT, G. *Middlemarch.* New York: Penguin, 1965. This classic of Realist fiction explores the psychology and growth in self-understanding of the principal characters, Dorothea Brooke and Dr. Lydgate.

FLAUBERT, G. *Madame Bovary.* Translated by A. Russell. New York: Penguin, 1961. One of the first Realist novels, and possibly the finest, Flaubert's work details Emma Bovary's futile attempts to find happiness in a stifling bourgeois world.

GASKELL, E. C. *North and South.* New York: Dutton, 1975. A portrait of economic and social disparities in mid-nineteenth-century England.

GILBERT, O., AND TRUTH, S. *The Narrative of Sojourner Truth.* Dover Thrift Editions, 1997. This autobiography, as told to a secretary, recounts the amazing life story of the nineteenth-century African American woman who endured thirty years of slavery in upstate New York, after which she became a leading abolitionist and a fighter for various reforms, including women's suffrage. Originally published in 1850.

HUGO, V. *Les Misérables.* Translated by L. Wraxall. New York: Heritage Press, 1938. A good English version of Hugo's epic novel of social injustice in early-nineteenth-century France.

MARX, K., AND ENGELS, F. *Basic Writings on Politics and Philosophy.* Edited by L. Feuer. Boston: Peter Smith, 1975. A representative selection of their prodigious writings, which challenged industrial capitalism in the mid–nineteenth century and provided the theoretical basis for socialism and communism.

MILL, J. S. *On Liberty.* New York: Norton, 1975. Mill's examination of the relationship between the individual and society.

———. *Utilitarianism.* Indianapolis: Hackett, 1978. A defense of the belief that the proper goal of government is to provide the greatest happiness for the greatest number.

SAND, G. *Indiana.* Translated by G. B. Ives. Chicago: Academy Chicago, 1977. Sand's first novel, with its Romantic themes and feminist message, established her as a writer of great promise.

TOLSTOY, L. *War and Peace.* Translated by L. and A. Maude. London: Oxford University Press, 1984. Tolstoy's epic novel traces the impact of the Napoleonic Wars on the lives of his Russian characters and explores such themes as the role of individual human beings in the flow of history.

WHITMAN, W. *The Complete Poems.* Edited by F. Murphy. New York: Viking Press, 1990. The complete poems of arguably the best poet yet produced in the United States. An authoritative edition compiled by a longtime Whitman scholar.

SUGGESTIONS FOR LISTENING

BRAHMS, JOHANNES. Brahms's four symphonies (1876, 1877, 1883, and 1885) demonstrate the disciplined style and majestic lyricism that made him the leader of the anti-Wagner school. Brahms also excelled in chamber music, a genre usually ignored by Romantic composers. His chamber works show him to be a worthy successor to Beethoven, especially in the Piano Quartet in G Minor, Op. 25 (late 1850s), the Clarinet Quintet in B Minor, Op. 115 (1891), and three string quartets, composed between 1873 and 1876.

SCHUMANN, ROBERT. Continuing the art-song tradition perfected by Schubert, Schumann composed song cycles such as *Dichterliebe (A Poet's Love)* (1840) and *Frauenliebe und Leben (A Woman's Love and Life)* (1840), both filled with heartfelt passion and set to verses by Romantic poets. Schumann also had much success with his works for solo piano, including the delightful *Kinderszenen (Scenes from Childhood)* (1839), which he called "reminiscences of a grown-up for grown-ups." Unlike the *lieder* and piano music, Schumann's other works are often neglected today, such as his four symphonies (1841, 1845–1846, 1850, 1851); two choral offerings, *Das Paradies und die Peri (Paradise and the Peri)* (1843) and *Der Rose Pilgefahrt (The Pilgrimage of the Rose)* (1851); incidental music for the stage (Byron's *Manfred*); and assorted chamber works.

VERDI, GIUSEPPE. Primarily a composer of opera, Verdi worked exclusively in the Romantic tradition, bringing to perfection the style of opera that alternated arias and recitatives. His operatic subjects are based mainly on works by Romantic authors, such as *Il Corsaro (The Corsair)* (1848), adapted from Lord Byron, and *La Traviata (The Lost One)* (1853), adapted from Alexandre Dumas the younger. Shakespeare, whom the Romantics revered as a consummate genius, inspired the librettos for *Otello* (1887) and *Falstaff* (1893). Like the Romantics generally, Verdi had strong nationalistic feelings that he expressed in, for example, *Les Vêpres Siciliennes (The Sicilian Vespers)* (1855) and *La Battaglia di Legnano (The Battle of Legnano)* (1849).

WAGNER, RICHARD. Wagner created a new form, music drama, that fused all the arts—a development that reflected his theory that music should serve the theater. His early style may be heard in *Der Fliegende Holländer (The Flying Dutchman)* (1842), which alternates arias and recitatives in the traditional way. By 1850, in *Lohengrin,* he was moving toward a more comprehensive operatic style, using continuously flowing music and the technique of recurring themes called leitmotifs. He reached his maturity with *Der Ring des Nibelungen (The Ring of the Nibelung),* written between 1853 and 1874; in this cycle of four operas, he focuses on the orchestral web, with the arias being simply one factor in the constantly shifting sounds. His works composed after 1853 pushed the limits of Classical tonality and became the starting point for modern music.

19

THE AGE OF EARLY MODERNISM
1871–1914

Between 1871 and 1914, the European continent enjoyed an almost unprecedented period of tranquility, free of military conflict and considered by many Westerners to be the new age predicted by Enlightenment thinkers. But hindsight exposes this period as one of rampant nationalism, aggressive imperialism, and growing militarism, culminating in the outbreak of World War I in 1914. The prolonged, violent nature of that global struggle ended the optimism of prewar Europe.

At the same time, the phenomenon known as "modern life" was emerging, with people sharing in the benefits of strong nation-states and of the Second Industrial Revolution. In the cultural realm, **Modernism** was born; this movement rejected both the Greco-Roman and the Judeo-Christian legacies and tried to forge a new perspective that was true to modern secular experience (Figure 19.1).

Modernism lasted about one hundred years, going through three distinct stages. During its first phase (1871–1914), which is treated in this chapter, artists, writers, and thinkers established the movement's principles through their creative and innovative works. The second phase, the zenith of Modernism (1914–1945), is the subject of Chapter 20; and the exhaustion and decline of the movement, the third phase (1945–1970), is covered in Chapter 21.

EUROPE'S RISE TO WORLD LEADERSHIP

The Age of Early Modernism, despite the prevailing mood of optimism, was an age of accelerated and stressful change. Beneath the period's tranquil

◀ **Detail** Vincent van Gogh. *The Starry Night.* 1889. Oil on canvas, 29 × 36¼" (73.7 × 92.1 cm). The Museum of Modern Art, New York. Acquired through the Lillie P. Bliss Bequest. Photograph © 1997 The Museum of Modern Art, New York.

580

Figure 19.1 UMBERTO BOCCIONI. *Unique Forms of Continuity in Space.* 1913. Bronze (cast 1931), 43⅞ × 34⅞ × 15¾" (111.2 × 88.5 × 40 cm). The Museum of Modern Art, New York. Acquired through the Lillie P. Bliss Bequest. Photograph © 1997 The Museum of Modern Art, New York. *Umberto Boccioni and his fellow Futurists were members of an Italian-based literary and artistic movement that typified Early Modernism's rejection of the past and set out to create a new concept of art. The Futurists called for the destruction of museums, libraries, and all existing art forms. In this striding bronze figure, Boccioni distorts form and space to create an airstreamed image of speed, the new modern icon.*

Figure 19.2 RAOUL DUFY. *July 14 in Le Havre.* 1906. Oil on canvas, 21½ × 14⅞". Collection of Mr. and Mrs. Paul Mellon. National Gallery, Washington, D.C. *This colorful depiction of Bastille Day, France's Independence Day, by Raoul Dufy (rah-uhl due-fee) (1877–1953), is a fitting symbol of nationalism and middle-class life in a provincial city. Dufy's blurred images of men and women hurrying down the street heighten the sense of hustle and bustle in this small but busy provincial city. Above the figures' heads the French flag flies front and center with other flags and banners fluttering nearby—France's tricolored flag a reminder of its revolutionary heritage. Le Havre, founded in the sixteenth century, was a busy industrial port on the Seine River. Dufy, a native of Le Havre, experimented briefly with Fauvism and Cubism before establishing his own unique style as a painter of recreational and festive events. He also was famous for his watercolors and prints depicting similar subjects.*

surface powerful forces were at work, namely imperialism, nationalism, and militarism, which were sowing the seeds that would lead to cataclysmic events after 1914 (see Chapter 20). Acting as a catalyst on these powerful forces was the middle class of central and western Europe (Figure 19.2).

Imperialism—the quest for colonies—began as a search for new markets and increased wealth. As Europe became a world power with a network of political and economic interests around the globe, rivalries among European states intensified, transforming most of them into armed camps. Combined with growing feelings of nationalism, imperialistic and militaristic impulses created an atmosphere that eventually led rival states to war.

The Second Industrial Revolution, New Technologies, and the Making of Modern Life

The Second Industrial Revolution differed from the first in several significant ways. First, Great Britain, the world's industrial leader since 1760, now faced strong competition from Germany and the United States. Second, science and research provided new and better industrial products and had a stronger influence than in the basically pragmatic first revolution. Finally, steam and water power were replaced by newer forms of industrial energy, such as oil and electricity. The internal combustion engine replaced the steam engine in ships and in the early 1900s gave rise to the automobile and the airplane.

Technology, the offspring of science, was also reshaping the world. The wireless superseded the telegraph, the telephone made its debut, and national and international postal services were instituted. Typewriters and tabulators transformed business practices. Ro-

Figure 19.3 MARY CASSATT. *Reading "Le Figaro."* 1878. Oil on canvas, 41 × 33". National Gallery, Washington, D.C. *Cassatt's woman reading a newspaper was a rare subject in the nineteenth century. Artists usually depicted women reading books rather than newspapers, which were identified with the man's world outside the home. The woman is the artist's mother, Katherine Cassatt, who is reading* Le Figaro, *one of Paris's leading newspapers. Rich and well educated, Mrs. Cassatt was a strong influence in her daughter's life and career. The formidable figure of the mother takes up much of the painting, and the mirror on the left reflects her and her surroundings. The artist has cropped the mirror, much in the style of a photograph, a popular technique among Early Modernist painters.*

tary presses printed thousands of copies of daily newspapers for an increasingly literate public (Figure 19.3).

The Second Industrial Revolution affected almost every aspect of the economy. In transportation, more efficient engines meant lower transportation costs and cheaper products. Refrigeration permitted perishable foods to be transported great distances without spoiling. Advertising became both a significant source of revenue for publishers and a powerful force in the consumer economy. Increased wealth meant more leisure for more people, and new recreations appeared, such as seaside resorts, music halls, movies, and bicycles—all contributing to the phenomenon known as modern life.

Industrialized cities, with their promises of well-paying jobs, comfortable lives, and noisy entertainments, drew residents of small towns and farms, and by 1900 nearly 30 percent of the people in the West lived in cities (Figure 19.4). As cities grew in in-

dustrialized countries, the standard of living improved. Consumers benefited from a general decline in prices and from steady wages and salaries. The period from 1900 to the outbreak of World War I in 1914 was a golden age for the affluent and leisured middle classes.

While the middle and upper classes enjoyed unprecedented prosperity, misery mounted among urban workers despite the creation of state-funded social welfare programs. Urban slums grew more crowded, and living conditions worsened. The presence of squalor in the midst of plenty pricked the conscience of many citizens, who began to work for better housing and less dangerous working conditions for laborers. When these reform efforts proved inadequate, labor unions arose, along with their best weapon, the strike.

One reform did succeed spectacularly: the founding of secular public education. Reformers claimed that public schools, financed by taxes and supervised by

Figure 19.4 CAMILLE PISSARRO. *The Great Bridge to Rouen.* 1896. Oil on canvas, 29³/₁₆ × 36½". Carnegie Museum of Art, Pittsburgh. Purchase. *Pissarro's painting captures the energy of Rouen and transforms this French river town into a symbol of the new industrial age. Contributing to the sense of vitality are the belching smokestack, the bridge crowded with hurrying people, and the dockworkers busy with their machinery. The fast pace is underscored by the Impressionist technique of "broken color," giving immediacy to the scene.*

state agencies, would prepare workers for jobs in industrialized society and create an informed and literate citizenry—two basic needs of modern life. An unanticipated result of the establishment of public school systems was that ties between children and their parents were loosened.

The status of women also changed dramatically. New employment opportunities opened for teachers, nurses, office workers, and sales clerks. Because some of these jobs required special skills, colleges and degree programs were developed to teach them to women. Many young women still turned to domestic service, but new household appliances reduced the need for servants. Female labor in factories was now regulated by state laws, but small shopkeepers continued to work long hours in family businesses (Figure 19.5).

Some women reformers, primarily from the middle class—for example, Emmeline Pankhurst (1858–1928) and Susan B. Anthony (1820–1906), leaders in the women's suffrage movement in Great Britain and the United States, respectively—advocated more freedom for women, continuing a tradition that had begun on a limited scale before 1871. These reformers launched successful campaigns to revise property and divorce laws, giving women greater control over their wealth

Figure 19.5 EYRE CROWE. *The Dinner Hour at Wigan.* 1874. Oil on canvas, 30 × 42¼". Manchester City Art Gallery, Manchester, England. *Social possibilities for English women expanded to some degree during this era. This painting depicts a factory scene in which the young female workers gain a brief respite from their tasks. A few talk together quietly, while others remain apart or finish a chore. They all seem dwarfed by the huge mill with the smokestacks in the background, a fitting symbol of industrial power.*

Figure 19.6 ANTON VON WERNER. *Proclamation of the German Empire on January 18, 1871 at the Hall of Mirrors in Versailles*. 1885. Oil on canvas, approx. 65¾ × 79½ ". Bismarck Museum, Friedrichsruhe, Germany. *This painting commemorates the moment when the German Empire was proclaimed and King William of Prussia became its first emperor. Von Werner uses reflections from the famed Hall of Mirrors at Versailles to make the stirring scene more theatrical, and added drama comes from the raised swords of the officers. The strong presence of the army was prophetic of the dominant role the military was destined to play in the German Empire.*

and their lives. In several countries, they founded suffrage movements, using protests and marches to dramatize their situation. The word *feminism* entered the English vocabulary in 1895. Following a vigorous, occasionally violent, campaign, women won the right to vote in Great Britain in 1918 and in the United States in 1920.

Response to Industrialism: Politics and Crisis

At the dawn of Early Modernism, the assumptions of liberalism in industrialized countries were being challenged from many quarters. Except in Britain and the United States, liberals were under siege in national legislatures both by socialists—who wanted more central planning and more state services for the workers—and by conservatives—who feared the masses and supported militant nationalism as a way to unify their societies. After 1900, political parties representing workers and trade unionists, which were strong enough to push successfully for laws to correct some social problems of industrialism, further threatened the liberals' hold on power.

Events also seemed to discredit liberal theory. Theoretically, under free trade the population ought to decline or at least stabilize, and the economy ought to operate harmoniously, but neither happened. Population was surging and industrial capitalism was erratic, leading many critics of liberal capitalism to conclude that the so-called laws of liberal economics did not work.

Domestic Policies in the Heavily Industrialized West Germany, France, Great Britain, and the United States all faced domestic problems during this period. Founded in 1871, the German Reich, or Empire, moved toward unity under the astute leadership of its first chancellor, Otto von Bismarck, and the new kaiser, or emperor, William I (r. 1871–1888), former king of Prussia (Figure 19.6). Despite the illusion of parliamentary rule, the tone of this imperial reich was conservative, militaristic, and nationalistic.

In France, the Third Republic was founded after the humiliating defeat of the Second Empire by Germany in 1871. Even though the government remained hopelessly divided between republicans and monarchists, it agreed on the need to correct the most glaring social injustices in an attempt to counteract the growing appeal of the workers' parties and socialism. The nation's liberal center gradually evaporated, creating bitter deadlocks between socialists and conservatives that no government could resolve.

Great Britain was more successful in solving its domestic problems during this period. Controlled by political parties that represented the upper and middle classes, the British government passed social legislation that improved the working and living conditions of many poor families and created opportunities for social mobility through a state secondary-school system. As in Germany and France, these reform efforts did not prevent workers from forming their own political party, the Labour party. Within a decade after World War I, it had gained enough support to elect a majority of Parliament and the prime minister.

SLICE OF LIFE
Winning the Right to Vote

LADY CONSTANCE LYTTON
Notes from a Diary

Lady Constance Lytton (1869–1923), the daughter of a former viceroy of India, was a leader of the women's suffrage movement in Great Britain. Arrested during a protest in Liverpool in 1910, she assumed the name and status of a working-class woman, Jane Warton, because she feared that her high social position would prompt the police to release her. As "Jane Warton," she went on a hunger strike and was force-fed by a doctor and wardresses (female guards), a horrifying tactic experienced by many suffragettes. This account is in her own words.

I was visited again by the Senior Medical Officer, who asked me how long I had been without food. I said I had eaten a buttered scone and a banana sent in by friends to the police station on Friday at about midnight. He said, "Oh, then, this is the fourth day; that is too long, I shall feed you, I must feed you at once," but he went out and nothing happened till about six o'clock in the evening, when he returned with, I think, five wardresses and the feeding apparatus. He urged me to take food voluntarily. I told him that was absolutely out of the question, that when our legislators ceased to resist enfranchising women then I should cease to resist taking food in prison. He did not examine my heart nor feel my pulse; he did not ask to do so, nor did I say anything which could possibly induce him to think I would refuse to be examined. I offered no resistance to being placed in position, but lay down voluntarily on the plank bed. Two of the wardresses took hold of my arms, one held my head and one my feet. One wardress helped to pour the food. The doctor leant on my knees as he stooped over my chest to get at my mouth. I shut my mouth and clenched my teeth. I had looked forward to this moment with so much anxiety lest my identity should be discovered beforehand, that I felt positively glad when the time had come. The sense of being overpowered by more force than I could possibly resist was complete, but I resisted nothing except with my mouth. The doctor offered me the choice of a wooden or steel gag; he explained elaborately, as he did on most subsequent occasions, that the steel gag would hurt and the wooden one not, and he urged me not to force him to use the steel gag. But I did not speak nor open my mouth, so that after playing about for a moment or two with the wooden one he finally had recourse to the steel. He seemed annoyed at my resistance and he broke into a temper as he plied my teeth with the steel implement.

He found that on either side at the back I had false teeth mounted on a bridge which did not take out. The superintending wardress asked if I had any false teeth, if so, that they must be taken out; I made no answer and the process went on. He dug his instrument down on to the sham tooth, it pressed fearfully on the gum. He said if I resisted so much with my teeth, he would have to feed me through the nose. The pain of it was intense and at last I must have given way for he got the gag between my teeth, when he proceeded to turn it much more than necessary until my jaws were fastened wide apart, far more than they could go naturally. Then he put down my throat a tube which seemed to me much too wide and was something like four feet in length. The irritation of the tube was excessive. I choked the moment it touched my throat until it had got down. Then the food was poured in quickly; it made me sick a few seconds after it was down and the action of the sickness made my body and legs double up, but the wardresses instantly pressed back my head and the doctor leant on my knees. The horror of it was more than I can describe.

I was sick over the doctor and wardresses, and it seemed a long time before they took the tube out. As the doctor left he gave me a slap on the cheek, not violently, but, as it were, to express his contemptuous disapproval, and he seemed to take for granted that my distress was assumed. At first it seemed such an utterly contemptible thing to have done that I could only laugh in my mind. Then suddenly I saw Jane Warton lying before me, and it seemed as if I were outside of her. She was the most despised, ignorant and helpless prisoner that I had seen. When she had served her time and was out of the prison, no one would believe anything she said, and the doctor when he had fed her by force and tortured her body, struck her on the cheek to show how he despised her! That was Jane Warton, and I had come to help her.

Interpreting This Slice of Life **Why** did the authorities force-feed Constance Lytton? **Why** did Lady Lytton assume the name of a working-class woman, and **what** does that reveal about English life? **Describe** the procedures and techniques used in force-feeding. **How** did Lady Lytton "see" Jane Warton at the end of her ordeal? **Explain** why the suffragettes used the hunger strike in their civil rights battle. **Compare and contrast** this battle for civil rights with recent civil rights struggles.

Figure 19.7 EDGAR DEGAS. *The Cotton Bureau in New Orleans.* 1873. Oil on canvas, 29⅛ × 36¼". Musée des Beaux-Arts, Pau, France. *By the third quarter of the nineteenth century, the United States was challenging English supremacy in world trade. The French painter Degas must have observed this scene—the interior of a cotton exchange in New Orleans—while visiting relatives in Louisiana. Whether consciously or not, Degas accurately depicted the social realities of this bourgeois work space: the capitalist idlers reading a newspaper or lounging against a wall and, in contrast, the paid employees intent on their work.*

Across the Atlantic, the United States began to challenge British industrial supremacy. America's rapidly expanding economy allowed big business to dominate politics at all levels until the reform movements of the early 1900s (Figure 19.7). These movements, spurred by America's democratic tradition, temporarily derailed the power of the large business conglomerates called trusts.

In the late nineteenth century, Europeans came to America in the largest migration of human population ever recorded. These immigrants—after painful adjustments, particularly in the crowded slums of the eastern cities—gradually entered the mainstream of American life. Largely from eastern and central Europe, they transformed the United States into a much richer ethnic society and made valuable contributions to the culture.

Domestic Policies in Central and Eastern Europe
The less industrialized states of central, southern, and eastern Europe faced more difficult problems. As the factory system began to appear in the region, these countries had no well-developed political and economic policies for handling the problems that came with industrialization. Because some regional leaders were stronger than the prime ministers, the Italian government allowed the northern regions to become industrialized while the southern regions, including Sicily, remained in a semifeudal condition. As a result, the north, driven by an expanding middle class,

moved far ahead of the agrarian south, where vast estates were worked by peasant labor.

In the Austro-Hungarian Empire, the government's biggest problem was ethnic unrest, a direct outgrowth of the denial of political freedom to Slavic minorities, notably the Czechs and the Slovaks. In 1867 the Austrian Germans had given political parity to the Hungarians, allowing them free rein within their land. But nothing was done to address the simmering discontent among the Slavs. Even while the region seethed with ethnic violence, its capital, Vienna, became a glittering symbol of Modernism. From *fin-de-siècle* ("end-of-the-century") Vienna came the cultural style called Expressionism and the psychology of Sigmund Freud.

Farther east, the Russian Empire slowly entered the industrial age, hampered by its vast size and its sluggish agrarian economy and its inefficient bureaucracy. Adding to Russia's woes were violent underground revolutionaries who despaired of any substantial reform in this autocratic society. In 1881 an anarchist assassinated the liberal czar Alexander II (r. 1855–1881), and his successors dismantled his reforms. Under them, Russia's economy worsened and the imperial ministers grew more reactionary. In 1905 Japan defeated Russia in the brief Russo-Japanese War (1904–1905), setting off a short-lived revolution led by under-paid factory workers and starving peasants. By promising relief, Czar Nicholas II (r. 1894–1917) weathered the storm, but few of his pledges were fulfilled. Instead, the state violently repressed dissent,

Figure 19.8 G. W. Bacon. *Battle of Omdurman*. 1898. Engraving. *In September 1898, an Anglo-Egyptian army of twenty-six thousand men, led by General H. H. Kitchener (1850–1916), annihilated Sudanese forces numbering about forty thousand, at Omdurman on the Nile River in Sudan. Within five hours, the British, armed with rifles, cannons, and machine guns, killed over ten thousand Sudanese troops and wounded about the same number, while losing fewer than four hundred soldiers. Leading one of the British units in the cavalry charge was the young Winston Churchill—whose glory days lay ahead. With this victory, the British extended their control of the Nile River farther south, and by 1914 they had solidified their position in Africa, controlling lands from Alexandria (in the north) to the Cape of Good Hope (in the south), and from the east to the west coast in sub-Saharan Africa (see Map 19.1).*

and, as a result, the imperial court grew dangerously isolated.

Imperialism and International Relations

In 1871 most European nations believed that domestic issues were more important than colonial matters and that internal law and order was the first priority. By 1914 those beliefs had been reversed. Domestic politics were no longer primary, and national interests tended to be calculated by each state's role in the global economy and in foreign affairs.

The Scramble for Colonies   Before 1875 the common wisdom was that a colony brought both benefits and

problems to a modern state, but after that year Western thinking abruptly changed. Europe's industrialized states began to compete for colonies and for trade rights around the world. To maintain their high standard of living, they had to find new markets, underdeveloped areas in which to invest capital, and cheap sources of raw materials. Given these needs, the continent of Africa was an imperialist's dream. Acquiring African lands through various means, including treaties with local chiefs, claims by missionaries and explorers, or victories by superior armies, the European states set up colonial governments, opened trading companies, and extracted raw materials, sharing the spoils of this product-rich continent (Figure 19.8). France and Britain got the best lands; Germany and Italy received the more barren, less commercially

LEARNING THROUGH MAPS

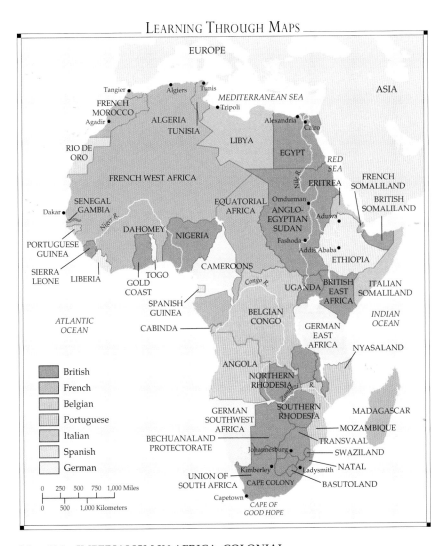

Map 19.1   IMPERIALISM IN AFRICA: COLONIAL STATES, 1914

This map shows Europe's colonies in Africa on the eve of World War I. **Notice** the movement of Europeans from the coastal lands of Africa in Map 15.1, Expansion of Europe, to the founding of colonies across the continent in this map. **Identify** the holdings of the European powers. **Which** country had the largest number of colonies? **Which** country had the smallest number? **Locate** centers of potential conflict among the colonial powers. **Which** two countries remained independent of European control? Source: Felix Gilbert, *The End of the European Era, 1890 to the Present*. New York: Norton, 1970, p. 23.

desirable areas (Map 19.1). In the Far East, imperialists competed for colonies in the South Pacific and China, making the Europeans rivals for land with the United States and Japan (the leading power in the Far East after military victories over China in 1895 and Russia in 1905) (Map 19.2).

Imperialism fomented many crises, particularly in Africa, but no major conflict occurred. In this mostly tranquil climate, people began to believe that peace depended on the secret alliances constructed by the major powers. The diplomatic pacts, reinforced by strong armies and navies, had originated after the

LEARNING THROUGH MAPS

Map 19.2 IMPERIALISM IN ASIA: COLONIAL STATES, 1914
This map shows Europe's expansion into Asia on the eve of World War I. **Compare** the small presence of Europeans in Asia in Map 15.1, Expansion of Europe, with their extensive holdings in this map. **Identify** holdings of the European powers. **Notice** that China, Japan, and the United States have become colonial powers. **Which** country was the dominant colonial power? **What** countries occupied islands in the Pacific Ocean? **Which** continent, Africa in Map 19.1 or Asia in this map, was more subject to European occupation? Source: Felix Gilbert, *The End of the European Era, 1890 to the Present*. New York: Norton, 1970, pp. 24–25.

Map 19.3   EUROPE ON THE EVE OF WORLD WAR I
This map shows the political divisions in Europe in 1914. **Identify** the member states of
the Triple Alliance and the Triple Entente. **Which** of the two alliances would have the
geographic advantage when defending its member states? **Which** small states might become battlegrounds if war broke out between the two alliances? **Locate** Sarajevo, the city
where an incident occurred that set off World War I. **Notice** the lost lands of the Ottoman Empire and the creation of nation-states on this map, compared with the same territories in Map 18.2, Europe in 1871.

Franco-Prussian War in 1871. By 1914 Europe was divided into two armed camps—France, Great Britain,
and Russia (called the Triple Entente) against Germany, Austria-Hungary, and Italy (known as the Triple
Alliance) (Map 19.3).

The Outbreak of World War I   In June 1914, an incident took place in Sarajevo (in modern Bosnia and
Herzegovina) for which diplomacy had no peaceful
remedy: the assassination of the heir to the Austro-
Hungarian throne, Archduke Francis Ferdinand
(1863–1914). The Austrians were convinced that Serbia, a Balkan state and an ally of Russia, was behind

the murder of the crown prince. They demanded a full
apology and punishment of the guilty parties. Serbia's
reply proved unsatisfactory and Austria declared war.

Austria's action set in motion the mobilization
plans required by the alliance system. Frantic efforts to
restore peace failed. By August 4, 1914, Russia, France,
and Britain were fighting Germany and Austria-
Hungary while Italy (a member of the Triple Alliance)
watched from the sidelines. Modern life—symbolized
by huge armies, military technology, and industrial
might—had plunged Europe and, later, much of the
world into the bloodiest war that civilization had yet
witnessed.

EARLY MODERNISM

As previously noted, at the dawn of the age of Modernism it was widely believed that the human race had turned a corner, that a golden era was about to begin. This sanguine outlook was fueled by the spread of self-government, new technology, and advances in science that held the promise of unlimited moral and material progress for humanity. As a result, there was everywhere a passion for novelty, a desire to cast off the dead hand of the past.

At the same time, however, a mood of uncertainty began to creep into the Modernist vocabulary and undercut the optimism. A few artists and thinkers, for whom rebellion was a primary response to the world, questioned traditional Western ethics, religion, customs, and other deeply held beliefs. They expressed their doubts in many ways, but chiefly through constant experimentation, through a desire to return to aesthetic fundamentals, and, especially among the painters, through a belief that the art process itself was more valuable than the completed work. As the pace of events accelerated in every area of life, a vigorous **avant-garde,** or vanguard, of writers, artists, and intellectuals pushed Western culture toward an elusive, uncertain future (see Figure 19.1).

Philosophy, Psychology, and Religion

Toward the end of the nineteenth century, new directions in philosophy and psychology reshaped these intellectual disciplines and fostered the shift to Modernism. These German-inspired ideas undercut cherished Western beliefs that dated from the Enlightenment—ideas about human rationality, universal moral order, and personal freedom. The creators of these seminal innovations were the philosopher Friedrich Nietzsche and the psychologists Sigmund Freud and Carl Jung. At the same time, religion, both mainstream and popular, though largely impervious to these intellectual trends, found it difficult to hew to traditional values and beliefs in the face of the growing secularization of society.

Nietzsche Friedrich Nietzsche [NEE-chuh] (1844–1900) was a prophet of Modernism who was notorious for his corrosive thought. He saw beyond the optimism of his times and correctly predicted the general disasters, both moral and material, that would afflict Western culture in the twentieth century. To him, the philosophies of the past were all false because they were built on nonexistent absolute principles. Denying moral certainty, Nietzsche asserted that he was the philosopher of the "perhaps," deliberately cultivating ambiguity. Nietzsche vehemently rejected middle-class and Judeo-Christian ideals, identifying them with "herd" or "slave" values. For the same reason, he heaped scorn on many of the "isms" of his day—liberalism, socialism, and Marxism—claiming that they appealed to humanity's lowest common denominator and were thus destroying Western civilization.

Nevertheless, there were affirmative, positive aspects to Nietzsche's thought. He believed in a new morality that glorified human life, creativity, and personal heroism. He forecast the appearance of a few *Übermenschen,* or supermen, who had the "will to power," the primeval urge to live beyond the herd and its debased values. He praised these supermen for living "beyond good and evil," for refusing to be bound by society's rules and mores.

Virtually unknown when he died, Nietzsche became one of the giants of twentieth-century thought. His radical thinking—notably in affirming that civilization itself is nothing more than a human invention—has touched nearly every phase of modern thought, including religion, philosophy, literary criticism, and psychology. An extreme individualist, he was contemptuous of the strong German state, though the Nazis in the 1930s used his writings to justify their theory of Aryan supremacy. His glorification of individualism was also a powerful stimulus to many artists, writers, and musicians.

Freud and Jung Rather than making a blanket condemnation of much of human morality and behavior, Sigmund Freud [FROID] (1856–1939) offered an approach to human psychology that could be used for further explorations into the study of the self. Part of the highly influential group of intellectuals and artists who flourished in Vienna around 1900, Freud, a neurologist, invented a new way of thinking about human nature that profoundly affected Western society.

Freud's analysis of the human mind challenged the Enlightenment's belief that human beings are fully rational. Freud argued that the human personality is the product of an intense internal struggle between instinctual drives and social reality. According to Freud, each psyche, or self, is composed of an *id*, a *superego,* and an *ego*. The id is the source of primitive, instinctual drives and desires, notably sex and aggression. The superego corresponds to the will of society internalized as the conscience. The ego represents the conscious public face that emerges from the conflict between the inborn instincts and the conscience and acts as the balancing component that establishes inner resolutions. In Freud's view, a true, lasting equilibrium among the three components of the psyche cannot be reached; the internal struggle is constant and inescapable. Those in whom the imbalance is pronounced suffer varying degrees of mental illness, ranging from mild neurosis to extreme psychosis. Even though Freud's theory tends toward determinism, he had hope for human freedom. For those who accepted their inescapable limitations, he believed that the truth about the human condition would liberate them from damaging habits of thought and enable them to function as morally free individuals—that is, free to make moral choices in full knowledge of the consequences of their actions.

Freud's greatest achievement was the founding of psychoanalysis, a type of therapy dedicated to the principle that once the roots of neurotic behavior are unraveled, a patient can lead a freer, healthier life. As part of treatment, he devised the "free association" method whereby his patients were asked to say, spontaneously and without inhibition, whatever came into their minds—memories, random observations, anything at all—and thus uncover traumas buried in their unconscious. He also studied his patients' dreams, which he thought were forms of wish fulfillment, a theory he set forth in *The Interpretation of Dreams* (1899). Freud's influence is pervasive today in Western culture, but critics have recently called into question not only his conclusions but also his ethics.

A challenge was made to Freud's views by a former associate, the Swiss psychologist Carl Jung [YOONG] (1875–1961). Jung developed a theory of a universal, collective unconscious, shared by all humans, that exists in conjunction with each individual's own "personal" unconscious. Jung speculated that the secrets of the unconscious could be revealed by studying archetypes, ancient images that recur again and again in human experience and appear in dreams, myths, and folk tales. His conception of archetypes opened a rich source of images and subjects for many Modernist artists and writers. Despite their differences, however, Freud and Jung agreed that the conscious mind is only a very small part of individual personality—a belief that is a cornerstone of Modernism.

Religious Developments The period 1870–1914 was one of the West's last great ages of religion, as religious values continued to motivate much of society. Evangelicalism, with its twin focus on personal salvation and faith-based truth, remained in control of mainline American Protestantism—Baptist, Congregational, Methodist, and Presbyterian—along with English Methodism. However, that changed in the 1880s, when adherents to the **Social Gospel**—stressing social betterment rather than personal piety—began to dominate mainline Protestantism. Social reform, rooted in Jesus' social teachings and the Jewish prophets' call for social justice (see Chapter 6), had always been a secondary goal of the evangelicals, extending back to John Wesley (see Chapter 17), but now it became the primary tenet of mainline Protestantism. The religious equivalent of progressive politics, the Social Gospel taught that the evils of the industrialized world could be ameliorated through social programs, such as settlement houses, soup kitchens, and various other outreach projects. In Europe, a similar development emerged in Inner Mission, a Lutheran program devoted to helping the industrial poor. Believers in the Social Gospel were called liberal Christians, because their optimistic perspective drew on key liberal ideas of the Enlightenment: free will, reason, and progress (see Chapter 16).

Contemporary evangelicals felt their faith betrayed by the rise of liberal Christianity in the United States. Thus, after 1880, a wing of the evangelical movement transformed itself, becoming the **fundamentalist** movement. The fundamentalists held fast to certain basic beliefs: the inerrancy of the Holy Bible, the need to be "born again," the truth of miracles, and the belief in the resurrection. In a broad sense, the fundamentalists are John Wesley's children, because like the founder of Methodism, they insisted on personal sanctification. Having lost control of mainline Protestantism, the fundamentalists founded an array of new sects, including the Church of God (1886), the Pentecostal Church (1901), the Church of God in Christ (1901)—a black Pentecostal church—and the Assemblies of God (1913). These churches, as well as other fundamentalist sects, shared the practice of "speaking in tongues," as a sign of the Holy Spirit's presence—derived from I Corinthians 12:8–10.

Meanwhile, in the Roman Catholic realm, the Vatican's strong stance against modern ideas (see Chapter 18) helped bring on the *Kulturkampf* (German, "Culture War"), from 1871 to 1878, between Germany and the Catholic Church. With Germany unified, the Protestant Chancellor Otto von Bismarck feared meddling by the church, especially on the part of Bavaria, a Catholic-majority state in southern Germany. Thus, he pushed a series of laws through the Reichstag, pointedly aimed at Catholic citizens, such as weakening church power over education, making civil marriages mandatory, and expelling the Jesuits from Germany. His plan failed, as Catholic representatives increased their numbers in the Reichstag, and, on the election of a new pope, Bismarck made peace with the church. Still, some German laws stayed in effect, such as the state's oversight of priests and the expulsion of the Jesuits, until 1917.

Although the 1878 compromise ended Germany's *Kulturkampf*, the popes thereafter until 1914 pursued a wavering policy toward new ideas and the upheavals in politics, economics, and society. On the one hand, they held the line against innovative ideas, such as by condemning **Modernism** (1907), a liberal movement within Catholicism (1850–1910), which applied new

Timeline 19.1   EARLY MODERNISM

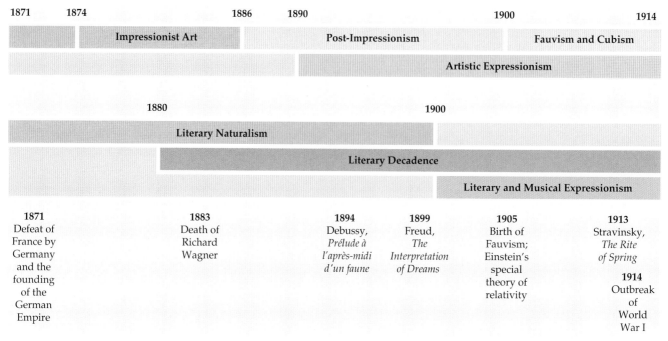

findings in history, philosophy, and psychology to church teachings. And, on the other hand, while opposing both socialism and the excesses of laissez-faire capitalism, they encouraged specific social reforms that led to social action, conducted by priests and lay Catholics in both Europe and overseas.

Literature

Three overlapping and contradictory styles characterize the literature of Early Modernism: Naturalism, Decadence, and Expressionism. The first of these, **Naturalism,** was inspired by the methods of science and the insights of sociology to focus on such issues as working-class unrest and women's rights. Naturalistic writers strove for objectivity and tended to see modern industrial society in a harsh light. **Decadent** writers rejected material values, scorned science, and were in flight from bourgeois society, which they identified with respectability and mediocrity. **Expressionism** was built on the premise that bourgeois culture had robbed the traditional vocabulary of the arts of its capacity to express the truth and therefore new methods and forms of expression must be sought. To a greater or lesser degree, these three styles share a disdain for middle-class life and values (Timeline 19.1).

Naturalistic Literature   The founder and chief exponent of Naturalism was Émile Zola [ZOH-luh]

(1840–1902), the French writer whose fame rests on the *Rougon-Macquart* series (1870–1893), twenty novels depicting the history of a single family under France's Second Empire. The novels treat socially provocative themes such as prostitution (*Nana*, 1880) and the horrifying conditions in the coal-mining industry (*Germinal*, 1884). They offer a richly detailed portrait of French society in the mid–nineteenth century and also illustrate Zola's belief in biological determinism. Whether the novels' characters became prostitutes or virtuous housewives, family men or drunken suicides, Zola traces their ultimate fates to inborn dispositions. Nevertheless, Zola was no rigid fatalist. His novels convincingly portray people fervently trying to control their destinies in an uncaring universe.

Another outstanding Naturalist was the Norwegian dramatist Henrik Ibsen (1828–1906). An important playwright, Ibsen helped to establish the **problem play,** dealing with social issues such as the public welfare versus private interest. This type of play became the staple of the modern theater and Ibsen its most eloquent practitioner. Ibsen lived mainly in Germany and Italy, writing about the middle-class Norwegian world he had fled, treating with frankness such previously taboo themes as venereal disease, suicide, and the decay of Christian values.

In *A Doll's House* (1879), Ibsen portrays a contemporary marriage and questions the wife's subservient role. Perhaps because of its controversial ending—the wife leaves her husband, asserting that her duties to herself are more sacred than her duties to him—this play created a tremendous first impression. In Ibsen's play, Nora is treated by her husband, Torvald, as a charming child whose sole purpose is to amuse him. When Nora borrows money to save Torvald's life, she deceives him about it because she knows how "painful and humiliating" it would be for him to know he owed her anything. But his reaction when he discovers it—condemning her bitterly and then forgiving her like a father—makes her realize she is living with a stranger. Faced with such lack of understanding, she deserts both husband and family, closing the door on bourgeois "decency." Ibsen's play was an international success, and its liberated heroine became the symbol of the new woman of the late 1800s.

The preeminent Naturalistic writer from eastern Europe was the Russian Anton Chekhov [CHEK-ahf] (1860–1904), a physician turned playwright and short-story writer, who found his subject in the suffocating life of Russia's small towns. He peopled his gently ironic plays with men and women in anguish over their ordinary lives, although his most arresting characters are those who endure disappointment without overt complaint. It is this latter quality that has made Chekhov's comedies, as these bittersweet plays are called, such favorites of both actors and audiences.

The Three Sisters (1901), a play that dramatizes the uneventful lives of a landowning family confined to the drab provinces, is characteristic of Chekhov's work. The characters conceal their depression behind false gaiety and self-deceit. His heroines, the three sisters, are bored, restless, and frustrated, not quite resigned to their mediocre existence. They talk constantly of a trip to Moscow, a journey longed for but never made. Today, Chekhov's plays suggest the dying world of Russia's out-of-touch ruling class, who were about to be swept away by the Marxist revolution of 1917.

An important Naturalistic writer in the United States was Kate Chopin [SHO-pan] (born Catherine O'Flaherty; 1851–1904), a short-story writer and novelist whose fiction reflected the general trend in nineteenth-century American literature away from Romanticism and toward Realism and Naturalism. A prevalent theme in Chopin's writings was a romantic awakening, usually by a female character. The setting for it was sketched out in **local color,** or regional details, and her method of tracking the action was Naturalistic—that is, she based plot twists on biological and socioeconomic factors. A St. Louis native, Chopin focused her stories and novels on **Creole** and **Cajun** life in Louisiana, a world that caught her imagination during a twelve-year-long marriage to a Creole planter and merchant.

The Awakening (1899) was Kate Chopin's masterpiece and the novel that abruptly ended her literary career, as she was stunned into silence by a hostile public reaction. A tale of adulterous passion, this novel is an American *Madame Bovary* (see Chapter 18). The story of Edna Pontellier, the Kentucky-born wife of a Creole husband, *The Awakening* explores a woman's passionate nature and its relation to self, marriage, and society. Edna rejects conventional morality, social duty, and personal obligations to her husband and children. She establishes her own home, earns money with her painting, accepts one lover, and pursues another. Ultimately, however, Edna's bid for freedom fails. She drowns herself—brought down by tradition, prejudice, and other societal pressures. Chopin's ending has been criticized for its shift to commonplace morality, but the novel nevertheless is an early attempt to deal with the issue of women's liberation. More than a simple Naturalist, Chopin is hailed today as a precursor of Post-Modernism (see Chapter 22) because of her keen interest in marginal people and feminist themes.

Decadence in Literature The Decadent movement began in France with Joris-Karl Huysmans [wees-MAHNS] (1848–1907), a follower of Zola's, who in 1884 broke with the social-documentary style of Naturalism and wrote the perverse novel *À rebours (Against Nature).* Paris was astonished by this partly autobiographical work. In it, Huysmans presents an exotic hero, Des Esseintes, bristling with vivid eccentricity and neurotic feelings and yet filled with inexpressible spiritual yearnings. Des Esseintes, hating modern life for its vulgarity and materialism, creates a completely encapsulated, silent world where he cultivates affected pleasures. He collects plants whose very nature is to appear diseased. He stimulates his senses with unusual sounds, colors, and smells, orchestrating them to music so that he experiences a sensory overload. And, in a violent rejection of Classicism, he embraces the crude Latin works of Late Rome.

In Great Britain, Oscar Wilde (1854–1900) was the center of the 1890s Decadent movement, with its generally relaxed view of morals and cynically amused approach to life (Figure 19.9). As with Huysmans, Wilde's outrageous manner can scarcely be separated from his literary achievements. Dressed in velvet and carrying a lily as he sauntered down London's main streets, Wilde gained notoriety as an **aesthete**—one unusually sensitive to the beautiful in art, music, and literature—even before he achieved fame as a dramatist of witty comedies of manners, such as *The Importance of Being Earnest* (1895). Wilde's only novel, *The Picture of Dorian Gray* (1894), features a hero immersed in exotic pleasures and secret vices, his youth preserved while his portrait ages horribly.

Today's most widely admired Decadent writer, the Frenchman Marcel Proust [PROOST] (1871–1922),

Figure 19.9 AUBREY BEARDSLEY. *The Dancer's Reward* from *Salomé.* 1894. Pen drawing, 9 × 6½″. Fogg Art Museum, Harvard University. *The visual counterpart to Wilde's decadent style in literature was Art Nouveau, especially as practiced by Aubrey Beardsley. Typical of his work is this black-and-white illustration for Wilde's play-poem* Salomé, *based on the biblical story of the dancer. In this print, depicting the climactic scene, Salomé grabs a lock of the hair of the beheaded John the Baptist, whose death she has ordered. With her left finger, she touches the blood as if to confirm that it is real. The device in the left corner of three vertical lines and three arrow- or heart-shaped forms is a signature adopted by Beardsley in 1893. The floral motif—the carnations on Salomé's cloak and at her throat—allude to Oscar Wilde's fondness for wearing flowers. Blending organic shapes and flowing lines with perverse themes, Beardsley's artificial style reveals Art Nouveau's affinity with an underworld of depravity.*

made his appearance at the end of this period. Starting in 1913 and concluding in 1927, Proust published a series of seven autobiographical novels collectively entitled *À la recherche du temps perdu* (*Remembrance of Things Past*). In this massive undertaking, he re-creates the world of upper bourgeois society that he had known as a young man but had deserted in 1903. Withdrawn into a cork-lined retreat reminiscent of Des Esseintes's silent hideaway in *À rebours,* Proust resurrected in the pages of his novels the aristocratic salons, the vulgar bourgeois world, and the riffraff of mistresses, prosti-

tutes, and rich homosexuals. Today, Proust's novels may be read in contradictory ways, as the supreme expression of a life lived for art or as the exemplification of a life empty of spiritual meaning.

Expressionist Literature   Expressionism, the third of these styles, was the only one that did not originate in France. Instead, it arose in Scandinavia in the works of the Swedish playwright August Strindberg and in central Europe in the fiction of Franz Kafka. Strindberg (1849–1912), having first achieved fame through Naturalistic drama, shifted to an Expressionist style in the 1890s. *The Dream Play* (first produced in 1907) is typical of his Expressionist dramas in employing generic figures with symbolic, all-purpose names ("Daughter," "Father," and so on), shadowy plots, and absurd fancies. In *The Dream Play,* time and place become meaningless, as, for instance, when a lovesick soldier suddenly becomes old and shabby and his bouquet of flowers withers before the audience's eyes. Strindberg's innovative techniques were meant not to obscure his meaning but rather to initiate the public into new ways of seeing and understanding life.

The ultimate pioneer of Expressionism was Franz Kafka (1883–1924), whose strange, boldly symbolic stories question traditional concepts of reality. One of Kafka's most striking achievements is the short story *Metamorphosis* (1919), in which the hero awakens to discover that while asleep he has been transformed into a giant insect—a vivid image of an identity crisis and a gripping parable of what happens to a person who is suddenly perceived to be totally different from other people.

Kafka's *The Trial,* a novel completed in 1914 and published in 1925, features a doomed main character with the generic name of Joseph K. An obscure minor government official, Joseph K. has his well-ordered world shattered when he is accused of a nameless crime. Unable to identify either his accusers or his misdeed and denied justice by the authorities, Joseph K. is eventually convicted by a mysterious court and executed by two bureaucrats in top hats. Kafka's faceless, powerless hero has become one of the most widely discussed figures of Modernism. In effect, Kafka transformed his own alienation—as a German-speaking Jew from the Czech-speaking, Protestant section of predominantly Roman Catholic Austria—into a modern Everyman victimized by forces beyond human control (Figure 19.10).

The Advance of Science

Biology and chemistry, in particular, made rapid advances around the turn of the century. In biology, the

Figure 19.10 EDVARD MUNCH. *The Scream.* 1893. Oil on canvas, 36 × 29″. Nasjonalgalleriet, Oslo. *The Expressionists, whether writers, artists, or musicians, responded to the uncertainty of the modern world with images of despair, anxiety, and helplessness. The work of the Norwegian painter Edvard Munch provides a visual counterpart to the bleak and brooding plays of Strindberg and the terrifying stories of Kafka. Munch, whose paintings reflect a nightmarish vision of life as a tormented existence never free from pain, once said, "I hear the scream in nature." The Scream is a visual metaphor of modern alienation. The skullheaded, sexless figure, with mouth open and hands over ears, seems to be ignored by the couple walking away in the background. Typical of Expressionism, Munch depicts the world as unnatural, as evidenced by the painting's swirling patterns of lines and colors. Masked and armed thieves stole Munch's* Scream *from its museum setting in 2004, and police recovered it, slightly damaged but repairable, in 2006.*

Austrian monk Gregor Johann Mendel (1822–1884) had summarized his groundbreaking research in 1865, but his findings, the basis for the new science of genetics, were ignored until three researchers, working independently, rediscovered his reports in 1900. By applying mathematics to biological theory, Mendel proved the existence of dominant and recessive traits, and using the laws of probability, he worked out the pattern for offspring over the generations. Subsequent research showed that Mendelian laws applied to virtually all animals and plants.

In chemistry, the outstanding development was radiochemistry, the study of radioactive materials. The founder of this new discipline was Marie Sklodowska Curie (1867–1934), a Polish physicist and the first scientist to be awarded two Nobel prizes. Working with her French husband, Pierre Curie (1859–1906), Madame Curie identified two new radioactive elements, polonium and radium. The isolation of radium stimulated research in atomic physics. Another contributor to radiochemistry was the German physicist Wilhelm Conrad Roentgen [RENT-guhn] (1845–1923), whose 1895 discovery of X rays led to their use in diagnostic medicine.

The discoveries in genetics and radiochemistry boosted the optimism and faith in progress that characterized this period, but developments in physics had the opposite effect, adding to the undercurrent of uncertainty and doubt that also existed. Three brilliant scientists—Max Planck, Niels Bohr, and Albert Einstein—launched a revolution that led other scientists to discard the previously accepted belief that Newton's laws of motion were universal.

Max Planck (1858–1947) laid the foundation for modern physics in 1900 with research in quantum theory. His research called into question the wave theory of radiation, which dated from the 1700s. Working with hot objects, Planck observed that the radiative energy that emanated from a heat source issued not in a smooth wave but in discrete bursts. He measured each burst of radiation and computed a mathematical formula for expressing the released energy, a unit that he called a *quantum*—a word meaning a specified amount, derived from the Latin *quanta*, or "how much." When Planck could not fit his quantum formula into traditional wave-theory physics, he realized the revolutionary nature of his discovery. Planck's quantum theory became a primary building block in the speculation of the second of the trio, Danish physicist Niels Bohr.

Bohr (1885–1962) was the prime mover in solving the mystery of the structure of the atom. When he began his research, the ancient Greek idea of the indivisible atom had already been laid to rest. Scientists in the early 1900s had proved that each atom is a neutral body containing a positive nucleus with negatively charged particles called electrons. And one researcher had speculated that electrons orbit a nucleus in much the same way that the planets move around the sun—suggesting a correspondence with Newtonian theory.

Until Bohr's theory of atomic structure was set forth in 1912, however, no one could explain how these miniature solar systems actually worked. Bohr's solution was based on bold assumptions: that an electron could revolve about a nucleus only in certain privileged orbits and that when it was in these orbits, it did not emit radiation. He concluded that an electron radiated only when it leaped from orbit to orbit. Using

Planck's quantum theory, he called these leaps quantum jumps, referring to the amount of radiative energy released. Bohr's discovery had tremendous consequences, leading eventually to the development of nuclear energy for weaponry and electrical generation.

German-born Albert Einstein (1879–1955) also did important theoretical work in atomic physics, but his most significant research in the early twentieth century involved the relationship between time and space. Newton had maintained that there existed absolute rest and absolute velocity, absolute space and absolute time. Einstein asserted that the only absolute in the universe is the speed of light, which is the same for all observers. He concluded that all motion is relative and that concepts of absolute space and time are meaningless. If two systems move with relatively uniform motion toward each other, there exist two different spaces and two different times. He called this finding the special theory of relativity. This theory replaces Newtonian absolute space with a grid of light beams that in effect determines the meaning of space in each situation. Einstein's special theory was the first step in a reformulation of scientific concepts of space and time.

The Modernist Revolution in Art

After 1871 a revolution began in the arts and architecture whose aim was to replace Renaissance ideals with Modernist principles. Although there were many trends within this revolution, in painting and sculpture it generally meant a shift from an art that reflected the natural world to one rooted in the artist's inner vision, from an art based on representational or naturalistic images to one devoted to nonrepresentational or nonobjective forms, and from an art focused on content to one dedicated to the process of creation itself. By the time the revolution in painting and sculpture was complete, artists had given up realism and made **abstraction** their ideal. In architecture, the Modernist revolution was less radical, though architects slowly turned away from the forms of the Greco-Roman and Gothic styles and created functional buildings devoid of decoration.

Impressionism   The stylistic innovation in painting known as **Impressionism** began in the 1870s. In spite of owing much to Realism and even to Romanticism, this new style marked a genuine break with the realistic tradition that had dominated Western art since the fourteenth century. The Impressionists wanted to depict what they saw in nature, but they were inspired by the increasingly fast pace of modern life to portray transient moments. They concentrated on the play of

light over objects, people, and nature, breaking up seemingly solid surfaces, stressing vivid contrasts between colors in sunlight and shade, and depicting reflected light in all its possibilities. Unlike earlier artists, they did not want to observe the world from indoors. They abandoned the studio, painting in the open air and recording spontaneous impressions of their subjects instead of making sketches outside and then moving indoors to complete the work from memory.

Some of the Impressionists' painting methods were influenced by technological advances. For example, the shift from the studio to the open air was made possible by the advent of cheap rail travel, which permitted easy access to the countryside or seashore, and by the discovery of chemical dyes and oils that allowed paint to be kept in tubes that the artists could carry with them.

Although Impressionism was a product of industrial society, it was at the same time indebted to the past. From Realism the Impressionist painters learned to find beauty in the everyday world. From the Barbizon painters (a group of French landscape painters active in the mid–nineteenth century) they took the practice of painting in the open air. From the Romantics they borrowed the techniques of "broken color"—splitting up complex colors into their basic hues—and of using subtle color shadings to create a shimmering surface effect (see Chapter 18).

Impressionism acquired its name not from supporters but from angry art lovers who felt threatened by the new painting. The term *Impressionism* was born in 1874, when a group of artists organized an exhibition of their paintings. Reaction from the public and the press was immediate, and derisive. Among the 165 paintings exhibited was *Impression: Sunrise,* by Claude Monet [moh-NAY] (1840–1926). Viewed through hostile eyes, Monet's painting of a rising sun over a misty, watery scene seemed messy, slapdash, and an affront to good taste (Figure 19.11). Borrowing Monet's title, art critics extended the term *Impressionism* to the entire exhibit. In response, Monet and his twenty-nine fellow artists in the exhibit adopted the name as a badge of their unity, despite individual differences. From then until 1886, Impressionism had all the zeal of a "church," as the painter Renoir put it. The Impressionists gave eight art shows. Monet was faithful to the Impressionist creed until his death, although many of the others moved on to new styles.

Monet wanted to re-create the optical sensations he experienced. Rejecting traditional content, he focused on light and atmosphere, simulating the visual effects of fog, haze, or mist over a landscape and, especially, over water. That this approach succeeded so well shows the harmony between Monet's scientific eye and painterly hand. His studies of changing light and atmosphere, whether depicting haystacks, the Rouen

Figure 19.11 CLAUDE MONET. *Impression: Sunrise.* 1872. Oil on canvas, 19½ × 25½". Musée Marmottan, Paris. *Monet's* Impression: Sunrise *illustrates the immediacy of Impressionism. From his window overlooking Le Havre harbor, he painted what he recorded in a letter to a friend: "sun in the mist and a few masts of boats sticking up in the foreground." The artist has transformed the substantial world of nature into fragmented daubs of broken color.*

cathedral, or water lilies (Figure 19.12), demonstrate Monet's lifelong devotion to Impressionism.

Unlike Monet, Auguste Renoir [REN-wahr] (1841–1919) did not remain faithful to the Impressionist movement. In the early 1880s, personal and aesthetic motives led him to move away from Impressionism and exhibit in the official Salon (when he could get his work accepted). In his modified style, he shifted from a soft-focus image to a concentration on form, a move that brought quick support from art critics and wealthy patrons.

Painted about the time of his break with Impressionism, *The Luncheon of the Boating Party* demonstrates Renoir's splendid mastery of form (Figure 19.13). Its subject is a carefree summer outing on a restaurant terrace on an island in the Seine, the company being composed of the painter's friends, including fellow artists, a journalist, the café owner, and an actress. *The Boating Party* shows that Renoir had not given up—nor would he ever—his Impressionist ties, for his stress in this work on the fleeting, pleasure-filled moment was basic to the style, as was his use of broken color in a natural background. Nevertheless, what remained central to Renoir's creed were the foreground figures, treated clearly and with substance.

In contrast to Monet and Renoir, whose careers bloomed in poverty, Berthe Morisot [mohr-ee-ZOH]

(1841–1895) was a member of the upper middle class. Her wealth and artistic connections—Fragonard was her grandfather and Manet her brother-in-law—allowed her to apply herself to painting and play an important role in the founding of the Impressionist school. In her work, she focused on atmosphere and the play of light on the human form, although she never sacrificed her subjects to the cause of color alone. Her subjects were modern life, though limited to the confined world of domestic interiors and gardens (Figure 19.14).

A few Americans also made significant contributions to Impressionism. The most important of them was Mary Cassatt [kuh-SAT] (1845–1926), a young woman who joined the Impressionist circle while studying painting in Paris. Cassatt was from a prosperous, well-connected Philadelphia family, and it was largely through her social ties that Impressionist painting was introduced to America. She suggested to her wealthy friends that this art was worth collecting, and some of the most notable Impressionist works in American museums are there because of her influence.

Cassatt, however, was not devoted exclusively to Impressionism. Like other artists of this era, she was fascinated by Japanese prints from French collections that were on exhibit in Paris in 1890, and she was the first to imitate all aspects, including color, of the

Figure 19.12 CLAUDE MONET. *Water Lilies.* Ca. 1920. Oil on canvas, 16′ × 5′ 15/16″. Carnegie Museum of Art, Pittsburgh. Acquired through the generosity of Mrs. Alan M. Scaife. *Knowledgeable about the art market and determined to escape a life of poverty, Monet produced nonthreatening works that appealed to conservative middle-class collectors. For these patrons, he painted natural scenes, such as water lilies, that evoked pleasant memories of simple rural values. Begun in 1899, the water lily series occupied him for the rest of his life. Setting up his easel in his splendid garden at Giverny and working at different times of the day, Monet captured the effect of changing sunlight on this beloved subject.*

◀ **Figure 19.13** AUGUSTE RENOIR. *The Luncheon of the Boating Party.* 1881. Oil on canvas, 51 × 68". The Phillips Collection, Washington, D.C. *Renoir's return to traditional values is reflected in this vivid painting. He uses the restaurant's terrace to establish conventional perspective, the left railing forming a diagonal line that runs into the distance. He balances the composition, weaving the young men and women into a harmonious ensemble, painting some standing and others sitting. He also employs colors effectively, using orange, blue, and black to offset the expanses of white in the tablecloth and the men's shirts and women's blouses.*

Figure 19.14 BERTHE MORISOT. *Laundresses Hanging Out the Wash.* 1875. Oil on canvas, 13 × 16". National Gallery of Art, Washington, D.C. Collection of Mr. and Mrs. Paul Mellon. *Morisot's* Laundresses Hanging Out the Wash, *shown with the Impressionists in 1876, was praised by critics for its clarity of color and handling of light. It depicts, from a high vantage point, a group of commercial washerwomen hanging out laundry in a garden. Morisot was one of the few Impressionists to depict urban workers, because, in rapidly urbanizing France, artists nostalgically focused on farm laborers at their tasks. Typical of her art, she emphasizes the flatness of the picture plane, which is unlike the three-dimensionality of paintings such as Renoir's* The Luncheon of the Boating Party *(see Figure 19.13). Her vigorous brushwork, making the painting difficult to decipher, gives a feeling of immediacy—the aim of Impressionist art.*

ENCOUNTER

The French Impressionists Meet Ukiyo-e *Art*

Japanese culture, having been closed to the West for more than 225 years, became an obsession among Europe's avant-garde in the late 1800s, once diplomatic and commercial relations were reestablished with the island kingdom. Soon there arose among cultural leaders the fashion Japonisme, a French term meaning "the love of all things Japanese."

Europeans, except for the Dutch, lost access to Japan in 1638, when Japan's military ruler, the shogun, closed the country to foreigners. Thereafter, the Dutch colony on Deshima, an island in Nagasaki harbor, operated as Japan's window on the world, conducting from there a highly regulated but lucrative two-way trade. The Dutch also kept Japan up-to-date on selected developments in the West through the import of scientific books and art prints (see Encounter in Chapter 14). Japan's isolationist policy began to crumble in 1853, in response to American gunboats demanding trade relations. At first, five ports were opened; others soon followed.

With trade renewed, Japanese culture flowed into the West. Especially impressive were woodblock prints, or *ukiyo-e* [U-kee-oy] ("pictures of the floating world")—then unknown in the West. Executed at first in black and white, *ukiyo-e* prints entered a golden age with the introduction of color in about 1770. When these prints reached Europe, their simple design and bold colors fascinated the Impressionist and Post-Impressionist painters.

Numerous artists, including Édouard Manet, Claude Monet, Pierre Renoir, Mary Cassatt (see Figure 19.15), Paul Cézanne, and Paul Gauguin, played with Japanese motifs in their works, but Vincent van Gogh had the greatest affinity with the *ukiyo-e* prints. Van Gogh especially admired and collected the prints of Andō Hiroshige [he-roh-SHE-ge] (1797–1858), with their flat areas of pure color and figures drawn with a few wispy lines. Hiroshige's *Sudden Shower at Ōhashi Bridge at Atake* (Encounter figure 19.1) inspired van Gogh's oil painting *The Bridge in the Rain (After Hiroshige)* (Encounter figure 19.2), one of three studies he made of Japanese prints. Van Gogh did more than "copy" the print; he transformed it by heightening the color contrasts and adding a decorative border. Learning from his *ukiyo-e* studies, van Gogh forged his own unique style of painting, thus establishing a link between Japanese and Western art.

Learning from the Encounter What historic event caused Japan to reopen its doors to the world? **What** role did trade play in this artistic encounter? **Define** *ukiyo-e* print. **What** was the appeal of *ukiyo-e* prints to Western artists? **Discuss** the influence of *ukiyo-e* prints on van Gogh's artistic style. **How** does art contribute to globalization?

---

ukiyo-e [U-kee-oy] prints—the woodcuts that had developed in Japan in the 1600s—as in *The Bath,* or *The Tub* (about 1891; Figure 19.15). A mother and child were a typical subject in Cassatt's art.

Post-Impressionism The rebellious, experimental spirit instilled by the Impressionists had freed art from the tyranny of a single style. Artists now moved in many directions, united only by a common desire to extend the boundaries of Impressionism. This ambition signified the triumph of the Modernist notion that art must constantly change in order to reflect new historical conditions—the opposite of the Classical ideal

of eternal truths. Impressionism was succeeded by **Post-Impressionism** (1886–1900), whose four most important artists were Georges Seurat, Paul Cézanne, Paul Gauguin, and Vincent van Gogh.

Like the Impressionists, Georges Seurat [suh-RAH] (1859–1891) painted the ordinary pleasures of Parisian life in a sunlit atmosphere, but his way of doing so was formulaic and theoretical, markedly different from the approach of, say, Monet. After studying scientific color theory, Seurat developed a technique known as **Pointillism** (or Divisionism), which meant applying to the canvas thousands of tiny dots of pure color juxtaposed in such a way that, when viewed from the

Encounter figure 19.1 ANDŌ HIROSHIGE. *Sudden Shower at Ōhashi Bridge at Atake.* Ca. 1857. Woodcut, approx. 13²⁄₅ × 8⁷⁄₁₀″. *Hiroshige created a new genre, the travelogue print, based on sketches made on the spot, in all weathers and at different times of day.* Sudden Shower at Ōhashi Bridge *is from the series* One Hundred Famous Views of Edo. *He boldly crops the composition, shows the human figures dwarfed by the setting, and uses unusual perspective—typical features of his art.*

Encounter figure 19.2 VINCENT VAN GOGH. *The Bridge in the Rain (After Hiroshige).* 1887. Oil on canvas, approx. 28³⁄₄ × 21¹⁄₄″. Van Gogh Museum, Amsterdam (Vincent van Gogh Foundation). *This painting shows the lessons van Gogh learned by copying Hiroshige's* ukiyo-e *print: strong, dark color to outline figures, bold color contrasts, cropping of the composition, and dramatic perspective. Van Gogh made these techniques his own in his later works.*

proper distance, they merged to form a natural, harmonious effect of color, light, and shade. His most famous Pointillist work is *A Sunday Afternoon on the Island of La Grande Jatte* (Figure 19.16), an affectionate, good-humored look at Parisians enjoying themselves. The technique may be novel and "scientific," but the composition is Classical and serene, with carefully placed and balanced figures and repeated curved shapes, visible in the umbrellas, hats, and other objects. Seurat's style led to a minor school of painters, but his influence was overshadowed by that of Cézanne.

Paul Cézanne [say-ZAN] (1839–1906), a pivotal figure in Western art, was the prophet of **abstraction** in Post-Impressionism and a precursor of Cubism. Abstraction is that trend in modern art that emphasizes shapes, lines, and colors independent of the natural world. With Édouard Manet, he was one of the founders of modern painting. He had exhibited with the original Impressionist group in 1874 but by 1878 had rejected the movement because its depiction of nature lacked substance and weight. He sought a new way to portray nature so as to reveal its underlying solidity and order. After experimentation, Cézanne concluded that nature was composed of such geometric forms as cylinders, spheres, cubes, and cones. By trying to reveal this idea in his works, he opened up a

Figure 19.15 MARY CASSATT. *The Bath,* or *The Tub.* Ca. 1891. Soft-ground etching with aquatint and drypoint on paper, 12⅜ × 8⅞″. National Museum of Women in the Arts, Washington, D.C. *This Cassatt print, in Japanese-inspired style, symbolizes the globalization of Western culture that was well under way in Early Modernism. The first of ten prints in a series, it is the only one that could be called a true imitation. It uses simple design, Japanese spatial pattern, flat areas of color, and a hint of Japanese facial features to create a Western version of a* ukiyo-e *print—except that it is made on a metal plate and not a woodblock. In the rest of this series, Cassatt adopted a more Western style, notably adding a complete background, such as wallpaper and windows. Her interest in Japanese prints coincided with Gauguin's experiments (see Figure 19.18) with Tahitian-inspired art; both are forerunners of Post-Modernism.*

new way of painting that has influenced art to the present day.

Cézanne's greatest works came after 1886, when he left Paris for his quiet home in Aix-en-Provence in southern France. Among his favorite subjects was the nearby mountain Mont Sainte-Victoire (Figure 19.17). Like many of his later works, *Mont Sainte-Victoire* points toward abstraction but never quite gives up representation. Amid the dense geometric forms in the picture's lower half, house shapes peek through daubs of green foliage, reminding the viewer that this is a realistic landscape. Later artists, such as Kandinsky and Malevich, took up Cézanne's challenge of telescoping the two-dimensional and the three-dimensional and created the first truly abstract paintings, the most visible signs of twentieth-century art (see Chapter 20).

The Post-Impressionist Paul Gauguin [go-GAN] (1848–1903) began the movement known as **primitivism**—the term used to describe the West's fascination with non-Western culture as well as pre-Renaissance art. Gauguin's eccentric personal life also made him a legendary figure of Modernism. Rejecting

the comforts of Parisian bourgeois life, he abandoned his career and his family and exiled himself to the French colony of Tahiti, living a decadent, bohemian existence.

Before moving to the South Pacific, Gauguin lived and painted among Breton peasants, inhabitants of Brittany in western France. He developed a personal style that favored flattened shapes and bright colors and avoided conventional perspective and modeling. He also became interested in non-Western, "primitive" religions, and many of his Tahitian works refer to indigenous beliefs and practices, as in *Manao Tupapau: The Spirit of the Dead Watching* (Figure 19.18). When exhibited in Paris, this painting created an uproar, for Western audiences were not accustomed to seeing dark-skinned nudes in art, and certainly not presented reclining on a bed, a customary pose for female nudes since the Renaissance (see Figure 16.7). Furthermore, the seated ghost at the left was a direct challenge to a secular worldview. Today, Gauguin's role in art has been reevaluated. He is now honored for his introduction of other cultural traditions into Western art, which

Figure 19.16 GEORGES SEURAT. *A Sunday Afternoon on the Island of La Grande Jatte.*
1884–1886. Oil on canvas, 6'9" × 10'1". Art Institute of Chicago. Helen Birch Bartlett
Memorial Collection, 1926. *Unlike most Impressionists, Seurat worked slowly and methodically. In the case of* La Grande Jatte, *he spent years organizing the canvas and then painting the thousands of dots required by the Pointillist technique. Such painstaking attention to detail was necessary to achieve the harmonious effect his finished paintings demonstrate.*

Figure 19.17 PAUL CÉZANNE. *Mont Sainte-Victoire.*
1904–1906. Oil on canvas, 28⅞ × 36¼". Philadelphia Museum of Art. George W. Elkins Collection. *Although Cézanne was the founder of the Post-Impressionist movement that culminated in abstraction, he had a conservative approach to art. He wanted to create paintings that had the solidity of the art in the museums, especially the works of the seventeenth-century painter Nicolas Poussin. Hence, Cézanne continued to rely on line and geometric arrangement as well as on color and light, simplifying his paintings into austere images of order and peaceful color. In this painting of Mont Sainte-Victoire—visible from his studio in Aix-en-Provence—Cézanne's closeness to abstract art may be seen. The distant mountain has a solid presence, but the houses, foliage, fields, and road disappear into a set of ambiguous forms and color planes. Cézanne's handling of the color planes, with their jagged edges and abrupt juxtapositions, inspired the Cubists to search for a new way to represent the world.*

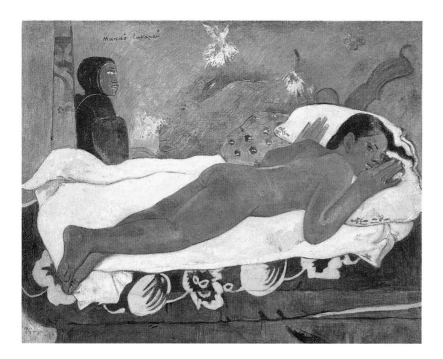

Figure 19.18 PAUL GAUGUIN. *Manao Tupapau: The Spirit of the Dead Watching.* 1892. Oil on burlap mounted on canvas, 28½ × 36⅜". Albright-Knox Art Gallery, Buffalo. A. Conger Goodyear Collection, 1965. *Gauguin wrote of this painting that he wanted to convey the presence of* tupapau, *or the Spirit of the Dead, as envisioned by the young girl on the bed. He implies her fear through the mixture of the yellow, purple, and blue colors; by the sparks of light, or phosphorescences, which symbolize the spirits of the dead; and by the ghost depicted as an old woman in the left background. He felt it necessary "to make very simple paintings, with primitive, childlike themes" and to use "a minimum of literary means" in order for western Europeans to understand how Tahitians viewed life and death.*

enriched its vocabulary, and for his expressive use of color.

With the Post-Impressionist Vincent van Gogh [van GO] (1853–1890), the tradition of Expressionism began to emerge in Western art, although he was not part of any of the various Expressionist schools of painters. "Expressionism" in his case meant that the work of art served as a vehicle for his private emotions to an unprecedented degree. Van Gogh sometimes allowed his moods to determine what colors to use and how to apply paint to canvas, a principle that led to a highly idiosyncratic style. Van Gogh's life was filled with misfortune, and even his painting had little recognition in his lifetime. In his early years, he was rebuffed in his efforts to do missionary work among poverty-stricken Belgian coal miners. All his attempts at friendship ended in failure, including a celebrated episode in the south of France with the painter Gauguin. Throughout his life, overtures to women resulted in utter humiliation. In the end, he became mentally unstable and committed suicide.

From his personal pain van Gogh created a memorably expressive style, however. Rejecting the smooth look of traditional painting and stirred by the colorful canvases of the Impressionists, he sometimes applied raw pigments with his palette knife or fingers instead of with a brush. His slashing strokes and brilliant colors often mirrored his mental states, giving the viewer a glimpse into his volatile personality. For instance, his *Self-Portrait* strongly suggests his mental agitation, through the dominance of the color blue and the swirling lines of paint (Figure 19.19). The anguish in his eyes is reinforced by the vortex of color framing the head and the deep facial lines. As a result, the portrait seethes with emotion.

Figure 19.19 VINCENT VAN GOGH. *Self-Portrait.* 1889. Oil on canvas, 25½ × 21¼". Musée d'Orsay, Paris. *Van Gogh's self-absorption is reflected in the thirty-six self-portraits he painted during his eleven-year artistic career. Anguished and prone to mental breakdown, he must have found a measure of reassurance in recording the subtle changes in his own countenance. A constant in all his likenesses is the haunted eyes, showing the inner torment from which he could never quite escape. The very execution of this work demonstrates van Gogh's passionate mood, as in the aggressive brushstrokes that congeal into a radiating pattern of energy lines covering the painting's surface. He painted this self-portrait in 1889, a year before he took his own life.*

The most memorable of van Gogh's paintings is *The Starry Night* (Figure 19.20). Executed in the last year of van Gogh's life, the painting depicts a tranquil village under an agitated sky filled with pulsating stars, an unnatural crescent moon, and whirling rivers of light. Intensifying the strange imagery is the grove of cypress trees (left foreground), rendered in the shape of flames. The ensemble of convoluted shapes and bold colors expresses the artist's inner turmoil. In a sense, van Gogh's works constitute his psychological signature; his style is perhaps the most easily recognizable one in Western art.

Fauvism, Cubism, and Expressionism   The preeminence of Paris as the hub of Western culture was enhanced by the arrival of Henri Matisse and Pablo Picasso in about 1900. These innovative and prolific artists emerged as the leaders of the pre–World War I generation, later dominating the art world in the twentieth century in much the same way that Ingres and Delacroix had in the nineteenth century.

Henri Matisse [ma-TEES] (1869–1954) rose to fame in 1905 as a leader of **Fauvism.** The Fauves—French for "wild beasts," a name their detractors gave to them—were a group of loosely aligned painters who exhibited together. Matisse's work, like that of his col-leagues, stemmed from the tradition of van Gogh, with color as its overriding concern. In *Open Window, Collioure,* Matisse painted a kaleidoscope of colors—pinks, mauves, bluish greens, bright reds, oranges, and purples—that derive not from the direct observation of nature but, rather, from the artist's belief that color harmonies can control the composition (Figure 19.21). The colors are "arbitrary" in the sense that they bear little resemblance to what one would actually see from the window, but they are far from arbitrary in their relation to one another—which was what interested Matisse.

Pablo Picasso [pih-KAH-so] (1881–1973), a talented young Spanish painter, was attracted to Paris's avant-garde art community in about 1900. In 1907 he proved his genius with *Les Demoiselles d'Avignon (The Young Ladies of Avignon),* perhaps the most influential painting of the twentieth century (Figure 19.22). This revolutionary work moved painting close to abstraction—the realization of Cézanne's dream. An unfinished work, *Les Demoiselles* reflects the multiple influences operating on Picasso at the time—the primitivism of African masks, the geometric forms of Cézanne, and the ancient sculpture of pre-Roman Spain. Despite its radical methods, this painting still has a conventional composition: five figures with a still life in the foreground.

Figure 19.20 VINCENT VAN GOGH. *The Starry Night*. 1889. Oil on canvas, 29 × 36¼" (73.7 × 92.1 cm). The Museum of Modern Art, New York. Acquired through the Lillie P. Bliss Bequest. Photograph © 1997 The Museum of Modern Art, New York. *Van Gogh's* The Starry Night *is a stunning symbol of the unstable world of Early Modernism. The whirling, luminous sky, formed with wild patches of color and tormented brushstrokes, reflects the psychic disturbance of the painter—an early example of Expressionist art. But van Gogh was more than an artist beset by personal demons; he wanted to follow Delacroix (see Chapters 17 and 18) and depict nature, using color and drawing, without slavishly copying reality. In van Gogh—as in his contemporary, the philosopher Nietzsche—psychic turmoil and artistic vision were virtually inseparable.*

Figure 19.21   Henri Matisse. *Open Window, Collioure.* 1905. Oil on canvas, 21¾ × 18⅛". Courtesy Mrs. John Hay Whitney, New York. *Like van Gogh, Matisse resisted quiet surface effects, preferring the look of paint applied in thick daubs and strips of varying length. His dazzling optical art was created by his use and placement of vibrant colors. In this painting, Matisse interprets the glorious view from his studio overlooking the Mediterranean.*

Nevertheless, with this painting Picasso redirected objective art beyond abstraction and into the development of nonobjective painting—thus overturning a standard founded in the Renaissance.

Les Demoiselles was the prelude to **Cubism,** one of the early-twentieth-century styles leading Western art toward abstraction. With his French colleague Georges Braque [BRAHK] (1882–1963), Picasso developed Cubism. This style of painting, which went through different phases at the hands of different artists, basically fragments three-dimensional objects and reassembles them in a pattern that stresses their geometric structure and the relationships of these basic geometric forms. Braque and Picasso worked so closely together that their paintings could sometimes not be separately identified, even, it is said, by the artists themselves.

An example of Picasso's Cubist style is *Portrait of Daniel-Henri Kahnweiler* (Figure 19.23). The subject was a Parisian art dealer who specialized in the works of Fauvism and Cubism, including those by Picasso and Braque. Kahnweiler wrote books on avant-garde movements and was a controversial figure on the international art scene for decades. Picasso immortalized him in this Cubist portrait, a fitting tribute to one who helped popularize the Cubist style.

With his adoption of Cubist methods, Picasso gave up Renaissance space completely, representing the subjects from multiple angles simultaneously and shaping the figures into geometric designs. He later added a new feature to Cubism when he applied bits and pieces of other objects to the canvas, a technique called **collage** (French for "pasting"). Collage nudged

Figure 19.22 PABLO PICASSO. *Les Demoiselles d'Avignon (The Young Ladies of Avignon).* Paris (June–July 1907). Oil on canvas, 8′ × 7′8″ (243.9 × 233.7 cm). The Museum of Modern Art, New York. Acquired through the Lillie P. Bliss Bequest. Photograph © 1997 The Museum of Modern Art, New York. *This painting's title derives from Picasso's native Barcelona, where Avignon Street ran through the red-light district. First intended as a moral work warning of the dangers of venereal disease (the figures still show provocative poses), the painting evolved over the months, changing as Picasso's horizons expanded. That he left the painting unfinished—like a scientist's record of a failed laboratory experiment—illustrates a leading trait of Modernism, the belief that truth is best expressed in the artistic process itself. A recent survey reveals that this painting is the most often reproduced work in art history textbooks.*

Cubism closer to pure abstraction; the flat plane of the painting's surface was now simply a two-dimensional showcase for objects.

Although Paris remained the capital of Western art, other cities were also the scene of aesthetic experiment. Oslo, Munich, Vienna, and Dresden became artistic meccas, especially for Expressionist painters who followed the path opened by van Gogh and the Fauves. In Munich, for example, Expressionism led to the formation of an international school of artists known as Der Blaue Reiter (The Blue Rider), named after a painting of the same name. Rejecting the importance of artistic content and refusing to paint "safe" objects, this group of painters concentrated on basics such as color and line, which were meant to express inner feelings. Founded by the Russian exile Wassily Kandinsky [kan-DIN-skee] (1866–1944) in 1911, this school made the first breakthrough to abstract art—nonrepresentational or nonobjective paintings that defy any sense of reality or connection to nature and

are, as the artist himself put it, "largely unconscious, spontaneous expressions of inner character, nonmaterial in nature." Kandinsky's "improvisations," as he labeled them, were free forms, possessing no objective content, consisting only of meandering lines and amorphous blobs of color (Figure 19.24). For all their seeming randomness, however, his paintings were planned to look that way. He consciously worked out the placement of the lines and the choices of color, leaving nothing to chance. He also linked the fluidity of painting with the lyricism of music, a connection suggested in this work by the meandering lines.

New Directions in Sculpture and Architecture Few sculptors of any consequence appeared in the 1871–1914 period and only one genius: Auguste Rodin [roh-DAN] (1840–1917). Rejecting the static Classicism of the mid–nineteenth century, Rodin forged an eclectic style that blended Romantic subject matter, Renaissance simplicity, and Gothic angularity with the radical

Figure 19.23 PABLO PICASSO. *Portrait of Daniel-Henri Kahnweiler.* 1910. Oil on canvas, 39⅝ × 25⅝". Gift of Mrs. Gilbert W. Chapman in memory of Charles B. Goodspeed. The Art Institute of Chicago, Chicago, IL. *This Cubist portrait represents Kahnweiler from several points of view at once, reshaping his image into a new structure of planes and shapes—typical of Cubist technique. Kahnweiler's head and hair, suit and torso, and crossed hands in his lap are visible, as are objects resting on a table to the left. Other parts of the painting seem indiscernible. Browns, grays, blacks, whites, and bluish tones accentuate the fragmented planes and shapes.*

changes under way in painting. In the sculpture *Eve* (Figure 19.25), he created a rough Gothic effect using modern means, torturing the surface, especially of the stomach and the head. The result was both Impressionistic (the play of light on the scored surfaces) and Expressionistic (the traces of Rodin's fingers on the bronze medium, which so dramatically suggest the intensity of the artist's involvement).

Having lagged behind the other arts for most of the century, architecture began to catch up in the 1880s. The United States led the way, notably in the works of the Chicago School. The skyscraper, perfected by Chicago-based architects, became synonymous with Modernism and modern life. Unlike Modernist paint-

ing and sculpture, the new architecture arose for practical reasons: dense populations and soaring real estate values.

Using the aesthetic dictum that "form follows function," the Chicago School solved design problems without relying on past techniques and traditions. This dictum means that a building ought to be a workable organism where the pressure of daily existence is channeled into a harmonious, functioning whole; in practical terms, the pressure is called function, the resultant building, form. The author of this dictum, Louis Sullivan (1865–1924), produced a masterly example of the Chicago School's style in the Wainwright Building in St. Louis, Missouri. Here, Sullivan used a

Figure 19.24 WASSILY KANDINSKY. *Improvisation 33 for "Orient."* 1913. Oil on canvas, 34¾ × 39¼". Stedelijk Museum, Amsterdam. *Kandinsky's radical Expressionism rested on the Romantic idea that serious art can function as a substitute for religion; the artist serves as a sort of "priest" who, through mystical insight, can tap into the divine. In 1912 he published his aesthetic beliefs in the treatise* Concerning the Spiritual in Art, *which became a fundamental text for modern artists. Later abstract artists, such as Robert Rauschenberg (see Chapter 21), ridiculed this theory as pretentious and showed that a nonrepresentational art that has no meaning outside itself is possible.*

Figure 19.25 AUGUSTE RODIN. *Eve.* 1881. Bronze, ht. 67". Rodin Museum, Philadelphia Museum of Art. *This life-size statue of Eve was originally conceived as half a pair, with Adam, to flank* The Gates of Hell, *Rodin's masterpiece, loosely based on Dante's* Inferno *(see Chapter 9). The figure of Eve owed much to Michelangelo's expressive forms, particularly that of Eve in* The Expulsion from the Garden of Eden *on the Sistine Chapel ceiling (see Chapter 12). Reflecting her dual roles as first mother and coauthor of original sin, Rodin's Eve is both voluptuous (beautiful face and curvaceous form) and ashamed (face averted and, in gestures of modesty, arms shielding breasts and left leg raised).*

Figure 19.26   Louis Sullivan. Wainwright Building. 1890–1891. St. Louis, Missouri. Photograph © Marvin Trachtenberg. *Purity became an identifying characteristic of Modernist style. It was apparent in Matisse's color experiments, in Picasso's abstract Cubist forms, and even in the Expressionist goal of unvarnished truth. In architecture, Louis Sullivan introduced the purity principle with his artistic credo that "form follows function." Originally built for a wealthy St. Louis businessman, this Early Modernist architectural icon deteriorated until the National Trust for Historic Preservation purchased it, thus saving it from the wrecking ball.*

steel frame, joining the horizontal and vertical girders, to create a towering grid, which became the exterior's defining pattern (Figure 19.26). Rather than covering the exterior walls with ornamentation or design elements, as was done in earlier steel skyscrapers, Sullivan left the girders exposed in order to give a sense of unity to the building. Vertical columns extend up the sides of the building, connecting the base—the two first floors—with the top floor. By making the building's exterior a grid, it became a visual expression of the structural frame underneath. Although Sullivan re-

jected the rich ornamentation of the nineteenth-century Gothic as well as the balanced decorations of Classicism, he nevertheless devised his own decorative scheme, which may be seen in the vertical and horizontal elements, for example, and the spaces (blocks) between the windows. In this building, Sullivan's one exception to his rule of pure functionality is in the decorative facade he used to "hide" the water tank and elevator machinery on its top floor.

Sullivan defined the public building for the twentieth century, and his disciple Frank Lloyd Wright

Figure 19.27 Frank Lloyd Wright. W. W. Willits House. 1902. Highland Park, Illinois. Copyright © Chicago Historical Society. *Between 1900 and 1910, Wright introduced his "prairie houses," named for the* Ladies Home Journal *article (1901) in which their designs first appeared. The Willits house, built in an affluent Chicago suburb, is a fine example of this Midwestern American style that became a model for domestic buildings all over the United States. Laid out in a cruciform shape, this dwelling has a central chimney core. The style's strong focus on horizontal lines, resulting in shifting planes of light across the facade, may be compared to the multiple perspectives of Cubism, the parallel development in painting.*

(1869–1959) did the same for domestic architecture in about 1910. In the Victorian era, architects had discovered that the middle-class demand for comfortable, spacious housing was an excellent source of income. This same class of patrons continued to demand well-built homes, and for them Wright created a new type of dwelling he called "organic," a term he coined to describe a building that was constructed of local woods and stone and therefore harmonized with the physical environment. Although unconventional in his own life, he was rather a Romantic about his bourgeois patrons. To strengthen domestic values, he planned houses that encouraged the inhabitants to identify with the natural surroundings; his structures also broke down the typical reliance on fixed interior walls to encourage fluid family relationships and a free flow of traffic. In time, Wright's style became standard for progressive architects throughout the United States, expressed in the exterior in strong horizontal lines, overhanging eaves, banks of windows, and a minimum of decorative detail (Figure 19.27).

Music: From Impressionism to Jazz

Richard Wagner died in 1883 (see Chapter 18), but in certain respects he is the commanding musical presence in Early Modernism. Most composers were either utilizing in their own way the harmonic advances he had made, working out the implications of those advances, or reacting to his influence by elaborately rejecting it. For example, a musical style influenced by Wagner was Impressionism, which was in part inspired by his shimmering, constantly alternating

Figure 19.28   Mathews Band. Lockport, Louisiana. Hogan Jazz Archive, Howard-Tilton Memorial Library, Tulane University. *Bands—both black and white—flourished in nineteenth-century America. Band concerts were part of town culture, as they played at local events, including picnics, holidays, and parades. For black musicians, playing in a band offered an opportunity to hone musical skills, earn cash, wear snappy clothes, and bask in the spotlight. Band culture, with its well-experienced musicians, became part of jazz culture, and in Dixieland jazz, the band component still remains strong today. The all-brass band pictured here was in Lockport, Louisiana, a village on Bayou Lafourche, near New Orleans. Note the region's vernacular-style building in the background: the wooden house, raised on blocks, for ventilation; the shallow porch with four plain wood supports; the central doorway with flanking windows; and the hinged wooden window covers.*

chords. The Impressionist composers did not stay under his tutelage, however. Where Wagner was philosophical and literary, seeking to fuse all the arts, the Impressionists explored sound for its own sake. Like Impressionist painters, Impressionist composers thought that all moments—no matter how real—were fleeting and fragmentary, and their musical compositions illustrated this principle. Their music, without conventional thematic development or dramatic buildup and release, often sounds veiled or amorphous when compared with the music of, for example, Haydn.

Claude Debussy [duh-byoo-SEE] (1862–1918), a French composer, founded the Impressionist style. He created constantly shifting colors and moods through such musical methods as gliding chords and chromatic scales derived from non-Western sources. Debussy's music represents the climax of the nineteenth-century interest in programmatic titles, large orchestras, rich chords, and relatively free rhythms and forms.

One of Debussy's programmatic works, *Prélude à l'après-midi d'un faune (Prelude to the Afternoon of a Faun)* (1894) is generally recognized as the first Impressionist orchestral masterpiece. This work, a musical setting of the Symbolist poem *"The Afternoon of a Faun"* (1876) by the French poet Stéphane Mallarmé (1842–1898), is a sensuous confection of blurred sounds and elusive rhythms. To achieve its mood of reverie, Debussy used a meandering musical line played by a soulful solo flute, backed by muted strings and delicately voiced brasses and woodwinds. Adding to the work's dreamy mood is its subtle **dynamics,** changes in the volume of sounds, as in the sudden shifts between *piano* (Italian, "soft") and *forte* (Italian, "loud").

Impressionist music produced a second major voice in France during this period: Maurice Ravel [ruh-VEL] (1875–1937), a composer loosely indebted to Debussy. Unlike Debussy, Ravel had a taste for the clear structure of Classical musical forms as well as established dance forms. Perhaps the most Impressionistic of Ravel's compositions is *Jeux d'eau (Fountains)* (1901), a programmatic work for piano marked by sounds evoking sparkling and splashing water. Even before Ravel wrote *Jeux d'eau*, his Classical inclinations were evident in *Pavane pour une infante defunte (Pavane for a Dead Princess)* (1899), a work for piano with a melancholy quality; here, the music captured the stately rhythm of the Baroque **pavane,** an English court dance of Italian origin. Dance also inspired Ravel's *Valses nobles et sentimentales (Waltzes Noble and Sentimental)* (1911), a work for piano based on the waltzes of Schubert (see Chapter 17) and the Parisian ballrooms of the 1820s, and *La Valse (The Waltz)* (1920), an orchestral work that is a sardonic homage to the waltzes of nineteenth-century Vienna. Ravel's best-known work, *La Valse* is in actuality an embittered metaphor in which the increasingly discordant sounds of the music represent the forces that generated the catastrophe of World War I.

A trend in opposition to Wagner was Expressionism, which developed simultaneously with Expressionist art in Vienna. Drawing on the insights of Freudian psychology, musical Expressionism offered a distorted view of the world, focusing on anguish and pain. Its most striking feature was its embrace of **atonality,** a type of music without major or minor keys. To the listener, atonal music sounds discordant and even disturbing, because it offers no harmonious frame of reference. It is characterized by wide leaps from one tone to another, melody fragments, interrupted rhythms, and violent contrasts. Rejecting traditional forms, Expressionist composers made experimentation central to their musical vision.

The founder and leader of the Expressionist school was Arnold Schoenberg [SHUHN-burg] (1874–1951), who gave up a Wagnerian style in about 1907 and moved toward atonality. At first, Schoenberg employed traditional musical forms, as in the Second String Quartet (1908), although no string quartet had ever sounded like his dissonant creation. Scored without a designated key and filled with snatches of melody, this work offered the listener no recognizable frame of reference. Violinists were required on occasion to play the most extreme notes of which their instruments were capable.

Besides traditional forms, Schoenberg also established a favorite compositional method of Expressionism: setting a literary text to music and following its changes in character and feeling. An influential example of Expressionist music with text was *Pierrot lunaire* (1912), based on Symbolist poems by a Belgian writer and scored for chamber quintet and (flute [and piccolo], clarinet [and bass clarinet], violin [and viola], cello, and piano) and voice. Though Schoenberg downplayed the source text's importance, the music's violent shifts and prevailing discord clearly complement the alienated psychology and shocking language of the Symbolist text. Instead of conventionally singing the text, the solo vocalist declaims, or chants, the words by combining speech and song.

"Moonstruck Pierrot," one of the twenty-one songs in the *Pierrot lunaire* cycle, features the poet as clown, made drunk with the beauty of the moonlight. Schoenberg's music conveys the poet's hyperbolic thoughts, as in, for example, the use of a **cadenza**—a passage with an improvised feel—to represent the streaming moonlight. He also establishes the main motive, a seven-note sequence for piano and violin, in the first line, which begins with "Den Wein" (German, "the wine")—a poetic metaphor for moonlight. The main motive and the Den Wein line are repeated in line 7 and line 13. The poetic text, like other songs in this cycle, is a **rondeau,** a thirteen-line French verse form dating from the Late Middle Ages.

Pierrot lunaire represents the extreme of Schoenberg's Expressionism before World War I. This work made him one of the two most highly respected composers of Early Modernism. Unwilling to rest on his laurels, he continued to experiment with innovative musical techniques (see Chapter 20).

The other outstanding twentieth-century musical genius active during this period was the Russian Igor Stravinsky [struh-VIN-skee] (1882–1971). Untouched by Wagnerism but attuned to the revolutionary events unfolding in the arts and in literature, Stravinsky acquired his reputation at about the same time as Schoenberg. In 1913 Stravinsky wrote the music for

The Rite of Spring, a ballet produced by Sergei Diaghilev [dee-AHG-uh-lef] (1872–1929) for the Ballets Russes in Paris. Stravinsky's music and the ballet's choreography tapped into the theme of primitivism in art that was currently the rage in the French capital. Stravinsky's pounding rhythms evoke a pagan ritual, using abrupt meter changes, a hypnotic beat, and furious **syncopation,** the musical technique of accenting a weak beat when a strong beat is expected. *The Rite of Spring* builds to an exhilarating—even frenetic—conclusion, entitled "The Sacrifice," with time signature changes in almost every measure, explosive beats on the drums, and blaring brasses. A sudden shift in dynamics brings a brief quieter interlude, marked by thrumming chords and silent beats, followed by a raucous, throbbing climax of drums and brasses. The "savage" music coupled with the erotic dancing created a scandal that made Stravinsky the leading avant-garde composer in the world. Despite his innovative rhythms, Stravinsky was no relentless experimenter. After World War I, Stravinsky, though touched by Modernism's influences, became the head of a Classical school that was centered in France and opposed the more extreme theories being introduced by Schoenberg through his work in Vienna.

As Western music moved away from ancient and medieval sources, a new tradition, **jazz,** rooted in African American tradition, began to emerge in the United States (Figure 19.28). The word *jazz,* originally a slang term for sexual intercourse, reflects the music's origins in the New Orleans sexual underworld. Jazz combined West African and African-Caribbean rhythms with Western harmony, along with an improvisatory call-and-response style rooted both in African songs and in gospel songs of the urban Protestant revival in the 1850s. Jazz drew on two other African American musical forms as well—ragtime, which was chiefly instrumental, and the blues, which originated as a vocal art.

Ragtime flourished from 1890 to 1920. The word *ragtime* is derived from the phrase "ragged time," the original name for this type of syncopated music perfected by black pianist and composer Scott Joplin (1868–1917) and based on a blend of African American rhythms and Western harmony. The **blues** grew out of the rural African American tradition of work songs and spirituals and evokes the pain to be found in life, love, poverty, and hard work. Blues and jazz are both powerfully expressive musical forms, considered specifically American contributions to world music.

The Legacy of Early Modernism

From the period of 1871–1914 come many of the trends that made the twentieth century such an exciting—and dangerous—era. The legacy of militant nationalism gave birth to the two great world wars that devastated the century. Nationalism remains a potent force, threatening to overturn state boundaries and governments. Imperialism, another legacy, had radically contradictory consequences. On the one hand, it exported Western peoples, values, and technology around the globe, bringing a higher standard of living and greater expectations for the future. On the other hand, it disturbed if not destroyed older ways of life and led to a series of wars as colonial peoples struggled to cast off the yoke of Western oppression. And militarism, a third legacy, made rivalry among states a perpetual source of anxiety and destruction.

On the cultural scene, the era of Early Modernism set the stage for the twentieth century. The rise of the masses led to a growing proletarization of culture. As a result, the middle classes were subjected to a cultural assault from urban workers in much the same way that aristocrats had been attacked and displaced by the middle classes. Technology fueled the rise of mass culture. A second legacy of this era was the avant-garde, whose leaders systematically tried to destroy the last vestiges of Judeo-Christian and Classical Greco-Roman traditions. In rejecting the Classical ideal of the search for eternal truths, artists followed the Impressionists' lead and continued to strive for change as a reflection of the new historical conditions that surrounded them. And finally, Early Modernism established the emotional and aesthetic climate of the century—its addiction to experimentalism, its love-hate relationship with uncertainty and restlessness, its obsession with abstraction, its belief in the hidden depths of the human personality, and its willingness to think the unthinkable.

KEY CULTURAL TERMS

Modernism
avant-garde
Social Gospel
fundamentalism
Modernism, in Catholicism
Naturalism
Decadence
Expressionism
problem play
local color
Creole
Cajun
aesthete
abstraction
Impressionism
ukiyo-e
Post-Impressionism

Pointillism
primitivism
Fauvism
Cubism
collage
dynamics
piano
forte
pavane
atonality
cadenza
rondeau
syncopation
jazz
ragtime
blues

SUGGESTIONS FOR FURTHER READING

CHEKHOV, A. P. *Plays.* Translated and edited by E. K. Bristow. New York: Norton, 1977. Excellent versions of Chekhov's most memorable plays: *The Sea Gull, Uncle Vanya, The Three Sisters,* and *The Cherry Orchard.*

CHOPIN, K. *The Awakening.* Edited by M. Culley. New York: Norton, 1976. The story of a sensual woman's coming of age that shocked the American public, whose outrage then silenced its author; with notes, excerpts from contemporary reviews, and essays in criticism. The novel was first published in 1899.

FREUD, S. *Civilization and Its Discontents.* Translated and edited by J. Strachey. New York: Norton, 1962. Freud's ideas about history and civilization, based on his psychological findings and theories; Strachey is the editor of the Standard Edition of Freud's complete works.

———. *The Interpretation of Dreams.* Translated and edited by J. Strachey. New York: Basic Books, 1955. Freud's seminal work about the role of the unconscious in human psychology and his new theory of psychoanalysis; considered by many scholars his most important work.

HUYSMANS, J.-K. *Against Nature.* Translated by R. Baldick. New York: Penguin, 1966. A superb English version of this curious work, first published in 1884.

IBSEN, H. *A Doll's House.* Translated by C. Hampton. New York: S. French, 1972. An excellent English version of Ibsen's most often performed play, the story of a woman's awakening to the facts of her oppressive marriage.

JUNG, C. G. *Basic Writings.* Edited with an introduction by V. S. de Laszlo. New York: Modern Library, 1959. A good selection of the most important works of the Swiss psychiatrist who explored the importance of myths and symbols in human psychology.

———. *Memories, Dreams, Reflections.* Edited by A. Jaffé. New York: Vintage, 1963. Jung's highly readable autobiography, in which he describes the origins of his theories.

KAFKA, F. *The Metamorphosis, The Penal Colony, and Other Stories.* Translated by W. and E. Muir. New York: Schocken Books, 1988. This volume contains the best of Kafka's brilliant short prose works, all concerned with anxiety and alienation in a hostile and incomprehensible world.

———. *The Trial.* Translated by W. and E. Muir. New York: Schocken Books, 1968. A definitive edition of Kafka's nightmare novel in which the lead character is tried and convicted of a crime whose nature he cannot discover.

NIETZSCHE, F. W. *The Portable Nietzsche.* Selected and translated by W. Kaufmann. New York: Penguin, 1976. A collection of the most important writings of the German philosopher, compiled by the American scholar who rescued Nietzsche from the charge of proto-Nazism into which his philosophy had fallen during the Nazi era.

PROUST, M. *Remembrance of Things Past.* Translated by C. K. Scott Moncrieff, T. Kilmartin, and A. Mayor. London: Chatto & Windus, 1981. Contains all seven volumes of Proust's monumental work, which portrays the early twentieth century as a transitional period with the old aristocracy in decline and the middle class on the rise.

WILDE, O. *The Picture of Dorian Gray.* New York: Oxford University Press, 1981. Wilde's only novel recounts the story of a man whose portrait ages and decays while he remains young and handsome despite a dissolute life; the most enduring work of the Decadent school of late-nineteenth-century English literature.

ZOLA, É. *Germinal.* Translated and with an introduction by L. Tancock. New York: Penguin, 1954. A Realist novel that exposes the sordid conditions in the French mining industry.

SUGGESTIONS FOR LISTENING

DEBUSSY, CLAUDE. Debussy's veiled, subtly shifting harmonies helped to found Impressionist music. Excellent examples of his style may be heard in the orchestral works *Prélude à l'après-midi d'un faune (Prelude to the Afternoon of a Faun)* (1894) and *Nocturnes* (1899); in the collections for piano called *Estampes (Prints)* (1913) and *Préludes* (1910–1913); and in the opera *Pelléas et Mélisande* (1902). Not all of his music was Impressionistic, however; for example, in the piano music called *Children's Corner* (1908), he blended Classical values with his typical harmonic structures.

JOPLIN, SCOTT. Typical of Joplin's ragtime compositions with a syncopated beat are "Maple Leaf Rag" (1899), "Sugar Cane Rag" (1908), and "Magnetic Rag" (1914). He also wrote a ragtime opera *Treemonisha* (1911), a failure in his lifetime but a modest success in recent revivals.

RAVEL, MAURICE. Working in the shadow of Debussy, Ravel was an Impressionist with Classical inclinations; where Debussy was rhapsodic, Ravel was restrained. The work for solo piano *Jeux d'eau (Fountains)* (1901) shows Ravel's Impressionist style to perfection. His Classicism is most evident in compositions indebted to dance forms, including two works for solo piano, *Pavane pour une infante defunte (Pavane for a Dead Princess)* (1899) and *Valses nobles et sentimentales (Waltzes Noble and Sentimental)* (1911), and two works for orchestra, *La Valse (The Waltz)* (1920) and *Boléro* (1928).

SCHOENBERG, ARNOLD. By the end of this period, in 1914, Schoenberg was recognized as the leader of Expressionist music, particularly with the atonal work *Pierrot lunaire (Moonstruck Pierrot)* (1912), scored for chamber quintet and voice. In earlier works, he was less radical, as in the Second String Quartet (1908), which fused Classical forms and fragmentary melodies. Only after 1923 did Schoenberg make a breakthrough to serial composition, the type of music with which he is most identified (see Chapter 20).

STRAVINSKY, IGOR. Stravinsky, who along with Schoenberg dominated twentieth-century music, also began writing music during this period, principally as a composer of ballet scores based on Russian folk tales and traditions. These were *The Firebird* (1910), *Petrushka* (1911), and *Le Sacre du printemps (The Rite of Spring)* (1913). With *Le Sacre,* he established his originality as a composer, especially in his innovative rhythms and his handling of folk themes.

Pinté mi retrato en el año de 1940
para el Doctor Leo Eloesser, mi médico y

20

THE AGE OF THE MASSES AND THE ZENITH OF MODERNISM

1914–1945

The events of the first half of the twentieth century are seen quite differently today than they were seen at the time. Historians are beginning to view World War I (1914–1918) and World War II (1939–1945) not as two separate conflicts but as a single struggle divided by a twenty-year peace. They believe that the Great Depression of the 1930s was not a signal that the capitalist system did not work but was simply an episode of economic downturn. And they know that the making of the masses into a historically powerful force was the most significant event of this time. The rise of the masses heralded the onset of a new phase of culture—the Age of the Masses—in which ordinary men and women from the lower middle class and the working class challenged bourgeois dominance in much the same way that the bourgeoisie had earlier challenged and eventually overcome the aristocracy.

The needs of this public led to the birth of mass culture, resulting in fresh forms of popular expression. Mass culture triggered negative responses in most serious artists, writers, and musicians, who preferred the difficult and somewhat remote style of Modernism. The leaders of Modernism, partly because of the extreme popularity of mass culture, now fashioned works that grew more and more revolutionary in form, constantly testing the limits of the arts. The period between 1914 and 1945 thus saw both the rise of mass culture and the zenith of Modernism.

◀ **Detail** FRIDA KAHLO. *Self-Portrait Dedicated to Dr. Eloesser.* 1940. Oil on masonite, 22¼ × 15¾". Private collection, U.S.A.

Figure 20.1 PABLO PICASSO. *Guernica.* 1937. Oil on canvas, 11'5½" × 25'5¾". Prado, Madrid. *Picasso's* Guernica *is a vivid symbol of the violent twenty years between World War I and World War II. Depicting the bombing of the unarmed town of Guernica by Nazi planes during the Spanish Civil War, the painting transforms the local struggle into an international battle between totalitarianism and human freedom—the issue that also dominated the age's ideological debates.*

THE COLLAPSE OF OLD CERTAINTIES AND THE SEARCH FOR NEW VALUES

Before World War I, liberal values guided most people's expectations. Between the outbreak of World War I and the end of World War II, however, the values of liberalism were severely tested and in some cases overthrown. Wars, revolutions, and social upheavals often dominated both domestic and foreign affairs. To those who clung to liberal ideals, the world seemed to have gone mad (Figure 20.1). In Russia, Italy, Germany, and Spain, individual rights became secondary to the needs of society or simply to the wishes of the ruling totalitarian party. The doctrine of laissez-faire also fell into discredit during the Depression of the 1930s, bringing capitalism itself into question and leading to the rise of state-controlled economies.

World War I and Its Aftermath

In 1914 came the war that nobody expected and that took an estimated ten million lives. On one side were the Central powers—Germany, Austria-Hungary (members of the Triple Alliance), Turkey, and Bulgaria. The principal war aim of these countries was to assert the power of the central European region, which had been eclipsed by western Europe for almost two hun-

dred years. Central Europe's new sense of importance was due to the unification of Germany in 1871, which had made the German Empire the most powerful industrial and military state on the Continent.

Opposed to the Central powers were the Allied forces: France, Russia, and Great Britain (members of the Triple Entente), joined in 1915 by Italy (a former member of the Triple Alliance). The Allies refused to allow the Central powers to revise the balance of power and, in particular, were determined to keep Germany from gaining new lands. The two sides found themselves bogged down in siege warfare that led to huge losses on the battlefield and appalling hardships at home (Figure 20.2).

In the spring of 1917, the stalemate between the two sides was upset by two key events. First, the United States entered the war on the Allied side, promising fresh troops and supplies (Figure 20.3). Second, revolution broke out in Russia, interrupting its war effort and eventually causing the newly formed Communist regime to make peace with the Central powers in 1918. The Germans launched a massive attack on the western front, but the Allies, supported by American troops, foiled the Germans and forced them to surrender in November 1918.

The peace that ended the war—the 1919 Treaty of Versailles—was based partly on a plan of the U.S. president, Woodrow Wilson (in office 1913–1921). The goal

Figure 20.2   PAUL NASH. *"We Are Making a New World."* 1918. Oil on canvas, 28 × 36". Imperial War Museum, London. *Paul Nash, one of Britain's official artists during World War I, made the reality of the war's destructive power evident to civilians at home. In his battle scenes, farmlands were turned into quagmires and forests into "no-man's lands." The artist's choice of the title for this painting mocks the politicians' promises that tomorrow will be better.*

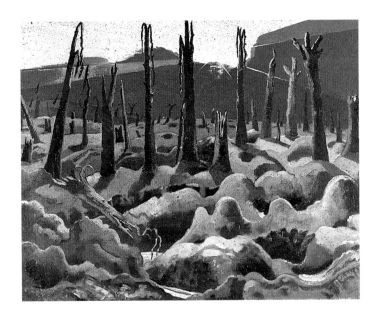

Figure 20.3   CHILDE HASSAM. *Allies Day. May, 1917.* 1917. Oil on canvas, 36½ × 30¼". Gift of Ethelyn McKinney in memory of her brother, Glen Ford McKinney, National Gallery, Washington, D.C. *Patriotic rituals, such as Bastille Day in France (see Figure 19.2), expanded readily during wartime to recognize nations allied to fight a common enemy. Upon the United States' entry into World War I, French, British, and American flags were displayed along New York City's Fifth Avenue. This outpouring of unity among the Allied forces and support for the war contrasts markedly with Paul Nash's ironic imagery (see Figure 20.2). Childe Hassam (1859–1935) studied in Paris before returning home to become America's leading Impressionist painter. In the style of a cropped photographic image, Hassam frames the flags with the tall buildings, on the left, which fade into the distance, and, on the right, only the thinnest edge of other buildings' facades. The painting's airy mood is heightened by the sunlight reflected on the buildings on the left.*

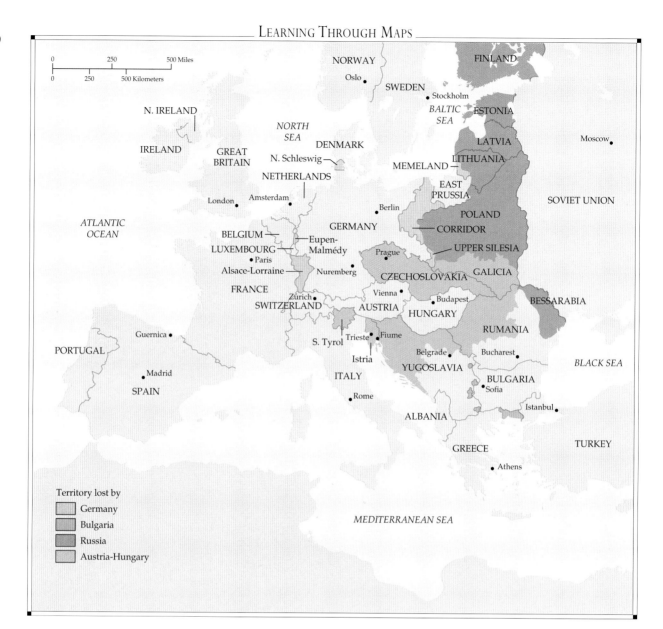

Map 20.1   EUROPE AFTER WORLD WAR I
This map shows Europe's political divisions in the early 1920s. **Notice** the territories lost by Germany, Bulgaria, Russia, and Austria-Hungary. **What** name was now given to Russia? **Which** countries lost the most territory? **How** did these lost lands affect European politics? **Observe** the increase in the size of countries in southeast Europe in this map, as compared with their smaller size in Map 19.3, Europe on the Eve of World War I. **Notice** that the Ottoman Empire in Map 19.3 has become Turkey in this map.

of Wilson's plan was to keep Europe safe from war, and it called for the self-determination of nations, democratic governments, and the establishment of the League of Nations, an international agency to maintain the peace. Despite the optimism surrounding its signing, the Versailles Treaty sowed the seeds of discord in Germany that contributed to World War II (Map 20.1). Defeated German officials and officers would later rally nationalistic feelings by denouncing the treaty as a humiliation for their country. The Versailles Treaty also prepared the ground for future troubles in the Middle East, particularly in turning over

Mesopotamia, that is, the provinces of Mosul, Baghdad, and Basra in the defunct Ottoman Empire, to British control. In Mesopotamia, where no single modern country had been before, the kingdom of Iraq would be formed in 1921, despite the deep fault lines among Shia and Sunni Muslims, Arabs, Kurds, Persians, and Assyrians (Figure 20.4).

Peace brought boom times to the economies of the victorious Allied forces, however. Britain and France returned to business as usual. The United States reverted to its prewar isolationism, and between 1924 and 1929 it exhibited the best and the worst of free

Figure 20.4 *The First Oil "Gusher" in the Middle East.* Kirkut, Iraq. October 14, 1927. © The British Petroleum Company plc, London. *The West entered the Age of Oil after World War I, and Britain's designs on Ottoman lands rested on educated hunches that vast pools of oil lay beneath the desert sands there. Signs of oil could be interpreted in swamp fires in Mosul and black sludge oozing out of the ground to make pools in Baghdad. However, it was in 1927 that the existence of underground oil, perhaps the largest field in the world, was confirmed by the eruption of oil, rising 140 feet above the derrick, as this anonymous photograph commemorates. Maneuvering to control this underground oil has been the burden of the history of Iraq ever since.*

The Great Depression of the 1930s

The Depression wiped out prosperity and brought mass unemployment, street demonstrations, and near starvation for many people. In Europe and the United States, governments were forced to take extreme measures to restore their economies. Great Britain and France had to discard free trade and move toward government-controlled economies. Under President Franklin Delano Roosevelt (in office 1933–1945) and his New Deal program, the United States followed a policy of state intervention to revitalize the economy (Figure 20.5). Roosevelt started public works projects,

enterprise—unprecedented prosperity and rampant greed.

The Central powers also rebuilt their economies in the 1920s. After a shaky start, Germany survived near bankruptcy to regain its status as the leading industrial state on the Continent. Under the Weimar Republic, Germany's first democratic parliamentary government, the country once again became a center for European culture, providing key leaders in avant-garde painting and literature. Conversely, Austria-Hungary was divided into separate nations, and its Slavic population dispersed among several states. Lacking a sound economic base, the one-time empire never fully recovered from its defeat.

As the 1920s drew to a close, a warning signal sounded: the crash of the New York stock market in October 1929. After the crash, the buoyant atmosphere of the twenties lingered for only a few months. Then economic depression in the United States, a key player in the world's economy, pulled down Europe's financial house.

Figure 20.5 DOROTHEA LANGE. *Migrant Mother, Nipomo, California.* 1936. Library of Congress. *Migrant workers were increasingly attracted to the vegetable fields of California during the Great Depression. Seasonal laborers, they harvested crops for very low wages under miserable working conditions and usually lived in crowded, unsanitary camps. This photograph shows a migrant mother, surrounded by three children, whose bleak future has been made worse by the failure of the pea crop. Dorothea Lange's poignant photographs, collected in* An American Exodus: A Record of Human Erosion *(1939), reflected her strong sense of social justice, her sympathy for the downtrodden, and her own life as the child of a broken home.*

622

ENCOUNTER

Civil Disobedience and the Campaign for Indian Independence

Once a country comes under the control of a foreign power, how does it recover its freedom? Warfare is the traditional method, as in the American Revolution, in which thirteen British colonies became the United States, independent of Great Britain. However, during the period between World War I and World War II, a new method of civil resistance emerged in British India, which came to be known as civil disobedience and which drew on Western and Eastern sources.

In the 1600s, Great Britain's rule in India extended only to trade and commerce, under the supervision of the British East India Company (see Encounter in Chapter 15). Then, in 1857, the Sepoy Rebellion—an uprising of Indian soldiers, known as sepoys—brought this phase of British-Indian history to an abrupt end. Brutally quelling the revolt, British leaders replaced the East India Company and brought India under direct rule by the British crown (Raj, or Reign—a Hindu word from Sanskrit, "king"). A secretary of state for India, a viceroy to India, and the Indian Civil Service were established to rule and operate India as part of the British Empire and for the benefit of Great Britain. The Raj continued what the East India Company had begun: fostering agriculture, building railroads and harbors, linking the country by telegraph, trying to change Indian customs and rituals, which the English considered barbaric, and founding schools to train Indians for lower positions in the Indian Civil Service.

Thereafter, many educated Hindus and Muslims, especially those who studied at Oxford and Cambridge, where they learned about Western politics and ideas, began to call for economic and social reforms as well as larger roles by Indians in Indian affairs. Founded in 1885, the National Indian Congress, modeled on Western political parties, began as an assembly where grievances could be aired and passed on to British officials, but it soon emerged as India's most influential reform group. As it grew more radical, the Congress blamed India's widespread poverty on the Raj. After 1900, the Congress allied itself with the newly formed All-India Muslim League, and, after World War I, their united front began to push for total independence. However, the British stood firm and the coalition frayed, as the Muslim minority held back out of fear that the Hindu-majority Congress would dominate India after independence was won.

What the National Indian Congress lacked was effective leadership—to unify its coalition with the Muslim League and to make their joint case for Indian independence—and that vacuum was filled with the return of Mohandas Karamchand Gandhi (1869–1948) to India in 1914. Gandhi, having studied law in London (1888–1891) and having become a civil rights lawyer in South Africa, fighting to protect fellow Indians from discrimination by white society (1893–1914), was the leader that this historic moment required. Moreover, while in South Africa, he had a moral and spiritual awakening, completing a process that began during his English sojourn. In his spiritual quest, he was influenced by an eclectic mixture of Western and Eastern sources, including the Russian Tolstoy's writings on Christianity, the American Thoreau's essay on civil disobedience, the Bible, the *Qur'an*, and, in particular, the *Bhagavad-Gita*, the Hindu religious classic on personal behavior. From these varied sources, Gandhi wove a complex creed, in which he repudiated materialism while embracing the doctrines of nonviolence (*ahimsa*) and civil disobedience (*satyagraha*, or "holding to the truth").

Gandhi now turned the Indian National Congress into an effective political weapon. And, through his understanding of his native land, he emerged as the voice and conscience of the Indian people. During the 1920s, he led a movement to boycott British goods and urged his countrymen to reject the British legal system and British-style education. He also opposed further industrialization, calling instead for Indians to return to cottage industries, such as spinning cloth for their clothes (Encounter figure 20.1).

India's hopes for self-rule were muddled by a 1937 British law, the Government of India Act, which made India a self-governing state within the British Empire, but it proved unworkable due to growing mistrust between Hindus and Muslims. During World War II, India remained loyal to the British Empire, in the face of threats of a Japanese invasion coupled with offers of liberation by Japanese troops. However, in 1942, when the war was going poorly for the Allies, Gandhi and other Congress leaders led protests and were arrested. Gandhi demanded immediate British withdrawal from India—a step that heightened what were already bad relations between him and the Raj.

In the postwar era, Gandhi played a key role in the negotiations that culminated in the granting of independence to the states of India (Hindu) and Pakistan (Muslim) in 1947. In this event's aftermath—as turmoil raged, caused by migrations of many Muslims and Hindus from one state to the other—Gandhi was assassinated by a deranged Hindu. Nevertheless, his peaceful approach to solving social, political, and economic issues lived on in the work of Martin Luther King Jr. and the 1960s civil rights movement (see Chapter 21), the protests of the Czechs and other central European peoples during the fall of communism (see Chapter 22), and civil disobedience in support of various causes around the world. During Gandhi's lifetime, Indian admirers, recognizing his special gifts, conveyed on him the honorific title Mahatma (mah-HAAT-mah), or Great-Souled.

Learning from the Encounter   Describe the political situation in India at the time of the Sepoy Rebellion. **Why** did the British crown take over India from the East India Company? **What** were some consequences of letting a few Indians be exposed to a Western education? **Discuss** the events and ideas that shaped Mahatma Gandhi's life. **Are** Gandhi's techniques useful in solving problems in the United States today?

Encounter figure 20.1   MARGARET BOURKE-WHITE. *Gandhi at the Spinning Wheel.* 1946. *In the 1930s Gandhi, as part of his campaign to drive the British from India, launched a program of village industries. Through this program, he encouraged fellow countrymen to gain economic independence from Britain as well as to identify themselves with India's crafts heritage. India historically is known as the home of the first spinning wheels. A man of his time, Gandhi used the media to advance his political agenda against British colonialism. In this photograph, which was widely reproduced in the media, he is depicted wearing a simple loin cloth while quietly reading a book. The photograph was shot by the American photographer Margaret Bourke-White, while on assignment for* Time *magazine.*

sponsored programs such as Social Security and unemployment insurance to benefit working people, and moved to regulate Wall Street and the banks. Depressed conditions hung on until World War II, however.

Germany suffered the most in Europe. Domestic problems, brought on in part by bank failures and rising unemployment, led to political crises that doomed the Weimar experiment in democracy and set the stage for the coming to power of the National Socialists, or Nazis, under Adolf Hitler.

While Europe suffered, Japan prospered. Since 1926 Japan had been ruled by Emperor Hirohito (r. 1926–1989), who was worshiped as a god, although actual power was wielded by military leaders and businessmen. In the 1930s, these groups pursued expansionist and militaristic policies, first taking over Manchuria and then making war on China. As the situation worsened in Europe in the late 1930s, Japan was able to take a free hand in Southeast Asia.

The Rise of Totalitarianism

With the peace treaty of 1919, democracy seemed triumphant in the West. By 1939, a mere twenty years later, most of the new democracies—including Germany, Austria, Hungary, Italy, Spain, Bulgaria, and Rumania—had become totalitarian. Totalitarianism on such a huge scale is a twentieth-century phenomenon, but its roots reach back to the policies of Robespierre during the French Revolution (see Chapter 17). Totalitarian governments control every aspect of the lives and thoughts of their citizens. Art, literature, and the press exist only in the service of the state. "Truth" itself becomes a matter of what the state says it is. Between the wars, totalitarianism emerged in two forms: Russian communism and European fascism.

Russian Communism   Russian communism was based on the writings of Karl Marx, whose theory was reinterpreted by the revolutionary leader V. I. Lenin (r. 1917–1924). Lenin accepted Marx's basic premise that economic conditions determine the course of history and his conclusion that history leads inevitably to a communist society run by and for the workers. Unlike Marx, Lenin believed that radical reform could occur only when a small, elite group—rather than a mass movement—seized power in the name of the people.

In 1917 Russia was plagued by an incompetent ruler, an inefficient military staff, a weak economy, and rising social and political discord. Revolution broke out in February, and a small band of Marxist communists—the Bolsheviks—seized control of the government in October. Led by Lenin, the Bolsheviks began to restructure the economy and the political system.

Under their plan, the state would control production and distribution, and soviets—or councils of workers, military personnel, and peasants—would restructure the social and economic order at the local level, as directed by the Communist party under Lenin.

After Lenin's death, Joseph Stalin (r. 1928–1953) eventually emerged as the sole ruler of the Union of Soviet Socialist Republics, as the Russian Empire was now called, and he proceeded to impose his will over the state with a vengeance. Production was increased and modernization accomplished through state-owned farms, factories, and heavy industry. No political party other than the Communist party was permitted, however, and Stalin was ruthless in dealing with his opponents and critics. He had them either murdered or imprisoned in a vast network of forced-labor camps, known as the Gulag, in the wilderness of Siberia. The number of Stalin's victims is beyond imagining: More than ten million men, women, and children met unnatural deaths in the period of forced collectivization of agriculture, 1929–1936, and millions more were murdered during purges and in the Gulag.

European Fascism   European fascism was based on the idea that the masses should participate directly in the state—not through a legislative or deliberative body such as a parliament, but through a fusion of the population into one "spirit." Fascism sought to bind the masses by appealing to nonrational sentiments about national destiny. Like communists, fascists believed that the individual was insignificant and the nation-state was the supreme embodiment of the destiny of its people.

In practice, fascism led to loss of personal freedom, as did communism, because its ideals of economic stability and social peace could be achieved only through dictatorship and tight control over the press, education, police, and the judicial system. Because of its idealistic nationalism, fascism was also hostile both to foreigners and to internal groups that did not share the majority's history, race, or politics. The movement's innate aggressiveness led to strong military establishments, which were used to conquer new lands in Europe and to win colonial empires. Fascism first appeared in Italy in the 1920s and then in Germany and Spain in the 1930s.

In Italy, a floundering economy and mounting national frustration led more and more people to follow the Fascists. Led by Benito Mussolini [moo-suh-LEE-nee] (r. 1922–1945), the Fascists dreamed of a revitalized Italy restored to its ancient glory. After seizing power in 1922, Mussolini achieved some success with his programs, and as the rest of Europe suffered through the Depression, his pragmatic policies gained admirers elsewhere.

Figure 20.6 Nuremberg Nazi Party Rally. 1933. *Under the skillful orchestration of their propaganda chief, Joseph Goebbels, the National Socialists staged massive demonstrations whose goal was to overpower the emotions of participants and observers alike. In this anonymous photograph, Nazi party members and private army units pass in review. In the 1930s, such demonstrations succeeded in uniting the German masses with the Nazi leader.*

Germany in the early 1930s was wracked by the Depression, unemployment, and political extremism, and in 1933 the German voters turned to the National Socialist (Nazi) party. Within three years, the Nazis had restored industrial productivity, eliminated unemployment, and gained the support of many business leaders and farmers. The success of the National Socialists depended ultimately on their *Führer,* or "leader," Adolf Hitler (r. 1933–1945), a middle-class Austrian and veteran who had hammered together a strong mass movement built on anti-Semitism and anticommunism. He used his magnetic personality to attract devoted followers with promises to restore Germany to prewar glory. From the beginning, the Nazis' ruthless treatment of political enemies, of the Jews, and of any dissidents aroused fears, but most Europeans ignored these barbaric acts, preferring to focus on the regime's successes (Figure 20.6).

Spain's agrarian economy and traditional institutions began to be strained by industrial growth in the 1920s, and in the early 1930s a coalition of reformers overthrew the king and created a secular republic with a constitution guaranteeing civil rights. Conservative forces plotted to restore monarchical rule and the church's influence. In 1936 civil war broke out. General Francisco Franco (r. 1939–1975) led the conservatives to victory in 1939, defeating an alliance of reformers. During hostilities, Hitler and Mussolini supplied Franco's fascist army with troops and equipment, and Stalin backed the losing faction. For the Germans and the Italians, Spain's civil war was a practice run for World War II. For example, the bombing of un-armed towns such as Guernica (see Figure 20.1) foreshadowed the indiscriminate bombing and killing of civilians that characterized the later war.

World War II: Origins and Outcome

The origins of World War II lay in the Treaty of Versailles (which many Germans denounced as a "dictated peace" that brought the loss of territory in France and Poland), the Great Depression, and nationalism. After less than a year in office, Hitler launched a campaign to revise the Versailles Treaty and engaged in a propaganda crusade that focused on Germany's glorious past. His regime, he boasted, was the Third Reich, or empire, which would last for a thousand years—like the centuries-long Holy Roman Empire (1000–1806) rather than the short-lived German Empire (1871–1918). In 1936 he marched troops into the Rhineland, the industrial heartland of Germany, which had been demilitarized by the Versailles Treaty. When the world failed to respond to this challenge, Hitler concluded that Germany's former enemies were weak, and he initiated a plan to conquer Europe. In the next two years, Europe watched as Hitler took Austria and Czechoslovakia. World War II began on September 1, 1939, when Germany invaded Poland; France and Britain responded with declarations of war.

Within nine months, the Nazis occupied most of western Europe. In the fall of 1940, the British, under their wartime leader Winston Churchill, were bravely holding on, taking the brunt of the German air raids.

Figure 20.7 MARGARET BOURKE-WHITE. Russian Tank Driver. 1941. *Photojournalism, a popular form in which the photograph rather than the text dominates the story, reached new heights during World War II, particularly in illustrated magazines such as* Life. *Margaret Bourke-White, one of the first women war journalists, was the only foreign correspondent–photographer present in the Soviet Union when the Germans invaded in June 1941. In this photograph, a Russian tank driver peers through his window with the cannon jutting out over his head—a vivid image of the integration of human beings into mechanized warfare.*

Unable to defeat England by air, Hitler turned eastward and invaded the Soviet Union in 1941 (Figure 20.7). Shortly thereafter, the Soviet Union and Great Britain became allies against Nazi Germany. Then, on December 7, 1941, Japan attacked Pearl Harbor, an American military base in the Pacific, and a few days later Germany and Italy followed Japan in declaring war on the United States. Japan's war motive was to eliminate the United States' naval presence in the Pacific region in order to be able to conquer and control Southeast Asia.

The war in Europe lasted until May 1945, when the combined armies of the Allied forces—Britain, the Soviet Union, and the United States—forced Germany to surrender. Italy had already negotiated an armistice with the Allies in September 1943 after anti-Fascists overthrew Mussolini and set up a republic. In the Pacific, where the Allies had captured key Japanese island strongholds, the war against Japan was brought to an abrupt end in August 1945, when the United States dropped atomic bombs on the Japanese cities of Hiroshima and Nagasaki (Figure 20.8). The more than two hundred thousand Japanese killed in these two raids climaxed the bloody six years of World War II, adding to its estimated thirty to fifty million deaths.

By 1945 the world had witnessed some of the most brutal examples of human behavior in history, but few people were prepared for the shock of the Nazi death camps. Gradually it became known to the world that the Nazis had rounded up the Jews of Germany and eastern Europe and transported them in cattle cars to extermination camps, where they were killed in gas chambers. The Nazis referred to their plan to eliminate the Jewish people as the Final Solution, but the rest of the world called it the Holocaust. This genocidal policy involved the murder of six million Jews out of a population of nine million, along with millions of other people the Nazis deemed undesirable, such as Gypsies and homosexuals (Figure 20.9).

In 1945, after six years of war, Germany and Japan lay in ruins. Italy escaped with less damage. France, partly occupied by the Germans for most of the war, was readmitted to the councils of the Allies. England, though victorious, emerged exhausted and in the shadow of her former allies, the United States and the Soviet Union. The old European order had passed away. The Soviet Union and the United States were now the two most powerful states in the world.

THE ZENITH OF MODERNISM

Modernism was the reigning cultural style during this turbulent interwar period. With its underlying spirit of skepticism and experimentation, it guided artists, writers, composers, filmmakers, designers, and

Figure 20.8 Carrier Planes over the U.S.S. *Missouri*. 1945. *Although the Japanese surrendered unconditionally on August 15, 1945, the formal signing of the surrender documents occurred in a ceremony on the deck of the U.S.S.* Missouri, *a battleship, in Tokyo Bay, on September 2, 1945—V-J Day. By then American troops were on the ground in Japan, and the supreme might of the Allies had been assembled to let the Japanese and the world know who had won the war. This message was delivered as squadrons of carrier planes flew over the victorious American fleet. The Allied forces, supplied with weapons and materials from the United States, proved that nations had to possess both military and industrial power if they expected to win wars.*

Figure 20.9 Nazi Death Camp in Belsen, Germany. 1945. *When the Nazis came to power in Germany in 1933, they secretly began to imprison their political enemies in concentration camps, where they were tortured or executed. By 1942 the Nazis had extended this secret policy across Europe to include minority civilians, particularly Jews. Photographs such as this one revealed to the world the atrocities committed by the Nazi regime.*

architects in their labors. But this style had limited emotional appeal, and an ever-growing general public felt isolated from avant-garde developments in art, music, and literature. When this wider audience was exposed to Modernist works, they often responded negatively, considering them incomprehensible, obscene, or decidedly provocative in some way. They turned instead to the increasingly available and affordable pleasures offered by **mass culture.**

Mass Culture, Technology, and Warfare

From its late-nineteenth-century beginnings, Modernism was both a product of and reaction against technology and warfare, and during the first half of the twentieth century, the three became even more intertwined. Technology and warfare often seemed inseparable as technology dictated how wars were fought and military planners, usually men whose experiences dated from an earlier time, seemed unable to adapt to the latest war technologies. And Modernism, holding a mirror up to the age, recorded and reflected the devastating impact of technology and warfare on society, exposing, in effect, the shaky foundations and boundaries of modern life. However, even mass culture, despite its mass appeal, seemed unable at times to resist the corrosive antics of the Modernist aesthetic.

Mass Culture and the New Technologies Like Modernism, mass culture was a direct outgrowth of industrialized society. Its roots reached back to the late nineteenth century, when skilled workers began to enjoy a better standard of living than had previously been possible for members of the lower classes. This new generation of consumers demanded products and amusements that appealed to their tastes: inexpensive, energetic, and easily accessible.

In response to their desires, entrepreneurs using new technologies flooded the market with consumer goods and developed new entertainments. Unlike the folk culture or popular culture of earlier times, modern mass culture was also mass-produced culture. The untapped consumers' market led to the creation or expansion of new industries, in particular automobiles, household products, and domestic appliances. Most forms of mass culture—the radio, newspaper comic strips and cartoons, professional sports, picture magazines, recordings, movies, and musical comedies—had originated before World War I, but now, between the wars, they came into their own. The 1920s was the golden age of Broadway's musical comedies, and radio reached its peak in the years between 1935 and 1955.

The spread of mass culture heightened the prestige of the United States, as it became known as the source of the most vigorous and imaginative popular works. The outstanding symbol of America's dominance of popular culture is Walt Disney (1901–1966), the creator of the cartoon figures of Mickey Mouse (1928) and other characters. By 1945 mass culture was playing an ever-growing role in the public and private lives of most citizens in the more advanced societies. A handful of creative people began to incorporate elements of mass culture into their works, using jazz in "serious" music or film in theatrical performances, for example. But in the main most artists, writers, and musicians stood apart from mass culture. Their isolation reflected an almost sacred commitment to the Modernist ideals of experimentation, newness, and deliberate difficulty. And some Modernists, especially among the visual artists, imbued these ideals with spiritual meaning.

Warfare The interdependency of technology and warfare accelerated in this violent era. In every nation the powerful industrial-military-state complex ordered the new weapons, mass-produced goods, and mobilized citizen armies. A new dictum now emerged: Only those states that successfully blended technology, warfare, and government can win wars. For example, the ties among the military, industry, and government were evident in the well-publicized Anglo-German naval rivalry of the early 1900s. This race to build the strongest battleships was a manifestation of imperialism and militant nationalism. And in the buildup to World War I, the military came to play the dominant role in this three-way relationship. To paraphrase one historian, the "twin processes" that distinguish the twentieth century now became the industrialization of war and the politicization of economics. The end result was to create fighting machines, which were out of control. Once elaborate preparations and detailed mobilization plans were set in motion, they could not be halted.

By 1914 industrialized nations had adopted new weapons such as the French 75 mm. field cannon, machine guns, and breech-loading rifles and had constructed rail systems that could be used in time of war. Thinking of yesterday's wars (see Chapter 18), military leaders at first believed that World War I would be swift and short. But, instead, World War I, because of retrograde thinking about military strategy and the new weaponry, turned out to be a war of indecisive battles, with huge losses on both sides. The lessons learned from this long, bitter struggle were that the next war would be fully mechanized with armored vehicles, tanks, and planes and that science and technology would play crucial roles.

Germany, Japan, and Italy, who took the lessons of World War I most to heart, did have the advantage in the first three years of World War II. But their natural resources, productivity, organizational skills, and resolve failed to match those of the Allied forces. Once the Allies' war machine was up and running, the tide of the war turned and the Axis powers were doomed to lose. Ultimately, Allied victory was made possible because of the well-oiled industrial-military-state complex, in which labor and management worked together, with occasional pressure from the government; bureaucracies smoothly supplied the logistics; states financed major scientific projects, such as the building of the first atomic bombs; and civilians willingly made sacrifices for the war effort.

Experimentation in Literature

Modernist writers between 1914 and 1945 maintained Early Modernism's dedication to experimentation, a stance that reflected their despair over the instability of their era. By challenging the traditional norms and methods of literature through their carefully composed experimental works, the Modernists were convinced that they could impose an order on the seeming randomness and meaninglessness of human existence.

The Novel   Depiction of the narrator's subjective consciousness was a principal concern of the Modernist novelists, who otherwise differed markedly from one another. The most distinctive method that arose from this concern was **stream-of-consciousness** writing, a method in which the narrative consists of the unedited thoughts of one of the characters, through whose mind readers experience the story. Stream-of-consciousness fiction differs from a story told in the first person—the grammatical "I"—by one of the characters (for example, Dickens's *David Copperfield*) in that it is an attempt to emulate the actual experience of thinking and feeling, even to the point of sounding fragmented, random, and arbitrary.

The Irish author James Joyce and the English writer Virginia Woolf were important innovators with the stream-of-consciousness technique. In his novel *Ulysses*, James Joyce (1882–1941) uses this device as a way of making the novel's characters speak directly to readers. For instance, no narrator's voice intrudes in the novel's final forty-five pages, which are the scattered thoughts of the character Molly Bloom as she sinks into sleep. This long monologue is a single run-on sentence without any punctuation except for a final period.

Despite the experimental style of *Ulysses*, Joyce aspired to more than technical virtuosity in this monumental work. He planned it as a modern version of the *Odyssey*, contrasting Homer's twenty-four books of heroic exploits with an ordinary day in the lives of three Dubliners. Joyce's sexual language, although natural to his characters, offended bourgeois morals. *Ulysses*, first published in France in 1922, became the era's test case for artistic freedom, not appearing in America or England until the 1930s.

Rejecting traditional narrative techniques, Virginia Woolf (1882–1941) experimented with innovative ways of exploring time, space, and reality. In her early novel *Jacob's Room* (1922), for example, she develops the title character through fragments of other people's comments about him. In *Mrs. Dalloway* (1925), she uses interior monologues to trace a woman's experiences over the course of a day in London. Like her contemporaries Joyce and Freud, Woolf was interested in examining the realities that lie below surface consciousness. Many consider *To the Lighthouse* (1927) Woolf's finest novel. In it she uses stream-of-consciousness to strip the story of a fixed point of view and capture the differing senses of reality experienced by the characters—in much the same way that the Cubist painters aimed at representing multiple views. To that end, she focuses on the characters' inner selves, creating diverse effects through interior monologues. For instance, one character's narrow, matter-of-fact mentality differs from his wife's emotional, free-ranging consciousness. A distinguished literary critic and the author of well-known feminist works such as *A Room of One's Own* (1929), Woolf gathered around her the avant-garde writers, artists, and intellectuals known as the Bloomsbury Group and founded, with her husband, Leonard Woolf, the Hogarth Press.

American writers also contributed experimental fiction to the Modernist revolution. By and large, these Americans made their first contacts with Europe during World War I and stayed on until the Great Depression drove them home (Figure 20.10). Ernest Hemingway (1899–1961) was the first of the Americans living abroad to emerge as a major literary star. His severely disciplined prose style relied heavily on dialogue, and he often omitted details of setting and background. His writing owed a debt to popular culture: From the era's hard-boiled detective fiction he borrowed a terse, world-weary voice to narrate his works, as in his 1926 novel, *The Sun Also Rises*. In this novel, he portrays his fellow American exiles as a "lost generation" whose future was blighted by World War I—a Modernist message. In Hemingway's cynical vision, politics is of little importance; what matter most are drinking bouts with male friends and casual sex with beautiful women.

William Faulkner (1897–1962) was another American who became one of the giants of twentieth-century literature. The stream-of-consciousness technique is central to his 1929 masterpiece, *The Sound and the Fury*. With a story line repeated several times but from

Figure 20.10 PABLO PICASSO. *Gertrude Stein.* 1906. Oil on canvas, 39¼ × 32". Metropolitan Museum of Art. Bequest of Gertrude Stein, 1946. *Talented Americans were introduced to Paris by American writer and expatriate Gertrude Stein, who made her studio a gathering place for the Parisian avant-garde. There she entertained Matisse and Picasso, composer Igor Stravinsky, writers Ernest Hemingway and F. Scott Fitzgerald, and many other brilliant exponents of Modernism. Stein was shocked at first by the starkness and brooding presence of Picasso's portrait of her, but she came to regard it as an accurate likeness, saying, "For me it is I, and it is the only reproduction of me which is always I."*

different perspectives, this novel is especially audacious in its opening section, which narrates events through the eyes of a mentally defective character. More important than his use of such Modernist devices was his lifelong identification with his home state of Mississippi, where, after a brief sojourn in Europe, he began to explore themes about extended families bound together by sexual secrets. Faulkner's universe became the fictional county of Yoknapatawpha, which he peopled with decaying gentry, ambitious poor whites, and exploited blacks. His artistic power lay in his ability not only to relate these characters to their region but also to turn them into universal symbols.

Although experimentalism was a highly visible aspect of Modernist fiction, not all Modernist writers were preoccupied with innovative methods. Other writers were identified with the Modernists because of their pessimistic viewpoints or their explosive themes. The Modernism of the British writer D. H. Lawrence (1885–1930), for example, was expressed in novels of sexual liberation. Frustrated by the coldness of sexual relations in bourgeois culture, Lawrence, the son of a miner, concluded that the machine age emasculated men. As an antidote, he preached a religion of erotic passion. He set forth his doctrine of sexual freedom most clearly in the 1928 novel *Lady Chatterley's Lover,* issued privately and quickly banned for its explicit language and scenes. Not until the 1960s, and only after bitter court battles, was this novel allowed to circulate freely. In the novel, the lovemaking episodes between Lady Chatterley, wed to an impotent aristocrat, and the lower-class gamekeeper Mellors were presented as models of sexual fulfillment with their mix of erotic candor and moral fervor.

Falling outside the Modernist classification is the English novelist and essayist George Orwell (1903–1950), who nevertheless was one of the major figures of the interwar period. Born Eric Blair to an established middle-class family, Orwell changed his name, rejected his background, lived and worked among the poor and downtrodden, and became a writer. He also became the conscience of his generation because he remained skeptical of all the political ideologies of his day. In the allegorical novel *Animal Farm* (1945), he satirized Stalinist Russia. In the anti-utopian novel *1984* (1948), he made totalitarianism the enemy, especially as practiced in the Soviet Union, but he also warned of the dangers of repression in capitalist society. What made Orwell remarkable in this age torn by ideological excess was his claim to be merely an ordinary, decent man. It is perhaps for this reason that today Orwell is claimed by socialists, liberals, and conservatives alike.

Poetry Modern poetry found its first great master in William Butler Yeats (1865–1939). His early poems are filled with Romantic mysticism, drawing on the myths of his native Ireland. By 1910 he had stripped his verses of Romantic allusions, and yet he never gave up entirely his belief in the occult or the importance of myth. As Irish patriots grew more hostile to their country's continued submersion in the United Kingdom, climaxing in the Easter Rebellion of 1916, Yeats's poems took on a political cast. His best verses came in the 1920s, when his primary sources were Irish history and Greco-Roman myth. Perhaps his finest lyric is "Sailing to Byzantium," a poem that conjures up the Classical past to reaffirm ancient wisdom and redeem the tawdry industrialized world.

T. S. Eliot (1888–1965) was another founder of Modern poetry. Reared in St. Louis and educated at Har-

Figure 20.11 JACOB LAWRENCE. *Migration Series, No. 58.* The original caption reads, "In the North the Negro had better educational facilities." 1940–1941. Tempera on gesso on composition board, 12 × 18". The Museum of Modern Art, New York. Gift of Mrs. David M. Levy. *Jacob Lawrence's* Migration Series, *a cycle of paintings commissioned by For-tune magazine, depicted the mass flight of African Americans from the American South to the North in their quest for a better life. Lawrence (1917–2000) was a Harlem resident and the son of black migrants. These works are simplistic in format (standard small size and common color scheme); nevertheless, they reveal Lawrence's knowledge of High Modernism, especially in the flatness and angularity of the figures and the unusual perspective. The painting titled No. 58 evokes a sense of rhythm by having the number sequence repeated by the young girls' arm and leg movements and their swaying dresses. This series established Lawrence as a serious artist, and in 1941 he became the first African American included in the permanent collection of New York's Museum of Modern Art.*

vard, Eliot moved to London in 1915, becoming an English citizen in 1927. He and Ezra Pound (1885–1972), another American exile, established a school of poetry that reflected the crisis of confidence that seized Europe's intellectuals after World War I. Like those of the Late Roman poets, Eliot's verses relied heavily on literary references and quotations.

"The Waste Land," published in 1922, showed Eliot's difficult, eclectic style; in 403 irregular lines, he quotes from or imitates thirty-five authors, including Shakespeare and Dante, adapts snatches from popular songs, and uses phrases in six foreign languages. Form matches content because the "waste land" itself repre-sents a sterile, godless region without a future, a sym-bol drawn from medieval legend but changed by Eliot into a symbol of the hollowness of modern life. In 1927

he moved beyond such atheistic pessimism, finding solace by being received into the Church of England—a step he celebrated in the poem "Ash Wednesday," published in 1930.

The black American poet Langston Hughes (1902–1967) also belongs with the outstanding Mod-ernists. Hughes drew inspiration from many sources, including Africa, Europe, and Mexico, but the ultimate power of his poetry came from the American experi-ence: jazz, spirituals, and his anguish as a black man in a white world. Hughes's emergence, like that of many African American writers, occurred during a popula-tion shift that began in 1914 when thousands of blacks from the American South settled in northern cities such as New York, Chicago, and Detroit in hopes of a better life (Figure 20.11).

At the same time that America's ethnographic map was being redrawn, a craze for Negro culture sprang up that was fueled by jazz and the avant-garde cult of primitivism. This craze sparked the Harlem Renaissance, a 1920s cultural revival in the predominantly black area of New York City called Harlem. Hughes was a major figure in this black literary movement. His earliest book of verses, *The Weary Blues* (1926), contains his most famous poem, "The Negro Speaks of Rivers." Dedicated to W. E. B. DuBois (1868–1963), the founder of the National Association for the Advancement of Colored People, Hughes's verse memorializes the deathless spirit of his race by linking black history to the rivers of the world.

Another outstanding figure of the Harlem Renaissance was Zora Neale Hurston (about 1901–1960), the most prolific African American woman writer of her generation. Poet, novelist, folklorist, essayist, Hurston made her literary task the exploration of what it means to be black and female in a white- and male-dominated society. An excellent example of her handling of this theme is the essay "How It Feels to Be Colored Me," published in 1928. In this short work, filled with self-mocking irony, she presents herself as torn between black and white culture and sometimes forced to choose between two then-current stereotypes: the "happy Negro" who performs for white folks for money and sheer joy and the "exotic primitive," the educated black who, despite a veneer of learning, remains "uncivilized." Nevertheless, she rejects both stereotypes as caused by being born black in a white culture. In certain moments, she claims to transcend race, though not gender: "I belong to no race nor time. I am the eternal feminine with its string of beads." Hurston's ideal is of a future, free of racism, in which African Americans no longer have to struggle with culturally imposed identities.

Drama   During the interwar years, drama moved in new directions in both Europe and America. An Expressionist in aesthetics and a Marxist in politics, the German Bertolt Brecht [BREKT] (1898–1956) blended a discordant style learned from the Berlin streets with his hatred of bourgeois society into what he called **"epic theater."** Rebelling against traditional theater, which he thought merely reinforced class prejudices, he devised a radical theater centered on a technique called the "alienation effect," whose purpose was to make the bourgeois audience uncomfortable (Figure 20.12). Alienation effects could take any form, such as outlandish props, inappropriate accents, or ludicrous dialogue. By breaking the magic spell of the stage, Brecht's epic theater challenged the viewers' expectations and prepared them for his moral and political message. A victim of Nazi oppression, Brecht fled first to Scandinavia and then to America, where he lived

for fifteen years before moving to East Berlin in 1952 to found a highly influential theater company.

A year before he officially embraced Marxism, Brecht teamed with the German-born composer Kurt Weill [WILE or VILE] (1900–1950) to create one of the best-known musicals in modern theater, *The Threepenny Opera* (1928). Loosely based on an eighteenth-century English opera, Brecht and Weill's Expressionist version was raucous, discordant, violent, and hostile to bourgeois values. The playwright, believing that bourgeois audiences wanted goodness to triumph over evil, made the hero a small-time hoodlum ("Mack the Knife") and then saved him at the last moment from a hanging that he richly deserved.

Besides such pathfinders as Brecht, this period also produced two major Modernist playwrights. The first of these was Jean Cocteau [kahk-TOE] (1889–1963), a French dramatist who helped to launch the French trend for modernizing the Greek classics. For example, Cocteau's *The Infernal Machine* (1934) updates Sophocles' *Oedipus*. In this modern retelling, the story is filled with Freudian overtones—Oedipus is portrayed as a "mother's boy"—and film clips are introduced for flashbacks. A second major Modernist was Eugene O'Neill (1888–1953), America's first dramatist to earn worldwide fame. Like Cocteau, O'Neill sometimes wrote new versions of Greek tragedies, as in *Mourning Becomes Electra* (1931), which was modeled on Aeschylus's *Oresteia*. O'Neill's best plays are his tense family dramas in which generations battle one another, as in *Long Day's Journey into Night,* staged posthumously in 1956.

Philosophy, Science, and Medicine

The Age of the Masses was a fertile period in philosophy, science, and medicine, when old certainties were under fire from, respectively, new schools of thought, a revolutionary way of looking at the world, and medical advances. However, certainty still reigned supreme in one highly visible aspect of science—the practical application of science as a cure for social ills. Indeed, this was the last period when blind faith in science still ruled, a trend that began with the Scientific Revolution and was sanctified by the Enlightenment's optimistic perspective (see Chapters 15 and 16).

Philosophy   During this period, the Idealist philosophy that had dominated Continental speculation since the early 1800s was replaced by two new schools of thought. First, in Austria and England, Ludwig Wittgenstein developed ideas that helped establish the logical positivist school, which became known after World War II as the analytical school. Second, in Germany, Martin Heidegger founded the existentialist

Figure 20.12 GEORGE GROSZ. *Tatlinis-tischer Planriss (Tatlinesque Diagram)*. 1920. Watercolor, India ink, and collage, approx. 16½ × 11½". Thyssen-Bornemisza Foundation Collection, Madrid, Spain. © 1997 Estate of George Grosz/Licensed by VAGA, New York, NY. *The works of German artist George Grosz (1893–1959) provide a visual counterpart to the dramas of Brecht. Grosz portrays bourgeois society as morally bankrupt, as in this painting of a brothel scene that shows a prostitute as a willing victim—note the prostitute's complicitous glance. Brecht makes the same point in the drama* Mother Courage *(1941) by presenting a businesswoman heroine interested only in making money even though it means sacrificing her sons in war. Grosz's* Tatlinistischer Planriss (Tatlinesque Diagram) *reflected the influence of Dada art, which was imported into Berlin from Zurich in late 1918, at the end of World War I. Typical of Berlin Dadaists, Grosz added a political message to this subversive art, and he underscored his corrosive vision with a brutal, unsentimental collage technique, using photographic and painted images and overlapping planes of color.*

This work also has affinities with Constructivism, the Russian avant-garde movement, especially in its title, which refers to Vladimir Tatlin (1885–1953), the Russian founder of Constructivism. Grosz met the avant-garde artist the year this work was made. While Tatlin's nonfigurative style did not influence Grosz, Grosz did share with Tatlin a disdain for bourgeois culture and elitist art, as depicted in this brothel scene. With the rise of the Nazis in 1932, Grosz fled his homeland for the United States.

school. Both schools tried to create new philosophies that were in harmony with Modernist developments.

The Austrian Ludwig Wittgenstein [VIT-guhn-stine] (1889–1951) believed that the West was in a moral and intellectual decline that he attributed to faulty language, for which, he surmised, current philosophical methods were to blame. Wittgenstein asserted that traditional philosophical speculation was senseless because, of necessity, it relied on language that could not rise above simple truisms.

Wittgenstein's solution to this intellectual impasse was to dethrone philosophy and make it simply the servant of science. He set forth his conclusion in his *Tractatus Logico-Philosophicus* in 1922. In this treatise, he reasoned that, although language might be faulty, there were mathematical and scientific tools for com-

prehending the world. He proposed that thinkers give up the study of values and morals and assist scientists in a quest for truth. This conclusion led to **logical positivism,** a school of philosophy dedicated to defining terms and clarifying statements.

Wittgenstein later rejected the idea that language is a flawed instrument and substituted a theory of language as games, in the manner of children's play. Nevertheless, it was the point of view set forth in the *Tractatus* that made Wittgenstein so influential in the universities in England between 1930 and 1960 and in America after World War II.

While Wittgenstein was challenging philosophy's ancient role, Martin Heidegger [HI-deg-uhr] (1889–1976) was assaulting traditional philosophy from another angle by founding modern **existentialism.** The result of Heidegger's extensive criticism, however, was to restore philosophy to its central position as the definer of values for culture. Heidegger's major work, *Being and Time*, was published in 1927. The focal point of his thinking was the peculiar nature of human existence (the source of the term *existentialism*) as compared with other objects in the world. In his view, human existence leads to anxiety, a condition that arises because of the consciousness that there is a future that includes choices and death. He noted that most people try to avoid facing their inevitable fate by immersing themselves in trivial activities. For a few, however, Heidegger thought that the existential moment offered an opportunity in which they could seize the initiative and make themselves into authentic human beings. "Authenticity" became the ultimate human goal: to confront death and to strive for genuine creativity—a typical German philosophical attitude shared with Goethe and Nietzsche.

Heidegger was among the twentieth century's foremost philosophers, but his political activities made him a controversial figure. He used his post as a German university professor to support the rise of Nazism in the 1930s. To hostile eyes, Heidegger's existential views—which acknowledged that individuals, powerless to reshape the world, could only accept it—seemed to support his political position. Indeed, some commentators have condemned existentialism for that reason.

Heidegger's best-known disciple, though one who rejected Nazism, was the French thinker Jean-Paul Sartre [SAHR-truh] (1905–1980). Sartre's major philosophical work, *Being and Nothingness* (1943), was heavily indebted to his mentor's concepts. From Heidegger came his definition of existentialism as an attitude characterized by concern for human freedom, personal responsibility, and individual choices. Sartre used these ideas to frame his guiding rule: Because human beings are condemned to freedom—that is, not free *not* to choose—they must take responsibility for their actions and live "without excuses." After 1945, Sartre rejected existentialism as overly individualistic and thereafter tended to support Marxist collectivist action.

Science   In the sciences, physics remained the field of dynamic activity. The breakthroughs made before World War I were now corroborated by new research that compelled scientists to discard the Newtonian model of the universe as a simple machine. They replaced it with a complex, sense-defying structure based on the discoveries of Albert Einstein and Werner Heisenberg (Figure 20.13).

Einstein was the leading scientist in the West, comparable to Newton in the eighteenth century. His special relativity theory, dating from 1905, overturned the Newtonian concept of fixed dimensions of time and space (see Chapter 19). In Einstein's view, absolute space and time are meaningless categories, since they vary with the situation. In 1915, he expanded this earlier finding into a general theory of relativity, a universal law based on complex equations that apply throughout the cosmos.

The heart of the general theory is that space is curved as a result of the acceleration of objects (planets, stars, moons, meteors, and so on) as they move through undulating trajectories. The earth's orbit about the sun is caused not by a gravitational "force" but by the curvature of space-time around the sun. In 1919 a team of scientists observed the curvature of space in the vicinity of the sun and confirmed that space curves to the degree that Einstein's theory had forecast. Since then, his general theory has survived many tests of its validity and has opened new paths of theoretical speculation.

The other great breakthrough of modern physics was the establishment of quantum physics. Before 1914 the German physicist Max Planck had discovered the quantum nature of radiation in the subatomic realm (see Chapter 19). Ignoring the classical theory that energy is radiated continuously, he proved that energy is emitted in separate units that he called *quanta*, after the Latin for "how much" (as in *quantity*), and he symbolized these units by the letter h.

Working with Planck's h in 1927, which by now was accepted as a fundamental constant of nature, the German physicist Werner Heisenberg [HIZE-uhn-berg] (1901–1976) arrived at the uncertainty principle, a step that constituted a decisive break with classical physics. Heisenberg showed that a scientist could identify either an electronic particle's exact location or its path, but not both. This dilemma led to the conclusion that absolute certitude in subatomic science is impossible because scientists with their instruments inevitably interfere with the accuracy of their own work—the uncertainty principle. The incertitude involved in quantum theory caused Einstein to remark, "God does not play dice with the world." Nevertheless, quantum theory joined relativity theory as a founding principle of modern physics.

A practical result of the revolution in physics was the opening of the nuclear age in August 1945. The American physicist J. Robert Oppenheimer [AHP-uhn-hi-muhr] (1904–1967), having made basic contributions to quantum theory, was the logical choice to head the team that built the first atomic bomb. Oppenheimer's other role as a member of the panel that advised that the atomic bombs be dropped on Japan raised ethical questions that divided the scientific community then and continue to do so.

Figure 20.13   ALBERTO GIACOMETTI. *Hands Holding the Void.* 1934. Plaster sculpture, original cast, ht. 61½". Yale University Art Gallery, New Haven, Connecticut. Anonymous gift. *The uncertainty of the modern world—as demonstrated by both physics and the economic and social realities of daily life—is poignantly symbolized in Giacometti's sculpture. His melancholy figure, clutching an invisible object, evokes the anguish humans suffered in no longer being able to expect answers from traditional sources, such as science and philosophy. Giacometti personally shared these fears as he created, in this Surrealistic work (inspired by his admiration for Egyptian sculpture), a semiseated female whose face is a mask. She seems to be, in the opinion of one critic, searching for what is truly human in a state of painful ignorance—the predicament of those in the modern world.*

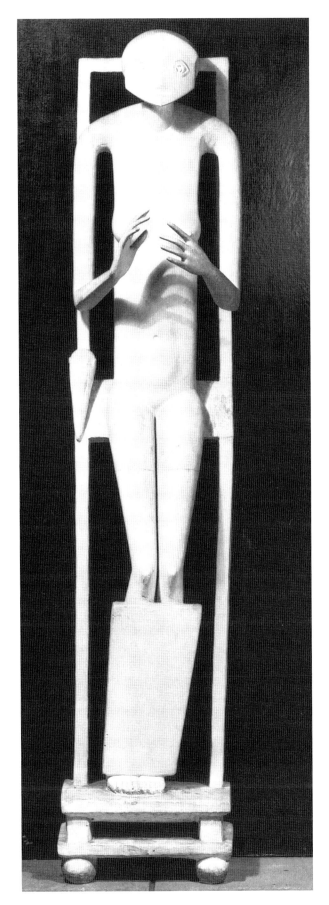

While debates divided the scientific community, many in the rest of society forcefully expressed their unquestioning trust in the pseudoscience behind the racist theories that then flourished across the West. These theories, which blamed social ills on innate racial differences, were rooted in the writings of Joseph-Arthur, Comte (Count) de Gobineau (go-be-no) (1816–1882), a French social theorist. Gobineau's claim that the white race—which he labeled the "Aryans," that is, the Germanic peoples, including the English— was superior to all others resonated across the political and social spectrum. Many people in the West came to share his view that the future of civilization depended on maintaining the racial purity and dominance of Aryan culture. Over time, Gobineau's theory, dressed up in many guises and justified by scientific research, had a powerful impact on Western society and history.

Germany was probably the country most affected by racist thought, as expressed in the eugenics (Greek, *eugenes,* "of good stock") movement, which called for the selective breeding of human beings. Nazi ideology, rooted in the myth of Aryan supremacy, led to a full-fledged eugenics program and eventually to genocide. Seeking Aryan racial purity, the Nazis created a forced sterilization program in the 1930s, in which doctors sterilized more than four hundred thousand people who were deemed genetically defective, including the mentally unfit, severe alcoholics, and the handicapped. The Aryan supremacy claim resulted in the Holocaust, the Nazi plan to eliminate Jews, whom German doctors believed to be carriers of many genetic disorders (see Slice of Life). After World War II, knowledge of the Holocaust helped discredit the eugenics movement.

The eugenics movement in the United States did not lead to genocide, but it did spark varied governmental policies. In 1924 a federal law was passed closing immigration from southern and eastern Europe, the Balkans, and Russia. Vice President Calvin Coolidge (1872–1933) justified this legislation thusly: "America

SLICE OF LIFE
The Face of Evil: A Nazi Death Camp

ELIE WIESEL
Night (2006)

In this excerpt from his autobiographical novel Night, *Wiesel (b. 1928) describes the arrival of his family at Auschwitz, a Nazi death camp, in 1944.*

The beloved objects that we had carried with us from place to place were now left behind in the wagon and, with them, finally, our illusions.

Every two yards, there stood an SS man, his machine gun trained on us. Hand in hand we followed the throng.

An SS came toward us wielding a club. He commanded:

"Men to the left! Women to the right!"

Eight words spoken quietly, indifferently, without emotion. Eight simple, short words. Yet that was the moment when I left my mother. There was no time to think, and I already felt my father's hand press against mine: we were alone. In a fraction of a second I could see my mother, my sisters, move to the right. Tzipora was holding Mother's hand. I saw them walking farther and farther away; Mother was stroking my sister's blond hair, as if to protect her. And I walked on with my father, with the men. I didn't know that this was the moment in time and the place where I was leaving my mother and Tzipora forever. I kept walking, my father holding my hand.

Behind me, an old man fell to the ground. Nearby, an SS man replaced his revolver in its holster.

My hand tightened its grip on my father. All I could think of was not to lose him. Not to remain alone.

The SS officers gave the order.

"Form ranks of fives!"

There was a tumult. It was imperative to stay together.

"Hey, kid, how old are you?"

The man interrogating me was an inmate. I could not see his face, but his voice was weary and warm.

"Fifteen."

"No. You're eighteen."

"But I'm not," I said. "I'm fifteen."

"Fool. Listen to what *I* say."

Then he asked my father, who answered:

"I'm fifty."

"No." The man now sounded angry. "Not fifty. You're forty. Do you hear? Eighteen and forty."

He disappeared into the darkness.

Interpreting This Slice of Life **Summarize** the events set forth in this excerpt from Wiesel's book. **What** is the significance of the inmate insisting that the son claim to be eighteen and the father to be forty? **Explain** what the narrator means by the word *illusions*, in the first sentence. **Relate** the narrator's experience with that of children caught in contemporary political upheavals.

---

must be kept American. Biological laws show . . . that Nordics deteriorate when mixed with other races." Only six senators voted against this exclusionary law. Further, by 1930, twenty-seven states had laws that allowed involuntary sterilization of the feebleminded and others deemed unfit—with the surgery performed usually at state-run psychiatric hospitals or homes for the mentally challenged. Eugenics programs also thrived in England and France. And, earlier, in 1901, Australia closed its doors to non-European immigrants, making itself a citadel of white culture.

Medicine Major medical events between 1900 and 1945 occurred mainly in two areas: identification of disease pathogens and the development of pharmaceuticals. Medical researchers, following Pasteur's discovery of germs (see Chapter 18), now identified many new pathogens—disease-causing agents—including the rickettsias, organisms that cause diseases such as typhus; protozoans, organisms that produce tropical illnesses such as malaria; and viruses, organisms that cause mumps, measles, and polio. New pharmaceuticals included aspirin (1899), the world's universal pain remedy today; arsphenamine (1910), an arsenic-based preparation, which was the first effective treatment for syphilis and the first chemotherapy; sulfonamide (1936), an antibacterial agent, used to cure septicemia (blood infection) and other infections; penicillin (discovered in 1928 and made available in injectable form in 1941), probably the West's most popular antibiotic, used against syphilis, meningitis, and other ills, until the rise of penicillin-resistant bacteria; and, finally, streptomycin (1944), the first successful treatment for infectious tuberculosis. Penicillin proved to be a great resource in World War II, its use helping to save many lives on the battlefield.

Timeline 20.1 HIGH MODERNISM, 1914–1945

1919	Neoclassical Music	
	1922	Serial Music
Constructivist Art	1922	Socialist Realist Art
1917	De Stijl	1932
	Cubism	
1915	Dada Art	1925	Surrealist Art
	Expressionist Art	
1919	Bauhaus	1933
	1929	International Style Architecture

World War I The Great Depression World War II

1914	1918	1922	1926	1929	1933	1936–1939	1939	1945
1915 Einstein's theory of relativity		Fascists take power in Italy; Joyce's *Ulysses*; Eliot's "The Waste Land"; Wittgenstein's *Tractatus Logico-Philosophicus*	Hemingway's *The Sun Also Rises*	Stock market crash	Nazis take power in Germany	Spanish Civil War		
	1917 Bolshevik Revolution in Russia		**1927** Heidegger's *Being and Time*; Heisenberg's uncertainty principle					

Art, Architecture, Photography, and Film

The art, architecture, photography, and film of the interwar period were driven by the same forces that were transforming literature and philosophy. Modernism reached its zenith in painting and architecture, photography came into its own as part of the mass media, and the movies became established as the world's most popular form of mass culture (Timeline 20.1).

Painting Painting dominated the visual arts in the interwar period. Painters launched new art movements every two or three years, although certain prevailing themes and interests could be discerned underneath the shifting styles: abstraction, primitivism and fantasy, and Expressionism. This era's most explosive art was produced within these stylistic categories. Picasso and Matisse, the two giants of twentieth-century art, continued to exercise their influence, yet they too worked within these three categories, all of which had arisen in the Post-Impressionist period.

ABSTRACTION The history of modern painting has been rewritten in the past forty-five years to accommodate the contributions of Soviet painters to abstract art. No one questions the primary role played by Picasso and Braque in Cubist paintings before World War I, but Soviet painters, beginning in 1917, moved beyond Cubism and toward full abstraction, thus staking out claims as early founders of modern abstract art. The most influential of these Soviet artists was Kasimir Malevich [mahl-YAY-vich] (1878–1935).

Influenced by the Cubists and the Futurists—an Italian school of artists who depicted forms in surging, violent motion—Malevich was already working in an abstract style when World War I began in 1914. Four years later, he was painting completely nonobjective canvases. Believing that art should convey ethical and philosophical values, he created a style of painting devoted to purity, in which he made line, color, and shape the only purposes in his art. He called this style **Suprematism,** named for his belief that the feelings are "supreme" over every other element of

Figure 20.14   KASIMIR MALEVICH. *Suprematist Composition.* 1916–1917. Oil on canvas, 29 × 36¼″ (73.7 × 92.1 cm). The Museum of Modern Art, New York. Photograph © 1997 The Museum of Modern Art. *Malevich's geometric style reflected his belief that abstract images had a spiritual quality comparable to that of religious icons. Thus, if approached in the proper spirit, an abstract form could become a meditation device that could lead the viewer's thoughts beyond the physical realm. For Malevich, the physical realm was no longer of use, and painting was a search for visual metaphors (mainly geometric elements) that could evoke awareness of unconscious and conscious experiences in the individual. His belief was typical of thinking among the German and Russian avant-garde in the early 1900s.*

life—"feelings," that is, expressed in a purely rational way.

Searching for a way to visualize emotions on canvas, Malevich adopted geometric shapes as nonobjective symbols, as in *Suprematist Composition* (Figure 20.14). In this painting, design has triumphed over representation. There are only geometric shapes of different sizes and varying lengths. The choice of the

geometric shapes reflects their role as basic elements of composition with no relation to nature. The qualities shown in Malevich's painting—flatness, coolness, and severe rationality—remain central to one branch of abstract art today.

Malevich's Suprematism helped to shape **Constructivism**, the first art style launched by Lenin's regime in 1917 and the last modern-art movement in Russia. Malevich's philosophical views, which were rooted in Christian mysticism, ran counter to the materialism of the Marxist government, however, and the flowering of abstraction in the Soviet Union was abruptly snuffed out in 1922. In that year, Lenin pronounced it a decadent form of bourgeois expression, and its leaders were imprisoned or exiled. In place of Constructivism, the Soviet leaders proclaimed the doctrine of **Socialist Realism,** which demanded the use of traditional techniques and styles and the glorification of the communist ideal. This type of realistic art also had greater appeal to the Soviet masses, who had been alienated by the abstract style of Constructivism.

A movement similar to Suprematism and Constructivism, called **de Stijl** [duh STILE] (The Style), originated in the Netherlands during this period and lasted from 1917 to 1932. De Stijl artists shared the belief that art should have spiritual values and that if artists were to revamp society along rational lines, from town planning to eating utensils, a more harmonious vision of life would result.

The de Stijl movement was led by the painter Piet Mondrian [MAHN-dree-ahn] (1872–1944), who after 1919 worked successively in Paris, London, and New York. He developed an elaborate theory to give a metaphysical meaning to his abstract paintings. A member of the Theosophists—a mystical cult that flourished in about 1900—he adapted some of their beliefs to arrive at a grid format for his later paintings, notably using the Theosophists' stress on cosmic duality, in which the vertical represented the male and the horizontal the female. His paintings took the form of a rectangle divided by heavy black lines against a white background. Into this highly charged field he introduced rectangles of the primary colors—blue, yellow, and red—which in his mystic vision stood as symbols of the sky, the sun, and dynamic union, respectively. After 1932 Mondrian began to tire of black but it was only with the coming of World War II, when he emigrated to New York City, that he was able to eliminate black. However, he remained faithful to the grid and the primary colors (Figure 20.15).

Despite the pioneering work of Suprematism and the de Stijl school, Cubism remained the leading art movement of this period, and Pablo Picasso was still the reigning Cubist. Picasso's protean genius revealed itself in multiple styles after 1920, but he continually

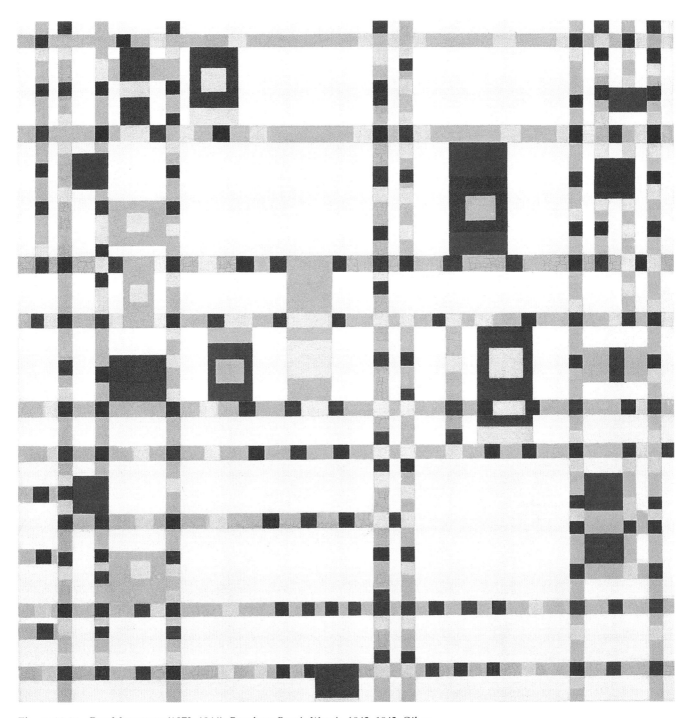

Figure 20.15   PIET MONDRIAN (1872–1944). *Broadway Boogie Woogie*. 1942–1943. Oil on canvas, 50 × 50". © 2007 Mondrian/Holtzman Trust c/o HCR International, Warrenton, VA. The Museum of Modern Art, New York. *Allied with those artists who identified abstract forms with spiritual values, Mondrian originated "the grid" as the ideal way to approach the canvas, allowing the verticals and horizontals to establish the painting area. In this painting, he pays homage to his new home and a dance craze of the era: The interaction of the colored lines evokes both the street map of Manhattan and the syncopated pattern of the Boogie Woogie. Mondrian's devotion to "the grid," along with his sparse use of color, gave rise to many of the dominant trends in art after World War II: two-dimensional images, geometric shapes, and "all over" paintings without a specific up or down.*

Figure 20.16 PABLO PICASSO. *The Three Musicians.* 1921. Oil on canvas, 6'8" × 6'2". Philadelphia Museum of Art. The A. E. Gallatin Collection. *This Cubist painting captures the energy of a musical performance. Here and there among the flattened shapes can be seen hints of musical instruments being fingered by disembodied hands. Only a little imagination is needed to bring this masked trio to life. The brilliant colors coupled with the broken and resynthesized forms evoke the jagged rhythms the musicians must have been playing.*

reverted to his Cubist roots, as in *The Three Musicians* (Figure 20.16). Like the rest of his works, this painting is based on a realistic source, in this case a group of masked musicians playing their instruments. The forms appear flattened, as if they were shapes that had been cut out and then pasted to the pictorial surface—the ideal of flatness so prized by Modern painters.

The most famous work of Picasso's long career also dates from this period: the protest canvas *Guernica*, painted in a modified Cubist style. Picasso named this painting for an unarmed town that had been bombed by the Nazi air force (in the service of Franco) during the Spanish Civil War. Picasso used every element in the work to register his rage against this senseless destruction of human life (see Figure 20.1). The black, white, and gray tones conjure up newspaper images, suggesting the casual way that newspapers report daily disasters. An all-seeing eye looks down on a scene of horror made visible to the world through the modern media—as symbolized by the electric bulb

that acts as a retina in the cosmic eye. Images of death and destruction—the mother cradling a child's body, the stabbed horse, the enraged bull, the fallen man, and the screaming woman—are made even more terrifying by their angular forms. In retrospect, *Guernica* was a watershed painting both topically and stylistically. The blending of Cubism with social protest was new—as was Franco's type of unbridled warfare. *Guernica* forecast even more horrifying events to come.

The American painter Georgia O'Keeffe (1887–1986) refused to follow European painters down the path to pure abstraction. Instead, she pursued a distinctively American type of abstraction, using American subjects drawn from nature, which she pared to their pure form and color; at the same time, she kept representation of the natural world as a primary goal of her art. A native of Wisconsin, O'Keeffe found a spiritual home in the American Southwest—Texas and especially New Mexico—whose sun-drenched, stark landscapes inspired some of her most famous images.

Sensitive to light, color, texture, and atmosphere, she registered in her paintings the previously hidden beauties of this desert world, as in *Cow's Skull with Calico Roses* (Figure 20.17). As early as the Renaissance, painters had occasionally used death's-heads as *memento mori* (reminders of death), but no artist before O'Keeffe had thought of presenting a cow's skull as an art subject. The already abstract form of the cow's skull, stripped bare of flesh, became even more abstract as she simplified it and presented it close-up with two roses nearby. The result is an image of shocking beauty.

PRIMITIVISM AND FANTASY   The Modernists' admiration for primitivism led to **Dada** [DAH-dah], the most unusual art movement of the twentieth century. Named for a nonsense word chosen for its ridiculous sound, Dada flourished in Zurich and Paris between 1915 and 1925, chiefly as unruly pranks by disaffected artists who wanted to "hurl gobs of spit in the faces of the bourgeoisie." They staged exhibits in public lavatories, planned meetings in cemeteries, and arranged lectures where the speaker was drowned out by a bell. Slowly it became evident that these outrageous acts conveyed the message that World War I had made all values meaningless. These artists could no longer support the spiritual claims and traditional beliefs of Western humanism. The Dada group embraced anti-art as the only ethical position possible for an artist in the modern era.

The most influential exponent of Dada was the French artist Marcel Duchamp [doo-SHAHN] (1887–1968), who abandoned Cubism in about 1915. His best-known Dada piece is the "definitely incomplete" work called *The Bride Stripped Bare by Her Bachelors, Even,* a mixture of oil, wire, and lead foil on two glass panels made between 1915 and 1923, sometimes called *The Large Glass* (Figure 20.18). Although it is certainly enigmatic, and in the eyes of many viewers it looked like a giant swindle, much is clear about *The Large Glass.* It has an erotic theme, typical of Dada art. Duchamp makes this theme manifest in the sculpture by devoting the upper half to the bride (the amorphous shape floating on the left) and her "apartment" (the stretch of gauze with three holes) and populating the lower "chamber" with the bachelors (the nine objects to the left) and their sex organ (the contraption made of a watermill, grinder, and other bits of metal). Linking the bride with the bachelors are tiny capillaries, or thin tubes, filled with oil—symbolic of fertilization with sperm. Duchamp's point seems to be similar to that of the novelist D. H. Lawrence: Sex in the machine age has become boring and mechanized.

Dada led to **Surrealism,** an art movement that began in the 1920s. Unlike Dada, Surrealism was basi-

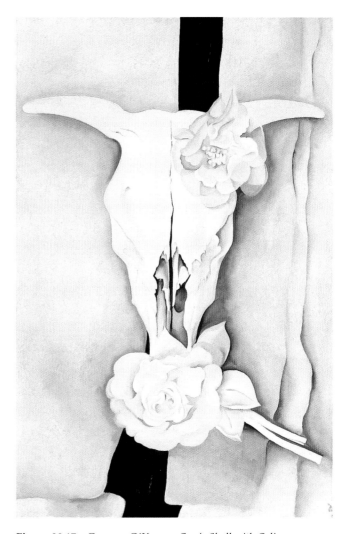

Figure 20.17 GEORGIA O'KEEFFE. *Cow's Skull with Calico Roses.* 1932. Oil on canvas, 36⁵⁄₁₆ × 24⅛". Art Institute of Chicago. Gift of Georgia O'Keeffe. *The simplified forms—the skull and the rose—link this painting to the period's trend to abstraction, but their placement so as to suggest the image of a "face" devouring a rose implies a connection with another development of this period, Surrealism, a style that delighted in realistic images with double meanings (see Figure 20.19). Whether intentional or not, O'Keeffe's overlapping of stylistic boundaries was typical of the fluid artistic scene in the years between the two world wars.*

cally a pictorial art. Inspired by Freud's teaching that the human mind conceals hidden depths, the Surrealists wanted to create a vision of reality that also included the truths harbored in the unconscious. They portrayed dream imagery, fantasies, and hallucinations in a direct fashion that made their paintings more startling than Dada. Among the leading Surrealists were Salvador Dali and Paul Klee.

The Spanish painter Salvador Dali [DAH-lee] (1904–1989) concentrated on subjects that surfaced from his lively imagination and often contained thinly

Figure 20.18 MARCEL DUCHAMP. *The Bride Stripped Bare by Her Bachelors, Even* (or *The Large Glass*). 1915–1923. Oil and lead wire on glass, 9'1¼" × 5'9⅛". Philadelphia Museum of Art. Bequest of Katherine M. Dreier. *Shortly after this legendary assemblage was built, the glass shattered. Duchamp repaired the work, replacing the glass with heavier panes and installing a reinforced frame. But effects of the accident are still apparent. Duchamp claimed to be delighted by these chance additions to his original design. In making this claim, he was the forerunner of the Modernist idea that chance should play a guiding role in art. After World War II, many artists began to incorporate random effects into their works.*

disguised sexual symbols. Probably his most famous work is the poetically named painting *The Persistence of Memory,* which depicts soft, melting watches in a desertlike setting (Figure 20.19). Sexual themes may be read in the limp images of watches—perhaps a reference to sexual impotence. Regardless of its meaning, the painting gives a strange twist to ordinary things, evoking the sense of a half-remembered dream—the goal of Surrealist art. Despite obvious painterly skills, Dali cultivated a controversial, even scandalous, personal image. His escapades earned him the public's ridicule, and the Surrealists even disowned him. From

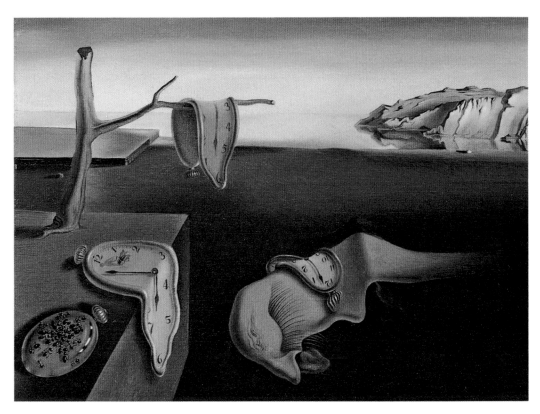

Figure 20.19 SALVADOR DALI. *The Persistence of Memory (Persistance de la mémoire)*. 1931. Oil on canvas, 9½ × 13" (24.1 × 33 cm). The Museum of Modern Art, New York. Given anonymously. Photograph © 1997 The Museum of Modern Art. *Dali liked to paint images that were actually optical illusions. In this painting, the watch depicted on the right is draped over an amorphous shape that, on inspection, appears to be that of a man. Dali's use of such optical effects reflected his often-stated belief that life is irrational.*

today's vantage point, however, Dali is admired for two reasons: for having created some of Modernism's most fantastic images and for being a link with the Pop artists of the 1960s (see Chapter 21).

The Swiss painter Paul Klee [KLAY] (1879–1940) may be grouped with the Surrealists, but he was too changeable to be restricted to a single style. He is best known for an innocent approach to art, which was triggered by his fondness for children's uninhibited scrawls. The childlike wonder portrayed in his whimsical works has made him a favorite with collectors and viewers. A professor from 1920 until 1930 at the Bauhaus, Germany's leading art institute between the wars, Klee created poetic images, rich in color and gentle wit, as in *Revolution of the Viaduct* (Figure 20.20). This painting depicts the breakup of a viaduct—a series of arches built to carry a road across a wide valley—when each arch, marching on thin "legs" and footlike bases, goes its own way. More than a cartoon, this whimsical work is Klee's allegorical response to

Europe's growing fascist culture—an atypical gesture by this usually apolitical artist. Klee equates the viaduct with the neo-Roman buildings favored by the Nazis as an expression of a homogeneous community ideal. The viaduct's breakup into individualized arches forecasts the downfall of Nazism. Klee thus espouses a quiet faith that fascist mass conformity may be undermined by the subversive acts of cultural revolutionaries—such as himself.

Klee's poetic images deeply impressed the Argentinean painter Xul Solar (zool so-LAHR) (born Oscar Agustin Alejandro Schulz) (1887–1963). Xul Solar's encounter with European art began during a twelve-year stay in France and Italy, where he mingled with the avant-garde, especially the Futurists (see Figure 19.1). But it was Klee and his childish sense of wonder that spoke directly to Xul Solar. When Xul Solar returned to Buenos Aires in 1924, his playfulness was soon evident in Neocriollismo ("New Creole-ism"), the movement he founded, along with its own Neo-Criollo language.

Figure 20.20 PAUL KLEE. *Revolution of the Viaduct.* 1937. Oil on canvas, 25⅝ × 19⅝". Kunsthalle, Hamburg. *Klee painted this work in the aftermath of the* Degenerate Art *exhibition, which opened in Munich in July 1937. Mounted by the Nazis to showcase what they called subversive art—art that encouraged "political anarchy and cultural anarchy"—the show was a frontal assault on Modernism. Klee, living in Switzerland after having been fired from his German teaching post in 1933, was represented by seventeen works in this show, displayed under the topics "confusion" and "insanity." Klee's* Revolution of the Viaduct *was part of the response of the international Modernist art world to the Nazi challenge.*

Mixing Portuguese and Spanish, Neo-Criollo was in part a sly call for unity among the nations of South America and in part an expression of his spiritual quest for a universal tongue. The name he now adopted, Xul Solar, has several meanings, including "solar light" and "light from the south." From this period stems his lifelong friendship with the writer Jorge Luis Borges (see Chapter 22). Xul Solar's paintings, usually executed in watercolors, combined a childlike quality with a visionary's sense of reality, as in *Drago* (Figure 20.21).

The Mexican painter Frida Kahlo [KAH-low] (1907–1954), famed for her unsettling self-portraits, might be classified with the Surrealists, though she is usually linked with the Mexican Muralists, the politically motivated artists who flourished between the

Figure 20.21 XUL SOLAR. *Drago.* 1927. Watercolor, approx. 10 × 12.6". Museo Xul Solar, Buenos Aires. *This small painting, filled with tiny national flags, schematic images of the sun, moon, and stars, religious symbols, and a lizard-like creature with two legs where the tail should be, portrays an alternate universe to that of Einstein and Newton. Drago suggests a dreamscape—hence, Xul Solar's art is sometimes linked with that of the Surrealists.*

Figure 20.22 FRIDA KAHLO. *Self-Portrait Dedicated to Dr. Eloesser.* 1940. Oil on masonite, 22¼ × 15¾". Private collection, U.S.A. *Kahlo reveals a Modernist sensibility in this likeness, which draws on multicultural sources, including Christianity and her indigenous Mexican heritage. The necklace of thorns, which makes her neck bleed, refers both to Christ's crown of thorns worn during the Crucifixion and to the Aztec prophetic ritual that required self-mortification with maguey thorns. The earring in the form of a hand—a gift from Picasso—symbolizes the hand of fate, and the jungle of oversized leaves evokes an image of nature out of control.*

two world wars and who painted mural (wall) cycles in public buildings to dramatize their socialist vision and solidarity with Mexico's native peoples. For most of her life, she was involved in a tempestuous marriage to Diego Rivera (1886–1957), a leading Mexican Muralist, but she was much more than the wife of a famous painter. Kahlo was an important artist in her own right, creating works that reflected her physical and spiritual suffering (she had polio at age six and was in a serious accident at eighteen). Today, she is known as an artist who turned private anguish into art with universal resonance.

Kahlo's *Self-Portrait Dedicated to Dr. Eloesser* (Figure 20.22) dates from a dark period in her life. Beset by marital and health problems and distraught over the assassination of her friend the Russian Marxist Leon Trotsky, who had been living in exile in Mexico, Kahlo was restored to health by the strict regimen of Dr. Eloesser of

San Francisco. In gratitude, she dedicated this work to him, as indicated by the flying banner, which reads, in part, "to my doctor and my best friend, with all my love." Despite this upbeat motif, the portrait reflects Kahlo's obsession with death and suffering.

EXPRESSIONISM The chief Expressionist painters in this era were Henri Matisse, a founder of Fauvism before World War I (see Chapter 19), and Max Beckmann, the heir to German Expressionism. In the 1930s, Matisse's art was distinguished by its decorative quality, a tendency since his Fauvist days. *Large Reclining Nude* shows his new style, which is characterized by a fresh approach to the human figure: enlarged, simplified, though clearly recognizable (Figure 20.23). The nude figure is depicted completely flat, without modeling or shading, so that it looks as if it has been cut out and glued to the gridded surface. Matisse has also

Figure 20.23   HENRI MATISSE. *Large Reclining Nude.* 1935. Oil on canvas, approx. 26 × 36⅓″. Baltimore Museum of Art. The Cone Collection. *Matisse's* Large Reclining Nude *established the archetypal images—a still life and a model in an interior—that Matisse painted for the rest of his life. It was also the first expression of his later style, which was characterized by the human figure's being simply another element in an overall design.*

abandoned the highly saturated colors of Fauvism and replaced them with cooler tones—in this case, a cotton-candy pink. Nevertheless, he stayed true to the leading Expressionist principle of distortion, as demonstrated by the nude figure's elongated body and dangling limbs.

Matisse was rebuked for concentrating on pretty subjects while the world slipped into anarchy. No such charge can be made against the German painter Max Beckmann (1884–1950), whose Expressionist paintings register horror at the era's turbulent events. *The Departure* is typical of his works, being concerned with both personal and spiritual issues (Figure 20.24). The struc-

ture of the painting—divided into three panels (a triptych) like a medieval altarpiece—suggests that it has religious meaning. It was the first of nine completed triptychs. Influenced by the mystical teachings of the German thinker Arthur Schopenhauer (1788–1860), East Asian philosophy, and the Jewish cabala (medieval writings), *The Departure* represents a yearning to be free of the horrors of earthly existence. In the side panels, Beckmann depicts images of cruelty, including bound human figures, one of whom is gagged, being subjected to torture—perhaps reflecting his fears of the rise of Nazism. In contrast, the central panel, in which a man, woman, and child are ferried across a lake by a

Figure 20.24   MAX BECKMANN. *The Departure*. 1932–1935. Oil on canvas, center panel 7′ ×
3′9″, side panels 7′ × 3′3″. The Museum of Modern Art, New York. *In* The Departure,
*Beckmann's Expressionism is revealed through the treatment of form and color. The flat, angular
figures, arranged into awkward positions, and the unusual perspective reinforce the painting's
disturbing theme. The dark hues of the side panel, appropriate for the violent images, contrast
with the bright colors of the central panel and its message of salvation.*

hooded boatman, evokes the theme of deliverance.
When the Nazis came to power in 1933, they declared
Beckmann a degenerate artist, confiscated his works,
and fired him from his academic post. In 1937 he
sought refuge in Amsterdam, where he managed to
survive World War II.

Architecture   In the 1920s and 1930s, architects continued their search for a pure style, free of decoration
and totally functional. Their research resembled a
mystical quest, stemming from the belief that new architecture could solve social problems by creating a
new physical environment—a recurrent theme in European Modernism.

This visionary conception of architecture was best
expressed in Germany's Bauhaus, an educational institution whose aim was to bring about social reform
through a new visual environment, especially in the
design of everyday objects. To that end, the school
brought together artists, craftspeople, and architects.
During its brief lifetime, which lasted from its founding in 1919 until 1933 when it was closed by the Nazis,
the Bauhaus, under Walter Gropius [GROH-pee-uhs]
(1883–1969), was the center of abstract art in Germany.
The Bauhaus affected later culture in two ways. First,
it developed a spartan type of interior decoration
characterized by all-white rooms and wooden floors,
streamlined furniture, and lighting supplied by banks

Figure 20.25 WALTER GROPIUS. The Bauhaus, Workshop Wing. 1925–1926. Dessau, Germany. Architectural Association Photo. © Petra Hodgson. *The Bauhaus (German, Architecture House) was an applied arts, architecture, and design school that operated from 1919 to 1933, when it was closed by the Nazis because of its supposed Jewish connections. Founded in Weimar in 1919, it moved to Dessau in 1925. Aspiring architects and designers trained in sculpture, painting, architecture, and crafts workshops, learning to design objects for a mass society, which would be both functional and aesthetically pleasing. Among the distinguished teachers were Paul Klee (see Figure 20.20) and Kandinsky (see Figure 19.24). The Bauhaus workshop wing, part of a three-building complex, was designed in the International style. Its front wall, constructed of glass and metal, became a defining architectural feature of office skyscrapers in the postwar period (see Figure 21.1).*

of windows by day and recessed lamps at night. Second, it introduced the **International style** in architecture, which is sleek, geometrical, and devoid of ornament (Figure 20.25).

The International style's most distinguished representative in the period between the wars was the Swiss architect Charles-Édouard Jeanneret, better known as Le Corbusier [luh kor-boo-ZYAY] (1887–1965). Le Corbusier's artistic credo was expressed in the dictum "A house is a machine for living." In pursuit of this ideal, he pioneered building methods such as prefabricated housing and reinforced concrete as ways to eliminate ordinary walls. His Savoye House, near Paris, became the prototype of private houses for the wealthy after World War II (Figure 20.26). The Savoye House was painted stark white and raised on columns, its ground floor had a curved wall, and its windows were slits. A painter before becoming an architect, Le Corbusier designed architecture that combined Cubism's abstractness (the raised box) with Constructivism's purity (whiteness).

Photography Between 1900 and 1945, photography continued to evolve within the two areas that emerged at the time of its birth: the photograph as a historical record and the photograph as a work of art (see Chapter 18). History-minded photographers wanted direct and realistic images, which would serve as records of their era for future generations, including documentary photographs, combat photographs, landscape scenes, urban scenes, industrial culture, and records of endangered social life (for example, village life and Native American rituals). In contrast, artistic photographers manipulated their final images, using soft-focus lenses and techniques borrowed from art and film, to create, for example, impressionistic photographs, photomontages (mixing photographs with words cut from newspapers), and photographs influenced by abstraction, Cubism, Dada, Surrealism, and other art styles of the era. Neither category is absolute, however, as aesthetic influences inevitably creep into historic photographs and artistic photographs do serve as historic records of the event that produced them.

Documentary photography, or photojournalism, was probably this period's most highly visible photographic genre. This was because newspapers and magazines, both part of the explosive growth of mass culture, seemed insatiable in their appetite for new images. Staid newspapers, like the *New York Times* and *The Times*, the English newspaper, resisted placing

Figure 20.26 LE CORBUSIER. Savoye House. 1929–1931. Poissy, near Paris. *Le Corbusier wanted to make a break with previous styles of architecture and create a new style in tune with the machine age. His design for the Savoye House realizes this ambition completely through its severe geometrical form, its absence of decoration except for architectural details, and its sparkling white walls. When finished, the Savoye House had the streamlined look associated with industrial machinery, an achievement much admired in the 1930s.*

photographs on the front page, but the tabloids and the regional press, eager to boost sales, plastered historic, lurid, and humorous photographs on the front page and sprinkled others liberally throughout their pages as a way to attract more readers. A milestone in photographic history occurred in 1936 with the founding of *Life* magazine—the brainchild of Henry Luce (1898–1967)—because it was the first general-audience magazine in which pictures dominated. With fifty-two issues each year, *Life* raised the demand for new photographs exponentially. *Life*'s success soon spawned rivals in the United States and similar-style magazines in Germany, England, France, and elsewhere.

Photojournalism, perhaps because it was still in its infancy and thus had little tradition, exerted a powerful attraction for women, including Margaret Bourke-White (1906–1971) and Dorothea Lange (1895–1965), two of the period's leading photojournalists. Bourke-White established her reputation with the Henry Luce group, starting in 1930. When *Life* was founded, she became one of four staff photographers who routinely circled the globe in search of a scoop. Her subjects, presented straightforwardly and directly, with just a hint of compassion, included Dust Bowl victims, southern sharecroppers, Czech life on the eve of the Nazi takeover, World War II (see Figure 20.7), Gandhi (see Encounter figure 20.1) and the partition of India, and the Korean War. Lange's fame rests primarily on her photographs for the Farm Security Administration (FSA), part of President Roosevelt's New Deal. Her photographs, made in extreme close-up, depict in uncomfortable detail lives wasted during the Depression (see

Figure 20.5). More than a documentary record, her photographs served a propaganda function, because they were commissioned by this federal agency to bring the plight of the rural poor to the attention of affluent America. Lange made other photographs, such as a record of the internment of Japanese Americans during World War II and a photo-essay on Mormon life for *Life* magazine, but none of them has the appeal of her New Deal portraits.

Film   Motion pictures—the movies—were immediately popular when they were introduced early in the twentieth century, and by the mid-1920s they had become the most popular mass entertainment, drawing larger audiences than the theater, vaudeville, and the music halls. The American film director D. W. Griffith (1875–1948) showed in such pioneering works as *The Birth of a Nation* (1915) and *Intolerance* (1916) that it was possible to make movies that were serious, sustained works of art. His technical innovations, such as crosscutting and the close-up, made more complex film narratives possible, but such attempts to develop the medium were rare. Although other directors quickly appropriated Griffith's techniques, few went beyond them, and the movies remained resolutely lowbrow. The present-day distinction between "movies" (the widest possible audience) and "films" (appealing to more educated, intellectual audiences) had not yet arisen.

One of the era's most inventive directors was the Russian Sergei Eisenstein [IZE-uhn-stine] (1898–1948), who introduced directorial techniques that had an enormous influence on the rise of art films. In *The Battleship Potemkin* (1925), he pioneered the montage technique, which consisted of highly elaborate editing patterns and rhythms. He developed the montage because he believed that the key element in films was the way the scenes were arranged, how they faded out and faded in, and how they looked in juxtaposition to one another. By focusing on the material of the film itself instead of highlighting the plot or the characters' psychology, Eisenstein showed his allegiance to the artistic aspect of moviemaking.

Perhaps the most controversial director of this period was Leni Riefenstahl [LAY-nee REE-fen-shtahl] (1902–2003), the German dancer and actress, who became Hitler's favorite moviemaker. Her masterpiece was *Triumph of the Will* (1934), an almost-two-hour-long documentary depicting the sixth Nazi Party Congress in Nuremberg, held in September 1934, which introduced the Nazi Party to the world (see Figure 20.6). The film's title was Hitler's own term, reflecting his borrowing from Nietzsche's philosophy (see Chapter 19). Made in black-and-white, this film lovingly depicted the Nazi pageant in all of its dramatic glory, including massed ranks of thousands of party members, torchlight parades, athletic displays by well-muscled young men, children marching in close ranks, and rituals involving flags emblazoned with swastikas. Riefenstahl made the film even more theatrical with new camera angles and creative editing. Although brilliant, this film showed how politics could subvert art, simply by making art the handmaid of a political agenda. After World War II, Riefenstahl was convicted as a war criminal for her Nazi propaganda and sentenced to four years in prison. Her career never recovered from the stigma of her support for the Nazi regime.

The United States (which eventually meant Hollywood, California) had dominated the motion picture industry since World War I, and the industry underwent important changes during the interwar years. Sound movies became technically feasible in the late 1920s, and in the early 1930s three-color cinematography processes were developed. Both of these technical developments became basic to the movies throughout the world, but other experiments, such as wide-screen and three-dimensional photography, were less successful. Another important development in this period was the descent on Hollywood of many German filmmakers in flight from the Nazis. In the Hollywood of the 1930s, these exiles helped to create some of the outstanding achievements in world cinema.

A sign of the excellence of Hollywood movies in these years is Orson Welles's *Citizen Kane* (1941), often called America's best film (Figure 20.27). An American, Welles (1915–1985) had learned from the German exiles and borrowed their Expressionist methods, such as theatrical lighting and multiple narrative voices. Welles's own commanding presence in the lead role also contributed to making this an unforgettable movie. But one of the hallmarks of the movie—its dark look, which underscores the brooding theme of unbridled lust for power—was in actuality a money-saving device to disguise the absence of studio sets. Is *Citizen Kane* a "film" or a "movie"? It is a measure of Welles's success that it is triumphantly both: Its frequent showing both on television and in theaters attests to its popularity, yet its discussion and analysis in film journals and books points to its high prominence as a film.

Music: Atonality, Neoclassicism, and an American Idiom

During the 1920s and 1930s, Western music was fragmented into two rival camps as a result of developments that had begun in the period before World War I (see Chapter 19). On one side was the Austro-German school headed by Arnold Schoenberg, who had introduced atonality before 1914 and in the 1920s

Figure 20.27 Still, from *Citizen Kane*. 1941. RKO. *This still from* Citizen Kane *conveys the megalomania of the film's hero, Charles Foster Kane, played by its director and star, Orson Welles. Kane is depicted standing before a huge portrait of himself. Such extreme vanity as displayed here was a typical propaganda method in the Age of the Masses. Totalitarian leaders of both the right and the left, including Hitler and Stalin, cultivated the cult of the personality through huge public portraits. Reflecting his democratic values, Welles's film satirized the rise and fall of citizen Kane, a self-absorbed newspaper mogul modeled on the newspaper publisher William Randolph Hearst (1863–1951). Part of the film's appeal stemmed from its innovative cinematography, which permitted deep-focus imagery, so that extreme foreground and background could be viewed simultaneously with equal clarity—a breakthrough that is suggested by this still.*

Figure 20.28 PABLO PICASSO. *Stravinsky*. 1920. Pencil on gray paper, 24⅜ × 19⅛". Musée Picasso, Paris. *Picasso's pencil sketch of Stravinsky is a perceptive character study. Long before Stravinsky became almost unapproachable, Picasso portrayed him as an aloof, self-absorbed young man. Stravinsky's cold demeanor is obvious in the tense posture, the harsh stare, and the clasped hands and crossed legs. Picasso's sketch also hints at Stravinsky's genius by exaggerating the size of his hands, perhaps to emphasize their role in the composer's creative life.*

pioneered serial music. On the other side was the French school led by Igor Stravinsky, who had experimented with primitive rhythms and harsh dissonances in the early 1900s but after World War I adopted a stern Neoclassical style.

Having abandoned tonality in 1909, Schoenberg in the 1920s introduced **serial music,** a method of composing with a **twelve-tone scale**—twelve tones that are related not to a tonal center in a major or minor key but only to each other. Lacking harmonious structure, serial music sounded dissonant and random and tended to create anxiety in listeners. As a result, serial music appealed to cult rather than mass audiences.

Lack of a huge responsive public did not halt Schoenberg's pursuit of atonality. His serial system culminated in *Variations for Orchestra* (1928), a composition that uses the Classical form of theme with variations. In 1933 he emigrated to America, where his devotion to atonality mellowed. Some of Schoenberg's later works mix twelve-tone writing with tonality.

Stravinsky, in exile from the Soviet Union after 1917, went to live in Paris, where he became the dominant figure of **Neoclassicism** in music, borrowing features from seventeenth- and eighteenth-century music (Figure 20.28). In his Neoclassical works, he abandoned many of the techniques that had become common to music since the Baroque period, such as Romantic emotionalism and programmatic composition as well as Impressionism's use of dense orchestral sounds. Austere and cool, his Neoclassical compositions used simple instrumental combinations and sounded harmonious. Stravinsky's works from this period made him the outstanding composer of the twentieth century.

Stravinsky originated Neoclassicism in 1919 with the ballet *Pulcinella* and brought the style to a close in 1951 with the opera *The Rake's Progress*. Between these two major works was one of his most admired compositions, the *Symphony of Psalms*, dating from 1930. *Pulcinella* and *The Rake's Progress* owe much to the music and comic operas of the Classical composers Pergolesi [per-GO-lay-see] (1710–1736) and Mozart (see Chapter 16), respectively, and the *Symphony of Psalms* follows a Baroque model in its small orchestra and musical structure. Despite borrowing forms and ideas, Stravinsky made them his own, introducing occasional dissonances and continuing to experiment with complex rhythmic patterns.

American music, meanwhile, was discovering its own idiom. Charles Ives (1874–1954) focused on American melodies, including folk songs, hymns, marches, patriotic songs, ragtime tunes, and music of his beloved New England. Working without models, Ives experimented with tonality and rhythm in ways similar to those of the European avant-garde. Typical of his work is the *Concord Sonata* for piano (1909–1915). Another American composer, Aaron Copland (1900–1990), had achieved some success by imitating European styles, but in the 1930s he began to develop a distinctive American style. His ballet scores *Billy the Kid* (1938), *Rodeo* (1942), and *Appalachian Spring* (1944), commissioned by choreographers Agnes de Mille (1909–1993) and Martha Graham (1893–1991), drew on hymns, ballads, folk tunes, and popular songs of the period. His delightful melodies, brilliant sound, jazzy experimentation, and upbeat rhythms ensured the popularity of these pieces.

Despite the overall folksy sound of *Appalachian Spring,* the only actual folk tune Copland used was "Simple Gifts," a hymn from the Shaker sect that expressed their faith in simple living. An eighteenth-century offshoot of the Quakers, known originally as "shaking Quakers," the Shakers showed religious fervor through ecstatic rituals, including speaking in tongues, dancing, and "shaking" of the body. Copland exploited this Shaker hymn, making it the theme of Section 7, "Simple Gifts," of his ballet score. Written in the Classical form of theme and variations, "Simple Gifts," begins with the sweet melody of the hymn's first two lines, "'Tis the gift to be simple, 'tis the gift to be free / 'Tis the gift to come down where we ought to

be." There are five variations, with the theme being varied through changes in key, tempo (slow to staccato), dynamics (soft to loud), instrument combinations, and tone color. In the concluding variation, Copland pulls out all stops, using the full orchestra playing ***fortississimo*** (a made-up term, "extremely loud"; abbreviated fff) to transform the simple melody into a majestic affirmation of the simple life.

A major American composer who cared less about developing a purely American idiom and more about exploring music's frontiers was George Antheil [an-TILE] (1900–1959). Living in Europe from 1922 to 1933, Antheil became part of the intellectual avant-garde who were intrigued by the machine-oriented culture of the Age of the Masses. In worshiping the machine, these artists and musicians followed in the steps of the Futurists, the Italian group who had raised "speed" to an artistic principle before World War I (see Figure 19.1). As part of the 1920s European scene, Antheil was led to incorporate industrial sounds—the music of the masses—into his compositions. Hence, his *Ballet mécanique (Mechanical Ballet)* (1924; revised 1952) included scoring for unusual "instruments" (electric bells, small wood propeller, large wood propeller, metal propeller, siren, and sixteen player pianos) as well as more traditional instruments (piano and three xylophones). Antheil claimed this incorporation of urban and industrial sounds as his goal in composing this iconoclastic work: "It is the rhythm of machinery, presented as beautifully as an artist knows how. . . . It is the life, the manufacturing, the industry of today."

The African American composer William Grant Still (1895–1978), who was born in the heart of the Old South, in Mississippi, also left his defining mark on this period. Still was uniquely positioned to make a major contribution to serious music. He was educated in both black and white institutions of higher learning, a student first of medicine and then of music composition and steeped in Western musical styles, both traditional and radically avant-garde, along with jazz idioms created by both white and black performers. His eclectic musical style used traditional Western musical forms infused with elements of jazz and various other forms of black musical expression, as well as popular music and orchestration. He wrote ballets, five symphonies, orchestral suites, symphonic poems, chamber works, songs, arrangements of spirituals, and operas, including *The Troubled Island* (1938), with a libretto by Langston Hughes, the first opera by an African American to be staged by a professional opera company (the New York City Opera).

Still's most popular work today is the *Afro-American Symphony* (1931), the first symphony by a black American to be performed by a major symphony orchestra. Still's symphony, though composed in a Western musical form, draws on elements of the African American heritage for its themes, rhythmic structures, and instrumentation. In the first part of the symphony's third movement, for example, the main theme, which appears after a brief introduction, is a four-note phrase that Still called the *hallelujah* motive, thereby evoking the central role played by gospel singing in African American life. Accompanying the *hallelujah* theme is a banjo playing on the offbeat—a jaunty reminder of the banjos in nineteenth-century black minstrel shows. The countermelody, a syncopated version of an African American spiritual, also was inspired by the African American church tradition. The playfulness of this section suggests a jubilant mood, based on the poem that Still quoted in a preface to this movement: "An' we'll shout ouah hallelujahs / On dat mighty reck'nin' day"—by Paul Laurence Dunbar (1872–1906), an African American poet. The "reck'nin' day" refers to the messianic hope for a day of jubilation at the time of Christ's second coming, when African Americans will be rewarded for their sufferings on earth. The jubilant mood is expressed through sudden shifts in dynamics, rhythm, tone color, register, and varied combinations of instruments.

During the Age of the Masses, jazz began to reach larger audiences, in part because of the development of the radio and the phonograph. Many jazz greats created their reputations in these years. The fame of the finest jazz composer, Duke Ellington (born Edward Kennedy Ellington; 1899–1974), dated from 1927 at Harlem's Cotton Club. Ellington's songs balanced superb orchestration with improvisation and ranged from popular melodies, such as "Sophisticated Lady"

(1932), to major suites, such as *Such Sweet Thunder* (1957), based on Shakespeare. Jazz's premiere female vocalist, Billie Holiday (1915–1959), whose bittersweet style was marked by innovative phrasing, also appeared then.

Ellington's "Mood Indigo" (1930), now a standard in the American songbook, shows him to be a master of jazz composition. He usually wrote for a fifteen- or sixteen-piece **swing band** orchestra, with himself on piano, creating music marked by syncopation and lush tone color. In "Mood Indigo," he used his music expressionistically to convey a gentle air of melancholy—hence its title. Introduced with a swelling crescendo that builds to a crashing climax, which is then repeated, this piece unfolds in typical popular song format: refrain, verse, refrain. The delicate blend of jauntiness and sadness invoked by the minor key gives it a haunting quality, which is heightened by the slow fade to silence at the end.

Two jazz performers whose careers extended well beyond this period are Louis Armstrong (1901–1971) and Ella Fitzgerald (1918–1996). Armstrong, better known as "Satchmo," became a goodwill ambassador for the United States with his loud and relaxed New Orleans–style trumpet playing. Ella Fitzgerald, a vocalist noted for her bell-like voice and elegant phrasing, became the peerless interpreter of jazz standards as well as pop tunes. In the next period, jazz fragmented into a host of styles and was a vital ingredient in the explosive birth of rock and roll, the popular music form originating in the 1950s that has since dominated popular music.

The Legacy of the Age of the Masses and High Modernism

The Age of the Masses has transformed material civilization in the West in both good and bad ways. It has given us the most destructive wars of history, the greatest economic depression since the fourteenth century, the most absolute forms of government since the Late Roman Empire, the first modern attempt to eliminate an entire people, the fully formed industrial-military-state complex, and a weapon capable of destroying the planet. At the same time, it has brought a better standard of living to most people in the West and given millions of Westerners their first taste of democracy.

This age has also had a contradictory impact on cultural developments. On the one hand, it saw the growth of a worldwide mass culture, led by American ingenuity, which began to dominate public and private life for most people. On the other hand, it inspired a revolt by Modernist artists, writers, and musicians to create works free of mass culture's influence. Their creations were experimental, perplexing, and often committed to what they defined as spiritual values. A few Modernists refused to become mass culture's adversaries, and these moderating voices pointed toward a healthier relationship between mass culture and the elitist tradition after World War II.

Besides the polarization of mass and high culture, this period left other cultural legacies. Films became ac-cepted as a serious art form, and they remain the greatest legacy of mass culture to the twentieth century. Photography was also now beginning to be accepted as a legitimate art form. Advances in medicine, especially in new pharmaceuticals, were ending the threat from many diseases and thus adding years to the expected human life span. It was also during this period that America emerged as a significant cultural force in the West, partly because of the tide of intellectuals flowing from Europe, partly because of America's growing political, economic, and military power, and partly because of excellent native schools of writers, musicians, and artists. And finally, a questioning mood became the normative way of looking at the world, replacing the certainty of previous centuries.

The Modernists had pioneered a questioning spirit in about 1900, and in this period the revolution in physics seemed to reinforce it. Einstein's conclusion that space and time are interchangeable was echoed by artists, writers, and musicians who focused on form to define content in their work. And Heisenberg's uncertainty principle seemed to reverberate everywhere—from Wittgenstein's toying with language to the highly personal narrative voices that dominated the novel to the constantly shrinking set of basic beliefs that characterized the period's religious thought and, ultimately, to the widespread belief that Western civilization had lost its course.

KEY CULTURAL TERMS

mass culture
stream-of-consciousness
epic theater
logical positivism
existentialism
Suprematism
Constructivism
Socialist Realism
de Stijl

Dada
Surrealism
International style
serial music
twelve-tone scale
Neoclassicism
fortississimo
swing band

SUGGESTIONS FOR FURTHER READING

BRECHT, B. *The Threepenny Opera.* English version by D. Vesey and English lyrics by E. Bentley. New York: Limited Editions Club, 1982. An excellent adaptation of Brecht's biting drama about the underworld in Victorian England; Bentley's lyrics capture the slangy flavor of the German play first staged in 1928.

COCTEAU, J. *The Infernal Machine and Other Plays.* Norfolk, Conn.: New Directions, 1964. Cocteau fuses Classicism with experimental methods in his Modernist plays; he updates the Oedipus legend, for example, by introducing Freudian ideas and using film clips to present flashbacks.

ELIOT, T. S. *Collected Poems, 1909–1962.* New York: Harcourt, Brace & World, 1963. Eliot, a pillar of Modernism, portrayed his times as exhausted and abandoned by God.

FAULKNER, W. *The Sound and the Fury.* New York: Modern Library, 1946. The most admired novel from the Yoknapatawpha series, Faulkner's monumental study of post–Civil War Mississippi society.

HEIDEGGER, M. *Being and Time.* Translated by J. Macquarrie and E. Robinson. New York: Harper, 1962. First published in 1927, this work helped launch the existentialist movement by portraying the universe as a meaningless place and human existence as a never-ending quest for authenticity.

HEMINGWAY, E. *The Sun Also Rises.* New York: Scribner's, 1970. Hemingway's semiautobiographical first novel, set in France and Spain in 1925.

HUGHES, L. *Selected Poems of Langston Hughes.* London: Pluto, 1986. Poetry by one of the twentieth century's outstanding writers.

JOYCE, J. *Ulysses*. New York: Penguin, 1986. This classic of Modernism uses a tapestry of narrative styles to portray a day in the lives of three middle-class citizens of Dublin.

LAWRENCE, D. H. *Lady Chatterley's Lover*. New York: Modern Library, 1983. A controversial work that poses sex as a panacea for the ills of contemporary industrialized life.

O'NEILL, E. *Three Plays: Desire Under the Elms, Strange Interlude, Mourning Becomes Electra*. New York: Vintage, 1961. O'Neill's trilogy of plays based on Aeschylus's *Oresteia* and involving a contemporary New England family.

ORWELL, G. *Animal Farm; Burmese Days; A Clergyman's Daughter; Coming Up for Air; Keep the Aspidistra Flying; 1984*. New York: Octopus/Heinemann, 1980. This volume contains Orwell's most significant writings, most of which convey the author's hatred of tyranny and his skepticism about the future of humanity.

SARTRE, J.-P. *Being and Nothingness: An Essay in Phenomenological Ontology*. Translated and with an introduction by H. E. Barnes. Abridged. New York: Citadel Press, 1956. Sartre sets forth his existentialist philosophy, focusing on such key ideas as individual freedom and personal responsibility.

WALKER, A., ed. *I Love Myself When I Am Laughing . . . And Then Again When I Am Looking Mean and Impressive: A Zora Neale Hurston Reader*. Introduction by M. H. Washington. Old Westbury, N.Y.: The Feminist Press, 1979. A judicious collection of Hurston's writings, including excerpts from novels (*Their Eyes Were Watching God*, 1936) and autobiography (*Dust Tracks on a Road*, 1942); essays ("How It Feels to Be Colored Me," 1928, "Crazy for Democracy," 1945); and short stories ("The Gilded Six-bits," 1933); with an admiring "afterword" by the celebrated writer Alice Walker.

WITTGENSTEIN, L. *Tractatus Logico-Philosophicus*. Translated by D. F. Pears and B. F. McGuiness, with an introduction by B. Russell. London: Routledge and Kegan Paul, 1974. An excellent English-language version of the treatise that led to logical positivism in philosophy.

WOOLF, V. *To the Lighthouse*. London: Hogarth Press, 1974. A typical Woolf novel in its stream-of-consciousness technique and its exquisitely detailed observations of contemporary thinking.

YEATS, W. B. *The Collected Poems of W. B. Yeats*. Edited by R. J. Finneran. New York: Collier Books, 1989. One of Modernism's leading voices, Yeats wrote poetry devoted to such themes as Celtic myth, the tragic violence of Irish history, and the mystical nature of human existence.

SUGGESTIONS FOR LISTENING

ANTHEIL, GEORGE. An American composer who worked in both experimental and traditional forms, Antheil lived in Europe in the 1920s and 1930s. His best-known experimental work is *Ballet mécanique (Mechanical Ballet)* (1924; revised 1952), scored for airplane propellers and other industrial noises. Recognizing that his mechanical aesthetic was at a dead end with this work, Antheil spent the rest of his career searching for a personal style: from Neoclassicism (1925–1927), as in the lyrical *Piano Concerto* (1926); to Americana experiments (1927–1942), as in the opera *Transatlantic* (1927–1928), a political farce about an American presidential election; to Neoromanticism (see Chapter 22), as in Symphony No. 4 (1942) and Symphony No. 5 (1947–1948), which blend melodic and rhythmic experiments with Classical forms.

COPLAND, AARON. Copland's most popular works incorporate folk melodies and pay homage to the American way of life. Copland used cowboy songs in the ballet scores *Billy the Kid* (1938) and *Rodeo* (1942); he incorporated variations on the Shaker hymn "Simple Gifts" in *Appalachian Spring* (1944), originally a ballet score that was later rearranged as a suite for symphony orchestra. His faith in the future of democracy is expressed most fully in the short, often-performed work "Fanfare for the Common Man."

ELLINGTON, EDWARD KENNEDY ("DUKE"). Ellington's jazz style blended careful orchestration with ample opportunity for improvisation. Many of his songs have become standards in the popular music repertory, such as "Creole Love Call" (1928), "Mood Indigo" (1934), "Don't Get Around Much Anymore" (1940), and "Sophisticated Lady" (1932). Less well known are his serious longer compositions, such as *Such Sweet Thunder* (1957) and *In the Beginning God* (1965), a religious work.

IVES, CHARLES. America's first great composer, Ives experimented with atonality, clashing rhythms, and dissonant harmony long before they became a standard part of twentieth-century music. He frequently drew on American themes, as in the *Concord Sonata* for piano (1909–1915) and the orchestral *Three Places in New England* (1903–1914; first performed in 1931), works that evoked the landscape of his native region. A good example of one of his atonal works is *The Unanswered Question* (1908), a short work for trumpet, four flutes, and strings.

SCHOENBERG, ARNOLD. During this period, Schoenberg, the leader of the school of atonality, originated serialism as a method of composing, as may be heard in *Variations for Orchestra* (1928), the unfinished opera *Moses and Aaron* (1932), and *Violin Concerto* (1936).

STILL, WILLIAM GRANT. Still's eclectic style usually relied on traditional Western musical forms while drawing on diverse elements of his African American background and hybrid educational experience, including jazz, popular music and orchestration, Negro spirituals, and Western avant-garde music. Notable achievements include the ballet *Lenox Avenue* (1937), the opera *The Troubled Island* (1938), with a libretto by Langston Hughes, and the *Afro-American Symphony* (1931).

STRAVINSKY, IGOR. Schoenberg's rival Stravinsky became the leader of Neoclassicism in music with the ballet *Pulcinella* (1919) and continued this musical style in such works as *Symphony of Psalms* (1930), the opera-oratorio *Oedipus Rex (Oedipus the King)* (1927), the Symphony in C (1940), and the opera *The Rake's Progress* (1951).

21

THE AGE OF ANXIETY AND LATE MODERNISM

1945–1970

Fear of nuclear war had a pervasive effect on attitudes and events after 1945 and led to an enormous buildup of weapons by the United States and the Soviet Union. This arms buildup in turn contributed to uncontrolled military spending at the expense of domestic programs. For some Westerners, anxiety about nuclear war produced a sense of absurdity and a mood of despair. Against the backdrop of these realities, the cultural style known as Late Modernism captured the anguish experienced by many artists, writers, and intellectuals.

FROM A EUROPEAN TO A WORLD CIVILIZATION

The end of World War II brought the cold war, an era of international tensions and conflicting ideologies. World relations were governed by a bipolar balance of power between the United States and the Union of Soviet Socialist Republics (USSR) (Figure 21.1). The American bloc included Western Europe, the British Commonwealth, and their former enemies Japan, West Germany, and Italy. The Soviet bloc embraced virtually all of Eastern Europe and, after 1949, when the Communists took power, China.

The cold war escalated for two main reasons. First, the superpowers extended their confrontations to the Third World, rushing in to influence events as the West's colonial empires fell and were replaced by struggling independent states. Second, the development of ballistic missiles capable of hurtling nuclear weapons across intercontinental distances raised the possibility of sudden strikes and mass destruction without warning.

◀ **Detail** ANDY WARHOL. *Mao.* 1973. Acrylic and silkscreen on canvas, 14'6⅞" × 11'4½". Art Institute of Chicago. Mr. and Mrs. Frank G. Logan Purchase Prize and Wilson L. Mead Funds.

Figure 21.1 WALLACE K. HARRISON INTERNATIONAL
COMMITTEE OF ARCHITECTS. United Nations Headquarters.
1949–1951. New York. *The decision to locate the United Nations
Headquarters in New York made that city the unofficial capital of
the free world—a term that was applied to the United States and
its allies during the cold war. And the choice of a "glass box" skyscraper for the United Nations Secretariat building helped to ensure that the International style would be the reigning style of
architecture in the postwar period, until about 1970.*

By the dawn of the 1970s, the West seemed balanced between the two superpowers and their respective blocs, despite sporadic ups and downs, and the
cold war loomed over the foreseeable future.

The Era of the Superpowers, 1945–1970

Between 1945 and 1970, the West followed two patterns. For the American bloc, democracy was the rule,
social welfare was slowly expanded, and the economies were booming. For the Soviet bloc, collectivist
regimes prevailed, social welfare was comprehensive, and the economies either stagnated or grew
slowly. The two systems emerged as seemingly inevitable consequences of World War II. With Germany
and Japan defeated, the ideological differences and
geopolitical viewpoints between the USSR and the
Western nations began to dominate the shape of the
postwar world.

Postwar Recovery and the New World Order The
chief Allied forces—the United States, Great Britain,
and the Soviet Union—began to plan for the postwar
era before World War II ended. They agreed to occupy
Germany and Japan, giving those nations representative forms of government and drastically curbing their
military systems. They joined with forty-eight other
countries in 1945 to found the United Nations, a peacekeeping and human rights organization dealing with
international disputes (Figure 21.1). They also prepared for worldwide economic recovery by establishing several transnational organizations, such as the
World Bank, which provides funds and technical assistance to developing countries for large-scale building projects, and the International Monetary Fund
(IMF), which fosters international monetary cooperation, encourages the expansion of international trade,
and attempts to stabilize exchange rates. However, the
Soviet Union refused to participate in these economic
arrangements.

When peace came in 1945, the Allies split Germany
into four occupied zones. In 1949 Britain, France, and
the United States united their zones into the Federal
Republic of Germany (West Germany), and the USSR
set up its zone as the German Democratic Republic
(East Germany). By 1969 West Germany, led by mod-
erates devoted to capitalism, had become Europe's
chief industrial power, and East Germany, under a collectivist regime, lagged far behind.

In Japan, the American victors imposed a democratic constitution that kept the emperor as a figure-
head; introduced a parliamentary system; gave the
vote to women, workers, and farmers; and virtually
eliminated the military. Between 1950 and 1973, under
this renovated system, Japan's gross domestic product
grew more than 10 percent a year on average, surpass-
ing that of any other industrialized nation.

By the early 1950s, both Great Britain and France
were enjoying moderate economic growth, although
each was beset by continuing labor unrest. Left-wing
governments in both countries nationalized major industries and founded national health-care systems, although conservatives periodically returned some
businesses to private hands.

France and West Germany recognized that in the
age of the superpowers the era of the small state was
over and that it was necessary to join forces to gain
economic stability. In 1957 they initiated a free-trade
zone that also included Belgium, the Netherlands,
Luxembourg, and Italy. Called the European Economic Community, or the Common Market, this organization became the driving force in Europe's
prosperity over the next decade.

A large reason for the formation of the Common
Market was that the USSR threatened to dominate Eu-

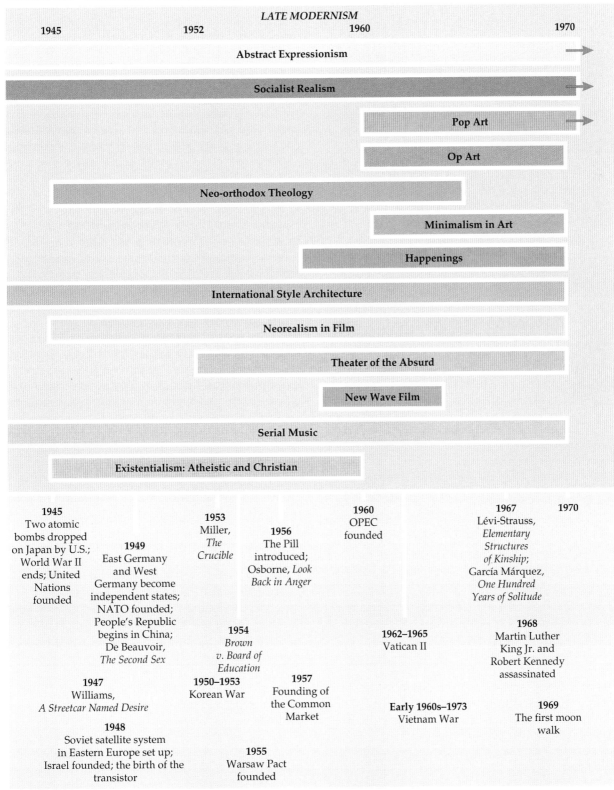

LATE MODERNISM

| 1945 | 1952 | 1960 | 1970 |

Abstract Expressionism

Socialist Realism

Pop Art

Op Art

Neo-orthodox Theology

Minimalism in Art

Happenings

International Style Architecture

Neorealism in Film

Theater of the Absurd

New Wave Film

Serial Music

Existentialism: Atheistic and Christian

1945
Two atomic bombs dropped on Japan by U.S.; World War II ends; United Nations founded

1947
Williams, *A Streetcar Named Desire*

1948
Soviet satellite system in Eastern Europe set up; Israel founded; the birth of the transistor

1949
East Germany and West Germany become independent states; NATO founded; People's Republic begins in China; De Beauvoir, *The Second Sex*

1953
Miller, *The Crucible*

1954
Brown v. Board of Education

1950–1953
Korean War

1955
Warsaw Pact founded

1956
The Pill introduced; Osborne, *Look Back in Anger*

1957
Founding of the Common Market

1960
OPEC founded

1962–1965
Vatican II

Early 1960s–1973
Vietnam War

1967
Lévi-Strauss, *Elementary Structures of Kinship*; García Márquez, *One Hundred Years of Solitude*

1968
Martin Luther King Jr. and Robert Kennedy assassinated

1969
The first moon walk

1970

rope. After World War II, Soviet troops occupied neighboring countries in Eastern Europe, ostensibly to provide a military shield for the USSR. By 1948 the Soviets had converted these countries into communist satellites, their industrial and agricultural systems tied to the Soviet economy. Thus, the USSR loomed more as a menace to than an ally of Western Europe.

The architect of the Soviet Union's rise to superpower status was Joseph Stalin, who was determined to keep the collectivist system free of the taint of

Figure 21.2 ANDY WARHOL. *Mao.* 1973. Acrylic and silk-screen on canvas, 14′6⅞″ × 11′4½″. Art Institute of Chicago. Mr. and Mrs. Frank G. Logan Purchase Prize and Wilson L. Mead Funds. *A feature of totalitarian societies in the twentieth century was the personality cult, the practice of giving a political leader heroic dimensions, thus making the leader the personification of the state. In Communist China, the cult of Mao Zedong established Mao as a secular god. American Pop artist Andy Warhol turned Mao's official photograph into a pop culture icon, suggesting that there was no difference between propaganda in a totalitarian state and media stardom in a free society.*

American domestic life was marked by a radical shift in mood from the 1950s to the 1960s. The 1950s were a decade of complacency and blandness. The 1960s, in contrast, were a turbulent decade around the world, of which the American experience was only a part. In the 1960s, millions of people protested against the Vietnam War, racism, and old ways of thinking. Hippies cultivated a bohemian lifestyle and contributed to the emergence of a counterculture that rejected mainstream values and traditions.

Racial prejudice was the most pressing domestic problem in the United States after World War II because it was so embedded in the nation's history. In 1954 the Supreme Court declared segregation in public schools unconstitutional. The next year, Rosa Parks (1913–2005), a black Alabaman, refused to move to the back of a bus as required by state law and was jailed. The social protest that was sparked by the jailing of Parks marked a watershed in American race relations. Rejecting a historically passive role, black citizens began to use the tactics of civil disobedience in their crusade to win equal rights. Nevertheless, the civil rights movement did not begin on a national scale until the 1960s. After some stalling, the federal government instigated changes in education, living conditions, and voting rights. In 1968 the civil rights struggle temporarily lost direction and momentum when its leader, Martin Luther King Jr., was assassinated, but new leaders arose in America's black community who have continued the struggle against racism.

The Cold War Hope for peace and cooperation among the victorious powers disappeared after 1945 as the USSR and the United States defined their respective spheres of influence. By 1949 an "iron curtain" had descended in Europe, dividing the West from the East (Map 21.1). In 1949 fear of a Soviet invasion led the Western democracies to form a military alliance called the North Atlantic Treaty Organization (NATO) with the United States as its leader. The Eastern bloc countered with the Warsaw Pact (1955), an alliance led by the Soviet Union. A race to stockpile weapons ensued, dividing the industrial world into armed camps. By 1955 a balance of terror seemed to have been reached because both the United States and the USSR possessed the atomic and hydrogen bombs. Nevertheless, the race for more weapons continued.

The East-West contest for power spread to other regions of the world. In 1949 Chinese Communists defeated the ruling Kuomintang party and commenced to build a socialist system under the leadership of Mao Zedong [MAU (D)ZE-DUHNG] (r. 1949–1976) (Figure 21.2). The struggle between the superpowers shifted to the Far East, where a limited war emerged between North and South Korea, which had been divided after

capitalism and the Western idea of freedom. He demanded extreme sacrifices from Soviet citizenry to bring their war-shattered economy up to the level of that of the advanced industrialized countries. After Stalin's death in 1953, his successors were more moderate, but they continued the policies of censorship and repression.

The United States took up the torch of free-world leadership in 1945, claiming to have earned this status because of crucial contributions to Allied victory. It further believed that the war had been a moral crusade for human freedom, and thus it should protect the rights of people everywhere. On the basis of these beliefs, the United States justified an activist foreign policy, and between 1945 and 1970 it was probably the wealthiest and most powerful country that ever existed.

LEARNING THROUGH MAPS

Map 21.1   EUROPE IN 1955
This map shows Europe at the height of the cold war. **Notice** the division of Europe between NATO and the Communist bloc. **Which** countries were not members of either alliance? **Which** countries would most likely be battlegrounds if war occurred between the two power blocs? **Notice** also the division between East Germany and West Germany. **Observe** the westward expansion of the Soviet Union in this map, as compared with the smaller Soviet Union on Map 20.1, Europe After World War I.

World War II into two independent states. In 1950 Soviet-dominated North Korea invaded South Korea to reunite the two states. Alarmed at this expansion of communism, the United States, under the auspices of the United Nations, sent troops in support of the South Koreans. Later in the year, China dispatched its soldiers to aid the North Koreans. After months of fighting, a stalemate resulted along the old borders, which were finally guaranteed in 1953 by an armistice. The Korean War ended in a draw, but it established one of the guiding principles of the nuclear age—that wars would not necessarily escalate into nuclear confrontations; they could be fought with conventional weapons rather than with nuclear arms.

Cold war tensions were heightened—and symbolized—by the Berlin Wall, which was built in 1961 by East Germany to prevent its citizens from going to West Berlin. Conceived as a way to save communism, this armed border only intensified divisions between Western and Eastern Europe (Figure 21.3). But the

severest strain on the superpower system was the Vietnam War, which erupted in the early 1960s. Originating as a civil war, it became a cold war contest when the United States joined South Vietnam to repel the communist troops invading from the north. For American soldiers, the war was doubly difficult to wage because it was fought in unfamiliar jungle terrain against a guerrilla army and because it became so violently unpopular at home. Protests culminated in confrontations at universities in Ohio and Mississippi, leaving six students killed in clashes with public authorities (Figure 21.4).

The Vietnam War was a turning point in world affairs. The United States withdrew from South Vietnam in 1973, thereby allowing its conquest by North Vietnam in 1975. Certain conclusions were quickly drawn from this setback to American might. First, the country's superpower status was cast into doubt, and its leaders became reluctant to exercise military power. Second, the war illustrated a new principle of foreign

Figure 21.3   The Brandenburg Gate. *Over 3.5 million refugees migrated to the West from the German Democratic Republic, or East Germany, between 1945 and 1961. In August 1961, East Germany constructed a wall of concrete and cinder blocks, reinforced with steel girders, and barbed wire strung on top that snaked through the city. From 1961 to 1989, the Berlin Wall symbolized the geopolitical and ideological conflicts between the East and the West. The Brandenburg Gate, in the background, is one of Berlin's historic landmarks.*

relations—namely, that even superpowers could not defeat small states by means of conventional warfare. Taken together, these post–Vietnam era principles suggested that the international influence of the United States was in decline and opened the door to new forms of global cooperation in the 1970s.

Emergence of the Third World   After 1945 Europe's overseas territories began to struggle for freedom and self-government, and by 1964 most of the empires had been replaced by independent countries—a process that has come to be called decolonization. In 1946 the United States let go of a former colony, the Philippines.

In 1947 Great Britain agreed to divide India into a Hindu-dominated state—India—and a separate Muslim state—Pakistan. The Dutch gave up the East Indies, which in 1950 became Indonesia. France tried to retain Indochina but in 1954 was driven out, and the former colony was divided into North and South Vietnam.

In the Middle East, Arab states were freed by France and Britain, who had dominated them since 1919. After 1945 the region was in continual turmoil because its oil was needed by the industrialized states, its geopolitical position in the eastern Mediterranean attracted the superpowers, and Islamic fundamentalism led to militant Arab nationalism. But the founding of Israel

Figure 21.4   The National Guard at Kent State, Ohio. 1970. *This photograph bears a striking resemblance to Goya's* Execution of the Third of May, 1808 *(see Figure 17.19), a painting that protested the killing of Spanish civilians by French soldiers. In the tense days after the Kent State deaths, this photograph served a similar function in American society as many people began to think of the dead students as martyrs to the anti–Vietnam War cause.*

Figure 21.5 Portraits of Queen Elizabeth II and Kwame Nkrumah, Accra, Ghana. *In 1957 the independent Republic of Ghana, in East Africa, was formed. Ghana was the first of Britain's African colonies to be granted independence. In 1961 Queen Elizabeth visited the new nation. Five years later, Nkrumah was overthrown by the army. The huge size of the double portraits suggests that Nkrumah was under the spell of the cult of personality.*

as a Jewish state in 1948, following World War II and the Holocaust, contributed the most to an unstable Middle East. Israel's founding resulted in the expulsion of more than a half million Arabs from Palestine, and the fate of these refugees has contributed to constant conflict in the region. The Israeli-Palestine conflict has served as a rallying cry for Arabs to destabilize and eliminate the state of Israel.

In Africa, nearly all colonies became free, although through often painful and costly transitions. In the 1960s, France concluded a bloody war in Algeria, relinquishing it and most of its other colonies in West Africa. The British withdrew gradually from East Africa, leaving behind bureaucracies that could serve the new states (Figure 21.5). In southern Africa, Rhodesia became Zimbabwe in 1980, achieving independence from Great Britain and gaining black majority rule.

One of the consequences of decolonization and the emergence of the Third World was the so-called North-South divide. Relationships between industrialized countries, which have been generally north of the Equator, and developing Third World countries, many located south of the Equator, became at this time a major issue in international politics. The newly independent but still developing countries quickly found themselves at a serious economic disadvantage. In 1964 the United Nations held a conference where plans were made to promote international trade to aid developing countries. Some progress was made in narrowing the North-South divide, but since then, over the years, the gap has widened.

Mass Culture In the postwar era, American mass culture began to serve as the common denominator of an emerging world civilization. American mass culture—with its democratic and energetic qualities, sexual content, and commitment to free expression—has attracted people around the globe. Scenes of American life, conveyed through television, movies, and advertising, have mesmerized millions, who imitate these images as far as they are able. The popularity of our clothing, food, and music has influenced behavior even in Eastern Europe, Russia, the Third World, and the Middle East.

The rise of a worldwide mass culture, in its infancy during Late Modernism, produced an insatiable demand for popular entertainment, along with a fascination with celebrities. Of the existing media when the period began, movies were perhaps best positioned to address this demand. American movies made many actors iconic presences around the world, for example, Marilyn Monroe (1926–1962) (see Figure 21.16). New forms of amusements, such as watching television, carrying transistor radios, listening to record albums, and attending rock concerts grew with the birth of new media. Contributing to this push for new types of entertainment was the abrupt shift in musical taste that occurred in the 1950s (see Encounter).

THE END OF MODERNISM

In 1947 the British-American author W. H. Auden published a poem entitled "The Age of Anxiety," which expressed the melancholy spirit of his times. He described a period caught between a frantic quest for certainty and a recognition of the futility of that search. Responding to the unparalleled violence of World War

II, Auden's anxious age was haunted by death and destruction, fueled by memories of the Holocaust in Europe and the two atomic bombs dropped on Japan. While relations between the Soviet Union and the United States deteriorated and World War III seemed inevitable, melancholy could and often did turn into despair. In this gloomy setting, Modernism entered its final phase.

Late Modernism, flourishing from 1945 until 1970, expressed the vision of a group of artists, writers, and thinkers who seemed almost overwhelmed by this despairing age. Existentialism—with its advice to forget the past and the future and to live passionately for the present—appeared to be the only philosophy that made sense. Paradoxically, diminished faith in humanity kept the Modernists at their creative tasks and prevented them from falling into hopeless silence.

Like earlier Modernists, Late Modernists thought of themselves as an elite. They were committed to saving what they considered worth saving in Western culture while destroying all in the past that was irrelevant, ignoring mass culture, and borrowing insights from depth psychology and non-Western sources. Armed with a sense of mission, they stripped their works down to the most basic components, abandoning strict rationality and making randomness the rule. They threw subject matter out the window and pressed experimentation to the extreme, reducing painting to lines and colors, sculpture to textures and shapes, and music to random collections of sound. Like earlier Modernists, they then invested these works with spiritual or metaphysical meaning by claiming that abstract paintings and sculptures were meditation devices and that music that mixed noise and harmony echoed the natural world.

Philosophy and Religion

Existentialism, born between the two world wars, dominated Western thought in the immediate postwar period. Two French writers, Jean-Paul Sartre and Albert Camus, were the chief voices of atheistic existentialism, though they expressed their ideas best through their novels and plays (see the section "The Literature of Late Modernism"). Theistic, or god-based, existentialism, also flourished, as a part of the religious thought of the times.

Postwar religious thought was dominated by **Neo-orthodoxy,** which had been founded by the Swiss Protestant thinker Karl Barth (1886–1968) in the aftermath of World War I. Claiming God was beyond human reason, Barth urged a return to traditional, or orthodox, Christian beliefs, such as original sin, the Trinity, the Resurrection, and even the Virgin

Birth, and rejected the more human-centered religion of liberal Protestantism, with its reliance on reason, which had been in ascendance since the late 1800s (see Chapter 19). Barth especially stressed the gulf between "wholly other" God and lowly humanity, a gulf only God could bridge—thus reviving the *via antiqua,* a Late Medieval theological position, which argued for the separation of reason and faith (see Chapter 10).

After 1945 and following Barth's lead, Neo-orthodoxy prospered in Western religious circles, especially in the writings of the German-born American Protestant Paul Tillich [TIL-ik] (1886–1965). Tillich's theology was forged in the crucible of twentieth-century calamities: His liberal Christian faith was shattered during World War I, while he served as a chaplain in the German army, and he fled Germany to the United States in 1933, after the Nazis barred him from university teaching—the first non-Jew to be purged. Once in the United States, he taught at prestigious divinity schools and eventually completed *Systematic Theology* (1951–1963), a three-volume work that explores linkages between culture and Christianity.

At the heart of Tillich's thought is his notion of God. He begins where the German proto-existentialist Nietzsche ends, with the "death of God" (see Chapter 19). For Tillich, though, the God who has died is the "personal" deity of liberal Christianity—an idea that leads some critics to accuse him of agnosticism or atheism. But Tillich insists that the authentic God exists: This infinite being is the "God behind God," the "ground of all being"—that is, the source for all existence and meaning in life.

Tillich thought of himself as a "boundary man," who stood on the threshold of two eras, when one way of life was dying and a new one was being born—an outlook that for many religious seekers seemed to sum up the Age of Anxiety. Catholics, Protestants, and existentialists, both atheistic and Christian, eagerly read his difficult works. Atheistic existentialists, while denying God's existence, nevertheless accepted Tillich's description of the human condition as hopeless without God. Christian existentialists fully accepted his description of the gulf separating humans from the "God behind God" and made a "leap of faith" to embrace the full panoply of orthodox Christian beliefs. "Leap of faith" was a phrase coined by the Danish thinker Søren Kierkegaard (1813–1855), whose works, despite being more than a century old, thrived in translation during Late Modernism—because of the popularity of Christian existentialism.

Two other major postwar religious thinkers, whose works attracted a wide-ranging audience, were the French Jesuit Teilhard de Chardin [tah-yahr duh shahr-dan] (1881–1955) and the German-Jewish religious philosopher Martin Buber (1878–1965). Teilhard, a geologist and paleontologist, blended science and religion in his philosophical writings, such as *The Phenomenon of Man* (1955), to set forth a Christianized view of evolution. For Teilhard, history is an evolutionary process with moral advances occurring at certain stages, such as the moment of Jesus' Incarnation, and the entire process is moving toward spiritual wholeness, when Jesus will return to earth—the Second Coming—to inaugurate the last stage of human redemption. Teilhard's most significant works were published after his death, because of their potential for controversy. In 1962, the Vatican warned believers against uncritical acceptance of his ideas.

Martin Buber was a commanding figure in the new state of Israel, having fled from Nazi Germany in 1938. Previously in Germany, he and Franz Rosenzweig (1886–1929) had translated the Hebrew Bible into German (1926–1937). Shortly after arriving in Jerusalem, Buber was appointed professor of social philosophy at Hebrew University, and later he was made the first president of the Israeli Academy of Sciences and Art. He also founded and became head of a college for training adult teachers. His best-known work, *I and Thou*, though first published in 1923, was among the Late Modern period's top religious best-sellers. In this work, using poetic language, Buber described the universe as comprising a three-tiered moral hierarchy: God, the Eternal Thou; the human, the I; and the rest of the world, the It—with the Eternal Thou making possible all human relationships. The ideal relation is that of I-Thou, between a human and God, a tie characterized by openness, mutuality, directness, and trust. He urged that all human-to-human relations be of the I-Thou type, to the fullest extent possible. The most problematic relation is that of I-It. A necessary evil when practiced between humans and the animal, plant, and natural worlds, the I-It relationship becomes morally wrong when used between humans, as it turns other people into objects for our use.

One remarkable milestone, with wide-ranging implications for religious culture, occurred under Late Modernism: reform of the Roman Catholic Church, initiated by Pope John XXIII (pope 1958–1963) and carried out by the Second Vatican Council (1962–1965), better known as Vatican II. Vatican II made dramatic changes within the church and the Catholic community, such as introducing vernacular language into the Mass, abolishing various dietary restrictions, and allowing greater lay participation in religious services. Even more dramatic changes were made in the church's views toward nonmembers: Eastern Orthodox and Protestant Christians were now no longer termed heretics but were regarded as brothers and sisters in Christ; friendly overtures were made to the

Jews along with expressions of regret for the anti-Semitism of the past; other world religions were addressed with praise for their spiritual quests; and peoples, everywhere, were assured of the church's repudiation of coercion in matters of faith. With its reforms, Vatican II became the most significant church council since the Council of Trent in the sixteenth century (see Chapter 13).

Political and Social Movements

In the 1960s, political and social movements, notably structuralism, feminism, and black consciousness, eclipsed existentialism. Unlike existentialism, with its focus on freedom and choice, **structuralism** affirms the universality of the human mind in all places and times; thus, human freedom is limited. Structuralists maintain that innate mental patterns cause human beings to interact with nature and one another in consistent and recurring ways, regardless of the historical period or the social setting. It follows that civilization (as represented in governments, social relations, and language, for example) and ideas (such as freedom, health, and beauty) arise from deep-seated modes of thought instead of from the environment or progressive enlightenment. Structuralists reason that not only is all knowledge conditioned by the mind but also civilization itself reflects the mind's inborn nature. By defining and analyzing the substrata of culture, they attempt to garner some understanding of the elemental nature of the human mind.

The two leading structuralists are Noam Chomsky [CHAHM-skee] (b. 1928), an American linguist, and Claude Lévi-Strauss [lay-vee-STRAUS] (b. 1908), a French anthropologist. Chomsky's *Syntactic Structures* (1957) prompted a revolution in linguistics, the scientific study of languages. He argues that below the surface form of sentences (that is, the grammar) lies a deeper linguistic structure that is intuitively grasped by the mind and is common to all languages. Similarly, Lévi-Strauss made war on empirical thinking with his 1967 study, *The Elementary Structures of Kinship*. He claimed that beneath the varied relations among clans in different societies exist certain kinship archetypes with such common themes as the incest taboo and marriage patterns. Chomsky and Lévi-Strauss imply the existence of common universal structures running through all minds and all societies that can be expressed as a general code. This conclusion gives a strong psychoanalytic cast to structuralist thought, because it leads researchers to focus on the subconscious mind.

Following Chomsky and Lévi-Strauss, other scholars have studied subsurface patterns in such disciplines as history, child development, and literature. No thinker has yet unified the various structuralisms into a coherent theory of mind. It is an intriguing coincidence, however, that the trend of thought that points to a universally shared mind-set parallels the rise of a global culture under Post-Modernism.

The revival of feminist thought has been another significant development in philosophy since World War II. The French thinker and novelist Simone de Beauvoir [duh boh-VWAHR] (1908–1986) sparked this revival, following the dry spell that set in after many Western women won the right to vote in the 1920s. In her 1949 treatise, *The Second Sex*, de Beauvoir argued that women are treated by men as "the Other," an anthropological term meaning a person or group accorded a different and lower existence. Drawing on personal anecdote and existentialist thought, she advised women who want independence to avoid marriage and, like men, create their own immortality (Figure 21.6).

De Beauvoir's message was heard around the world, but it was especially in the United States that women heeded her. America's best-known feminist in the 1960s was Betty Friedan (1921–2006). She awakened the dormant women's movement with *The Feminine Mystique* (1963), arguing that society conspired to idealize women and thus discourage them from competing with men. In 1966 she founded the National Organization for Women (NOW), a pressure group that has attracted millions of members. According to its founding manifesto, NOW supports women's "equal partnership with men" and is committed to "integrating women into the power, privileges, and responsibilities of the public arena." Friedan did not always agree with the more radical feminists of the 1970s, and in 1982 she showed that she was still a moderate in *The Second Stage*, a book that advocated men's liberation as a condition for women's equality.

Like feminism, the black consciousness movement has grown and flourished since 1945 (Figure 21.7). The earliest significant theorist of black identity was Frantz Fanon [fah-NOHN] (1925–1961), a psychiatrist from French Martinique who practiced medicine among the Arabs of Algeria. An eyewitness to French colonialism and oppression, Fanon became convinced that the West had doomed itself by abandoning its own moral ideals. By the late 1950s, Fanon had begun to justify black revolution against white society on the basis of existential choice and Marxism. In 1961, in *The Wretched of the Earth*, he issued an angry call to arms, urging nonwhites to build a separate culture. Some black leaders in America welcomed Fanon's message in the 1960s, as did Third World thinkers who turned their backs on Western ideologies in the 1970s.

America in the 1960s produced a radical black voice in Malcolm X (1925–1965), the pseudonym of Malcolm Little. A fiery personality, he made sharp ideological shifts, moving from advocacy of black separatism to a call for an interracial civil war and, after his conversion to orthodox Islam, to support of racial harmony. Assassinated allegedly by former colleagues, he remains today a prophetic voice for many African Americans who want a clearer sense of their history, culture, and accomplishments in a predominantly white society.

In the turbulent 1960s, Malcolm X's voice was overpowered by that of Martin Luther King Jr. (1929–1968), a visionary who dreamed of a world free from racial discord. Probably the most famous black figure in Western history, King was an advocate of civil disobedience—based on Christian teachings, the writings of the New England philosopher and abolitionist Henry David Thoreau, and the example of India's liberator, Gandhi. An inspirational leader and a superb orator, King galvanized blacks, along with many whites, into the Southern Christian Leadership Conference, organized by ministers to end segregation in American life, notably in schools and universities. Though King was assassinated before his dream was fully realized, his vision of an integrated society lives on, but the movement has taken many directions.

Science and Technology

Although important theories were developed in biology and physics during the postwar period, the spectacular advances in applied science affected people more directly and immediately. From the late 1940s through the 1960s, the life and manners of populations around the world were irretrievably altered by the inventions coming out of laboratories and research centers and by the scientific by-products of the cold war. The origin of many of these discoveries and inventions dates from World War II, when there were scientific breakthroughs induced by war, among them, radar, the jet engine, rockets, and the atomic bomb.

One of the first inventions in the postwar era was the transistor, a semiconductor for controlling electronic impulses. Unveiled in 1948, the transistor quickly began to replace the vacuum tube, which had previously been proven unreliable in the fast-growing telephone industry. The transistor soon had other commercial uses, such as in hearing aids and small, or pocket, radios. In the 1960s, mass-produced transistor radios were manufactured by Japanese companies, successfully launching the information age—marked by miniaturization and mobility.

Figure 21.6   JUDY CHICAGO. *The Dinner Party.* 1979. Installation view. Multimedia, china painting on porcelain, needlework, 48 × 48 × 48' installed. © Judy Chicago. *The rebirth of feminism led some women artists to adopt explicit feminist themes in their art, as in the works of Judy Chicago (born Gerowitz, 1939). Chicago abandoned Abstract Expressionism in the late 1960s, at about the same time she changed her name, thereafter devoting her art to the feminist cause.* The Dinner Party, *her most ambitious project to date, is dedicated to leading historical and mythological women of Western civilization. In this work, she arranges a triangular-shaped dining table with thirty-nine places decorated in individual styles, honoring such famous women as Sappho and Sojourner Truth (inset; see also Chapter 18).*

Figure 21.7 ROMARE BEARDEN. *The Prevalence of Ritual: Baptism.* 1964. Collage on board,
9 × 12″. The Hirshhorn Museum and Sculpture Garden, Smithsonian Institution, Washington, D.C. © Romare Bearden Foundation/Licensed by VAGA, New York, NY. *Romare
Bearden (1914–1988), the United States' most honored post–World War II black painter, blended
Modernism with elements from his cultural heritage. In the 1960s, he developed a style reminiscent of Cubism that used collage and flattened, angular figures and that drew on his personal experiences, as in this collage of a baptismal scene—an allusion to the important role of churches in
the black American tradition. Bearden places the person to be baptized in the center of the composition, a large hand over his head. The references to African masks suggest that this ritual unites
an ancient way of life with the present.*

During World War II, atomic scientists believed that atomic energy could be harnessed for peaceful purposes. Some of these scientists helped build a nuclear reactor plant in Idaho that, in 1951, successfully generated electricity. In the 1950s, the first commercial nuclear power stations started operations to generate electrical power. By 1970, forty-two plants were producing about 4.5 percent of the electricity used in the United States. Meanwhile, other nations began their own nuclear power programs. For many countries, nuclear power seemed to be the most promising alternative to fossil fuels and the answer to the growing need for new sources of energy.

The rivalry between the United States and the Soviet Union also manifested itself in science and technology. In 1957 the Soviets took a dramatic leap in the "space race" by launching the first globe-circling satellite, *Sputnik.* Four years later, in 1961, the Soviet Union sent the cosmonaut Yury Gagarin (1934–1968) around the earth. Shocked by the Soviet lead, the United States sent its first satellite into space in 1958 and put John Glenn (b. 1921) into orbit in 1962. President John Kennedy (in office 1961–1963), determined to win the contest, promised that the United States would have a man on the moon before the end of the sixties. In July 1969, two astronauts walked on the surface of the moon (see Slice of Life). Making the "space race" possible were advancements in telecommunications, rocketry, and the miniaturization of controlling and guidance systems.

SLICE OF LIFE
Humans in Space: "One Giant Leap for Mankind"

NEIL ARMSTRONG AND EDWIN E. ALDRIN
Recollections of the Moon Landing and Transmittals of the Astronauts' Voices

The intersecting of science, technology, and the human spirit was played out before a worldwide audience in July 1969 when the American astronauts Neil Armstrong (b. 1930) and Edwin E. Aldrin (b. 1930) walked on the moon. The event transcended cold war politics, as earthlings realized that Armstrong's first steps on the moon were monumental: They ushered in a new age. As Armstrong said, "That's one small step for man, one giant leap for mankind." And, with this, opportunities opened and fears were raised about the future of the planet and space travel.

NEIL ARMSTRONG: The most dramatic recollections I had were the sights themselves. Of all the spectacular views we had, the most impressive to me was on the way to the Moon, when we flew through its shadow. We were still thousands of miles away, but close enough, so that the Moon almost filled our circular window. It was eclipsing the Sun, from our position, and the corona of the Sun was visible around the limb of the Moon as a gigantic lens-shaped or saucer-shaped light, stretching out to several lunar diameters. It was magnificent, but the Moon was even more so. We were in its shadow, so there was no part of it illuminated by the Sun. It was illuminated only by earthshine. It made the Moon appear blue-grey, and the entire scene looked decidedly three-dimensional. . . .

[*After touchdown*] The sky is black, you know. It's a very dark sky. But it still seemed more like daylight than darkness as we looked out the window. It's a peculiar thing, but the surface looked very warm and inviting. It was the sort of situation in which you felt like going out there in nothing but a swimming suit to get a little sun. From the cockpit, the surface seemed to be tan. It's hard to account for that, because later when I held this material in my hand, it wasn't tan at all. It was black, grey and so on. It's some kind of lighting effect, but out the window the surface looks much more like light desert sand than black sand. . . .

EDWIN E. ALDRIN [*On the moon*]: The blue color of my boot has completely disappeared now into this—still don't know exactly what color to describe this other than grayish-cocoa color. It appears to be covering most of the lighter part of my boot . . . very fine particles. . . .

[*Later*] The Moon was a very natural and pleasant environment in which to work. It had many of the advantages of zero gravity, but it was in a sense less *lonesome* than Zero G, where you always have to pay attention to securing attachment points to give you some means of leverage. In one-sixth gravity, on the Moon, you had a distinct feeling of being *somewhere*. . . . As we deployed out experiments on the surface we had to jettison things like lanyards, retaining fasteners, etc., and some of these we tossed away. The objects would go away with a slow, lazy motion. If anyone tried to throw a baseball back and forth in that atmosphere he would have difficulty, at first, acclimatizing himself to that slow, lazy trajectory; but I believe he could adapt to it quite readily. . . .

Odor is very subjective, but to me there was a distinct smell to the lunar material—pungent, like gunpowder or spent cap-pistol caps. We carted a fair amount of lunar dust back inside the vehicle with us, either on our suits and boots or on the conveyor system we used to get boxes and equipment back inside. We did notice the odor right way.

Interpreting This Slice of Life **How** does Neil Armstrong describe the sights as they approach the moon? **What** are some of the advantages and disadvantages of being on the moon? In **what** ways did these landings and subsequent trips to the moon affect our society? **What** are the implications in humans taking future trips to the moon and beyond? **Explain.**

Medicine

Breakthroughs in medicine changed the patterns of behavior and raised the living standards for millions of people everywhere. While most discoveries saved lives, some had social and moral implications that spilled over into societal and gender issues, which were beginning to surface in the United States and around the world.

The invention of a safe birth control pill in 1956 triggered a sexual revolution, which, by the late 1960s, was part of the social unrest and rejection of many accepted moral codes and personal behavior patterns for many Americans. This newly found sexual freedom, popular in the 1960s and 1970s, grew more restricted in the 1980s with the advent of AIDS (see Chapter 22).

Other developments in medicine benefited the public without generating social and moral debates. In the

1950s, polio was eradicated through vaccines developed by the American physicians Jonas Salk (1914–1995) and Albert Sabin (1906–1993). Innovative surgical methods, radiation treatment, and chemotherapy drastically reduced cancer mortality. In the biological sciences, in 1953, Francis Crick (1916–2004) and James Watson (b. 1928) reported their discovery of the structure of DNA (deoxyribonucleic acid), the chemical substance ultimately responsible for determining individual hereditary characteristics. The implications of this discovery would not be fully understood until later (see Chapter 22).

The Literature of Late Modernism: Fiction, Poetry, and Drama

Despite Late Modernism's prevailing mood of despair, this period produced a veritable cacophony of voices in fiction, poetry, and drama. After World War II, literary culture flourished along the New York–London–Paris axis, though voices from beyond that axis occasionally were able to break through and be heard. African American writers continued to make their presence felt on the international stage. The avant-garde was still very much alive, as writers pushed the boundaries of literary art. There also emerged new schools of writing and theater, based on rival theories, seeking to connect with audiences. The names of many of these writers have become household names, and their works today are lauded as classics. In retrospect, this period was a golden age of literature.

Fiction   France's leading postwar thinkers, Jean-Paul Sartre and Albert Camus, were among Late Modernism's outstanding voices. In a trio of novels called *Roads to Freedom*, published between 1945 and 1950, Sartre interwove Marxist collectivist beliefs with existentialism's focus on the individual. Although accepting the existentialist view that life is cruel and must be confronted, he portrayed his characters as cooperating for a new and better world, presumably one in which they would be able to live in harmony. Sartre also wrote a series of plays on current issues that are infrequently performed today. His most successful drama, and perhaps his most enduring literary work, was *No Exit* (1944), which shows how three characters turn their lives into living hells because of their unfortunate choices in desperate situations.

Like Sartre, the Algerian-born writer and thinker Albert Camus [kah-MOO] (1913–1960) wrote novels, plays, and philosophical works that mirrored his political thinking and personal values. His finest literary work was *The Fall* (1956), a novel published at the height of his reputation as one of the West's main moral voices. In 1957 he was awarded the Nobel Prize in Literature, an honor that Sartre declined in 1964. Written as a single rambling monologue, *The Fall* portrays an anguished, self-doubting central character who accuses himself of moral fraud. When admirers recognized Camus himself in the narrator's voice, they were shocked because they were unwilling to accept this harsh self-judgment. Whether this self-mocking confession heralded Camus's move toward God—as some critics have maintained—can never be known, for an auto accident prematurely ended his life.

Existentialism's rejection of bourgeois values and its affirmation of identity through action appealed to black writers in the United States. As outsiders in a white-dominated society, these writers identified with the French thinkers' call to rebellion. The first black author to adopt an existential perspective was Richard Wright (1908–1960), whose outlook was shaped by his birth on a Mississippi plantation. His works, such as his novel *Native Son* (1940) and his autobiography, *Black Boy* (1945), were filled with too much rage at racism to be accepted by white literary critics in the 1940s. His later years were spent in Paris, where he further developed his interest in existentialism.

The most successful black American author of this time was James Baldwin (1924–1987), who began to write during a self-imposed exile in France (1948–1957), where he had fled from racial discrimination. In a series of novels and essays, he explored the consequences of growing up black in a predominantly white world. In his first novel, *Go Tell It on the Mountain* (1953), he drew on his Christian beliefs to mute his anger against the injustices that he believed blacks daily endured. This novel, which held out hope for an integrated society, established the literary theme that he pursued until Martin Luther King Jr.'s assassination caused his vision to darken. In later novels, such as *No Name in the Street* (1972), he regretfully accepted violence as the only path to racial justice for black Americans.

In postwar fiction, existentialism sometimes took second place to a realistic literary style that concentrated on exposing society's failings. Three major writers who blended existential despair with Realism's moral outrage were Norman Mailer (b. 1923), Doris Lessing (b. 1919), and Alexander Solzhenitsyn [sol-zhuh-NEET-suhn] (b. 1918). Their goal was to uncover the hypocrisy of their age.

Mailer, an American, drew on his experience as a soldier in World War II to capture the horror of modern war in his first and finest novel, *The Naked and the Dead* (1948). This work portrays a handful of enlisted men, a microcosm of America, as victims of their leaders' bad choices. He describes their officers as pursuing fantasies of glory, inspired by a notion that the world is godless and without lasting values. In the late

1960s, Mailer began to write as a journalist, eventually achieving so much fame that today his essays overshadow his novels. His best journalism is the book-length essay *The Armies of the Night* (1968), an account of the October 1967 peace march on Washington, D.C., in which he participated. This book won Mailer a Pulitzer Prize.

Lessing, a white eastern African writer, used Realism to show the contradictions at work in her homeland, Rhodesia (modern Zimbabwe), between blacks and whites, British and Dutch, British and colonials, capitalists and Marxists, and, always, women and men. In the *Children of Violence* series (1950–1969), consisting of five novels, she presents the story of the rise of black freedom fighters and the diminishing of white control in what was then a British colony. This disintegrating world serves as a backdrop to the existential struggle for self-knowledge and independence by the main character, Martha Quest. In her best-known novel, *The Golden Notebook* (1962), Lessing addresses, among other issues, the socialization process that stifles women's creativity. Her concerns, however, are not just female identity but also the moral and intellectual fragmentation and confusion she sees in the modern world. In recent years, she has turned to science fiction to address these issues.

The Russian Solzhenitsyn writes realistic novels that praise the Russian people while damning Marxism, which he regards as a "Western heresy," opposed to Orthodox Christianity. His short novel *One Day in the Life of Ivan Denisovich* (1962) reflects his own rage at being unjustly imprisoned under Stalin. This novel, published during Nikita Khrushchev's (in office 1958–1964) de-Stalinization drive, offers an indelible image of the tedium, harassment, and cruelty of life in a forced-labor camp. And yet Ivan Denisovich remains a Soviet John Doe, dedicated to Marxism, his work, and his comrades (Figure 21.8).

When Solzhenitsyn's later books, which were banned in the Soviet Union until its fading years, revealed his hatred for communism, he was deported, in 1974. Choosing exile in the United States, he settled in a Vermont hideaway from which he expressed moral disgust with the West for its atheistic materialism and softness toward the Soviet system. His values—Christian fundamentalism and Slavophilism, or advocacy of Russia's cultural supremacy—resemble those of Russia's great nineteenth-century preexistentialist novelist Dostoevsky. Believing that communism was finally dead, Solzhenitsyn returned to his homeland in 1994, but he has not become a moral force in post-Soviet Russia.

Poetry Many Late Modernist poets used a private language to such a degree that their verses were often unintelligible to ordinary people and thus did not have a wide audience. A few who used more conventional verse styles, however, earned a large readership. Of this latter group, the Welsh poet Dylan Thomas (1914–1953) was the most famous and remains so today. Thomas's poems mirror the obscurity favored by the Modernist critics, but what makes his works so memorable is their glorious sound. With their strong emotional content, jaunty rhythms, and melodious words, they are perfect to read aloud.

Better known than Thomas's poems, though, is his verse play *Under Milk Wood* (1954), arguably the best-loved poetic work of Late Modernism. Unlike the poems, this verse play is direct and imbued with simple emotions. Originally a play for radio, it presents a typical day in a Welsh village, a world Thomas knew well, having grown up in such a place. His portrait of the colorful speech and intertwined lives of the eccentric villagers has moved millions of listeners, evoking for them bittersweet memories of their own youth.

A Late Modernist poet who was able to be experimental and yet win a large audience was the American writer Allen Ginsberg (1926–1997), the most significant poet produced by the **Beat Generation** of the 1950s. Like Dylan Thomas, he had an ear for colloquial speech, and his ability to construct new forms to convey iconoclastic views was unequaled by any other poet of his time. His most famous poem is "Howl" (1956), a work of homage to rebel youth and illicit drugs and sex. Overcoming censorship, this poem of Ginsberg's opposed capitalist, heterosexual, bourgeois society and became the anthem of the Beat Generation.

Drama Late Modern drama spawned multiple trends. There were experimental plays, filled with theatrical innovations and philosophic allusions: "social problem" plays, written in the naturalistic tradition of Ibsen and Shaw; Realist-style plays, dealing with class conflict; and lyrical plays, driven by poetic language and rich characterization.

During Late Modernism, the most radical changes in literature took place in drama. Sharing existentialism's bleak vision and determined to find new ways to express that outlook, a group of dramatists called the **Theater of the Absurd** emerged. The absurdists shifted the focus of their plays away from the study of the characters' psychology to stress poetic language and abandoned realistic plots to concentrate on outrageous situations. A typical absurdist play mixed tragedy with comedy, as if the playwright thought that the pain of existence could be tolerated only if blended with humor.

Samuel Beckett (1906–1989), an Irish writer who lived in Paris, was the best-known dramatist of absurdist theater. His *Waiting for Godot* (1952) is a play in

Figure 21.8 VITALY KOMAR AND ALEKSANDER MELAMID. *Stroke (About March 3, 1953).* 1982–1983. Oil on canvas, 6′ × 3′11″. Collection of Evander D. Schley. Courtesy Ronald Feldman Fine Arts, New York. Photo credit: D. James Dee. *The two Russian émigré painters Komar and Melamid—who work as a team—painted this work,* Stroke, *soon after arriving in the United States. In it, they depict the lonely death of Stalin and the discovery of his body by a member of his inner circle. The artists subtly criticize both Stalin and the Soviet system in the way the official stares unmoved at the dead tyrant. Komar and Melamid show their Post-Modernist tendencies in their use of elements from earlier styles of art, such as the theatrical lighting and unusual perspective typical of Caravaggio (see Chapter 14).*

which almost nothing "happens" in the conventional sense of that word. Combining elements of tragedy and farce, *Waiting for Godot* broke new ground with its repetitive structure (the second act is almost a replica of the first), its lack of scenery (the stage is bare except for a single tree), and its meager action (the characters engage in futile exchanges based on British music hall routines). What plot there is also reinforces the idea of futility, as the characters wait for the mysterious Godot, who never appears.

In later years, Beckett's works explored the dramatic possibilities of silence, as in the one-act drama *Not I*

(1973). In this play, a voice—seen only as a mouth illuminated in a spotlight—tries to, but cannot, stop talking. Beckett's plays portrayed human consciousness as a curse; yet, at the same time, his works affirmed the human spirit's survival in the face of despair.

Another member of the absurdist school was Eugene Ionesco [e-oh-NES-ko] (1909–1994), the Romanian-born French playwright, whose plays were purely absurdist in style and explored themes similar to Beckett's, such as social isolation and the breakdown in language. Rejecting Naturalism, with its focus on ordinary folk struggling to bring order to their everyday lives, Ionesco created a non-naturalistic theater, using surreal methods, bizarre speech patterns, and nonrational modes of thought. So hostile were his plays to the Naturalist style that they have been called anti-plays. After establishing his reputation with a series of short, one-act plays, such as *The Lesson* (1952), he graduated to longer plays and became a leading light of the Theater of the Absurd. Ionesco's most enduring full-length play is *Rhinoceros* (1959), a play with conformity as its theme. In it, people in a small town are being turned into rhinoceroses. At first, this evokes horror—in themselves and in others—but, eventually, as the entire town is transformed, everyone takes delight in their new skins. Ironically, the play ends with the anti-hero, too stupid to become a rhinoceros, glorying in his humanity.

In the late 1950s, when his plays were first performed, England's Harold Pinter (b. 1930) was often grouped with the absurdist playwrights. Soon, however, it became apparent that he belonged to no particular school but, instead, was creating his own style. Today, **Pinteresque** is a term denoting a dramatic style marked by enigmatic plots, underwritten characters, and, especially, the liberal use of silences in the dialogue.

For Pinter, a play often begins with a room, occupied by one or more characters. Dramatic tension is introduced by the arrival of a stranger, who throws all into confusion, upsetting routines and calling relationships into question, as seen, for example, in *The Homecoming* (1965), perhaps Pinter's best-known play. In this play, a professor brings his wife home to meet his father and two brothers in London. The wife's presence sparks sexual tensions among family members, who compete for her attention. The play ends, surprisingly, with the wife's joining the all-male household and the husband turning a blind eye. In 2005, Pinter was awarded the Nobel Prize for Literature.

In addition to the absurdist playwrights, other significant Late Modernist dramatists included the American Arthur Miller (1915–2005), the British John Osborne (1929–1994), and the American Tennessee Williams (1911–1983).

Arthur Miller was the master of the "social problem" play, a genre that originated with Ibsen in Early Modernism (see Chapter 19). Significantly, Miller adapted Ibsen's 1881 play *Enemy of the People* into English in 1951, because of its strong defense of minority rights. Most of Miller's early works, which established his reputation as an activist playwright, addressed social concerns, including *All My Sons* (1947), about a corrupt factory owner in wartime; *Death of a Salesman* (1951), about false social values; and *The Price* (1968), about a failed relationship between two brothers. So did his masterpiece, *The Crucible* (1953), in which he uses the story of a 1692 witch trial in Salem, Massa-

chusetts, to symbolize the Communist investigation then being undertaken by the Un-American Activities Committee of the U.S. House of Representatives. *The Crucible*, Miller's most-performed play, is almost unique among his works in being set in the past.

John Osborne's fame rests primarily on a single work: the Realist drama *Look Back in Anger* (1956). Filled with working-class rage against the leaders of postwar British society, this play centers on a tormented hero, Jimmy Porter, and two compliant, apron-wearing, middle-class women, who cater to his every mood and whim. Osborne's play was the opening salvo in a movement that was quickly named the **Angry Young Men.** Osborne's scathing words, uttered by Jimmy Porter, seemed to speak for a generation, who lamented their country's failure to maintain its empire and England's place in the sun. *Look Back in Anger* caused a revolution on the British stage, as elitist dramas gave way to plays dealing with class conflict and working-class themes.

The lyrical dramas of Tennessee Williams (born Thomas Lanier Williams) addressed a wholly different set of issues, mainly furtive sex and family secrets—reflecting perhaps his homosexuality—and penned-up violence—a legacy of his upbringing in the Deep South. Adding to the intensity of his plays is the romantic speech of his characters, many of whom are self-deluded. His many masterpieces include *The Glass Menagerie* (1944), about a domineering mother; *A Streetcar Named Desire* (1947), about forbidden sexual desire; *Cat on a Hot Tin Roof* (1955), about sexual frustration; and *The Night of the Iguana* (1961), about a wayward clergyman. Of these, *A Streetcar Named Desire* stands out for its indelible portraits of the fading southern belle Blanche, who uses gentility as both a veil and a weapon, and the crude Stanley, who is impatient with romantic drivel. Both of them are victims, in a way, of a world in transition. By 1965, Williams's most creative period was over, but his lyrical drama made him the poet of Late Modernism.

Late Modernism and the Arts

In the postwar art world, leadership shifted from Paris to New York. The end of Parisian dominance had been predicted since the swift fall of France to the Nazis in 1940, and the economic and military superiority of the United States at the war's end ensured that America's largest city would be the new hub of Western culture. New York's cultural leaders were divided in 1945, however. On one side stood those who wanted to build on the native school of American art, which was realistic and provincial. On the other side was a group ready to take up the mantle of leadership of the West's

Figure 21.9 JACKSON POLLOCK. *Blue Poles.* 1952. Oil, enamel, and aluminum paint, 6'11" × 16'. Collection, Australian National Gallery, Canberra. *This painting is virtually unique among Pollock's drip canvases by having a recognizable image, the eight long, vertical, dark blue "poles." He achieved this effect by first swirling paint onto the canvas and then applying a stick covered in blue pigment onto its surface. His refusal to use traditional methods reflects his belief that rational approaches to art are flawed and his faith that subconscious feelings, when released, reveal hidden truths—an attitude typical of the Abstract Expressionists.*

avant-garde. The chief institutional ally of this latter group, which soon dominated the field, was the Museum of Modern Art (MOMA) in New York City, founded principally by the Rockefeller family in 1929. Ironically, the New York connection was also nurtured in the experimental atmosphere of North Carolina's Black Mountain College (closed in 1956), which proved to be a way station for many avant-garde artists (as well as poets, musicians, and dancers) on the road to success in Manhattan.

In determining the direction of Modern art, the New York artists had to contend with various forces: the domination of painting by Picasso, whose restless experimentation seemed to define art's leading edge; the prevalence of psychological theories that encouraged artists to experiment with spontaneous gestures and to seek insights from primitive peoples and from religious experience; and the cardinal need for constant newness. These forces had all been at work in Modernism since 1900, but as a result of World War II, the Holocaust, and the postwar arms race, the need to dispel illusions was greater and the level of despair higher.

Painting Shortly after 1945, an energetic style of painting came to dominate Late Modernism and still plays a major role: **Abstract Expressionism,** sometimes called **Action Painting.** Like earlier Modernists, the Abstract Expressionists made spiritual claims for their

work, saying their spontaneous methods liberated the human spirit. One of the founders of Abstract Expressionism was the American Jackson Pollock (1912–1956), who launched this style with his "drip paintings," created between 1947 and 1950. Influenced by Jungian therapy to experiment with spontaneous gestures, Pollock nailed his canvases to the floor of his studio and dripped loops of house paint onto them from buckets with holes punched in their bottoms (Figure 21.9). The drip canvases led to a new way of looking at art in terms of randomness, spontaneity, "alloverness," and stress on the actual physical process of painting. Pollock's tendency to move around the canvas during its execution also introduced the idea of the artist interacting with the artwork.

Another founder of Abstract Expressionists was the Dutch-born Willem de Kooning (VIL-uhm duh KOO-ning) (1904–1997). De Kooning studied art and worked as a commercial artist in Holland before coming to the United States as a stowaway in 1926. His earliest art—still lifes and figures—showed the influence of Cubism and Picasso and, later, Surrealism. By 1945 he had created a new style, using male figures and abstract elements. In 1948 he established his reputation with a one-man show of abstract black-and-white paintings, using enamel house paints—a revolutionary gesture. These were followed by more abstract works in which he introduced color. By then, de Kooning was defining himself as an Action Painter.

Figure 21.10 WILLEM DE KOONING. *Woman and Bicycle.* 1953. Oil on canvas, 6′4½″ × 4′1″. Collection. Whitney Museum of American Art, New York. *De Kooning's female, with her bulging eyes, double set of exaggerated teeth, and extended breasts, fills over half the canvas. Her threatening appearance is heightened by the artist's slashing brushstrokes and vivid colors, especially in the flesh tones and dress. Feminist critics have observed that this painting alludes to one of a male's basic fears: large and monstrous women out to conquer and subdue him. Many women see this painting and the series as an insult to their bodies and female identity. Some art critics interpret this painting from a formalist perspective, viewing the image as secondary to the work's meaning and focusing more on de Kooning's handling of paint and use of colors.*

In 1950 de Kooning painted a controversial series on women. These paintings caused a furor, which has not fully subsided today. To other Abstract Expressionists, de Kooning seemed to be breaking ranks with their techniques and imagery, and many critics especially faulted his rendition of the female form and features (Figure 21.10). For the next ten years, the mid-fifties to the mid-sixties, de Kooning moved from painting women to landscapes and back to women again. His return to the female form—which some art critics and feminists read as satirizing women's bodies—generated more controversy.

The first generation of Abstract Expressionists was attracted by the movement's energy, rawness, and seriousness. An outstanding recruit to the new art was Mark Rothko [RAHTH-koh] (1903–1970), a Russian émigré who painted in a style very different from Pollock's. A mystic, Rothko envisioned eliminating pigment and canvas and suspending clouds of shimmering colors in the air. After 1950 he settled for creating huge paintings that focused on no more than two or three fields of color (Figure 21.11).

By the mid-1950s, a new generation of Abstract Expressionists had emerged in New York, the most important of whom were Helen Frankenthaler [FRANK-un-thahl-uhr] (b. 1928), Frank Stella (b. 1936), Jasper Johns (b. 1930), and Robert Rauschenberg [RAU-shun-buhrg] (b. 1925). Following in Pollock's footsteps, Frankenthaler adopted a method of spilling pigment onto canvas from coffee cans. By guiding the paint's flowing

Figure 21.11 MARK ROTHKO. *Ochre and Red on Red.* 1954. Oil on canvas, 7'8⅝" × 5'3¾". The Phillips Collection, Washington, D.C. *In his paintings, Rothko aims to create secular icons for a nonreligious age, a spiritual theory inherited from the Russian Constructivist tradition. Accordingly, he banishes all references to nature from his art and focuses on fields of color floating in space—timeless, universal images.*

Figure 21.12 HELEN FRANKENTHALER. *Jacob's Ladder.* 1957. Oil on unprimed canvas, 9'5⅜" × 5'9⅞" (287.9 × 177.5 cm). The Museum of Modern Art, New York. Gift of Hyman N. Glickstein. Photograph © 1997 Museum of Modern Art, New York. *Frankenthaler's staining method—pouring paint onto a canvas—illustrates the tension between spontaneity and control typical of Abstract Expressionism. On the one hand, this technique leads naturally to surprises because of the unpredictable flow of the paint. On the other hand, the artist exercises control over the process, from choosing the colors and thickness of the paint to manipulating the canvas during the staining. In effect, she becomes both a participant in and the creator of the final work of art.*

into asymmetrical forms, called shaped canvases. These geometric shapes, curves, and intersecting patterns of bright colors established his reputation and made him one of the most popular artists of the late 1960s (Figure 21.13). Unlike many other Late Modernist artists, Stella became an important figure in Post-Modern art (see Chapter 22).

Jasper Johns and Robert Rauschenberg found Abstract Expressionism too constricting and overly serious, however. Although Johns did not abandon Expressionism, he added ordinary objects to his works, as in *Target with Plaster Casts* (1955) (Figure 21.14). In this work, Johns painted a banal image below a row of wooden boxes enclosing molds of body parts. A basic feature of his art is the contrast between the precisely rendered human parts (above) and the painterly target (below). Johns's fascination with such tensions paved the way for the self-contradicting style of Post-Modernism. Similarly, Rauschenberg abandoned pure painting to become an **assemblage** artist, mixing found objects with junk and adding a dash of paint. In *Monogram*, he encircled a stuffed goat with a rubber tire and splashed the goat's head with color, thus turning ready-made objects into an abstract image (Figure 21.15).

Both Johns and Rauschenberg, with their playful attack on serious art, opened the door for the **Pop Art** movement. Rejecting the Modernist belief that spiritual values may be expressed in nonrealistic works, the Pop artists frankly admitted that they had no spiritual, metaphysical, or philosophic purpose—they simply created two-dimensional images. Even though a kind of Pop Art developed in London in the 1950s, it was not until a new generation of New York artists began to explore commercial images in the early 1960s that the movement took off.

The most highly visible Pop artist was Andy Warhol (1927–1987), a former commercial artist who was fascinated by the vulgarity and energy of popular culture. Warhol's deadpan treatment of mass culture

trajectory, she stained the canvas into exquisite, amorphous shapes that, though completely flat, seem to suggest a third dimension (Figure 21.12).

Frank Stella, after graduating from Princeton University, began as an Abstract Expressionist but quickly found the style too confining. While experimenting with various styles, Stella gave birth to a technique called **hard-edge**—a term used to describe the nonpainterly effect created by strips of color separated by precise clear edges. To achieve this, Stella made black paintings patterned at first with white stripes and then later with colored stripes. In the mid-sixties, he enhanced the visual effect of his hard-edged paintings by working with canvases that were fashioned

678

Figure 21.13 FRANK STELLA. *Tahkt-i-Sulayman I.* 1967. Polymer and fluorescent paint on canvas, 10'¼" × 20'2¼". Menil Collection, Houston. *This painting, with its curving lines, is part of Stella's* Protractor Series—*a term based on the drafting instrument, usually shaped as a semicircle. The outlines of the protractor are repeated horizontally and vertically across the canvas and interlace with one another. The warmer variations of reds and pinks are balanced by the cooler shades of blues and greens. Stella's subject is purely abstract, colors and lines only, with no hint of any natural or human forms. The name for this work is inspired by the name of a royal palace in medieval Persia.*

Figure 21.14 JASPER JOHNS. *Target with Plaster Casts.* 1955. Encaustic on canvas with plaster cast objects, 51 × 44 × 3½". Courtesy Leo Castelli Gallery, New York. © Jasper Johns/ Licensed by VAGA, New York, NY. *Johns is a key figure in the transitional generation of painters between the Abstract Expressionists and the Pop artists. He rebelled against the pure abstraction of the older movement, yet he shied away from embracing mass culture images as directly as did the younger school of painters. His* Target with Plaster Casts *is typical of his playful, witty style. In this work, he makes a visual play on words, juxtaposing a bull's-eye with plaster casts of body parts, each of which has been a "target"—that is, a subject for artists to represent throughout history.*

Figure 21.15 ROBERT RAUSCHENBERG. *Monogram*. 1959. Multimedia construction, 4 × 6 × 6′. Moderna Museet, KSK, Stockholm. Art © Robert Rauschenberg/Licensed by VAGA, New York, NY. *In his glorification of junk, Rauschenberg helped to open the door to Post-Modernism. In works such as* Monogram, *he showed that anything, no matter how forlorn, even a stuffed goat and a discarded automobile tire, could be used to make art. Such irreverence reflected a democratic vision in which no object is seen as having greater artistic merit than any other.*

icons became legendary, whether they were Campbell's Soup cans, Coca-Cola bottles, or Marilyn Monroe (Figure 21.16). By treating these icons in series, much in the same way that advertisers blanket the media with multiple images, he conveyed the ideas of repetitiveness, banality, and boredom. An artist who courted fame, Warhol recognized America's obsession with celebrity in his often-quoted line, "In the future everyone will be famous for fifteen minutes."

With the New York School commanding the art world, European artists seemed to disappear into the shadows. One group, however, shared the stage with the New York group for a brief moment in the 1960s: the practitioners of **Op Art.** Embracing the abstract ideal of Abstract Expressionism, Op Art concentrated on abstract, mathematical forms, which were visually stimulating to the eyeball, such as whirling effects, moiré silklike surfaces, or lingering afterimages. Perhaps the best-known Op artist is Bridget Riley (b. 1931), a British painter whose theory of perception owes much to that of Georges Seurat, the founder of Pointillism (see Chapter 19). Riley's Untitled (1964) (Figure 21.17), made during her formative period, is executed in black-and-white, which was typical of her style at the time. The more steadily the viewer studies the image, the greater the vibrating effect on the eye.

Sculpture Among the major sculptors working in the postwar period, the British sculptor Henry Moore (1898–1986) was the only one who did not attempt to translate into sculptural form what was taking place in the world of painting. Moore established his reputation before World War II, in the 1930s, when he was identified with Surrealism and Constructivism (see

Figure 21.16 ANDY WARHOL. *Marilyn Monroe.* 1962. Oil, acrylic, and silkscreen enamel on canvas, 20 × 16″. *Warhol's portrait of Marilyn Monroe, America's most famous postwar sex symbol, was typical of his style, which placed little value on originality. Working from a photograph supplied by her Hollywood studio, he merely used his brushes and paint to exaggerate the image that studio hairdressers and cosmetologists had already created. His commercial approach to portraiture made him the most celebrated society artist of his generation.*

Artist's Proof

To Christopher Parler
Bridget Riley '66

Figure 21.17 BRIDGET RILEY. Untitled. 1964. Screenprint, 20 × 4″. Museum of Modern Art, New York. Abby Aldrich Rockefeller Fund. *Bridget Riley is typical of Op artists in her reliance on prints—a strategy to democratize art by making it available to an extended audience, in contrast to the implied elitism of original oil paintings. Riley also seems to prefer silkscreen printing, a commercial method for reproducing art images, especially those with a so-called hard edge, as in her works.*

Chapter 20). His artistic ideal was guided by the "truth to materials" argument and by the principle of exposing the complete sculptural form. By "truth to materials," Moore meant that he often used a material in its natural state, such as wood or stone. Even some of his bronze castings had a rough texture, an unfinished and unpolished quality that made them seem more natural. Moore, in trying to reveal the complete sculptural form, abandoned the traditional solid mass of a work to create, within his sculpture, "voids, holes, and hollows." Cutting into the solid forms, he hollowed them out to allow interplay between the solid mass and the open areas.

In the 1930s, Moore slowly won over the skeptical public, who had initially rejected his works. During World War II, he continued to sculpt and, at the same time, sketched a series of "shelter drawings," which depicted Londoners huddled in the underground subway stations during the "blitz"—the Nazi bombing of England. His sketches and sculptures enhanced his reputation in the United Kingdom and abroad.

After the war, Moore increasingly worked in bronze, casting huge sculptures to be installed in sculpture gardens, in parks, and in front of public buildings (Figure 21.18). Many of them represented the humanistic tradition and images characteristic of his postwar sculptures—a mother and child, a reclining nude, a fallen warrior, or a family group. By the time of his death, Moore was considered one of the leading sculptors of the postwar period and his monumental works part of the urban landscape amid the era's prosperity and growth.

Abstract Expressionist painting had its equivalent in sculpture in the works of several Americans, notably David Smith (1906–1965); Louise Nevelson (1899–1988),

Figure 21.18   HENRY MOORE. *Reclining Figure.* 1957–1958. Roman travertine, length 16'8". UNESCO Building, Paris. *Moore made the reclining female nude with her "open" body one of his trademarks. The UNESCO figure, with its rough surface, reflects Moore's appreciation for the effect of climate on natural stones and his admiration for ancient sculptures weathered over time. While most of his female figures were cast in bronze, this one is carved in marble.*

a Russian émigré; and Eva Hesse (1936–1970), a German émigrée. David Smith's point of departure, however, differed from that of the painters in that he drew inspiration from the symbols of primitive cultures, as in *Cubi XIX*, a geometric work that, according to the artist, represents an altar with a sacrificial figure (Figure 21.19). If the viewer is unaware of the intended meaning, however, this stainless steel work has the inaccessible look of a Pollock drip canvas. In contrast, the wooden sculptures of Louise Nevelson are not about representation at all but are simple compositions fashioned from old furniture and wooden odds and ends (Figure 21.20). The use of found objects allowed Nevelson to realize the Abstract Expressionist's goal of spontaneous art devoid of reference to the artist's life. Eva Hesse followed Nevelson in opposing representational art, but Hesse's art owed more to **minimalism,** a trend that stripped art to its basics and then worked on that. Hesse ultimately found that goal too simplistic. In her short career, she created a small body of abstract works, filled with wit, irony, and ideas, as in *Hang Up* (1966) (Figure 21.21); the punning title refers to a neurotic condition as well as the means for mounting a picture.

Pop Art was an influence in the sculptures of George Segal (1924–2000) and Claes Oldenburg (b. 1929). Segal's ghostly works are plaster casts of live subjects, such as his dual portrait of Robert and Ethel Scull, leading patrons of the Pop Art movement (Figure 21.22).

Figure 21.19   DAVID SMITH. *Cubi XIX.* 1964. Stainless steel, 9'5⅛" × 21¾" × 20¾". Photo © Tate Gallery / Art Resource, NY. Art © Estate of David Smith / Licensed by VAGA, New York, NY. *Smith's ability as a sculptor of enormous and rather destructive energies shines through in the monumental* Cubi *series, the last artworks he made before his accidental death. A machinist by training, Smith liked to work with industrial metals, welding and bending them into geometric units to meet his expressive needs. His desire to shape mechanical images into expressive forms related him to the Abstract Expressionist movement in painting.*

Segal himself rejected the Pop Art label—pointing out that his sculptures have expressionistic surfaces, like Rodin's works (see Chapter 19)—but his method reduces the body to a cartoon form and thus relates it to popular culture. In contrast, Oldenburg embraced consumer culture while manufacturing sly, humorous reproductions of familiar objects—typewriters, electric fans, toilets, bathtubs, and pay telephones (Figure 21.23). These collapsed sculptures of ordinary objects—made of vinyl or canvas and stuffed with foam rubber or kapok—served as opposite images of the manufactured goods. Oldenburg's humor in depicting American productivity complemented the Pop Art painters who similarly were mocking material, consumer society.

While American sculpture flourished, the controversial German sculptor Joseph Beuys [BOYS] (1921–1986) was shaking up the art establishment at home and developing a theoretically based style, which helped shape the Post-Modernist movement after 1970 (see Chapter 22). Beuys's dramatic impact on sculpture was similar to that of John Cage's influence on Western music.

Beuys's first sculptures, made from animal fat and felt, reflected his miraculous escape during World War II, when he, a pilot in the German air force, was taken from his downed plane by rescuers who thrust his cold body into these substances for protection. His use of unconventional materials echoed artistic choices then being made by members of the Abstract Expressionist school. His greatest notoriety, and the source of his enduring influence, came in the 1960s with his staged performances—reminiscent of "happenings" then under way in New York and a forecast of the performance art of the 1970s (see Chapter 22). Beuys's masterwork, preserved on film, is *How to Explain Pictures to a Dead Hare* (1965). In this staged piece, Beuys, his head smeared with honey, cradled a dead rabbit while wandering through an art gallery and talking about the paintings to the unseeing beast (Figure 21.24). This radical piece of Performance Art clearly reflected Beuys's artistic credo: opposition to the old concept of art as a unique object and support for the dismantling of the dealer-critic-museum system. A political radical whose views harkened back to Early Modernism, he sought to blend artistic freedom with social revolution. Beuys's visionary theatrics led to the revival of German Expressionism—one of the major developments in Western art today (see Chapter 22).

Architecture   In Late Modernist architecture, the Finnish-born Eero Saarinen [E-ro SAAR-uh-nen] (1910–1961) and the German-born Ludwig Mies van der Rohe [mees van duh ROH] (1886–1969) were two of the most influential architects. Both made important,

though quite distinct, contributions after World War II as they experimented with materials and designs.

Eero Saarinen came from a family of architects and sculptors. After graduating from Yale University, he joined, in the late 1930s, his father's architectural firm in Michigan. He followed the International style throughout his career, but, in the last decade of his life, he began to experiment with the style's basic rectilinear format, specifically by introducing eye-catching sculptural forms and designs. Reinforced and prestressed concrete, which had been available for many years (see Chapter 20), provided Saarinen with the materials to bring to fruition his sculptural-based buildings.

Saarinen's approach was to define a structure by its specific purpose, such as an organized sports arena (ice hockey rink) or a building for transportation (airline terminal), and then create a design that would both serve and symbolize the building's function. In the Dulles International Airport, outside Washington, D.C., and the TWA terminal at Kennedy International Airport in New York City (Figure 21.25), Saarinen achieved the sense and symbolism of flight. Two other powerful artistic legacies of Saarinen's creative genius were his 360-foot-high Gateway Arch in St. Louis (completed after his death) and his award-winning furniture designs.

Mies van der Rohe, in comparison with Saarinen, had a greater impact on Late Modernist architecture with his International style buildings in New York and other American cities. The last head of the Bauhaus, Germany's premier design school before World War II, Mies closed its doors in 1933 and moved to the United States in 1938 (see Chapter 20). In the 1950s, he captured the world's attention with a glass skyscraper, New York's Seagram Building (Figure 21.26). Based on the artistic creed "less is more," this building's design is simple, a bronze skeletal frame on which are hung tinted windows—the building's only decorative feature. The implementation of his ideals of simplicity

Figure 21.20   LOUISE NEVELSON. *Sky Cathedral.* 1958. Assemblage: wood construction, painted black, 11'1¼" × 10'1¼" × 1'6" (343.9 × 305.4 × 45.7 cm). Museum of Modern Art, New York. Gift of Mr. and Mrs. Ben Mildwoff. Photograph © 1997 Museum of Modern Art, New York. *Though a Modernist, Nevelson anticipated Post-Modernism by combining genres, as in this freestanding wall that integrates architecture, sculpture, and painting. She divided the wall into a grid, stuffed found objects into the wall's compartments, and painted the finished work black.*

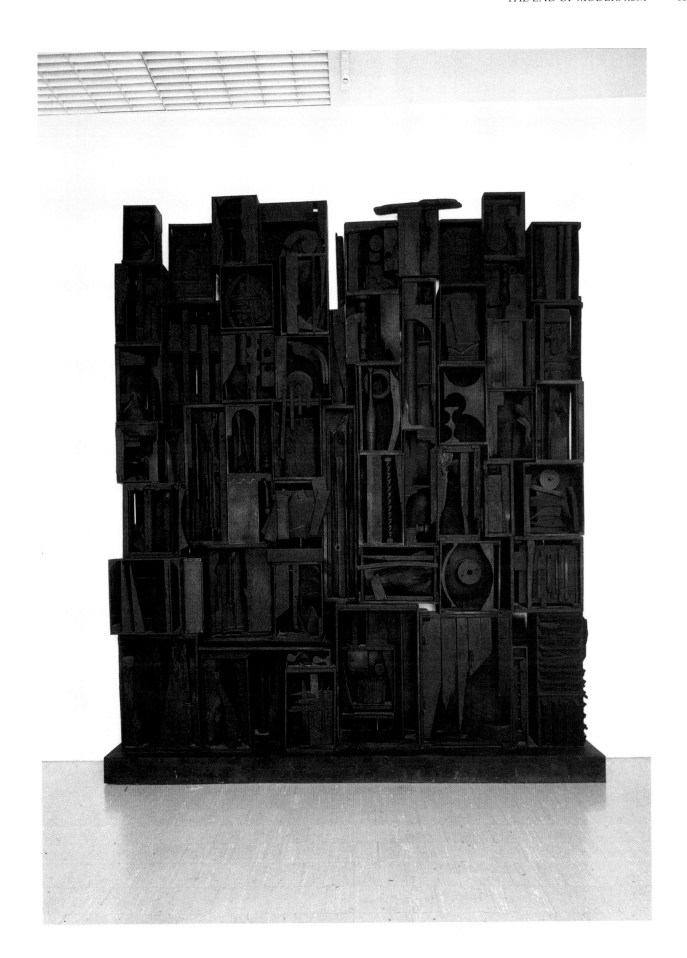

Figure 21.21 EVA HESSE. *Hang Up*. 1966. Acrylic on cord and cloth, wood and steel, 72 × 84 × 78". Through prior gifts of Arthur Keating and Mr. and Mrs. Edward Morris, 1988.130. © Estate of Eva Hesse. The Art Institute of Chicago. *Hesse, in a playful mood, presents only the painting's frame and "hang up" cord, thus forcing the viewer to consider how these objects qualify as art. And if this work is art, then a question arises: What about the rest of the museum's paintings, are their frames and cords art, too? There's also aggressive wit in the thrusting pattern made by the cord as it pushes into the viewing space. Another innovation in this work is the use of acrylic, a manufactured fiber, whose pliability gives the cord its unusual form.*

Figure 21.22 GEORGE SEGAL. *Robert and Ethel Scull*. 1965. Plaster, canvas, wood, and cloth, 8 × 6 × 6'. Private collection. Courtesy Sidney Janis Gallery, New York. Photograph © Geoffrey Clements. Art © George and Helen Segal Foundation/ Licensed by VAGA, New York, NY. *Unlike his fellow Pop artists, Segal looks at the world through existential eyes. Where Warhol glamorized his celebrity subjects, Segal portrays his wealthy patrons, the Sculls, as beset by anxiety. He conveys their boredom and depression through fixed facial expressions and heavy limbs while keeping their appearances generalized. His modeling technique, which requires subjects not to move until the plaster dries, reinforces the melancholy image.*

Figure 21.23 CLAES OLDENBURG. *Soft Pay-Telephone*. 1963. Vinyl, filled with kapok, mounted on a painted wood panel, 46 × 19 × 9". Solomon R. Guggenheim Museum, New York. Gift, Ruth and Philip Zierler, in memory of their dear departed son, William S. Zierler. *Oldenburg claims that his soft forms possess many identities, thus allowing a variety of interpretations. His allusions to the sensual and erotic in the shape and contours of* Soft Pay-Telephone *are evident. The sagging vinyl, filled with material from the kapok tree, presents in a humorous way one of the most used objects in communication in the 1960s, which now is becoming a museum piece itself.*

Figure 21.24 Joseph Beuys in performance. *How to Explain Pictures to a Dead Hare*. Galerie Schmela, Dusseldorf, Germany. 1965. *This photograph of Joseph Beuys holding forth during a performance in 1965 is an iconic image of Late Modernism. More than an artist, Beuys considered himself a shaman, that is, a priest able to communicate with the gods and perform healing rituals—a view that harkened back to primitive times. Thus, his acts were, in effect, shamanistic rituals, mysterious to outsiders but therapeutic for the initiated. In this belief, he was part of the 1960s assault against consumer culture; he particularly denied that art should be a marketable commodity. Indeed, his artistic activity left no body of artworks to be sold. Rather, there are films and photographs of performances and otherwise only props and personal belongings, as in the cargo vest above. Beuys tapped into the period's longing for meaning, as he became in demand as a personality.*

and restraint also led him to geometrize the building, planning its structural relationships according to mathematical ratios. So successful was Mies van der Rohe's "glass box" building that skyscrapers built according to similar designs dominate the skylines of cities around the world.

Happenings

Happenings was the term given to theatrical skits created by painters, sculptors, musicians, dancers, actors, and friends, performing odd and sometimes ridiculous actions. Happenings were planned so as to give the appearance of spontaneity; often involving chance elements, these experimental events—changeable, irreproducible, and explosive—were staged so as to make the audience a participant in the performance. Were they serious or meant to be viewed as satires? Or were they a "put-on"?—the much-abused critical term, dating from the period, inspired by the off-putting behavior of jazz performers toward unsophisticated fans. Whatever their meaning, happenings could have thrived only in the 1960s, when much of the West's traditional culture was under assault from within the establishment. Some older critics often

Figure 21.25 EERO SAARINEN. Trans-World Airline (TWA) Terminal, Kennedy International Airport. 1962. New York City. Ezra Stoller © Esto. *The terminal's exterior is designed to give the impression of a bird in flight. Saarinen accomplished this by installing a reinforced concrete roof anchored by two soaring beams, or cantilevers, which flare up and out on both ends and are connected by a lower center section, with the whole roof resting on giant Y-shaped pillars. Inside, curving stairways and supports add to the exterior's sense of a bird soaring. The sculptural design helped define the purpose of the building and enhanced the anticipation and adventure of flying. This terminal is no longer in use, and its future remains in doubt.*

Figure 21.26 LUDWIG MIES VAN DER ROHE AND PHILIP JOHNSON. Seagram Building. 1954–1958. New York City. Ezra Stoller © Esto. *Mies's decision to use bronze-tinted windows as virtually the only decorative feature of the Seagram Building's simple geometrical design had a profound impact on his contemporaries. Following his lead, other architects made the high-rise skeleton-frame building with tinted windows the most recognizable symbol of Late Modernism.*

Figure 21.27   ALLAN KAPROW. Scene, from *18 Happenings in 6 Parts*. 1959. *This photograph shows the artist Allan Kaprow playing a musical instrument in the first happening for which he wrote the script and John Cage the music. At the time, Kaprow was studying music with Cage, whose aleatory ideas are evident in the event's program. During each of the event's six parts, three happenings took place simultaneously, with the ringing of a bell signaling when to begin and end. Audience members were given cards of written instructions, which told them when to applaud and when to shift seats and move from gallery to gallery.*

sniffed at the entire concept, denying its originality and instead connecting it to Dada (see Chapter 20) and Dada's wild cabaret shows during World War I in Europe. The first happening probably was held at Black Mountain College, in the early fifties, featuring the avant-garde artist Robert Rauschenberg. The artist credited with organizing the first happening in New York City was the painter Allan Kaprow (b. 1927), who, according to legend, staged *18 Happenings in 6 Parts* (1959) (Figure 21.27), along with the composer John Cage and Robert Rauschenberg. Kaprow is also credited with coining the term *happening*.

Late Modern Music

The major musical styles that were dominant before World War II persisted in Late Modernism. New York was the world's musical capital, and musical styles were still polarized into tonal and atonal camps, led by Stravinsky and Schoenberg, respectively. After Schoenberg's death in 1951, however, Stravinsky abandoned tonality and adopted his rival's serial method. Stravinsky's conversion made twelve-tone serialism the most respected type of atonal music, though other approaches to atonality sprang up, notably in the United States. Under Late Modernism, this dissonant style became the musical equivalent of the spontaneous canvases painted by Pollock and the Abstract Expressionist school.

Despite embracing the dissonance and abstraction of serialism, Stravinsky filled his Late Modernist works with energy and feeling, the touchstones of his musical style. Two of his finest serial works are *Agon* (1957), a score for a ballet with no other plot than a competition among the dancers, and *Requiem Canticles* (1968), a religious service for the dead, marked by austere solemnity.

Dissonance also characterizes the music of Krzystof Penderecki [pahn-duhr-ETS-key] (b. 1933), a member of the "Polish School" who is anything but a doctrinaire Modernist. Committed to an older musical ideal,

688

ENCOUNTER

The Globalization of Popular Music

The West has had international music since Hellenistic Greece and ancient Rome, a time when popular singers were treated much like today's rock stars. Later, church music, music commissioned by rich and powerful patrons, and music composed for elites, such as opera audiences, dominated international music, until about 1800, when the marketplace began to reshape musical expression (though it remained within the confines of Western forms). The rise of global music did not begin until after 1945.

Global music emerged between 1945 and 1970, powered by many forces, such as improved technology, international relations, and popular preferences. New media, such as radio, film, and television, transformed the world into a "global village," a term dating from this era. The potential audience for this global village was broadened by rapid advances in the recording industry, which were fueled by a postwar economic boom in the West, Japan, and parts of the Third World. After 1948, the superpowers fostered global music, with the Soviets exporting classical music and the Americans a mixture of classical, pop, and jazz.

Since the 1930s, big bands had dominated American popular music. Usually composed of approximately twenty musicians and led by an instrument-playing conductor, the big bands of the era played love ballads, swing tunes, and jazzy pop, in concerts, at nightclubs, and in recording studios. The Big Band sound often recast African American music and song for its predominantly white audiences. As the Big Band era gave way to rock and roll, American popular music in the mid-fifties became infused with revolutionary styles and sounds. In rock and roll, music drew from both the white and black sounds, from country music and from rhythm and blues, from rockabilly and from gospel and jazz; and overlaying it all was an uninhibited sexual tone. The sound of rock and roll—gritty, loud, and urgent—reflected its mixed heritage outside the mainstream. Rock and roll's first outlets were bars, records, and radio, but soon small bands of five to eight musicians performed in concerts and on tours, playing to

hordes of screaming fans, especially teenagers. In these early years, one performer soon emerged who epitomized the revolution taking place in popular music—Elvis Presley (1935–1977), the first king of rock and roll.

In the mid-sixties, rock and roll evolved into rock, a more sophisticated but less sexy global style, embodied most famously by the Beatles (active 1959–1970). Soon, rock had wiped most other musical styles off the map or forced local styles to adapt new features to survive, such as driving rhythms, wailing vocals, and youthful angst.

Even though most influences flowed outward, some rock stars, for example, the Beatle George Harrison (1943–2001) were drawn to non-Western music. Enamored of Eastern mysticism, Harrison persuaded the Beatles to fly to India in 1967 to meditate for a week—a fact loudly reported in the world's media. More important, he played a sitar, an Indian lute, in the song "Norwegian Wood" (1965)—a first for rock and roll. He studied the sitar with Ravi Shankar (b. 1920), India's most famous musician, and their friendship helped make Shankar one of the first non-Western superstars of global music. By the 1960s, global music was the cornerstone of a worldwide youth culture.

Along with rock and roll, but of lesser note, two other musical forms helped the rise of global music: folk music, especially non-Western, and dance music, mainly from Latin America with African rhythms. Non-Western folk music showed its power by creating a few global stars, for example, the South African Miriam Makeba (b. 1932), singing Xhosa and Zulu songs. Dance music contributed a Latin beat with African overtones to global music, including many new steps: the *rumba* (early twentieth century), an Afro-Cuban dance rooted in the West Indies; the Argentine *tango* (reinvented in the late 1930s), of Hispano-African origin; the *samba* (early 1940s), a Brazilian blend of syncopation with African steps; the *mambo* ("voodoo priestess") (1943), a mix of swing and Afro-Cuban rhythms; the *cha-cha-cha* (1954), a Cuban off-

he believes that music, above all things, must speak to the human heart. Nevertheless, he has been a constant innovator, seeking especially to create new sounds through the unconventional use of stringed instruments and the human voice. Marked by Classical restraint, his compositions are clearly structured works permeated by fluctuating clouds of sounds, as in *Threnody for the Victims of Hiroshima* (1960), scored for

fifty-two stringed instruments. (A threnody is a song of lamentation.) Reflective of the melancholy mood of Late Modernism, this work conjures up the eerie minutes, in 1945 at Hiroshima, between the dropping of the atomic bomb and its detonation. Penderecki achieves unearthly effects through the use of **glissando** (the blending of one tone into the next in scalelike passages) in an extremely high register and spring of the mambo; and the *bossa nova* (Portuguese, "new wave") (late 1950s), a Brazilian blend of samba and jazz.

A fitting symbol of the global music then emerging is the African American jazz trumpeter Louis "Satchmo" Armstrong (Encounter figure 21.1), who toured the world tirelessly after 1947, earning the nickname "Ambassador Armstrong" (see Chapter 20). Ambassador Armstrong lives on in recordings such as "What a Wonderful World" (1968), which celebrates Satchmo's simple faith at the height of the 1960s rebellion.

Learning from the Encounter   What is the difference between an international music culture and a global music culture? **What** forces contributed to the rise of a global music culture after 1945? **Evaluate** the significance of each of these forces. **What** role did rock and roll play in the rise of a global music culture? **Discuss** the impact of folk music and dance music on global music culture. **Why** is Louis Armstrong a "fitting symbol" of early global music? **Who** today best represents global music in our contemporary culture?

Encounter figure 21.1   Louis Armstrong in performance. Accra, Ghana. 1956. *In this photograph, Louis Armstrong, bending on the left, is shown in performance in Accra, capital of the African state of Ghana. On the stage with him are Edmund Hall and Trummy Young, two of his musicians. In concerts such as this, Armstrong, with his Dixieland music, could easily be seen as an ambassador of the free world to those yearning for independence. A year later, in 1957, Ghana gained its independence from the British Empire.*

by the string players' bowing their instruments in abnormal ways.

The most influential Late Modernist was John Cage (1912–1992), whose unusual, even playful, approach to music opened the door to Post-Modernism. Briefly Schoenberg's student, Cage gained most of his controversial notions—in particular, his goal of integrating noise into music—from the enigmatic teachings of Zen

Buddhism. A work that demonstrates this goal is called *4'33" (Four Minutes and Thirty-three Seconds).* The title describes the time period for which the performer is to sit immobile before a piano keyboard so that the concert hall sounds, in effect, become the music during the performer's silence. Cage's spirited experiments made him the darling of the avant-garde. Along with assemblage artists, choreographers, and sculptors, he helped to break down the divisions among the art forms—in anticipation of a Post-Modernist development.

Film

Film was perhaps the most important art form of Late Modernism, holding its own against the upstart—television—though the outcome of the competition for market share between the two media is now in doubt. Filmmaking grew more international in scale, with the trend moving toward a global cinema. Hollywood flexed its muscles more and more as the period unfolded, but studios in Europe and elsewhere played major roles in this expanding world market of mass entertainment.

In Rome, Cinecittà—Italy's largest motion picture studio—was rebuilt, after being devastated during the war. At Cinecittà, the first postwar film movement was born, **Neorealism,** which trained an unforgiving eye on the gritty life of postwar Italy. The director Roberto Rosselini (1906–1977) founded this movement with *Open City* (1945), an unsparing portrait of Italy's chaotic capital in the war's last days, as the Italian underground fought Nazi occupiers in retreat. Perhaps the greatest of the Neorealists was Federico Fellini (1920–1993), who adopted a satirical style as his art progressed, taking images from the circus and often using the actress Giulietta Masina (1921–1994), his wife, as his muse. This he did in the incomparable *Julieta of the Spirits* (1965), a hilarious romp through the consumer-driven, erotically charged Italy that had emerged in the 1960s.

Similarly, Japan's film industry was rebuilt after the war, thus helping its national economy to recover and ensuring a Japanese presence in the global culture then being born. Daiei Films in Tokyo cleverly inaugurated a successful marketing campaign to export their films to the West, through means of seeking awards in film festivals, which now functioned as international marketplaces for film distributors. Daiei's success began at the prestigious Venice Film Festival in 1951, when *Roshomon*—a dramatic film, directed by Akira Kurosawa [kur-uh-SAH-wah] (1910–1998), recounted a particular event from the shifting perspectives of its several characters. *Roshomon* won the top prize and at the same time introduced the world to Japanese cinema. A stream of films followed, usually falling into the category of **art film,** featuring unusual narrative structures, blood and gore with an uplifting humanist message, and dramatic camera work, and the whole suffused with the personal vision of the director.

Art films also dominated the French film industry. In the 1950s, France's influential journal of film criticism *Cahiers du Cinéma* began to use the term *auteur*

(French, "author") to denote those directors who "wrote" with their cameras as they made their films. *Auteurs* were distinguished from mere directors, who simply made movies by collaborating with screenwriters, cinematographers, editors, costume designers, set designers, lighting technicians, musicians, and so on, much in the style of an orchestra conductor with various musicians. Auteurist theory inspired France's first postwar film movement, *Nouvelle Vague,* or the French **New Wave** (late 1950s to early 1960s). Adopting experimental methods, New Wave directors used "jump cuts"—rapid changes of scenes—freeze frames, and ambiguous time sequences to create idiosyncratic films, such as *The 400 Blows* (1959), directed by François Truffaut (1932–1984). Unique among these directors was the politically minded Jean-Luc Godard (b. 1930), whose *Week End* (1967) is a serio-comic satire of "the weekend from hell."

Sweden, neutral during World War II, now enjoyed a film boom, largely through the multilayered works of Ingmar Bergman (b. 1918). Bergman's angst-ridden characters, torn between love of life and the certainty of death, were consummate exemplars of Late Modernism. Drawing on his strict Lutheran upbringing, Bergman created a powerful series of films, set both in the bleak feudal past and in the equally bleak, though different, world of the modern middle class. The greatest of these are *The Seventh Seal* (1957), which presents a harrowing vision of the medieval plague, culminating in a chess game between the Crusader hero and Death (Figure 21.28), and *Winter Light* (1963), part of the *Silence of God* trilogy, which offers a portrait of a Protestant pastor adrift in the personal and political ambiguities of modern life.

Other important film centers during this period included Moscow, London, and Calcutta, in India. Yet, while the rest of the world produced art films, Hollywood stayed with the tried and true: genre movies, defined by drama or setting, such as westerns (late forties to early fifties); *film noir* (French, "dark film"), a style of crime film marked by harsh lighting, hard-boiled heroes, and existential angst (late forties to early fifties); musicals (until 1967); social problems (entire period); and romantic comedies (entire period). Some of the genres, by their nature, produced escapist movies with formulaic plots, stereotyped characters, and predictable outcomes. One representative of Hollywood's creative genius, while still working within the confines of a genre—the musical—is the incomparable *Singing in the Rain* (1952), co-directed by Stanley Donen (b. 1924) and the film's star, Gene Kelly (1912–1996). While the movie breaks no new ground, it has become the gold standard by which other musicals are judged, because of the perfect ease with which it realizes each of the disparate elements of the filmic art.

Figure 21.28   The Devil and the Knight. Still, from *The Seventh Seal*. Ingmar Bergman, director. 1957. *Various scenes in the film depict the ongoing chess match (as here) between the Devil (Bengt Ekerot) and the returning crusader knight, Antonius Block (Max von Sydow). Antonius plays chess for his soul, even as he reveals much about his feelings for God, religion, and life. The title,* The Seventh Seal, *is taken from the biblical book of Revelation, where the opening of seven seals heralds the end of the world. Revelation 8:1 states: "The Lamb then broke the seventh seal, and there was silence in heaven for about half an hour." Bergman's allegorical movie vividly represents this dramatic passage with its depiction of a world beset by plague, violence, and death.*

Besides genre movies, another trend in film in the United States, and elsewhere, was the rise of the documentary. The documentary style was made possible by the invention of the portable handheld camera in 1959, thus allowing the recording of ordinary people and events in real time. Documentaries attracted a cult following because of the immediacy of their subjects, which were often "ripped from newspaper headlines." Two early examples are *Don't Look Back* (1967), directed by New Yorker D. A. Pennebaker (b. 1925), about the 1965 concert tour of Great Britain by the then-emerging singer Bob Dylan (b. 1941), and *Titicut Follies* (1967), an exposé of the horrors of a mental hospital in Massachusetts, directed by New Yorker Frederick Wiseman (b. 1930). U.S. documentary films appeared at the same time as the French movement called *cinéma vérité* ("direct cinema"). Both the French and the Americans shared values with Italy's Neorealists, especially in their preference for truth over art.

A further development that changed film was the rise of film festivals for showcasing new releases. The Venice Film Festival came first, in 1932, but after the war, festivals were established in Cannes, France (1947), Berlin (1951), London (1956), and Karlovy Vary, in the Czech Republic (1965). In the United States, the film industry remained aloof from festivals during this period, preferring to market itself through other means, but other important changes in the U.S. film industry were the genesis of art house cinemas and university film societies, showing foreign films and catering to selected audiences. Around the globe, film distribution systems were set up to specialize in old films, and movie houses showing "classic" films grew in popularity.

The Legacy of the Age of Anxiety and Late Modernism

The 1945–1970 period began with a war-weary world hoping for peace and ended in a standoff between two superpowers capable of destroying the human race. Although this international rivalry permeated nearly every phase of life in this Age of Anxiety, including the arts and humanities, it was the visual arts, especially painting, that seemed to continue to develop independently of these events, following their own path as one artistic style quickly succeeded another.

In the mid-1950s, fear gripped the world as the United States and the Soviet Union, armed with atomic and hydrogen bombs and long-range missiles, seemed positioned to go to war. But as one crisis followed another, the adversaries found ways to avoid a military showdown. In the competition for economic supremacy, the USSR and its eastern European satellites lost the race. By the early 1970s, the West had surged ahead in manufacturing, productivity, and marketing to produce a consumer society and a burgeoning middle class that were the envy of the world.

In the immediate postwar era, some Western intellectuals embraced existentialism, while others turned to Christian existentialism or Neo-orthodoxy. The vast majority of believers remained with traditional religious faiths, seeking answers and solace in an increasingly secular society. Protestant churches confronted the changing world in their separate denominations, while the Roman Catholic Church convened a council. By the late 1960s, structuralism and a materializing hedonism in popular culture, which were challenging the tenets of Christian and middle-class values, indicated future unrest.

Scientific discoveries and inventions were, as they always had been, a mixed blessing. Most were beneficial in their initial stages, raising the standard of living or, in the case of medicine and medical practices, improving the lives of people in many societies. The United States, in its desire to be a world leader, added universities and research centers to the already existing industrial-military-state complex, creating a military establishment capable of wielding huge economic, political, and even spiritual influence—as President Dwight Eisenhower (in office 1953–1961) famously cautioned. This amalgamation of knowledge and power for the benefit of a nation, a trait of Western societies since the Scientific Revolution, has become an accepted way of life in most industrialized countries and has increasingly shaped contemporary society.

Late Modernism, like bipolar international relations and rising economic trends, emerged out of the traumas and experiences of World War II. The United States, with New York City as the hub, became the West's cultural leader, as the "arts capital" label shifted from Europe to America. Painting, sculpture, architecture, and literature flourished in the United States with only an occasional voice from Western Europe or the Soviet Union being heard on the international level. Abstract Expressionism was the first art style of the restless and rebellious postwar generation of New York painters and sculptors, followed by an ever-changing series of styles: Pop Art, Op Art, minimalism, and other schools. The rapid shift in styles represented Modernism with a vengeance: the ideal of newness, leading to the "shock of the new." Films witnessed a rebirth after the war and, along with television, competed for a worldwide audience, whose attention spans were growing shorter and shorter. In the arts and popular culture, the United States was outdistancing the Soviet Union, as American clothes, music, Hollywood movies, and celebrities won the hearts of young people around the world. The United States, with its materialistic society, relaxed lifestyle, and rock and roll music, was now the force driving the emergent global culture.

Regardless of events in the arts and elsewhere, the cold war defined the Age of Anxiety. The crises that brought both superpowers to the brink of war, the efforts of the United States and the Soviet Union to gain support among Third World countries, and the deep-seated ideological differences between their political and economic systems seemed to indicate that the cold war would last for decades. Likewise, the divide between rich and poor countries, which had begun in the 1960s, signaled more widening in the future. Finally, innovations in the arts foreshadowed more changes to come in styles, techniques, and materials after 1970.

KEY CULTURAL TERMS

Late Modernism
Neo-orthodoxy
Structuralism
Beat Generation
Theater of the Absurd
Pinteresque
Angry Young Men
Abstract Expressionism
Action Painting
hard-edge

assemblage art
Pop Art
Op Art
minimalism
happening
glissando
Neorealism
art film
auteur
Nouvelle Vague (New Wave)

SUGGESTIONS FOR FURTHER READING

The Autobiography of Malcolm X. With the assistance of A. Haley. Secaucus, N.J.: Castle Books, 1967. In his own words, Malcolm X describes his rise from obscurity to become a powerful figure posing radical solutions to racial problems.

BALDWIN, J. *Go Tell It on the Mountain*. New York: Grossett and Dunlap, 1953. A novel representative of Baldwin's early optimism about reconciliation of the black and white races.

———. *No Name in the Street*. New York: Dial Press, 1972. A novel representative of Baldwin's bitterness after the murder of Martin Luther King Jr.

BECKETT, S. *Waiting for Godot.* Edited and with an introduction by H. Bloom. New York: Chelsea House Publishers, 1987. The central image of Beckett's absurdist play—pointless waiting—has become a metaphor for the disappointed hopes of Late Modernism.

CAMUS, A. *The Fall.* Translated by J. O'Brien. New York: Knopf, 1957. Camus's most autobiographical novel, dealing with self-deceit and spiritual yearning.

CHOMSKY, N. *Syntactic Structures.* The Hague: Mouton, 1957. The work that revolutionized linguistics by claiming that there is a structure that lies hidden beneath the surface of language.

DE BEAUVOIR, S. *The Second Sex.* Translated and edited by H. M. Parshley. New York: Vintage, 1974. One of the books that helped launch the feminist revival by arguing that women must abandon "femininity" and create their own immortality just as men do.

FANON, F. *The Wretched of the Earth.* Translated by C. Farrington. New York: Grove Press, 1968. Fanon's groundbreaking study of racism and colonial liberation; a classic of modern revolutionary theory.

FRIEDAN, B. *The Feminine Mystique.* New York: Norton, 1963. The first acknowledgment of housewives' dissatisfaction with their role and desire for a career, this work was a milestone in the rebirth of feminism in the United States.

GINSBERG, A. *Collected Poems, 1947–1980.* New York: Harper & Row, 1984. A Late Modernist, Ginsberg wrote poetry that reflected his openness to diversity and his passion for freedom.

KING, M. L., JR. *A Testament of Hope: The Essential Writings of Martin Luther King, Jr.* New York: Harper & Row, 1986. A good introduction to the thought of the most influential black American in history.

LESSING, D. *Children of Violence.* (Includes *Martha Quest, A Proper Marriage, A Ripple from the Storm, Landlocked.*) New York: Simon and Schuster, 1964–1966. *The Four-Gated City.* New York: Knopf, 1969. Covering the period between the 1930s and 1960s, this series is Lessing's literary meditation on the transformation of her colonial homeland, Rhodesia, into the black state of Zimbabwe. *Martha Quest,* the focal point of this quintet of novels, is the author's surrogate witness to these turbulent events.

LÉVI-STRAUSS, C. *The Elementary Structures of Kinship.* Translated by J. H. Bell and others. Boston: Beacon Press, 1969. A classic of social anthropology, this work established that there are only a few basic patterns of kinship relationships in all societies.

MAILER, N. *The Naked and the Dead.* New York: Rinehart, 1948. Mailer's novel of World War II, his first and best work.

SARTRE, J.-P. *The Age of Reason* and *The Reprieve.* Translated by E. Sutton. *Troubled Sleep.* Translated by G. Hopkins. New York: Knopf, 1947, 1947, and 1950. Sartre's trilogy of novels, called *The Roads to Freedom,* demonstrates existentialism in action.

———. *No Exit and Three Other Plays.* Translated by L. Abel and S. Gilbert. New York: Vintage, 1976. *No Exit* is Sartre's most famous drama, illustrating his idea that "hell is other people" because they strive to define us and see us as objects; also includes *Dirty Hands, The Respectful Prostitute,* and *The Flies.*

SOLZHENITSYN, A. *One Day in the Life of Ivan Denisovich.* Translated by R. Parker. New York: Dutton, 1963. Published with permission of the Soviet authorities, this novel revealed the existence of Stalin's slave labor camps.

THOMAS, D. *The Collected Poems of Dylan Thomas.* New York: New Directions, 1953. The finest lyric poet of the Late Modern period, Thomas wrote on such themes as sex, love, and death.

———. *Under Milk Wood, A Play for Voices.* New York: New Directions, 1954. A verse play set in a mythical Welsh village that comes to symbolize a lost world in an urbanized age.

WRIGHT, R. *Black Boy: A Record of Childhood and Youth.* New York: Harper, 1945. Wright's description of his rise from sharecropper status to international renown.

———. *Native Son.* New York: Grossett and Dunlap, 1940. Wright's most celebrated novel, the powerful story of the violent consequences of racism in the life of a young black man.

SUGGESTIONS FOR LISTENING

CAGE, JOHN. After the late 1950s, Cage's music came to be characterized by wholly random methods that he called *aleatory* (from the Latin *alea,* "dice"), as represented by *4'33"* (*Four Minutes and Thirty-three Seconds*) (1952), *Variations IV* (1963), and *Aria with Fonatana Mix* (1958).

PENDERECKI, KRZYSTOF. Penderecki, an eclectic composer, draws inspiration from diverse sources, including Stravinsky and Classical and church music. Reflective of the turbulence of contemporary Poland, his music centers on themes of martyrdom, injustice, and persecution. The first work that made him an international musical star was *Threnody for the Victims of Hiroshima* (1960), a piece for orchestra that uses stringed instruments and human voices in unusual ways. Perhaps his masterpiece is the more traditional oratorio *Passion and Death of Our Lord Jesus Christ According to St. Luke,* more commonly called "The St. Luke Passion" (1966), which incorporates Gregorian chant, folk music, nonverbal choral sounds, and modified serialism. He also has had success with operas, as in the simultaneously dissonant and lyrical *Paradise Lost* (1978), based on Milton's epic poem (see Chapter 14).

STRAVINSKY, IGOR. After 1951 Stravinsky replaced his Neoclassical style with the technique of serial music, as in the song *In Memoriam Dylan Thomas* (1954), the ballet *Agon* (1954–1957), and the orchestral works *Movements* (1959) and *Orchestral Variations* (1964).

22

THE CONTEMPORARY WORLD
Globalization, Terror, and Post-Modernism
1970–

After 1970, as the twentieth century was coming to a close, the West entered a period of extremes, marked by rapid shifts in the popular mood, oscillating from optimism to pessimism and back again. Politically, the collapse of the Soviet Union and the eastern bloc generated elation, but, at the same time, the revival of old ethnic loyalties and hatreds led to despair. Economically, higher oil prices made oil-producing countries wealthier but endangered the affluence enjoyed by the industrialized world. The shifting of industry from the West to cheaper labor markets further raised hopes and fears. Social issues, once local in scope, now became global problems: the specter of food shortages and famines sparked by population explosions; the threat of job loss caused by new labor-saving technology; and the potential for environmental calamities to the earth's ecosystem produced in the wake of surging growth in developing countries. In the 1990s, the cumulative effects of the fall of communism, the growing prosperity of the West, the revolutions in the electronic and telecommunications industries, and the migrations of populations from undeveloped countries to the industrialized world hastened what was already under way: globalization. And globalization helped to define the emerging cultural style, Post-Modernism, with its vision of a unified, multicultural world.

Underlying these developments was a renewed sense of hope that marked the beginning of the twenty-first century. However, that optimism quickly faded as economic crises increased, conflicts in the Middle East intensified, and terrorism spread around the globe, including direct attacks on the United States. The apparent abrupt changes in the contemporary world, at this stage

◀ **Detail** FRANK O. GEHRY. Guggenheim Museum. 1997. Bilbao, Spain. © David Young-Wolff / Photo Edit.

of history, can be divided into two phases: toward a new global order, 1970–2001; and the Age of Terror, 2001–present.

TOWARD A NEW GLOBAL ORDER, 1970–2001

The early 1970s marked a turning point in history, not only for Western civilization but also for the world. The balance of political power began to shift from the bipolar, superpower model to a multipolar system that included Japan, China, and Western Europe. This global shift began when the superpowers moved toward *détente,* a French term meaning "a waning of hostility." By the early 1970s, détente had produced several arms-limitation treaties between the USSR and the United States, creating a favorable climate for a reappraisal of cold war attitudes and a reduction of other global ideological battles. China, a previously closed country, began to open slowly to interaction with the United States and other Western countries. In addition, the industrialized nations began to experience energy shortages that revealed their dependence on the oil-producing countries, which had formerly exerted little influence on world events.

National Issues and International Realignment

In the early 1970s, the standard of living declined for most citizens in Western Europe and the United States when the Organization of Petroleum Exporting Countries (OPEC), a cartel of the oil-rich states of the Middle East, raised prices. As a result, most Western nations went into a recession that resulted in rising unemployment and inflation. The migration of Turks, North Africans, and Arabs to Europe as "guest workers" restructured the labor market and intensified socioeconomic tensions in many European countries. In the Soviet Union, it was becoming clear that the state-controlled economy could no longer produce both arms and consumer goods.

The 1970s were a time of political drift in the United States in the wake of the Watergate scandal and President Richard Nixon's (in office 1969–1974) resignation; in contrast, the 1980s brought dramatic changes both nationally and internationally. The government adopted laissez-faire economic policies and experienced an economic turnaround. The nation paid for this prosperity, however, with increased spending, a huge national debt, and a shift in foreign trade from creditor to debtor status. The gap between rich and poor also widened, leading to increasing polarization in American society.

Two events, both setbacks for détente, clouded the international scene: a Soviet invasion of Afghanistan in 1979 in support of local Communist leaders and the founding in 1980 of Solidarity in Poland, a labor movement that pushed for economic reform. The Polish government, supported by the USSR, ruthlessly suppressed the movement. Cold war sentiments revived, ongoing disarmament talks between the superpowers broke down, and an intensified arms race seemed imminent.

The international tension dissipated in 1985 with the appearance of Mikhail Gorbachev [GOR-bah-chof] (in office 1985–1991) as the new moderate leader of the Soviet Union, whose economic policies had proved to be unproductive and who had fallen behind capitalist nations. He introduced a new era of détente and helped guide the cold war to a peaceful close. His overtures to the United States resulted in limited arms reductions and opened communication between the two superpowers.

The Fall of Communism

Within the Soviet Union, Gorbachev initiated reforms in the state bureaucracy and the Communist party that were designed to raise the standard of living. His plans dramatically altered the course of history in the USSR, Eastern Europe, and the world. Gorbachev's domestic reforms contributed to the breakup of the centralized structure of the USSR, as some member states declared their independence and others gained more local control. From the old Soviet system, following more than seventy years of communism, a desperately weakened Russia reemerged, shorn of its vast empire yet still managing to retain some ethnic republics through a commonwealth arrangement (Map 22.1).

After 1989 Gorbachev's policies toward the satellite states led to the dissolution of the communist bloc in Eastern Europe, symbolized by the destruction of the Berlin Wall (Figure 22.1). Newly independent, these former communist states, including Russia itself, still struggle to maintain their social welfare programs and worker protection legislation and at the same time to move toward democratic government and a market economy. Within Russia, which is increasingly subject to ethnic and regional crises, Boris Yeltsin (in office

Figure 22.1   Fall of the Berlin Wall. 1989. *Given the Soviet Union's previous use of force in Eastern Europe, no one had predicted that the collapse of the communist states would be so quick and bloodless. The most symbolic event of this extraordinary period was the dismantling of the wall that separated East Berlin from West Berlin.*

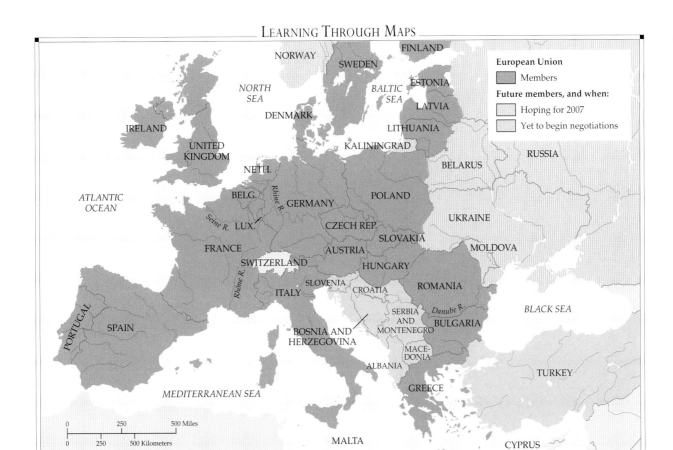

Map 22.1   EUROPE IN 2007

This map shows the member countries of the European Union as of 2004. **Note** those countries awaiting membership in 2007. **Observe** which current member states of the E.U. are former members of the Communist bloc, as shown on Map 21.1, Europe in 1955. **Identify** the countries that have thus far not begun negotiations for membership in the E.U. **Why** do you think these countries have failed to begin their negotiations for E.U. membership? **Speculate** on Russia's attitude toward the expansion of the E.U. to the borders of Russia.

Figure 22.2 Bhopal Disaster. Bhopal, India, 1984. *A husband carries his wife's body by the deserted chemical factory—the source of the lethal disaster. A toxic gas spread over the city during the night of December 3, 1984. With so many deaths, mass cremations followed over the next few days. More than twenty thousand people eventually died from related diseases caused by the disaster.*

1991–1999) tried to steer a course in uncharted political waters between the nationalists and communists, who wanted to restore their country's former imperial and economic systems, and the reformers, who wanted to expand the marketplace economy and ensure political freedom. With Vladimir Putin (in office 1999–) as president, Russia seems ready to become involved in international trade and diplomacy, while dismantling earlier democratic reforms and centralizing political power.

During the 1980s, some unforeseen events either hinted at future trends or directly altered the course of history. In 1984, in Bhopal, India, a chemical company accident released a toxic gas that killed nearly 2,500 residents (Figure 22.2). Two years later, the town of Chernobyl, Ukraine, was abandoned after a meltdown at a nuclear power plant. While these disasters underscored worldwide environmental issues, they also contributed to a maturing vision that nations had to cooperate to prevent future calamities as well as to address the growing threats not only to humans but to the biosphere as well.

Nevertheless, the collapse of the Soviet Union overshadowed all other events in the 1980s and changed the course of history in the late twentieth century—

and beyond. The downfall of the Soviet system set off a chain of events that ended its control of eastern and central Europe and rebalanced the power structure in Europe, marked the demise of communism, and left the United States the "winner" of the cold war. The euphoria generated by the fall of communism and the expectancy of a "new world order" quickly became linked with market-based economies, which were now replacing the discredited state-run models. The implications of these political and economic transformations gave further proof that the world was shrinking and that globalization would be the defining trend in the 1990s (Timeline 22.1).

The Post–Cold War World

Because of the startling changes after 1989, the long-awaited multipolar system of international politics did not materialize, as the United States was now the world's lone superpower. Other countries, which were to be part of this multipolar group, faced nearly intractable problems. Russia, stripped of its satellites, was beset with lawlessness and corruption and its leader, President Putin, has seemed determined to

Timeline 22.1   CULTURAL STYLES, 1970–PRESENT

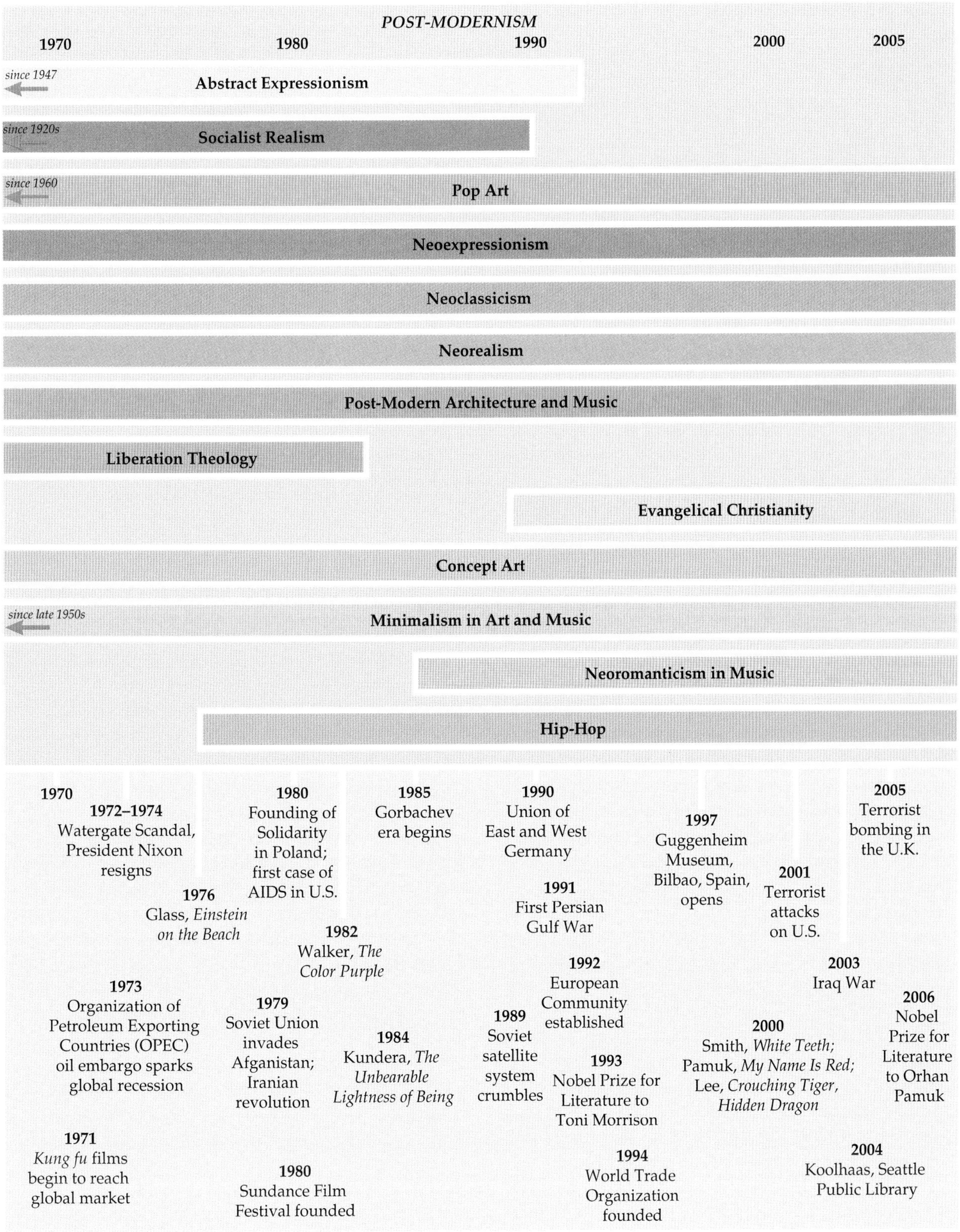

POST-MODERNISM

| 1970 | 1980 | 1990 | 2000 | 2005 |

since 1947
← **Abstract Expressionism**

since 1920s
Socialist Realism

since 1960
← **Pop Art**

Neoexpressionism

Neoclassicism

Neorealism

Post-Modern Architecture and Music

Liberation Theology

Evangelical Christianity

Concept Art

since late 1950s
← **Minimalism in Art and Music**

Neoromanticism in Music

Hip-Hop

1970

1972–1974
Watergate Scandal,
President Nixon
resigns

1976
Glass, *Einstein
on the Beach*

1973
Organization of
Petroleum Exporting
Countries (OPEC)
oil embargo sparks
global recession

1971
Kung fu films
begin to reach
global market

1980
Founding of
Solidarity
in Poland;
first case of
AIDS in U.S.

1982
Walker, *The
Color Purple*

1979
Soviet Union
invades
Afganistan;
Iranian
revolution

1984
Kundera, *The
Unbearable
Lightness of Being*

1980
Sundance Film
Festival founded

1985
Gorbachev
era begins

1989
Soviet
satellite
system
crumbles

1990
Union of
East and West
Germany

1991
First Persian
Gulf War

1992
European
Community
established

1993
Nobel Prize for
Literature to
Toni Morrison

1994
World Trade
Organization
founded

1997
Guggenheim
Museum,
Bilbao, Spain,
opens

2001
Terrorist
attacks
on U.S.

2000
Smith, *White Teeth;*
Pamuk, *My Name Is Red;*
Lee, *Crouching Tiger,
Hidden Dragon*

2005
Terrorist
bombing in
the U.K.

2003
Iraq War

2006
Nobel
Prize for
Literature
to Orhan
Pamuk

2004
Koolhaas, Seattle
Public Library

Figure 22.3 Protester Standing in Front of Tanks. Tiananmen Square, Beijing, China, 1989. *In the 1980s, the Chinese government abandoned its isolationist policy, engaged in international trade, and sent its young people to study abroad to prepare them to be future leaders of China. Having seen life outside China, they returned home and began to demand more freedom, which the authoritarian government would not permit. This struggle, between the government and the youth, climaxed in Tiananmen Square, the symbol of Chinese Communist power, during the pro-democracy demonstrations that were watched, as they unfolded, on television around the world.*

amass more power at the expense of earlier promising economic and democratic trends. Japan failed to recover from the downturn of its financial markets, starting in the early 1990s. China, in spite of its phenomenal economic growth of 8 to 12 percent a year, has had a number of domestic crises, in particular with some citizens calling for a more open and democratic society. Public demonstrations led Chinese authorities to crack down on protesters, led by university students, in Beijing's Tiananmen Square in June 1989 (Figure 22.3).

As other nations concentrated on domestic issues, the United States basked in its role as the world's only superpower because of its military superiority, its central role in international relations, and its consumer society that helped propel a global economic boom. Contributing to America's role as world leader was its unwillingness to work in full harmony with the United Nations. Convinced that the U.N. was dominated by Third World interests, the United States preferred to act alone, through coalitions of its own choosing, or to work with established regional alliances.

Throughout the 1990s, economic globalization further increased because of the spread of free-market systems, but volatility in financial markets led to social and political unrest and brought into question some of the assumptions of laissez-faire capitalism. In the early 1990s, the economies of the Pacific Rim countries, except for Japan (whose economy struggled with stag-

gering deficits, sustained deflation, and interest rates approaching near zero), were booming, but by 1998, the euphoria had waned. Paralleling globalization has been the rise of regional economic alliances, such as the formation of the European Union into a free-trade zone. The E.U. instituted its own currency, the Euro, which has become an alternative to the American dollar in the international monetary system. The Euro has also made Europe more competitive in the global market. The creation of the North Atlantic Free Trade Association (NAFTA) among Canada, the United States, and Mexico became a model for other countries that have established similar regional economic groups. Fueling these changes are fast-paced technological advances, such as the Internet and electronic commerce, which are revolutionizing the way the world conducts its business.

In 1994 the World Trade Organization (WTO) was founded to promote free trade. The WTO encourages nations to settle their trade disputes, and it is empowered to enforce such settlements. Over 123 nations, including China, are members. The WTO, along with the World Bank, the International Monetary Fund (IMF), and regional trade associations, has increased global wealth and reduced global poverty. However, not all countries have benefited from globalization and free trade, and some voters have been choosing leaders who oppose these institutions and are openly critical of free-market economics. In these disaffected coun-

Figure 22.4 The Carinski Bridge in Mostar, Bosnia and Herzegovina. 1996. *The reopening of the Carinski Bridge in 1996 symbolized the hope for peace and reconciliation between the Croatians and Muslims in Mostar. However, the ancient feuds linger among the various ethnic groups in the Balkans. In 1999, to the south in Kosovo, the Yugoslav Serbs attempted to drive out the Kosovo Muslims. A coalition of United Nations and NATO forces intervened, and the Yugoslav troops withdrew. Joint U.N. and NATO peacekeeping units now occupy the territory, but the area remains unstable.*

tries, such as Venezuela and Greece, globalization has become identified with the United States, giving rise to anti-American and antiglobalization sentiments and generating a new form of populism, advocating the rights and well-being of a nation's citizenry in reaction to the multinational corporations and the power of the developed nations.

From about 1995 to 2001, the world's economy was driven by that of the United States. Recovering from a mild recession in the early 1990s, the American stock market rose sharply. The rally was based on "dot-com" companies—mainly in communications and technology, funded by venture capitalists—that had sprung up across the country. Speculation and greed, as with the stock market craze of the 1920s, ran the market up to new heights, until the bubble burst in 2001, leaving the companies broke and investors angry. At the same time, American businesses began to outsource many white-collar jobs to developing nations, following the lead of factory owners who had earlier moved plants overseas to countries with cheap labor. Now, corporations were hiring foreign engineers, computer technicians, and software designers for jobs formerly done by office workers in the United States.

In addition to the economic fallout from the end of the cold war, regional nationalism and ethnic violence, which had been suppressed during the era of the superpowers (1945–1970s), now resurfaced. In the 1990s, with the disintegration of Yugoslavia, wars broke out among the newly formed states along ethnic and religious lines. Eventually, as Europe dithered over what to do, the United States decided to act. After a series of

air strikes, the fighting ended and the warring factions were brought to the peace table, where they accepted a series of accords, thus bringing a wary peace to the region (Figure 22.4).

The other nations that came out of the Soviet Union's orbit in the 1990s fared better. Since 1995, most of the newly formed central and eastern European countries have transformed their economies from state socialism to variations of free-market capitalism. They have drafted constitutions, set up federated systems, formed political parties, and installed democratically elected governments. Most of these countries have turned away from Russia and toward Western Europe, seeking membership in the European Union and NATO (see Map 22.1).

The changes taking place across the European landscape in the nineties were matched by events in the Middle East. Tensions and wars in that region had mounted during the cold war. Israel won wars against its neighbors in 1967 and 1973, and in the late 1970s, conditions seemed to improve when Egypt and Israel signed peace treaties. Just when it seemed that these treaties might pave the way for further negotiations and an easing of tensions in that area, the Iranian revolution occurred. Iran's shah was deposed in 1979, and a theocratic government was established. While heartening to the faithful, the formation of an Islamic state let the world know that a militant, if not radical, Islamic movement had been born.

The Middle East was further destabilized when Iraq, under Saddam Hussein [sa-DAHM hu-SANE] (r. 1979–2003) invaded Iran in 1980. Believing Iran weak under its new revolutionary government, Hussein calculated a quick and easy victory. However, the war, with high casualties on both sides, dragged on until 1988. Two years later, the Iraqis invaded Kuwait, which soon led to the 1991 Gulf War. A coalition of Western and Muslim states, led by the United States, drove the Iraqis from Kuwait. Although defeated, Hussein remained in power throughout the decade.

THE AGE OF TERROR, 2001–

Two iconic American buildings—symbolic of the far-reaching economic, military, and cultural power of the reigning superpower—became the target of anti-Americanism on September 11, 2001. Previous terrorist attacks had targeted overseas military bases, the World Trade Center (1993), and embassies in Africa (1998), but those paled in comparison to the devastating assault on the Twin Towers of the World Trade Center in New York City (Figure 22.5) and the Pentagon in Washington, D.C. The attacks, commonly referred to as "9/11," were organized by radical Muslims from the Middle East, who used America's open-door policy and their own technological know-how for their destructive scheme.

The United States and other nations soon began to understand and react to the changes triggered by these acts of terrorism: fighting an elusive band of revolutionaries, with no particular state identity and no visible government, and, thus, having no way to determine when, and if, the war is won. A small radical Islamic sect, al Qaeda [al KAY-duh] (Arabic, "the base"), was widely believed to be behind the attacks. These developments, affecting nearly every phase of life in the United States as well as in much of the West, have probably altered the course of history for at least the first half of the twenty-first century.

After the initial shock of 9/11, the United States retaliated. Its leaders were convinced that the government in Afghanistan—the Taliban, an Islamic fundamentalist group—was harboring al Qaeda and its head, Osama bin Laden [o-SAH-mah bin LAHD-en] (b. 1957). U.S. forces invaded the country in October 2001. The Taliban-led government fell in a few weeks, and America and its allies occupied the capital and parts of the country. A new constitution was drafted, and elections held as a first step toward democracy, but Afghanistan remains volatile, with ethnic rivalries, systemic poverty, and a resurgent Taliban movement.

In March 2003, the United States, supported by Britain and a few other nations, invaded Iraq. President George W. Bush (in office 2001–) reasoned that Saddam Hussein's dictatorship had to be overthrown, claiming he possessed weapons of mass destruction,

Figure 22.5   Proposed World Trade Center Project. 2004. New York. *The 2001 destruction of the Twin Towers of the World Trade Center complex presented a challenge and an opportunity to rebuild the area. After years of public debates, political pressures, and lawsuits, the authorities chose the plan of the Berlin-based Studio Libeskind in 2004. The Polish-born American Daniel Libeskind's (LEE-behs-kihnd) (b. 1946) model shows Freedom Tower to the left, an open area and plaza for the memorial to the 9/11 victims, and a cluster of five surrounding buildings. Freedom Tower, the centerpiece of the project, will be a 1,500-foot skyscraper with a 276-foot-tall spire, making it taller than the Twin Towers. Construction of the subway station and transportation hub started in late 2005. A 9/11 museum and a performing arts center, designed by Frank Gehry, are being planned.*

which were about to be unleashed on the world. Although the initial fighting lasted only weeks and Saddam Hussein was captured in December 2003, the war has dragged on for over three years, proving costly in lives and expenditures (Figure 22.6). The U.S. public is deeply divided over the war, which overshadows other events and shapes public discourse today. Unlike the cold war, which was a by-product of twentieth-century events, this conflict is deeply rooted in history, going back to the twelfth-century Crusades (see Chap-

Figure 22.6 American Soldiers Examine an Iraqi Child. 2005. *This scene—American soldiers examining a wounded Iraqi child during a U.S. government–sponsored community health outreach program—recalls similar images from the United States' recent wars—from World War II to the Vietnam War. This picture also illustrates the dilemma of an army fighting on foreign soil. The soldiers are warriors waging a war against the enemy and, at the same time, protectors of the innocent victims of warfare. Throughout history, armies have come as liberators and remained as occupiers, which often turns them from friend to foe.*

Figure 22.7 *An Anti-American Painting.* 2006. Tehran, Iran. *The United States' "stars and stripes," in the shape of a revolver, expresses the growing hostility against America in Iran and other parts of the Muslim world. The contrast between the painted protest and the arabesque patterns on the wall is heightened by the woman strolling down the street. Her traditional attire emphasizes the cultural gulf between American women and Muslim women. The shadows of the trees frame the photograph, giving it an artistic touch that catches the eye while sending an obvious message to the viewer.*

ter 9). After the flowering of Islamic civilization (see Chapter 8), the Muslims experienced centuries of humiliation as they fell victims to European power. In the past decade, some of Islam's religious and political leaders have capitalized on the ensuing resentment, calling on their followers to avenge past misdeeds by "the Western infidels" and to reestablish a theocratic Muslim empire. Whether recent events will result in a "clash of civilizations" remains to be seen. Whatever its final resolution, tensions between the West and Islam are now more intense than ever before, and more violence and bloodshed seem likely in the near future (Figure 22.7).

THE BIRTH OF POST-MODERNISM

In the early 1970s, Late Modernism (see Chapter 21) was challenged by a new movement that became known as **Post-Modernism.** Characterized by a cautious optimism and an interest in reinterpreting past styles, Post-Modernism reflects a search for more positive responses to the world than Late Modernism had.

Having grown to maturity after World War II and feeling that Late Modernism's anxiety was outdated, the Post-Modernists embraced mass culture and preferred a more playful approach to creativity (Figure 22.8). And, having witnessed the cold war's rivalry between the two superpowers, which ranged over the entire world, the Post-Modernists envisioned a global culture, free from military threat. In part because the United States is unique among the nations of the earth in being a microcosm of global society, and in part because affluence has made its consumers the driving force in the world's economy, American artists and scholars have played a key role in establishing the culture of Post-Modernism. The emergence of the United States as the only superpower has also enhanced its presence in Post-Modernism. Thus, the spread of Post-Modernism around the world leads to a paradox: American culture, especially popular culture, values, and technology, is eagerly adopted abroad, but with this adoption come voices denouncing America's cultural imperialism as well as its military strength and economic power.

The Post-Modernists' cultural vision causes them to look in two directions at the same time—forward to an emerging global civilization that is many voiced and

Figure 22.8 NAM JUNE PAIK. *My Faust-Channel 5-Nationalism.* 1989–1991. Twenty-five Quasar 10-inch televisions, three Sony laser disc players, Neogothic wood frame with base, 104 × 50 × 32". Private Collection, Seoul. *Designed by the Korean American artist Nam June Paik, this artwork is a playful commentary on war as a form of national religion. Housed in a Neogothic frame, inspired by medieval altarpieces, the art is filled with military objects, such as bombs, jackboots, and helmets, as well as television screens and laser disc players. By covering the top and sides of the frame with flags from many of the world's nations, Paik suggests that all countries make sacred cults of their military establishments.*

democratic, and backward to the roots of the Western tradition. This vision embraces the works of women, minority group members, and representatives of the Third World, even as it reexamines both Classical and pre-Classical civilizations. This global vision was thrown into doubt after 9/11, when the day's tragic events inaugurated the Age of Terror.

Medicine, Science, and Technology

In the Age of Globalization, advances in science and technology have had a greater impact than in the past. Not only have science and technology accelerated and directed change around the globe, but they have also become integral parts of the world's economy, international affairs, and the military-industrial complex of most nations. Only time will determine the ultimate value of recent inventions and discoveries.

Medicine The health and well-being of most humans have improved since 1970. New drugs and surgical procedures have saved and prolonged life for millions in industrialized nations. National and international organizations have worked together to distribute drugs and build medical facilities in the world's poor regions. A number of childhood diseases have been eradicated through inoculations.

Organ transplants and the use of artificial organs have prolonged life for many people otherwise without hope. But these practices have also embroiled the medical profession in ethical controversy, including charges that only a few can afford these procedures and that they drain the financial resources of the health-care system. Likewise, new methods in human reproduction, such as test-tube fertilization and surrogate parenting, although helping a few, have raised moral dilemmas and led to court cases involving questions such as: When a couple divorces, which of the two has a legal right to a fertilized egg? With surrogate parenting, does a surrogate mother have parental rights? When a sperm donor is used, does the donor have a legal right to protect his identity from his offspring?

Despite breakthroughs in medicine that have saved millions of lives, some places around the globe are still threatened by fatal diseases, and worldwide epidemics are always possible. In the 1980s, AIDS (acquired immune deficiency syndrome) arrived and quickly spread into certain sections of society. AIDS, along with an increase of other sexually transmitted diseases, not only slowed down the sexual revolution but also wiped out segments of the population. In sub-Saharan Africa, AIDS has devastated many communities where there are few hospitals or clinics. Attitudes and perceptions in Africa have exacerbated the problem either by denying the existence of the disease or by rejecting modern medical practices. In some areas, the most productive age groups have been decimated, leaving behind a generation of orphans, many probably infected with the disease (Figure 22.9).

Fatal infectious diseases have also become a threat. Easily transmitted, and with millions of international travelers as carriers, they can spread rapidly around

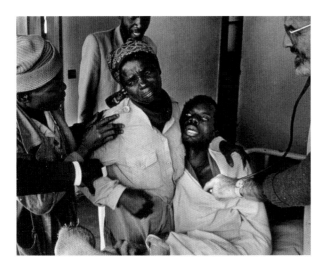

Figure 22.9 AIDS Patient Dies from Kidney Failure While Surrounded by Family Members. Mission Hospital, Southern Africa. 2002. Gideon Mendel/Network—Saba. *According to a recent study, three million people died of AIDS in 2005. Two million of them were from sub-Saharan Africa. The United Nations and some of its members, including the United States, have increased their efforts to combat AIDS. However, the approach of the United States "faith-based" organizations—no condoms and sexual abstinence—have stirred up controversies among Americans and world health authorities. About forty million humans are living with AIDS or HIV (human immunodeficiency virus), which affects the immune system and leads to AIDS.*

the world. Especially worrisome have been the influenza viruses, such as "bird flu," originating and moving out of Asia. The World Health Organization (WHO) and national health units work together, monitoring the paths of these diseases and cooperating to contain and eradicate them. However, their lethal potential and rapid transmission will continue to challenge the international medical profession.

Science Advances in genetics, based on the discovery of DNA, are now revealing basic information about the origins of life. Researchers have decoded the human genome, composed of perhaps three billion units of DNA, arranged into twenty-three pairs of chromosomes. In biogenetics, scientists have cloned animal and plant products and organs, as well as whole sheep and mice, their most spectacular achievement. As in medicine, these breakthroughs raise serious ethical questions, such as: What use will be made of the genome map? Should attempts be made to clone humans? Are genetically modified fruits and vegetables safe for human consumption? Despite attempts to resolve these questions within the scientific community, their final resolution will probably be determined within the legal system.

Technology In many ways the inventions and improvements of machines in business and communications have had a more direct and immediate impact on society and individuals than advances in medicine and science. The new devices have evolved from the miniaturized integrated circuit invented around 1959, which had its origins in transistors (see Chapter 21), and the founding of the microchip industry, starting in the 1970s. The microchip replaced the transistor and all of its components with a single integrated circuit, or chip, thus making it possible to further reduce the size of machines, in particular, the computer.

The introduction of communication satellites, a by-product of the U.S. space program of the 1960s, has made a global culture possible. Multinational corporations are linked by these satellites, and individuals all over the world watch televised events at the same time thanks to satellite communication.

Perhaps most important, the computer and the Internet have revolutionized life on every level, making previously unimaginable quantities of data immediately accessible, simplifying complex tasks, and transforming the traditional habits of personal and public life around the globe. Consumers, through e-commerce, purchase goods and services directly and, through e-trade, buy and sell stocks and bonds without brokers. Scholars, researchers, and students, through IT (information technology), access journals, books, libraries, and databases to keep up with areas of expertise. From Web sites, businesses place orders, restock inventories, and sell to customers. Individuals can e-mail friends and family, keep up with current events, and pursue interests and hobbies. These developments have contributed to "cocooning," a mode of living in which people center their lives in their homes, surrounded by electronic devices, and venture out into the public domain for amusement and social contact less and less.

In contrast, the cell, or mobile, telephone has expanded social contact by allowing people to discuss business or private matters anyplace and anytime. Yet, like many other miniaturized electronic devices, the cell phone has tethered the wandering individual to the communication network, like a puppet on a string. The microchip has also made it possible for the entertainment industry to produce many new products, and, in turn, portable TVs, radios, and CD players offer even more mobility, privacy, and pleasure to consumers. However, some buyers with alternate agendas, such as terrorists, have utilized these inventions to construct an effective and sophisticated global network that allows them to carry on their destructive work and to deliver their messages to a worldwide audience. For better and for worse, e-mails, blogs, and text messages whiz around the world in seconds. These instant forms of communicating can galvanize opinions, appeal for international aid in time of crisis, or stir up groups and set off riots or demonstrations.

Technology and globalization are, likewise, central to the growth of many emerging economies. Technology, since the dawn of the Industrial Revolution, has given developing nations the means to catch up with the more advanced ones. Just as Germany and the United States eventually bypassed Great Britain (see Chapter 19), today poor countries with access to models of productivity and technology can close the gap and sell their manufactured goods to richer, consumer nations. The Pacific Rim countries did this in the 1970s and 1980s. China, rapidly moving up the technology ladder, will be a partner or a rival to the more advanced industrialized nations. India is also developing as a player in international trade and commerce.

Since 1995, the earth's ecology and the way technology and industry interface with the climate has become a global issue. In the 1980s, studies and incidents showed that the emission of certain gases, including carbon dioxide, were creating a "greenhouse effect," or the warming of the earth's surface, which might melt the polar ice and raise sea levels. In the early 1990s, a few nations, alarmed by the prospect of global warming, agreed to reduce their industrial emissions. Later, in 1997, 141 countries ratified the Kyoto Protocol. The treaty, which mandates specific reductions of polluting greenhouse gases, went into effect in 2005. However, the United States refused to sign, asserting that the treaty's demands would cripple its economy and predicting the failure of most industrialized nations to meet its emission standards.

Another breakthrough is under way in nanotechnology, which seeks to characterize and manipulate materials on the atomic level, with the aim of building microscopically small devices. This breakthrough follows the post-1945 trend toward miniaturization (see Chapter 21). (*Nano* [Greek, "dwarf"] in the international scientific vocabulary means "one-billionth part of.") Since this cutting-edge research focuses on the behavior of atoms, both singly and· in clusters, the outcome of this new path is unclear. Research is still in the dream state, though stain-resistant textiles using nanotechnology, for example, are already available. Current research holds the promise of future benefits in varied fields, including health care, the environment, and communications.

Philosophy and Religion

Since the 1970s, most intellectual trends have been confined to academic circles and small groups of think-

ers, while religious ideas and movements have caught the attention of the world. The two primary subjects of academic and literary debate have been Post-Structuralism and Deconstruction. **Post-Structuralism,** growing out of Structuralism (see Chapter 21), offers varied ways to understand and interpret literary texts. **Deconstruction** is a method of criticism that focuses on reading, rhetoric, and aspects of language. In the wider world, organized religious groups have dominated the news around the globe. They have entered the political arena, often playing a pivotal role in international affairs and expressing their views on economic, social, and cultural issues.

Philosophy Thomas Kuhn, Roland Barthes, and Jacques Derrida were leading thinkers in the Post-Modern era, though most of their writings appeared earlier. Their ideas gave rise to ongoing debates about timeless issues, such as how humans communicate, understand, and explore the unknown and comprehend their own existence and the meaning of life. Kuhn's ideas were easily understood and quickly adopted by the intellectual community, but the difficult works of Barthes and Derrida were not as accessible and remain unfamiliar to the general public.

The American scientist Thomas Kuhn (1922–1996) was a student of the history of science, exploring the assumptions and methods of scientific research. In *The Structure of Scientific Revolutions* (1962), Kuhn reasoned that throughout the history of science, research has been framed by a paradigm—an unconsciously agreed-on pattern of thought in each scientific discipline—that limits scientists to operating within its boundaries. For Kuhn, no basic changes can occur in science until a series of findings are made that render the existing paradigm unworkable, resulting in a **paradigm shift.** When a paradigm shift occurs, one worldview is exchanged for another, as occurred, for example, when earth-centered astronomy gave way to sun-centered astronomy (see Chapter 15). A paradigm shift, in turn, sparks new experiments that test basic assumptions and generate more questions. Kuhn's paradigm-shift argument was soon adopted by other disciplines, including the social sciences, economics, and business school curriculums, and it has now entered into the mainstream of Western thought.

While Roland Barthes [BART] (1915–1980) bridged the Structuralism and Post-Structuralism movements, he, in contrast to Kuhn, attracted a select group of followers and his influence was confined to a small audience. In books on linguistics and language, Barthes, as a Structuralist, asserted that every language has its own structure, or "code," capable of being "decoded." In later works, Barthes, as a Post-Structuralist, argued that any theory or explanation, such as that used in understanding or decoding a language or literary work, requires its own theory of meaning or explanation. This necessitates a further set of codes and explanations or a series of discourses. Although his quirky style, wit, and allusions and his eclectic interests made Barthes difficult to understand, his ideas had a profound impact on both literary and cultural criticism in France and the United States. But what bothered many of his critics were the implications of his thought. Since Barthes reasoned that there were no certainties in understanding a text, there were, therefore, no overarching concepts (such as science) or political or economic systems (such as democracy or socialism or capitalism). Critics charged that his analysis led to extreme relativism or even **nihilism**—the denial of objective truth.

Jacques Derrida [deh-RE-dah] (1930–2004), a French philosopher and linguist, was another voice of Post-Modernism and the founder of Deconstruction. His book *Of Grammatology* (1967) established his reputation as a seminal thinker. Derrida defined Deconstruction as a new type of reading practice, which "deconstructed" a text, claiming that a text, whether it be a novel, philosophical essay, or history book, could be read in many ways and could have so many meanings that it possessed no ultimate meaning. He argued that speech and writing, as they were deconstructed, could not be analyzed as they were subject to how they were read and who was the reader. Deconstruction became another way to destabilize and displace the former methods of understanding what was said or read or thought to be the "truth." Like the critics of Post-Structuralism, the enemies of Deconstruction concluded that it was one more assault on the West's self-evident truths and fundamental principles—which were rooted in scientific methods, empiricism, and rationalism.

Religion and Religious Thought   After 1970 religious beliefs and organizations tried, as in the past, to adjust to a rapidly changing world. On the one hand, the faithful utilized the latest technology for learning purposes, to spread the faith, and to defend themselves, but, on the other hand, some rejected or attacked scientific and cultural changes that they believed to be threats to their values and beliefs. Christianity and Islam, the world's most popular religions, adopted similar patterns of acceptance or repudiation, but they varied in their respective strategies and tactics for accommodating their faiths to modernity and the Post-Modern world.

In Latin America in the late 1960s, **liberation theology** became a driving force in the struggle against poverty and the oppression of the poor everywhere. Inspired by Vatican II (see Chapter 21), this school of thought was founded primarily by Roman Catholic intellectuals and appealed especially to Catholic clergy who lived and worked among the dispossessed. Mixing Christian social justice with Marxist rhetoric, advocates of liberation theology called for reform of the economic and political systems along with planned Christian-based communities that allowed the poor to work together to improve their living and working conditions. As liberation theology grew into a movement, its revolutionary ideas appeared to threaten the stability of some Latin American countries. In the 1980s, the Catholic Church withdrew its support for the movement and military regimes wiped out many of its communities, killing some priest-leaders. But liberation theology survived as an underground movement in poverty-stricken regions of the world.

In the United States, the sense of Christian social justice reached new heights in the civil rights movement in the late 1960s. But the assassination of Martin Luther King Jr. in 1968, the acceleration of the Vietnam War, and cultural upheaval at home ended this phase of religious activism. Partly in reaction to these events, and partly due to the revival and restructuring of the evangelical wing of Protestantism (see Chapter 19), institutionalized religion in the United States took on a different hue. This shift was brought about for many reasons. In the 1960s and 1970s, a small band of charismatic, fundamentalist preachers, led by Billy Graham (b. 1918), capitalized on the rapid growth of television to deliver their revival messages. Some of these TV evangelists reached celebrity status, and their followers donated generously to build campus-style religious centers, large sanctuaries, and colleges. These preachers touched the hearts and minds of many who were disgusted with the direction in which mainstream America was moving. For them, what they called the coarsening of American life was slowly undermining society's values and morals—thus threatening their vision of a Christian America and their own personal faith. By the early 1990s, these groups—now calling themselves evangelicals—had coalesced into the National Association of Evangelicals and, through their political involvement, were affecting the outcome of elections. Known variously as the "Religious Right" or the "Christian Conservatives," they joined with the Republican party to form a powerful force in American politics. Through the media and the ballot box, they continue to proclaim their beliefs about many issues of modern life, including stem cell research, evolution, abortion, homosexuality, and same-sex marriages. Their participation in politics has sparked heated debates over the relationship between government and religion and raised, once again, concerns about the "wall" that has separated church and state in the United States for more than two hundred years.

Unlike in the United States, organized religion in western Europe has continued to decline as a social and cultural force. Many urban churches have been converted to secular uses, the ranks of Roman Catholic priests and nuns are in steep decline, and membership in Protestant churches has dwindled. However, in Africa and Asia, both the Roman Catholic and Protestant churches, especially the evangelicals, are on the rise. They have won many converts to their faiths, expanded mission programs, and built churches, schools, and hospitals. Bishops and cardinals from African and Asian countries make up an increasingly large percentage of the Roman Catholic hierarchy, which indicates that the Roman Catholic Church will be less Eurocentric in the future.

The papacy of John Paul II (pope, 1978–2005) typified the challenges facing not only the Roman Catholic Church but all organized religion in the late twentieth century. A cardinal from then-communist Poland, he was the first non-Italian pope in 455 years. An engaging, bright, and energetic man, he took advantage of the news media and the jet plane, making highly publicized visits to nearly every country on the globe and traveling more than 742,000 miles. He reached out to other faiths and played a key role in bringing down the communist regime in his native Poland, which turned out be the opening phase of the fall of the USSR (Figure 22.10). He also strengthened papal power, undermined some Vatican II reforms (see Chapter 21), and held firm to the church's traditional stands on most gender and social issues—positions not pleasing to reform-minded Catholics. The humanity and political acumen so evident in his early years gave way to a more autocratic style and a conservative theology, which reflected not only his aging but also the church's response to its more globalized membership and an increasingly secular world.

Islam, the world's other major religion, has also been under siege in the contemporary world, particularly with the rise of Islamic radicalism. In 1979, in Iran, the ayatollahs—learned Shi'ite scholars—led a revolution against the shah's regime and set up the Islamic Republic of Iran. In Afghanistan, after an Afghani victory against the Soviets (1988) and an inconclusive civil war (1992–1996), the Taliban (r. 1996–2001), a local Islamist movement, emerged the winner and established a strict Muslim theocracy. The Taliban gave Osama bin Laden a safe haven from which to operate his al Qaeda network. Other radical Muslim groups—such as the Muslim Brotherhood in Egypt, Hezbollah in Lebanon, and Hamas, which won political power in Palestine in early 2006—attract Muslims who see them as alternatives to dysfunctional regimes, the sworn enemies of Israel, or as the strident voices of anti-Americanism who are willing to take

Figure 22.10   Pope John Paul II in Poland. 1979. *Soon after being elected pope, Karol Wojtyla [voy-TIH-wah] returned to his homeland. His June 1997 visit to Poland was a bold gesture. The leader of the Roman Catholic Church was warmly received, and he met with many organizations, including Solidarity, the underground labor movement that, in 1989, helped overthrow the communist government in Poland. In retrospect, the pope's trip was seen as an important step in the ending of the cold war.*

on the "Great Satan" (the United States), or as all of the above.

The radical Muslims have been further motivated by their knowledge of how European Crusaders conquered and humiliated their ancestors (see Chapter 9), by geopolitics and the recognition of their pivotal location on the globe, by the oil that has enriched their countries and raised Arab national pride, and by recent reinterpretations of the *Qur'an*. The most influential reinterpretation was done by Sayyid Qutb [si-YID KU-tahb] (1906–1966), an Egyptian intellectual. In his *Qur'anic* commentary, *In the Shade of the Qur'an* (thirty volumes, starting in 1954), and the brief *Milestones* (1964), Qutb advised the faithful on how Allah wanted them to live in the modern world. And, most important, this father of modern Islamic terrorism also laid out a revolutionary plan that called for a *jihad*, an armed struggle against the Infidels (the West) and their puppets—the secular Muslim ruling elites. In this *jihad*, the Near Enemy (Muslim secular rulers) and the

Far Enemy (the United States and its European allies) would have to be destroyed. Osama bin Laden answered Qutb's call to arms and has converted many Muslims to his version of Qutb's ideology. After expelling the Infidels, this modern-day *jihad* must purify the Muslim lands of erring communities, kill the Far Enemies, and found a new Islamic empire based on the past, back to the time of the Prophet and the founding of Islam. Whatever ultimate fate awaits al Qaeda, the "franchising" of al Qaeda cells has spread throughout the world, as may be seen in recent terrorist attacks in Europe.

The Literature of Post-Modernism

Post-Modernist literature is notable for the inclusion of new literary voices drawn from diverse sources, including Latin America, central and eastern Europe, and the Islamic world, as well as minorities, assimilated colonial peoples, and new immigrants. Taken together, these new voices signal a shift away from the dominance of the New York–London–Paris cultural axis and the rise of a more global culture.

Fiction   In the late 1960s, for the first time, Latin American authors attracted international acclaim. Most of these writers were distinguished by left-wing political opinions and devotion to a literary style called **"magic realism,"** which mixed realistic and supernatural elements. The ground had been prepared for the magic realists by the Argentine author Jorge Luis Borges [BOR-hays] (1899–1986), whose brief, enigmatic stories stressed fantasy and linguistic experimentation.

The outstanding representative of the magic realist school is Gabriel García Márquez [gahr-SEE-uh MAHR-kays] (b. 1928) of Colombia, who received the 1982 Nobel Prize for Literature—the first Latin American novelist to be so honored. His *One Hundred Years of Solitude* (1967) is among the most highly acclaimed novels of the postwar era. Inspired by William Faulkner's (see Chapter 20) fictional county of Yoknapatawpha, Mississippi, García Márquez invented the town of Macondo as a symbol of his Colombian birthplace. Through the eyes of an omniscient narrator—probably an unnamed peasant—who sees Macondo as moving toward a predestined doom, he produced a hallucinatory novel that blends details from Latin American history with magical events, such as a character's ascent into heaven. The novel's pessimism is typical of the magic realist school.

While Latin America's authors were enjoying international renown for the first time, the writers of central and eastern Europe—another new center of Post-Modernism—were renewing an old tradition. From the early 1800s until communist regimes were installed in the early twentieth century, the finest writers of central and eastern Europe had often been honored in the West. The revival of the literature of this region was heralded by the 1950s cultural thaw initiated by Soviet leader Khrushchev (see Chapter 21), but this thaw proved premature, since controversial writers were either silenced or forced to seek refuge in the West.

Exile was the choice of the novelist Milan Kundera [KOON-deh-rah] (b. 1929) of communist Czechoslovakia, who moved to France after his first novel, *The Joke* (1969), put him in disfavor with Czech authorities. Kundera's style has affinities with magic realism, notably the blending of fantasy with national history, but unlike the Latin American authors, he uses fantasy to emphasize moral themes, never for its own sake. He is also more optimistic than the magic realists, hinting that the power of love can lead to a different and better life. Indeed, Kundera tends to identify sexual freedom with political freedom.

The equation of sexual and political freedom is certainly the message of Kundera's finest novel to date, *The Unbearable Lightness of Being* (1984). He made the center of this work two historic events—the coming of communism to Czechoslovakia in 1948 and its reimposition after the 1968 uprising. He describes the obsessive and ultimately destructive behavior of his main characters as they try to define their sexual natures in the repressive Czech state. Although his novel shows how insignificant human existence is in the face of political repression, he refuses to despair. That his characters struggle for sexual fulfillment, even when faced with overpowering odds, is his way of affirming the strength of human nature. Ultimately, Kundera endorses the humanist belief that the human spirit can be diminished but never broken. The novel was made into a popular art film in 1988, directed by Philip Kaufman (b. 1936), with an international cast.

A belief in the power of the human spirit, similar to Kundera's, is apparent in the work of the American writer Alice Walker (b. 1944). In her poetry, essays, and fiction, she brings a positive tone to her exploration of the African American experience. Her novel *The Color Purple* (1982) is the story of a black woman abused by black men and victimized by white society. The literary device she uses to express this woman's anguish is an old one, a story told through an exchange of letters. What is unique is that in some letters the suffering woman simply pours out her heart to God—an unexpected but moving twist in the skeptical atmosphere of the postwar world. *The Color Purple* also draws on Walker's feminist consciousness, showing that the heroine's survival depends on her solidarity with other black women. Winner of the 1983 Pulitzer Prize, *The Color Purple* was transformed into an award-winning

ENCOUNTER

Continental Drift: Demography and Migration

Prehistoric evidence reveals that the size and density of human populations (demography) and their movement from one geographic area to another (migration) have always been part of the human experience. And from the time humans invented writing, they began to record their hopes and fears as they roamed the globe. Thus, today's migrations and demography, while closely linked to the Age of Globalization, are not new to the humanistic tradition, but simply the latest chapter of an ancient tradition.

The world's expanding population and shifting patterns of migration are continuations of past trends, but they also may indicate the global community's future destiny. Statistics show that today's migrants are exerting strong pressures on national and local governments, along with human service agencies, and increasing tensions within countries and between nations. Making these pressures more acute are the earth's constricted livable areas, the finite supply of natural resources, and the varied ethnic, racial, cultural, religious, and ideological differences between the migrants and their adopted lands.

Since the 1500s, migrations, both voluntary and forced, have accelerated over time, with each new generation affecting the growth of commerce and the ethnic and racial character of target nations' peoples. Migrations in the 1600s and 1700s were closely tied to the first phase of global expansion, and immigrants in this wave were mainly slaves from Africa shipped to the New World and a smaller number of white Europeans sent to convict settlements overseas, as in Australia. In the 1800s, the "Great Migration" occurred, when, between 1845 and 1914, forty-one million immigrants settled in North and South America, though most came from Europe to the United States. In the twentieth century, many nations placed restrictions on immigration, but desperate people, especially those seeking work and political asylum, continued to find new homelands.

Since the 1970s, the patterns of immigration have been Vietnamese war refugees to the United States and some Asian nations following the Vietnam War; legal and illegal workers from Latin America to the United States (Encounter figure 22.1); ex-colonials returning "home" to Europe as the colonial system broke down; guest workers from southern Europe and Muslim countries to Europe; Asian "temporary" workers to the oil-exporting countries; and eastern Europeans to western Europe with the collapse of communism. The flow of people around the world has put pressures along many borders, such as between eastern and western European nations, among some Asian countries, and along the Mexican–United States border. Regardless of efforts to control or stop the flow, immigration will surely continue. And many immigrants have recorded their stories in fiction, plays, and films—thus contributing to the multiculturalism of Post-Modernism.

Demographic studies show that the world's population is approaching seven billion, and the projection is for over nine billion by 2050. The largest numbers will be in Asia (5.4 billion) and Africa (2 billion), followed by Latin America (806 million), Europe (603 million), and North America (438 million). However, diseases, such as AIDS in Africa, flu epidemics from Asia, or some other lethal illness, could change these forecasts. Twenty of the most populous cities are on the five largest land masses: twelve in Asia, five in Latin America, two in Europe, and one in North America (New York). Other demographic shifts are taking place that will bring more challenges. In rich countries, the population is aging and the working population is

---

film in 1985, directed by Stephen Spielberg, and in 2005 it became a successful Broadway musical.

Toni Morrison, another American writer, was the first African American to win the Nobel Prize for Literature. Awarded in 1993, the prize recognized her for a group of novels that explore the plight of black people in American society. Except for *The Song of Solomon* (1977), which has a male narrator, her novels focus on female characters who are victims of a racist society. For example, in her first novel, *The Bluest Eye* (1970), a young black girl, attracted by the standard of white beauty, yearns to have blue eyes. Morrison also shows how violence is a central part of the black experience, as, for instance, in *Sula* (1973), when a grandmother, wanting to support her family, deliberately injures herself in order to collect insurance money. Inspired by her sense of an African heritage, she draws on folklore, mythology, and sometimes the supernatural, as in *Beloved* (1987), where a ghost is the central character. Along with racism and violence, Morrison imbues her novels with spiritual longing, thus offering hope for a more just society in the future.

Maxine Hong Kingston (b. 1940) has enriched Post-Modernism by bringing Chinese Americans into

Encounter figure 22.1   Mexican Migrants. 1986. *Mexican migrants, desperately seeking to enter the United States, travel across deserts or pay smugglers to get them across the border. The United States faces a growing dilemma with the large influx of illegal immigrants from Central and Latin America, and politicians cannot agree on how to solve the problem. Agribusiness, many farmers, and low-paying companies need these migrants, legal or illegal, as cheap laborers. But their arrival has overloaded state and local welfare agencies, aroused suspicion and distrust, and heightened prejudices. Some civilian groups, such as the Minuteman project, have begun vigilante patrols along the borders in an effort to capture those trying to slip into the United States and the government has approved the building of a 700-mile wall to discourage illegal entry.*

declining, while in poor countries, the population is growing and a larger percentage of this population is young people.

These population trends and movements are changing the face of the West. National identity is being questioned today, and the contradictory answers to this issue can be polarizing in an ethnically and racially mixed society. For example, France in 2006, with a population that is 10 percent Muslim, largely the result of immigration from former colonies, has been beset by urban unrest among Arab youth and divisive protests over the ban of religious headscarves in public schools and the lack of jobs and economic opportunities. The future of the West will be determined in large part by how Westerners respond to the challenges of globalization and two of its most powerful stimulants: demography and migrations.

Learning from the Encounter   What are some of the broad issues brought about by demographic changes and immigration? **How** have the major migrations since the seventeenth century affected the growth of nations? **Discuss** the patterns of migrations since the 1970s. **What** do the demographic studies tell us about the world's populations? Give **examples** of how these developments affect American society and your own life.

American literature through her autobiographical books, a novel, short stories, and articles. Her avowed aim as a writer has been to "claim America," meaning to show that the Chinese have the right to belong through their labor in building the country and supporting themselves. In staking out this claim, she was influenced by the poet William Carlos Williams (1883–1963), a Modernist who envisioned an American culture distinct from Europe and fashioned from indigenous materials and forms. Kingston's writings not only celebrate Chinese strength and achievement but also serve to avenge wrongs—by calling exploitation, racism, and ignorance by their true names.

The daughter of Chinese immigrants whose language was Say Yup, a dialect of Cantonese, Kingston has used her own life as a paradigm of the Chinese American experience. Drawing on childhood stories told in the immigrant community, she wrote two works that summarize her Chinese heritage: *The Woman Warrior: Memoirs of a Girlhood Among Ghosts* (1976), dealing with matriarchal influence, and *China Men* (1980), telling of the patriarchal side.

As Post-Modern literature grew more pluralistic, a major voice was missing, one that represented overseas peoples, drawn to Europe from former colonies. When the colonial system ended, in the Late Modern era, the mother countries were very relaxed toward former subjects, granting them easy access for travel, work, and settlement—which constituted one of the major migration movements of the late twentieth century. For example, between 1991 and 2001, half of the 2.2 million people added to Britain's population were born outside of Britain. Assimilation was always the goal of the relaxed immigration policy, but barriers—cultural, philosophical, and often legal—worked to undermine that goal. And European elites tended to ignore the new immigrants, once settled. Now, with the dawn of the new millennium, this neglected world found a commanding voice: the English-born Zadie Smith (born Sadie Smith) (b. 1975).

Smith, educated within the British establishment at Cambridge University, made a stunning debut with *White Teeth* (2000), an evocative novel about multicultural London. In highly ironic prose, Smith presents the lives of three overlapping families—all outsiders in a way—over three generations: a working-class family of Muslim Bengalis; a working-class family similar to the author's, with a white English father and a Jamaican-born wife; and an educated, middle-class family of British Jews. A hugely ambitious work, brilliantly realized, *White Teeth* addresses many of today's major topics, such as ethnic and racial identity, terrorism, and assimilation.

The terrorist attacks on New York and Washington, D.C., in 2001 made Westerners eager for knowledge about Islamic culture, by writers from within that world. Previously, translations of Islamic works of fiction had appeared regularly in the West, though their style and themes usually echoed Western fiction, as in *The Cairo Trilogy* (1956–1957), about three generations of Egyptians between World War I and the early 1950s, by the Nobel laureate Naguib Mahfouz [MAH-fooz] (b. 1911). Now, after 9/11, the audience expanded dramatically, to address the burgeoning desire for Islamic books.

The most profound voice yet to emerge in Islam is that of the controversial Turkish writer Orhan Pamuk [PAH-muk] (b. 1952). His first novel, *The White Castle* (1985), about the ironies of modernization, made him a writer to watch. Later works confirmed that judgment. Today, Western readers often hail him as the "conscience of his nation," because his themes echo basic Turkish dilemmas: Western or Islamic identity, secularism or religion, and freedom or authority. While Pamuk's novels are filled with ambiguity, his words to the Swiss press landed him in trouble in 2005. His offense was his use of the word "genocide" to describe Turkey's killing of Armenians in 1915–1917 and his claim that thirty thousand Kurds had been killed by Turks since 1985. He was charged with insulting Turkey's national character. In early 2006 the charges were dropped. Still in doubt is Turkey's looming membership in the Euro-

pean Union, which demands that all member countries meet Europe's standards of free speech.

Of Pamuk's novels, *My Name Is Red* (2000) has excited the most global attention. It is a murder mystery, and much more. Learned, ironic, erotic, and deeply steeped in the literary methods of the Modernist novel, *My Name Is Red* focuses on a circle of artists—all miniaturists—at the court of the Ottoman sultan Murat III (r. 1574–1594), a great patron of the arts. When one artist goes missing, a chain of events is unleashed, ending with the death of the murderer. Adding to the novel's allure are tidbits of Ottoman history, references to miniaturist styles across the Islamic world, and, of special note, meditations on the stir that arose when Western painting was introduced to the Ottoman court (see Encounter figure 11.1). The novel's narrative unfolds in a Modernist style, as each of its fifty-nine chapters is told from a shifting perspective, including those of several characters, a dog, a gold coin, and the color red. *My Name Is Red* won the International IMPAC Dublin Literary Award in 2003. In 2006 Pamuk received the Nobel Prize for Literature, the first Turkish writer to be honored with this award.

Poetry   Poetry has, by and large, experienced a fallow period after 1970. The already tiny audience for poetry has grown smaller still, in response to the explosive growth of mass media, shifting demographics, and the obscurity of most verse. It has also thus far resisted globalization, largely because, as is often said, "Poetry in translation does not travel well." However, one major poet, writing in English, has emerged: Derek Walcott (b. 1930), the West Indian poet.

Walcott's writings reflect his personal situation, first as a youth on the remote volcanic island of St. Lucia, and second as a mature black writer, torn between island culture and his new American homeland. Author of numerous plays and books of poetry, Walcott became world famous with *Omeros* (1990), a book-length poem that revisited Homer's *Iliad* and *Odyssey*, transposing their setting to the Caribbean in the 1900s and drawing on their themes of war and homecoming, respectively. Dante's *Divine Comedy* was another major influence on Walcott, providing him with the theme of salvation and the three-line verse form in which the poem is composed. In *Omeros*, Walcott blended imagery and diction, redolent of the lush tropics, with anguish for the paradisiacal world he had lost. Walcott was awarded the Nobel Prize for Literature in 1992, the third black author to be so honored.

Drama   Drama, like poetry, has not become global. Avant-garde theater has nearly withered away but has not disappeared. Few great dramatists have emerged. Having been politicized by the 1960s, most dramatists made sociopolitical issues central in their work. Thus, the theater, often diagnosed as "the glorious invalid," has been ailing much of the time. However, there have been two rays of hope: the comedies of the Italian team Dario Fo (b. 1926) and Franca Rame (b. 1929) and the rise of comedy troupes.

In Fo-Rame, from 1959 to 1970, Fo was the leader, writing, directing, designing sets and costumes, and, sometimes, composing music. Rame, his wife, muse, and leading lady, assisted at all levels. Nurtured in socialist families in Italy, the pair were drawn to "popular theater," which catered to ordinary people. Their early plays were little more than comic revues, satirizing postwar Italy. In response, the church and the state began a campaign to censor them, which has not subsided. Over time, as their satire became fiercer, their fame grew, along with controversy. In the 1960s, Fo and Rame took their act to Italian television, where they became sensations. From 1970 to 1985, they performed with a theatrical collective (based in Milan and presenting plays there and all over Italy and around the world), for which Fo wrote plays, including *Accidental Death of an Anarchist* (1970), which established his international reputation. This provocative play, based on a real-life event, raised the question: Did a police suspect leap to his death or was he pushed? Blending drama with comedy, this full-length, tragic farce used techniques from **commedia dell'arte** (Italian, "comedy of art"), a theatrical form from the sixteenth to the eighteenth century, involving clowns, puppets, and stock figures; absurdist drama; and Fo's own imagination. In 1997, for his work as a playwright, Dario Fo was awarded the Nobel Prize for Literature.

Theater troupes, offering evenings of inventive wit, social satire, and music, originated in England. The British group that pioneered this trend was Beyond the Fringe (1960–1963), a four-person team, featuring the actor and musician Dudley Moore (1935–2002). Their example later inspired the Monty Python Flying Circus (1969–1974), led by the hilarious John Cleese (b. 1939), the master of "silly walks." The success of Beyond the Fringe was confined mainly to concert halls and television, while Monty Python's reach extended further, ranging over all of mass culture. Both groups made topical satire their forte, mocking religion, the state, and popular fads. But what made Monty Python so special was its surrealism, an influence from absurdist theater. The current popularity of sociopolitical satire in the West is a testament to the enduring influence of these two groups.

Post-Modernism and the Arts

By 1970 the arts had already begun to change, as artists and architects moved beyond Late Modernism, which seemed to have dissolved into weak minimalist schools (see Chapter 21). In Post-Modernism, the "shock of the new" gave way to the "shock of the old." Seeking a way out of Late Modernism's chaotic pessimism and its focus on abstraction, Post-Modern artists were more optimistic and revived earlier styles, although always with added layers of meaning, nuance, or irony. Realism made a triumphant return to art, flourishing as **Neorealism,** a style based on photographic clarity of detail; as **Neoexpressionism,** a style that offers social criticism and focuses on nontraditional painting methods; and as **Neoclassicism** (not to be confused with the Neoclassicism of the late eighteenth century), which had been dormant since the early twentieth century and pronounced dead by the Late Modernists. Neoclassicism is the most striking style within Post-Modernism, in both painting and architecture, perhaps because it looks so fresh to modern eyes. In addition to these various forms of realism, Modernist abstraction remains a significant facet of Post-Modernism. In their openness to artistic possibilities and their refusal to adopt a uniform style, the Post-Modernists very much resemble the Post-Impressionists of the late nineteenth century.

Painting An outstanding Neorealist painter is the American Philip Pearlstein (b. 1924), who specializes in nonidealized nudes. Starting in the 1960s, he made his chief subject human bodies beyond their prime, perhaps as a way of reflecting the melancholy of the age. His nudes are rendered in stark close-up, the bodies at rest like hanging meat, and with cropped heads and limbs as in a photograph (Figure 22.11). His works seem to parody the "centerfold sexuality" that accompanied the sexual revolution brought on in part by the birth control pill.

Whereas Neorealism tends to neutrality or moral subtlety, Neoexpressionism uses realism to create paintings that are overtly socially critical. The outstanding Neoexpressionist and the most highly regarded painter among the Post-Modernists is the German artist Anselm Kiefer [KEE-fuhr] (b. 1945), whose expressive tendencies owe much to his older countryman Joseph Beuys (see Chapter 21). Kiefer's works have blazed new trails with nontraditional painting materials, including dirt, tar, and copper threads. Existential anguish is alive in his works, which tend to focus on apocalyptic images of a blasted earth—a chilling reference to the threat of nuclear destruction (Figure 22.12). Post-Modern optimism may nevertheless be read in his borrowings from Mesopotamia and Egypt, which affirm the continuity of Western culture from its earliest stages to the present. In his apocalyptic vision, personal references, and historical allusions, Kiefer is perhaps the contemporary artist closest to the German Expressionists of the early twentieth century.

In the United States, an early convert to Neoexpressionism was Susan Rothenberg [ROTH-en-berg]

Figure 22.11 PHILIP PEARLSTEIN. *Female on Eames Chair, Male on Swivel Stool.* 1981. Watercolor, 60 × 40″. Collection of Eleanor and Leonard Bellinson. Courtesy Donald Morris Gallery, Birmingham, Mich. *Pearlstein's refusal to glamorize his nude subjects is part of a democratizing tendency in Post-Modernism. Just as some Post-Modernist authors borrow freely from mass-circulation genres such as mystery and science fiction, so Pearlstein focuses attention on bodily features like sagging breasts and bulging veins that had been overlooked by realistic painters.*

(b. 1945). Sensing the tidal shift under way in art, she abandoned 1960s minimalism for a more expressive style, starting in 1973. Until 1980, she painted one subject: the horse. Her horse paintings have a contrived feeling about them; a Rothenberg horse is not so much a living presence as a representation of her deep feelings—an artistic credo she shares with van Gogh (see Chapter 19). In *Butterfly* (1976), the horse's midsection coincides with the crossing of a giant *X*, thus giving shape to the composition (Figure 22.13). Although the animal is shown in a running pose, its body is made flat through the design and the painterly effects, in the manner of the Action painter Willem de Kooning (see Figure 21.10).

The British painter Sue Coe (b. 1951), who now lives and works in the United States, is another important Neoexpressionist whose art serves social and political causes. Daughter of a working-class London family, she is a counterculturalist who came of age in the stormy 1960s. Committed to feminist and overtly political art, she does not espouse any specific ideology but simply confronts injustice wherever she sees it. She once described her creed in these words: "If you remove your armies from other people's countries, I won't paint war." In a broad sense, she wants her art to be a tool for change, to bear witness to the vices of capitalist and urban society, as in *Modern Man Followed by the Ghosts of His Meat* (Figure 22.14), one of the works in her indictment of the meat industry and its shocking treatment of animals. Although the message constantly threatens to overpower the art, Coe's paintings are meant to move viewers to share the artist's concerns and thus work for reform.

A painter who embraced elements of Neorealism and Neoexpressionism, along with other artistic trends, to forge a unique personal style is the Colombian artist Fernando Botero (b. 1932). In the manner of the Neorealists, Botero populates his canvases with human and animal shapes, though he makes each figure grossly overweight. In the manner of Neoexpressionists, he adopts exaggerated effects—the inflated figures—to reveal his negative feelings for his middle-class subjects, but, unlike the Neoexpressionists, he creates highly varnished canvases, devoid of visible brushstrokes and textured surfaces. The rotund figures are flat, brightly colored, and boldly outlined—as in Colombian folk art. And he gives each work a political subtext, a mission he borrowed from the Mexican muralist Diego Rivera (see Chapter 20). *Dancing in Colombia* (1980), with its robust musicians, is typical of Botero's style, but the dancers, rendered in a smaller scale, are fairly unusual (Figure 22.15). This scene mocks the smug middle class, who party while drug lords destroy their country.

A painter who uses Neoclassicism to make subtle commentary on art history is Peter Blake (b. 1920). In *The Meeting,* or *"Have a Nice Day, Mr. Hockney,"* he depicts a meeting of three 1960s British Pop artists who in the 1980s joined the ranks of Post-Modernism (Figure 22.16). This new version of Courbet's *The Meeting,* or *"Bonjour Monsieur Courbet"* (see Figure 18.12) is both an ironic comment on contemporary Neoclassicism and a classical composition in itself. The three artists depicted here are, from left to right, Howard Hodgkin (b. 1932), Peter Blake, and David Hockney (b. 1937), the last-named grasping a huge paintbrush. Blake's *Meeting* abounds in ironic juxtapositions: age versus youth, Old World versus the New, the aesthetic life versus consumerism, work versus play, and

Figure 22.12 ANSELM KIEFER. *Osiris and Isis.* 1985–1987. Diptych, mixed media on canvas, 12′6″ × 18′4½″ × 6½″. **Courtesy Marian Goodman Gallery, New York.** *Kiefer drew on an ancient Egyptian myth (see Figure 4.8) to give shape to his fears of modern technology. He represents Isis, the goddess who restored her husband-brother Osiris to life, as an electronic keyboard at the top of a pyramid. He adds actual copper wires to connect the circuit board to broken bits of ceramics, his symbol of Osiris's fragmented body. In Kiefer's Post-Modern imagination, technology has become a deity with the capacity to destroy or create.*

Figure 22.13 SUSAN ROTHENBERG. *Butterfly.* 1976. Acrylic on canvas, 69½ × 83″. National Gallery, Washington, D.C. Gift of Perry R. and Nancy Lee Bass. 1995.6.1. *While Rothenberg's choice of the horse as a subject may reflect her personal feelings, the horse is among the oldest images in the Western canon, dating from the prehistoric cave art of France. The horse was revered as a noble beast in aristocratic cultures that have flourished from antiquity until modern times, and their art has reflected that view. Even in the modern liberal democracies of the 1800s, the horse, while no longer prized as in the past, was still judged valuable as a work animal or a romantic beast and was represented as such in art. Only with the coming of Modernist abstraction did the horse cease to appeal to artists. Rothenberg's art thus restores the horse to a central place in the canon, with the image now purged of elitist and utilitarian overtones.*

Figure 22.14 Sue Coe. *Modern Man Followed by the Ghosts of His Meat.* 1990. Copyright © 1990 Sue Coe. Courtesy Galerie St. Etienne, New York. *This is one of the works in the protest booklet* Meat: Animals and Industry *by Sue Coe and her sister Mandy, inspired by visits to slaughterhouses and factory farms. This work is in the vein of an editorial cartoon inspired by a Dickens novel. Coe prefers to work with graphic arts ("handmade, mechanically reproduced images") because they engage the viewer more directly and allow the artist to reach a larger audience than do more traditional means.*

Figure 22.15 Fernando Botero. *Dancing in Colombia.* 1980. Oil on canvas, 74 × 91". Metropolitan Museum of Art, New York. Anonymous Gift, 1983 (1983.251). *Botero's use of "fatness" to depict Colombia's ruling middle class springs from the socialist belief that the wealthy feast while the poor starve—a visual equivalent of the English slang "fat cat." Because famine has largely ended in the industrialized world, Botero's symbolism may be meaningless for some people. Yet, many can still resonate to the rotund shapes, viewing them simply satirically, because of the obesity epidemic in the United States and elsewhere in the West.*

Figure 22.16 PETER BLAKE. *The Meeting,* or *"Have a Nice Day, Mr. Hockney."* 1981–1983. Oil on canvas, 39 × 49". Tate Gallery. *Blake brings Classicism up-to-date by applying its features and principles to a contemporary California setting. He fills the sun-drenched scene with double-coded references, including the pose of the girl in the right foreground (borrowed partly from a skating magazine and partly from Classical sculpture), the dog (an allusion to American youth culture and Alberti's Renaissance artistic theory), and the winged hat of the person in the Dodgers shirt (a contemporary sports emblem and a symbol of the god Mercury). The result is a hybrid scene, marked by the ironic contrast between the grave and self-contained central figures and the "cool" teenagers in the background.*

timeless present versus fleeting moment. Blake's Post-Modernism fuses rival traditions, the eternal values of Classicism and the transience of Pop Art.

Modernist abstraction continues to have a powerful impact on Post-Modernism. The most brilliant current disciple of abstraction is Frank Stella (b. 1936), a painter who has produced an immense and varied body of work. A minimalist in the 1950s, painting striped canvases (see Figure 21.13), he became a forerunner of Neoexpressionism in the 1970s, using gaudy color and decorative effects. He has remained true to abstract ideals, as in *Norisring,* one of the *Shard* series, which uses the scraps left over from other works (Figure 22.17). Fully abstract and nonrepresentational, this work is nevertheless Post-Modernist, since it combines

the genres of painting and sculpture—an ambition of many Post-Modernists.

Among the Post-Modern painters who remain devoted to Late Modern abstraction is Samuel Gilliam (b. 1933), an African American. Gilliam began as an Abstract Expressionist and a color field painter, covering the entire canvas with color and emphasizing solid areas of color on a monumental scale. Later in his career, Gilliam explored new artistic outlets. A series of experiments led him to create multicolored soaked and stained canvases, draping and wrapping them in space, and shaping them into three-dimensional sculptural works (Figure 22.18). Gilliam's large "draped" paintings were hung in public places—subway stations, airports, and libraries—and became part of the

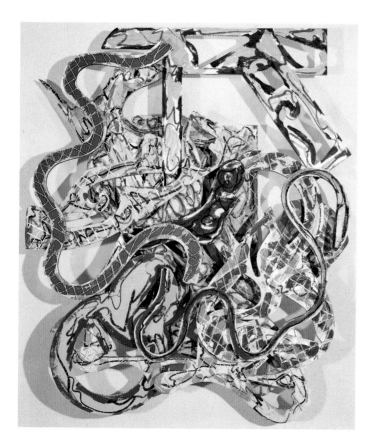

Figure 22.17   FRANK STELLA. *Norisring (XVI, 3X).* 1983. Mixed media on etched aluminum, 6'7" × 5'7" × 1'3". Collection of Ann and Robert Freedman. Courtesy Knoedler & Company, New York. *Largely because of his lively intelligence, Stella has stayed on the cutting edge of Post-Modernism. He has kept abstraction alive almost single-handedly at a time when realist styles are dominant. His 1960s innovation, the shaped canvas, allowed him to replace the rectilinear canvas with an abstract form (see Figure 21.13). By the early 1980s, he had transformed the shaped canvas into a blend of sculpture and painting, as in the* Circuits *series.*

installation art movement (see below). They are also on view in many art museums. Gilliam continues to experiment in diverse media, using computers to create images, combining colors, textures, spaces, and materials, such as plastics and aluminum, and linking his earlier styles with his latest innovations. Using his own handmade paper, Gilliam hand-painted works of mixed media, including cutouts, stitching, and collages, which combine colors and textures and are testaments to his innovative spirit. He and Romare Bearden (see Chapter 21) are recognized as the leading African American painters after World War II.

Defying easy categorization is the German painter Gerhard Richter (b. 1932), whose style-shifting images make him the art world's chameleon. This protean artist's paintings range over the Post-Modernist spectrum, from abstraction to a kind of realism, with stops in between, including photo-realism (a painting style that mimics the clarity of a photograph) and Op Art, often working in two styles at once. He further complicates his art through varied means, such as choosing banal subjects (two lighted candles) and blurring realistic images (to suggest faded photographs). Per-

Figure 22.18   SAM GILLIAM. *All Cats Are Grey at Night.* 1996. Acrylic on canvas, 65 × 44 × 8" (installed, variable). Collection of Patrick Everett. Photo: Mark Gulezian/Quicksilver. *Gilliam, who was a member of the Washington Color School of the 1960s, moved beyond Abstract Expressionism, redefining its traditions and techniques to experiment and create his own style. According to one critic, Gilliam has brought back "the pleasure of texture and the optical qualities of painting." In his "drapes"—as these works are called—he blends colors, softening them on the surface and balancing them in the hanging of the canvas, thus combining colors and texture.*

Figure 22.19 GERHARD RICHTER. *Betty.* 1988. Oil on canvas, 40¼ × 28½". St. Louis Art Museum. © Gerhard Richter. *Richter's jarring portrait of Betty—with face averted—sparks a multilayered interpretation. In existential terms, the subject expresses the isolation of modern life. In an art historical sense, the depiction of the back of the head evokes the method of Renaissance sculptors in fully finishing their figures in the round (see Figure 11.11). In Modernist terms, the provocative pose is a challenge to viewers' basic assumptions about art (see Figure 21.21). A feminist reading could interpret the subject as rejecting the "male gaze" of the painter. And in Freudian terms, the pose could reflect an estrangement between subject (his wife?) and artist. Richter's silence about his motives here leaves the meaning of the work open. Thus, Richter's* Betty *stands as a masterpiece of Post-Modernist ambiguity.*

haps his most arresting image is *Betty* (1988) (Figure 22.19), a portrait of a woman whose face is hidden from the artist's (and the viewer's) gaze. This perverse image, with its slightly blurred effect, while charming, forces the viewer to question the artistic intent of this most enigmatic of Post-Modern artists.

Sculpture Like painters, Post-Modernist sculptors began to work with realistic forms. For example, serving as complements to the Neorealist paintings of Philip Pearlstein are the sculptures of the American John De Andrea (b. 1941). Typically, De Andrea uses traditional poses, as in *Sphinx* (Figure 22.20). But his human figures are fully contemporary, suggestive of young upwardly mobile professionals ("yuppies") who have taken off their clothes. Whether or not his works are satirical, De Andrea manages to capture in sculptural form the erotic quality considered so desirable by modern advertising, movies, and mass media.

Minimalism, an art movement that originated in the 1950s and 1960s (see Chapter 21), showed great staying power after 1970, particularly among sculptors who drew inspiration from its reductionist tendencies. Minimalist sculptors explored issues of medium, form, and meaning, as in the works of Dan Flavin (1933–1996). Flavin, rejecting the traditional materials of sculpture, made light the principal medium in his art (Figure 22.21). Because his usual light source was fluorescent tubes, this choice impacted the final form of his works. And, because of the centrality of technology in his art, each work's meaning is fairly literal and not personal—a pervasive feature of minimalism.

The minimalist aesthetic also inspired the spare form of the Vietnam Veterans' Memorial, in Washington, D.C., designed by Maya Ying Lin (b. 1959), the daughter of Chinese immigrants. Winner of a national contest for the design—two highly polished black granite walls set at angles so as to form a giant V—Lin rejected traditional images of fallen warriors (see Figure 4.12) and chose instead an unconventional and understated tribute to those who had died. In her artistic

Figure 22.20 JOHN DE ANDREA. *Sphinx.* 1987. Polyvinyl, oil paint, life-size. Courtesy ACA Galleries, New York. *Unlike Pearlstein, who uses nudity to register his disgust, De Andrea designs his polyvinyl nudes to celebrate the glossy lives of the upper middle class. The bodies of his nude subjects convey what today's consumer culture urges everyone to be: healthy, sleek, athletic, and sexy.*

Figure 22.21 DAN FLAVIN. *Untitled (For Ellen).* 1975. Pink, blue, and green fluorescent light, ht. 88¼". As installed at the Des Moines Art Center, Des Moines. 1994. *Just as video art added a new medium—sound—to the sculptural art, so did Dan Flavin's works in light. By making light his medium, Flavin shifted the aesthetic focus from sculpture's traditional concerns— texture and presence—to mood and atmosphere. In* Untitled, *which is installed in a corner niche of an otherwise empty gallery, the glowing lights evoke feelings of safety and pleasure. Adding a personal touch to this abstract piece is the subtitle,* For Ellen, *whose memory presumably has inspired the cheery colors of pink, blue, and green.*

Figure 22.22 MAYA YING LIN. Vietnam Veterans' Memorial. 1982. Black granite, 250' length (each wing). Washington, D.C. *The vertex of the V-shaped memorial is set in such a way that makes it possible to view the Washington Monument and then turn to see the Lincoln Memorial—the shrines that honor America's two most admired presidents. The Vietnam Veterans' Memorial, although controversial when built, has had a healing effect, bringing the nation together after a war that bitterly divided its citizens. Every day, visitors come to pay their respects, leaving flowers, photographs, letters, and military medals. The seemingly endless list of names reminds the viewer of the terrible costs of war.*

vision, the memorial was to appear "as a rift in the earth," which would lift up and then recede—a hint of the environmental art principles then being born. On the memorial's two walls are carved the names of the Vietnam War's casualties, the more than fifty-eight thousand American men and women killed or missing, arranged not alphabetically but by the war year for each death. Perusing the names gives a striking representation of the rhythm of the conflict, as the fighting intensified in the late 1960s and early 1970s and then wound down to its end, in 1974. Built on the northwest side of the National Mall, this monument has become one of the most hallowed and visited places in the United States (Figure 22.22).

In contrast to the solemnity and timelessness of Lin's outdoor sculptures are the entertaining and transitory works of Christo (b. 1935) and his wife, Jeanne-

Claude (b. 1935). Their creations are often identified with environmental art, a type of art that is related to nature, usually site specific and sometimes ephemeral (see "Environmental Art"), and also with **conceptual art,** a type of art in which the idea or concept is more important than the means employed to complete it. Conceptual art, which began in the 1960s, is often a vehicle for sociopolitical ideas. Regardless of how Christo and Jeanne-Claude's works are defined, they overawe the viewer, relate to the landscape, bring out crowds and the media, and stir up controversy (Figure 22.23).

Their monumental projects require years of planning, the cooperation and approval of government agencies and private institutions, the employment of hundreds of workers, and the purchase of vast quantities of materials, usually roping, steel rods, and fabrics. Christo and Jeanne-Claude accept no funding or donations for these million-dollar events and pay for them from the sales of their own works, including postcards, scale models, and other personalized items. Their wrapping a building, stringing a nylon fence along a coastline, or decorating a park or environmental site becomes a public spectacle. Yet each art event lasts for only a few weeks and is then dismantled—to be remembered through photographs, on film, or in the minds of those who witnessed it. The environment

Figure 22.23 CHRISTO AND JEANNE-CLAUDE. Image, from *The Gates*. 2005. Central Park, New York. *The Gates in Central Park lasted for two weeks, a typical time period for a Christo project. Seventy-five hundred gates—free-hanging, saffron-colored fabric panels—were positioned ten to fifteen feet apart along the footpaths for a total of twenty-three miles. The winter landscape, with the bare trees and blanket of snow, and the rows of saffron-colored panels, gave the effect of a brightly colored river running through Central Park where an individual could walk for miles enjoying the interplay between nature and the art. The artists, who developed the concept in 1979, worked with government and civic groups to gain their approval. Christo and Jeanne-Claude, according to their arrangements, paid for the $21-million-dollar project.*

Figure 22.24 RACHEL WHITEREAD. *Untitled (Yellow Bath)*. 1996. Cast made of rubber and polystyrene. Luhring Augustine Gallery, New York. *Whiteread's wide-ranging eye has led her to sculpt many household objects, including mattresses, chairs and tables, bookshelves, and bathtubs. Her works are more than mere representations; she makes a cast of the spaces around an object, trying to capture traces of a human presence. In its new incarnation, Whiteread's bathtub has been compared to a sarcophagus. Such an interpretation is acceptable to the artist, as she is on record as comparing her casting technique to the making of a death mask. Indeed, there is a faint air of melancholy about Whiteread's sculptures, since they seem to affirm human mortality.*

returns to its pre-event state and the art has disappeared—thus, only the idea or the memory remains of this transitory happening.

Another important Post-Modernist sculptor is Rachel Whiteread (b. 1964), one of the "Brit Pak" or, more seriously, the YBA, Young British Artists. The YBA has traded in the low-key style of older British art for an art that is attention grabbing and often associated with scandal. Unlike the works of many of this British school, Whiteread's sculptures are deeply serious and modest in execution. Inspired by American minimalist art of the 1960s and 1970s, her works usually represent simple ideas using familiar, everyday objects (Figure 22.24). She works in various media, including plaster, concrete, resin, and rubber.

Installation Art   Enjoying a vogue today is **installation art,** a boundary-challenging type of art born in the 1960s that creates architectural tableaux [tah-BLOZ]—depictions of a scene, as on a stage, with silent and motionless characters—using objects drawn from and making references to artistic sources (such as music, painting, sculpture, and theater) and the workaday world (such as everyday tasks, media images, and foodstuffs); the work may include a human presence. One of the most gifted installation artists is the American Ann Hamilton (b. 1956), who is known for her sensory works layered with meaning. The piece *mantle,* installed at the Miami Art Museum in 1998 (Figure 22.25), filled up a second-floor gallery and had as its human focus a woman performing a household task before an open window—an homage to Dutch genre art, which often pictured women in similar poses. The task the seated woman is performing—sewing sleeves onto the bodies of wool coats—gives rise to the piece's name (a mantle is, among other things, a sleeveless garment). Multiple wires dangle down the gallery's wall into a mound of sixty thousand cut flowers displayed on a 48-foot-long table behind the woman. This mountainous display of slowly decaying flowers is a memento mori, or a reminder of death—a frequent theme of Renaissance art. Hamilton's growing reputation led to her choice as the American representative at the prestigious Venice Art Bienniale in 1999.

Figure 22.25   ANN HAMILTON. View of *mantle*. Miami Art Museum. 1998. *Installation art has affinities with other innovative art forms, but it lacks the centrality of the videotaped image, as in video art, or a strong musical component, as in performance art. In* mantle, *there was a minor musical aspect: Radio receivers, placed amid the flowers, transmitted musical and other sounds during the event. Feminist in perspective, this installation may be interpreted as an ironic comment on the male-dominated art world, because, until recently, this world discouraged women from becoming artists and limited their artistic choices mainly to domestic chores, such as making clothes. In the photograph, Ann Hamilton is the woman sewing; volunteers and paid attendants performed this task when the artist was absent.*

Environmental Art   A new art form that emerged after 1970 was **environmental art.** Environmental structures were constructed with native materials, such as stone, mud, water, and plants, so as to appear as if made by nature. Part landscape design, part engineering, and part minimalist art, this sculpture began in response to Modernism's wish to erase the boundary between art and life, as in Robert Smithson's *Spiral Jetty* (1970) (Figure 22.26). What made environmental sculpture Post-Modern was its politics, as the works, in effect, expressed solidarity with the environmental cause.

Video Art   Nam June Paik (1932–2006) was virtually the founder of video art and certainly the most influential artist working in this medium during his lifetime. **Video art** is made with a video monitor, or monitors, and may be produced using computerized programs or with handheld cameras; the work may be ephemeral or permanent. Working with videotapes beginning in 1959, Paik evolved from an artist intent on being entertaining into one devoted to serious issues in his projects and, starting in the 1980s, embracing political ideas. A sophisticated work that represent his political beliefs is *My Faust (Stations): Religion* (1989–1991), which is part of a series of thirteen individual multimonitor installations (see Figure 22.8). Rich in allusions, this work refers to the thirteen channels available at the time for Manhattan television viewers, and the word *stations* in the title, reinforced by the Neogothic altarpieces, suggests Christianity's

Stations of the Cross, the thirteen stages of Jesus' journey to his crucifixion. The character Faust was a symbol of both restlessness and relentless seeking of knowledge, even to the loss of the soul (see Chapter 17). Thus, Paik's *My Faust* suggests humanity's pact with the devil for secular power and glory.

Architecture   By the mid-1960s, Late Modernism was moving toward Post-Modernism, as avant-garde architects experimented with new structural forms and built with new materials. In particular, the unadorned "glass box"—the centerpiece of Late Modernism's reigning architectural style—was cast aside in favor of decorative exteriors and various **claddings,** or covers or overlays on the exterior walls.

Also contributing to the rise of Post-Modern architecture was a new way of thinking about a building. In Late Modernism, a building was usually a monument, a timeless structure like a painting or a sculpture. But in Post-Modernism, a building is one piece of a historic urban landscape, for good or ill. If the setting is thriving, then a new building should harmonize with its neighbors, but if the area is in decline, then the new edifice can act as a catalyst to help revitalize the urban space. Thus, performing arts centers, opera houses, athletic arenas, and museums became agents of change, the nucleus around which restaurants, theaters, shops, apartments, and condominiums are built. A building itself becomes a place not only to see but also to experience urban life. For example, a new museum now functions as an educational center, sponsors varied entertainments, features a fancy restaurant, and serves as a repository for art.

The chief exponent of Post-Modern architecture is the American Robert Venturi (b. 1925), whose ideas are summarized in his book *Complexity and Contradiction in Architecture* (1966). Rejecting Modernist architecture, which he thinks inhuman because of its starkness, he attempts to create buildings that express the energy and ever-changing quality of contemporary life. Fascinated by mass culture, he is inspired by popular styles of architecture, such as Las Vegas casinos and motels in the form of Indian tepees—a kitsch style sometimes called "vernacular." A work that enshrines his love of the ordinary is his Guild House, a retirement home in a lower-middle-class section of Philadelphia (Figure 22.27). Faceless and seemingly artless, this building is indebted to popular culture for its aesthetic appeal; for instance, the wire sculpture on the roof looks like a television antenna, and the recessed entrance and the sign evoke memories of old-time movie houses. Venturi's playful assault on Modernism opened the door to the diversity of Post-Modernism. In 1991, Venturi received the Pritzker Architecture Prize, considered the profession's highest honor.

Among the architects who have spanned both Late Modernism and Post Modernism and who recognize

Figure 22.26 ROBERT SMITHSON. *Spiral Jetty.* 1970. Rock, salt crystals, earth, and water, diameter 1,500'. Great Salt Lake, Utah. © Estate of Robert Smithson/Licensed by VAGA, New York. *Smithson's mission, derived from minimalist aesthetics, was to blur the boundary between art and nature, as in* Spiral Jetty. *Constructed of materials native to the Great Salt Lake region, the jetty gives little hint of its human origin, except for the spiral form. And even that form has altered over time, as the lake's water levels have risen and fallen. By creating art that is subject to the same climatic and geologic forces as its site, Smithson reminds viewers of the transience of all human endeavor. Thus, an air of gentle melancholy pervades his works.*

Figure 22.27 ROBERT VENTURI. Guild House. 1965. Philadelphia. *Venturi's aesthetic aim is to transform the ordinary into the extraordinary. He followed this democratic ideal in Guild House, where he took a "dumb and ordinary" (his term) concept and tried to give it a monumental look. His ironic intelligence and his perverse delight in mass culture have made him a guiding spirit of Post-Modernism.*

Figure 22.28   I. M. PEI. Rock and Roll Hall of Fame and Museum. 1998. Cleveland,
Ohio. *The Rock and Roll Hall of Fame and Museum is only one of several museums I. M. Pei
has designed over the past few years. These structures are functioning testaments to his goal to
bring together the arts and education. The museum's transparent pyramids at the entrance invite
the public to enjoy the sights, the sounds, and the experience. Pei's design sets the building's vertical, horizontal, and circular sections by the shore of Lake Erie, thus converting the lake's surface
into a reflecting pool.*

the relationships between urban life and architecture is
I. M. Pei [PAY] (b. 1917). Pei, born in China, came to the
United States in his teens to study architecture. Among
his teachers was Walter Gropius [GROH-pe-us]
(1883–1969), of Bauhaus fame, who had fled from Nazi
Germany (see Chapter 20). After completing his studies, Pei founded his own firm in 1955. He and his partners designed some of the most significant buildings
of the late twentieth century, including the John F.
Kennedy Library in Boston, the Morton H. Myerson
Symphony Center in Dallas, the East Building of the
National Gallery in Washington, D.C., and the Rock
and Roll Hall of Fame and Museum in Cleveland (Figure 22.28). He and his sons have also taken their talents to China, where they built hotels and huge
business complexes, such as the Bank of China Tower,
in Hong Kong. Pei has designed museums not just to
be repositories for art but as educational and social
centers, and to make them more accessible and welcoming for a broader audience—a Post-Modern trend
to democratize the arts. Pei was awarded the Pritzker
Architecture Prize in 1983.

One of the strains in Post-Modern architecture is
high tech, a style that uses industrial techniques and
whose roots stretch back to the Crystal Palace (see Figure 18.6) and the Eiffel Tower. Richard Rogers (b. 1933)
of England and Renzo Piano (b. 1937) of Italy launched
this revival with the Pompidou Center in Paris, which
boldly displays its factory-made metal parts and transparent walls (Figure 22.29). Commissioned by France
to restore Paris's cultural position over New York, the
Pompidou Center has spawned many imitations as
well as a style of interior decoration. Piano was
awarded the Pritzker Architecture Prize in 1998.

One of the most controversial buildings in Post-
Modern architecture is the thirty-seven-story, pink
granite headquarters building of American Telephone
and Telegraph, executed in a Neoclassical style (Figure
22.30). Designed by Philip C. Johnson (1906–2006), an
American disciple of Mies van der Rohe, this building
was a slap in the face to the Modernist ideal because it
used Classical forms. AT&T Headquarters has a base,
middle, and top, corresponding to the foot, shaft, and
capital of a Greek column—the basic element of Greco-

Figure 22.29 RICHARD ROGERS AND RENZO PIANO. The Georges Pompidou Center for Art and Culture. 1971–1977. Paris. *Designed in a gaudy industrial style and erected in the heart of a quiet section of Paris called Beaubourg, the Pompidou Center was controversial from the start, as it was planned to be. Its showy appearance sharply contrasted with the historic styles of neighboring structures—a contrast that has become a guiding ideal of Post-Modernist architects. The furor that greeted the Pompidou Center on its opening has occurred in other places where city governments have placed colorful and brash high-tech temples amid their more traditional buildings.*

Figure 22.30 PHILIP C. JOHNSON AND JOHN BURGEE. American Telephone and Telegraph Headquarters. 1979–1984. New York. © Peter Mauss/Esto. *Although Classical rules were followed in the planning of Johnson and Burgee's AT&T Headquarters, it was built using Modernist methods. Like Modernist structures, the building has a steel frame to which exterior panels are clipped. Despite its Modernist soul, the physical presence of this Post-Modernist building conveys the gravity and harmony customarily associated with Classical architecture.*

Roman building style. As a final blow to Modernist purity, Johnson topped his building with a split pediment crown (a triangular shape whose apex is split, usually so as to form a semicircle—a typical feature of Classical architecture), causing a hostile critic to compare it to an eighteenth-century Chippendale highboy (a tall chest of drawers set on a legged base). Notwithstanding the furor surrounding its creation, this building heralded the resurgence of Neoclassicism in the Post-Modernist age. Johnson was the first recipient of the Pritzker Architecture Prize, in 1979.

The Guggenheim Museum in the Basque city of Bilbao, Spain, designed by the American Frank Gehry (b. 1929), was recognized immediately as a classic when it opened in 1997. Hired by city officials to build the museum as part of a civic rejuvenation project, Gehry chose a building site on the Nervion River, which has played a major role in the city's history. Gehry's design is in the form of a rose, or "metallic flower," with a rotunda at its center and the petals spiraling in waves of centrifugal force (Figure 22.31). Typical of Gehry's expressionist handling of flexible materials, strips of

Figure 22.31 FRANK O. GEHRY. Guggenheim Museum. 1997. Bilbao, Spain. *Gehry is famed for pushing the boundaries of architecture, which has often been confined by set rules, because he, as a friend of painters and sculptors, sees himself as both an artist and an architect. Thus, the Bilbao Guggenheim has been labeled sculptural architecture, considered a work of art in itself. Gehry relied on a sophisticated computer program to achieve the building's dramatic curvature, and he chose metal titanium to sheathe the exterior, thereby giving it a gleaming, wavy-in-a-strong-wind appearance.*

metal ripple and flare outward into the city. Within the Baroque interior are exhibition spaces, an auditorium, a restaurant, a café, retail space, and an atrium that functions as a town square. The choice of a rose, the symbol of the Virgin Mary, was appropriate for Catholic Spain. Gehry, by shifting this emblem from a church to a museum, transformed it into an ambiguous sign of the Post-Modern period. In 1989, Gehry was awarded the Pritzker Architecture Prize.

Two of architecture's brightest new stars are Rem (born Remmet) Koolhaas (b. 1944), of the Netherlands, and Zaha Hadid (b. 1950), an Iraqi-born British citizen.

Both were awarded the Pritzker Architecture Prize, Koolhaas in 2000 and Hadid in 2004, the first woman to receive it. Their lives overlapped in London, when Hadid worked at the Office for Metropolitan Architecture (OMA), which Koolhaas co-founded in 1975. Koolhaas moved OMA to Rotterdam in the early 1980s, but Hadid remained in London, now her home.

Rebelling against Late Modernism's belief that architecture could be an agent for social transformation, Koolhaas and Hadid created non-utopian styles that connected with their urban settings. For both, a building is one part of a city, but cities, not buildings, are the basic units of the emerging global culture. Koolhaas set these ideas in motion in his 1975 treatise, *Delirious New York, A Retroactive Manifesto for Manhattan*—a call to arms to refashion the urban landscape. Koolhaas's Seattle Central Library (2004) (Figure 22.32), set atop one of the hills overlooking Puget Sound, is a beautiful realization of his ideal: A building should harmonize with its immediate urban context. Hadid pursued a similar goal in the Rosenthal Center for Contemporary Art (2003), in Cincinnati, which fits seamlessly into its setting (Figure 22.33)—her best work to date.

Film

After 1970 the film industry, now globalized, was under siege from many, often interrelated forces, including technological innovations, a volatile marketplace, evolving film tastes, and the steady loss of audiences to television viewing. Although the American film remained paramount globally, the Hollywood studio system, ailing since 1955, began to break down. The first casualty was the once-great MGM Studios in 1973, though its fortunes revived into a more compact company in 1980.

Old Hollywood soon gave way to the new, as film studios shrank and movie screens grew wider, to counter the assault from television. Studios devised creative strategies to lower costs, such as shooting films abroad or sharing expenses with foreign companies. New film distribution systems arose, offering new formats, such as videos and DVDs, both for rent and for sale, and television showed an unquenchable demand for movies on the small screen. A few small companies made a specialty of art films. For example, Miramax Films (1979–2005), with appealing works

Figure 22.32 REM KOOLHAAS. Seattle Central Library. 2004. Seattle. *Despite a restless façade, Seattle's Central Library is meant to be used rather than viewed as a monument, according to the architect, Koolhaas. In his aesthetic vision, the cascading levels and thrusting angles echo the hilly terrain of the city's downtown. Inside, a soaring atrium welcomes visitors and psychedelic green-yellow escalators beckon patrons to explore. Besides escalators and elevators, an innovative pathway spirals through the eleven-level structure. Generous windows overlook the surrounding cityscape and allow interplay between the indoors and outside. Koolhaas's masterpiece reinvents the Modernist "glass box," making the library's exterior and interior into an exuberant fantasy, but, like many Post-Modern libraries, a place to enjoy and to meet.*

Figure 22.33 Zaha Hadid. Rosenthal Center for Contemporary Art. 2003. Cincinnati. *Hadid's bold design—dramatic color contrasts, elongated horizontal lines, and interplay of shadow and light—gives a fresh look to the corner site of the Rosenthal Center. Yet the building fits easily into the Cincinnati setting, as its dramatic facade makes linkages with the nearby buildings (right, left, and rear). The street-level floor, articulated by a combination of glass walls and columns, is reminiscent of Early Modernism.*

such as the historic comedy *Shakespeare in Love* (1998), directed by John Madden (b. 1949), became a leading global brand. The new Hollywood also spawned auteurist directors, including the New York–based Woody Allen (b. 1935), who directed urban neurotic art films such as *Annie Hall* (1977), and Clint Eastwood (b. 1930), who directed the Post-Modern western *Unforgiven* (1992). A strong sign that Hollywood had changed was the warm welcome given the founding of what is now the Sundance Film Festival, in 1980, by the actor Robert Redford (b. 1937). The festival is a national and international showcase for art films, independent films, and documentaries. Today, most Hollywood studios have an art house division that specializes in films for a niche market—a small segment of the market, but valuable for its power to influence popular taste.

Nonetheless, in the new Hollywood, filmmakers continued to make genre films, keeping them fresh with new technologies, such as DTS Digital Sound in *Jurassic Park* (1993), directed by Steven Spielberg (b. 1946); computer-generated graphics in *Toy Story* (1995), a collaboration between Pixar Studios and Disney; and digital video cameras in *Star Wars: Episode II—Attack of the Clones* (2002), directed by George Lucas (b. 1944). Of special note is *Titanic* (1997), the disaster film directed by James Cameron (b. 1954), which shows Hollywood's newest quandary: It was the most expensive film ever made and the highest-grossing film of all time.

A final major change in Hollywood after 1970 was that films began to represent more closely the ethnic and racial pluralism of the United States. The trend began with *Sweet Sweetback's Baadasssss Song!* (1971), directed by Melvin Van Peebles (b. 1932), which led, in turn, to the **blaxploitation film** genre—crime films featuring a swaggering black hero and catering to black audiences. Van Peebles's commercially successful works paved the way for other black directors, such as Spike (born Shelton) Lee (b. 1957), with his urban drama *Do the Right Thing* (1989), a study of racially charged violence. As African Americans joined the Hollywood mainstream, Hispanics and Asian Americans followed suit. However, after 9/11, Arab Americans and other Americans of Middle Eastern descent were rarely depicted favorably in films—a source of grievance for these groups.

The seismic shifts shaking the American film industry were felt around the globe. Although audiences declined sharply, those viewers who remained were more youthful. As Asia's economies soared (in Japan, from the 1970s to the 1990s, and in China, India, and South Korea, from the 1990s on), their youthful audiences became a driving force in the market, as in the rise of the martial arts film genre. Japanese cinema retained a strong hold on world cinema. For example, Akira Kurosawa's (1910–1998) *Ran* (1985), Shakespeare's *King Lear* transposed to feudal Japan, experienced international acclaim and technicians there introduced the IMAX wide-screen format (1970)—a popular format for movies in most large cities today.

Film industries in Australia and China also joined the global film community. Australia's film boom produced art films of exquisite beauty, often based on real-life events, mixing gritty details with magic realism, such as *Picnic at Hanging Rock* (1975), a haunting tale of a school outing that ends tragically, directed by Peter Weir (b. 1944). Weir later was summoned to Hollywood—a path now taken by many foreign directors. Australian film remains highly influential today, as in *Moulin Rouge* (2001), directed by Baz Luhrmann (b. 1962), which almost single-handedly revived the musical genre. And Australia's top directors and actors move easily between Australia and Hollywood.

China's rise to global eminence in film was equally spectacular, despite the use of a lowly genre inspired by ancient fighting rituals—the martial arts film. The revival began in Hong Kong, where martial arts films were entrenched by 1955. The regional genre went global in *The Big Boss* (1971), starring Bruce Lee (born Lee Jun Fan, in San Francisco) (1940–1973) and directed by Wei Lo (1918–1996). This film featured fighting with bare fists—*kung fu*, a Cantonese term, hence, the kung fu genre. With Hong Kong's films burgeoning, mainland China's film world reawakened in the mid-1980s, when a new generation of filmmakers emerged who preferred art films to genre films. The group's leader was Zhang Yimou (b. 1951), whose films, while controversial in China, were greeted as revelations and earned many awards abroad, as, for example, *Raise the Red Lantern* (1991), a heartbreaking tale of forced marriages, multiple wives, and intrigue. The proof that China's films were truly global came when *Crouching Tiger, Hidden Dragon* (2000), a martial arts film directed by Taiwan's Ang Lee (b. 1954), won the Academy Award for Best Foreign Language Film (Figure 22.34).

Post-Modern Music

In the 1960s, some innovative composers rejected Late Modernist atonality for its unemotional quality and its apparent devotion to harsh sounds. In place of atonality, they founded a Post-Modern style devoted to making music more emotionally appealing, though they remained committed to experimental methods. Among

the most notable composers working within this style is the American Philip Glass (b. 1937), who has made it his mission to return exuberance to music. He has pursued this goal while working in a minimalist tradition, although he draws on varied sources, including classical Indian music, African drumming, and rock and roll. Much of Glass's music is written for **synthesizer,** a machine with a simple keyboard that can duplicate the sounds of up to twelve instruments simultaneously. He composes with simple tonal harmonies, pulsating rhythms, unadorned scales, and, above all, lilting arpeggios, the cascading sounds produced by playing the notes of a chord in rapid sequences.

A Glass piece is instantly recognizable for its repetitiveness and obsessive quality, as in "Vessels," from the score for the documentary film *Koyaanisqatsi* (1983), a Hopi term meaning "life out of balance." In this choral work, sung without a text, Glass manipulates human voices into a thrilling dialogue, much as earlier composers had used groups of instruments. A cluster of higher voices creates a constantly shifting pattern of undulating tones, against which a group of lower voices forges a forward-moving wall of sound. Glass's kaleidoscopic music provides a haunting accompaniment to the time-lapse photography used in the documentary film.

A composer of symphonies, chamber works, film scores, and dance pieces, Glass has gained the widest celebrity for his operas. His first opera, *Einstein on the Beach* (1976), produced in collaboration with the equally controversial American director Robert Wilson (b. 1941), was staged at New York's Metropolitan Opera, a rarity in recent times for a living composer. In their kaleidoscopic work, Glass and Wilson redefined the operatic form, staging a production lasting four

Figure 22.34 Still, from *Crouching Tiger, Hidden Dragon.* 2000. Crouching Tiger, Hidden Dragon *featured several Asian superstars, along with relative unknowns, such as Zhang Ziyi (b. 1979) (pictured above, center). Zhang plays a young woman, a runaway, who is on a quest involving honor and revenge. Her character—central to the complex story—blends Eastern martial arts with Western feminist aspirations—a mixture that appealed to a global audience. Ironically, while Westerners were drawn to the over-the-top fighting scenes—actors on wires, moving in seemingly gravity-less space—Chinese viewers were critical, finding the spectacle unrealistic.*

and one-half hours without intermission and with Glass's driving music set to Wilson's texts with no recognizable plot, no formal arias, and no massed choruses. So successful was this venture that Glass followed it with operas based on other remarkable figures, *Satyagraha* (1978), dealing with the life of Gandhi, India's liberator (see Encounter in Chapter 20), and *Akhnaten* (1984), focusing on the Egyptian pharaoh who is sometimes called the first monotheist (see Chapter 1). Glass's interests took an even more multicultural turn in 1998 with the premiere and world tour of his multimedia opera *Monsters of Grace,* with a libretto based on the thirteenth-century mystical poetry of the Persian poet Jalal ad-Din ar-Rumi (see Chapter 8). In 2000, Glass returned to Western themes with *In the Penal Colony*—a "pocket opera" he terms it, that is, a short, compact opera with few characters and simple staging—based on Kafka's short story. Western themes became intensely political in his opera *Waiting for the Barbarians* (2005), with a libretto based on the 1980 novel by Nobel laureate John M. Coetzee [KUUT-zee] (b. 1940), a South African novelist of German and English descent. The opera's setting and plot—a frontier town of an unnamed "Empire," which is awaiting the attack of the "barbarians"—evokes the Iraq War and the threat of terrorism.

One of the best-known living composers is the American John Adams (b. 1947). Like many other composers of his generation, Adams is a minimalist, but he stands out for his resonant sounds and firm grasp of musical form. He has written for a wide range of media, including orchestra, opera, video, film, and dance, and he has composed both electronic and instrumental music. His operas, *Nixon in China* (1987), *The Death of Klinghoffer* (1991), *I Was Looking at the Ceiling and Then I Saw the Sky* (1998), and *Doctor Atomic* (2005), based on historical events, have been viewed by more audiences than any other operas in recent history. Two orchestral works, *The Chairman Dances,* adapted from *Nixon in China,* and *Shaker Loops* (1996), have been called "among the best known and most frequently performed of contemporary American music" by one critic. In 2001 Adams returned to his minimalist roots with *Guide to Strange Places,* a twenty-minute pulsing orchestral work, divided into five sections with alternating fast and slow movements. Two years later, this piece became the score for a ballet of the same name, choreographed by Peter Martins (b. 1946), the Danish-born ballet master of the New York City Ballet, the eighth collaboration between Adams and Martins. Adams frequently conducts some of the world's most prestigious orchestras.

Three major composers with reputations for bold inventiveness and diverse influences demonstrate the multiple styles of Post-Modern music. They are the Hungarian-born Austrian Gyorgy Ligeti [LIG-uh-tee] (1923–2006), the American John Corigliano [koh-RIG-li-ah-no] (b. 1938), and the Chinese-born Tan Dun (b. 1957).

Ligeti's music, rooted in the minimalist aesthetic, has evolved over the course of his career. In his early works, he showed the mischievous spirit of John Cage, as in *Future of Music* (1961), a piece in which the performer and the audience simply gaze at one another for a set time. Later, he briefly drew on **electronic music** (music involving electronic processing, picked up from varied sound sources and requiring the use of loudspeakers in concert), pioneered by the French-born American composer Edgar Varese (1883–1965). In the mid-1960s, Ligeti abandoned melody, rhythm, and harmony to fashion a unique sound, as in *Atmospheres* (1966)—his most frequently heard work to date. In *Atmospheres,* he invented "micropolyphony," to create shifting masses of sound, notable for their density and texture. In 1968, the director Stanley Kubrick (1928–1999) used passages from this work to evoke the future in the film *2001: A Space Odyssey.* A restless genius, Ligeti continued to experiment, as in the opera *Le Grand Macabre* (1976; revised 1999), blending pop culture, satire, mock operatic music, and the peasant paintings of Pieter Bruegel (see Chapter 13). This ironic valentine to Post-Modernism has been called by critics an "anti-opera," "musical comedy of the absurd," and "an apocalyptic romp" (Figure 22.35).

Corigliano belongs to the **Neoromantic** wing of Post-Modern music. His works, composed in varied mediums, including orchestral, chamber, opera, and film, show an ever-evolving style, filled with rich expressiveness and innovative technique. He is perhaps best known today for the film score of *The Red Violin* (1999), directed by the Canadian François Girard (b. 1963). Following the three-hundred-year-history of "the red violin," Corigliano's haunting score (finished in 1997) draws on diverse musical styles, such as classical, pop, and folk, covering a global odyssey from Italy to Austria to Britain to China to Canada. Using the score's central motif, he expanded it into *The Red Violin Chaconne* (1997), an independent work for violin and orchestra. (A chaconne, originally an eighteenth-century Spanish court dance, is a musical form that features variations on a harmonic progression, rather then variations on a melody.)

Tan Dun (surname, Tan) is a rising presence on the global music scene. Or, as John Cage has said, Tan is a musical force "as the East and the West come together as our one home." A graduate of Beijing's Central Conservatory (1981) and of New York's Columbia University (PhD, 1993), he developed an eclectic style that reflects deep familiarity with the music of both cultures. In orchestral and chamber music, opera, and

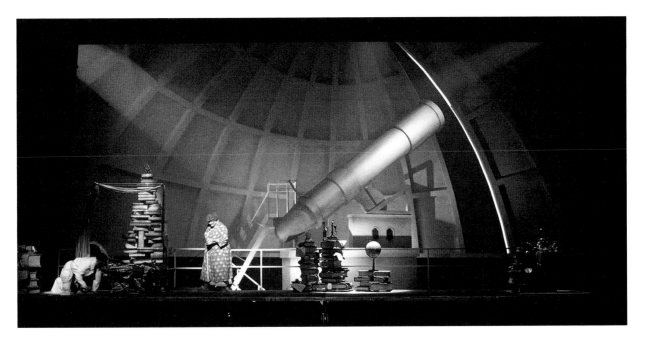

Figure 22.35 Scene, from *Le Grand Macabre*. *By blithely mixing periods and styles, Ligeti's Le Grand Macabre has established itself as a satiric work that plays fast and loose with operatic tradition. The setting, to quote the composer, is "the run-down but nevertheless carefree and thriving principality of Breughelland [Ligeti's term] in an 'anytime' century." The hero is Death (Le Grand Macabre) and the subject is living in the shadow of the apocalypse. In this world, Death gets no respect, as the cunning peasant inhabitants pursue sex, alcohol, and political advancement. In the scene above, an astrologer peers through a telescope—a device not yet invented in Bruegel's time.*

film scores, he blends Chinese musical, historical, and cultural traditions with historic Western styles, including Classical, minimalist, and popular music forms. Global audiences first became acquainted with Tan's dramatic music in Ang Lee's film *Crouching Tiger, Hidden Dragon* (2000), for which his score was awarded an Oscar. His most ambitious work to date, the opera *Marco Polo* (1995), fuses a Western avant-garde musical form—an opera within an opera—with pan-Asian multicultural elements: Peking Opera from China, kabuki theater from Japan, shadow puppet theater from Indonesia, and face painting from Tibetan ritual. Period musical instruments from Europe, India, Tibet, and China add to the multicultural fusion. In this multilayered story, the travel of Marco Polo from West to East is symbolic of the real-life trip of the Italian adventurer, the global encounter now under way within the Post-Modern world, and Tan Dun's own spiritual journey.

In Post-Modern chamber music, stringed instruments still dominated, but the woodwinds were now heard more and more. The woodwind family (clarinets, oboes, bassoons, and flutes) came late to orchestra membership; thus, music composed especially for them lagged behind in the repertory. A few composers wrote for woodwinds early on, but it was not until the late 1900s that conditions were ripe for significant concertizing by woodwind ensembles. A woodwind group whose popular success is making them a pres-

ence in global music is the Imani Winds, founded in 1997. A boundary-defying ensemble, Imani Winds blends traditional chamber pieces with African and Latino music, ranging from Maurice Ravel (see Chapter 19) to the Argentine tango composer Astor Piazzolla (1921–1992) to Swahili spirituals. The new popularity of woodwind music follows in the footsteps of the Canadian Brass, founded in 1970, who raised the global profile of the brass family (varied horns, including the tuba). Through stage concerts, television appearances, and fifty or more recordings, the Canadian Brass have become world famous, successfully bridging the gap between chamber music and popular music.

Performance Art

Laurie Anderson (b. 1947) is a key artist in **performance art**—a democratic type of mixed-media art born in the 1960s that ignores artistic boundaries, happily mixing high art (such as music, painting, and theater) and popular art (such as rock and roll, film, and fads) to create a unique, irreproducible artistic experience. Anderson's performance art consists of sing-and-tell story-songs about mundane events of daily life, which somehow take on unearthly significance. These monologues are often tinged with humor and are delivered in a singsong voice backed up by mixed-media images, strange props, and varied electronic media, including electronic musical instruments, photo projection, manipulated video, and devices that alter the sound of her voice. Central to the performance is her stage persona, rather like Dorothy in *The Wizard of Oz*, in which she gazes with wide-eyed wonder on the modern technological world. A gifted violinist, she intends her music to play only a supporting role in her art, though her recordings—for example, *The Ugly One with the Jewels* (1995), based on a work called *Readings from the New Bible* (1992–1995)—have found eager listeners. In *Songs and Stories from "Moby Dick"* (1999), based on Herman Melville's nineteenth-century novel, she broke new ground by composing for male voices as well as her own (Figure 22.36).

The American Cindy Sherman (b. 1954) has also created a body of performance art, but without music. Sherman first attracted notice in the 1970s with photographs of herself in elaborately staged poses, evocative of old movie scenes. Although these photographs focused on women as victims, their ambiguous nature made her controversial, especially to feminists. In the eighties, she made a series *History Portraits*, in which she impersonated famous art subjects. In the nineties, she made photographs using pornographic subjects,

mock fashion images, and fairy-tale characters (Figure 22.37). Sherman's art, with its staged and rather tacky quality, seeks to dethrone high art and bring it down to earth for today's audiences.

Mass Culture

The information boom has been the explosive force Americanizing the world and transforming it into a global village, with television providing the initial means of transformation. As the earth has shrunk, more electronic gear—the videocassette recorder, the compact-disc player, the digital recorder, the camcorder, the computer—has reduced the individual's world even more, turning each home into a communications center. The global information highway, including the Internet and the World Wide Web, and developments in international communications technology, such as the cellular telephone, have made the world even smaller.

With this information explosion, critics have labeled our era the Age of Infotainment, that is, a blend of information and entertainment, a phenomenon that can be observed across the mass media. Older ways of

Figure 22.36 WILLIAM STRUHS. Laurie Anderson performing at the Spoleto Festival U.S.A., June 1999. *Laurie Anderson, second from left, whose works virtually define performance art, is pictured here in the midst of a performance of* Songs and Stories from "Moby Dick" *at the Spoleto Festival U.S.A., held in Charleston, South Carolina. Her nineteenth-century costume, the stovepipe top hat and frock coat, reflects the time period of Melville's famous novel. The setting of the performance, with its alienating effects created by electronic means, suggests the technological world that is the principal concern of her art. For example, on a background screen are projected, among other things, constantly shifting lines and words of Melville's text, letters of the alphabet, blown-up images of the performers, and dictionary definitions; similarly, in addition to instrumental music, there are songs, chanted passages, and spoken words, some of whose sounds are deliberately distorted by electronic means.*

Figure 22.37 Cindy Sherman. *Untitled #298*. Photograph, 73 × 49½". 1994. *In this photograph from the* Fairy Tale Series, *Sherman impersonates a medieval wizard, standing in profile against a star-filled "sky" and wearing a blonde wig and flowing robe whose inner lining is emblazoned with skulls. The props have been assembled by Sherman, based on some plan of her own, making this photograph a unique image. Works such as this bring into question the creating of art when there is no preexisting prototype. Interpretation of Sherman's art is difficult, as she is dismissive of what critics say, calling their analyses "a kind of side effect."*

transmitting information, such as newspapers, magazines, and radio, have declined, while newer outlets, such as television and computers, have grown. Even new formats for information are under siege; for example, the nightly televised news has taken second place to the 24-hour news network format pioneered by CNN in the early 1980s. Today, CNN reaches more than two billion people globally. CNN itself is now challenged by start-up news channels around the world. Plans are afoot for a pan-African news channel, using French and English, and Qatar-based Al Jazeera, the global voice of the Arabs, plans to begin a broadcast in English in 2006.

Similar changes are under way in entertainment. Old types of amusements, such as radio and comic strips, have been joined by innovative means of media coverage, including cable television with MTV, and all-sports channels. These changes have given birth to extravagantly popular figures: Michael Jackson (b. 1958), superstar of the mid-1980s, Madonna (b. 1959), queen of popular songs in the early 1990s, and Eminem (born Marshall Mathers III in 1972), a white rapper and the king of pop music at the dawn of the new millennium. As entertainment continues to evolve, probably the most highly visible and influential development in recent years has been the birth of hip-hop—the voice of the people in the street.

The rise of hip-hop began in the 1970s. With origins in break dancing, graffiti art, rap rhyming, and disc jockeys playing with turntables and "scratch" effects, **hip-hop** music emerged in black and Hispanic America, spoken in either English or Spanish. By 2001, hip-hop was paramount in American pop music, largely because of the same forces mainstreaming African Americans in Hollywood films and on television. Today, hip-hop has spread to Mexico, much of Latin America, parts of Canada, and the Far East. Only time will tell if this is simply a fad or if hip-hop will be an enduring product of a civilization that is truly pluralistic and global.

❧ A SUMMING UP

Since the dawn of history, humans have discovered that understanding their own times, while necessary, can be difficult and unpredictable. Few have possessed either the ability to make sense of their own history or the wisdom to know what will endure. Predicting how today's events and trends will determine the course of history in the twenty-first century is well nigh impossible.

Nonetheless, considering the current breathtaking changes in the political, social, and economic realms, we offer two contradictory interpretations of the near future. On the one hand, in our Post-Modern era, we see a new vision of the world—global and democratic, embracing the contributions, tastes, and ideas of men and women from many races and countries and borrowing freely from high culture and mass culture. In this optimistic view, the world continues to take its lead from Western civilization, largely because of its proven capacity to adapt and survive. On the other hand, in light of the mounting tensions around the world, these trends toward unity seem mere illusions. In our pessimistic view, the future may be filled with renewed disruptions and clashes among societies, which could manifest themselves in various ways, ranging from economic sanctions to armed conflicts to terrorist campaigns.

When we consider our past, as we have in this book, one major lesson is clear: The long term in history is unpredictable. For example, five thousand years ago in 3000 B.C.E., who could have predicted that the fledgling Egyptian and Mesopotamian societies

SLICE OF LIFE
Who Are the Islamic Terrorists?

DAVID BROOKS
Trading Cricket for Jihad

The journalist David Brooks (b. 1964) is an astute observer of current events. In this 2005 op-ed piece, he goes against the common wisdom of the origin of today's Islamic terrorists. Brooks believes that Islamic terrorists, rather than originating in dysfunctional regimes in the Arab world, are homegrown within the West—as in the famous Pogo comic strip: "We have met the enemy and he is us." The CIE is the Council on Islamic Education, and Salafism is a fundamentalist school of Islam that calls for a return to the values of early Muslim times.

Nothing has changed during the war on terror as much as our definition of the enemy.

In the days after Sept. 11, it was commonly believed that the conflict between the jihadists and the West was a conflict between medievalism and modernism. Terrorists, it was said, emerge from cultures that are isolated from the West. They feel disoriented by the pluralism of the modern age and humiliated by the relative backwardness of the Arab world. They are trapped in stagnant, dysfunctional regimes, amid mass unemployment, with little hope of leading productive lives.

Humiliated and oppressed, they lash out against America, the symbol of threatening modernity. Off they go to seek martyrdom, dreaming of virgins who await them in the afterlife.

Now we know that story line doesn't fit the facts.

We have learned a lot about the jihadists, from Osama bin Laden down to the Europeans who attacked the London subways [in July 2005]. We know, thanks to a database gathered by Marc Sageman, formerly of the C.I.E., that about 75 percent of anti-Western terrorists come from middle-class or upper-middle-class homes. An amazing 65 percent have gone to college, and three-quarters have professional or semiprofessional jobs, particularly in engineering or science.

Whether they have moved to Egypt, Saudi Arabia, England, or France, these men are, far from being medieval, drawn from the ranks of the educated, the mild, and the multilingual.

The jihadists are modern psychologically as well as demographically because they are self-made men (in traditional societies there are no self-made men). Rather than deferring to custom, many of them have rebelled against local authority figures, rejecting their parents' bourgeois striving and moderate versions of Islam, and their comfortable lives.

They have sought instead some utopian cause to give them an identity and their lives meaning. They find that cause in a brand of Salafism that is not traditional Islam but a modern fantasy version of it, an invented tradition. They give up cricket and medical school and take up jihad.

In other words, the conflict between the jihadists and the West is a conflict within the modern, globalized world. The extremists are the sort of utopian rebels modern societies have long produced.

In his book, "Globalized Islam," the French scholar Olivier Roy points out that today's jihadists have a lot in common with the left-wing extremists of the 1930s and 1960s. Ideologically, Islamic neofundamentalism occupies the same militant space that was once occupied by Marxism. It draws the same sorts of recruits (educated second-generation immigrants, for example), uses some of the same symbols and vilifies some of the same enemies (imperialism and capitalism).

Roy emphasizes that the jihadists are the products of globalization, and its enemies. . . .

The first implication [of this new definition] is that democratizing the Middle East, while worthy in itself, may not stem terrorism. Terrorists are bred in London and Paris as much as anywhere else.

Second, the jihadists' weakness is that they do not spring organically from the Arab or Muslim world. They claim to speak for the Muslim masses, as earlier radicals claimed to speak for the proletariat. But they don't. . . .

Third, terrorism is an immigration problem. Terrorists are spawned when educated, successful Muslims still have trouble sinking roots into their adopted homelands. Countries that do not encourage assimilation are not only causing themselves trouble, but endangering others around the world as well.

Interpreting This Slice of Life What, according to Brooks, is the common belief about the origins of the Islamic terrorists? **What** does Brooks believe to be the correct cause of the current wave of terrorism? **Define** *jihadist.* **Compare and contrast** the jihadists with the left-wing extremists of the 1930s and 1960s, as set forth in Olivier Roy's scholarly study. **Is** Brooks's point of view persuasive? **Explain. Are** there other social or political problems affected by immigrant groups not fitting into their adopted homelands?

would become cradles of civilization, leaving enduring cultural forms before falling into decay? Or in 2000 B.C.E., who could have foreseen that a rejuvenated Egypt and Mesopotamia would eventually be undermined by Iron Age invaders? Or would it have been possible to guess in 1000 B.C.E., a time of disarray and decline in the eastern Mediterranean, that first Greece and later Rome would evolve into the civilizations that became the standard in the West? Or at the dawn of the Christian era, with the Roman Empire at its height, who would have dared forecast that Roman power would spread so widely but then collapse, to be succeeded by three separate and distinct civilizations—Islam, Byzantium, and the West? Or in 1000 C.E., who could have anticipated that the backward West would become the constantly revolutionizing industrial giant whose culture would dominate the world? Drawing a lesson from this quick survey, we readily admit that

we cannot know what this millennium will bring. Perhaps all we can say is that, based on past history, civilization as we know it is likely to undergo fundamental change, for good or ill, as a consequence of some currently unforeseen technological, political, religious, economic, or social innovation.

Underneath these tensions, uncertainties, conflicts, and daily crises flows the challenge of modern life and below that current what makes us human: the search for spiritual guidance, the curiosity to explore, the satisfaction to comprehend, the genius to express our creative talents, and the past to guide us. These common threads of human existence, like an abiding faith, prove that the human spirit survives and, ultimately, prevails. The Mesopotamians and Greeks recognized these immortal qualities in mortals. Whatever the future, we will continue to hold to these humanistic values.

The Legacy of the Contemporary World

After 1970, the world seemed to turn a corner, leaving the immediate past behind. One after another, old traditions, habits, and principles, in place for generations, fell by the wayside and were quickly replaced by new truths, arrangements, and loyalties. During this period, the cold war ended and the Age of Terror was born. Instead of rivalry between two superpowers, the world now faces a war between the West and Islam, which threatens to become a clash of civilizations. Bipolar diplomacy has now yielded to a world with one superpower—the United States—and the solid bloc of Western powers has fragmented into an American group and a European Union group. With the United States as the reigning superpower, its democratic institutions and free-market economy have become widely imitated by much of the world. However,

the revival of militant nationalism and ethnic warfare, the reaction against globalization in some poorer countries in the form of populism, and, most recently, the spread of terrorism threaten the triumph of liberal democracy and free-market economics. At the same time, the prospect of endless progress stretching into the unforeseeable future has given way to the hope of modest growth limited by the earth's dwindling natural resources. The division of the world into three parts after World War II—the West, the Soviet bloc, and the Third World—has now evolved into an emerging global civilization, interconnected via technology, the United Nations and its various agencies, multinational corporations, film, mass media, mass culture, tourism, and assorted nongovernmental organizations (NGOs).

KEY CULTURAL TERMS

Post-Modernism
Post-Structuralism
Deconstruction
paradigm shift
nihilism
liberation theology
magic realism
commedia dell'arte
Neorealism
Neoexpressionism
Neoclassicism
conceptual art

installation art
environmental art
video art
cladding
high tech
blaxploitation film
synthesizer
electronic music
Neoromanticism
performance art
hip-hop

SUGGESTIONS FOR FURTHER READING

BARTHES, R. *Elements of Semiology.* London: Cape, 1967. Translated by A. Lavers and C. Smith. Semiology, the study of signs and their meaning, was an invention of Barthes, used by him in the reading and interpretation of texts.

DERRIDA, J. *Of Grammatology.* Baltimore: Johns Hopkins University Press, 1997. Translated by G. C. Spivak. An updated version of Derrida's difficult 1967 work, which established deconstructionist theory.

FO, D. *Accidental Death of an Anarchist.* New York: S. French, 1987. Translated by S. Cowan. A deeply political play, Fo's tragic farce entertains even as it raises questions about Italy's police and court system.

GARCÍA MÁRQUEZ, G. *One Hundred Years of Solitude.* New York: Cambridge University Press, 1990. A classic of Post-Modernism that mixes magical happenings with realistic events in the mythical Colombian town of Macondo.

KINGSTON, M. H. *China Men.* New York: Knopf, 1980. Dealing with Kingston's patriarchal heritage, this autobiographical work complements *The Woman Warrior,* which focuses on matriarchal influences.

———. *The Woman Warrior: Memoirs of a Girlhood Among Ghosts.* New York: Knopf, 1976. A novel dealing with the confusion of growing up Chinese American in California; the "ghosts" of the subtitle refer to both the pale-faced Americans and the legendary female avengers brought to life by immigrant tales.

KUHN, T. *The Structure of Scientific Revolution.* Chicago: University of Chicago Press, 1996. Kuhn's thesis, now an established principle, is that revolutions occur in science only after sufficient discrepancies arise to challenge the ruling paradigm in a scientific field. First published in 1970.

KUNDERA, M. *The Unbearable Lightness of Being.* Translated by M. H. Heim. New York: Harper & Row, 1984. A novel that explores the anguish of life under communism in Eastern Europe.

MORRISON, T. *Beloved.* New York: Plume, 1998. First published in 1987, *Beloved* widened Morrison's audience after it was made into a movie. Morrison transformed a true incident from pre–Civil War America into a haunting and complex story with the dimensions of a Greek tragedy.

PAMUK, O. *My Name Is Red.* New York: Vintage, 2002. Translated by E. M.Goknar. A literary tour de force, set in the sixteenth-century Ottoman Empire, that blends murder mystery, court intrigue, and art history, with a meditation on differences between Western and Muslim civilizations.

SMITH, Z. *White Teeth.* New York: Vintage, 1990. Using story lines from three families of diverse ethnic, racial, and religious heritages, which intersect and overlap, this novel uncovers the melting pot that post-imperial Britain is today.

WALCOTT, D. *Omeros.* New York: Farrar, Straus & Giroux, 1990. An epic treatment of Caribbean culture, drawing on Homer's *Iliad* (war), and *Odyssey* (homecoming) and Dante's *Divine Comedy* (salvation), composed in a Dante-esque verse form.

WALKER, A. *The Color Purple.* New York: Harcourt Brace Jovanovich, 1982. An uplifting novel that describes the central black female character's rise from degradation to modest dignity. The heroine's awkward but poignantly moving letters reveal the difficulty and the ultimate heroism of her victory.

SUGGESTIONS FOR LISTENING

ADAMS, JOHN. Adams, a minimalist, has emerged as one of the freshest composers working today. Noted for resonant sounds and strong mastery of form, his music embraces a wide array of media, including orchestral music, as in *Harmonium* (1997) and *Guide to Strange Places* (2005), and especially opera, as in *Nixon in China* (1987), *The Death of Klinghoffer* (1991), *I Was Looking at the Ceiling and Then I Saw the Sky* (1998), and *Doctor Atomic* (2005).

ANDERSON, LAURIE. The premier performance artist of our time, Anderson has come a long way since 1973's *Duets on Ice,* when, dressed in a kilt and skating on ice, she played duets with herself on the violin (it had been altered to play a prerecorded solo) on Manhattan street corners, the duration of the piece dependent on the melting ice. More recent performances are memorialized through records such as *Mister Heartbreak* (1984); *Sharkey's Day* (1984), based on a Bauhaus work by Oskar Schlemmer; *Strange Angels* (1989), taken from the performance piece entitled *Empty Places; The Ugly One with the Jewels* (1995), generated by the performance called *Stories from the New Bible* (1992–1995); and *Life on a String* (2001), inspired by the material in *Songs and Stories from "Moby Dick"* (1999), based on Herman Melville's novel. Her most popular work to date—almost 900,000 copies sold—is *O Superman* (1980), a single record that was later incorporated into the epic-length *United States I–IV* (1983).

CANADIAN BRASS. Founded in 1970, the Canadian Brass, a quintet, successfully established the concert format for horn instruments through their success. In more than fifty recordings, they have made themselves a place at the table of world music. Two representative CDs are *Go for Baroque* (1973–1974) and *People of Faith* (2006).

CORIGLIANO, JOHN. Corigliano's deeply emotional music evokes the Romantic era, with its soaring themes, lush tones, and rhythmic energy. A prolific award-winning composer, he has written orchestral works (such as *Concerto for Clarinet and Orchestra* [1977]), chamber pieces (such as *Phantasmagoria,* for cello and piano [2000]), one opera (*Ghosts of Versailles* [1999]), and film scores (such as *Altered States* [1997]) and was awarded the 2001 Pulitzer Prize in Music for his Symphony No. 2. In his most famous work for orchestra, Symphony No. 1 (1999), Corigliano registered his anger and sorrow over the loss of friends to AIDS; the piece's third movement includes a twelve-minute cantata—thus evoking the choral singing in Beethoven's Ninth Symphony (see Chapter 17). Corigliano's most mainstream work remains the film score for *The Red Violin* (1999)—for which he won an Oscar.

GLASS, PHILIP. Glass's pulsating rhythms and cascading sounds have made him a popular and successful figure in Post-Modern music. He is best known for his operas, including *Einstein on the Beach* (1976), *Satyagraha* (1978), *Akhnaten* (1984), *Monsters of Grace* (1998), and *Waiting for the Barbarians* (2005), and for his film scores, such as those for *Koyaanisqatsi* (1983), *Mishima* (1985), *Kundun* (1998), the classic silent film *Dracula* (1999), *The Hours* (2002), and *The Illusionist* (2006).

IMANI WINDS. A newly founded woodwind group, Imani Winds has reached a surprisingly large audience. The group has a global sound, mixing traditional chamber music with African and Latino music. Their recordings are *Umoja* (Swahili, "unity") (2002) and *The Classical Underground* (2005).

LIGETI, GYORGI. Ligeti's eclectic range extends over the Post-Modern landscape, including the Cage-like *Future of Music* (1961), the electronic music of *Articulation* (1958), the New Age music of *Atmospheres* (1966) and *Lux Aeterna (Eternal Light),* the "anti-opera" *Le Grand Macabre* (1976; rev. 1999), the pulsing *Clocks and Clouds* (1972–1973), and the world music–inspired *Études for Piano* (3 vols., 1985–2001).

TAN DUN. Tan Dun, trained in music in both China and the United States, is the most global composer working today. His music draws on varied styles: from the West, Classical, experimental, and popular; and from China, Peking opera and traditional and folk music. He is also multicultural in his instrument choices, ranging over the musical history of both cultures, including nontraditional and organic instruments, such as bowls of water amplified to make sounds, as in *Water Passion After St. Matthew* (2000). His eclectic output includes the opera *Marco Polo* (1995), the orchestral piece *Tea: A Mirror of Soul* (2002), and for multimedia, *The Map: Concerto for Cello, Video and Orchestra* (2002). His fame rests primarily on his film scores: *Crouching Tiger, Hidden Dragon* (2000) and *Hero* (2004).

GLOSSARY

Italicized words within definitions are defined in their own glossary entries.

abstract art   Art that presents a subjective view of the world—the artist's emotions or ideas—or art that presents *line, color,* or shape for its own sake.

Abstract Expressionism   Also known as *Action Painting,* a nonrepresentational artistic style that flourished after World War II and was typified by randomness, spontaneity, and an attempt by the artist to interact emotionally with the work as it was created.

abstraction   In Modern art, nonrepresentational or nonobjective forms in sculpture and painting that emphasize shapes, *lines,* and *colors* independent of the natural world.

a cappella [ah kuh-PEL-uh]   From the Italian, "in chapel style"; music sung without instrumental accompaniment.

Action Painting   Another name for *Abstract Expressionism.* Action Painting referred to an artist's use of agitated motions while applying paint to canvas, such as Jackson Pollock's "drip paintings" or Willem de Kooning's slashing strokes. Inspired by *Surrealism's* reliance on automatic responses as a way to release the creative unconscious.

adab [ah-DAHB]   An Arabic term. Originally, it meant good manners or good conduct. In the eighth century, it appeared as a literary *genre;* later, it indicated the possession of athletic skills and literary knowledge and applied especially to the elite. Today, *adab* refers to the whole of literature.

aesthete   One who pursues and is devoted to the beautiful in art, music, and literature.

aisles   The side passages in a church on either side of the central *nave.*

Alexandrianism [al-ig-ZAN-dree-an-ism]   A literary style developed in the *Hellenistic* period, typically formal, artificial, and imitative of earlier Greek writing.

ambulatory [AM-bue-la-tor-e]   A passageway for walking found in many religious structures, such as outdoors in a *cloister* or indoors around the *apse* or the *choir* of a church.

Anglicanism   The doctrines and practices of the Church of England, which was established in the early sixteenth century under Henry VIII.

Angry Young Men   A late 1950s and early 1960s literary movement in Great Britain, composed of novelists and playwrights, whose works expressed frustration and anger over their country's loss of empire and declining status on the world's stage. Most of the Angry Young Men were part of an emerging meritocracy, having been born in the lower classes but educated in the universities, including Oxford and Cambridge.

anthropomorphism [an-thro-po-MOR-fizm]   The attributing of humanlike characteristics and traits to nonhuman things or powers, such as a deity.

antiphon [AN-te-fon]   In music, a short prose text, chanted by unaccompanied voices during the Christian *liturgy.*

apocalypse [uh-PAHK-uh-lips]   In Jewish and early Christian thought, the expectation and hope of the coming of God and his final judgment; also closely identified with the last book of the New Testament, Revelation, in which many events are foretold, often in highly symbolic and imaginative terms.

apse   In architecture, a large projection, usually rounded or semicircular, found in a *basilica,* usually in the east end; in Christian *basilicas,* the altar stood in this space.

aquatint   An early type of color print, made with a metal plate, which attempted to replicate the effect of a watercolor; originated in the Netherlands in about 1650. The golden age of the aquatint was from about 1770 to 1850. The print's name derives from nitrous oxide *(aqua fortis),* a chemical used in the printmaking process.

arabesque [air-uh-BESK]   Literally, "Arabian-like"; decorative lines, patterns, and designs, often floral, in Islamic works of art.

arcade   A series of arches supported by *piers* or columns, usually serving as a passageway along a street or between buildings.

Archaic style   The style in Greek sculpture, dating from the seventh century to 480 B.C.E., that was characterized by heavy Egyptian influence; dominated by the *kouros* and *kore* sculptural forms.

architectural paintings   A type of wall painting, which created the optical illusion of either a wall opening or the effect of looking through a window; popular in imperial Rome.

architrave [AHR-kuh-trayv]   The part of the *entablature* that rests on the *capital* or column in Classical *post-beam-triangle construction.*

aria [AH-ree-uh]   In music, an elaborate *melody* sung as a solo or sometimes a duet, usually in an *opera* or an *oratorio,* with an orchestral accompaniment.

ars nova   Latin, "new art"; a style of music in fourteenth-century Europe. It used more secular themes than the "old art" music of earlier times, which was closely identified with sacred music.

art film   A film *genre* marked by unusual narrative structures, violent action, and uplifting themes; associated with directors indebted to *auteurist* theory.

art song (*lied*)   In music, a *lyric* song with *melody* performed by a singer and instrumental accompaniment usually provided by piano; made popular by Schubert in the nineteenth century.

ashlar [ASH-luhr]   A massive hewn or squared stone used in constructing a fortress, palace, or large building.

assemblage art   An art form in which the artist mixes and/or assembles "found objects," such as scraps of paper, cloth, or junk, into a three-dimensional work and then adds paint or other decorations to it.

ataraxia [at-uh-RAK-see-uh]   Greek, "calmness"; in *Hellenistic* philosophy, the state of desiring nothing.

atonality [ay-toe-NAL-uh-tee]   In music, the absence of a *key* note or tonal center and the use of the *tones* of the chromatic *scale* impartially.

atrium [AY-tree-uhm]   In Roman architecture, an open courtyard at the front of a house; in Christian *Romanesque* churches, an open court, usually colonnaded, in front of the main doors of the structure.

attic   The topmost section or crown of an arch.

audience   The group or person for whom a work of art, architecture, literature, drama, film, or music is intended.

aulos   In music, a reed woodwind instrument similar to the oboe, usually played in pairs by one player as the double aulos; used in Greek music.

autarky [AW-tar-kee]   Greek, "self-sufficient"; in *Hellenistic* thought, the state of being isolated and free from the demands of society.

auteur [oh-TURR]   French, "author"; a film director who imposes a personal style. The *auteurist* director "writes" with the camera to express a personal vision.

avant-garde [a-vahn-GARD]   French, "advance guard"; writers, artists, and intellectuals who push their works and ideas ahead of more traditional groups and movements.

baldacchino [ball-duh-KEE-no]   An ornamental structure in the shape of a canopy, supported by four columns, built over a church altar, and usually decorated with statues and other ornaments.

balustrade   In architecture, a rail and the row of posts that support it, as along the edge of a staircase or around a dome.

baptistery   A small, often octagonal structure, separated from the main church, particularly in Europe, where baptisms are performed.

bard   A tribal poet-singer who composed and recited works, often of the *epic poetry* genre.

Baroque [buh-ROKE]   The prevailing seventeenth-century artistic and cultural style, characterized by an emphasis on grandeur, opulence, expansiveness, and complexity.

barrel vault   A ceiling or *vault* made of sets of arches placed side by side and joined together.

basilica [buh-SILL-ih-kuh]   A rectangular structure that included an *apse* at one or both ends; originally a Roman building used for public purposes, later taken over by the Christians for worship. The floor plan became the basis of nearly all early Christian churches.

bay   A four-cornered unit of architectural space, often used to identify a section of the *nave* in a *Romanesque* or *Gothic* church.

bel canto [bell KAHN-toe]   Italian, "beautiful singing"; a style of singing characteristic of seventeenth-century Italian *opera* stressing ease, purity, and evenness of *tone* along with precise vocal technique.

Beat Generation   A literary movement in the United States, from about 1950 to 1970, made up of poets, novelists, and playwrights, who stood apart from the mainstream literary establishment, as reflected in their use of street language, experimental forms of literary expression, and liberal use of alcohol and drugs. While expressing solidarity with society's downtrodden—the source of the term *Beat*—the Beats criticized capitalism, bourgeois society and values, and the nuclear arms race.

blank verse   Unrhymed iambic pentameter (lines with five feet, or units, each consisting of an unaccented and an accented syllable).

blaxploitation film   A crime film *genre* that features a swaggering black hero, catering to black audiences.

blind arcade   A decorative architectural design that gives the appearance of an open *arcade* or window but is filled in with some type of building material such as stone or brick.

blues   A type of music that emerged around 1900 from the rural African American culture, was originally based on work songs and religious spirituals, and expressed feelings of loneliness and hopelessness.

Byzantine style [BIZ-uhn-teen]   In painting, decoration, and architecture, a *style* blending Greco-Roman and oriental components into a highly stylized art form that glorified Christianity, notably in domed churches adorned with *mosaics* and polished marble; associated with the culture of the Eastern Roman Empire from about 500 until 1453.

cadenza [kuh-DEN-zah]   In music, a *virtuoso* passage, usually for a solo instrument or voice, meant to be improvised or to have an improvised feeling.

Cajun   A descendant of French pioneers, chiefly in Louisiana, who in 1755 chose to leave Acadia (modern Nova Scotia) rather than live under the British crown.

calligraphy   Penmanship or handwriting, usually done with flowing lines, used as a decoration or as an enhancement of a written work; found in Islamic and Christian writings.

Calvinism   The theological beliefs and rituals set forth in and derived from John Calvin's writings, placing emphasis on the power of God and the weakness of human beings.

campanile   From the Latin "campana," bell; a bell tower, especially one near but not attached to a church; an Italian invention.

canon   A set of principles or rules that are accepted as true and authoritative for the various arts or fields of study; in architecture, it refers to the standards of proportion; in painting, the prescribed ways of painting certain objects; in sculpture, the ideal proportions of the human body; in literature, the authentic list of an author's works; in religion, the approved and authoritative writings that are accepted as divinely inspired, such as the *scriptures* for Jews and Christians; and in religious and other contexts, certain prescribed rituals or official rules and laws. In music, a canon is a *composition* in which a *melody* sung by one voice is repeated exactly by successive voices as they enter.

canzone [kan-ZOH-nee]   Latin, "chant"; a type of love poem popular in southern France during the twelfth and thirteenth centuries.

capital   In architecture, the upper or crowning part of a column, on which the *entablature* rests.

cathedral   The church of a bishop that houses a cathedral, or throne symbolizing the seat of power in his administrative district, known as a diocese.

causality   The idea that one event "causes" another; the relation between a cause and its effect.

cella [SELL-uh]   The inner sanctum or walled room of a *Classical* temple where sacred statues were housed.

chanson [shahn-SAWN]   French, "song"; a fourteenth- to sixteenth-century French song for one or more voices, often with instrumental accompaniment. Similar to a *madrigal*.

chanson de geste [shahn-SAWN duh zhest]   A poem of brave deeds in the *epic* form developed in France during the eleventh century, usually to be sung.

character   A person in a story or play; someone who acts out or is affected by the *plot*.

chiaroscuro [key-ahr-uh-SKOOR-oh]   In painting, the use of dark and light contrast to create the effect of modeling of a figure or object.

Chinese Rococo   A variation of the European *Rococo*, characterized by oriental shapes, materials, techniques, and design elements.

Chinoiserie (shen-WAZ-uh-ree)   French, "Chinois," China. A *style* and taste in the West for Chinese culture, embracing the decorative arts and, to a lesser extent, Chinese writings; most influential from 1740 to 1770, but lingering until about 1850.

chivalric code   The rules of conduct, probably idealized, that governed the social roles and duties of aristocrats in the Middle Ages.

chivalric novel   A Late Medieval literary form that presented romantic stories of knights and their ladies; the dominant literary form in Spain from the Late Middle Ages into the *Renaissance*.

choir   In architecture, that part of a *Gothic* church in which the service was sung by singers or clergy, located in the east end beyond the *transept;* also, the group of trained singers who sat in the choir area.

chorus   In Greek drama, a group of performers who sang and danced in both *tragedies* and *comedies*, often commenting on the action; in later times, a group of singers who performed with or without instrumental accompaniment.

Christian humanism   An intellectual movement in sixteenth-century northern Europe that sought to use the ideals of the *Classical* world, the tools of ancient learning, and the morals of the Christian *scriptures* to rid the church of worldliness and scandal.

chthonian deities [THOE-nee-uhn]   In Greek religion, earth gods and goddesses who lived underground and were usually associated with peasants and their religious beliefs.

civic humanism   An Italian *Renaissance* ideal, characterized by dedicated and educated citizens who served as administrators and civil servants in their cities; inspired by the period's *Classical* revival.

civilization   The way humans live in a complex political, economic, and social structure, usually in an urban environment, with some development in technology, literature, and art.

cladding   In architecture, a covering or overlay of some material for a building's exterior walls.

Classic, or Classical   Having the forms, values, or standards embodied in the art and literature of Greek and Roman *civilization;* in music, an eighteenth-century style characterized by simplicity, proportion, and an emphasis on structure.

Classical Baroque style   A secular variation of the *Baroque* style that was identified with French kings and artists, was rooted in *Classical* ideals, and was used mainly to emphasize the power and grandeur of the monarchy.

Classicism   A set of aesthetic principles found in Greek and Roman art and literature emphasizing the search for perfection or ideal forms.

clavier [French, KLAH-vyay; German, KLAH-veer]   Any musical instrument having a keyboard, such as a piano, organ, or harpsichord; the term came into general usage with the popularity of Bach's set of studies entitled *The Well-Tempered Clavier.*

clerestory windows [KLEER-stor-ee]   A row of windows set along the upper part of a wall, especially in a church.

cloister   In architecture, a covered walkway, open on one side, which is attached to the four walls of buildings that face a quadrangle; originated in medieval church architecture. Also, a monastery or convent dedicated to religious seclusion.

codex [KO-deks] (plural, **codices**)   The earliest form of a bound book, made of parchment pages, dating from about the first century B.C.E. in pagan Rome.

collage [koh-LAHZH]   From the French *coller,* to "glue"; a type of art, introduced by Picasso, in which bits and pieces of materials such as paper or cloth are glued to a painted surface.

color   Use of the hues found in nature to enhance or distort the sense of reality in a visual image.

commedia dell'arte [kuh-MAY-de-uh del-AR-teh]   Italian, "comedy of art"; an Italian theatrical *genre* from the sixteenth century, using puppets and stock characters, with a strong streak of improvisation. Highly influential later on live theater in Italy and elsewhere.

comedy   A literary *genre* characterized by a story with a complicated and amusing *plot* that ends with a happy and peaceful resolution of all conflicts.

comedy of manners   A humorous play that focuses on the way people in a particular social group or class interact with one another, especially regarding fashions and manners.

composition   The arrangement of constituent elements in an artistic work; in music, composition also refers to the process of creating the work.

concerto [kuhn-CHER-toe]   In music, a *composition* for one or more soloists and *orchestra,* usually in a symphonic *form* with three contrasting movements.

conceptual art   A *Late Modern* art movement in which the concept or idea of the proposed art is more important than the means for its execution.

congregational or Friday mosque   A type of *mosque* used for Friday prayers, inspired by Muhammad's original example. Characterized by a central courtyard along with a domed fountain for ablutions; found across the Islamic world.

consort   A set of musical instruments in the same family, ranging from bass to soprano; also, a group of musicians who entertain by singing or playing instruments.

Constructivism   A movement in nonobjective art, originating in the Soviet Union and flourishing from 1917 to 1922 and concerned with planes and volumes as expressed in modern industrial materials such as glass and plastic.

content   The subject matter of an artistic work.

context   The setting in which an artistic work arose, its own time and place. Context includes the political, economic, social, and cultural conditions of the time; it can also include the personal circumstances of the artist's life.

contrapposto [kon-truh-POH-stoh]   In sculpture and painting, the placement of the human figure so the weight is more on one leg than the other and the shoulders and chest are turned in the opposite direction from the hips and legs.

convention   An agreed-upon practice, device, technique, or form.

Corinthian   The third Greek architectural order, in which temple columns are slender and *fluted,* sit on a base, and have *capitals* shaped like inverted bells and decorated with carvings representing the leaves of the acanthus bush; this style was popular in *Hellenistic* times and widely adopted by the Romans.

cornice   In architecture, the crowning, projecting part of the *entablature.*

cosmopolitan   From Greek, "cosmos," world, and "polis," city; a citizen of the world, that is, an urban dweller with a universal, or world, view.

Counter-Reformation   A late-sixteenth-century movement in the Catholic Church aimed at reestablishing its basic beliefs, reforming its organizational structure, and reasserting itself as the authoritative voice of Christianity.

countersubject   In music, in the *fugue,* a contrasting variant to the *subject;* played in tandem with the *subject,* either below or above it.

covenant   In Judaism and Christianity, a solemn and binding agreement or contract between God and his followers.

Creole   An ambiguous term, sometimes referring to descendants of French and Spanish settlers of the southern United States, especially Louisiana; used by Kate Chopin in her short stories and novels in this sense. In other contexts, *Creole* can refer either to blacks born in the Western Hemisphere (as distinguished from blacks born in Africa) or to residents of the American Gulf states of mixed black, Spanish, and Portuguese ancestry.

crescendo [krah-SHEN-doh]   In music, an increase in volume.

cruciform [KROO-suh-form]   Cross-shaped; used to describe the standard floor plan of a church.

Cubism   A *style* of painting introduced by Picasso and Braque in which objects are broken up into fragments and patterns of geometric structures and depicted on the flat canvas as if from several points of view.

culture   The sum of human endeavors, including the basic political, economic, and social institutions and the values, beliefs, and arts of those who share them.

cuneiform [kue-NEE-uh-form]   Wedge-shaped characters used in writing on tablets found in Mesopotamia and other ancient *civilizations.*

Cynicism   A *Hellenistic* philosophy that denounced society and its institutions as artificial and called on the individual to strive for *autarky.*

Dada [DAH-dah]   An early-twentieth-century artistic movement, named after a nonsense word that was rooted in a love of play, encouraged deliberately irrational acts, and exhibited contempt for all traditions.

Decadence   A late-nineteenth-century literary *style* concerned with morbid and artificial subjects and themes.

Deconstruction   In *Post-Modern* literary analysis, a set of practices for analyzing and critiquing a text in order to "deconstruct" its actual meaning and language.

deductive reasoning   The process of reasoning from the general to the particular—that is, beginning with an accepted premise or first statement and, by steps of logical reasoning or inference, reaching a conclusion that necessarily follows from the premise.

Deism [DEE-iz-uhm]   A religion based on the idea that the universe was created by God and then left to run according to *natural laws,* without divine interference; formulated and practiced in the eighteenth century.

de Stijl [duh STILE]   Dutch, "the style"; an artistic movement associated with a group of early-twentieth-century Dutch painters who used rectangular forms and primary colors in their works and who believed that art should have spiritual values and a social purpose.

devotio moderna [de-VO-tee-oh mo-DER-nuh]   The "new devotion" of Late Medieval Christianity that emphasized piety and discipline as practiced by lay religious communities located primarily in northern Europe.

Diaspora [dye-AS-puhr-uh]   From the Greek, "to scatter"; the dispersion of the Jews from their homeland in ancient Palestine, a process that began with the Babylonian Captivity in the sixth century B.C.E. and continued over the centuries.

Dionysia [DYE-uh-NYSH-ee-ah]   Any of the religious festivals held in ancient Athens honoring Dionysus, the god of wine; especially the Great Dionysia, celebrated in late winter and early spring in which *tragedy* is thought to have originated.

divining   Predicting the future by "reading," or interpreting, the entrails of an animal or the behavior of birds; practiced by ancient Roman priests and religious leaders.

Doric   The simplest and oldest of the Greek architectural orders, in which temple columns have undecorated *capitals* and rest directly on the *stylobate.*

drum   In architecture, a circular or polygonal wall used to support a dome.

drypoint   In art, the technique of incising an image, using a sharp, pointed instrument, onto a metal surface or block used for printing. Also, the print made from the technique.

dynamics   In music, changes in the volume of a sound.

Early Renaissance style   A *style* inspired by *Classical* rather than *Gothic* models that arose among Florentine architects, sculptors, and painters in the late fourteenth and early fifteenth centuries.

electronic music   Music produced using electronic means, usually with a *synthesizer* and/or a computer.

empiricism   The process of collecting data, making observations, carrying out experiments based on the collected data and observations, and reaching a conclusion.

engraving   In art, the technique of carving, cutting, or etching an image with a sharp, pointed instrument onto a metal surface overlaid with wax, dipping the surface in acid, and then printing it. Also, the print made from the technique.

Enlightenment   The eighteenth-century philosophical and cultural movement marked by the application of reason to human problems and affairs, a questioning of traditional beliefs and ideas, and an optimistic faith in unlimited progress for humanity, particularly through education.

entablature [en-TAB-luh-choor]   In architecture, the part of the temple above the columns and below the roof, which, in *Classical* temples, included the *architrave,* the *frieze,* and the *pediment.*

entasis [EN-ta-sis]   In architecture, convex curving or enlarging of the central part of a column to correct the optical illusion that the column is too thin.

environmental art   A *Post-Modern* art form that uses the environment, including stone, earth, and water, so as to create a natural-looking artwork. Environmental art is ephemeral, as it tends to revert to its primary elements over time—thus echoing the ever-changing world of nature.

epic   A poem, novel, or film that recounts at length the life of a hero or the history of a people.

epic poetry   Narrative poetry, usually told or written in an elevated style, that recounts the life of a hero.

epic theater   A type of theater, invented by Brecht, in which major social issues are dramatized with outlandish props and jarring dialogue and effects, all designed to alienate middle-class *audiences* and force them to think seriously about the problems raised in the plays.

Epicureanism [ep-i-kyoo-REE-uh-niz-uhm]   A *Hellenistic* philosophy, founded by Epicurus and later expounded by the Roman Lucretius, that made its highest goals the development of the mind and an existence free from the demands of everyday life.

episode   In music, a short transitional section played between the *subject* and the *countersubject;* used in *fugal* composition.

eschatology [es-kuh-TAHL-uh-jee]   The concern with final events or the end of the world, a belief popular in Jewish and early Christian communities and linked to the concept of the coming of a *Messiah.*

evangelicalism   Historically, a nineteenth-century Protestant movement, mainly in the United States, which grew out of the Methodist tradition and emphasized personal piety and the working of the Holy Spirit. Evangelicalism dominated mainline Protestant America until about 1870. Today, evangelicalism is a term used for describing Protestants who emphasize *fundamentalism,* biblical inerrancy, and conservative social values.

evangelists   From the Greek *evangelion,* a term generally used for those who preach the Christian religion; more specifically, the four evangelists, Matthew, Mark, Luke, and John, who wrote about Jesus Christ soon after his death in the first four books of the New Testament.

evolution   The theory, set forth in the nineteenth century by Charles Darwin, that plants and animals, including humans, evolved over millions of years from simpler forms through a process of natural selection.

existentialism [eg-zi-STEN-shuh-liz-uhm]   A twentieth-century philosophy focusing on the precarious nature of human existence, with its uncertainty, anxiety, and ultimate death, as well as on individual freedom and responsibility and the possibilities for human creativity and authenticity.

Expressionism   A late-nineteenth-century literary and artistic movement characterized by the expression of highly personal feelings rather than of objective reality.

fan vaulting   A decorative pattern of *vault* ribs that arch out or radiate from a central point on the ceiling; popular in English *Perpendicular* architecture.

Faustian [FAU-stee-uhn]   Resembling the character Faust in Goethe's most famous work, in being spiritually tormented, insatiable for knowledge and experience, or willing to pay any price, including personal and spiritual integrity, to gain a desired end.

Fauvism [FOH-viz-uhm]   From the French "fauve," wild beast; an early-twentieth-century art movement led by Matisse and favoring exotic colors and disjointed shapes.

fête galante [fet gah-LAHNN]   In *Rococo* painting, the *theme* or scene of aristocrats being entertained or simply enjoying their leisure and other worldly pleasures.

First Great Awakening   The period of religious revivalism among Protestants that placed emphasis on a direct and personal relationship with God and undermined the traditional role and power of the established churches; centered mainly in the British American colonies during the 1730s and 1740s.

First Romanesque   The first stage of *Romanesque* architecture, about 1000–1080. First Romanesque churches had high walls, few windows, and flat wooden roofs, and were built of stone rubble and adorned with *Lombard bands* and *Lombard arcades.* Begun along the Mediterranean, in the area ranging from Dalmatia, across Northern Italy and Provence, to Catalonia.

Flamboyant style [flam-BOY-uhnt]   A Late French *Gothic* architectural style of elaborate decorations and ornamentation that produce a flamelike effect.

Florid Baroque style   A variation of the *Baroque* style specifically identified with the Catholic Church's patronage of the arts and used to glorify its beliefs.

fluting   Decorative vertical grooves carved in a column.

flying buttress   An external masonry support, found primarily in *Gothic* churches, that carries the thrust of the ceiling, or *vault,* away from the upper walls of the building to an external vertical column.

forms   In music, particular structures of arrangements of elements, such as *symphonies,* songs, concerts, and *operas.* In painting and sculpture, **form** refers to the artistic structure rather than to the material of which an artwork is made.

forum   In Rome and many Roman towns, the public place, located in the center of the town, where people gathered to socialize, transact business, and administer the government.

forte [FOR-tay]   Italian, "loud." A musical term.

fortississimo [fawrh-tis-ISS-e-moh]   In music, extremely loud; abbreviated fff.

Fourth Century style   The sculptural *style* characteristic of the last phase of the *Hellenic* period, when new interpretations of beauty and movement were adopted.

fresco   A painting done on wet or dry plaster that becomes part of the plastered wall.

friars   Members of a thirteenth-century mendicant (begging) monastic order.

frieze [FREEZ]   A band of painted designs or sculptured figures placed on walls; also, the central portion of a temple's *entablature* just above the *architrave.*

fugue [fewg]   In music, a *composition* for several instruments in which a *theme* is introduced by one instrument and then repeated by each successively entering instrument so that a complicated interweaving of themes, variations, *imitations,* and echoes results; this compositional technique began in the fifteenth century and reached its zenith in the *Baroque* period in works by Bach.

fundamentalism   Historically, an American Protestant movement that broke free of the *evangelicals* from about 1870 to 1970, stressing biblical inerrancy, "speaking in tongues," and opposition to certain modern scientific trends, such as evolution and higher criticism. Today, fundamentalism is often aggregated with *evangelicalism* and other socially conservative religious movements.

gallery   In architecture, a long, narrow passageway or corridor, usually found in churches and located above the *aisles,* and often with openings that permit viewing from above into the *nave.*

gargoyle [GAHR-goil]   In architecture, a water spout in the form of a grotesque animal or human, carved from stone, placed on the edge of a roof.

genre [ZHON-ruh]   From the French, "a kind, a type, or a class"; a category of artistic, musical, or literary composition, characterized by a particular *style, form,* or *content.*

genre subject   In art, a scene or a person from everyday life, depicted realistically and without religious or symbolic significance.

geocentrism   The belief that the earth is the center of the universe and that the sun, moon, and stars revolve around it.

ghazal [GUZ-l]   A short *lyric,* usually dealing with love, composed in a single rhyme and based on the poet's personal life and loves.

glissando [gle-SAHN-doe] (plural, **glissandi**)   In music, the blending of one *tone* into the next in scalelike passages that may be ascending or descending in character.

goliards [GOAL-yuhrds]   Medieval roaming poets or scholars who traveled about reciting poems on topics ranging from moral lessons to the pains of love.

Gospels   The first four books of the New Testament (Matthew, Mark, Luke, and John), which record the life and sayings of Jesus Christ; the word itself, from Old English, means "good news" or "good tales".

Gothic style   A *style* of architecture, usually associated with churches, that originated in northern France and whose three phases—Early, High, and Late—lasted from the twelfth to the sixteenth century. Emerging from the *Romanesque* style, Gothic is identified by pointed arches, *ribbed vaults, stained-glass* windows, *flying buttresses,* and carvings on the exterior.

Greek cross   A cross in which all the arms are of equal length; the shape used as a floor plan in many Greek or Eastern Orthodox churches.

Gregorian chant   A style of *monophonic* church music sung in unison and without instrumental accompaniment and used in the *liturgy;* named for Pope Gregory I (590–604).

groined vault, or cross vault   A ceiling, or *vault,* created when two *barrel vaults,* set at right angles, intersect.

happening   A *Late Modern* theatrical development, combining skits with outrageous events and involving performances by painters, actors, musicians, and audience members, so as to give the impression of spontaneity.

hard-edge   In *Late Modern* painting, a technique used in color paintings, by which the areas of *color* are precisely delineated from one another.

harmony   The simultaneous combination of two or more *tones*, producing a chord; generally, the chordal characteristics of a work and the way chords interact.

heliocentrism   The belief that the sun is the center of the universe and that the earth and the other planets revolve around it.

Hellenic [hell-LENN-ik]   Relating to the time period in Greek civilization from 480 to 323 B.C.E., when the most influential Greek artists, playwrights, and philosophers, such as Praxiteles, Sophocles, and Plato, created their greatest works; associated with the *Classical* style.

Hellenistic [hell-uh-NIS-tik]   Relating to the time period from about 323 to 31 B.C.E., when Greek and oriental or Middle Eastern cultures and institutions intermingled to create a heterogeneous and *cosmopolitan civilization.*

hieroglyphs [HI-uhr-uh-glifs]   Pictorial characters used in Egyptian writing, which is known as hieroglyphics.

High Classical style   The *style* in Greek sculpture associated with the ideal physical form and perfected during the zenith of the Athenian Empire, about 450–400 B.C.E.

higher criticism   A rational approach to Bible study, developed in German Protestant circles in the nineteenth century, that treated the biblical *scriptures* as literature and subjected them to close scrutiny, testing their literary history, authorship, and meaning.

High Renaissance   The period from about 1495 to 1520, often associated with the patronage of the popes in Rome, when the most influential artists and writers of the *Renaissance,* including Michelangelo, Raphael, Leonardo da Vinci, and Machiavelli, were producing their greatest works.

high tech   In architecture, a *style* that uses obvious industrial design elements with exposed parts serving as decorations.

hip hop   In *Post-Modern* popular culture, after 1970, an eclectic trend among African Americans and Hispanic Americans, drawing on break dancing, graffiti art, rap rhyming, and disc jockeys playing with turntables and "scratch" effects; highly influential on today's youth culture, popular music, film, and dance styles.

holiness   A nineteenth-century American Protestant movement, which came out of the Methodist tradition, emphasizing holy living and the need to be "born again" as a true disciple of Jesus Christ; part of the *fundamentalist* movement after 1870.

Homeric epithet   A recurring nickname, such as "Ox-eyed Hera," used in Homer's *Iliad* or *Odyssey.*

homo faber   Latin, "human fabricator"; an anthropological term used to describe humans as creators of tools and machines.

hubris [HYOO-bris]   In Greek thought, human pride or arrogance that leads an individual to challenge the gods, usually provoking divine retribution.

humanism   An attitude that is concerned with humanity, its achievements, and its potential; the study of the *humanities*; in the *Renaissance*, identified with *studia humanitatis.*

humanities   In the nineteenth century, the study of Greek and Roman languages and literature; later set off from the sciences and expanded to include the works of all Western peoples in the arts, literature, music, philosophy, and sometimes history and religion; in *Post-Modernism* extended to a global dimension.

hymn   From the Greek and Latin, "ode of praise of gods or heroes"; a song of praise or thanksgiving to God or the gods, performed both with and without instrumental accompaniment.

idealism   In Plato's philosophy, the theory that reality and ultimate truth are to be found not in the material world but in the spiritual realm.

idée fixe [ee-DAY FEEX]   French, "fixed idea"; in music, a recurring musical *theme* that is associated with a person or a concept.

ideogram [ID-e-uh-gram]   A picture drawn to represent an idea or a concept.

idyll   A relatively short poem that focuses on events and *themes* of everyday life, such as family, love, and religion; popular in the *Hellenistic Age* and a standard form that has been periodically revived in Western literature throughout the centuries.

illuminated manuscript   A richly decorated book, painted with brilliant colors and gold leaf, usually of sacred writings; popular in the West in the Middle Ages.

illusionism   The use of painting techniques in *Florid Baroque* art to create the appearance that decorated areas are part of the surrounding architecture, usually employed in ceiling decorations.

imitation   In music, a technique in which a musical idea, or motif, is presented by one voice or instrument and is then followed immediately by a restatement by another voice or instrument; the effect is that of a musical relay race.

impasto [ihm-PAHS-toe]   In painting, the application of thick layers of pigment.

Impressionism   In painting, a *style* introduced in the 1870s, marked by an attempt to catch spontaneous impressions, often involving the play of sunlight on ordinary events and scenes observed outdoors; in music, a style of *composition* designed to create a vague and dreamy mood through gliding melodies and shimmering *tone colors.*

impressionistic   In art, relating to the representation of a scene using the simplest details to create an illusion of reality by evoking subjective impressions rather than aiming for a totally realistic effect; characterized by images that are insubstantial and barely sketched in.

incunabula   (singular, **incunabulum**)   The collection of books printed before 1500 C.E.

inductive reasoning   The process of reasoning from particulars to the general or from single parts to the whole and/or final conclusion.

installation art   A boundary-challenging type of art born in the 1960s that creates architectural tableaux, using objects drawn from and making references to artistic sources (such as music, painting, sculpture, and theater) and the workaday world (such as everyday tasks, media images, and foodstuffs) and that may include a human presence. Associated with the work of Ann Hamilton.

International style   In twentieth-century architecture, a *style* and method of construction that capitalized on modern materials, such as ferro-concrete, glass, and steel, and that produced the popular "glass box" skyscrapers and variously shaped private houses.

Ionic   The Greek architectural order, developed in Ionia, in which columns are slender, sit on a base, and have *capitals* decorated with scrolls.

isorhythm   In music, a unifying method based on rhythmic patterns rather than *melodic* patterns.

Italo-Byzantine style [ih-TAL-o-BIZ-uhn-teen]   The *style* of Italian *Gothic* painting that reflected the influence of *Byzantine* paintings, *mosaics,* and icons.

iwan [eye-van]   In Islamic architecture, a vaulted hall. In the 4-*iwan mosque,* one *iwan* was used for prayers and the other three for study or rest.

jazz   A type of music, instrumental and vocal, originating in the African American community and rooted in African, African American, and Western musical forms and traditions.

Jesuits [JEZH-oo-its]   Members of the Society of Jesus, the best-organized and most effective monastic order founded during the *Counter-Reformation* to combat Protestantism and spread Roman Catholicism around the world.

jihad [JEE-HAD]   Originally, this Arabic term meant "to strive" or "to struggle" and, as such, was identified with any pious Muslim combating sin and trying not to do evil. In modern times, radical Islamic states and groups have given the term new meaning as "Holy War" and have used it to justify military and other violent action against their enemies. A central belief in Islam.

key   In music, a tonal system consisting of seven *tones* in fixed relationship to a tonic, or keynote. Since the *Renaissance, key* has been the structural foundation of the bulk of Western music, down to the *Modernist* period.

keystone   The central stone at the top of an arch that locks the other stones in place.

koine [KOI-nay]   A colloquial Greek language spoken in the *Hellenistic* world that helped tie together that *civilization.*

kore [KOH-ray]   An *Archaic* Greek standing statue of a young draped female.

kouros [KOO-rus]   An *Archaic* Greek standing statue of a young naked male.

Late Gothic style   A *style* characterized in architecture by ornate decoration and tall cathedral windows and spires and in painting and sculpture by increased refinement of details and a trend toward naturalism; popular in the fourteenth and fifteenth centuries in central and western Europe.

Late Mannerism   The last stage of the *Mannerist* movement, characterized by exaggeration and distortion, especially in painting.

Late Modernism   The last stage of *Modernism,* characterized by an increasing sense of existential despair, an attraction to non-Western cultures, and extreme experimentalism.

lay   A short *lyric* or narrative poem meant to be sung to the accompaniment of an instrument such as a harp; based on Celtic legends but usually set in feudal times and focused on courtly love *themes,* especially adulterous passion. The oldest surviving lays are those of the twelfth-century poet Marie de France.

leitmotif [LITE-mo-teef]   In music, and especially in Wagner's *operas,* the use of recurring *themes* associated with particular characters, objects, or ideas.

liberalism   In political thought, a set of beliefs advocating certain personal, economic, and natural rights based on assumptions about the perfectibility and autonomy of human beings and the notion of progress, as first expressed in the writings of John Locke.

liberation theology   A reform movement, which began in the late 1960s among Roman Catholic priests and nuns in Latin America, blending Christian teachings on social and economic justice with Marxist theory. After this movement went global, the Vatican withdrew its support in the 1980s, though liberation theology remains an underground force in some parts of the world today.

libretto [lih-BRET-oh]   In Italian, "little book"; the text or words of an *opera,* an *oratorio,* or a musical work of a similar dramatic nature involving a written text.

line   The mark—straight or curved, thick or thin, light or dark—made by the artist in a work of art.

Linear A   In Minoan *civilization,* a type of script still undeciphered that lasted from about 1800 to 1400 B.C.E.

Linear B   In Minoan *civilization,* an early form of Greek writing that flourished on Crete from about 1400 until about 1300 B.C.E. and lasted in a few scattered places on the Greek mainland until about 1150 B.C.E.; used to record commercial transactions.

liturgical drama   Religious dramas, popular between the twelfth and sixteenth centuries, based on biblical stories with musical accompaniment that were staged in the area in front of the church, performed at first in Latin but later in the *vernacular languages;* the mystery plays (*mystery* is derived from the Latin for "action") are the most famous type of liturgical drama.

liturgy   A rite or ritual, such as prayers or ceremonies, practiced by a religious group in public worship.

local color   In literature, the use of detail peculiar to a particular region and environment to add interest and authenticity to a narrative, including description of the locale, customs, speech, and music. Local color was an especially popular development in American literature in the late nineteenth century.

logical positivism   A school of modern philosophy that seeks truth by defining terms and clarifying statements and asserts that metaphysical theories are meaningless.

logos [LOWG-os]   In *Stoicism,* the name for the supreme being or for reason—the controlling principle of the universe—believed to be present both in nature and in each human being.

Lombard arcades   In architecture, a sequence of decorative *arcades* beneath the eaves of a building. First used in churches in Lombardy (North Central Italy). A defining feature of the *First Romanesque.*

Lombard bands   In architecture, a web of vertical bands or buttresses along the sides of a building. First used in churches in Lombardy (North Central Italy). A defining feature of the *First Romanesque.*

luminism   In nineteenth-century American landscape painting, a group of artists, who were inspired by the vastness of the American west and influenced by *Transcendentalism,* approached their work by consciously removing themselves from their paintings.

lute   In music, a wooden instrument, plucked or bowed, consisting of a sound box with an elaborately carved sound hole and a neck across which the (often twelve) strings pass. Introduced during the High Middle Ages, the lute enjoyed a height of popularity in Europe from the seventeenth to eighteenth century.

Lutheranism   The doctrine, *liturgy,* and institutional structure of the church founded in the sixteenth century by Martin Luther, who stressed the authority of the Bible, the faith of the individual, and the worshiper's direct communication with God as the bases of his new religion.

lyre   In music, a handheld stringed instrument, with or without a sound box, used by ancient Egyptians, Assyrians, and Greeks. In Greek culture, the lyre was played to accompany song and recitation.

lyric   A short subjective poem that expresses intense personal emotion.

lyric poetry   In Greece, verses sung and accompanied by the *lyre;* today, intensely personal poetry.

Machiavellianism [mahk-ih-uh-VEL-ih-uhn-iz-uhm]   The view that politics should be separated from morals and dedicated to the achievement of desired ends through any means necessary ("the end justifies the means"); derived from the political writings of Machiavelli.

madrasah [mah-DRASS-ah]   An Arabic term meaning a religious school for advanced study; a forerunner of the Islamic university. Today, *madrasahs* are schools for Islamic youth, and their curriculum is based on the *Qur'an.*

madrigal [MAD-rih-guhl]   A *polyphonic* song performed without accompaniment and based on a secular text, often a love *lyric;* especially popular in the sixteenth century.

maenad [MEE-nad]   A woman who worshiped Dionysus, often in a state of frenzy.

magic realism   A literary and artistic *style* identified with Latin American *Post-Modernism* that mixes realistic and supernatural elements to create imaginary or fantastic scenes.

Mannerism   A cultural movement between 1520 and 1600 that grew out of a rebellion against the *Renaissance's* artistic norms of symmetry and balance; characterized in art by distortion and incongruity and in thought and literature by the belief that human nature is depraved.

maqamah [mah-kah-mah]   In Arabic, "assembly." A Muslim literary *genre,* intended for educated readers, that recounted stories of rogues and con men; filled with wordplay, humor, and keen usage of Arabic language and grammar. Created by al-Hamadhani in the tenth century.

Mass   In religion, the ritual celebrating the Eucharist, or Holy Communion, primarily in the Roman Catholic Church. The Mass has two parts, the Ordinary and the Proper; the former remains the same throughout the church year, whereas the latter changes for each date and service. The Mass Ordinary is composed of the Kyrie, Gloria, Credo, Sanctus, and Agnus Dei; the Mass Proper includes the Introit, Gradual, Alleluia or Tract, Sequence, Offertory, and Communion. In music, a musical setting of certain parts of the Mass, especially the Kyrie, Gloria, Credo, Sanctus, Benedictus, and Agnus Dei. The first complete Mass Ordinary was composed by Guillaume de Machaut [mah-SHOH] (about 1300–1377) in the fourteenth century.

mass culture   The tastes, values, and interests of the classes that dominate modern industrialized society, especially the consumer-oriented American middle class.

medallion   In Roman architecture, a circular decoration often found on triumphal arches enclosing a scene or portrait; in more general architectural use, a tablet or panel in a wall or window containing a figure or an ornament.

medium   The material from which an artwork is made.

melody   A succession of musical *tones* having a distinctive shape and rhythm.

melisma   In music, in *plainsong,* a style of singing in which a group of notes is sung to the same syllable; the opposite of *syllabic* singing.

Messiah   A Hebrew word meaning "the anointed one," or one chosen by God to be his representative on earth; in Judaism, a savior who will come bringing peace and justice; in Christianity, Jesus Christ (*Christ* is derived from a Greek word meaning "the anointed one").

metope [MET-uh-pee]   In architecture, a panel, often decorated, between two *triglyphs* on the *entablature* of a *Doric* Greek temple.

mezzotint   Also known as half-tone. An early type of color print, made with a metal plate, characterized by subtle gradations of shadings and clear definition of *line;* developed in about 1650 in the Netherlands.

microtone   In music, an interval, or distance between a sound (pitch) on a scale, that is smaller than a semi*tone*—

the smallest interval in mainstream Western music prior to *jazz.* Muslim music uses a microtonal system.

minaret   In Islamic architecture, a tall, slender tower with a pointed top, from which the daily calls to prayer are delivered; located near a *mosque.*

minbar [min-bar]   In Muslim *mosque* architecture, a pulpit with steps, sometimes on wheels for portability; used by a cleric for leading prayers and giving sermons.

miniature   A small painting, usually of a religious nature, found in *illuminated manuscripts;* also, a small portrait.

minimalism   A trend in *Late Modern* and *Post-Modern* art, architecture, and music which found beauty in the bare essentials and thus stripped art, buildings, and music to their basic elements. The minimalist aesthetic was a strong influence in the architecture of Mies van der Rohe, many art styles, including *conceptual art, environmental art,* and *Op Art,* and the music of Philip Glass.

minstrel   A professional entertainer of the twelfth to the seventeenth century; especially a secular musician; also called "jongleur."

minuet and trio   In music, a *Classical* music form, based on two French court dances of the same name, dating from the seventeenth and eighteenth centuries; often paired in the third section of *symphonies* in the *Classical* period. Typically, the minuet was in ¾ time and with a moderate *tempo,* while the trio provided contrast but had no standard form.

Modernism   A late-nineteenth- and twentieth-century cultural, artistic, and literary movement that rejected much of the past and focused on the current, the secular, and the revolutionary in search of new forms of expression; the dominant style of the twentieth century until 1970. In Roman Catholic Church history, *Modernism* was a liberal movement among progressive churchpeople, 1850 to 1910, which applied new findings in history, philosophy, and psychology to traditional church teachings; condemned by the Vatican in 1907.

modes   A series of musical *scales* devised by the Greeks and believed by them to create certain emotional or ethical effects on the listener.

monophony [muh-NOF-uh-nee]   A *style* of music in which there is only a single line of melody; the *Gregorian chants* are the most famous examples of monophonic music.

monotheism   From the Greek *monos,* single, alone, and the Greek *theos,* god; the belief that there is only one God.

mood   In music, the emotional impact of a *composition* on the feelings of a listener.

mosaic   An art form or decoration, usually on a wall or a floor, created by inlaying small pieces of glass, shell, or stone in cement or plaster to create pictures or patterns.

mosque   A Muslim place of worship, often distinguished by a dome-shaped central building placed in an open space surrounded by a wall.

motet   A multivoiced song with words of a sacred or secular text, usually sung without accompanying instruments; developed in the thirteenth century.

mural   A wall painting, usually quite large, used to decorate a private or public structure.

muse   In Greek religion, any one of the nine sister goddesses who preside over the creative arts and sciences.

music drama   An *opera* in which the action and music are continuous, not broken up into separate *arias* and *recitatives,* and the music is determined by its dramatic appropriateness, producing a work in which music, words, and staging are fused; the term was coined by Wagner.

narrative voice In literature, the *narrator,* a key element in fiction. An omniscient narrator, usually in the third person, knows everything about the *plot* and *characters,* regardless of time and place—typical of nineteenth-century novels. In *Modernist* fiction, the narrative voice tends to be disjointed, unreliable, and often in the first person.

narrator The speaker whose voice we hear in a story or poem.

narthex The porch or vestibule of a church, usually enclosed, through which worshipers walk before entering the *nave.*

Naturalism In literature, a late-nineteenth-century movement inspired by the methods of science and the insights of sociology, concerned with an objective depiction of the ugly side of industrial society.

natural law In *Stoicism* and later in other philosophies, a body of laws or principles that are believed to be derived from nature and binding on human society and that constitute a higher form of justice than civil or judicial law.

natural philosophy Science based on philosophical speculation and experiments or data, founded in Ionian Greece in the sixth century B.C.E.; a term that embraced both science and philosophy until about 1800 C.E.

nave The central longitudinal area of a church, extending from the entrance to the *apse* and flanked by *aisles.*

Neoclassical style In the late eighteenth century, an artistic and literary movement that emerged as a reaction to the *Rococo* style and that sought inspiration from ancient *Classicism.* In the twentieth century, between 1919 and 1951, *Neoclassicism* in music was a style that rejected the emotionalism favored by *Romantic* composers as well as the dense orchestral sounds of the *Impressionists;* instead, it borrowed features from seventeenth- and eighteenth-century music and practiced the ideals of balance, clarity of texture, and nonprogrammatic works.

Neoclassicism In the late third century B.C.E., an artistic movement in the disintegrating *Hellenistic* world that sought inspiration in the Athenian Golden Age of the fifth and fourth centuries B.C.E.; and, since 1970, *Neoclassicism* has been a highly visible submovement in *Post-Modernism,* particularly prominent in painting and architecture, that restates the principles of *Classical* art—balance, harmony, idealism.

Neoexpressionism A submovement in *Post-Modernism,* associated primarily with painting, that offers social criticism and is concerned with the expression of the artist's feelings.

Neolithic Literally, "new stone"; used to define the New Stone Age, when human *cultures* evolved into agrarian systems and settled communities; dating from about 10,000 or 8000 B.C.E. to about 3000 B.C.E.

Neo-orthodoxy A twentieth-century Protestant movement, dedicated to recentering orthodox theology in Christian thought and emphasizing the central role played by God in history. Founded after World War I in opposition to the *Social Gospel.*

Neo-Platonism A philosophy based on Plato's ideas that was developed during the Roman period in an attempt to reconcile the dichotomy between Plato's concept of an eternal World of Ideas and the ever-changing physical world; in the fifteenth-century *Renaissance,* it served as a philosophical guide for Italian humanists who sought to reconcile Late Medieval Christian beliefs with *Classical* thinking.

Neorealism A submovement in *Post-Modernism* that is based on a photographic sense of detail and harks back to many of the qualities of nineteenth-century *Realism.*

Neoromanticism A *Post-Modern* movement in music, starting after 1970, which rejects *atonality* and draws inspiration from the music of the *Romantic* period.

New Comedy The style of comedy favored by *Hellenistic* playwrights, concentrating on gentle satirical *themes*—in particular, romantic *plots* with stock *characters* and predictable endings.

nihilism The denial of any objective ground of truth, and, in particular, of moral truths.

Nominalism [NAHM-uh-nuhl-iz-uhm] In medieval thought, the school that held that objects were separate unto themselves but could, for convenience, be treated in a collective sense because they shared certain characteristics; opposed to *Realism.*

Northern Renaissance The sixteenth-century cultural movement in northern Europe that was launched by the northward spread of Italian *Renaissance* art, culture, and ideals. The Northern Renaissance differed from the Italian Renaissance largely because of the persistence of the *Late Gothic style* and the unfolding of the *Reformation* after 1520.

Nouvelle Vague French, "New Wave"; a *Late Modern* movement in French film, featuring innovative narrative structures and various experimental cinematic techniques. French word for "New Wave" films in the post–World War II period which experimented with new ways to capture scenes and events.

octave In music, usually the eight-tone interval between a note and a second note of the same name, as in C to C.

oculus [AHK-yuh-lus] The circular opening at the top of a dome; derived from the Latin word for "eye."

Old Comedy The style of *comedy* established by Aristophanes in the fifth century B.C.E., distinguished by a strong element of political and social satire.

oligarchy From the Greek *oligos,* "few"; a state ruled by the few, especially by a small fraction of persons or families.

Olympian deities In Greek religion, sky gods and goddesses who lived on mountaintops and were worshiped mainly by the Greek aristocracy.

Op Art A *Late Modern* art movement, using *abstract,* mathematically based forms to create stimulating images for the eyes, such as optical patterns, lingering images, and whirling effects.

opera A drama or play set to music and consisting of vocal pieces with *orchestral* accompaniment; acting, scenery, and sometimes *choruses* and dancing are used to heighten the dramatic values of operas.

oratorio A choral work based on religious events or *scripture* employing singers, *choruses,* and *orchestra,* but without scenery or staging and performed usually in a church or a concert hall.

orchestra In Greek theaters, the circular area where the *chorus* performed in front of the audience; in music, a group of instrumentalists, including string players, who play together.

organum [OR-guh-nuhm] In the ninth through the thirteenth centuries, a simple and early form of *polyphonic* music consisting of a main *melody* sung along with a *Gregorian chant;* by the thirteenth century it had developed into a complex multivoiced song.

Orientalizing A phase of Greek art, particularly Greek vase painting, lasting from about 700 to 530 B.C.E., which drew inspiration from Near Eastern art, including artistic techniques, vessel forms, decorative motifs, and subjects.

Paleolithic Literally, "old stone"; used to define the Old Stone Age, when crude stones and tools were used; dating from about 2,000,000 B.C.E. to about 10,000 B.C.E.

pantheism The doctrine of or belief in multitudes of deities found in nature; a recurrent belief since prehistoric times. Prominent in nineteenth-century Romanticism.

pantomime In Roman times, enormous dramatic productions featuring instrumental music and dances, favored by the masses; later, a type of dramatic or dancing performance in which the story is told with expressive or even exaggerated bodily and facial movements.

paradigm shift The exchange of one worldview or perspective for another, as, for example, the shift from earth-centered astronomy to sun-centered astronomy between 1550 and 1700; a **paradigm** is an unconsciously agreed-on pattern of thought in a scientific discipline and, by extension, any shared set of beliefs and habits of thought; a term coined by Thomas Kuhn.

parchment A writing surface, prepared from calf-, sheep-, and goatskins, developed in ancient Pergamum. Parchment's supple surface allowed the storing of writing on both sides of a page and thus opened the door to the first books.

pastoral A type of *Hellenistic* poetry that idealized rural customs and farming, especially the simple life of shepherds, and deprecated urban living.

pavane [puh-VAHN] A sixteenth- and seventeenth-century English court dance of Italian origin; the dance is performed by couples to stately music. Ravel based *Pavane for a Dead Princess* (1899) on this *Baroque* dance form.

pediment In *Classical*-style architecture, the triangular-shaped area or gable at the end of the building formed by the sloping roof and the *cornice*.

pendentive [pen-DEN-tiv] In architecture, a triangular, concave-shaped section of *vaulting* between the rim of a dome and the pair of arches that support it; used in Byzantine and Islamic architecture.

performance art A democratic type of mixed-media art born in the 1960s that ignores artistic boundaries, mixing high art (such as music, painting, and theater) and popular art (such as rock and roll, film, and fads), to create a unique, nonreproducible, artistic experience. Associated with the work of Laurie Anderson.

peristyle [PAIR-uh-stile] A colonnade around an open courtyard or a building.

Perpendicular style The highly decorative *style* of *Late Gothic* architecture that developed in England at the same time as the *Late Gothic* on the European continent.

Persian miniature A style of *miniature* painting that flourished in Persia from the thirteenth to the seventeenth century; characterized by rectangular designs, the depiction of the human figure as about one-fifth the height of the painting, and refined detail.

perspective A technique or formula for creating the illusion or appearance of depth and distance on a two-dimensional surface. **Atmospheric perspective** is achieved in many ways: by diminishing color intensity, by omitting detail, and by blurring the lines of an object. **Linear perspective,** based on mathematical calculations, is achieved by having parallel lines or lines of projection appearing to converge at a single point, known as the *vanishing point,* on the horizon of the flat surface and by diminishing distant objects in size according to scale to make them appear to recede from the viewer.

philosophes [FEEL-uh-sawfs] A group of European thinkers and writers who popularized the ideas of the *Enlightenment* through essays, novels, plays, and other works, hoping to change the climate of opinion and bring about social and political reform.

phonogram A symbol used to represent a syllable, a word, or a sound.

Physiocrats [FIZ-ih-uh-kratz] A group of writers, primarily French, who dealt with economic issues during the *Enlightenment,* in particular calling for improved agricultural productivity and questioning the state's role in economic affairs.

piano Italian, "soft." In music, softly. Also, the usual term for *pianoforte.*

pianissimo Italian, "very softly," a musical term.

pianoforte [pee-an-o-FOR-tay] A piano; derived from the Italian for "soft/loud," terms used to describe the two types of sound emitted by a stringed instrument whose wires are struck with felt-covered hammers operated from a keyboard.

picaresque novel From the Spanish term for "rogue." A type of literature, originating in sixteenth-century Spain, that recounted the comic misadventures of a roguish hero who lived by his wits, often at the expense of the high and mighty; influenced novel writing across Europe, especially in England, France, and Germany, until about 1800; the anonymous *Lazarillo de Tormes* (1554) was the first picaresque novel.

pictogram A carefully drawn, often stylized, picture that represents a particular object.

pier In architecture, a vertical masonry structure that may support a *vault,* an arch, or a roof; in *Gothic* churches, piers were often clustered together to form massive supports.

Pietà [pee-ay-TAH] A painting or sculpture depicting the mourning Virgin and the dead Christ.

Pietism A religious reform movement among German Lutherans, which stressed personal piety, along with support for social programs for the poor; part of the general religious ferment of western Europe in the late 1600s and early 1700s and a catalyst for the *First Great Awakening* in British Colonial America in the 1700s.

pilaster [pih-LAS-tuhr] In architecture, a vertical, rectangular decorative device projecting from a wall that gives the appearance of a column with a base and a *capital;* sometimes called an applied column.

Pinteresque In the theater, a dramatic style, attributed to the British playwright Harold Pinter; characterized by enigmatic *plots* and, especially, long pauses in the dialogue.

Platonism The collective beliefs and arguments presented in Plato's writings stressing especially that actual things are copies of ideas.

plainsong Also called *plainchant.* In music, the *monophonic* chant sung in the *liturgy* of the Roman Catholic Church.

plot The action, or arrangement of incidents, in a story.

podium In architecture, a low wall serving as a foundation; a platform.

poetry Language that is concentrated and imaginative, marked by meter, rhythm, rhyme, and imagery.

Pointillism [PWANT-il-iz-uhm] Also known as Division-ism, a *style* of painting, perfected by Seurat, in which tiny dots of paint are applied to the canvas in such a way that when they are viewed from a distance they merge and blend to form recognizable objects with natural effects of color, light, and shade.

polyphony [puh-LIF-uh-nee] A style of musical *composition* in which two or more voices or melodic lines are woven together.

polytheism [PAHL-e-the-iz-uhm]   The doctrine of or belief in more than one deity.

Pop Art   An artistic *style* popular between 1960 and 1970 in which commonplace commercial objects drawn from *mass culture*, such as soup cans, fast foods, and comic strips, became the subjects of art.

portico   In architecture, a covered entrance to a building, usually with a separate roof supported by columns.

post-and-lintel construction   A basic architectural form in which upright posts, or columns, support a horizontal lintel, or beam.

post-beam-triangle construction   The generic name given to Greek architecture that includes the post, or column; the beam, or lintel; and the triangular-shaped area, or *pediment*.

Post-Impressionism   A late-nineteenth-century artistic movement that extended the boundaries of *Impressionism* in new directions to focus on structure, composition, fantasy, and subjective expression.

Post-Modernism   An artistic, cultural, and intellectual movement, originating in about 1970, that is more optimistic than *Modernism*, embraces an open-ended and democratic global *civilization*, freely adapts elements of high culture and *mass culture*, and manifests itself chiefly through revivals of earlier styles, giving rise to *Neoclassicism*, *Neoexpressionism*, and *Neorealism*.

Post-Structuralism   In analytical theory, a set of techniques, growing out of *structuralism*, which were used to show that meaning is shifting and unstable.

Praxitelean curve [prak-sit-i-LEE-an]   The graceful line of the sculptured body in the *contrapposto* stance, perfected by the *Fourth Century style* sculptor Praxiteles.

primitivism   In painting, the "primitives" are those painters of the Netherlandish and Italian schools who flourished before 1500, thus all Netherlandish painters between the van Eycks and Dürer and all Italian painters between Giotto and Raphael; more generally, the term reflects modern artists' fascination with non-Western art forms, as in Gauguin's Tahitian-inspired paintings. In literature, primitivism has complex meanings; on the one hand, it refers to the notion of a golden age, a world of lost innocence, which appeared in both ancient pagan and Christian writings; on the other hand, it is a modern term used to denote two species of cultural relativism, which either finds people isolated from civilization to be superior to those living in civilized and urban settings, as in the cult of the Noble Savage (Rousseau), or respects native peoples and their cultures within their own settings, yet accepts that natives can be as cruel as Europeans (the view expressed by Montaigne).

problem play   A type of drama that focuses on a specific social problem; the Swedish playwright Ibsen was a pioneer of this *genre*, as in *A Doll's House* (1879), concerning women's independence.

program music   Instrumental music that depicts a narrative, portrays a *setting*, or suggests a sequence of events; often based on other sources, such as a poem or a play.

prose   The ordinary language used in speaking and writing.

proverb   A pithy saying, thought to convey folk wisdom or a general truth.

Puritanism   The beliefs and practices of the Puritans, a small but influential religious group devoted to the teachings of John Calvin; they stressed strict rules of personal and public behavior and practiced their beliefs in England and the New World during the seventeenth century.

putti [POOH-tee]   Italian, plural of *putto*; in painting and sculpture, figures of babies, children, or sometimes angels.

qasida [kah-SEE-dah]   In Arabic, "ode." An ode composed in varied meters and with a single rhyme; that is, all lines end in the same rhyming sound. The leading poetic *genre* in Muslim literature.

qiblah [kee-blah]   In Islamic *mosque* architecture, a niche, often richly decorated, pointing the direction for prayer, that is, toward the Kaaba in Mecca.

ragtime   A type of instrumental music, popularized by African Americans in the late nineteenth and early twentieth centuries, with a strongly syncopated rhythm and a lively *melody*.

Rayonnant [ray-yo-NAHNN]   A decorative *style* in French architecture associated with the High *Gothic* period, in which walls were replaced by sheets of *stained glass* framed by elegant stone *traceries*. Also called *Radiant*.

Realism   In medieval philosophy, the school that asserted that objects contained common or universal qualities that were not always apparent to the human senses but that were more real or true than the objects' physical attributes; opposed to *Nominalism*. In art and literature, a mid- to late-nineteenth-century style that focused on the everyday lives of the middle and lower classes, portraying their world in a serious, accurate, and unsentimental way; opposed to *Romanticism*.

recitative [ress-uh-tuh-TEEV]   In music, a rhythmically free but often stylized declamation, midway between singing and ordinary speech, that serves as a transition between *arias* or as a narrative device in an *opera*.

Reformation   The sixteenth-century religious movement that looked back to the ideals of early Christianity, called for moral and structural changes in the church, and led ultimately to the founding of the various Protestant churches.

refrain   In music, a recurring musical passage or phrase; called *ritornello* in Italian.

regalia   Plural in form, often used with a singular verb. The emblems and symbols of royalty, as the crown and scepter.

relief   In sculpture, figures or forms that are carved so that they project from the flat surface of a stone or metal background. **High relief** projects sharply from the surface; **low relief**, or **bas relief**, is more shallow.

Renaissance [ren-uh-SAHNS]   From the French for "rebirth"; the artistic, cultural, and intellectual movement marked by a revival of *Classical* and *humanistic* values that began in Italy in the mid-fourteenth century and had spread across Europe by the mid-sixteenth century.

representational art   Art that presents a likeness of the world as it appears to the naked eye.

Restrained Baroque style   A variation of the *Baroque* style identified with Dutch and English architects and painters who wanted to reduce *Baroque* grandeur and exuberance to a more human scale.

revenge tragedy   A type of play popular in sixteenth-century England, probably rooted in Roman *tragedies* and concerned with the need for a family to seek revenge for the murder of a relative.

ribbed vault   A masonry roof with a framework of arches or ribs that reinforce and decorate the *vault* ceiling.

rocaille [roh-KYE]   In *Rococo* design, the stucco ornaments shaped like leaves, flowers, and ribbons that decorate walls and ceilings.

Rococo style [ruh-KOH-koh]   An artistic and cultural *style* that grew out of the *Baroque* style but that was more intimate and personal and emphasized the frivolous and superficial side of aristocratic life.

romance   A story derived from legends associated with Troy or Celtic culture but often set in feudal times and centered on *themes* of licit and illicit love between noble lords and ladies.

Romanesque style [roh-muhn-ESK]   A *style* of architecture, usually associated with churches built in the eleventh and twelfth centuries, that was inspired by Roman architectural features, such as the *basilica,* and was thus Roman-like. Romanesque buildings were massive, with round arches and *barrel* or *groined vault* ceilings, and had less exterior decoration than *Gothic* churches.

Romanticism   An intellectual, artistic, and literary movement that began in the late eighteenth century as a reaction to *Neoclassicism* and stressed the emotional, mysterious, and imaginative side of human behavior and the unruly side of nature.

rondeau [RON-doh], pl. (rondeaux)   A French verse form, consisting of 13 lines, or sometimes 10 lines, dating from the Late Middle Ages.

rose window   A large circular window, made of *stained glass* and held together with lead and carved stones set in patterns, or *tracery,* and located over an entrance in a *Gothic cathedral.*

sacred music   Religious music, such as Gregorian chants, *masses,* and hymns.

sarcophagus [sahr-KAHF-uh-guhs] (plural, **sarcophagi**)   From the Greek meaning "flesh-eating stone"; a marble or stone coffin or tomb, usually decorated with carvings, used first by Romans and later by Christians for burial of the dead.

satire   From the Latin, "medley"—a cooking term; a literary *genre* that originated in ancient Rome and was characterized by two basic forms: (a) tolerant and amused observation of the human scene, modeled on Horace's style, and (b) bitter and sarcastic denunciation of all behavior and thought outside a civilized norm, modeled on Juvenal's style. In modern times, a literary work that holds up human vices and follies to ridicule or scorn.

satyr-play [SAT-uhr]   A comic play, often featuring sexual *themes,* performed at the Greek drama festivals along with the *tragedies.*

scale   A set pattern of *tones* (or notes) arranged from low to high.

scenographic [see-nuh-GRAF-ik]   In *Renaissance* architecture, a building style that envisioned buildings as composed of separate units; in the painting of stage scenery, the art of *perspective* representation.

scherzo [SKER-tso]   From the Italian for "joke"; a quick and lively instrumental *composition* or movement found in *sonatas* and *symphonies.*

scholasticism   In medieval times, the body or collection of knowledge that tried to harmonize Aristotle's writings with Christian doctrine; also, a way of thinking and establishing sets of arguments.

Scientific Revolution   The seventeenth-century intellectual movement, based originally on discoveries in astronomy and physics, that challenged and overturned medieval views about the order of the universe and the theories used to explain motion.

scripture   The sacred writings of any religion, as the Bible in Judaism and Christianity.

Second Romanesque   The second and mature stage of *Romanesque* architecture, about 1080–1200. Second Romanesque churches were richly decorated and built on a vast scale, including such features as double *transepts,* double *aisles,* crossing towers, and towers at the ends of the *transepts;* associated with Cluniac monasticism.

secular music   Nonreligious music, such as *symphonies,* songs, and dances.

serenade   In music, a lighthearted piece, intended to be performed outdoors in the evening; popular in the eighteenth and nineteenth centuries.

serial music   A type of musical composition based on a *twelve-tone scale* arranged any way the composer chooses; the absence of a tonal center in serial music leads to *atonality.*

setting   In literature, the background against which the action takes place; in a representational artwork, the time and place depicted.

Severe style   The first sculptural style of the *Classical* period in Greece, which retained stylistic elements from the *Archaic* style.

sfumato [sfoo-MAH-toh]   In painting, the blending of one *tone* into another to blur the outline of a form and give the canvas a smokelike appearance; a technique perfected by Leonardo da Vinci.

shaft graves   Deep pit burial sites; the dead were usually placed at the bottom of the shafts; a burial practice in Mycenaean Greece.

skene [SKEE-nee]   A small building behind the *orchestra* in a Greek theater, used as a prop and as a storehouse for theatrical materials.

Skepticism   A *Hellenistic* philosophy that questioned whether anything could be known for certain, argued that all beliefs were relative, and concluded that *autarky* could be achieved only by recognizing that inquiry was fruitless.

slave narrative   A literary *genre,* either written by slaves or told by slaves to secretaries, which emerged prior to the American Civil War; the genre was launched by the *Narrative of the Life of Frederick Douglass, an American Slave* (1845); the harsh details of the inhumane and unjust slave system, as reported in these narratives, contributed to *Realist* literature.

social contract   In political thought, an agreement or contract between the people and their rulers defining the rights and duties of each so that a civil society might be created.

Social Gospel   A Protestant movement, mainly in the United States, whose heyday was from 1880 to 1945, which stressed social improvement rather than personal piety; the religious equivalent of *liberal* politics.

socialism   An economic and political system in which goods and property are owned collectively or by the state; the socialist movement began as a reaction to the excesses of the factory system in the nineteenth century and ultimately called for either reforming or abolishing industrial capitalism.

Socialist Realism   A Marxist artistic theory that calls for the use of literature, music, and the arts in the service of the ideals and goals of socialism and/or communism, with an emphasis in painting on the realistic portrayal of objects.

solipsism   In philosophy, the sense that only one's self exists or can be known.

sonata [soh-NAH-tah]   In music, an instrumental *composition,* usually in three or four movements.

sonata form   A musical *form* or structure consisting of three (or sometimes four) sections that vary in *key, tempo,* and *mood.*

stained glass   An art form characterized by many small pieces of tinted glass bound together by strips of lead, usually to produce a pictorial scene of a religious theme; developed by *Romanesque* artists and a central feature of *Gothic* churches.

stele [STEE-lee]   A carved or inscribed vertical stone pillar or slab, often used for commemorative purposes.

stereobate   In Greek architecture, the stepped base on which a temple stands.

Stoicism [STO-ih-sihz-uhm]   The most popular and influential *Hellenistic* philosophy, advocating a restrained way of life, a toleration for others, a resignation to disappointments, and a resolution to carry out one's responsibilities. Stoicism appealed to many Romans and had an impact on early Christian thought.

stream-of-consciousness   A writing technique used by some modern authors in which the narration consists of a *character's* continuous interior monologue of thoughts and feelings.

structuralism   In *Post-Modernism,* an approach to knowledge based on the belief that human behavior and institutions can be explained by reference to a few underlying structures that themselves are reflections of hidden patterns in the human mind.

studia humanitatis [STOO-dee-ah hu-man-ih-TAH-tis] **(humanistic studies)**   The Latin term given by *Renaissance* scholars to new intellectual pursuits that were based on recently discovered ancient texts, including moral philosophy, history, grammar, rhetoric, and poetry. This new learning stood in sharp contrast to medieval *scholasticism.*

Sturm und Drang [STOORM oont drahng]   German, "Storm and Stress"; a German literary movement of the 1770s that focused on themes of action, emotionalism, and the individual's revolt against the conventions of society.

style   The combination of distinctive elements of creative execution and expression, in terms of both *form* and *content.*

style galant [STEEL gah-LAHNN]   In *Rococo* music, a *style* of music developed by French composers and characterized by graceful and simple *melodies.*

stylobate [STY-luh-bate]   In Greek temples, the upper step of the base that forms a platform on which the columns stand.

Sublime [suh-BLIME]   In *Romanticism,* the term used to describe nature as a terrifying and awesome force full of violence and power.

subject   In music, the main *theme.*

Suprematism [suh-PREM-uh-tiz-uhm]   A variation of *abstract art,* originating in Russia in the early twentieth century, characterized by the use of geometric shapes as the basic elements of the composition.

Surrealism [suh-REE-uhl-iz-uhm]   An early-twentieth-century movement in art, literature, and theater, in which incongruous juxtapositions and fantastic images produce an irrational and dreamlike effect.

swing band   A 15- to 16-member orchestra, which plays ballads and dance tunes; dominated popular music in the United States and in large cities in western Europe, from the early 1930s until the early 1950s.

syllabic   In music, in *plainsong,* a style of musical setting in which one note is set to each syllable.

symbolic realism   In art, a *style* that is realistic and true to life but uses the portrayed object or person to represent or symbolize something else.

symphony   A long and complex *sonata,* usually written in three or four movements, for large *orchestras;* the first movement is traditionally fast, the second slow, and the third (and optional fourth) movement fast.

syncopation [sin-ko-PAY-shun]   In music, the technique of accenting the weak beat when a strong beat is expected.

syncretism [SIN-kruh-tiz-uhm]   The combining of different forms of religious beliefs or practices.

synthesizer [SIN-thuh-size-uhr]   An electronic apparatus with a keyboard capable of duplicating the sounds of many musical instruments, popular among *Post-Modernist* composers and musicians.

tabula rasa [TAB-yuh-luh RAH-zuh]   "Erased tablet," the Latin term John Locke used to describe the mind at birth, empty of inborn ideas and ready to receive sense impressions, which Locke believed were the sole source of knowledge.

technique   The systematic procedure whereby a particular creative task is performed.

tempo   In music, the relative speed at which a *composition* is to be played, indicated by a suggestive word or phrase or by a precise number such as a metronome marking. (A metronome is a finely calibrated device used to determine the exact tempo for a musical work.)

terza rima [TER-tsuh REE-muh]   A three-line stanza with an interlocking rhyme scheme (*aba bcb cdc ded,* and so on), used by Dante in his *Divine Comedy.*

texture   In a musical composition, the number and nature of voices or instruments employed and how the parts are combined.

theater of the absurd   A type of theater that has come to reflect the despair, anxieties, and absurdities of modern life and in which the characters seldom make sense, the plot is nearly nonexistent, bizarre and fantastic events occur onstage, and *tragedy* and *comedy* are mixed in unconventional ways; associated with *Late Modernism.*

theme   The dominant idea of a work; the message or emotion the artist intends to convey; used in music, literature, and art.

theme and variations   In music, a *technique* in which a musical idea is stated and then repeated in variant versions, with modifications or embellishments; used in independent works or as a single movement in a *symphony, sonata,* or chamber work.

theocracy   From the Greek *theos,* "god"; a state governed by a god regarded as the ruling power or by priests or officials claiming divine sanction.

theology   The application of philosophy to the study of religious truth, focusing especially on the nature of the deity and the origin and teachings of an organized religious community.

tone   A musical sound of definite pitch; also, the quality of a sound.

tone color   In music, the quality of a sound, determined by the overtones; used for providing contrasts.

tracery   Ornamental architectural work with lines that branch out to form designs, often found as stone carvings in *rose windows.*

tragedy   A serious and deeply moral drama, typically involving a noble protagonist brought down by excessive pride (hubris) and describing a conflict between seemingly irreconcilable values or forces; in Greece, tragedies were performed at the festivals associated with the worship of Dionysus.

Transcendentalism   A literary and philosophical movement that emphasized the spiritual over the material, the metaphysical over the physical, and intuition over empiricism. Its central tenet identified God or the divine spirit (Transcendence) with Nature; popular in early and mid-nineteenth-century New England.

transept In church architecture, the crossing arm that bisects the *nave* near the *apse* and gives the characteristic *cruciform* shape to the floor plan.

tremolo In music, the rapid repetiton of two pitches in a chord, so as to produce a tremulous effect.

triglyph [TRY-glif] In Greek architecture, a three-grooved rectangular panel on the *frieze* of a *Doric* temple; triglyphs alternated with *metopes*.

trill In music, the rapid alternation of two notes, a step apart; used as a musical embellishment.

triptych [TRIP-tik] In painting, a set of three hinged or folding panels depicting a religious story, mainly used as an altarpiece.

trope [TROHP] In *Gregorian chants*, a new phrase or *melody* inserted into an existing chant to make it more musically appealing; also called a turn; in literature, a figure of speech.

troubador [TROO-buh-door] A composer and/or singer, usually an aristocrat, who performed *secular* love songs at the feudal courts in southern France.

twelve-tone scale In music, a fixed *scale* or series in which there is an arbitrary arrangement of the twelve *tones* (counting every half-tone) of an octave; devised by Arnold Schoenberg.

tympanum [TIM-puh-num] In medieval architecture, the arch over a doorway set above the lintel, usually decorated with carvings depicting biblical themes; in *Classical*-style architecture, the recessed face of a *pediment*.

ukiyo-e [oo-key-yoh-AY] A type of colorful Japanese print, incised on woodblocks, that is characterized by simple design, plain backgrounds, and flat areas of color. Developed in seventeenth-century Japan; admired by late-nineteenth-century Parisian artists, who assimilated it to a Western style that is most notable in the prints of Mary Cassatt.

Utilitarianism [yoo-til-uh-TARE-e-uh-niz-uhm] The doctrine set forth in the social theory of Jeremy Bentham in the nineteenth century that the final goal of society and humans is "the greatest good for the greatest number."

vanishing point In linear *perspective*, the point on the horizon at which the receding parallel lines appear to converge and then vanish.

vault A ceiling or roof made from a series of arches placed next to one another.

vernacular language [vuhr-NAK-yuh-luhr] The language or dialect of a region, usually spoken by the general population as opposed to the wealthy or educated elite.

vernacular literature Literature written in the language of the populace, such as English, French, or Italian, as opposed to the language of the educated elite, usually Latin.

via antiqua [VEE-uh ahn-TEE-kwah] The "old way," the term used in Late Medieval thought by the opponents of St. Thomas Aquinas to describe his *via media*, which they considered outdated.

via media [VEE-uh MAY-dee-ah] The "middle way" that St. Thomas Aquinas sought in reconciling Aristotle's works to Christian beliefs.

via moderna [VEE-uh moh-DEHR-nah] The "new way," the term used in Late Medieval thought by those thinkers who opposed the school of Aquinas.

video art A type of art made with a video monitor or monitors; produced using either computerized programs or handheld cameras; can be ephemeral or permanent.

virtuoso [vehr-choo-O-so] An aristocratic person who experimented in science, usually as an amateur, in the seventeenth century, giving science respectability and a wider audience; later, in music, a person with great technical skill.

voussoir [voo-SWAR] A carved, wedge-shaped stone or block in an arch.

woodcut In art, the technique of cutting or carving an image onto a wooden block used for printing; originated in the Late Middle Ages. Also, the print made from the technique.

word painting In music, the illustration of an idea, a meaning, or a feeling associated with a word, as, for example, using a discordant *melody* when the word *pain* is sung. This technique is especially identified with the sixteenth-century *madrigal*; also called word illustration or madrigalism.

ziggurat [ZIG-oo-rat] A Mesopotamian stepped pyramid, usually built with external staircases and a shrine at the top; sometimes included a tower.

CREDITS

lon Collection, USA/© Bridgeman Art Library; **17.14, 17.15,** © Clore Collection, Tate Gallery, London/Art Resource, NY; **17.16,** © Jörg P. Anders/Bildarchiv Preussischer Kulturbesitz/Art Resource, NY; **17.17,** © Scala/Art Resource, NY; **17.18,** Museum of Fine Arts, Boston. Bequest of William P. Babcock. Photograph © The Museum of Fine Arts, Boston (B4165.43); **17.19, 17.20,** © Erich Lessing/Art Resource, NY; **17.21,** © Réunion des Musées Nationaux/Art Resource, NY; **17.22,** © AKG Images; **17.23,** Courtesy of the John Carter Brown Library at Brown University; **17.24,** © AKG Images **Chapter 18 CO18,** © Erich Lessing/Art Resource, NY; **18.1,** © Réunion des Musées Nationaux/Art Resource, NY; **18.2,** © Ronald Sheridan/Ancient Art & Architecture Collection; **18.3,** Courtesy Museum of Fine Arts, Boston. Henry Lillie Pierce Fund. Photograph © Museum of Fine Arts. Boston (99.22); **18.4,** Edouard Manet. Alabama and Kearsarge. John G. Johnston Collection, 1917. © Philadelphia Museum of Art. Cat. 1027.; **18.5,** Royal Holloway and Bedford New College, Surrey/© Bridgeman Art Library; **18.6,** © Victoria & Albert Museum/Art Resource, NY; **18.7,** © Hulton Archive/Getty Images; **Encounter 18.1,** Courtesy Georgia State Parks and Historic Sites. Photo by Robb Helfrick; **Encounter 18.2,** © National Portrait Gallery, Smithsonian Institution/Art Resource, NY; **18.8,** The Courtauld Institute Gallery, Somerset House, London; **18.9,** Louvre, Paris, France/Lauros-Giraudon/© The Bridgeman Art Library; **18.10,** © Réunion des Musées Nationaux/Art Resource, NY; **18.11,** The Metropolitan Museum of Art, Bequest of Maria DeWitt Jesup, 1915. (15.30.61). Photograph © 1992 The Metropolitan Museum of Art; **18.12,** © Réunion des Musées Nationaux/Art Resource, NY; **18.13,** © Erich Lessing/Art Resource, NY; **18.14,** © The British Museum; **18.15,** The Metropolitan Museum of Art, Bequest of Mrs. H.O. Havemeyer, 1929. The H.O. Havemeyer Collection. (29.100.129). Photograph © 1992 The Metropolitan Museum of Art; **18.16,** Courtesy Museum of Fine Arts, Boston. Gift of Quincy Adams Shaw through Quincy A. Shaw, Jr. and Mrs. Marian Shaw Haughton. Photograph © Museum of Fine Arts, Boston (17.1485); **18.17,** The Metropolitan Museum of Art, Gift of Cornelius Vanderbilt, 1887. (87.25). Photograph by Schecter Lee © 1997 The Metropolitan Museum of Art; **18.18,** © Réunion des Musées Nationaux/Art Resource, NY; **18.19,** Library of Congress (62-5803); **18.20,** © Victoria & Albert Museum/Art Resource, NY; **18.21,** © Private Collection/Bridgeman Art Library **Chapter 19 CO19,** Vincent van Gogh, *The Starry Night,* (1889). Oil on canvas. 29 x 34¼″ (73.7 x 92.1 cm). Acquired through the Lillie P. Bliss Bequest. The Museum of Modern Art, NY. Digital image © The Museum of Modern Art, NY/ Licensed by Scala/Art Resource, NY; **19.1,** Umberto Boccioni (1882-1916). *Unique Forms of Continuity in Space.* 1913. Bronze. 43⅞ x 34⅞ x 15¼″. Acquired through the Lillie P. Bliss Bequest. (231.1948). The Museum of Modern Art, New York. Digital Image © The Museum of Modern Art, NY/Licensed by Scala/Art Resource, NY; **19.2,** Collection of Mr. and Mrs. Paul Mellon, Image © 2006 Board of Trustees, National Gallery of Art, Washington, 1906, oil on canvas, .546 x .378 (21½ x 14⅞); framed: .638 x .473 x .036 (25⅛ x 18⅝ x 1⁷⁄₁₆). 1985.64.13; **19.3,** © Christie's London/Artothek; **19.4,** © Carnegie Museum of Art, Pittsburgh, Museum Purchase; **19.5,** Eyre Crowe, *The Dinner Hour at Wigan,* © Manchester City Art Galleries; **19.6,** © The Granger Collection, New York; **19.7,** © Erich Lessing/Art Resource, NY; **19.8,** © The Art Archive/Ellen Tweedy; **19.9,** Courtesy of the Fogg Art Museum, Harvard University Art Museums, Bequest of Grenville L. Winthrop. © President and Fellows of Harvard College; **19.10,** Photo: J. Lathion, © Nasjonalgalleriet; **19.11,** © Réunion des Musées Nationaux/Art Resource, NY; **19.12,** © Carnegie Museum of Art, Pittsburgh, Acquired through the generosity of Mrs. Alan M. Scaife; **19.13,** The Phillips Collection, Washington, D.C.; **19.14,** Collection of Mr. and Mrs. Paul Mellon. Photograph © Board of Trustees, National Gallery of Art, Washington; **Encounter 19.1,** The Whitworth Art Gallery, The University of Manchester; **Encounter 19.2,** Amsterdam, Van Gogh Museum (Vincent Van Gogh Foundation); **19.15,** Mary Cassatt (American, 1844-1926) *The Bath,* 1891. Soft-ground etching with aquatint and drypoint on paper. 12⅜ x 9⅞. National Museum of Women in the Arts. Gift of Wallace and Wilhelmina Holladay; **19.16,** Helen Birch Bartlett Memorial Collection, 1926.224. © 2003 Art Institute of Chicago. All rights reserved.; **19.17,** Paul Cezanne, *Mont Sainte-Victorie.* 27½ x 35¼″. Philadelphia Museum of Art, The George W. Elkins Collection. Photo by Graydon Wood, 1995; **19.18,** Albright-Knox Art Gallery, Buffalo, NY. A. Conger Goodyear Collection, 1965; **19.19,** © Réunion des Musées Nationaux/Art Resource, NY; **19.20,** Vincent van Gogh, *The Starry Night,* (1889). Oil on canvas. 29 x 34¼″ (73.7 x 92.1 cm). Acquired through the Lillie P. Bliss Bequest. The Museum of Modern Art, NY. Digital image © The Museum of Modern Art, NY/Licensed by Scala/ Art Resource, NY; **19.21,** Open Window, Collioure, Collection of Mr.

and Mrs. John Hay Whitney, Image © 2006 Board of Trustees, National Gallery of Art, Washington, 1905, oil on canvas, .553 x .460 (21¾ x 18⅛); framed: .711 x 6.22 x .051 (28 x 24½ x 2) © 2007 Succession H. Matisse, Paris/Artists Rights Society (ARS), New York; **19.22,** Pablo Picasso (1881-1973). *Les Demoiselles d'Avignon.* 1907. Oil on canvas, 8′ x 7′8″. Acquired through the Lille P. Bliss Bequest. (333.1939). The Museum of Modern Art, New York. Digital Image © The Museum of Modern Art, NY/Licensed by Scala/Art Resource, NY. © 2007 Estate of Pablo Picasso/Artists Rights Society (ARS), New York; **19.23,** Pablo Picasso, Spanish, 1881-1973, *Daniel-Henry Kahnweiler,* 1910, oil on canvas, 101.1 x 73.3 cm, Gift of Mrs. Gilbert W. Chapman in memory of Charles B. Goodspeed, 1948.561, The Art Institute of Chicago. Photography © The Art Institute of Chicago. © Estate of Pablo Picasso/ Artists Rights Society (ARS), New York; **19.24,** Stedelijk Museum, Amsterdam. © 2007 Artists Rights Society (ARS), New York/ADAGP, Paris; **19.25,** Augustine Rodin. *Eve.* 67 x 18½ x 23¼″. The Rodin Museum, Philadelphia. Gift of Jules E. Mastbaum. **19.26,** © Marvin Trachtenberg; **19.27,** © Chicago Historical Society; **19.28,** The William Ransom Hogan Archive of New Orleans Jazz, Tulane University **Chapter 20 CO20,** Courtesy of Mary-Anne Martin/Fine Art, New York. © 2003 Banco de México, Diego Rivera & Frida Kahlo Museums Trust. Av. Cinco de Mayo No. 2, Centro, Del. Cuauhtémoc 06059, Mexico, D.F.; **20.1,** Photo © AKG Images. © 2007 Estate of Pablo Picasso/ Artists Rights Society (ARS), New York; **20.2,** © Imperial War Museum, London/The Bridgeman Art Library; **20.3,** Gift of Ethelyn McKinney in memory of her brother Glenn Ford McKinney, © 2006 Board of Trustees, National Gallery of Art, Washington, 1917, oil on canvas, .927 x .768 (36½ x 30¼); framed 1.108 x .943 x .064 (43⅝ x 37⅛ x 2½). 1943.9.1; **20.4,** © British Petroleum Company plc, London; **20.5,** Courtesy Library of Congress, 62-95653; **Encounter 20.1,** © Margaret Bourke-White/Time Life Pictures/Getty Images; **20.6,** © AP/Wide World Photos; **20.7,** © Margaret Bourke-White/Time Life Pictures/ Getty Images; **20.8,** © Corbis; **20.9,** © AP/Wide World Photos; **20.10,** The Metropolitan Museum of Art, Bequest of Gertrude Stein, 1947 (47.106). Photograph © 1996 The Metropolitan Museum of Art. © 2007 Estate of Pablo Picasso/Artists Rights Society (ARS), New York; **20.11,** Jacob Lawrence (1917-2000). "In the North the African American had more educational opportunities." Panel 58 from *The Migration Series.* (1940-41; text and titled revised by the artist, 1993) Tempera on gesso on composition board, 12 x 18″ (30.5 x 45.7 cm). Gift of Mrs. David M. Levy. The Museum of Modern Art, New York. Digital Image © The Museum of Modern Art, NY/Licensed by Scala/Art Resource, NY. © 2007 The Jacob and Gwendolyn Lawrence Foundation, Seattle/ Artists Rights Society (ARS), New York; **20.12,** © Museo Thyssen-Bornemisza. Madrid; **20.13,** Photo: Yale University Art Gallery. © 2007 Artists Rights Society (ARS), New York/ADAGP, Paris; **20.14,** Stedelijk Museum, Amsterdam; **20.15,** Piet Mondrian, Dutch, 1872-1944. *Broadway Boogie Woogie,* 1942-43. Oil on canvas. 50 x 50″ (127 x 127 cm). Given anonymously. The Museum of Modern Art, NY. Digital image © The Museum of Modern Art, NY/Licensed by Scala/Art Resource, NY. © 2007 Mondrian/Holtzman Trust c/o HCR International Warrenton, VA; **20.16,** Philadelphia Museum of Art. The A.E. Gallatin Collection. © 2007 Estate of Pablo Picasso/Artists Rights Society (ARS), New York; **20.17,** Georgia O'Keeffe, American, 1887-1986, *Cow's Skull with Calico Roses,* oil on canvas, 1932, 92.2 x 61.3 cm, Gift of Georgia O'Keeffe, 1947.712. Photograph © 2000 The Art Institute of Chicago, All Rights Reserved. © 2007 The Georgia O'Keeffe Foundation; **20.18,** Marcel Duchamp, *The Bride Stripped Bare by Her Bachelors,* Even (The Large Glass) Front View. 109¼ x 69¼. Philadelphia Museum of Art, Bequest of Katherine S. Dreier. © 2007 Artists Rights Society (ARS), New York/ ADAGP, Paris/Succession Marcel Duchamp; **20.19,** Salvador Dali (1904-1989). *The Persistence of Memory.* 1931. Oil on canvas, 9½ x 13″. (162.1934). Given anonymously. The Museum of Modern Art, New York. Digital Image © The Museum of Modern Art, NY/Licensed by Scala/Art Resource, NY. © 2007 Salvador Dali, Gala-Salvador Dali Foundation/Artists Rights Society (ARS), New York; **20.20,** Photo © Artothek. © 2007 Artists Rights Society (ARS), New York/VG Bild-Kunst, Bonn; **20.21,** All rights reserved by Pan Klub Foundation. Xul Solar Museum; **20.22,** Courtesy of Mary-Anne Martin/Fine Art, New York. © 2003 Banco de México, Diego Rivera & Frida Kahlo Museums Trust. Av. Cinco de Mayo No. 2, Centro, Del. Cuauhtémoc 06059, Mexico, D.F.; **20.23,** The Baltimore Museum of Art, The Cone Collection, formed by Dr. Claribel Cone and Mrs. Etta Cone of Baltimore, Maryland. © 2007 Succession H. Matisse, Paris/Artists Rights Society (ARS), New York; **20.24,** Max Beckmann (1884-1950). *Departure.* 1932-33. Oil on canvas, triptych, center panel, 7′¾″ x 45⅜″; side panels each 7′¾″ x 39¼″. Given anonymously (by exchange). (6.1942.a-c). The Museum

INDEX

Page numbers in *italics* indicate pronunciation guides; pages numbers in **boldface** indicate illustrations. For readers using the two-volume set of *The Western Humanities*, page numbers 1–383 (Chapters 1–12) refer to material in Volume I: *Beginnings through the Renaissance* and page numbers 384–736 (Chapters 11–22) refer to material in Volume II: *The Renaissance to the Present*.